Sixth Joint Conference on Lexical and Computational Semantics (*SEM 2017)

Vancouver, Canada
3 – 4 August 2017

ISBN: 978-1-5108-4562-6

*SEM 2017: The Sixth Joint Conference on Lexical and Computational Semantics

Proceedings of the Conference

August 3-4, 2017
Vancouver, Canada

*SEM 2017 is sponsored by:

The Association for Computational Linguistics

Introduction

Preface by the General Chair

The 2017 edition of *SEM, the 6th in the annual series, took on as its theme "representations of meaning", an area of acute interest in the field for the past several years. The conference program shows that this year's *SEM has been especially successful in covering its theme from a broad range of perspectives, including various flavors of distributional, lexical, and formal/linguistic semantics. Thus, the 2017 conference meets the overall goal of the *SEM series, by bridging across relatively independent communities approaching the computational modeling of semantics from different angles. Hopefully, the diversity of the program will provide not only something of interest to a broad audience of NLP researchers, but also serve to stimulate new ideas and synergies that can significantly impact the field.

As always, *SEM would not have been possible without the active involvement of our community. Aside from our dedicated program committee, to whom we give an extended acknowledgement further in this introduction, we are very thankful to Eduardo Blanco (Publicity Chair) and Sandro Pezzelle (Publication Chair) for their efficiency and hard work in making the conference a visible event, from website to proceedings. We are particularly grateful to ACL SIGLEX, who made it possible to offer two exciting keynotes, and to SIGLEX and Lexical Computing for supporting the annual Adam Kilgarriff Award for the best paper at *SEM 2017. Our keynote speakers, Yejin Choi and Katrin Erk, are owed special thanks for taking part in the selection of the best paper.

On behalf of the Program Committee Chairs, to whom we owe the greatest debt for the excellence of the program, and myself as General Chair, I invite you to explore, exploit, and enjoy the diversity of perspectives on the computational modeling of semantics that *SEM 2017 strives to provide.

Nancy Ide,
General Chair of *SEM 2017

Preface by the Program Chairs

We are pleased to present this volume containing the papers accepted at the Sixth Joint Conference on Lexical and Computational Semantics (*SEM 2017, co-located with ACL in Vancouver, Canada, on August 3-4, 2017).

*SEM received a record number of submissions this year, which allowed us to compile a diverse and high-quality program. The number of submissions was over one hundred (107). After we had discarded some papers due to formal issues, 101 papers were reviewed for the conference, (52 long and 49 short). Out of these, 36 papers were accepted (22 long, 14 short). Thus, the acceptance rate was 35.6% overall, 42.3% for the long papers and 28.6% for the short submissions. Some of the papers were withdrawn after acceptance, due to multiple submissions to other conferences (the 2017 schedule was particularly complicated, with significant intersection of *SEM with EMNLP, CoNLL, IWCS and other venues). The final number of papers in the program is 30.

Submissions were reviewed in 9 different areas: Representations of Meaning (special topic of interest), Distributional Semantics, Semantics for Applications, Lexical Semantics, Lexical Resources and Ontologies, Discourse and Dialogue, Semantic Parsing and Semantic Role Labeling, Multimodal Semantics, Formal and Linguistic Semantics. The most prolific areas were Distributional Semantics (19 submitted papers), Representations of Meaning (15), and Semantics for Applications (15).

The papers were evaluated by a program committee of 14 area chairs from Asia, Europe and North America, assisted by a panel of 167 reviewers. Each submission was reviewed by three reviewers, who were furthermore encouraged to discuss any divergence in evaluation. The papers in each area were subsequently ranked by the area chairs. The final selection was made by the program co-chairs after an independent check of all reviews and discussion with the area chairs. Reviewers' recommendations were also used to shortlist a set of papers nominated for the Adam Kilgarriff Award. These papers were judged by a committee chaired by Nancy Ide.

The final *SEM 2017 program consists of 17 oral presentations and 13 posters, as well as two keynote talks by Yejin Choi ("From Naive Physics to Connotation: Modeling Commonsense in Frame Semantics", joint keynote with SemEval 2017) and Katrin Erk ("What do you know about an alligator when you know the company it keeps?").

We are deeply thankful to all area chairs and reviewers for their help in the selection of the program, for their readiness in engaging in thoughtful discussions about individual papers, and for providing valuable feedback to the authors. We are also grateful to Eduardo Blanco for his precious help in publicizing the conference, and to Sandro Pezzelle for his dedication and thoroughness in turning the program into the proceedings you now have under your eyes. Last but not least, we are indebted to our General Chair, Nancy Ide, for her continuous guidance and support throughout the process of organizing this installment of *SEM.

We hope you enjoy the conference!

Aurélie Herbelot & Lluís Màrquez,
Program Co-Chairs of *SEM 2017

*SEM 2017 Chairs and Reviewers

General Chair:

Nancy Ide, Vassar College, USA

Program Co-Chairs:

Aurélie Herbelot, University of Trento, Italy
Lluís Màrquez, Qatar Computing Research Institute, Qatar

Publication Chair:

Sandro Pezzelle, University of Trento, Italy

Publicity Chair:

Eduardo Blanco, University of North Texas, USA

Area Chairs:

Representations of meaning
Tim Baldwin, University of Melbourne, Australia
Louise McNally, Universitat Pompeu Fabra, Spain

Semantics for applications
Roser Morante, Vrije Universiteit Amsterdam, the Netherlands
Mark Sammons, University of Illinois at Urbana-Champaign, USA

Lexical semantics, figurative language
Diana Inkpen, University of Ottawa, Canada
Ekaterina Shutova, University of Cambridge, UK

Distributional semantics
Alessandro Lenci, University of Pisa, Italy
Islam Beltagy, University of Texas at Austin, USA

Coreference, discourse and dialogue
Raquel Fernández, University of Amsterdam, the Netherlands
Nianwen Xue, Brandeis University, USA

Lexical resources, linked data, ontologies
Simone Paolo Ponzetto, University of Mannheim, Germany

Formal and linguistic semantics
Laura Rimell, University of Cambridge, UK

Semantic parsing and semantic role labeling
Luke Zettlemoyer, University of Washington, USA

Semantics in multimodal approaches
Angeliki Lazaridou, DeepMind

Reviewers:

Eneko Agirre, Alan Akbik, Marianna Apidianaki, Ron Artstein, Yoav Artzi, Valerio Basile, Roberto Basili, Beata Beigman Klebanov, Meriem Beloucif, Farah Benamara, Andrew Bennett, Luciana Benotti, Luisa Bentivogli, Jonathan Berant, Raffaella Bernardi, Chris Biemann, Eduardo Blanco, Gemma Boleda, Georgeta Bordea, Ellen Breitholz, Julian Brooke, Elia Bruni, Paul Buitelaar, Luana Bulat, Elena Cabrio, Hiram Calvo, Nicoletta Calzolari, Jose Camacho-Collados, Xavier Carreras, Jorge Carrillo-de-Albornoz, Tommaso Caselli, Kai-Wei Chang, Emmanuele Chersoni, Christos Christodoulopoulos, Grzegorz Chrupała, Philipp Cimiano, Stephen Clark, Alexis Conneau, Inés Crespo, Mauro Dragoni, Kevin Duh, Katrin Erk, Stefan Evert, Cécile Fabre, Ingrid Falk, Stefano Faralli, Anna Feldman, Tim Fernando, Diego Frassinelli, Daniel Fried, Michael Färber, Aldo Gangemi, Spandana Gella, Anna Lisa Gentile, Jonathan Ginzburg, Roxana Girju, Dan Goldwasser, Jorge Gracia, Iryna Gurevych, Hannaneh Hajishirzi, Luheng He, Iris Hendrickx, Eric Holgate, Veronique Hoste, Julian Hough, Julie Hunter, Allan Jabri, Sujay Kumar Jauhar, Richard Johansson, David Jurgens, Laura Kallmeyer, Hans Kamp, Yoshihide Kato, Ruth Kempson, Casey Kennington, Douwe Kiela, Halil Kilicoglu, Manfred Klenner, Ekaterina Kochmar, Alexander Koller, Parisa Kordjamshidi, Valia Kordoni, Zornitsa Kozareva, Sebastian Krause, Germán Kruszewski, Gourab Kundu, Tom Kwiatkowski, Ákos Kádár, Man Lan, Gabriella Lapesa, Dan Lassiter, Gianluca Lebani, Omer Levy, Annie Louis, Junhua Mao, Alda Mari, Erwin Marsi, Shigeki Matsubara, Louise McNally, Oren Melamud, Tristan Miller, Shachar Mirkin, Saif Mohammad, Alessandro Moschitti, Smaranda Muresan, Preslav Nakov, Vivi Nastase, Vincent Ng, Malvina Nissim, Sebastian Padó, Alexis Palmer, Martha Palmer, Denis Paperno, Panupong Pasupat, Ellie Pavlick, Maciej Piasecki, Mohammad Taher Pilehvar, Massimo Poesio, Hoifung Poon, Christopher Potts, Rashmi Prasad, Laurette Pretorius, Laurent Prévot, Matthew Purver, Marek Rei, Martin Riedl, Mathieu Roche, Stephen Roller, Marco Rospocher, Michael Roth, Alla Rozovskaya, Josef Ruppenhofer, Attapol Rutherford, Magnus Sahlgren, Mark Sammons, Enrico Santus, Roser Saurí, Natalie Schluter, Sabine Schulte im Walde, Diarmuid Ó Séaghdha, Jennifer Sikos, Carina Silberer, Yangqiu Song, Vivek Srikumar, Evgeny Stepanov, Stan Szpakowicz, Idan Szpektor, Niket Tandon, Joel Tetreault, Ivan Titov, Sara Tonelli, Yulia Tsvetkov, Lyle Ungar, Shyam Upadhyay, Tim Van de Cruys, Eva Maria Vecchi, Erik Velldal, Marc Verhagen, Yannick Versley, Aline Villavicencio, Chuan Wang, Grégoire Winterstein, Feiyu Xu, Nianwen Xue, Torsten Zesch, Pierre Zweigenbaum

Invited Talk: From Naive Physics to Connotation: Modeling Commonsense in Frame Semantics

Yejin Choi
(Joint Invited Speaker with SemEval 2017)

University of Washington, USA

Abstract

Intelligent communication requires reading between the lines, which in turn, requires rich background knowledge about how the world works. However, learning unspoken commonsense knowledge from language is nontrivial, as people rarely state the obvious, e.g., "my house is bigger than me." In this talk, I will discuss how we can recover the trivial everyday knowledge just from language without an embodied agent. A key insight is this: The implicit knowledge people share and assume systematically influences the way people use language, which provides indirect clues to reason about the world. For example, if "Jen entered her house", it must be that her house is bigger than her. I will discuss how we can model a variety of aspects of knowledge – ranging from naive physics to connotation – adapting the representations of frame semantics.

Invited Talk: What Do You Know About an Alligator When You Know the Company It Keeps?

Katrin Erk

University of Texas at Austin, USA

Abstract

How can people learn about the meaning of a word from textual context? If we assume that lexical knowledge has to do with truth conditions, then what can textual (distributional) information contribute? I will argue that at the least, an agent can observe how textual contexts co-occur with concepts that have particular properties, and that the agent can use this information to make inferences about unknown words: "I don't know what an alligator is, but it must be something like a crocodile". I will further argue that this inference can only be noisy and partial, and is best described in probabilistic terms.

Table of Contents

What Analogies Reveal about Word Vectors and their Compositionality
Gregory Finley, Stephanie Farmer and Serguei Pakhomov 1

Learning Antonyms with Paraphrases and a Morphology-Aware Neural Network
Sneha Rajana, Chris Callison-Burch, Marianna Apidianaki and Vered Shwartz 12

Decoding Sentiment from Distributed Representations of Sentences
Edoardo Maria Ponti, Ivan Vulić and Anna Korhonen 22

Detecting Asymmetric Semantic Relations in Context: A Case-Study on Hypernymy Detection
Yogarshi Vyas and Marine Carpuat 33

Domain-Specific New Words Detection in Chinese
Ao Chen and Maosong Sun 44

Deep Learning Models For Multiword Expression Identification
Waseem Gharbieh, Virendrakumar Bhavsar and Paul Cook 54

Emotion Intensities in Tweets
Saif Mohammad and Felipe Bravo-Marquez 65

Deep Active Learning for Dialogue Generation
Nabiha Asghar, Pascal Poupart, Xin Jiang and Hang Li 78

Mapping the Paraphrase Database to WordNet
Anne Cocos, Marianna Apidianaki and Chris Callison-Burch 84

Semantic Frame Labeling with Target-based Neural Model
Yukun Feng, Dong Yu, Jian Xu and Chunhua Liu 91

Frame-Based Continuous Lexical Semantics through Exponential Family Tensor Factorization and Semantic Proto-Roles
Francis Ferraro, Adam Poliak, Ryan Cotterell and Benjamin Van Durme 97

Distributed Prediction of Relations for Entities: The Easy, The Difficult, and The Impossible
Abhijeet Gupta, Gemma Boleda and Sebastian Padó 104

Comparing Approaches for Automatic Question Identification
Angel Maredia, Kara Schechtman, Sarah Ita Levitan and Julia Hirschberg 110

Does Free Word Order Hurt? Assessing the Practical Lexical Function Model for Croatian
Zoran Medić, Jan Šnajder and Sebastian Padó 115

A Mixture Model for Learning Multi-Sense Word Embeddings
Dai Quoc Nguyen, Dat Quoc Nguyen, Ashutosh Modi, Stefan Thater and Manfred Pinkal 121

Aligning Script Events with Narrative Texts
Simon Ostermann, Michael Roth, Stefan Thater and Manfred Pinkal 128

The (too Many) Problems of Analogical Reasoning with Word Vectors
Anna Rogers, Aleksandr Drozd and Bofang Li 135

Semantic Frames and Visual Scenes: Learning Semantic Role Inventories from Image and Video Descriptions
Ekaterina Shutova, Andreas Wundsam and Helen Yannakoudakis.........................149

Acquiring Predicate Paraphrases from News Tweets
Vered Shwartz, Gabriel Stanovsky and Ido Dagan...155

Evaluating Semantic Parsing against a Simple Web-based Question Answering Model
Alon Talmor, Mor Geva and Jonathan Berant...161

Logical Metonymy in a Distributional Model of Sentence Comprehension
Emmanuele Chersoni, Alessandro Lenci and Philippe Blache 168

Double Trouble: The Problem of Construal in Semantic Annotation of Adpositions
Jena D. Hwang, Archna Bhatia, Na-Rae Han, Tim O'Gorman, Vivek Srikumar and Nathan Schneider..178

Issues of Mass and Count: Dealing with 'Dual-Life' Nouns
Tibor Kiss, Francis Jeffry Pelletier, Halima Husic and Johanna Poppek.....................189

Parsing Graphs with Regular Graph Grammars
Sorcha Gilroy, Adam Lopez and Sebastian Maneth...199

Embedded Semantic Lexicon Induction with Joint Global and Local Optimization
Sujay Kumar Jauhar and Eduard Hovy..209

Generating Pattern-Based Entailment Graphs for Relation Extraction
Kathrin Eichler, Feiyu Xu, Hans Uszkoreit and Sebastian Krause.........................220

Classifying Semantic Clause Types: Modeling Context and Genre Characteristics with Recurrent Neural Networks and Attention
Maria Becker, Michael Staniek, Vivi Nastase, Alexis Palmer and Anette Frank...............230

Predictive Linguistic Features of Schizophrenia
Efsun Sarioglu Kayi, Mona Diab, Luca Pauselli, Michael Compton and Glen Coppersmith....241

Learning to Solve Geometry Problems from Natural Language Demonstrations in Textbooks
Mrinmaya Sachan and Eric Xing 251

Ways of Asking and Replying in Duplicate Question Detection
João António Rodrigues, Chakaveh Saedi, Vladislav Maraev, João Silva and António Branco . 262

Conference Program

August 3rd, 2017

9:00–10:30   **Session S1: Invited Talk (Jointly with SemEval) and Best Paper Award**

9:00–9:15   *Opening Remarks*

9:15–10:15   *Invited Talk: From Naive Physics to Connotation: Modeling Commonsense in Frame Semantics*
Yejin Choi

10:15–10:30   *Announcement of the Adam Kilgarriff Best Paper Award*

10:30–11:00   *Coffee Break*

11:00–12:30   **Session S2: Distributional Semantics**

11:00–11:30   *What Analogies Reveal about Word Vectors and their Compositionality*
Gregory Finley, Stephanie Farmer and Serguei Pakhomov

11:30–12:00   *Learning Antonyms with Paraphrases and a Morphology-Aware Neural Network*
Sneha Rajana, Chris Callison-Burch, Marianna Apidianaki and Vered Shwartz

12:00–12:30   *Decoding Sentiment from Distributed Representations of Sentences*
Edoardo Maria Ponti, Ivan Vulić and Anna Korhonen

12:30–14:00   *Lunch Break*

14:00–15:30   Session S3: Lexical Semantics and Lexical Resources

14:00–14:30   *Detecting Asymmetric Semantic Relations in Context: A Case-Study on Hypernymy Detection*
Yogarshi Vyas and Marine Carpuat

14:30–15:00   *Domain-Specific New Words Detection in Chinese*
Ao Chen and Maosong Sun

15:00–15:30   *Deep Learning Models For Multiword Expression Identification*
Waseem Gharbieh, Virendrakumar Bhavsar and Paul Cook

15:30–16:00   *Coffee Break*

16:00–16:30   Session S4: Lexical Semantics and Lexical Resources (continued)

16:00–16:30   *Emotion Intensities in Tweets*
Saif Mohammad and Felipe Bravo-Marquez

16:30–18:00   Session S5: Poster Session

Deep Active Learning for Dialogue Generation
Nabiha Asghar, Pascal Poupart, Xin Jiang and Hang Li

Mapping the Paraphrase Database to WordNet
Anne Cocos, Marianna Apidianaki and Chris Callison-Burch

Semantic Frame Labeling with Target-based Neural Model
Yukun Feng, Dong Yu, Jian Xu and Chunhua Liu

Frame-Based Continuous Lexical Semantics through Exponential Family Tensor Factorization and Semantic Proto-Roles
Francis Ferraro, Adam Poliak, Ryan Cotterell and Benjamin Van Durme

Distributed Prediction of Relations for Entities: The Easy, The Difficult, and The Impossible
Abhijeet Gupta, Gemma Boleda and Sebastian Padó

Comparing Approaches for Automatic Question Identification
Angel Maredia, Kara Schechtman, Sarah Ita Levitan and Julia Hirschberg

Does Free Word Order Hurt? Assessing the Practical Lexical Function Model for Croatian
Zoran Medić, Jan Šnajder and Sebastian Padó

A Mixture Model for Learning Multi-Sense Word Embeddings
Dai Quoc Nguyen, Dat Quoc Nguyen, Ashutosh Modi, Stefan Thater and Manfred Pinkal

Aligning Script Events with Narrative Texts
Simon Ostermann, Michael Roth, Stefan Thater and Manfred Pinkal

The (too Many) Problems of Analogical Reasoning with Word Vectors
Anna Rogers, Aleksandr Drozd and Bofang Li

Semantic Frames and Visual Scenes: Learning Semantic Role Inventories from Image and Video Descriptions
Ekaterina Shutova, Andreas Wundsam and Helen Yannakoudakis

Acquiring Predicate Paraphrases from News Tweets
Vered Shwartz, Gabriel Stanovsky and Ido Dagan

Evaluating Semantic Parsing against a Simple Web-based Question Answering Model
Alon Talmor, Mor Geva and Jonathan Berant

August 4th, 2017

9:00–10:30   **Session S6: Invited Talk and Distributional Semantics**

9:00–10:00   *Invited Talk: What Do You Know About an Alligator When You Know the Company It Keeps?*
Katrin Erk

10:00–10:30   *Logical Metonymy in a Distributional Model of Sentence Comprehension*
Emmanuele Chersoni, Alessandro Lenci and Philippe Blache

10:30–11:00   *Coffee Break*

11:00–12:30   **Session S7: Linguistic and Formal Semantics**

11:00–11:30   *Double Trouble: The Problem of Construal in Semantic Annotation of Adpositions*
Jena D. Hwang, Archna Bhatia, Na-Rae Han, Tim O'Gorman, Vivek Srikumar and Nathan Schneider

11:30–12:00   *Issues of Mass and Count: Dealing with 'Dual-Life' Nouns*
Tibor Kiss, Francis Jeffry Pelletier, Halima Husic and Johanna Poppek

12:00–12:30   *Parsing Graphs with Regular Graph Grammars*
Sorcha Gilroy, Adam Lopez and Sebastian Maneth

12:30–14:00   *Lunch Break*

August 4th, 2017 (continued)

14:00–15:30   **Session S8: Representations of Meaning**

14:00–14:30   *Embedded Semantic Lexicon Induction with Joint Global and Local Optimization*
Sujay Kumar Jauhar and Eduard Hovy

14:30–15:00   *Generating Pattern-Based Entailment Graphs for Relation Extraction*
Kathrin Eichler, Feiyu Xu, Hans Uszkoreit and Sebastian Krause

15:00–15:30   *Classifying Semantic Clause Types: Modeling Context and Genre Characteristics with Recurrent Neural Networks and Attention*
Maria Becker, Michael Staniek, Vivi Nastase, Alexis Palmer and Anette Frank

15:30–16:00   *Coffee Break*

16:00–17:30   **Session S9: Semantics for Applications**

16:00–16:30   *Predictive Linguistic Features of Schizophrenia*
Efsun Sarioglu Kayi, Mona Diab, Luca Pauselli, Michael Compton and Glen Coppersmith

16:30–17:00   *Learning to Solve Geometry Problems from Natural Language Demonstrations in Textbooks*
Mrinmaya Sachan and Eric Xing

17:00–17:30   *Ways of Asking and Replying in Duplicate Question Detection*
João António Rodrigues, Chakaveh Saedi, Vladislav Maraev, João Silva and António Branco

17:30–17:40   *Closing Remarks*

What Analogies Reveal about Word Vectors and their Compositionality

Gregory P. Finley
EMR.AI*
San Francisco, CA
gregpfinley@gmail.com

Stephanie Farmer
Department of Linguistics
Macalester College
Saint Paul, MN
sfarmer@macalester.edu

Serguei V.S. Pakhomov
College of Pharmacy
University of Minnesota
Minneapolis, MN
pakh0002@umn.edu

Abstract

Analogy completion via vector arithmetic has become a common means of demonstrating the compositionality of word embeddings. Previous work have shown that this strategy works more reliably for certain types of analogical word relationships than for others, but these studies have not offered a convincing account for why this is the case. We arrive at such an account through an experiment that targets a wide variety of analogy questions and defines a baseline condition to more accurately measure the efficacy of our system. We find that the most reliably solvable analogy categories involve either 1) the application of a morpheme with clear syntactic effects, 2) male–female alternations, or 3) named entities. These broader types do not pattern cleanly along a syntactic–semantic divide. We suggest instead that their commonality is distributional, in that the difference between the distributions of two words in any given pair encompasses a relatively small number of word types. Our study offers a needed explanation for why analogy tests succeed and fail where they do and provides nuanced insight into the relationship between word distributions and the theoretical linguistic domains of syntax and semantics.

1 Introduction

In recent years, low-dimensional vectors have proven an efficient and fruitful means of representing words for numerous computational applications, from calculating semantic similarity to serving as an early layer in deep learning architectures (Baroni et al., 2014; Schnabel et al., 2015; LeCun et al., 2015). Despite these advances, however, strategies for representing meaning compositionally with a vector model remain limited. Given the difficulties in training representations of composed meaning (for example, most possible phrases will be rare or unattested in training data), achieving an accurate means of building complex lexical or phrasal representations from lower-order ones would be a decisive coup in computational semantics.

Another promising avenue of compositional semantics is the representation of concepts that do not map easily to lexemes. A simple averaging of two vectors may yield a concept that is semantically akin to both, and the arithmetic difference between word vectors has been said to represent the relationship between two terms. The ability to model knowledge unbounded by linguistic labels is an exciting prospect for natural language processing and artificial intelligence more broadly.

A common test of the compositional properties of word vectors is complete-the-analogy questions. Word vector arithmetic has achieved surprisingly high accuracy on this type of task. A flurry of recent studies have applied this test under various conditions, but there has been limited focus on defining precisely what types of relations vectors can capture, and less still on explaining these differences. As such, there remains a major gap in our understanding of distributional semantics. Our original experimental work improves upon prior methods by 1) targeting a wide variety of analogy questions drawn from several available resources and 2) defining a baseline condition to control for differences in "difficulty" between questions. These considerations enable an analysis that constitutes a major step towards a comprehensive, theoretically grounded account for the

---

* This work was done while the first author was a post-doctoral research associate at the University of Minnesota.

1

*Proceedings of the 6th Joint Conference on Lexical and Computational Semantics (*SEM 2017)*, pages 1–11,
Vancouver, Canada, August 3-4, 2017. ©2017 Association for Computational Linguistics

observed phenomena. To begin, however, we present a brief review of the analogy problem as usually posed.

2 Background

Several computational approaches have been proposed for representing the meaning of words (and holistic phrases) in terms of their co-occurrence with other words in large text corpora. Some of these, such as latent semantic analysis (Landauer and Dumais, 1997), focus on developing semantic representations based on theories of human cognition, whereas others, such as random indexing (Kanerva, 2009) and word embeddings (Bengio et al., 2003; Mikolov et al., 2013a) focus more on computational efficiency. Despite differences in purpose and implementation, all current distributional semantic approaches rely on the same basic principle of using similarity between co-occurrence frequency distributions as a way to infer the strength of association between words. For many practical purposes, such as information indexing and retrieval and semantic clustering, these approaches work remarkably well.

There is no obvious best way to compose these types of representations into larger arbitrary linguistic units, although it does seem that certain regularities exist between terms that surface through vector subtraction (Mikolov et al., 2013c; Levy et al., 2014). Why should this be the case? Consider the relationships between a difference vector $w_b - w_a$ and other words in the vocabulary: $w_b - w_a$ will be orthogonal to words that co-occur equally frequently with w_a and w_b, highly similar to words that co-occur only with w_b, and dissimilar (negative) to words that co-occur only with w_a.[1] If a word's context is a fair representation of its meaning, as is the key tenet of the distributional hypothesis, then this vector difference should isolate crucial differences in meaning.

Analogy tasks have been used to test how well vector differences capture consistent semantic differences. Four-word proportional analogies, typically written as $w_1{:}w_2{::}w_3{:}w_4$, feature two pairs of words such that the relationship between w_1 and w_2 is the same as between w_3 and w_4. If these words are represented with vectors, then, it is assumed that the differences between each pair are

roughly equal:

$$w_2 - w_1 \approx w_4 - w_3 \tag{1}$$

In the most popular version of this task, a system is given the first three words in the analogy and asked guess the best candidate for w_4. Solving for w_4,

$$w_4 \approx w_3 + w_2 - w_1 \tag{2}$$

and thus a system selects its hypothesis w_{hyp} from the vocabulary V—typically excluding w_1, w_2 and w_3—by finding the word with maximum angular (cosine) similarity to the hypothesis vector (expressed as vector dot product, assuming all word vectors are unit length):

$$w_{hyp} = \arg\max_{w \in V} \left(w \cdot (w_3 + w_2 - w_1)\right) \tag{3}$$

We call this algorithm 3COSADD following Levy *et al.* (2014). Levy and Goldberg (2014) note that this strategy is equivalent to finding the word in the lexicon that is the best match for w_3 and w_2 while also being most distant from w_1. This reframing suggests that it may not be necessary at all to represent ineffable concepts through intermediate stages of vector composition; 3COSADD could be solving analogies simply through term similarity. Indeed, words in a pair sharing some relation tend to be similar to each other; when they are extremely similar, the difference between w_2 and w_1 is negligible, and the task becomes trivial.

Linzen (2016) makes this observation as well and goes on to demonstrate that accuracy falls to near zero across the board when not excluding w_1, w_2, and w_3 from contention in the hypothesis space, which shows how strongly dependent 3COSADD is upon vector similarity. We agree wholeheartedly with that paper's claim that it is important to measure the consistency of vector differences in a way that is mindful of the typically high similarity between paired terms.

2.1 Analogy Test Sets

Several categorized sets of semantic and syntactic analogies are publicly available. One of the earliest was published by Microsoft Research (Mikolov et al., 2013c) and consists of 16 categories of inflectional morphological relations for English nouns, verbs, and adjectives. The most commonly reported test set, which we refer to as the Google set, is included with the distribution of

---

[1] These assertions are supported by the distributivity of a dot product, which is the standard calculation for similarity, over addition: $w_x \cdot (w_b - w_a) = w_x \cdot w_b - w_x \cdot w_a$.

the word2vec tool (Mikolov et al., 2013a). The Google set comprises 14 categories, mostly involving inflectional or geographical relationships between terms. Categories are grouped into a "semantic" and a "syntactic" subset, and results are often reported averaged over each rather than by category. This practice is rather problematic in our view, as the syntactic/semantic division is quite coarse and even questionable in some cases. We explore the relationship between syntax, semantics, and morphology in detail later on.

The "Better Analogy Test Set" (BATS) is a large set developed to contain a balanced sampling of a wide range of categories (Gladkova et al., 2016). BATS features 40 categories of 50 word pairs each, covering inflectional and derivational morphology as well as several semantic relations.

The relational similarity task in SemEval-2012 featured relations between word pairs targeting a massive range of lexical semantic relationships (Jurgens et al., 2012). By drawing on the aggregated results of the task's participants, we have extracted highly representative pairs for each relation to build an analogy set.

2.2 Accounting for Analogy Performance

In addition to those already cited, numerous other recent papers have evaluated word embeddings by benchmarking on analogy questions (Mikolov et al., 2013b; Garten et al., 2015; Lofi et al., 2016). There is some consensus regarding performance across question types: systems do well on questions of inflectional morphology (especially so for English (Nicolai et al., 2015)), but far less reliably so for various non-geographical semantic questions—although some gains in performance are possible by adjusting the embedding algorithms used or their hyperparameters (Levy et al., 2015), or by training further on subproblems (Drozd et al., 2016).

Amongst all of these findings, however, we found lacking a cohesive, thorough, and satisfying account of why vector arithmetic works where it does to solve analogies. To that end, we conducted an experiment to arrive at such an explanation, with some notable departures from previously used methods. We included a wide range of available test data, which is key because individual sets usually feature some bias towards one type or a few types of question, and benchmarkers often report nothing more than accuracy averaged over an entire set (Schnabel et al., 2015). Additionally, we define a baseline, which is critical not only to gauge effectiveness, but also to understand the mechanism behind solving analogies using compositional methods.

In the following sections we present the design of the experiment, baseline condition, and question sets; a discussion of how performance on analogy questions breaks down by broad category; and finally, a theoretical accounting for the observed patterns and the implications for distributional semantics.

3 Method

3.1 Word Embeddings

We used word embeddings trained on the plain text of all articles from Wikipedia as of September 2015, processed to remove all punctuation and case distinctions. We tested the word2vec and GloVe (Pennington et al., 2014) training algorithms. Results were qualitatively very similar between the two, although word2vec scored slightly higher on our metrics. Due to space considerations, we discuss only the word2vec results.

Hyperparameters were set as recommended for analogy tasks by the developers: 200-dimensional vectors, continuous bag-of-words sampling, 8-word window size. (We also tested a skip-gram model in word2vec and saw only slight and occasional differences—more subtle even than those seen between word2vec and GloVe.)

3.2 Test Set

We used a pooled set of analogy questions comprising the Google, Microsoft, SemEval 2012, and BATS test sets. At test time, any analogies that featured a word absent from our lexicon were discarded. (Note that the Microsoft categories testing the English possessive enclitic 's were not tested, as preprocessing for our vector training corpus removed all punctuation.) The sizes of each set following the removal of out-of-vocabulary analogies are given in Table 1.

Note that the BATS and SemEval data sets feature a number of word pairs in each category but not four-word analogy questions. We simply took every possible pair of pairs from the same category, so long as this did not result in an analogy in which w_1 and w_2 were the same word or in which w_4 was not unique. Some pairs in BATS have more than one correct answer; for uniformity

Source	Categories	Analogies
Microsoft Research	14	7,000
Google (word2vec)	14	19,544
SemEval2012	79	30,082
BATS	40	95,625
Total	**147**	**152,251**

Table 1: Summary of test data sources.

with other test sets, we use only the first answer provided for each of these pairs.

For SemEval, we used the "platinum standard" data distribution, which includes rankings of word pairs in each category based on how well they represent the relationship as defined. We took only the best half of pairs from that ranking to generate the test set. This was necessary because pairs lower down the list tend to poorly represent the relationship, or even to represent its opposite.

3.3 Measures

Virtually all existing studies of automated analogy solving report accuracy as the main measure. Accuracy is indeed a relevant measure when the goal is to simulate human performance on a particular task. Our purpose, however, is to understand the nature of semantic representations and account for when vector arithmetic does and does not function well as a model of relationships.

For every analogy question, we calculate the ranking of the correct w_4 in the hypothesis space—that is, the ordering of all words in the lexicon in descending order of the result of the 3CosAdd hypothesis function (3). A "correct" answer would correspond to a ranking of 1.

Accuracy is a coarse measure in that it is insensitive to any ranking other than 1. Rather than accuracy, we borrow a measure from information retrieval (Voorhees, 1999)—the reciprocal of rank (RR) averaged across analogy questions in each category, which is always a positive fraction in the range:

$$\frac{1}{||V||} \leq RR \leq 1 \qquad (4)$$

Numerically, RR acts as a "softer" version of accuracy, with rankings other than 1 contributing somewhat to the average.

Besides being coarse, accuracy is also an uncontrolled measure in that it is insensitive to differences in analogy "difficulty," by which we mean the prior degree of similarity between sin-

gle word vectors. An example: nominal plural analogies, such as *dog:dogs::horse:horses*, often achieve high accuracy, but this may follow naturally from the high similarity between most singular nouns and their plural forms—indeed, for both of these pairs, the singular and plural forms are the closest terms to each other in our trained vector space.

To measure the efficacy of vector arithmetic in a manner controlled for variances in prior vector similarity, we propose a baseline, defined for each analogy as the best ranking between the word most similar to w_2 and the word most similar to w_3:

$$rank_{base} = \min(rank(\arg\max_{w \in V}(w \cdot w_2)),$$
$$rank(\arg\max_{w \in V}(w \cdot w_3))) \qquad (5)$$

For the above example, as *dog* is the most similar word to *dogs*, there is no improvement to be made upon baseline. Likewise, for the analogy *banana:yellow::sky:blue*, baseline would likely be high because *yellow* and *blue* are very similar.

Consistent with reporting RR for 3CosAdd, we report baseline reciprocal rank (BRR). We suspect that using RR will be especially illustrative for baseline, where there may be many "near misses" that are informative but would all be reduced to zero if measuring only accuracy.

Our baseline is similar to the so-called Only-B baseline tested by Linzen (2016), except that the latter considers only w_3. We include w_2 because this term has just as much effect on the 3CosAdd hypothesis as w_3. Note that our baseline would not itself be implementable as a solving strategy because it presumes access to w_4 to select between w_2 and w_3; nevertheless, we contend that it is helpful to define the baseline as we have done to account for those categories in the test data where all w_2 and w_4 are drawn from a small semantic cluster—most notably, the color example in the previous paragraph. (Overall, 16–18% of analogies across our test sets show similarity to w_2 as a better baseline than to w_3.)

Improvement is defined as the difference between 3CosAdd RR and baseline RR, a measure we will refer to as reciprocal rank gain (RRG). RRG is more sensitive to shifts in rank that might not result in perfect accuracy. Analogies that show improvement from a very poor rank to first place will show a gain of nearly 1, whereas moving from second to first place is only 0.5 (and moving from poor rank to second is nearly 0.5). If 3COSADD yields a worse hypothesis, this will be reflected as a negative RRG.

We also tested other solving methods suggested by Levy and Goldberg (Levy et al., 2014), 3COS-MUL and PAIRDIRECTION, although we do not report them here—results with the former were virtually indistinguishable from 3COSADD, and poorer overall with the latter.

The raw results of our similarity experiments, as well as source code to replicate all steps of the experiments and analysis, can be downloaded at `https://github.com/gpfinley/analogies`.

4 Results

Most broadly, we confirm prior findings that vector arithmetic can be used to solve analogy questions, with a mean RRG of .165 across all questions in all categories ($t = 187$, $p \ll .01$). For a more nuanced analysis, we sorted analogy tests into four broad supercategories of analogical relationship: 30 categories of inflectional morphology, 12 of derivational morphology, 10 of named entities, and 95 of semantics of non-named entities (79 of which are from SemEval).

The gain in RR from baseline for all categories is presented visually in Figure 1, where they are grouped into our four supercategories for ease of interpretation. (See the appendix for the names of the top performing categories.) Each individual category is represented by a line between its BRR and 3COSADD RR. Within each supercategory, we also consider intermediate groupings of categories, and these are visualized by differences in line stroke in the figure. Note that some patterns are evident between and within supercategories:

- **Inflectional:** Although all inflectional categories show positive RRG, adjectival and verbal inflection shows reliably higher RRG than nominal inflection.

- **Derivational:** Derivational morphemes whose primary function is to shift syntactic class (*-tion*, *-ment*, *-ly*, *-ness*) show on average higher RRG than those with stronger regular semantic consequences (*-less*, *-able*, *over-*, adjectival *un-*, repetitive *re-*, agentive *-er*).

- **Named entities:** All categories—and particularly those dealing with country capitals—show high RRG.

- **Lexical:** Analogy relationships based on gender difference exhibit high RRG, while most other categories have low or even negative RRG.

We performed a linear regression analysis to predict RRG as a function of supercategory ($F = 24600$, $p \ll .01$, $R^2 = .39$). The model is summarized in Table 4. (Note that the model contains no intercept term, so the coefficient for each supercategory is equivalent to its mean RRG.) A positive RRG can be demonstrated with high statistical significance for all supercategories except lexical semantics.

We also investigated possible effects of word frequency on analogy performance. Multicollinearity poses a major challenge here: the frequencies of all four words in an analogy are highly correlated, and frequency can change dramatically across category. A comprehensive analysis of this complex problem is beyond the scope of this study, although we did find that the difference between an analogy's w_4 frequency and the mean w_4 frequency in that category correlates positively with RRG, although this effect is subtle ($r = .016$, $t = 6.28$, $p \ll .01$).

5 Discussion

It is clear from our results that vector arithmetic is a better approach for certain types of analogy questions than for others. Almost as clear is the hierarchy of the four broad types of questions that we have defined: excellent performance for inflection and named entities, with decidedly mixed results for derivational morphology and poorer still for lexical semantics—with the notable exception of male–female analogies. Below, we account for these patterns in the context of two domains of linguistic theory: the interaction between morphology and syntax, and the type-theoretic difference between individuals and sets.

5.1 Morphology and Syntax

Verbal and adjectival inflection show much more improvement over baseline than nominal inflection. It may simply be that the nominal categories have too high a baseline value to show much evidence of improvement by 3COSADD. It is also possible, however, that the nominal plural has fewer syntactic implications than verbal and adjectival morphology: nouns in non-subject position do not participate in number agreement in

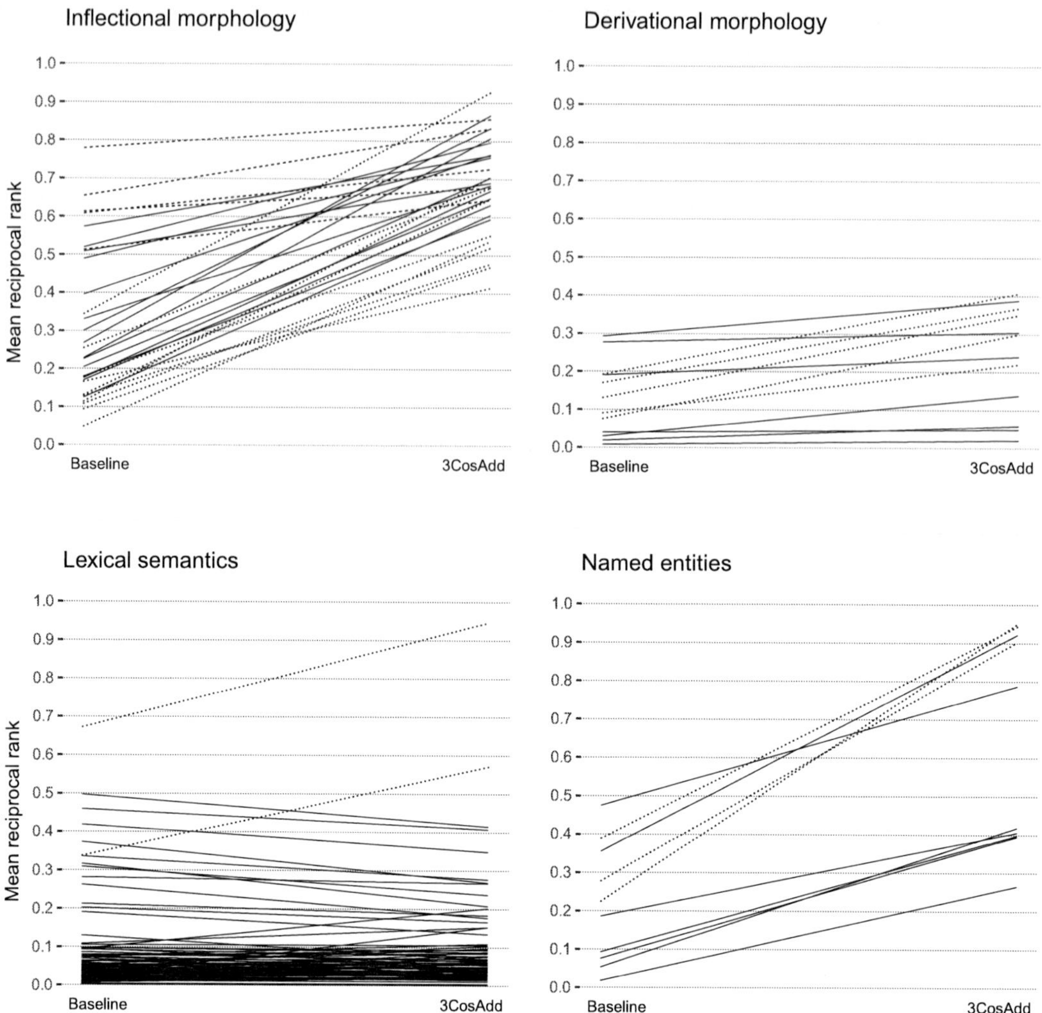

Figure 1: Mean reciprocal rank shifts between baseline and 3CosAdd for four supercategories. Each line is a single category of analogy questions ("country - capital" or "male - female," for example). Some lines are differentiated by stroke type (dotted, solid, or dashed), the meaning of which is idiosyncratic to each supercategory: for inflectional, dashed lines are for nouns, dotted lines for adjectives, and solid lines for verbs; for derivational, dotted lines are for morphemes that change syntactic class with minimal semantic impact (e.g., *-ly*, as opposed to *re-*); for named entities, dotted lines are for country capitals; for lexical semantics, dotted lines are for gender relationships. Within supercategory, the difference in RRG between categories of different stroke types is significant in every case ($|t|$ between 14.5 and 58.7, $p \ll .01$).

English, so the plurality of many nouns in a text has little syntactic consequence.

Derivational morphology might be expected to perform worse than inflectional morphology for a number of reasons. Even for highly productive morphemes, derivation tends to have more id-iosyncratic meaning (Haspelmath and Sims, 2010, 100). For example, although 'recruitment' refers to the act of recruiting, 'government' refers to a governing body rather than the act of governing; similarly, the adverb 'sadly' can be used as a sentential adverb (expressing the speaker's attitude

SUPERCATEGORY	ESTIMATE	STD ERROR	t
Inflectional	.345	.0015	228 ***
Derivational	.106	.0018	57.7 ***
Lexical semantics	−.000	.0012	−0.293
Named entities	.420	.0020	207 ***

Table 2: Summary of regression model for reciprocal rank gain as a function of analogy supercategory. All starred levels are highly significant ($p \ll .01$).

about the statement) as well as a manner adverb, whereas 'angrily' cannot. These semantic characteristics introduce lexically dependent variance that is far less pronounced for inflection.

From our results with derivational sets, there is evidence of a trend in which morphemes with predominantly syntactic consequences are better handled than those with stronger semantic consequences (see dotted/solid lines in Figure 1). Significant further experimental work is needed to quantify the syntactic versus semantic effects of derivational morphemes.

We predict that such work would support the notion of a continuum between morphemes with only syntactic effects and those with only (lexically) semantic effects. Those towards the syntactic end of the continuum will tend to be better captured by vector offsets in distributional representations. There would be a partial overlap between this continuum and the inflectional–derivational continuum in that derivational morphology tends to have more idiosyncratic meanings and is less relevant to syntax. There would be differences as well, especially as regards the property that word class-changing morphology is more derivational: the repetitive *re-* in English, for example, may be considered less derivational than the deverbal nominalizer *-ment* because it does not change word class, but *re-* has virtually no syntactic consequences for the verb to which it affixes.

5.2 Semantics: Named Entities as Individuals

Our results show that analogy sets containing named entities are more readily solvable than those that contain other lexical categories (common nouns, verbs, etc.).

A possible explanation for this is that named entities have a single real-world referent—there is, for instance, only one Amsterdam—while there is a large set of real-world referents that correspond to a common noun like 'dog'. We would expect the co-occurrences of 'dog', then, to be more diverse than those of a named entity like 'Amsterdam'.

The distinction drawn here between named entities and other parts of speech is analogous to the distinction between words of type e ("individuals") and words of type $\langle e, t \rangle$ in Montagovian set-theoretic semantics (Montague, 1973). According to Montague, proper names (arguments of type e) denote *individuals*, while verbs and common nouns (predicates of type $\langle e, t \rangle$) denote *sets* of individuals. Thus, 'Amsterdam' denotes an individual, while 'dog' denotes the set of dogs.

To better appreciate how this distinction might lead to "fuzzier" representations for some words, consider that training a vector on separate references to numerous members of a set of individuals is akin to a massive case of pseudo-polysemy—the vector can only capture the average of all referents rather than a single, clear referent. Polysemy is a well-known problem in training word vectors (Reisinger and Mooney, 2010), although this case of multiple referents has not been considered before to our knowledge.

Overall, named entity categories show very good RRG results, especially when both terms in a pair are named entities (as opposed to 'name - occupation', say). Country capitals show excellent performance in particular. In the broader history of this line of reserach, it is worth noting that the composition of the Google test set plays to this strength: country capital questions constitute over a quarter of its analogies (and over half of those in the "semantic" set, as noted by Gladkova *et al.* (2016)). As our experiments and others have demonstrated, however, the vector arithmetic approach struggles for most semantic questions.

Given the enormous influence of word2vec, it is worth asking whether prevailing knowledge in this field has been influenced by a selective focus on easier tasks. As further illustration of this point, note that the classic go-to example, *king:queen::man:woman*, is drawn from the sole category in lexical semantics with any clear positive result in our experiments.

As a matter of fact, we should address the exceptional performance on analogies in male–female categories; why, of all lexical semantic sets, do we see such high performance here? We suspect these categories does well for the same reason that inflectional analogies do well: English features gender agreement with some personal pronouns—and, of course, with coreferential gendered terms—so there are concrete and regular distributional consequences of a noun's semantic gender.

5.3 A Unified Account

A recurrent thread in our accounting for all categories is that 3CosAdd does well with relationships that have predictable effects on distribution—i.e., nearby terms and their morphology and syntax (although all morphology is effectively suppletive for these embeddings). This is especially evident with inflectional morphology, and true as well for certain types of derivational morphology as well as classes that participate in agreement, such as gender.

Relations between named entities are not governed by syntactic differences as inflectional relationships are, but there is a certain *distributional* parallel between the two: terms with a single referent will generally exhibit a less blurred co-occurrence profile than those with multiple referents; similarly, the difference between two realizations of the same root (e.g. 'hot' and 'hotter') will be highly non-orthogonal primarily with words of syntactic relevance, which is also a small set. The common theme is clear: the smaller the set of unique word types that co-occur with either word 1 or word 2 but not both (i.e.,the symmetric difference), the more cleanly the relationship between word 1 and word 2 can be captured.

Recall that our results also suggest that analogy questions containing frequent words are easier to solve with vector arithmetic than those containing less frequent words. We suspect that this is because the distributional representations of frequent words are more robust and less noisy. We believe, however, that more targeted investigation into the effects of frequency might qualify this generalization. For instance, it is reasonable to assume that a word's frequency correlates with the diversity of its co-occurrence, and that this diversity could

signal distinct word senses, which are notoriously tricky for distributional representations. This is a ripe topic for further study.

5.4 Challenges

One challenge in interpreting our results is that categories with seemingly identical relations can show marked discrepancies in performance: note the differences between Google 'comparative' and Microsoft 'JJ_JJR', which examine the same inflectional relationship but show rather different levels of performance. Similarly, note the extreme difference in baseline rank for Google 'gender' (called 'family' in the original set) and BATS 'male - female' categories. Clearly, lexical choices make a significant difference and can even overshadow the inter-category differences that we are trying to measure. Note that in both of the above examples, the version of the category featuring more unique word types showed lower baseline *and* lower gain.

The explanations we put forward here may need to be extended to address other types of relationships that we did not evaluate. One particular interesting example might be Linzen *et al.*'s (2016) tests of analogies between quantifiers across domains—e.g., *everything:nothing::always:never*—which show intriguingly mixed results.

6 Conclusion

We evaluated syntactic and semantic analogy questions from a large and highly diverse test set using metrics more controlled and more sensitive than accuracy. Inspecting the results across categories, we were able to account for the differences in performance we observed across types of word relationships in terms that are consistent with the distributional training objectives of word embeddings.

Vector arithmetic with word embeddings is most effective when co-occurrence are limited to a small number of words, either by syntactic regularities or ease of semantic representation. It is possible to account for both of these by considering distributional phenomena directly.

Still, questions remain—do our negative results reflect the failure of word vectors to model semantic nuances, or the failure of vector arithmetic to capture them, or is the semantic data simply too noisy for current methods? Further experiments with special attention paid to smoothing lexical semantic representations will be key to solving this problem.

Acknowledgments

This work was partially supported by a University of Minnesota Academic Health Center Faculty Development Award and by the National Institute of General Medical Sciences (GM102282).

References

Marco Baroni, Georgiana Dinu, and German Kruszewski. 2014. Dont count, predict! a systematic comparison of context-counting vs. context-predicting semantic vectors. In *Proceedings of the ACL*. pages 238–247.

Yoshua Bengio, Réjean Ducharme, Pascal Vincent, and Christian Jauvin. 2003. A neural probabilistic language model. *Journal of Machine Learning Research* 3(Feb):1137–1155.

Aleksandr Drozd, Anna Gladkova, and Satoshi Matsuoka. 2016. Word embeddings, analogies, and machine learning: Beyond king − man + woman = queen. In *Proceedings of COLING 2016, the 26th International Conference on Computational Linguistics*. pages 3519–3530.

Justin Garten, Kenji Sagae, Volkan Ustun, and Morteza Dehghani. 2015. Combining distributed vector representations for words. In *Proceedings of NAACL-HLT*. pages 95–101.

Anna Gladkova, Aleksandr Drozd, and Satoshi Matsuoka. 2016. Analogy-based detection of morphological and semantic relations with word embeddings: what works and what doesnt. In *Proceedings of NAACL-HLT*. pages 8–15.

Martin Haspelmath and Andrea Sims. 2010. *Understanding Morphology*. Routledge.

David A Jurgens, Peter D Turney, Saif M Mohammad, and Keith J Holyoak. 2012. Semeval-2012 task 2: Measuring degrees of relational similarity. In *Proceedings of the First Joint Conference on Lexical and Computational Semantics (*SEM)*. pages 356–364.

Pentti Kanerva. 2009. Hyperdimensional computing: An introduction to computing in distributed representation with high-dimensional random vectors. *Cognitive Computation* 1(2):139–159.

Thomas K Landauer and Susan T Dumais. 1997. A solution to plato's problem: The latent semantic analysis theory of acquisition, induction, and representation of knowledge. *Psychological review* 104(2):211.

Yann LeCun, Yoshua Bengio, and Geoffrey Hinton. 2015. Deep learning. *Nature* 521(7553):436–444.

Omer Levy and Yoav Goldberg. 2014. Neural word embedding as implicit matrix factorization. In Z. Ghahramani, M. Welling, C. Cortes, N. D. Lawrence, and K. Q. Weinberger, editors, *Advances in Neural Information Processing Systems 27*, Curran Associates, Inc., pages 2177–2185.

Omer Levy, Yoav Goldberg, and Ido Dagan. 2015. Improving distributional similarity with lessons learned from word embeddings. *Transactions of the Association for Computational Linguistics* 3:211–225.

Omer Levy, Yoav Goldberg, and Israel Ramat-Gan. 2014. Linguistic regularities in sparse and explicit word representations. In *Proceedings of CoNLL*. pages 171–180.

Tal Linzen. 2016. Issues in evaluating semantic spaces using word analogies. In *Proceedings of the 1st Workshop on Evaluating Vector Space Representations for NLP*.

Tal Linzen, Emmanuel Dupoux, and Benjamin Spector. 2016. Quantificational features in distributional word representations. In *Proceedings of the Fifth Joint Conference on Lexical and Computational Semantics (*SEM)*. pages 1–11.

Christoph Lofi, Athiq Ahamed, Pratima Kulkarni, and Ravi Thakkar. 2016. Benchmarking semantic capabilities of analogy querying algorithms. In *Database Systems for Advanced Applications*. Springer, pages 463–478.

Tomas Mikolov, Kai Chen, Greg Corrado, and Jeffrey Dean. 2013a. Efficient estimation of word representations in vector space.

Tomas Mikolov, Ilya Sutskever, Kai Chen, Greg S Corrado, and Jeff Dean. 2013b. Distributed representations of words and phrases and their compositionality. In C. J. C. Burges, L. Bottou, M. Welling, Z. Ghahramani, and K. Q. Weinberger, editors, *Advances in Neural Information Processing Systems 26*, Curran Associates, Inc., pages 3111–3119.

Tomas Mikolov, Wen-tau Yih, and Geoffrey Zweig. 2013c. Linguistic regularities in continuous space word representations. In *Proceedings of NAACL*. pages 746–751.

Richard Montague. 1973. The proper treatment of quantification in ordinary English. In K. J. J. Hintikka, M. E. Moravcsik, and P. Suppes, editors, *Approaches to Natural Language: Proceedings of the 1970 Stanford Workshop on Grammar and Semantics*, Dordrecht.

Garrett Nicolai, Colin Cherry, and Grzegorz Kondrak. 2015. Morpho-syntactic regularities in continuous word representations: A multilingual study. In *Proceedings of NAACL*. pages 129–134.

Jeffrey Pennington, Richard Socher, and Christopher D Manning. 2014. Glove: Global vectors for word representation. In *Proceedings of EMNLP*. volume 14, pages 1532–1543.

Joseph Reisinger and Raymond J Mooney. 2010. Multi-prototype vector-space models of word meaning. In *Proceedings of NAACL*. pages 109–117.

Tobias Schnabel, Igor Labutov, David Mimno, and Thorsten Joachims. 2015. Evaluation methods for unsupervised word embeddings. In *Proceedings of EMNLP*.

Ellen M Voorhees. 1999. The trec-8 question answering track report. In *NIST Special Publication 500-246: The Eighth Text REtrieval Conference*. pages 77–82.

Appendix: Mean Rank by Category

CATEGORY	RR	CATEGORY	BRR	CATEGORY	RRG
G:capital	.950	G:plural	.711	**G:capital**	.750
G:capital-all	.945	noun - plural_reg	.674	**country - capital**	.659
G:gender	.933	*G:gender*	.618	verb_inf - 3pSg	.604
G:nationality-adj	.917	noun - plural_irreg	.603	G:superlative	.600
country - capital	.909	NN_NNS	.596	**G:capital-all**	.584
G:comparative	.896	G:pres-participle	.566	VBZ_VB	.580
verb_inf - 3pSg	.843	*X is opp. dir. from Y*	.535	G:comparative	.578
G:plural	.841	verb_inf - Ving	.496	VB_VBZ	.573
noun - plural_reg	.835	**G:city-in-state**	.486	**G:nationality-adj**	.548
VB_VBZ	.818	NNS_NN	.484	JJS_JJR	.536
verb_inf - Ving	.783	verb_Ving - Ved	.478	JJR_JJS	.496
VBZ_VB	.781	G:past-tense	.463	VBD_VB	.470
G:city-in-state	.774	*X, Y same category*	.462	VBD_VBZ	.469
G:pres-participle	.755	*antonyms - binary*	.436	VBZ_VBD	.465
G:plural-verbs	.752	G:plural-verbs	.371	verb_inf - Ved	.465
G:past-tense	.739	**G:nationality-adj**	.369	VB_VBD	.443
G:superlative	.713	**G:capital-all**	.361	JJ_JJR	.443
NN_NNS	.710	*things - color*	.340	JJ_JJS	.426
VBD_VB	.677	verb_Ving - 3pSg	.336	adj - comparative	.422
verb_Ving - Ved	.670	*can't X and Y at same time*	.320	verb_3pSg - Ved	.400
noun - plural_irreg	.662	G:comparative	.317	G:plural-verbs	.381
verb_Ving - 3pSg	.661	*male - female*	.317	adj - superlative	.373
JJ_JJR	.659	*antonyms - gradable*	.306	**name - occupation**	.340
JJS_JJR	.653	*G:opposite*	.292	verb_Ving - 3pSg	.325
NNS_NN	.626	*X, Y two kinds in category*	.283	JJR_JJ	.321
VBD_VBZ	.623	*X and Y are contrary*	.279	*G:gender*	.316
VB_VBD	.621	*un+adj_reg*	.268	**name - nationality**	.312
verb_inf - Ved	.604	**country - capital**	.250	**G:city-in-state**	.288
VBZ_VBD	.571	*X, Y similar type of thing*	.245	verb_inf - Ving	.287
adj - comparative	.570	VB_VBZ	.245	**country - language**	.278
male - female	.557	verb_inf - 3pSg	.239	G:past-tense	.276
verb_3pSg - Ved	.553	*X will become Y*	.239	**G:currency**	.246
JJR_JJS	.543	JJ_JJR	.217	*male - female*	.240
JJ_JJS	.520	*G:adj-to-adverb*	.208	*verb+tion_irreg*	.240
adj - superlative	.468	VBD_VB	.207	*verb+ment_irreg*	.231
JJR_JJ	.437	*re+verb_reg*	.207	JJS_JJ	.228
X is opp. dir. from Y	.421	VBZ_VB	.201	**UK_city - county**	.219
G:adj-to-adverb	.402	**G:capital**	.200	*G:adj-to-adverb*	.195
name - occupation	.389	*synonyms - exact*	.199	*adj+ly_reg*	.192
JJS_JJ	.376	VB_VBD	.178	verb_Ving - Ved	.192
⋮		⋮		⋮	

Table 3: The top 40 categories for reciprocal rank using 3COSADD (RR), baseline reciprocal rank (BRR), and reciprocal rank gain (RRG = RR − BRR) as calculated from embeddings trained on Wikipedia text using word2vec. Categories based on inflectional morphology are in plain text, derivational morphology in *italics*, named entity semantics in **bold**, and lexical in ***bold italic***. Sources for analogy questions can be identified from category names: those starting with 'G:' are from the Google set; in all capital letters, the Microsoft set; with reference to 'X' and 'Y', the SemEval set; all others, BATS. Some category names are abbreviated from their original names.

Learning Antonyms with Paraphrases
and a Morphology-Aware Neural Network

Sneha Rajana[*] Chris Callison-Burch[*] Marianna Apidianaki[*Ψ] Vered Shwartz[Φ]
[*]Computer and Information Science Department, University of Pennsylvania, USA
[Ψ]LIMSI, CNRS, Université Paris-Saclay, 91403 Orsay
[Φ]Computer Science Department, Bar-Ilan University, Israel
`{srajana,ccb,marapi}@seas.upenn.edu` `vered1986@gmail.com`

Abstract

Recognizing and distinguishing antonyms from other types of semantic relations is an essential part of language understanding systems. In this paper, we present a novel method for deriving antonym pairs using paraphrase pairs containing negation markers. We further propose a neural network model, *AntNET*, that integrates morphological features indicative of antonymy into a path-based relation detection algorithm. We demonstrate that our model outperforms state-of-the-art models in distinguishing antonyms from other semantic relations and is capable of efficiently handling multi-word expressions.

1 Introduction

Identifying antonymy and expressions with contrasting meanings is valuable for NLP systems which go beyond recognizing semantic relatedness and require to identify specific semantic relations. While manually created semantic taxonomies, like WordNet (Fellbaum, 1998), define antonymy relations between some word pairs that native speakers consider antonyms, they have limited coverage. Further, as each term of an antonymous pair can have many semantically close terms, the contrasting word pairs far outnumber those that are commonly considered antonym pairs, and they remain unrecorded. Therefore, automated methods have been proposed to determine for a given term-pair (x, y), whether x and y are antonyms of each other, based on their occurrences in a large corpus.

Charles and Miller (1989) put forward the co-occurrence hypothesis that antonyms occur together in a sentence more often than chance. However, non-antonymous semantically related words

Paraphrase Pair	Antonym Pair
not sufficient/insufficient	sufficient/insufficient
insignificant/negligible	significant/negligible
dishonest/lying	honest/lying
unusual/pretty strange	usual/pretty strange

Table 1: Examples of antonyms derived from PPDB paraphrases. The antonym pairs in column 2 were derived from the corresponding paraphrase pairs in column 1.

such as hypernyms, holonyms, meronyms, and near-synonyms also tend to occur together more often than chance. Thus, separating antonyms from pairs linked by other relationships has proven to be difficult. Approaches to antonym detection have exploited distributional vector representations relying on the distributional hypothesis of semantic similarity (Harris, 1954; Firth, 1957) that words co-occurring in similar contexts tend to be semantically close. Two main information sources are used to recognize semantic relations: path-based and distributional. Path-based methods consider the *joint* occurrences of the two terms in a given sentence and use the dependency paths that connect the terms as features (Hearst, 1992; Roth and Schulte im Walde, 2014; Schwartz et al., 2015). For distinguishing antonyms from other relations, Lin et al. (2003) proposed to use antonym patterns (such as *either X or Y* and *from X to Y*). Distributional methods are based on the *disjoint* occurrences of each term and have recently become popular using word embeddings (Mikolov et al., 2013; Pennington et al., 2014) which provide a distributional representation for each term. Recently, combined path-based and distributional methods for relation detection have also been proposed (Shwartz et al., 2016; Nguyen et al., 2017). They showed that a good path representa-

*Proceedings of the 6th Joint Conference on Lexical and Computational Semantics (*SEM 2017)*, pages 12–21,
Vancouver, Canada, August 3-4, 2017. ©2017 Association for Computational Linguistics

tion can provide substantial complementary information to the distributional signal for distinguishing between different semantic relations.

While antonymy applies to expressions that represent **contrasting** meanings, paraphrases are phrases expressing the **same** meaning, which usually occur in similar textual contexts (Barzilay and McKeown, 2001) or have common translations in other languages (Bannard and Callison-Burch, 2005). Specifically, if two words or phrases are paraphrases, they are unlikely to be antonyms of each other. Our first approach to antonym detection exploits this fact and uses paraphrases for detecting and generating antonyms (*The dementors caught Sirius Black/ Black could not escape the dementors*). We start by focusing on phrase pairs that are most salient for deriving antonyms. Our assumption is that phrases (or words) containing negating words (or prefixes) are more helpful for identifying opposing relationships between term-pairs. For example, from the paraphrase pair (caught/*not* escape), we can derive the antonym pair (caught/escape) by just removing the negating word 'not'.

Our second method is inspired by the recent success of deep learning methods for relation detection. Shwartz et al. (2016) proposed an integrated path-based and distributional model to improve hypernymy detection between term-pairs, and later extended it to classify multiple semantic relations (Shwartz and Dagan, 2016) (LexNET). Although LexNET was the best performing system in the semantic relation classification task of the CogALex 2016 shared task, the model performed poorly on synonyms and antonyms compared to other relations. The path-based component is weak in recognizing synonyms, which do not tend to co-occur, and the distributional information caused confusion between synonyms and antonyms, since both tend to occur in the same contexts. We propose *AntNET*, a novel extension of LexNET that integrates information about negating prefixes as a new morphological pattern feature and is able to distinguish antonyms from other semantic relations. In addition, we optimize the vector representations of dependency paths between the given term pair, encoded using a neural network, by replacing the embeddings of words with negating prefixes by the embeddings of the base, non-negated, forms of the words. For example, for the term pair *unhappy/joyful*,

we record the negating prefix of ***unhappy*** using a new path feature and replace the word embedding of *unhappy* with *happy* in the vector representation of the dependency path between *unhappy* and *sad*. The proposed model improves the path embeddings to better distinguish antonyms from other semantic relations and gets higher performance than prior path-based methods on this task. We used the antonym pairs extracted from the Paraphrase Database (PPDB) (Ganitkevitch et al., 2013; Pavlick et al., 2015b) in the paraphrase-based method as training data for our neural network model.

The main contributions of this paper are:

- We present a novel technique of using paraphrases for antonym detection and successfully derive antonym pairs from paraphrases in the PPDB, the largest paraphrase resource currently available.

- We demonstrate improvements to an integrated path-based and distributional model, showing that our morphology-aware neural network model, AntNET, performs better than state-of-the-art methods for antonym detection.

2 Related Work

Paraphrase Extraction Methods Paraphrases are words or phrases expressing the same meaning. Paraphrase extraction methods that exploit distributional or translation similarity might however propose paraphrase pairs that are not meaning equivalent but linked by other types of relations. These methods often extract pairs having a related but not equivalent meaning, such as contradictory pairs. For instance, Lin and Pantel (2001) extracted 12 million "inference rules" from monolingual text by exploiting shared dependency contexts. Their method learns paraphrases that are truly meaning equivalent, but it just as readily learns contradictory pairs such as *(X rises, X falls)*. Ganitkevitch et al. (2013) extract over 150 million paraphrase rules from parallel corpora by pivoting through foreign translations. This multilingual paraphrasing method often learns hypernym/hyponym pairs, due to variation in the discourse structure of translations, and unrelated pairs due to misalignments or polysemy in the foreign language. Pavlick et al. (2015a) added interpretable semantics to PPDB (see Section 3.1 for

Method	#pairs
(x,y) from paraphrase ($\tilde{x}$,y)/(x,$\tilde{y}$)	80,669
(x, paraphrase(y)), (paraphrase(x), y)	81,221
(x, synset(y)), (synset(x), y)	692,231

Table 2: Number of unique antonym pairs derived from PPDB at each step. Paraphrases and synsets were obtained from PPDB and WordNet respectively.

Source	#pairs
WordNet	18,306
PPDB	773,452

Table 3: Number of unique antonym pairs derived from different sources. The number of pairs obtained from PPDB far outnumbers the antonym pairs present in EVALution and WordNet.

details) and showed that paraphrases in this resource represent a variety of relations other than equivalence, including contradictory pairs like *nobody/someone* and *close/open*.

Pattern-based Methods Pattern-based methods for inducing semantic relations between a pair of terms (x, y) consider the lexico-syntactic paths that connect the joint occurrences of x and y in a large corpus. A variety of approaches have been proposed that rely on patterns between terms in a corpus to distinguish antonyms from other relations. Lin et al. (2003) used translation information and lexico-syntactic patterns to extract distributionally similar words, and then filtered out words that appeared with the patterns 'from X to Y' or 'either X or Y' significantly often. The intuition behind this was that if two words X and Y appear in one of these patterns, they are unlikely to represent a synonymous pair. Roth and Schulte im Walde (2014) combined general lexico-syntactic patterns with discourse markers as indicators for the specific semantic relations between word pairs (e.g. contrast relations might indicate antonymy and elaborations may indicate synonymy or hyponymy). Unlike previous pattern-based methods which relied on the standard distribution of patterns, Schwartz et al. (2015) used patterns to learn word embeddings. They presented a symmetric pattern-based model for representing word vectors in which antonyms are assigned to dissimilar vector representations. More recently, Nguyen et al. (2017) presented a pattern-based neural network model that exploits lexico-syntactic patterns from syntactic parse trees for the task of distinguishing between antonyms and synonyms. They applied HypeNET Shwartz et al. (2016) to the task of distinguishing between synonyms and antonyms, replacing the direction feature with the distance in the path representation.

3 Paraphrase-Based Antonym Derivation

Existing semantic resources like WordNet (Fellbaum, 1998) contain a much smaller set of antonyms compared to other semantic relations (synonyms, hypernyms and meronyms). Our aim is to create a large resource of high quality antonym pairs using paraphrases.

3.1 The Paraphrase Database

The Paraphrase Database (PPDB) contains over 150 million paraphrase rules covering three paraphrase types: lexical (single word), phrasal (multiword), and syntactic restructuring rules, and is the largest collection of paraphrases currently available. PPDB . In this paper, we focus on lexical and phrasal paraphrases up to two words in length. We examine the relationships between phrase pairs in the PPDB focusing on phrase pairs that are most salient for deriving antonyms.

3.2 Antonym Derivation

Selection of Paraphrases We consider all phrase pairs from PPDB (p_1, p_2) up to two words in length such that one of the two phrases either begins with a negating word like *not*, or contains a negating prefix.[1] We chose these two types of paraphrase pairs since we believe them to be the most indicative of an antonymy relationship between the target words. There are 7,878 unordered phrase pairs of the form (p'_1, p_2) where p'_1 begins with 'not', and 183,159 phrases of the form (p'_1, p_2) where p'_1 contains a negating prefix.

Paraphrase Transformation For paraphrases containing a negating prefix, we perform morphological analysis to identify and remove the negating prefixes. For a phrase pair like *un*happy/sad, an antonymy relation is derived between the base form of the negated word, without the negation prefix, and its paraphrase (happy/sad). We use

---

[1] Negating prefixes include *de, un, in, anti, il, non, dis*

Unrelated	Paraphrases	Categories	Entailment	Other relation
much/worthless	correct/that's right	Japan/Korea	investing/ increased investment	twinkle/dark
disability/present	simply/merely	black/red	efficiency/ operational efficiency	naw/not gonna
equality/gap	till/until	Jan/Feb	valid/equally valid	access/available

Table 4: Examples of different types of non-antonyms derived from PPDB.

MORSEL (Lignos, 2010) to perform morphological analysis and identify negation markers. For multi-word phrases with a negating word, the negating word is simply dropped to obtain an antonym pair (e.g. different/*not* identical → different/identical). Some examples of PPDB paraphrase pairs and antonym pairs derived from them are shown in Table 1. The derived antonym pairs are further expanded by associating the synonyms (from WordNet) and lexical paraphrases (from PPDB) of each phrase with the other phrase in the derived pair. While expanding each phrase in the derived pair by its paraphrases, we filter out paraphrase pairs with a PPDB score (Pavlick et al., 2015a) of less than 2.5. In the above example, **un***happy/sad*, we first derive *happy/sad* as an antonym pair and expand it by considering all synonyms of *happy* as antonyms of *sad* (e.g. *joyful/sad*), and all synonyms of *sad* as antonyms of *happy* (e.g. *happy/gloomy*). Table 2 shows the number of pairs derived at each step using PPDB. In total, we were able to derive around 773K unique pairs from PPDB. This is a much larger dataset than existing resources like WordNet and EVALution as shown in Table 3.

Analysis We performed a manual evaluation of the quality of the extracted antonyms by randomly selecting 1000 pairs classified as 'antonym' and observed that the dataset contained about 63% antonyms. Errors mostly consisted of phrases and words that do not have an opposing meaning after the removal of the negation pattern. For example, the equivalent pair *till/until* that was derived from the PPDB paraphrase rule *not till/until*. Other non-antonyms derived from the above methods can be classified into unrelated pairs (background/figure), paraphrases or pairs that have an equivalent meaning (admissible/permissible), words that belong to a category (Africa/Asia), pairs that have an entailment relation (valid/equally valid) and pairs that are related but not with an antonym relationship (twinkle/dark). Table 4 gives some examples of

categories of non-antonyms.

Annotation Since the pairs derived from PPDB seemed to contain a variety of relations in addition to antonyms, we crowdsourced the task of labelling a subset of these pairs in order to obtain the true labels.[2] We asked workers to choose between the labels: antonym, synonym (or paraphrase for multi-word expressions), unrelated, other, entailment, and category. We showed each pair to 3 workers, taking the majority label as truth.

4 LSTM-Based Antonym Detection

In this section we describe AntNET, a long short term memory (LSTM) based, morphology-aware neural network model for antonym detection. We first focus on improving the neural embeddings of the path representation (Section 4.1), and then integrate distributional signals into our network resulting in a combined method (Section 4.2).

4.1 Path-Based Network

Similarly to prior work, we represent each dependency path as a sequence of edges that leads from x to y in the dependency tree. We use the same path-based features proposed by Shwartz et al. (2016) for recognizing hypernym relations: lemma and part-of-speech (POS) tag of the source node, the dependency label, and the edge direction between two subsequent nodes. Additionally, we also add a new feature that indicates whether the source node is negated.

Rather than treating an entire dependency path as a single feature, we encode the sequence of edges using a long short term memory network (Hochreiter and Schmidhuber, 1997). The vectors obtained for the different paths of a given (x, y) pair are pooled, and the resulting vector is used for classification. The overall network structure is depicted in Figure 1.

---

[2] 5884 pairs were randomly chosen and were annotated on www.crowdflower.com

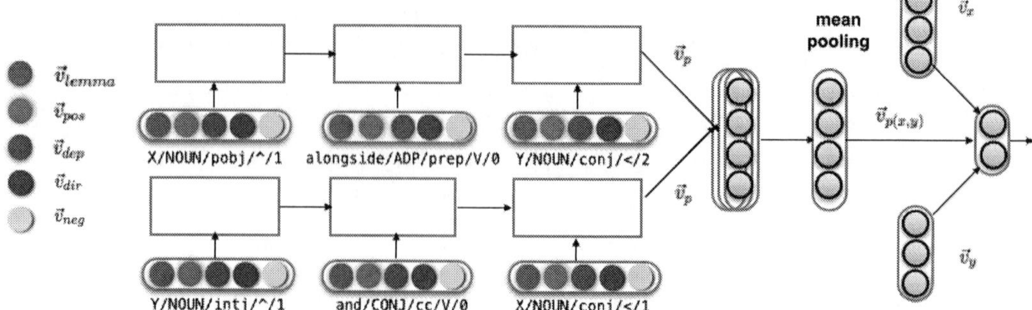

Figure 1: Illustration of the AntNET model. Each pair is represented by several paths and each path is a sequence of edges. An edge consists of five features: lemma, POS, dependency label, dependency direction, and negation marker.

Edge Representation We denote each edge as $lemma/pos/dep/dir/neg$. We are only interested in checking if x and/or y have negation markers but not the intermediate edges since negation information for intermediate lemmas is unlikely to contribute to identifying whether there is an antonym relationship between x and y. Hence, in our model, neg is represented in one of three ways: *negated* if x or y is negated, *not-negated* if x or y is not negated, and *unavailable* for the intermediate edges. If the source node is negated, we replace the lemma by the lemma of its base, non-negated, form. For example, if we identified *unhappy* as a 'negated' word, we replace the lemma embedding of *unhappy* by the embedding of *happy* in the path representation. The negation feature will help in separating antonyms from other semantic relations, especially those that are hard to distinguish from, like synonyms.

The replacement of a negated word's embedding by its base form's embedding is done for a few reasons. First, words and their polar antonyms are more likely to co-occur in sentences compared to words and their negated forms. For example, *Neither happy nor sad* is probably a more common phrase than *Neither happy nor unhappy*, so this technique will help our model to identify an opposing relationship between both types of pairs, *happy/unhappy* and *happy/sad*. Second, a common practice for creating word embeddings for multi-word expressions (MWEs) is by averaging over the embeddings of each word in the expression. Ideally, this is not a good representation

for phrases like *not identical* since we lose out on the negating information obtained from *not*. Indicating the presence of *not* using a negation feature and replacing the embedding of *not identical* by *identical* will increase the classifier's probability of identifying *not identical/different* as paraphrases and *identical/different* as antonyms. And finally, this method helps us distinguish between terms that are seemingly negated but are not in reality (e.g. *invaluable*). We encode the sequence of edges using an LSTM network. The vectors obtained for all the paths connecting x and y are pooled and combined, and the resulting vector is used for classification. The vector representation of each edge is the concatenation of its feature vectors:

$$\vec{v}_{edge} = [\vec{v}_{lemma}, \vec{v}_{pos}, \vec{v}_{dep}, \vec{v}_{dir}, \vec{v}_{neg}]$$

where $\vec{v}_{lemma}, \vec{v}_{pos}, \vec{v}_{dep}, \vec{v}_{dir}, \vec{v}_{neg}$ represent the vector embeddings of the negation marker, lemma, POS tag, dependency label and dependency direction, respectively.

Path Representation The representation for a path p composed of a sequence of edges $edge_1, edge_2, .., edge_k$ is a sequence of edge vectors: $p = [\vec{edge}_1, \vec{edge}_2, ..., \vec{edge}_k]$. The edge vectors are fed in order to a recurrent neural network (RNN) with LSTM units, resulting in the encoded path vector $\vec{v}_p$.

Classification Task Given a lexical or phrasal pair (x, y) we induce patterns from a corpus where each pattern represents a lexico-syntactic path connecting x and y. The vector representation for each term pair (x, y) is computed as the weighted average of its path vectors by applying average pooling as follows:

$$\vec{v}_{p(x,y)} = \frac{\sum_{p \in P(x,y)} f_p . \vec{v}_p}{\sum_{p \in P(x,y)} f_p} \quad (1)$$

$\vec{v}_{p(x,y)}$ refers to the vector of the pair (x, y); $P(x, y)$ is the multi-set of paths connecting x and y in the corpus and f_p is the frequency of p in $P(x, y)$. The vector $\vec{v}_{p(x,y)}$ is then fed into a neural network that outputs the class distribution c for each class (relation type), and the pair is assigned to the relation with the highest score r:

$$c = softmax(MLP(\vec{v}_{p(x,y)})) \quad (2a)$$
$$r = argmax_i c[i] \quad (2b)$$

MLP stands for Multi Layer Perceptron and can be computed with or without a hidden layer (equations 4 and 5 respectively).

$$\vec{h} = tanh(W_1 . \vec{v}_{p(x,y)} + b_1) \quad (3)$$

$$MLP(\vec{v}_{p(x,y)}) = W_2 . \vec{h} + b_2 \quad (4)$$

$$MLP(\vec{v}_{p(x,y)}) = W_1 . \vec{v}_{p(x,y)} + b_1 \quad (5)$$

W refers to a matrix of weights that projects information between two layers; b is a layer-specific vector of bias terms and $\vec{h}$ is the hidden layer.

4.2 Combined Path-Based and Distributional Network

The path-based supervised model in Section 4.1 classifies each pair (x, y) based on the lexico-syntactic patterns that connect x and y in a corpus. Inspired by the improved performance of Shwartz et al.'s (2016) integrated path-based and distributional method over a simpler path-based algorithm, we integrate distributional features into our path-based network. We create a combined vector representation using both the syntactic path features and the co-occurrence distributional features of x and y for each pair (x, y). The combined vector representation for (x, y), $\vec{v}_{c(xy)}$, is computed by simply concatenating the word embeddings of x ($\vec{v}_x$) and y ($\vec{v}_y$) to the path-based feature vector $\vec{v}_{p(x,y)}$:

$$\vec{v}_{c(xy)} = [\vec{v}_x, \vec{v}_{p(x,y)}, \vec{v}_y] \quad (6)$$

5 Experiments

We experiment with the path-based and combined models for antonym identification by performing two types of classification: binary and multiclass classification.

Train	Test	Val	Total
5,122	1,829	367	7,318

Table 5: Number of instances present in the train/test/validation splits of the crowdsourced dataset.

5.1 Dataset

Neural networks require a large amount of training data. We use the labelled portion of the dataset that we created using PPDB, as described in Section 3. In order to induce paths for the pairs in the dataset, we identify sentences in the corpus that contain the pair and extract all patterns for the given pair. Pairs with an antonym relationship are considered as positive instances in both classification experiments. In the binary classification experiment, we consider all pairs related by other relations (entailment, synonymy, category, unrelated, other) as negative instances. We also perform a variant of the multiclass classification with three classes (antonym, other, unrelated). Due to the skewed nature of the dataset, we combined category, entailment and synonym/paraphrases into one class. For both classification experiments, we perform random split with 70% train, 25% test, and 5% validation sets. Table 5 displays the number of relations in our dataset. Wikipedia[3] was used as the underlying corpus for all methods and we perform model selection on the validation set to tune the hyper-parameters of each method. We apply grid search for a range of values and pick the ones that yield the highest F_1 score on the validation set. The best hyper-parameters are reported in the appendix.

5.2 Baselines

Majority Baseline The majority baseline is achieved by labelling all the instances with the most frequent class occuring in the dataset i.e. FALSE (binary) or UNRELATED (multiclass).

---

[3]We used the English Wikipedia dump from May 2015 as the corpus.

Model	Binary			Multiclass		
	P	**R**	**F$_1$**	**P**	**R**	**F$_1$**
Majority baseline	0.304	0.551	0.392	0.222	0.472	0.303
SP baseline	0.661	0.568	0.436	0.583	0.488	0.344
Path-based SD baseline	0.723	0.724	0.722	0.636	0.675	0.651
Path-based AntNET	0.732	0.722	0.713	0.652	0.687	0.661**
Combined SD baseline	0.790	0.788	0.788	0.744	0.750	0.738
Combined AntNET	**0.803**	**0.802**	**0.802***	**0.746**	**0.757**	**0.746***

Table 6: Performance of the AntNET models in comparison to the baseline models.

Feature	Model	Binary			Multiclass		
		P	**R**	**F$_1$**	**P**	**R**	**F$_1$**
Distance	Path-based	0.727	0.727	0.724	0.665	0.692	0.664
	Combined	0.789	0.788	0.788	0.732	0.743	0.734
Negation	Path-based	0.732	0.722	0.713	0.652	0.687	0.661
	Combined	**0.803**	**0.802**	**0.802**	**0.746**	**0.757**	**0.746**

Table 7: Comparing the novel negation marking feature with the distance feature proposed by Nguyen et al. (2017).

Distributed Baseline The method proposed by Schwartz et al. (2015) uses symmetric patterns (SPs) for generating word embeddings. The authors automatically acquired symmetric patterns (defined as a sequence of 3–5 tokens consisting of exactly 2 wildcards and 1–3 words) from a large plain-text corpus, and generated vectors where each co-ordinate represented the co-occurrence in symmetric patterns of the represented word with another word of the vocabulary. For antonym representation, the authors relied on the patterns suggested by (Lin et al., 2003) to construct word embeddings containing an antonym parameter that can be turned on in order to represent antonyms as dissimilar, and that can be turned off to represent antonyms as similar. To evaluate the SP method on our data, we used the pre-trained SP embeddings[4] with 500 dimensions. We use the SVM classifier with RBF kernel for the classification of word pairs.

Path-based and Combined Baseline Since AntNET is an extension of the path-based and combined models proposed by (Shwartz and Dagan, 2016) for classifying multiple semantic relations, we use their models as additional baselines. Because their model used a different dataset that contained very few antonym instances, we repli-

cated the baseline (SD) with the dataset and corpus information as in Sectionn 5.1 rather than comparing to the reported results.

5.3 Results

Table 6 displays the performance scores of AntNET and the baselines in terms of precision, recall and F_1. Our combined model significantly[5] outperforms all baselines in both binary and multiclass classifications. Both path-based and combined models of AntNET achieve a much better performance in comparison to the majority class and SP baselines.

Comparing the path-based methods, the AntNET model achieves a higher precision compared to the path-based SD baseline for binary classification, and outperforms the SD model in precision, recall and F_1 in the multiclass classification experiment. The low precision of the SD model stems from its inability to distinguish between antonyms and synonyms, and between related and unrelated pairs which are common in our dataset, causing many false positive pairs such as *difficult/harsh*, *bad/cunning*, *finish/far* which were classified as antonyms.

Comparing the combined models, the AntNET model outperforms the SD model in precision, recall and F_1, achieving state-of-the-art results for antonym detection. In all the experiments, the

---

[4]`https://homes.cs.washington.edu/`
`~roysch/papers/sp_embeddings/sp_`
`embeddings.html`

[5]We used paired t-test. *$p < 0.1$, **$p < 0.05$

performance of the model in the binary classification task was better than in the multiclass classification. Multiclass classification seems to be inherently harder for all methods, due to the large number of relations and the smaller number of instances for each relation. We also observed that as we increased the size of the training dataset used in our experiments, the results improved for both path-based and combined models, confirming the need for large-scale datasets that will benefit training neural models.

Effect of the Negation-marking Feature   In our models, the novel negation marking feature is successfully integrated along the syntactic path to represent the paths between x and y. In order to evaluate the effect of our novel negation-marking feature for antonym detection, we compare this feature to the distance feature proposed by Nguyen et al. (2017). In their approach, they integrate the distance between related words in a lexico-syntactic path as a new pattern feature, along with lemma, POS and dependency for the task of distinguishing antonyms and synonyms. We re-implemented this model by making use of the same information regarding dataset and patterns as in Section 5.1 and then replacing the direction feature in the SD models by the distance feature.

The results are shown in Table 7 and indicate that the negation marking feature and the replacement of the embeddings of negated words by the ones of their base forms enhance the performance of our models more effectively than the distance feature does, across both binary and multiclass classifications. Although, the distance feature has previously been shown to perform well for the task of distinguishing antonyms from synonyms, this feature is not very effective in the multiclass setting.

5.4   Error Analysis

Figure 2 displays the confusion matrices for the binary and multiclass experiments of the best performing AntNET model. The confusion matrix shows that pairs were mostly assigned to the correct relation more than to any other class.

False Positives   We analyzed the false positives from both the binary and multiclass experiments. We sampled about 20% false positive pairs and identified the following common errors. The majority of the misclassification errors stem from antonym-like or near-antonym relations: these are

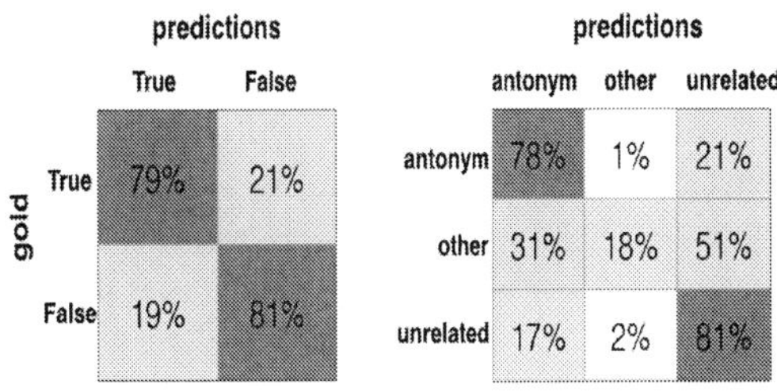

Figure 2: Confusion matrices for the combined AntNET model for binary (left) and multiclass (right) classifications. Rows indicate gold labels and columns indicate predictions. The matrix is normalized along rows, so that the predictions for each (true) class sum to 100%.

relations that could be considered as antonymy but were annotated by crowd-workers as other relations because they contain polysemous terms, for which the relation holds in a specific sense. For example: *north/south* and *polite/sassy* were labelled as *category* and *other* respectively. Other errors stem from confusing antonyms and unrelated pairs.

False Negatives   We again sampled about 20% false positive pairs from both the binary and multiclass experiments and analyzed the major types of errors. Most of these pairs had only few co-occurrences in the corpus often due to infrequent terms (e.g. *cisc/risc* which define computer architectures). While our model effectively handled negative prefixes, it failed to handle negative suffixes causing incorrect classification of pairs like *spiritless/spirited*. A possible future work is to simply extend this model to handle negative suffixes as well.

6   Conclusion

In this paper, we presented an original technique for deriving antonyms using paraphrases from PPDB. We also proposed a novel morphology-aware neural network model, AntNET, which improves antonymy prediction for path-based and combined models. In addition to lexical and syntactic information, we suggested to include a novel morphological negation-marking feature.

Our models outperform the baselines in two relation classification tasks. We also demonstrated that the negation marking feature outperforms previously suggested path-based features for this task.

Since our proposed techniques for antonymy detection are corpus based, they can be applied to different languages and relations. The paraphrase-based method can be applied to other languages by extracting the paraphrases for these languages from the PPDB and using a morphological analysis tool (e.g. Morfette for French (Chrupala et al., 2008)) or by looking up the negation prefixes in a grammar book for languages that do not dispose of such a tool. The LSTM-based model could also be used in other languages since the method is corpus based, but we would need to create a training set for new languages. This would not however be too difficult; the training set used by the model is not that big (the one used here was around 6000 pairs) and could be easily labelled through crowdsourcing.

We release our code and the large-scale dataset derived from PPDB, annotated with semantic relations.

Acknowledgments

This material is based in part on research sponsored by DARPA under grant number FA8750-13-2-0017 (the DEFT program). The U.S. Government is authorized to reproduce and distribute reprints for Governmental purposes. The views and conclusions contained in this publication are those of the authors and should not be interpreted as representing official policies or endorsements of DARPA and the U.S. Government.

This work has also been supported by the French National Research Agency under project ANR-16-CE33-0013 and partially supported by an Intel ICRI-CI grant, the Israel Science Foundation grant 880/12, and the German Research Foundation through the German-Israeli Project Cooperation (DIP, grant DA 1600/1-1).

We would like to thank our anonymous reviewers for their thoughtful and helpful comments.

References

Colin Bannard and Chris Callison-Burch. 2005. Paraphrasing with Bilingual Parallel Corpora. In *Proceedings of the 43rd Annual Meeting on Association for Computational Linguistics (ACL'05)*. Stroudsburg, PA, pages 597–604.

Regina Barzilay and Kathleen R. McKeown. 2001. Extracting Paraphrases from a Parallel Corpus. In *Proceedings of the 39th Annual Meeting on Association for Computational Linguistics (ACL'01)*. Toulouse, France, pages 50–57.

Walter G. Charles and George A. Miller. 1989. Contexts of antonymous adjectives. *Applied Psychology* 10:357–375.

Grzegorz Chrupala, Georgiana Dinu, and Josef van Genabith. 2008. Learning Morphology with Morfette. In *Proceedings of the Sixth International Conference on Language Resources and Evaluation (LREC'08)*. Marrakech, Morocco, pages 2362–2367.

Christiane Fellbaum, editor. 1998. *WordNet: an electronic lexical database*. MIT Press.

J. R. Firth. 1957. A synopsis of linguistic theory, 1930–1955. In *Studies in Linguistic Analysis*, Basil Blackwell, Oxford, United Kingdom, pages 1–32.

Juri Ganitkevitch, Benjamin Van Durme, and Chris Callison-Burch. 2013. PPDB: The Paraphrase Database. In *Proceedings of the 2013 Conference of the North American Chapter of the Association for Computational Linguistics: Human Language Technologies (NAACL/HLT)*. Atlanta, Georgia, pages 758–764.

Zellig S. Harris. 1954. Distributional structure. *Word* 10(23):146–162.

Marti Hearst. 1992. Automatic acquisition of hyponyms from large text corpora. In *Proceedings of the 14th International Conference on Computational Linguistics (COLING'92)*. Nantes, France, pages 539–545.

Sepp Hochreiter and Jurgen Schmidhuber. 1997. Long short-term memory. *Neural Computation* 9(8):1735–1780.

Constantine Lignos. 2010. Learning from Unseen Data. In *Proceedings of the Morpho Challenge 2010 Workshop*. Aalto University School of Science and Technology, Helsinki, Finland, pages 35–38.

Dekang Lin and Patrick Pantel. 2001. DIRT - Discovery of Inference Rules from Text. In *Proceedings of the Seventh ACM SIGKDD International Conference on Knowledge Discovery and Data Mining (KDD'01)*. San Francisco, California, pages 323–328.

Dekang Lin, Shaojun Zhao, Lijuan Qin, and Ming Zhou. 2003. Identifying synonyms among distributionally similar words. In *Proceedings of the Eighteenth International Joint Conference on Artificial Intelligence (IJCAI '03)*. Acapulco, Mexico, pages 1492–1493.

Tomas Mikolov, Ilya Sutskever, Kai Chen, Greg Corrado, and Jeffrey Dean. 2013. Distributed Representations of Words and Phrases and their Compositionality. In *Proceedings of the 26th International Conference on Neural Information Processing Systems (NIPS'13)*. Lake Tahoe, Nevada, pages 3111–3119.

Kim Anh Nguyen, Sabine Schulte im Walde, and Ngoc Thang Vu. 2017. Distinguishing antonyms and synonyms in a pattern-based neural network. In *Proceedings of the 15th Conference of the European Chapter of the Association for Computational Linguistics (EACL'17)*. Valencia, Spain, pages 76–85.

Ellie Pavlick, Johan Bos, Malvina Nissim, Charley Beller, Benjamin Van Durme, and Chris Callison-Burch. 2015a. Adding Semantics to Data-Driven Paraphrasing. In *The 53rd Annual Meeting of the Association for Computational Linguistics (ACL'15)*. Beijing, China, pages 1512–1522.

Ellie Pavlick, Pushpendre Rastogi, Juri Ganitkevich, and Chris Callison-Burch Ben Van Durme. 2015b. PPDB 2.0: Better paraphrase ranking, fine-grained entailment relations, word embeddings, and style classification. In *Proceedings of the 53rd Annual Meeting of the Association for Computational Linguistics (ACL'15)*. Beijing, China, pages 425–430.

Jeffrey Pennington, Richard Socher, and Christopher Manning. 2014. GloVe: Global Vectors for Word Representation. In *Proceedings of the 2014 Conference on Empirical Methods in Natural Language Processing (EMNLP'14)*. Doha, Qatar, pages 1532–1543.

Michael Roth and Sabine Schulte im Walde. 2014. Combining Word Patterns and Discourse Markers for Paradigmatic Relation Classification. In *Proceedings of the 52nd Annual Meeting of the Association for Computational Linguistics (ACL'14)*. Baltimore, MD, pages 524–530.

Roy Schwartz, Roi Reichart, and Ari Rappoport. 2015. Symmetric Pattern Based Word Embeddings for Improved Word Similarity Prediction. In *Proceedings of the Nineteenth Conference on Computational Natural Language Learning (CoNLL'15)*. Beijing, China, pages 258–267.

Vered Shwartz and Ido Dagan. 2016. CogALex-V Shared Task: LexNET - Integrated Path-based and Distributional Method for the Identification of Semantic Relations. In *Proceedings of the 5th Workshop on Cognitive Aspects of the Lexicon (CogALex-V)*. Osaka, Japan, pages 80–85.

Vered Shwartz, Yoav Goldberg, and Ido Dagan. 2016. Improving Hypernymy Detection with an Integrated Path-based and Distributional Method. In *Proceedings of the 54th Annual Meeting of the Association for Computational Linguistics (ACL'16)*. Berlin, Germany, pages 2389–2398.

A Supplemental Material

For deriving antonyms using PPDB, we used the XXXL size of PPDB version 2.0 found in http://paraphrase.org/.

To compute the metrics in Tables 6 and 7, We used scikit-learn with the "averaged setup", which computes the metrics for each relation and reports their average weighted by support (the number of true instances for each relation). Note that it can result in a F_1 score that is not the harmonic mean of precision and recall.

During preprocessing we handled removal of punctuation. Since our dataset only contains short phrases, we removed any stop words occurring at the beginning of a sentence (Example: a man → man) and we also removed plurals. The best hyperparameters for all models mentioned in this paper are shown in Table 8. The learning rate was set to 0.001 for all experiments.

Model	Type	Dropout
SD-path	Binary	0.2
SD-path	Multiclass	0.4
SD-combined	Binary	0.4
SD-combined	Multiclass	0.2
ASD-path	Binary	0.0
ASD-path	Multiclass	0.2
ASD-combined	Binary	0.0
ASD-combined	Multiclass	0.2
AntNET-path	Binary	0.0
AntNET-path	Multiclass	0.2
AntNET-combined	Binary	0.4
AntNET-combined	Multiclass	0.2

Table 8: The best hyper-parameters in every model.

Decoding Sentiment from Distributed Representations of Sentences

Edoardo Maria Ponti
ep490@cam.ac.uk

Ivan Vulić
iv250@cam.ac.uk

Anna Korhonen
alk23@cam.ac.uk

Language Technology Lab, University of Cambridge

Abstract

Distributed representations of sentences have been developed recently to represent their meaning as real-valued vectors. However, it is not clear how much information such representations retain about the polarity of sentences. To study this question, we decode sentiment from unsupervised sentence representations learned with different architectures (sensitive to the order of words, the order of sentences, or none) in 9 typologically diverse languages. Sentiment results from the (recursive) composition of lexical items and grammatical strategies such as negation and concession. The results are manifold: we show that there is no 'one-size-fits-all' representation architecture outperforming the others across the board. Rather, the top-ranking architectures depend on the language and data at hand. Moreover, we find that in several cases the additive composition model based on skip-gram word vectors may surpass supervised state-of-art architectures such as bidirectional LSTMs. Finally, we provide a possible explanation of the observed variation based on the type of negative constructions in each language.

1 Introduction

Distributed representations of sentences are usually acquired in an unsupervised fashion from raw texts. Those inferred from different algorithms are prone to grasp parts of their meaning and disregard others. Representations have been evaluated thoroughly, both intrinsically (interpretation through distance measures) and extrinsically (performance on downstream tasks). Moreover, several methods have been considered, based on both the compo-

sition of word embeddings (Milajevs et al., 2014; Marelli et al., 2014; Sultan et al., 2015) and direct generation (Hill et al., 2016). The evaluation was focused solely on English, and it rarely concerned other languages (Adi et al., 2017; Conneau et al., 2017). As a consequence, many 'core' methods to learn distributed sentence representations are largely under-explored in a variety of typologically diverse languages, and still lack a demonstration of their usefulness in actual downstream tasks.

In this work, we study how well distributed sentence representations capture the *polarity of a sentence*. To this end, we choose the Sentiment Analysis task as an extrinsic evaluation protocol: it directly detects the polarity of a text, where polarity is defined as the attitude of the speaker with respect to the whole content of the string or one of the entities mentioned therein. This attitude is measured quantitatively on a scale spanning from negative to positive with arbitrary granularity. As such, polarity consists in a crucial part of the meaning of a sentence, which should not be lost.

The polarity of a sentence depends heavily on a complex interaction between lexical items endowed with an intrinsic polarity, and morphosyntactic constructions altering polarity, most notably negation and concession. The interaction is deemed to be recursive, hence some approaches take into account word order and phrase boundaries in order to apply the correct composition (Socher et al., 2013). However, some languages lack continuous constituents: contiguous spans of words do not correspond to syntactic subtrees, making composition unreliable (Ponti, 2016). Moreover, the expression of negation varies across languages, as demonstrated by works in Linguistic Typology (Dahl, 1979, *inter alia*). In particular, negation can appear as a bounded morpheme or a free morpheme; it can precede or follow the verb; it can 'agree' or not in polarity with indefinite pronouns; it can alter the expression of verbal

22

*Proceedings of the 6th Joint Conference on Lexical and Computational Semantics (*SEM 2017)*, pages 22–32,
Vancouver, Canada, August 3-4, 2017. ©2017 Association for Computational Linguistics

categories (e.g. tense, aspect, or modality).

We explore a series of methods endowed with different features: some hinge upon word order, others on sentence order, others on neither. We evaluate these unsupervised representations using a Multi-Layer Perceptron which uses the generated sentence representations as input and predicts sentiment classes (positive vs. negative) as output. Training and evaluation are based on a collection of annotated databases. Owing to the variety of methods and languages, we expect to observe a variation in the performance correlated with the properties of both.

Moreover, we establish a ceiling to the possible performances of our method based on decoding unsupervised distributed representations. In fact, we offer a comparison between this and supervised deep learning architectures that achieve state-of-art scores in the Sentiment Analysis task. In particular, we also evaluate a bi-directional LSTM (Li et al., 2015) on the same task. These models have advantage over distributed representations as: i) they are specialised on a single task rather than built as general-purpose representations; ii) their recurrent nature allows to capture the sequential composition of polarity in a sentence. However, since training these models requires large amounts of annotated data, resource scarcity in other languages hampers their portability.

The aim of this work is to assess which algorithm for distributed sentence representations is the most appropriate for capturing polarity in a given language. Moreover, we study how language-specific properties have an impact on performance, finding an explanation in Language Typology. We also provide an in-depth analysis of the most relevant features by visualising the activation of hidden neurons. This will hopefully contribute to advancing the Sentiment Analysis task in the multilingual scenarios. In § 2, we survey prior work on multilingual sentiment analysis. Afterwards, we present the tested algorithms for generating distributed representations of sentences in § 3. In § 4, we sketch the dataset and the experimental setup. Finally, § 5 examines the results in light of the sensitivity of the algorithms and the typology of negation.

2 Multilingual Sentiment Analysis

The task of sentiment classification is mostly addressed through supervised approaches. However, these achieve unsatisfactory results in resource-lean languages because of the scarcity of resources to train dedicated models (Denecke, 2008). This afflicts state-of-art deep learning architectures even more compared to traditional machine learning algorithms (Chen et al., 2016). As a consequence, previous work resorted to i) language transfer or ii) joint multilingual learning. The former adapts models from a source resource-rich language to a target resource-poor language; the latter infers a single model portable across languages. Approaches based on distributed representations induced in an unsupervised fashion do not face the difficulty resulting from resource scarcity: they are portable to other tasks and languages. In this section we survey deep learning techniques, adaptive models, and unsupervised distributed representations for sentiment classification in a multilingual scenario. The last approach is the focus of this work.

Deep learning algorithms for sentiment classification are designed to deal with compositionality. Hence, they often rely on recurrent networks tracing the sequential history of a sentence, or special compositional devices. Recurrent models include bi-directional LSTMs (Li et al., 2015), possibly enriched with context (Mousa and Schuller, 2017). On the other hand, Socher et al. (2013) put forth a Recursive Neural Tensor Network, which composes representations recursively through a single tensor-based composition function. Subsequent improvements of this line of research include the Structural Attention Neural Networks (Kokkinos and Potamianos, 2017), which adds structural information around each node of a syntactic tree.

When supervised monolingual models are not feasible, language transfer can bridge between multiple languages, for instance through supervised latent Dirichlet allocation (Boyd-Graber and Resnik, 2010). Direct transfer relies on word-aligned parallel texts where the source language text is either manually or automatically annotated. The sentiment information is then projected onto the target text (Almeida et al., 2015), also leveraging non-parallel data (Zhou et al., 2015). Chen et al. (2016) devised a multi-task network where an adversarial branch spurs the shared layers to learn language-independent features. Finally, Lu et al. (2011) learned from annotated examples in both the source and target language. Alternatively, sentences from other languages are translated into English and assigned a sentiment based on lexical resources (Denecke, 2008) or supervised methods

(Balahur and Turchi, 2014).

Finally, cross-lingual sentiment classification can leverage on shared distributed representations. Zhou et al. (2016) captured shared high-level features across aligned sentences through autoencoders. In this latent space, distances were optimised to reflect differences in sentiment. On the other hand, Fernández et al. (2015) exploited bilingual word representations, where vector dimensions mirror the distributional overlap with respect to a pivot. Le and Mikolov (2014) concatenated sentence representations obtained through variants of Paragraph Vector and trained a Logistic Regression model on top of them.

Previous studies thus demonstrated that sentence representations retain information about polarity, and that they partly alleviate the drawbacks of deep architectures (single-purposed and data-demanding). Hence, the Sentiment Analysis tasks seems convenient to compare different sentence representation architectures. Nonetheless, a systematic evaluation has never taken place for this task, and a large-scale study over typologically diverse languages has not been attempted for any of the algorithms reviewed. We intend to fill these gaps, considering the methods to generate sentence representations outlined in the next section.

3 Distributed Sentence Representations

Word vectors can be combined through various compositional operations to obtain representations of phrases and sentences. Mitchell and Lapata (2010) explored two operations: addition and multiplication. Notwithstanding their simplicity, they are hardly outperformed by more sophisticated operations (Rimell et al., 2016). Some of these compositional representations based on matrix multiplication were also evaluated on sentiment classification (Yessenalina and Cardie, 2011). Alternatively, sentence representations can be induced directly with no intermediate step at the word level. In this paper, we focus on sentence representations that are generated in an unsupervised fashion. Furthermore, they are 'fixed', that is, they are not fine-tuned for any particular downstream task, since we are interested in their intrinsic content.[1]

---

[1]This excludes methods concerned with phrases, like the ECO embeddings (Poliak et al., 2017), or requiring structured knowledge, like CHARAGRAM (Wieting et al., 2016a).

3.1 Algorithms

We explore several methods to generate sentence representations. One exploits a compositional operation (addition) over word representations stemming from a Skip-Gram model (§ 3.1.1). Others are direct methods, including FastSent (§ 3.1.2), a Sequential Denoising AutoEncoder (SDAE, § 3.1.3) and Paragraph Vector (§ 3.1.4). Note that FastSent relies on sentence order, SDAE on word order, and Paragraph Vector on neither. All these algorithms were trained on cleaned-up Wikipedia dumps.

The choice of the algorithms was based on following criteria: i) their performance reported in recent surveys (n.b., the surveys were limited to English and evaluated on other tasks), most notably Hill et al. (2016) and Milajevs et al. (2014); ii) the variety of their modelling assumptions and features encoded. The referenced surveys already hinted that the usefulness of a representation is largely dependent on the actual application. Shallower but more interpretable representations can be decoded with spatial distance metrics. Others, more deep and convoluted architectures, outperform the others in supervised tasks. We inquire whether the generalisation is tenable also in the task of Sentiment Analysis targeting sentence polarity.

3.1.1 Additive Skip-Gram

As a bottom-up method, we train word embeddings using skip-gram with negative sampling (Mikolov et al., 2013). The algorithm finds the parameter θ such that, given a pair of a word w and a context c, the model discriminates correctly whether it belongs to a set of sentences S or a set of randomly generated incorrect sentences S':

$$\prod_{(w,c) \in S} p(S = 1 | w, c, \theta) \prod_{(w,c) \in S'} p(S' = 0 | w, c, \theta)$$

The representation of a sentence was obtained via element-wise addition of the vectors of the words belonging to it (Mitchell and Lapata, 2010).

3.1.2 FastSent

The FastSent model was proposed by Hill et al. (2016). It hinges on a sentence-level distributional hypothesis (Polajnar et al., 2015; Kiros et al., 2015). In other terms, it assumes that the meaning of a sentence can be inferred by the neighbour sentences in a text. It is a simple additive log-linear model conceived to mitigate the computational expensiveness of algorithms based on a similar assumption.

Hence, it was preferred over SkipThought (Kiros et al., 2015) because of i) these efficiency issues and ii) its competitive performances reported by Hill et al. (2016). In FastSent, sentences are represented as bags of words: a context of sentences is used to predict the adjacent sentence. Each word w corresponds to a source vector u_w and a target vector v_w. A sentence S_i is represented as the sum of the source vectors of its words $\sum_{w \in S_i} u_w$. Hence, the cost C of a representation is given by the softmax $\sigma(x)$ of a sentence representation and the target vectors of the words in its context c.

$$C_{S_i} = \sum_{c \in S_{i-1} \cup S_{i+1}} \sigma(\sum_{w \in S_i} u_w, v_c) \qquad (1)$$

This model does not rely on word order, but rather on sentence order. It encodes new sentences by summing over the source vectors of their words.

3.1.3 Sequential Denoising AutoEncoder

Sequential Denoising AutoEncoders (SDAEs) combine features of Denoising AutoEncoders (DAE) and Sequence-to-Sequence models. In DAE, the input representation is corrupted by a noise function and the algorithms learns to recover the original (Vincent et al., 2008). Intuitively, this makes the model more robust to changes in input that are irrelevant for the task at hand. This architecture was later adapted to encode and decode variable-length inputs, and the corruption process was implemented in the form of dropout (Iyyer et al., 2015). In the implementation by Hill et al. (2016),[2] the corruption function is defined as $f(S|p_o, p_x)$. S is a list of words (a sentence) where each has a probability p_o to be deleted, and the order of the words in every distinct bigram has a probability p_x to be swapped. The architecture consists in a Recurrent Layer and predicts $p(S|f(S|p_o, p_x))$.

3.1.4 Paragraph Vector

Paragraph Vector is a collection of log-linear models proposed by Le and Mikolov (2014) for paragraph/sentence representation. It consists of two different models, namely the Distributed Memory model (DM) and the Distributed Bag Of Words model (DBOW). In DM, the ID of every distinct paragraph (or sentence) is mapped to a unique vector in a matrix D and each word is mapped to a unique vector in matrix W. Given a sentence i and

a window size k, the vector $D_{i,}$ is used in conjunction with the concatenation of the vectors of the words in a sampled context $\langle w_{i_1}, \ldots, w_{i_k} \rangle$ to predict the next word through logistic regression:

$$p(W_{i_{k+1}} | \langle D_i, W_{i_1}, \ldots, W_{i_k} \rangle) \qquad (2)$$

Note that the sentence ID vector is shared by the contexts sampled from the same sentence. On the other hand, DBOW focuses on predicting the word embedding W_{i_j} for a sampled word j belonging to sentence i given the sentence representation D_i. As a result, the main difference between the two Paragraph Vector models is that the first is sensitive to word order (represented by the word vector concatenation), whereas the second is insensitive with respect to it. These models store a representation for each sentence in the training set, hence they are memory demanding. We use the *gensim* implementation of the two models available as Doc2Vec.[3]

3.2 Hyper-parameters

The choice of the models' hyper-parameters was based on two (contrasting) criteria: i) conservativeness with those proposed in the original models and ii) comparability among the models in this work. In particular, we ensured that each model had the same sentence vector dimensionality: 300. The only exception is SDAE: we kept the recommended value of 2400. Paragraph Vector DBOW and SkipGram were trained for 10 epochs, with a window size of 10, a minimum frequency count of 5, and a sampling threshold of 10^{-5}. FastSent was set as having a minimum count of 3, and no sampling. The probabilities in the corruption function of the SDAE were set as $p_o = 0.1$ (deletion) and $p_x = 0.1$ (swapping). The dimension of the RNN (GRU) hidden states (and hence sentence vector) was 2400, whereas single words were assigned 100 dimensions. The learning rate was set to 0.01 without decay, and the training lasted 7.2 hours on a NVIDIA Titan X GPU. The main properties of each algorithm are summarised in Table 1.

Algorithm	WO	SO
Additive SkipGram		
ParagraphVec DBOW		
FastSent		✓
Sequential Denoising AutoEncoder	✓	

Table 1: Sensitivity to Word or Sentence Order.

---

[2] `https://github.com/fh295/SentenceRepresentation`

[3] `https://radimrehurek.com/gensim/models/doc2vec.html`

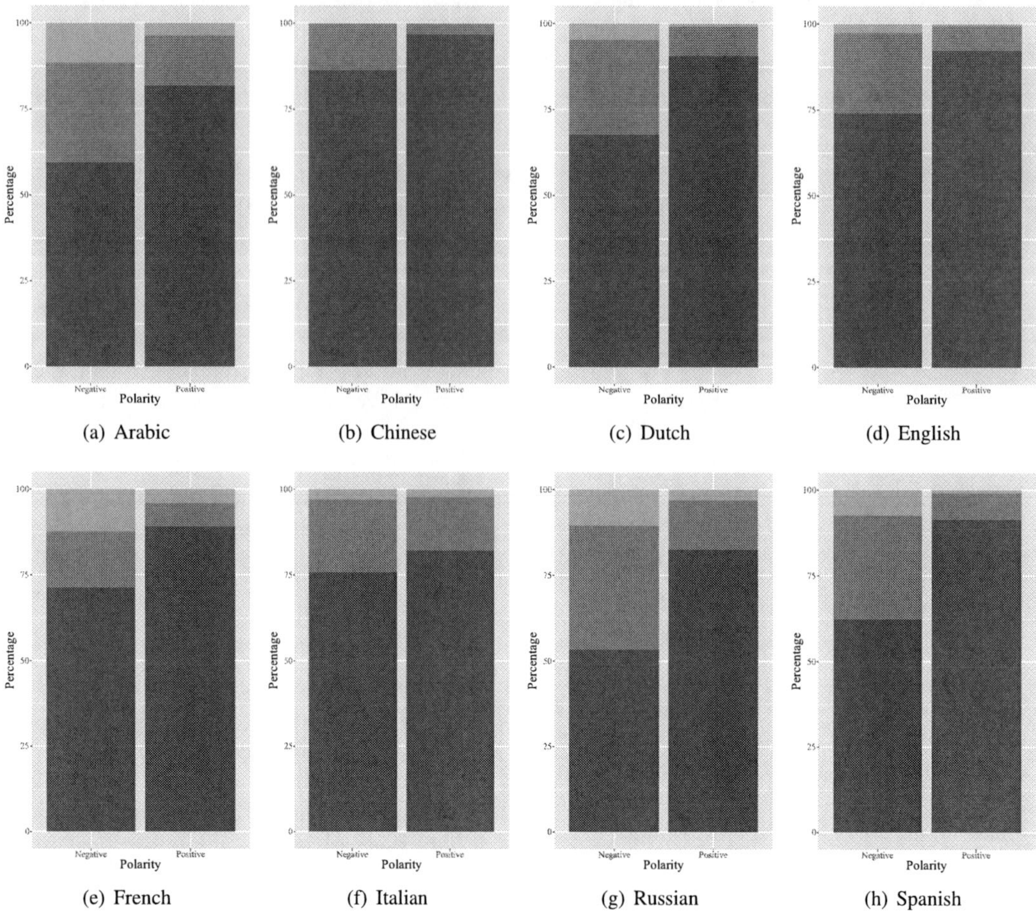

Figure 1: Percentages of negative (left) and positive (right) sentences with the same amount of negative grammatical markers. A count of 0 is represented in dark blue, 1 in light blue, and 2 or more in green.

4 Experimental Setup

Now, we evaluate the quality of the distributed sentence representations from § 3 on Sentiment Analysis. In § 4.1 we introduce the datasets of all the considered languages, and the evaluation protocol in § 4.2. Finally, to provide a potential performance ceiling, we compare the obtained results with those of a deep, state-of-art classifier, outlined in § 4.3.

4.1 Datasets

The data for training and testing are sourced from the SemEval 2016: Task 5 (Pontiki et al., 2016). These datasets provide customer reviews in 8 languages labelled with Aspect-Based Sentiment, i.e., opinions about specific entities or attributes rather than generic stances. The languages include Arabic (hotels domain), Chinese (electronics), Dutch (restaurants and electronics), English (restaurants and electronics), French, Russian, Spanish, and Turkish (restaurants all). We mapped the labels to an overall polarity class (positive or negative) by selecting the majority class among the aspect-based sentiment classes for a given sentence. Note that no general sentiment for the sentence was included in this pool. Moreover, we added data for Italian (tweets) from the SENTIPOLC shared task in EVALITA 2016 (Barbieri et al., 2016). We discarded neutral stances from the corpus, and retained only positive and negative ones. Table 2 shows the final size of the dataset partitions and the Wikipedia dumps. In Figure 1, we report the percentage of sentences with the same amount of negative grammatical markers (e.g. the word *not* and the suffix *n't* in English) based on their polarity class. We discuss the impact of the variation of these percentages on the results in § 5.

Language	Wikipedia Dumps	Train	Test
Arabic	3406732	4570	1163
Chinese	8067971	2593	1011
Dutch	11860559	2169	683
English	30000002	3584	1102
French	26024881	1410	534
Italian	15338617	4588	512
Russian	16671224	2555	835
Spanish	22328668	1553	646
Turkish	3622336	1008	121

Table 2: Size of the data partitions (# sentences).

4.2 Evaluation Protocol

After mapping each sentence in the dataset to its distributed representation, we fed them to a Multi-Layer Perceptron (MLP), trained to detect the sentence polarity. In the MLP, a logistic regression layer is stacked onto a 60-dimensional hidden layer with a hyperbolic tangent activation. The weights were initialised from the random *xavier* distribution Glorot and Bengio (2010). The cross-entropy loss was normalised with the L2-norm of the weights scaled by $\lambda = 10^{-3}$. The optimisation with gradient descent ran for 20 epochs with early stopping. Batch size was 10 and the learning rate 10^{-2}.

4.3 Comparison with State-of-Art Models

In addition to unsupervised distributed sentence representations, we test a bi-directional Long Short-Term Memory neural network (bi-LSTM) on the same task. This is a benchmark to compare against results of deep state-of-art architectures. The choice is based on the competitive results of this algorithm and on its sensitivity to word order. The accuracy of this architecture is 45.7 for 5-class and 85.4 for 2-class Sentiment Analysis on the standard dataset of the Stanford Sentiment Treebank.

The importance of word order is evident from the architecture of the network. In a recurrent model, the word embedding of a word w_t at time t is combined with the hidden state h_{t-1} from the previous time step. The process is iterated throughout the whole sequence of words of a sentence. This model can be extended to multiple layers. LSTM is a refinement associating each time epoch with an input, control and memory gate, in order to filter out irrelevant information (Hochreiter and Schmidhuber, 1997). This model is bi-directional if it is split in two branches reading simultaneously the sentence in opposite directions (Schuster and Paliwal, 1997).

Contrary to the evaluation protocol sketched in § 4.2, the bi-LSTM does not utilise unsupervised sentence representations. Rather, it is trained directly on the datasets from § 4.1. The optimisation ran for 20 epochs, with a batch size of 20 and a learning rate of $5 \cdot 10^{-2}$. The 60-dimensional hidden layer had a dropout probability of 0.2. Crucially, the word embeddings were initialised with the Skip-Gram model described in § 3.1.1. Since performance tends to vary depending on the initialisation, this ensures a fair comparison.

5 Results

The results are displayed in Figure 2. Weighted F1 scores were preferred over accuracy scores, since the two classes (positive and negative) are unbalanced. We decoded the unsupervised representations multiple times through different initialisation of the MLP weights, hence we report both the mean value and its standard deviation. The results are not straightforward: there is no algorithm outperforming the others in each language; unexpectedly not even the bi-LSTM used as a ceiling. However, the variation in performance follows certain trends, depending on the properties of languages and algorithms. We now examine: i) how performance is affected by the properties of the algorithms, such as those summarised in Table 1; ii) how typological features concerning negation and the text domain could make polarity harder to detect; iii) the interaction between negation and indefinite pronouns, by visualising the contribution of each word to the predicted class probabilities.

5.1 Feature Sensitivity of the Algorithms

The state-of-art bi-LSTM algorithm chosen as a ceiling is not the best choice in some languages (Italian, and Turkish). In these cases, it is always surpassed by the same model: additive Skip-Gram. The drop in Italian is possibly linked to its dataset in specific, since all the algorithms behave similarly badly. Turkish is possibly challenging for a recursive model because of the sparsity of its vocabulary. These cases, however, are not isolated: averaged word embeddings outperformed LSTMs in text similarity tasks (Arora et al., 2016) and provide a strong baseline in English (Adi et al., 2017).

In any case, the general high performance of additive Skip-Gram is noteworthy: it shows that a simple method achieves close-to-best results in almost every language among decoded distributed

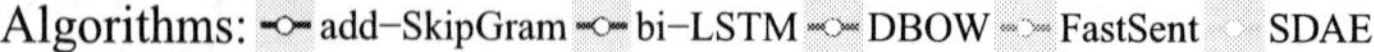

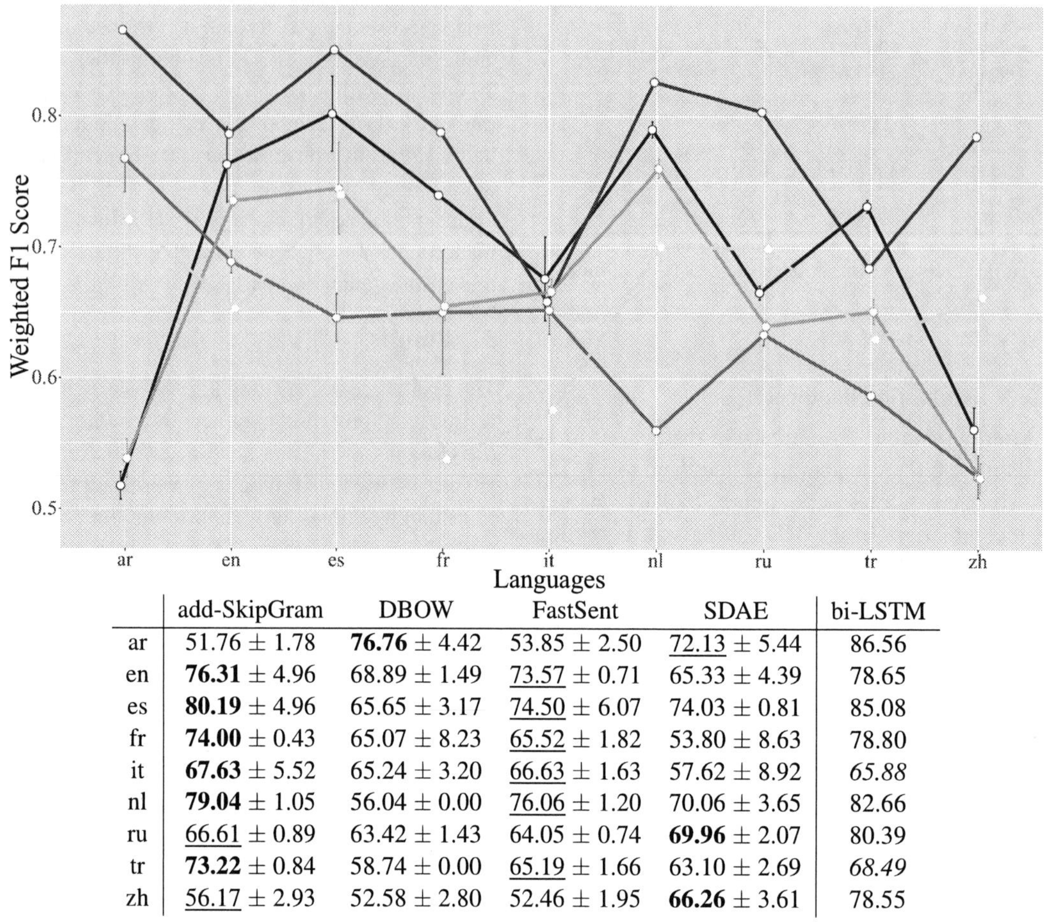

	add-SkipGram	DBOW	FastSent	SDAE	bi-LSTM
ar	51.76 ± 1.78	**76.76** ± 4.42	53.85 ± 2.50	<u>72.13</u> ± 5.44	86.56
en	**76.31** ± 4.96	68.89 ± 1.49	<u>73.57</u> ± 0.71	65.33 ± 4.39	78.65
es	**80.19** ± 4.96	65.65 ± 3.17	<u>74.50</u> ± 6.07	74.03 ± 0.81	85.08
fr	**74.00** ± 0.43	65.07 ± 8.23	<u>65.52</u> ± 1.82	53.80 ± 8.63	78.80
it	**67.63** ± 5.52	65.24 ± 3.20	<u>66.63</u> ± 1.63	57.62 ± 8.92	*65.88*
nl	**79.04** ± 1.05	56.04 ± 0.00	<u>76.06</u> ± 1.20	70.06 ± 3.65	82.66
ru	<u>66.61</u> ± 0.89	63.42 ± 1.43	64.05 ± 0.74	**69.96** ± 2.07	80.39
tr	**73.22** ± 0.84	58.74 ± 0.00	<u>65.19</u> ± 1.66	63.10 ± 2.69	*68.49*
zh	<u>56.17</u> ± 2.93	52.58 ± 2.80	52.46 ± 1.95	**66.26** ± 3.61	78.55

Figure 2: Results of 5 different algorithms on 9 languages. Values report the mean Weighted F1 Score and the standard deviation. The best results per language are given in bold and the second-best is underlined. Data points where the ceiling is outperformed are in italics.

representations. This result is in line with other findings: Wieting et al. (2016b) showed that word embeddings, once retrained and decoded by linear regression, beat many methods that generate sentence representations directly.

Moreover, the second-best method for languages is always FastSent, which is the only one hinging upon neighbouring sentences as features. This demonstrate that sentiment is encoded not only within a sentence, but also in its textual context. As a consequence, a relatively small and accessible dataset (Wikipedia) is sufficient to provide a reliable model in most languages. Nonetheless, the varying size of the dumps affects FastSent as well as the other unsupervised algorithms: limited data hinders them from learning faithful representations,

as in Arabic, Chinese, and Turkish (see Table 2).

In general, algorithms sensitive to the same features behave similarly, e.g. SDAE and bi-LSTM. They follow the same trend in relative improvements from one language to another. The generally low performance of SDAE could depend on the limited training time, which was necessary to evaluate the algorithm on the whole set of languages.

5.2 Typology of Negation and Domain

In some languages, the scores are very scattered: this fluctuation might be due to their peculiar morphological properties. In particular, Arabic is an introflexive language, Chinese is a radically isolating language, and Turkish an agglutinative language. On the other hand, the algorithms achieve better

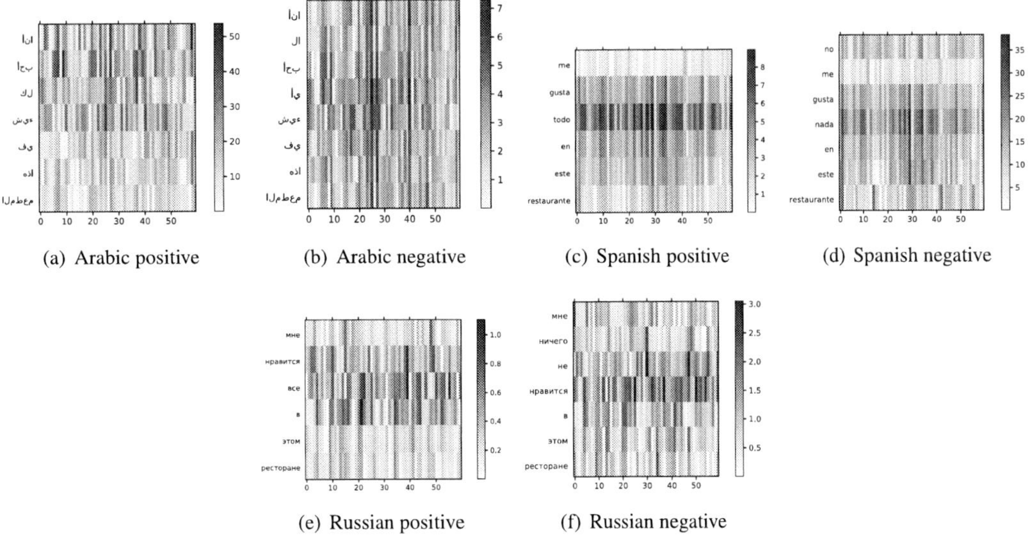

(a) Arabic positive   (b) Arabic negative   (c) Spanish positive   (d) Spanish negative

(e) Russian positive   (f) Russian negative

Figure 3: Visualization of the derivative of the class scores with respect to the word embeddings.

scores in the fusional languages, save Italian.

A fine-grained analysis shows also that the performance is affected by the typology of the negation in each language, although negative markers appear in a reduced number of examples (see Figure 1). Semantically, negation is crucial in switching or mitigating the polarity of lexical items and phrases. Morpho-syntactically, negation is expressed through several constructions across the languages of the world. Constructions differ in many respects, which are classified as feature-value pairs in databases like the World Atlas of Language Structures (Dryer and Haspelmath, 2013).[4]

Negation can affect the declarative verbal main clauses. In fact, negative clauses can be: i) symmetric, i.e., identical to the affirmative counterpart except for the negative marker; ii) asymmetric, i.e. showing structural differences between negative and affirmative clauses (in constructions or paradigms); iii) showing mixed behaviour. Alterations concern for instance finiteness, the obligatory marking of unreality status, or the expression of verbal categories. Secondly, negation interacts with indefinite pronoun (e.g. *nobody, nowhere, never*). Negative indefinites can i) co-occur with standard negation; ii) be forbidden in concurrence;

iii) display a mixed behaviour. Finally, the relation of the negative marker with respect to verb is prone to change. Firstly, it can be either an affix or a prosodically independent word. Secondly, its position can be anchored to the verb (preceding, following, or both). Thirdly, negation can be omitted, doubled or even tripled.

Performances seem to suffer the ambiguity in mapping between a negative marker and negative meaning. In fact, the bi-LSTM achieves lower scores in languages with asymmetric constructions (Chinese, English, and Turkish): the additional changes in the sentence construction and/or verb paradigm might create noise. Additional reasons of difficulty may occur when negation is doubled (French) or affixed (Turkish), since this makes negation redundant or sparse. On the other hand, add-SkipGram appears to be sensitive to the presence of negation: according to the counts in Figure 1, when this is too pervasive (Arabic and Russian) or rare (Chinese), the scores tend to decrease.

These comments on the results based on linguistic properties can also suggest speculative solutions for future work. For algorithms based on sentence order, it is not clear whether the problem lies in the lack of wider collections of texts in some languages, or rather on the maximum amount of information about polarity that is learnt through a sentence-level distributional hypothesis. On the other hand, impairments of the other algorithms seem to be linked

---

[4]The features considered here for negation are 113A 'Symmetric and Asymmetric Standard Negation', 114A 'Subtypes of Asymmetric Standard Negation', 115A 'Negative Indefinite Pronouns and Predicate Negation', and 143A 'Order of Negative Morpheme and Verb'.

with redundancies and noise. Filtering out words that contribute to this effect might benefit the quality of the representation. Moreover, the sparsity due to cases where negation is an affix might be mitigated by introducing character-level features.

The other inherent source of variation is the text domain, on which the difficulty of the task depends (Glorot et al., 2011). Although the unstructured nature of tweets could hinder the quality of the sentence representations in Italian, however, no clear effect is evident based on the other domains.

5.3 Visualisation

Since languages vary in the "polarity agreement" between verbs and indefinite pronouns, algorithms may weigh these as features differently. We analyse their role through a visualizasion of the activation in the hidden layer of the bi-LSTM. In particular, we approximated the objective function through a linear function, and estimated the contribution of each word to the true class probability by computing the prime derivative of the output scores with respect to the embeddings. This technique is presented and detailed by Li et al. (2015). The visualised hidden layers are shown in Figure 3, whereas the sentences used as input are glossed in Ex. (3) (Arabic), Ex. (4) (Spanish), and Ex. 5 (Russian).

(3) *'ana 'uhibu kl shay' fi hadha*
1SG like.NPST.1SG every thing in this
almataeim / 'ana la 'uhibu
restaurant / 1SG not.NPST like.NPST.1SG
'ayu shay' fi hadha almataeam
any thing in this restaurant

(4) *me gust-a todo en est-e*
1SG.DAT like-3SG everything in this-SG
restaurant-e / no me gust-a
restaurant-SG / not 1SG.DAT like-3SG
nada en est-e restaurant-e
nothing in this-SG restaurant-SG

(5) *mne nráv-itsja vs-jo v*
1SG.DAT like.IMPV-PRS.3SG all-NOM.SG in
ét-om restoráne / mne
this-PREP.SG restaurant-PREP.SG / 1SG.DAT
ni-čevó ne nráv-itsja v
nothing-GEN not like.IMPV-PRS.3SG in
ét-om restorán-e
this-PREP.SG restaurant-PREP.SG

The two compared sentences correspond to the translation of two English sentences. The first is positive: 'I like everything in this restaurant'; the second is negative: 'I don't like anything in this restaurant'. These include a domain-specific but sentiment-neutral word that plays the role of a touchstone. The more a cell tends to blue, the higher its activation. In some languages (e.g. Arabic), the sentiment verb elicits a stronger reaction in the positive polarity, whereas the indefinite pronoun dominates in the negative polarity. In several other languages (e.g. Spanish), indefinite pronouns are more relevant than any other feature. In Russian, only sentiment verbs always provoke a reaction. These differences might be related to the "polarity agreement" of these languages, which happens always, sometimes, and never, respectively. In some other languages, however, no evidence is found of any similar activation pattern.

6 Conclusion

In this work, we examined how much sentiment polarity information is retained by distributed representations of sentences in multiple typologically diverse languages. We generated the representations through various algorithms, sensitive to different properties from training corpora (e.g, word or sentence order). We decoded them through a simple MLP and compared their performance with one of the state-of-art algorithms for Sentiment Analysis: bi-directional LSTM. Unexpectedly, for some languages the bi-directional LSTM is outperformed by unsupervised strategies like the addition of the word embeddings obtained from a Skip-Gram model. This model, in turn, surpasses more sophisticated algorithms for most of the languages. This demonstrates i) that no algorithm is the best across the board; and ii) that some simple models are to be preferred even for downstream tasks, which partially contrasts with the conclusions of Hill et al. (2016). Moreover, representation algorithms sensitive to word order have similar trends, but they do not always achieve performance superior to algorithms based on the sentence order. Finally, some properties of languages (i.e. their type of negation) appear to have an impact on the scores: in particular, the asymmetry of negative and affirmative clauses and the doubling of negative markers.

Acknowledgements

This work was supported by the ERC Consolidator Grant LEXICAL (648909). The authors would like to thank the anonymous reviewers for their helpful suggestions and comments.

References

Yossi Adi, Einat Kermany, Yonatan Belinkov, Ofer Lavi, and Yoav Goldberg. 2017. Fine-grained analysis of sentence embeddings using auxiliary prediction tasks. In *Proceedings of ICLR*. http://arxiv.org/abs/1608.04207.

Mariana SC Almeida, Cláudia Pinto, Helena Figueira, Pedro Mendes, and André FT Martins. 2015. Aligning opinions: Cross-lingual opinion mining with dependencies. In *Proc. of the Annual Meeting of the Association for Computational Linguistics*.

Sanjeev Arora, Yingyu Liang, and Tengyu Ma. 2016. A simple but tough-to-beat baseline for sentence embeddings. In *ICLR 2017*.

Alexandra Balahur and Marco Turchi. 2014. Comparative experiments using supervised learning and machine translation for multilingual sentiment analysis. *Computer Speech & Language* 28(1):56–75.

Francesco Barbieri, Valerio Basile, Danilo Croce, Malvina Nissim, Nicole Novielli, and Viviana Patti. 2016. Overview of the evalita 2016 sentiment polarity classification task. In *Proceedings of Third Italian Conference on Computational Linguistics (CLiC-it 2016) & Fifth Evaluation Campaign of Natural Language Processing and Speech Tools for Italian. Final Workshop (EVALITA 2016)*.

Jordan Boyd-Graber and Philip Resnik. 2010. Holistic sentiment analysis across languages: Multilingual supervised latent dirichlet allocation. In *Proceedings of the 2010 Conference on Empirical Methods in Natural Language Processing*. Association for Computational Linguistics, pages 45–55.

Xilun Chen, Ben Athiwaratkun, Yu Sun, Kilian Weinberger, and Claire Cardie. 2016. Adversarial deep averaging networks for cross-lingual sentiment classification. *arXiv preprint arXiv:1606.01614*.

Alexis Conneau, Douwe Kiela, Holger Schwenk, Loïc Barrault, and Antoine Bordes. 2017. Supervised learning of universal sentence representations from natural language inference data. *CoRR* abs/1705.02364. http://arxiv.org/abs/1705.02364.

Östen Dahl. 1979. Typology of sentence negation. *Linguistics* 17(1-2):79–106.

Kerstin Denecke. 2008. Using sentiwordnet for multilingual sentiment analysis. In *Data Engineering Workshop, 2008. ICDEW 2008. IEEE 24th International Conference on*. pages 507–512.

Matthew S. Dryer and Martin Haspelmath, editors. 2013. *WALS Online*. Max Planck Institute for Evolutionary Anthropology, Leipzig. http://wals.info/.

Alejandro Moreo Fernández, Andrea Esuli, and Fabrizio Sebastiani. 2015. Distributional correspondence indexing for cross-lingual and cross-domain sentiment classification. *Journal of Artificial Intelligence Research* 55:131–163.

Xavier Glorot and Yoshua Bengio. 2010. Understanding the difficulty of training deep feedforward neural networks. In *Aistats*. volume 9, pages 249–256.

Xavier Glorot, Antoine Bordes, and Yoshua Bengio. 2011. Domain adaptation for large-scale sentiment classification: A deep learning approach. In *Proceedings of the 28th international conference on machine learning (ICML-11)*. pages 513–520.

Felix Hill, Kyunghyun Cho, and Anna Korhonen. 2016. Learning distributed representations of sentences from unlabelled data. *arXiv preprint arXiv:1602.03483*.

Sepp Hochreiter and Jürgen Schmidhuber. 1997. Long short-term memory. *Neural computation* 9(8):1735–1780.

Mohit Iyyer, Varun Manjunatha, Jordan L Boyd-Graber, and Hal Daumé III. 2015. Deep unordered composition rivals syntactic methods for text classification. In *ACL (1)*. pages 1681–1691.

Ryan Kiros, Yukun Zhu, Ruslan R Salakhutdinov, Richard Zemel, Raquel Urtasun, Antonio Torralba, and Sanja Fidler. 2015. Skip-thought vectors. In *Advances in neural information processing systems*. pages 3294–3302.

Filippos Kokkinos and Alexandros Potamianos. 2017. Structural attention neural networks for improved sentiment analysis. In *EACL 2017*.

Quoc V Le and Tomas Mikolov. 2014. Distributed representations of sentences and documents. In *ICML*. volume 14, pages 1188–1196.

Jiwei Li, Xinlei Chen, Eduard Hovy, and Dan Jurafsky. 2015. Visualizing and understanding neural models in nlp. *arXiv preprint arXiv:1506.01066*.

Bin Lu, Chenhao Tan, Claire Cardie, and Benjamin K Tsou. 2011. Joint bilingual sentiment classification with unlabeled parallel corpora. In *Proceedings of the 49th Annual Meeting of the Association for Computational Linguistics: Human Language Technologies-Volume 1*. Association for Computational Linguistics, pages 320–330.

Marco Marelli, Luisa Bentivogli, Marco Baroni, Raffaella Bernardi, Stefano Menini, and Roberto Zamparelli. 2014. Semeval-2014 task 1: Evaluation of compositional distributional semantic models on full sentences through semantic relatedness and textual entailment. *SemEval-2014*.

Tomas Mikolov, Ilya Sutskever, Kai Chen, Greg S Corrado, and Jeff Dean. 2013. Distributed representations of words and phrases and their compositionality. In *Advances in neural information processing systems*. pages 3111–3119.

Dmitrijs Milajevs, Dimitri Kartsaklis, Mehrnoosh Sadrzadeh, and Matthew Purver. 2014. Evaluating neural word representations in tensor-based compositional settings. *idea* 10(47):39.

Jeff Mitchell and Mirella Lapata. 2010. Composition in distributional models of semantics. *Cognitive science* 34(8):1388–1429.

Amr El-Desoky Mousa and Björn Schuller. 2017. Contextual bidirectional long short-term memory recurrent neural network language models: A generative approach to sentiment analysis. In *EACL 2017*.

Tamara Polajnar, Laura Rimell, and Stephen Clark. 2015. An exploration of discourse-based sentence spaces for compositional distributional semantics. In *Workshop on Linking Models of Lexical, Sentential and Discourse-level Semantics (LSDSem)*. page 1.

Adam Poliak, Pushpendre Rastogi, M Patrick Martin, and Benjamin Van Durme. 2017. Efficient, compositional, order-sensitive n-gram embeddings. *EACL 2017* page 503.

Edoardo Maria Ponti. 2016. Divergence from syntax to linear order in ancient greek lexical networks. In *The 29th International FLAIRS Conference*.

Maria Pontiki, Dimitrios Galanis, Haris Papageorgiou, Ion Androutsopoulos, Suresh Manandhar, Mohammad Al-Smadi, Mahmoud Al-Ayyoub, Yanyan Zhao, Bing Qin, Orphée De Clercq, Véronique Hoste, Marianna Apidianaki, Xavier Tannier, Natalia Loukachevitch, Evgeny Kotelnikov, Nuria Bel, Salud María Jiménez-Zafra, , and Gülsen Eryigit. 2016. Semeval-2016 task 5: Aspect based sentiment analysis. In *Proceedings of the 10th International Workshop on Semantic Evaluation, SemEval*. volume 16.

Laura Rimell, Jean Maillard, Tamara Polajnar, and Stephen Clark. 2016. Relpron: A relative clause evaluation dataset for compositional distributional semantics. *Computational Linguistics* .

Mike Schuster and Kuldip K Paliwal. 1997. Bidirectional recurrent neural networks. *IEEE Transactions on Signal Processing* 45(11):2673–2681.

Richard Socher, Alex Perelygin, Jean Y Wu, Jason Chuang, Christopher D Manning, Andrew Y Ng, Christopher Potts, et al. 2013. Recursive deep models for semantic compositionality over a sentiment treebank. In *Proceedings of the conference on empirical methods in natural language processing (EMNLP)*. Citeseer, volume 1631, page 1642.

Md Arafat Sultan, Steven Bethard, and Tamara Sumner. 2015. Dls@ cu: Sentence similarity from word alignment and semantic vector composition. In *Proceedings of the 9th International Workshop on Semantic Evaluation*. pages 148–153.

Pascal Vincent, Hugo Larochelle, Yoshua Bengio, and Pierre-Antoine Manzagol. 2008. Extracting and composing robust features with denoising autoencoders. In *Proceedings of the 25th international conference on Machine learning*. ACM, pages 1096–1103.

John Wieting, Mohit Bansal, Kevin Gimpel, and Karen Livescu. 2016a. Charagram: Embedding words and sentences via character n-grams. *arXiv preprint arXiv:1607.02789* .

John Wieting, Mohit Bansal, Kevin Gimpel, and Karen Livescu. 2016b. Towards universal paraphrastic sentence embeddings. In *ICLR 2017*.

Ainur Yessenalina and Claire Cardie. 2011. Compositional matrix-space models for sentiment analysis. In *Proceedings of the Conference on Empirical Methods in Natural Language Processing*. Association for Computational Linguistics, pages 172–182.

Guangyou Zhou, Tingting He, Jun Zhao, and Wensheng Wu. 2015. A subspace learning framework for cross-lingual sentiment classification with partial parallel data. In *Proceedings of the international joint conference on artificial intelligence, Buenos Aires*.

Xinjie Zhou, Xianjun Wan, and Jianguo Xiao. 2016. Cross-lingual sentiment classification with bilingual document representation learning .

Detecting Asymmetric Semantic Relations in Context:
A Case-Study on Hypernymy Detection

Yogarshi Vyas and **Marine Carpuat**
Department of Computer Science
University of Maryland
yogarshi@cs.umd.edu and marine@cs.umd.edu

Abstract

We introduce WHiC[1], a challenging testbed for detecting hypernymy, an asymmetric relation between words. While previous work has focused on detecting hypernymy between word types, we ground the meaning of words in specific contexts drawn from WordNet examples, and require predictions to be sensitive to changes in contexts. WHiC lets us analyze complementary properties of two approaches of inducing vector representations of word meaning in context. We show that such contextualized word representations also improve detection of a wider range of semantic relations in context.

1 Introduction

Language understanding applications like question answering (Harabagiu and Hickl, 2006) and textual entailment (Dagan et al., 2013) benefit from identifying semantic relations between words beyond synonymy and paraphrasing. For instance, given *"Anand plays chess."*, and the question *"Which game does Anand play?"*, successfully answering the question requires knowing that *chess* is a kind of *game*, i.e. *chess* entails *game*. Such lexical entailment relations are asymmetric (*chess* $\implies$ *game*, but *game* $\not\implies$ *chess*), and detecting their direction accurately is a challenge.

While prior work has defined lexical entailment as a relation between word types, we argue that it is better defined between word meanings illustrated by examples of usage in context. Ignoring context is problematic since entailment might hold between some senses of the words, but not others. Consider the word *game* in the following contexts:

1. The championship *game* was played in NYC.
2. The hunters were interested in the big *game*.

Given the sentence, *Anand is the world* chess *champion*, chess $\implies$ game in the first context, while chess $\not\implies$ game in the second context.

Lexical entailment encompasses several semantic relations, with one important relation being *hypernymy* (Roller et al., 2014; Shwartz et al., 2016). In this work, we focus on hypernymy detection in context, and show that existing resources can be leveraged to automatically create test beds for evaluation. We introduce "Wordnet Hypernyms in Context" (WHiC, pronounced *which)*, a large dataset, automatically extracted from Word-Net (Fellbaum, 1998) using examples provided with synsets. Crucially, WHiC includes challenging negative examples that assess the ability of models to detect the direction of hypernymy.

We use WHiC to determine the effectiveness of existing supervised models for hypernymy detection (Roller and Erk, 2016) applied to representations, not only of word types, but of words in context. Such contextualized representations are induced in two ways: the first is based on Context2Vec, a BiLSTM model that embeds contexts and words in the same space (Melamud et al., 2016); the second aims to capture geometric properties of the context in a standard word embedding space built using GloVe (Pennington et al., 2014).

We show that the two contextualized representations improve performance over context-agnostic baselines. The structure of WHiC lets us show that they have complementary properties: Context2Vec-based models have higher recall and tend to identify directionality much better than Glove-based models. We also show that the context-aware representations improve performance on identifying a broader range of semantic relations (Shwartz and Dagan, 2016).

---

[1]https://github.com/yogarshi/whic

33

*Proceedings of the 6th Joint Conference on Lexical and Computational Semantics (*SEM 2017)*, pages 33–43,
Vancouver, Canada, August 3-4, 2017. ©2017 Association for Computational Linguistics

Words (w_l, w_r)	Exemplars (c_l, c_r)	Does $w_l \implies w_r$?
staff, *stick*	c_l = He walked with the help of a wooden *staff*. c_r = The kid had a candied apple on a *stick*.	Yes
staff, *body*	c_l = The hospital has an excellent nursing *staff*. c_r = The whole *body* filed out of the auditorium.	Yes
staff, *stick*	c_l = The hospital has an excellent nursing *staff*. c_r = The kid had a candied apple on a *stick*.	No

Table 1: Examples of the context-aware hypernymy detection task

2 Detecting Hypernymy in Context

2.1 Task Definition

We frame hypernymy detection in context as a binary classification task. Each example consists of a 4-tuple (w_l, w_r, c_l, c_r), where w_l and w_r are word types, and c_l and c_r are sentences which illustrate each word usage. The example is treated as positive if $w_l \implies w_r$, given the meaning of each word exemplified by the contexts, and negative otherwise, as can be seen in Table 1.

As mentioned in Section 1, hypernymy is only one specific case of lexical entailment. The nature of entailment relations captured out-of-context can be broader depending on the test beds considered[2]. These relations can include synonymy, hypernymy, some meronymy relations, and also cause-effect relations.

2.2 Motivation

The need to study hypernymy detection in context is important due to several reasons. First, many downstream tasks which might benefit from detecting hypernyms will have words appearing in specific contexts. Second, existing definitions (and, by extension, annotations) of lexical entailment do not explicitly or consistently address polysemy. For instance, the substitutional definition for entailment by Zhitomirsky-Geffet and Dagan (2009) asks the reader to think of a natural sentence that provides the missing context to the two words being considered, thus constraining the possible senses of the two words. On the other hand, Turney and Mohammad (2013) propose a relational definition, inviting the reader to imagine a semantic relation that connects the two words and constrains their possible senses. In contrast, we propose to detect hypernymy between word meanings described by specific contexts.

Lexical entailment or hypernymy in context is also different from recognizing textual entailment (RTE). RTE (Dagan et al., 2006, 2013) involves detecting entailment relations between sentences, while hypernymy is a relation between words. Additionally, the two contexts c_l and c_r in our task can be very different, unlike in textual entailment, where the premise and hypothesis are usually related. For instance, the first example in Table 1 illustrates a scenario where the hypernymy relation holds between *staff* and *stick*, but there is no entailment relationship between the two sentences. On the other hand, the sentence "*Children smile and wave at the camera.*" entails "*There are children present.*", but there is no meaningful hypernymy relationship between words in the two sentences.

Finally, the proposed task is also related to, but different from word sense disambiguation (WSD). Unlike WSD, this task eschews an explicit sense inventory, instead relying on the provided contexts to decide the specific relation between the words. This might provide a more natural way to think about word senses for (untrained) human annotators (Erk et al., 2013). WSD can in principle be used as a preprocessing step to address hypernymy detection in context, but it is not required. Also, WSD remains a challenging task (Moro and Navigli, 2015) and it might introduce errors early in the preprocessing pipeline.

2.3 WHiC : A Dataset for Lexical Entailment in Context

We require a dataset to study hypernymy detection in context to satisfy the following desiderata: (1) the dataset should make it possible to assess the sensitivity of context-aware models to contexts that signal different word senses, and (2) the dataset should help quantify the extent to which models detect the asymmetric direction of hypernymy, rather than symmetric semantic similarity.

---

[2]We refer the reader to Turney and Mohammad (2013) and Shwartz et al. (2017) for comprehensive surveys of supervised and unsupervised methods for the out-of-context task.

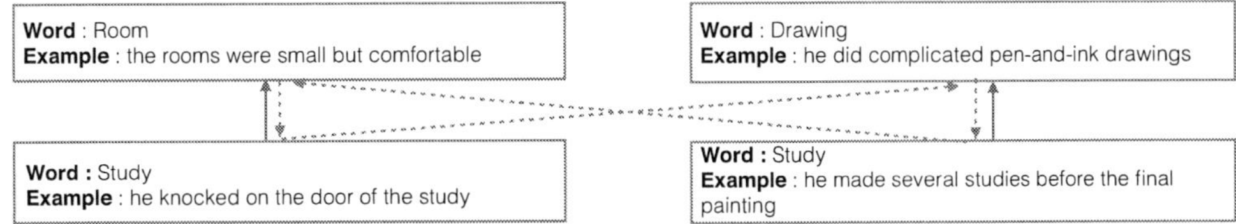

Figure 1: Sample dataset creation process based on two synsets of the word *study*. The green/solid lines indicate positive examples, while the red/dashed lines indicate negative examples

Existing datasets for lexical entailment (Baroni and Lenci, 2011; Baroni et al., 2012; Kotlerman et al., 2010) have driven progress on the **out of context** task only, and are therefore insensitive to context changes. In addition, they include a variety of negative examples without controlling for entailment direction. For instance, Baroni and Lenci (2011) use cohyponyms and random words as negative examples. Since cohyponyms are words that share a common hypernym (for example, *salsa* and *tango* are cohyponymys with respect to *dance*), hypernymy does not hold between them in any direction. On the other hand, random examples (also used by Baroni et al. (2012)) are likely to be detected using symmetric semantic similarity rather than asymmetric hypernymy detection.

Shwartz and Dagan (2016) recently introduced CONTEXT-PPDB, a dataset for fine-grained lexical inference in context. This dataset consists of word pairs along with a pair of sentential contexts, with a label indicating the semantic relation between the two words in the given contexts. However, since CONTEXT-PPDB only consists of ~3700 sentence pairs, it provides only a smaller number of annotated examples per relation, making it difficult to train large supervised models on (we return to this dataset in Section 5).

We address these gaps by introducing, WHIC, a large dataset automatically derived from Word-Net (Fellbaum, 1998). WordNet groups synonyms into *synsets* and defines semantic relations such as hypernymy and meronymy between these synsets. Most synsets are further accompanied by one or more short sentences illustrating the use of the members of the synset. WHIC uses these example sentences as context for the words, and the hypernymy relations to draw candidate word pairs. The process starts from a seed list of words W and proceeds as follows (see Figure 1) :

1. For all word types $w \in W$ obtain synsets S_w.

2. For each synset $i \in S_w$, pick a hypernym synset s_h^i, with a corresponding word form w_h^i. Also obtain c^i and c_h^i which are example sentences corresponding to w^i and w_h^i respectively - (w^i, w_h^i, c^i, c_h^i) serves as a positive example. Repeat this process for all hypernyms (solid/green arrows in Figure 1).

3. **Permute** the positive examples to get negative examples. From (w^i, w_h^i, c^i, c_h^i) and (w^j, w_h^j, c^j, c_h^j), generate negative examples (w^i, w_h^j, c^i, c_h^j) and (w^j, w_h^i, c^j, c_h^i) (longer dashed/red arrows in Figure 1).

4. **Flip** the positive examples to generate negative examples. From (w^i, w_h^i, c^i, c_h^i) generate the negative example (w_h^i, w^i, c_h^i, c^i) (shorter dashed/red arrows in Figure 1).

We run this process using the 9000 most frequent words from Wikipedia as W (after filtering the top 1000 as stopwords). This yields a total of 5239 positive examples, 12303 negative examples from Step 3, and 5239 negative examples from Step 4.

WHIC satisfies the desiderata outlined above. The dataset has a well-defined focus, since we only pick hypernym-hyponym pairs. The negative examples generated in Steps 3 and 4 require discriminating between different word senses and entailment directions. Finally, with over 22000 examples distributed over 6000 word pairs, the dataset is large enough to train large supervised models. We define a 70/5/25 train/dev/test split, and ensure that each set contains different word pairs, to avoid memorization and overfitting (Levy et al., 2015).

3 Representing Words and their Contexts for Entailment

How can we construct representations of the meaning of target words w_l and w_r, and their respective exemplar contexts c_l and c_r?

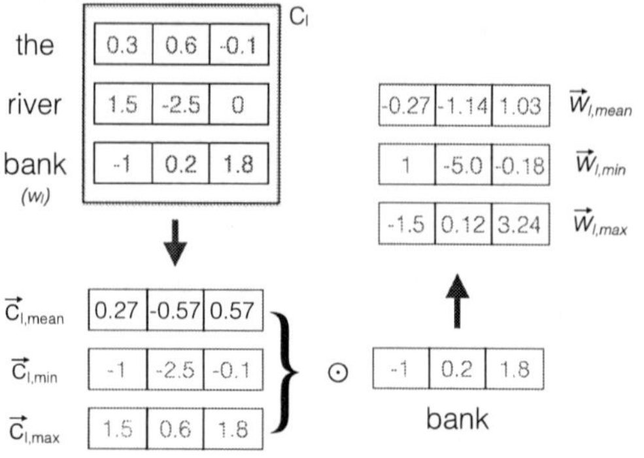

Figure 2: Constructing word-in-context representations for "bank", in the context "the river bank". ⊙ indicates element-wise multiplication.

We will construct representations for c_l, and c_r, and create context-aware representations for w_l and w_r by "masking" their word embeddings with the embeddings for c_l and c_r (Section 3.3). We compare two approaches to representing c_l and c_r. The first (Section 3.1) builds on standard representations for word types, which have proven useful for detecting lexical entailment and other semantic relations out of context (Baroni et al., 2012; Kruszewski and Baroni, 2015; Vylomova et al., 2016; Turney and Mohammad, 2013). The second approach (Section 3.2) uses a recurrent neural model to embed words and contexts in the same space, allowing direct comparisons between them.

3.1 Creating Context Representations from Word Type Representations

Given an example (w_l, w_r, c_l, c_r), let $\vec{w}_l$ and $\vec{w}_r$ refer to the context-agnostic representations of w_l and w_r, and let C_l and C_r represent the matrices obtained by row-wise stacking of the context-agnostic representations of words in c_l and c_r respectively.

Following Thater et al. (2011); Erk and Padó (2008), we apply a filter to word type representations to highlight the salient dimensions of the exemplar context, emphasizing relevant dimensions and downplaying unimportant ones. However, while prior work represents context by averaging word vectors, we propose richer representations that better capture the salient geometrical properties of the exemplar context that might get lost by averaging.

We construct fixed length representations for the contexts c_l and c_r by running convolutional fil-

ters over C_l and C_r. Specifically, we calculate the column-wise maximum, minimum and the mean over the matrices C_l and C_r, as done by Tang et al. (2014) for supervised sentiment classification. This yields three d-dimensional vectors for c_l ($\vec{c}_{l,max}$, $\vec{c}_{l,min}$, $\vec{c}_{l,mean}$), and three d-dimensional vectors for c_r ($\vec{c}_{r,max}$, $\vec{c}_{r,min}$, $\vec{c}_{r,mean}$). Computing the maximum and minimum across all vector dimensions captures the exterior surface of the "instance manifold" (the volume in embedding space within which all words in the instance reside), while the mean summarizes the density per-dimension within the manifold (Hovy, 2015).

3.2 LSTM-based Context Representations: Context2Vec

An alternative approach to contextualizing word representations is to directly compare the representations of words with representations of contexts. This can be done using Context2Vec (Melamud et al., 2016), a neural model that, given a target word and its sentential context, embeds both the word and the context in the same low-dimensional space using a BiLSTM, with the objective of having the context predict the target word via a log-linear model. This model approaches the state-of-the-art on lexical substitution, sentence completion, and supervised word sense disambiguation. For each example (w_l, w_r, c_l, c_r), we extract the word type representations $\vec{w}_{l,c2v}$ and $\vec{w}_{l,c2v}$ from Context2Vec, as well as the context representations $\vec{c}_{l,c2v}$, and $\vec{c}_{r,c2v}$.

3.3 Context-aware Masked Representations

Given these two methods to learn representations for words and their contexts, we also learn context aware word representations for the target words. We transform initial context-agnostic representations for target word types by taking an element-wise product of the word type vectors with vectors representing the context.

Specifically, for the context representations learned in Section 3.1, we take an element-wise product of the word type vectors ($\vec{w}_*$) with ($\vec{c}_{*,max}$, $\vec{c}_{*,min}$, $\vec{c}_{*,mean}$) where $* \in \{l, r\}$. This yields three d-dimensional vectors for w_l ($\vec{w}_{l,max}$, $\vec{w}_{l,min}$, $\vec{w}_{l,mean}$), and three for w_r ($\vec{w}_{r,max}$, $\vec{w}_{r,min}$, $\vec{w}_{r,mean}$). We refer to our final word-in-context representations for w_l and w_r as $\vec{w}_{l,mask}$ and $\vec{w}_{r,mask}$ respectively, where $\vec{w}_{l,mask}$ is the concatenation of $\vec{w}_{l,max}$, $\vec{w}_{l,min}$, $\vec{w}_{l,mean}$, and $\vec{w}_{r,mask}$ is also similarly constructed.

For the word and context representations obtained from Context2Vec (Section 3.2), we create the context-aware representations $\vec{w}_{l,c2v,mask}$ by vector multiplication between $\vec{w}_{l,c2v}$ and $\vec{c}_{l,c2v}$. We also obtain $\vec{w}_{r,c2v,mask}$ similarly.

4 Comparing Words and Contexts for Entailment

Given the word, context, and word-in-context representations described above, we predict entailment via supervised classification.

Our classifier is the *Hypernymy-Feature detector* (Roller and Erk, 2016), which is the current state-of-the-art supervised model for detecting hypernymy on several datasets. This model aims to overcome the shortcomings of previous supervised hypernymy detection models, which used linear classifiers on top of concatenation of the two vectors representing the target words. These models only captured notions of *prototypicality* without modeling the interactions between the two words; that is, they guessed that (*animal, sofa*) is a positive example because *animal* looks like a hypernym (Levy et al., 2015).

Instead, the *H-Feature detector* model trains a linear classifier using concatenation, as described above, and then removes this prototypical information from the word vectors by projecting them on a hyperplane orthogonal to the separating hyperplane learned by the linear classifier. By repeating this process, one can learn multiple classifiers, each of which increases the models representational power. In each iteration i, four features are extracted to represent the word pair, based on the current representations of the word pair $(\vec{x}, \vec{y})$ and the hyperplane $\vec{p}_i$ learned in the current iteration :

1. The similarity between $\vec{x}$ and the hyperplane, $\vec{x}.\vec{p}_i$
2. The similarity between $\vec{y}$ and the hyperplane, $\vec{y}.\vec{p}_i$
3. The similarity between the two words, $\vec{x}.\vec{y}$
4. The similarity between the difference of the two words, and the hyperplane, $(\vec{y} - \vec{x}).\vec{p}_i$

Features 1 and 2 capture similarities like the one included in the concatenation classifier. The third feature aims to overcome the shortcomings of the concatenation model by directly modeling the similarities between the two target words. Finally, the fourth feature captures the distributional inclusion hypothesis (Geffet and Dagan, 2005) – if word v is a hypernym of u, then the set of features of u are included in the set of features of v – by intuitively capturing whether y includes x (Roller et al., 2014).

5 Experimental Set-up

Tasks In addition to WHIC, we evaluate our context-aware representations on CONTEXT-PPDB. As mentioned in Section 2.3, CONTEXT-PPDB is a dataset for fine-grained lexical inference in context that captures other semantic relations beyond hypernymy. It has been created using 375 word pairs from a subset of the English Paraphrase Database (Ganitkevitch et al., 2013; Pavlick et al., 2015). These word pairs are semi-automatically labeled with semantic relations out-of-context. Shwartz and Dagan (2016) augmented them with examples of word usage in context, and re-annotated the word pairs given the extra contextual information. The final dataset consists of 3750 words/contexts tuples with a corresponding semantic label, one of which is entailment.

All our experiments are with the default train/dev/test splits on both datasets.

Contextualized Word Representations To obtain the Context2Vec representations, we use an existing 600-dimensional model trained on ukWaC (Ferraresi et al., 2006). We use 600 dimensional GloVe embeddings trained on the same corpus to create $\vec{w}_l$, $\vec{w}_r$, C_l, and C_r, and allow for a controlled comparison with Context2Vec. Context2Vec representations are significantly more expensive to train: Melamud et al. (2016) indicate that training requires ~30 hours on a Tesla K80 GPU, while the GloVe embeddings can be trained on the exact same amount of data in less than 7 hours on a CPU.

Supervised Lexical Entailment Classifier We use an SVM with an RBF kernel for WHIC and Logistic Regression for CONTEXT-PPDB as implemented in Scikit-Learn [3] as our classifiers, to allow for exact comparisons with past work on CONTEXT-PPDB. We use default parameters, except for adding class weights in the WHIC experiments to account for the unbalanced data. For WHIC we use features derived from the H-Feature

---

[3]http://scikit-learn.org

model described in Section 4. For CONTEXT-PPDB we simply concatenate the representations and use them directly as the features. We evaluate the predictions using F1 score.

6 Experiments on WHiC

In our first set of experiments, we evaluate the two models described in Section 3 on WHiC under a variety of combinations.

6.1 Overall Results

Results are summarized in Table 2. Supervised models[4] outperform the baseline that always predict that hypernymy holds ("All True Baseline") by up to 16 F-score points. Context-aware models outperform context-agnostic models by up to 3 points[5]. GloVe and Context2Vec models yield similar F1, both when used as word type representations alone, and when combined with masked representations. However, GloVe and Context2Vec representations capture complementary information: GloVe yields slightly better precision while Context2Vec models yield significantly better recall. The best performance overall is obtained by a hybrid model that uses word-type representations from Context2Vec and masked context-aware representations derived from GloVe.

Additionally using Context2Vec vectors directly ($\vec{c}_{l,c2v}, \vec{c}_{r,c2v}$) performs much worse than using them as masks ($\vec{w}_{l,c2v,mask}, \vec{c}_{r,c2v,mask}$). This highlights the benefit of using context to influence the word type representation rather than to directly compare word and context representations.

Finally, there is no benefit in using the context-aware masked representations without the word type representations: using just the masked representations by themselves does worse than using them in combination with the word type representations.

Overall, the scores in Table 2 highlight the challenging nature of WHiC, and leave scope for improvement with potentially better models for context-aware representations.

| Supervised Model Config. | | | | |
Word-type	Context-aware	P	R	F
GloVe	None	44	60	51
GloVe	GloVe Masks	42	73	53
None	GloVe Masks	32	64	43
C2V	None	40	73	52
C2V	C2V Masks	41	73	52
None	C2V Masks	30	94	45
C2V	C2V Contexts	23	10	14
None	C2V Contexts	8	2	3
C2V Words	GloVe Masks	41	**78**	**54**
GloVe Words	C2V Masks	**44**	64	52
All True Baseline		24	100	38

Table 2: Results on WHiC. a) Word type indicates (GloVe or Context2Vec (C2V)) H-Features extracted from context-agnostic representations. b) Context aware indicates H-Features extracted from the context-aware representations described in Section 3.

6.2 Sensitivity to context

To determine the sensitivity of our models to context changes, we evaluate on the balanced subset of WHiC comprised of positive examples and negative examples created by permuting contexts in Step 3 of the dataset creation process. We analyze the predictions using a modified version of precision, recall and F-score, defined as the precision, recall, and F1-score calculated over each (w_l, w_r) word pair, and then averaged over all word pairs. We call these measures the Macro-P/R/F1.

Table 3 shows that context-aware representations generally improve performance on all three metrics, but the gain is larger on recall. Again we observe that models using Context2Vec word types and masks have a better Macro-R than the corresponding GloVe models. Overall, the masked representations obtained from Context2Vec perform the best on these metrics, closely followed by the overall best model that uses the Context2Vec word type representations and the masked representations from GloVe.

Finally, note that the all-true baseline surprisingly does as well as the best context-aware model on this metric. However, it cannot detect the direction of hypernymy (Section 6.3), and the structure of WHiC allows us to distinguish these two factors.

---

[4]We also tried two unsupervised context-agnostic baselines using cosine similarity and balAPinc (Kotlerman et al., 2010) but they trivially predicted all pairs as entailing

[5]A statistically significant difference with $p < 0.01$ under the McNemar's test (McNemar, 1947)

| Supervised Model Config. | | Context sensitivity | | | Directionality |
Word Type rep.	Context-aware rep.	Macro-P	Macro-R	Macro-F	Pairwise Acc.
GloVe	None	13	28	17	59
GloVe	GloVe Masks	17	35	22	71
None	GloVe Masks	13	30	18	59
C2V	None	15	35	21	71
C2V	C2V Masks	16	35	21	72
None	C2V Masks	**18**	**45**	**25**	62
C2V	C2V Contexts	5	5	4	9
None	C2V Contexts	1	1	1	1
C2V	GloVe Masks	17	37	23	**76**
GloVe	C2V Masks	14	29	19	63
All True Baseline		18	50	25	0

Table 3: Macro-P/R/F1 and Pairwise accuracy, are intended to capture context-awareness (Section 6.2) and directionality-discrimination abilities (Section 6.3) of the models, respectively.

6.3 Sensitivity to Entailment Direction

Next, we evaluate to what extent the models capture the direction of hypernymy using the balanced subset of WH1C that consists of all positive examples and flipped negative examples generated in Step 4 in the dataset creation process. We measure directionality by looking at the fraction of pairs $((w_l, w_r, c_l, c_r), (w_r, w_l, c_r, c_l))$ where both examples are correctly labeled, i.e. the former is labeled as $\implies$ and the latter as $\not\implies$. We call this metric the pairwise accuracy.

As seen in Table 3, the best pairwise accuracy is again obtained by the hybrid model using word type representations from Context2Vec and the masked representations from GloVe. Overall Context2Vec models do a better job at capturing directionality than GloVe.

6.4 Nature of Contextualized Masks

We also hypothesized that masked contextualized representations based on the full volume of the context using min and max operations (Section 3.1) better capture salient context dimensions than the more usual vector averaging approach. We test this hypothesis empirically by replacing masked word-in-context representations $\vec{w}_{l,mask}$ and $\vec{w}_{r,mask}$ by two other ways to capture context. In the first method, we use the mean of the contexts $(\vec{c}_{l,mean}, \vec{c}_{r,mean})$. In the second method, we use $(\vec{w}_{l,mean}, \vec{w}_{r,mean})$, i.e. the masked representations calculated by using only the mean of the context, and not the max and min.

Table 4 shows that our preferred method outperforms the two alternatives on WH1C, with our proposed representations outperforming the other methods by 3 F1 points. Additionally, this increase in performance also comes with significant improvement in detection of asymmetric relations.

6.5 Summary

Overall, both Context2Vec and Glove representations improve performance over context-agnostic baselines. Using masking to contextualize word type representations works better than just using the context representations as is. The best performing model is a hybrid model that uses word type representations from Context2Vec and masked representations from GloVe. Analysis enabled by the structure of the dataset shows that all masked representations are sensitive to changes in meaning indicated by glosses from distinct WordNet synsets. However, the more expensive Context2Vec representations do a better job at recall and direction of hypernymy.

7 CONTEXT-PPDB

We now experiment on CONTEXT-PPDB to test the ability of contextualized representations to capture semantic relations beyond hypernymy, to aid future work on recognizing other contextualized relationships.

Shwartz and Dagan (2016) establish a baseline of 67 F1 on this dataset using rich features characterizing word pairs drawn from PPDB as

Dataset	Representations	P	R	F	Context sensitivity	Directionality
WHiC	$\vec{c}_{l,mean},\vec{c}_{r,mean}$	**45**	59	51	17	58
	$\vec{w}_{l,mean},\vec{w}_{r,mean}$	43	62	51	18	61
	$\vec{w}_{l,mask},\vec{w}_{r,mask}$	42	**73**	**53**	**22**	**71**

Table 4: Impact of masks on WHiC measured by Precision (P), Recall (R), F-Measure (F), context sensitivity (Macro-F1) and directionality (Pairwise accuracy). Replacing our contextualized representations by a mean representation of the context, or a contextualized representation based only on the mean, leads to drops in performance.

Word Type	P	R	F
Baseline	68	70	67
++ context-aware rep.s	72	72	**72**

Table 5: Results on CONTEXT-PPDB. Baseline indicates the previous state of the art result on this dataset (Shwartz and Dagan, 2016)

Label	Baseline	++ Context-aware Rep.s
Equivalence	76	76
Entailment	79	**87**
Alternation	55	55
Other-related	12	**28**
Independent	77	**78**

Table 6: Performance of the baseline and augmented model on all semantic relations in CONTEXT-PPDB measured using per-class F1

well as similarity scores between words and contexts. The PPDB features notably include scores for likelihood of context-agnostic entailment labels, distributional similarities, and probabilities of the word pair being paraphrases, among other scores. Additionally, word representation features are used: given two word/context pairs (w_x, c_x, w_y, c_y), GloVe vectors are used to represent w_x and w_y, as well as words in c_x and c_y, and are used to extract the following feature, which capture the most salient word/context similarities between the two pairs :

$$\{\max_{w \in c_y} \vec{w_x} \cdot \vec{w}, \max_{w \in c_x} \vec{w_y} \cdot \vec{w}, \max_{w \in c_x, w' \in c_y} \vec{w} \cdot \vec{w'}\}$$

We augment this system with contextualized word representations. We use the GloVe based masked representations, as they can be obtained with a negligible computation cost in addition the features already included in the baseline, and as the labels denote a mix of directional and non-directional relations. This remarkably yields an improvement ~5 F1 points compared to the previous state-of-the-art (Table 5). Breaking down results per label (Table 6) shows an increase of 8 F1 points for the entailment class. This improvement again stems from a large increase in recall, mirroring the behavior observed on WHiC. The diverse "other-related" category also benefits from context-aware representations.

8 Related Work

WordNet and lexical entailment The "is-a" hierarchy of WordNet (Fellbaum, 1998) is a prominent source of information for unsupervised detection of hypernymy and entailment (Harabagiu and Moldovan, 1998; Shwartz et al., 2015), as well as a source of various datasets (Baroni and Lenci, 2011; Baroni et al., 2012). WHiC is inspired by the latter line of work, except that we extract exemplar contexts from WordNet in addition to relations between words.

Modeling word meaning in context Prior models for the meaning of a word in a given context aimed to capture semantic equivalence in tasks such as lexical substitution, word sense disambiguation or paraphrase ranking, rather than asymmetric relations such as entailment. One line of work (Dinu and Lapata, 2010; Reisinger and Mooney, 2010) views each word as a set of latent word senses. These models rely on token representations for individual occurrences of a word and then choose a set of token vectors based on the current context. An alternate set of models (Erk and Padó, 2008; Thater et al., 2011; Dinu et al., 2012) avoids defining a fixed set of word senses, and instead contextualizes word type vectors as we do here. These models share the idea of using an element-wise multiplication to apply a context mask to word type representations. The nature of the context representation varies: Erk and Padó (2008) use inverse selectional preferences; Thater et al. (2010) combine a first order co-occurrence based representation for the context with a second order representation for the target, Thater et al. (2011) rely on syntactic dependencies to define context. Apidianaki (2016) shows that bag-of-word context representation within a small context window works as well as syntactic definitions of context for ranking paraphrases in context.

Our use of convolution is motivated by success of similar models on sentence classification tasks. Tang et al. (2014) uses convolution over embedding matrices for unigrams, bigrams, and trigrams, while Hovy (2015) uses just unigrams. However, all these works use the resulting representations to predict properties of the sentence (e.g., sentiment), rather than to contextualize target word representations.

In-context lexical semantic tasks Besides entailment, other lexical semantic tasks studied in context include lexical substitution (McCarthy and Navigli, 2007) and cross-lingual lexical substitution (Mihalcea et al., 2010). The focus of these tasks and their related datasets is on synonymy and translation equivalence, since they require one to predict substitutes for a target word instance, which preserve its meaning in a given sentential context. On the other hand, the focus of this work and WHiC is on detecting more fine-grained relations via lexical entailment. Another related task is that of paraphrase ranking (Apidianaki, 2016). The work by Apidianaki (2016) is also notable because of their successful use of models of word-meaning in context from Thater et al. (2011), which is closely related to our work.

9 Conclusion

We introduced WHiC, a dataset to evaluate lexical entailment in context, providing exemplar sentences to ground the meaning of words being considered for entailment, and challenging examples designed to capture entailment direction accurately.

We showed that supervised models developed for context-agnostic lexical entailment can address the context-aware task to some extent, when replacing word representations with a contextualized version. We compared two contextualized representations including (1) a simple context-aware representation based on the geometry of word embeddings, and (2) Context2Vec, a more expensive BiLSTM-based model that yields representations of words and their context in the same space. Both improve performance over context-agnostic models, and have complementary properties: models using Context2Vec are more accurate at discriminating the direction of entailment. They also have a better recall when measured using metrics designed to test sensitivity to context. Finally, we also showed that contextualized representations can improve detection of other semantic relations in context.

While encouraging, the performance of models considered leave substantial room for improvement. For instance, it remains to be seen whether richer features for the supervised models and richer context representations can improve sensitivity to context, and whether the nuances of the task can be better captured with annotations on a graded scale, following previous work on word meaning in context (Erk et al., 2013).

Acknowledgements

The authors thank the anonymous reviewers for their comments, as well as the members of the CLIP lab at UMD and Mona Diab for many conversations which helped shape this paper. We also thank Vered Shwartz for help with data and code for CONTEXT-PPDB, and Stephen Roller for help with the H-Feature detector code.

References

Marianna Apidianaki. 2016. Vector-space models for PPDB paraphrase ranking in context. In *Proceedings of EMNLP 2016*. Austin, TX, USA, pages 2028–2034.

Marco Baroni, Raffaella Bernardi, Ngoc-Quynh Do, and Chung-chieh Shan. 2012. Entailment above the word level in distributional semantics. In *Proceedings of EACL 2012*. pages 23–32. http://dl.acm.org/citation.cfm?id=2380822.

Marco Baroni and Alessandro Lenci. 2011. How we BLESSed distributional semantic evaluation. In *Proceedings of the GEMS 2011 Workshop on GEometrical Models of Natural Language Semantics*. pages 1–10. http://dl.acm.org/citation.cfm?id=2140490.2140491.

Ido Dagan, Oren Glickman, and Bernardo Magnini. 2006. The PASCAL Recognising Textual Entailment Challenge. In *Proceedings of the First*

International Conference on Machine Learning Challenges: Evaluating Predictive Uncertainty Visual Object Classification, and Recognizing Textual Entailment. Springer-Verlag, Southampton, UK, MLCW'05, pages 177–190.

Ido Dagan, Dan Roth, Mark Sammons, and Fabio Massimo Zanzotto. 2013. *Recognizing Textual Entailment: Models and Applications*. Morgan & Claypool Publishers.

Georgiana Dinu and Mirella Lapata. 2010. Measuring Distributional Similarity in Context. In *Proceedings of EMNLP 2010*. Cambridge, MA, USA, pages 1162–1172. http://eprints.pascalnetwork.org/archive/00008156/.

Georgiana Dinu, Stefan Thater, and Sören Laue. 2012. A comparison of models of word meaning in context. In *Proceedings of NAACL-HLT 2012*. pages 611–615.

Katrin Erk, Diana McCarthy, and Nicholas Gaylord. 2013. Measuring Word Meaning in Context. *Computational Linguistics* 39(3).

Katrin Erk and Sebastian Padó. 2008. A structured vector space model for word meaning in context. In *Proceedings of EMNLP 2010*. Honolulu, HA, USA, October, pages 897–906. https://doi.org/10.3115/1613715.1613831.

Christiane Fellbaum, editor. 1998. *WordNet: An Electronic Lexical Database*. MIT Press.

Adriano Ferraresi, Eros Zanchetta, Marco Baroni, and Silvia Bernardini. 2006. Introducing and evaluating ukWaC , a very large web-derived corpus of English. In *Proceedings of the 4th Web as Corpus Workshop*.

Juri Ganitkevitch, Benjamin Van Durme, and Chris Callison-Burch. 2013. PPDB : The Paraphrase Database. *Proceedings of NAACL-HLT 2013* (June):758—-764. http://cs.jhu.edu/ ccb/publications/ppdb.pdf.

Maayan Geffet and Ido Dagan. 2005. The Distributional Inclusion Hypotheses and Lexical Entailment. In *Proceedings of ACL 2005*. Ann Arbor, MI, June, pages 107–114.

Sanda Harabagiu and Andrew Hickl. 2006. Methods for Using Textual Entailment in Open-Domain Question Answering. *Proceedings of ACL* (July):905–912. https://doi.org/10.3115/1220175.1220289.

Sanda Harabagiu and Dan Moldovan. 1998. Knowledge processing on an extended wordnet. *WordNet: An electronic lexical database* 305:381–405.

Dirk Hovy. 2015. Demographic Factors Improve Classification Performance. In *Proceedings of ACL-IJCNLP 2015*. Beijing, China, pages 752–762.

Lili Kotlerman, Ido Dagan, Idan Szpektor, and Maayan Zhitomirsky-Geffet. 2010. Directional Distributional Similarity for Lexical Inference. *Natural Language Engineering* 16(4):359–389. https://doi.org/10.1017/S1351324910000124.

German Kruszewski and Marco Baroni. 2015. Deriving Boolean structures from distributional vectors. *Transactions of ACL* 3:375–388.

Omer Levy, Steffen Remus, Chris Biemann, and Ido Dagan. 2015. Do Supervised Distributional Methods Really Learn Lexical Inference Relations? In *NAACL HLT 2015*. pages 970–976.

Diana McCarthy and Roberto Navigli. 2007. SemEval-2007 Task 10: English Lexical Substitution Task. In *Proceedings of SEMEVAL 2007*. pages 48–53. https://doi.org/10.1007/s10579-009-9084-1.

Quinn McNemar. 1947. Note on the sampling error of the difference between correlated proportions or percentages. *Psychometrika* 12(2):153–157.

Oren Melamud, Jacob Goldberger, and Ido Dagan. 2016. context2vec: Learning Generic Context Embedding with Bidirectional LSTM. In *Proceedings of CoNLL 2016*. Berlin, Germany, pages 51–61.

Rada Mihalcea, Ravi Sinha, and Diana McCarthy. 2010. SemEval-2010 Task 2: Cross-Lingual Lexical Substitution. In *Proceedings of SemEval 2010 (ACL 2010)*. Uppsala, Sweden, July, pages 9–14.

Andrea Moro and Roberto Navigli. 2015. Semeval-2015 task 13: Multilingual all-words sense disambiguation and entity linking. *Proc. of SemEval-2015* .

Ellie Pavlick, Pushpendre Rastogi, Juri Ganitkevitch, Benjamin Van Durme, and Chris Callison-Burch. 2015. PPDB 2.0: Better paraphrase ranking, fine-grained entailment relations, word embeddings, and style classification. *Proceedings of ACL-IJCNLP 2015* pages 425–430.

Jeffrey Pennington, Richard Socher, and Christopher D Manning. 2014. GloVe: Global Vectors for Word Representation. In *Proceedings of EMNLP 2014*. Doha, Qatar, pages 1532–1543. https://doi.org/10.3115/v1/D14-1162.

Joseph Reisinger and Raymond J Mooney. 2010. Multi-Prototype Vector-Space Models of Word Meaning. In *Proceedings of NAACL 2010*. Los Angeles, CA, June, pages 109–117.

Stephen Roller and Katrin Erk. 2016. Relations such as Hypernymy: Identifying and Exploiting Hearst Patterns in Distributional Vectors for Lexical Entailment. *Proceedings of EMNLP 2016* http://arxiv.org/abs/1605.05433.

Stephen Roller, Katrin Erk, and Gemma Boleda. 2014. Inclusive yet Selective: Supervised Distributional Hypernymy Detection. *Proceedings of COLING 2014* pages 1025–1036.

Vered Shwartz and Ido Dagan. 2016. Adding Context to Semantic Data-Driven Paraphrasing. In *Proceedings of *SEM 2016*. Berlin, Germany, pages 108–113.

Vered Shwartz, Yoav Goldberg, and Ido Dagan. 2016. Improving Hypernymy Detection with an Integrated Pattern-based and Distributional Method. In *Proceedings of ACL 2016*.

Vered Shwartz, Omer Levy, Ido Dagan, and Jacob Goldberger. 2015. Learning to Exploit Structured Resources for Lexical Inference. In *Proceedings of CoNLL 2015*. Beijing, China, pages 175–184. http://www.aclweb.org/anthology/K15-1018.

Vered Shwartz, Enrico Santus, and Dominik Schlechtweg. 2017. Hypernyms under Siege: Linguistically-motivated Artillery for Hypernymy Detection. In *Proceedings of EACL 2017*. Valencia, Spain.

Duyu Tang, Furu Wei, Nan Yang, Ming Zhou, Ting Liu, and Bing Qin. 2014. Learning Sentiment-Specific Word Embedding. In *Proceedings of ACL 2014*. Baltimore, MD, USA, pages 1555–1565. https://doi.org/10.3115/1220575.1220648.

Stefan Thater, Hagen Fuerstenau, and Manfred Pinkal. 2010. Contextualizing Semantic Representations Using Syntactically Enriched Vector Models. In *Proceedings of ACL 2010*. Uppsala, Sweden, July, pages 948–957. http://eprints.pascal-network.org/archive/00008090/.

Stefan Thater, Hagen Fürstenau, and Manfred Pinkal. 2011. Word Meaning in Context : A Simple and Effective Vector Model. In *Proceedings of IJCNLP 2011*. Chiang Mai, Thailand, pages 1134–1143.

Peter Turney and Saif Mohammad. 2013. Experiments with three approaches to recognizing lexical entailment. *Natural Language Engineering* 1(1):1–42. https://doi.org/10.1017/S1351324913000387.

Ekaterina Vylomova, Laura Rimell, Trevor Cohn, and Timothy Baldwin. 2016. Take and Took, Gaggle and Goose, Book and Read: Evaluating the Utility of Vector Differences for Lexical Relation Learning. In *Proceedings of ACL 2016*. Berlin, Germany, pages 1671–1682.

Maayan Zhitomirsky-Geffet and Ido Dagan. 2009. Bootstrapping Distributional Feature Vector Quality. *Computational Linguistics* (November 2008).

Domain-Specific New Words Detection in Chinese

Ao Chen[1], Maosong Sun[1]

[1]Department of Computer Science and Technology,
State Key Lab on Intelligent Technology and Systems,
National Lab for Information Science and Technology, Tsinghua University, China
`chenao3220@gmail.com, sms@mail.tsinghua.edu.cn`

Abstract

With the explosive growth of Internet, more and more domain-specific environments appear, such as forums, blogs, MOOCs and etc. Domain-specific words appear in these areas and always play a critical role in the domain-specific NLP tasks. This paper aims at extracting Chinese domain-specific new words automatically. The extraction of domain-specific new words has two parts including both new words in this domain and the especially important words. In this work, we propose a joint statistical model to perform these two works simultaneously. Compared to traditional new words detection models, our model doesn't need handcraft features which are labor intensive. Experimental results demonstrate that our joint model achieves a better performance compared with the state-of-the-art methods.

1 Introduction

Accompanying with the development of Internet, many new specific domains appear, such as forums, blogs, Massive Open Online Courses (MOOCs) and etc. There are always a group of important words in these domains, which are known as domain-specific words. Domain-specific words include two types as shown in Table 1. The first ones are rare and unambiguous words which will seldom appear in other domains such as "栈顶"(stack top) and "二叉树"(binary tree). These words may cause word segmentation problems. For example, if we do not recognize "栈顶"(stack top) as a word, the segmentation "栈顶 运算符 是 乘号"(the operator at stack top is multiplication sign) will be like "栈 顶运 算符 是 乘号". In this case, "栈顶" means "stack top"

Domain words	Translation	Type
栈顶	stack top	1
二叉树	binary tree	1
复杂度	complexity	2
遍历	iterate	2

Table 1: Examples of domain-specific word in data structure domain

and "运算符" means "operator", but in the segmentation result, "顶运" is segmented into a word in mistake and will bring lots of problems to the further applications.

The other type is common and ambiguous words which have specific new meanings in this domain, such as "复杂度"(complexity) and "遍历"(iterate). These words often play important roles in domain-specific tasks. For example，in MOOCs which are typical domain-specific environments, there is an Automated Navigation Suggestion(ANS)(Zhang et al., 2017) task which suggests a time point for users when they want to review the front contents of the video. With the help of the recognition of this type of words, we can easily give higher weights to those domain-specific contents.

After extracting these two type of words, we can also use them for creating ontologies, term lists, and in the Semantic Web Area for finding novel entities(Färber et al., 2016). Besides, in MOOCs area it will also benefit Certification Prediction(CP)(Coleman et al., 2015) (which predicts whether a user will get a course certification or not), Course Recommendation(CR)(Aher and Lobo, 2013) and so on by providing textual knowledge.

Researchers have made great efforts to extract domain-specific words. Traditional new word detection methods usually employ statistical methods according to the pattern that new words ap-

*Proceedings of the 6th Joint Conference on Lexical and Computational Semantics (*SEM 2017)*, pages 44–53,
Vancouver, Canada, August 3-4, 2017. ©2017 Association for Computational Linguistics

pear constantly. Such methods like Pointwise Mutual Information(Church and Hanks, 1990), Enhanced Mutual Information(Zhang et al., 2009), and Multi-word Expression Distance(Bu et al., 2010). These methods focus on extracting the first type of domain-specific words and conduct post-processing to discover the second type of words. Deng et al. proposed a statistical model Top-Words(Deng et al., 2016) to extract the first type of words, it can imply some of these statistical measures into the model itself. Besides, it designs a feature called relative frequency to extract the second type of domain-specific words. TopWords is based on a Word Dictionary Model(WDM)(Ge et al., 1999; Chang and Su, 1997; Cohen et al., 2007) in which a sentence is sampled from a word dictionary. To extract the second type of words, it needs to train its model on a common background corpus which is expensive and time-consuming.

To address these issues, we propose a Domain TopWords model by assuming that a sentence is sampled from two word dictionaries, one for common words and the other for domain-specific words. Besides, we propose a flexible domain score function to take the external information into consideration, such as word frequencies in common background corpus. Therefore, the proposed model can extract these two types of words jointly. The main contributions of this paper are summarized as follows:

- We propose a novel Domain TopWords model that can extract both two types of domain-specific words jointly. Experimental results demonstrate the effectiveness of our model.

- Our model achieves a comparable performance even with much less information comparing to the origin TopWords model.

The rest of the paper is structured as follows: the related work will be introduced in section 2. Our model will be introduced in section 3, including model definition and the algorithm details. Then we will present the experiments in section 4. Finally, the work is summarized in section 5.

2   Related work

New word detection as a superset of new domain-specific word detection has been investigated for a long time. New word detection methods mainly contain two directions: the first ones conduct the word segmentation and new word detection jointly. Most of them are supervised models, typical models include conditional random fields proposed by Peng et al. (2004). These supervised models cannot be used in domain-specific words detection directly, due to the lack of annotated domain-specific data. In addition, there are also some unsupervised models, such as Top-Words proposed by Deng et al. (2016). However, it needs time-consuming post-processing to extract the second type of domain-specific words.

Another type treats new word detection as a separate task. This line of methods can be mainly divided into three genres. The first genre is usually preceded by part-of-speech tagging, and treats the new word detection task as a classification problem or directly extracts new words by semantic rules. For example, Argamon et al. (1998) segments the POS sequence of a multi-word into small POS tiles, and then counts tile frequency in both new words and non-new words on training sets, then uses these counts to extract new word. Chen and Ma (2002) uses statistical rules to extract new Chinese word. GuoDong (2005) proposes a discriminative Markov Model to detect new words by chunking one or more separated words. However, these supervised models usually need expert knowledge to design linguistic features and lots of annotated data which are expensive and unavailable in the new arising domains.

The second genre employs user behavior data to detect new words. User typing behavior in Sogou Chinese Pinyin input method which is the most popular Chinese input method is used to detect new words by Zheng et al. (2009). Zhang et al. (2010) proposed to utilize user query log to extract new words. However, these works are usually limited by the availability of the commercial resources.

The third genre employs statistical features and has been extensively studied. In this type of works, new word detection is usually considered as multi-word expression extraction. The measurements of multi-word association are crucial in this type of work. Traditional measurements include: Pointwise Mutual Information (PMI) (Church and Hanks, 1990) and Symmetrical Conditional Probability (SCP) (da Silva and Lopes, 1999). Both these two measures are proposed to measure bi-gram association. Among all 84 bigram association measurements, PMI has been reported to be the best in Czech data(Pecina, 2005). To measure arbitrary of n-grams, some works separate n-grams into two parts and adopt the existing bi-gram based measurements directly. Some other n-gram based measures are also proposed, such as Enhanced Mutual Information (EMI) Zhang et al. (2009). And Multi-word Expression Distance (MED) was proposed by Bu et al. (2010) which based on the information distance theory. The MED measure was reported superior performance to EMI, SCP and other measures. And a pattern based framework which integrates these statistical features together to detect new words was proposed by Huang et al. (2014).

3 Methodology

In this section, we propose a Domain TopWords model. We introduce the Word Dictionary Model(Ge et al., 1999; Chang and Su, 1997; Cohen et al., 2007) and TopWords model proposed by Deng et al. (2016) in subsection 3.1 and 3.2. Then we introduce our Domain TopWords model in subsection 3.3, 3.4 and 3.5. At last, we introduce the modified EM algorithm for our model in 3.6.

3.1 Word Dictionary Model

Word Dictionary Model (WDM) is a unigram language model. It treats a sentence as a sequence of basic units, i.e., words, phrases, idioms, which in this paper are broadly defined as "words". Let $D = \{w_1, w_2, \ldots, w_N\}$ be the vocabulary (dictionary) which contains all interested words, then the sentence can be represented as $S_i = w_{i_i} w_{i_2} \ldots w_{i_j}$. And each word is a sequence of characters. Let $A = \{a_1, \ldots, a_p\}$ be the basic characters of the interested language which in English contain only 26 letters but may include thousands of distinct Chinese characters. Then the words can be represented as $w_i = a_{i_1} a_{i_2} \ldots a_{i_j}$. WDM treats each sentence S as a sampling of words from D with the sampling probability θ_i for word w_i. Let $\theta = (\theta_1, \theta_2, \ldots \theta_N)$ be the sampling probability of the whole D, then the probability of sampling a specific sentence with length K is:

$$P(S|D, \theta) = \prod_{k=1}^{K} \theta_k \qquad (1)$$

3.2 TopWords

TopWords algorithm based on WDM is introduced in Deng et al. (2016), and is used as an unsupervised Chinese text segmentation and new word discovery method. In English texts, words are split by spacing, but in Chinese, there is no spacing between words in a sentence. For unsegmented Chinese text T, let C_T denote the set of all possible segmentations under the dictionary D. Then, under WDM, we have the probability of a Chinese text T:

$$P(T|D, \theta) = \sum_{S_i \in C_T} P(S_i|D, \theta) \qquad (2)$$

Then the likelihood of the parameter θ under the given corpus G is:

$$
\begin{aligned}
L(\theta|D, G) &= P(G|D, \theta) \\
&= \prod_{T_j \in G} P(T_j|D, \theta) \\
&= \prod_{j=1}^{n} \sum_{S_i \in C_{T_j}} P(S_i|D, \theta)
\end{aligned}
\qquad (3)
$$

where θ_{i_k} is the sampling probability of k-th word w_{i_k} in segmentation S_i, n is the number of sentences in the corpus G. Then the value of θ can be estimated by the maximum-likelihood estimate(MLE) as follows:

$$\theta^* = \arg\max_{\theta} \prod_{j=1}^{n} \sum_{S_i \in C_{T_j}} P(S_i|D, \theta) \qquad (4)$$

The MLE value of θ can be computed by the EM algorithm.

After extracting the first type of domain-specific words, the author proposes a measure called relative frequency to extract the second type of domain-specific words. The relative frequency ϕ_i^k of word w_i in domain k can be estimated as follows:

$$\phi_i^k = \frac{\theta_i^k}{\sum_{j=1}^{K} \theta_i^j} \qquad (5)$$

θ_i^k is estimated probability of word w_i from the kth domain.

3.3 Domain Word Dictionary Model

To add the ability to discover domain-specific words, we first use a Domain Word Dictionary Model (D-WDM) instead of the origin WDM model. D-WDM regards a sentence as a sampling from two word dictionaries, one is the common background word dictionary D^c and the other is the domain word dictionary D^d. So a word w_i in a sentence S is sampling first with probability φ to determine which dictionary it is from, and then with probability θ_i^t from D^d or D^c. So the probability of sampling in D-WDM a specific sentence with length K is:

$$P(S_i|D,\theta,\varphi) = \prod_{k=1}^{K_i}(\varphi\theta_{i_k}^c + (1-\varphi)\theta_{i_k}^d) \quad (6)$$

where

$$\theta = (\theta^c, \theta^d) \quad (7)$$

3.4 Domain TopWords

The main difference between Domain TopWords(D-TopWords) and TopWords is that D-TopWords is under the D-WDM model. So there are two word dictionaries, one for common words and the other for the domain-specific words. So the likelihood of θ with the given corpus G under the D-WDM model is:

$$L(\theta|D,G,\varphi) = \prod_{T_j \in G}\sum_{S_i \in C_{T_j}} P(S_i|D,\theta,\varphi)$$

$$= \prod_{j=1}^{n}\sum_{S_i \in C_{T_j}}\prod_{k=1}^{K_i}(\varphi\theta_{i_k}^c + (1-\varphi)\theta_{i_k}^d)$$

$$(8)$$

where the parameter φ need to be fixed. If the φ is adapted, the model will converge at a point which maximize the probability difference of the words between the initial θ_d and θ_c.

However, in the D-WDM model, there is no difference between the domain dictionary D_d and the common dictionary D_c except the parameter φ. So if we use pure EM algorithm to estimate the parameter θ^c and θ^d, it is obvious that the algorithm cannot determine whether a word should be sampled from D_c or D_d. And even though the model has the ability to distinguish the two kinds of words, it can not find out which words are domain-specific words either if we only use the domain-specific corpus. So we must add the common background corpus knowledge into our model and denote this function as domain score function σ.

Domain TopWords model uses an optimized probability function of a segmentation which can take the background knowledge into consideration. The probability of a segmentation S_i of a sentence as follows:

$$P(S_i|T;D,\theta,\varphi,\sigma) = \frac{Q(S_i|T;D,\theta,\varphi)}{\sum_{S_i \in C_T} Q(S_i|T;D,\theta,\varphi)}$$

$$(9)$$

$$Q(S_i|T;D,\theta,\varphi,\sigma) = \prod_{k=1}^{K_i}(\varphi\theta_{i_k}^c + (1-\varphi)\theta_{i_k}^d\sigma_{i_k})$$

$$(10)$$

is the score of the sampled segmentation S_i of T. $P(S_i|T;D,\theta,\varphi,)$ is the nomorlized version of $Q(S_i|T;D,\theta,\varphi,\sigma)$. σ_{i_k} is the domain score of the word w_{i_k}.

3.5 Selection of domain score σ

As mentioned above, we need a domain score function σ to tell our model how to distinguish whether a word is a common word or a domain-specific word. This function has several choices, i.e., the frequency of the word in a large background corpus, matches of specific templates, and so on. And we find that statistical features, like left(right) entropy and mutual information, are useless as the background knowledge function because the D-TopWords model itself has taken this part of features into consideration. We introduce some choices of the σ function and evaluate the effects in our experiment.

Constant Score The first choice of σ function is a constant function which returns a constant number for all words. This means there is no encouragement for any word so that we will get a θ^d which has almost the same word distribution as θ^c. We denote D-TopWords with constant σ function as D-TopWords+Const.

Background Frequency Score It is a natural idea that uses the reciprocal of the frequency of the word in a common background corpus. This σ function encourages words with low background frequency to be sampled from θ^d. The detailed function is as follows:

$$\sigma(w) = \sqrt{\frac{P}{Fre(w)}} \quad (11)$$

where P is a constant. The parameter P need to be tuned according to the size of the domain corpus, in our experiments we choose 900 to get a domain score in the range of 1-10 for domain words. And $Fre(w)$ is the frequency of word w in background corpus. We denote the result as D-TopWords+Fre.

RF Score We use the reciprocal of word probability in the dictionary of the origin TopWords method estimated with common background corpus as our domain score. We denote this function as RF function respect to the relative frequency in TopWords. The detailed function is as follows:

$$\sigma(w) = \sqrt{\frac{1}{WP(w) \times 10^5}} \quad (12)$$

where the $WP(w)$ is the word probability of word w in the dictionary of origin TopWords model. We denote the result as D-TopWords+RF.

3.6 EM estimation of θ

The parameter θ will be estimated by the EM algorithm as we will show below. In the beginning, we add all the words in vocabulary to θ and default values will be set for both θ^c and θ^d before EM steps. We employ a "top-down" strategy to discover words, and this is the reason why this method is called TopWords. It adds all words into its dictionary at first and then drops the words whose probability is close to zero (e.g., $< 10^{-8}$, and we use this value in our experiments). A good choice of the default value for θs is the normalized frequency vector of the words in the corpus.

Next, we will show the EM algorithm for our D-TopWords model. Let $\theta^{(r)}$ be the estimated value of θ at the r-th iteration. Then the E-step and the M-step can be computed as follows. The E-step computes the Q-function:

$$Q(\theta|\theta^{(r)}) = E_{S|G,\theta^{(r)}}[logL(\theta; G, S)]$$

$$= \sum_{j=1}^{n} \sum_{S \in C_{T_j}} P(S|T_j; D, \theta^{(r)}) \quad (13)$$

$$logP(S|D, \theta)$$

and the M-step maximizes $Q(\theta|\theta(r))$ so as to update θ_d and θ^c as follows

$$\theta^{c(r+1)} = (c_1^{(r)}, \ldots, c_N^{(r)}, n)/(n + \sum_i (c_i^{(r)}))$$

$$\theta^{d(r+1)} = (d_1^{(r)}, \ldots, d_N^{(r)}, n)/(n + \sum_i (d_i^{(r)}))$$

$$(14)$$

where

$$c_i^{(r)} = \sum_{T_j \in G} c_i(T_j)$$

$$c_i(T_j) = \sum_{S \in T_j} c_i(S) \cdot P(S|T_j; D, \theta^{(r)}) \cdot \quad (15)$$

$$\frac{\varphi \theta_i^{c(r)}}{\varphi \theta_i^{c(r)} + (1 - \varphi)\theta_i^{d(r)} \sigma_i}$$

$c_i(S)$ is the number of occurrences of w_i which is sampled from common dictionary in sentence S, and

$$d_i^{(r)} = \sum_{T_j \in G} d_i(T_j)$$

$$d_i(T_j) = \sum_{S \in T_j} d_i(S) \cdot P(S|T_j; D, \theta^{(r)}) \cdot \quad (16)$$

$$\frac{(1 - \varphi)\theta_i^{d(r)}}{\varphi \theta_i^{c(r)} + (1 - \varphi)\theta_i^{d(r)} \sigma_i}$$

$d_i(S)$ is the number of occurrences of w_i which is sampled from domain dictionary D_d in sentence S.

In the experiment, we found that because of the lack of domain-specific data the model tends to get long words and short segmentation. We add a segmentation length related factor to reduce this tendency, then our Q function of segmentation S_i becomes:

$$Q(S_i|\theta) = \alpha^{K_i} \prod_{k=1}^{K_i} (\varphi \theta_{i_k}^c + (1 - \varphi)\theta_{i_k}^d \sigma_{i_k}) \quad (17)$$

α is a constant parameter. K_i is the length of the segmentation S_i.

4 Experiments

In this section, we first perform an experiment to compare our method to several baselines. And

$top\ K\ words \Rightarrow$	**100**	**200**	**400**	**700**
Huang et al.(2014)	0.435	0.413	0.378	0.353
D-TopWords+Const	0.266	0.162	0.152	0.150
TopWords+Fre	0.630	0.576	0.495	0.412
D-TopWords+Fre	0.719	0.664	0.573	0.504
TopWords+RF	0.759	0.679	0.601	0.548
D-TopWords+RF	**0.795**	**0.705**	**0.615**	**0.553**

Table 2: Discovering new words in data structure domain (MAP)

then we perform parameter analysis to demonstrate how the parameters will affect our model. At last, we conduct some case studies to analysis these methods in details.

4.1 Data Preparation

We use transcripts of an online course called Data Structure from Xuetangx.com. Xuetangx.com is one of the biggest MOOC platforms in China. These transcripts are a total of 55,045 lines, including 655312 Chinese characters in it and totally 1,792 different characters.

We segment the corpus by characters and count the frequency of character-based n-grams from unigram up to 7-gram. We drop words with the frequency less than 5 and result in a 55,452 lines n-gram list. The resulted n-gram list is very sparse (close to 1:170) and most of the results are obviously meaningless (like "这样一" which means "one such"). We asked two annotators to label these n-grams. These two annotators are requested to judge whether an n-gram is a domain-specific word or not, it takes almost one week to annotate these n-grams. If there is a disagreement in these annotations, the annotators will discuss the final annotation and result in a 12.6% disagreement ratio. Most of the disagreements are like "访问"(visit) and "插入"(insert) which are somewhat ambiguous. Finally, we use a relatively strict standard, this results in 326 domain-specific words. The final annotated file can be accessed in our Github repo[1].

We use YUWEI corpus as our common background corpus. This corpus is developed by the National Language Commission, which contains 25,000,309 words with 51,311,659 characters.

4.2 Evaluation Metric

The output of our method is a ranked list, so we use mean average precision (MAP) as one of our

evaluation metrics. The MAP value is computed as follows:

$$MAP(K) = \frac{\sum_{k=1}^{K} P(k) \times rel(k)}{\sum_{k=1}^{K} rel(k)} \quad (18)$$

where the $P(k)$ is the precision of the top k words, $rel(k)$ is a indicator function which return 1 when word at rank k is a domain-specific word and 0 otherwise. K is the length of the result list. When we get a list whose elements are all domain-specific words, the $MAP(K)$ will be 1.

We will also display the precision-recall curves of our results.

4.3 Discovering New Words

4.3.1 Experiment Settings

We compare different settings of our method with two baselines. The first baseline is pattern-based unsupervised new word detection method, which is proposed by Huang et al. (2014). The following statistical features are taken into consideration: left pattern entropy (LPE), normalized multi-word expression distance (NMED), enhanced mutual information (EMI). We implement both character based and word-based version, and the word-based version outperforms character based version. We use the optimal parameter setting in Huang's method, which is the LPE+NMED setting in their paper. And we use annotated words to extract the candidate patterns which is a pretty good treatment for this method.

The second baseline is origin TopWords method which has been mentioned in above section. We first run the TopWords method in the domain-specific corpus, and then use a function to rerank the word dictionary θ. We use two functions to rerank the dictionary. The first one is the background frequency function and we denote this version as TopWords+Fre. The second one is the standard relative frequency method, we use the dictionary θ_B of TopWords method run in background

[1]http://github.com/dreamszl/dtopwords

D-TopWords+Fre	TopWords+Fre	Huang et al.
具体来说(specifically speaking)	接下来(next)	确实(indeed)
请注意(attention please)	换而言之(in other words)	至少(at least)
换而言之(in other words)	具体来说(specifically speaking)	对齐位置(alignment position)
字符(character)	同学们好(hello students)	顺序性(succession)
括号(brackets)	我们(we)	诸如此类(and so on)

Table 3: Top 5 wrong results of D-TopWords+Fre, TopWords+Fre and Huang et al.'s method

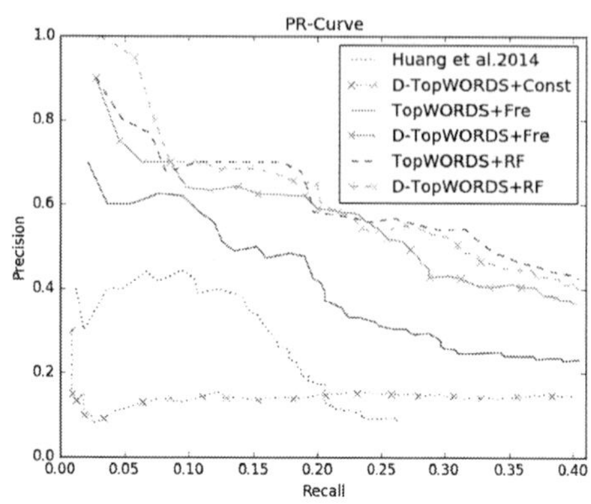

Figure 1: PR-Curves of our methods and two baselines

corpus to rerank θ. We denote this version as TopWords+RF.

4.3.2 Result and Analysis

(1) The MAP values of all the methods are shown in Table 2, and the PR-curves are shown in Figure 1. From the results, we can see our D-TopWords+RF and TopWords+RF achieve the best performance. Our D-TopWords+RF achieves better performance than TopWords+RF method, especially when the recall is lower our D-TopWords+RF outperforms TopWords+RF obviously as shown in Figure 1. In the actual application scenario, our model is more practical as the top results returned by the model are more important.

(2) Our D-TopWords methods achieve better performance than the corresponding TopWords results. We expect that our D-TopWords model can use the external information more effectively and accurately. Our D-TopWords model will give more weights to the probability whether a sequence can be a word or not, and the TopWords model will more reliable on the external information.

(3) More than that, our D-TopWords+Fre methods is significantly better than TopWords+Fre model and comparable to the D-TopWords+RF and TopWords+Rf model. The external background information RF takes the probability a sequence can be a word or not into consideration, however, our D-TopWords can consider this information in the model itself. So RF information is relative redundancy than Fre information to our D-TopWords model. The RF information needs to be trained on the common background corpus when the common background corpus is large it will take a very long time.

(4) We perform experiments of Huang et al.'s method with different domain score functions and all of these result in a poor performance. With the recall raising the precision decreases sharply, we suppose that it is because such statistical features based models cannot deal with low-frequency words well. However, our model can deal with this kind of words better by using the context information. And our model can hold a better balance between the probability whether a sequence can be a word or not and the domain score, which is hard for Huang et al.'s method.

4.4 Parameter Tuning

Table 5 shows how the performance changes with different α which is the segmentation length related parameter and φ which is the dictionary weight parameter. As we can see, the performance gets better when φ increases and get the best result when φ is 0.9. φ represents the probability a word is sampled from the common dictionary, so it means that a word is sampled from the common dictionary with a 90% possibility and domain-specific dictionary with 10%.

It achieves the best performance when φ is set as 0.9 and α is set as 100. Looking into the results, we found α determines the length of the words in θ. When α chooses a smaller value the results tend to be longer, when α chooses bigger value the results tend to be shorter. And when the size of cor-

Data Structure	*University Chemistry*	*Nuclear Physics*
遍历(iterate)	过程当中(in the process)	衰变(decay)
关键码(key code)	平衡常数(equilibrium constant)	活度(activity)
递归(recursive)	配合物(complex)	放射源(redioactive source)
具体来说(specifically speaking)	解离(dissociation)	γ 射线(γ-ray)
复杂度(complexity)	吉布斯自由能(Gibbs free energy)	去表示(to express)
BST (binary search tree)	杂化轨道(hybrid track)	入射粒(incident grain)
左孩子(left child)	孤对电子(lone paired electron)	MeV (MeV)
运算符(operator)	电极电势(electrode potential)	靶核(target nucleus)
数据结构(data structure)	同学们好(hello students)	半衰期(half-life period)
B 树(B tree)	反应速率(reaction rate)	核素(species)

Table 4: Top 10 results of D-TopWords+Fre in three courses

φ \ α	10	50	100	500	1000
0.3	0.243	0.344	0.389	0.416	0.429
0.5	0.323	0.441	0.479	0.529	0.516
0.7	0.405	0.513	0.559	0.593	0.483
0.9	0.437	0.672	0.719	0.547	0.448
0.99	0.306	0.470	0.479	0.519	0.447

Table 5: MAP of top 100 results'performance with different α and φ, under the D-TopWords+Fre model.

pus increasing, a smaller α value will get better performance. We set α as 10 when estimates θ of the common background corpus.

4.5 Case study

(1) The top five wrong results of D-TopWords+RF and TopWords+RF are similar. There are some wrong results appearing in top 100 results in TopWords+RF but not in D-TopWords+RF such as "大家注意"(everybody attention). After inspecting the common dictionary θ_c in D-TopWords+RF, we find both "大家"(everybody) and "注意"(attention) are in high ranks. We suppose that the usage of Domain Word Dictionary Model helps to deal with this type of sequences better.

(2) The teacher of this course uses "换而言之"(in other words), "具体来说"(specifically speaking) very frequently, so the TopWords+Fre and D-TopWords+Fre cannot recognize them. And the wrong results "接下来"(next) and "同学们好"(hello students) rank lower in our method compared to TopWords+Fre method (i.e., 25 and 41 vs 4 and 13). We suppose that it is because our method can keep a better balance of the domain

score and the probability that a sequence be a new word. And we inspect other wrong results which have a similar situation, these words all have a much lower rank in our method. So these phenomena confirm our assumption that our model achieves better performance in the sequences that with low frequency in background corpus but cannot be a word.

(3) The wrong result "我们"(we) doesn't appear in the domain dictionary θ_d, but appears at rank 7 in the θ_c dictionary in our model. There are also some results appearing in a high rank in TopWords+Fre method, but in a low rank in our D-TopWords+Fre method. For example, 比如说(for example) ranks in 39 in TopWords+Fre but rank in 574 in D-TopWords+Fre, "这么样"(the same as it) ranks in 31 in TopWords+Fre but ranks in 2759 in D-TopWords+Fre, "也就是"(that's it) ranks in 53 in TopWords+Fre but not appear in our method, and so on. We suppose that the usage of Domain Word Dictionary Model is the reason that our model can reach a better performance in these type of words.

(4) The first 10 results (D-TopWords+Fre) in *Data Structure* course and two other courses are shown in table 4.

5 Conclusion

We propose a pure unsupervised D-TopWords model to extract new domain-specific words. Compared to traditional new word extraction model, our model doesn't need handcrafted lexical features or statistical features and starts from the unsegmented corpus. Compared to the origin TopWords model, our model can reach a better performance with the same information and can reach a comparable performance with only background corpus frequency information to the Top-Words model with the relative frequency which is expensive and time-consuming.

Our D-TopWords model adds the ability to distinguish whether a word from common dictionary or domain dictionary to the origin TopWords model. We add a domain score parameter to let our model which can take the external information easily and efficiently. Experiments show that due to our modification our model can use much less external information to reach a comparable performance to the origin TopWords model.

Ackonwledgements

I am very grateful to my friends in THUNLP lab and the reviewers for giving many suggestions in the course of my thesis writing. This work is supported by Center for Massive Online Education, Tsinghua University, and XuetangX (http://www.xuetangx.com/), the largest MOOC platform in China.

References

Sunita B Aher and LMRJ Lobo. 2013. Combination of machine learning algorithms for recommendation of courses in e-learning system based on historical data. *Knowledge-Based Systems* 51:1–14.

Shlomo Argamon, Ido Dagan, and Yuval Krymolowski. 1998. A memory-based approach to learning shallow natural language patterns. In *Proceedings of the 17th international conference on Computational linguistics-Volume 1*. Association for Computational Linguistics, pages 67–73.

Fan Bu, Xiaoyan Zhu, and Ming Li. 2010. Measuring the non-compositionality of multiword expressions. In *Proceedings of the 23rd International Conference on Computational Linguistics*. Association for Computational Linguistics, pages 116–124.

Jing-Shin Chang and Keh-Yih Su. 1997. An unsupervised iterative method for chinese new lexicon extraction. *Computational Linguistics and Chinese Language Processing* 2(2):97–148.

Keh-Jiann Chen and Wei-Yun Ma. 2002. Unknown word extraction for chinese documents. In *Proceedings of the 19th international conference on Computational linguistics-Volume 1*. Association for Computational Linguistics, pages 1–7.

Kenneth Ward Church and Patrick Hanks. 1990. Word association norms, mutual information, and lexicography. *Computational linguistics* 16(1):22–29.

Paul Cohen, Niall Adams, and Brent Heeringa. 2007. Voting experts: An unsupervised algorithm for segmenting sequences. *Intelligent Data Analysis* 11(6):607–625.

Cody A Coleman, Daniel T Seaton, and Isaac Chuang. 2015. Probabilistic use cases: Discovering behavioral patterns for predicting certification. In *Proceedings of the Second (2015) ACM Conference on Learning@ Scale*. ACM, pages 141–148.

J Ferreira da Silva and G Pereira Lopes. 1999. A local maxima method and a fair dispersion normalization for extracting multi-word units from corpora. In *Sixth Meeting on Mathematics of Language*. pages 369–381.

Ke Deng, Peter K Bol, Kate J Li, and Jun S Liu. 2016. On the unsupervised analysis of domain-specific chinese texts. *Proceedings of the National Academy of Sciences* page 201516510.

Michael Färber, Achim Rettinger, and Boulos El Asmar. 2016. On emerging entity detection. In *Knowledge Engineering and Knowledge Management: 20th International Conference, EKAW 2016, Bologna, Italy, November 19-23, 2016, Proceedings 20*. Springer, pages 223–238.

Xianping Ge, Wanda Pratt, and Padhraic Smyth. 1999. Discovering chinese words from unsegmented text (poster abstract). In *Proceedings of the 22nd annual international ACM SIGIR conference on Research and development in information retrieval*. ACM, pages 271–272.

Zhou GuoDong. 2005. A chunking strategy towards unknown word detection in chinese word segmentation. In *International Conference on Natural Language Processing*. Springer, pages 530–541.

Minlie Huang, Borui Ye, Yichen Wang, Haiqiang Chen, Junjun Cheng, and Xiaoyan Zhu. 2014. New word detection for sentiment analysis. In *ACL (1)*. pages 531–541.

Pavel Pecina. 2005. An extensive empirical study of collocation extraction methods. In *Proceedings of the ACL Student Research Workshop*. Association for Computational Linguistics, pages 13–18.

Fuchun Peng, Fangfang Feng, and Andrew McCallum. 2004. Chinese segmentation and new word detection using conditional random fields. In *Proceedings of the 20th international conference on Computational Linguistics*. Association for Computational Linguistics, page 562.

Han Zhang, Maosong Sun, Xiaochen Wang, Zhengyang Song, Jie Tang, and Jimeng Sun. 2017. Smart jump: Automated navigation suggestion for videos in moocs. In *Proceedings of the 26th International Conference on World Wide Web Companion*. International World Wide Web Conferences Steering Committee, pages 331–339.

Wen Zhang, Taketoshi Yoshida, Xijin Tang, and Tu-Bao Ho. 2009. Improving effectiveness of mutual information for substantival multiword expression extraction. *Expert Systems with Applications* 36(8):10919–10930.

Yan Zhang, Maosong Sun, and Yang Zhang. 2010. Chinese new word detection from query logs. In *International Conference on Advanced Data Mining and Applications*. Springer, pages 233–243.

Yabin Zheng, Zhiyuan Liu, Maosong Sun, Liyun Ru, and Yang Zhang. 2009. Incorporating user behaviors in new word detection. In *IJCAI*. Citeseer, volume 9, pages 2101–2106.

Deep Learning Models For Multiword Expression Identification

Waseem Gharbieh and **Virendra C. Bhavsar** and **Paul Cook**
Faculty of Computer Science, University of New Brunswick
Fredericton, NB E3B 5A3 Canada
{waseem.gharbieh,bhavsar,paul.cook}@unb.ca

Abstract

Multiword expressions (MWEs) are lexical items that can be decomposed into multiple component words, but have properties that are unpredictable with respect to their component words. In this paper we propose the first deep learning models for token-level identification of MWEs. Specifically, we consider a layered feedforward network, a recurrent neural network, and convolutional neural networks. In experimental results we show that convolutional neural networks are able to outperform the previous state-of-the-art for MWE identification, with a convolutional neural network with three hidden layers giving the best performance.

1 Introduction

Multiword expressions (MWEs) are lexical items that can be decomposed into multiple component words, but have properties that are idiomatic, i.e., marked or unpredictable, with respect to properties of their component words (Baldwin and Kim, 2010). MWEs include a wide range of phenomena such as noun compounds (e.g., *speed limit* and *monkey business*), verb–particle constructions (e.g., *clean up* and *throw out*), and verb–noun idiomatic combinations (e.g., *hit the roof* and *blow the whistle*), as well as named entities (e.g., *Prime Minister Justin Trudeau*) and proverbs (e.g., *Two wrongs don't make a right*). One particular challenge for natural language processing (NLP) is MWE identification — i.e., to identify which tokens in running text correspond to MWEs so that they can be analyzed accordingly. The challenges posed by MWEs have led to them to be referred to as a "pain in the neck" for NLP (Sag et al., 2002); nevertheless, incorporating knowledge of MWEs into NLP applications can lead to improvements in tasks including machine translation (Carpuat and Diab, 2010), information retrieval (Newman et al., 2012), and opinion mining (Berend, 2011).

Recent work on token-level MWE identification has focused on methods that are applicable to the full spectrum of kinds of MWEs (Schneider et al., 2014a), in contrast to earlier work that tended to focus on specific kinds of MWEs (Uchiyama et al., 2005; Fazly et al., 2009; Fothergill and Baldwin, 2012). Deep learning is an emerging class of machine learning models that have recently achieved promising results on a range of NLP tasks such as machine translation (Bahdanau et al., 2015; Sutskever et al., 2014), named entity recognition (Lample et al., 2016), natural language generation (Li et al., 2015), and sentence classification (Kim, 2014). Such models have, however, not yet been applied to broad-coverage MWE identification.

In this paper we propose the first deep learning models for broad-coverage MWE identification. Specifically, we propose and evaluate a layered feedforward network, a recurrent neural network, and two convolutional neural networks. We compare these models against the previous state-of-the-art (Kirilin et al., 2016) and several more-traditional supervised machine learning approaches. We show that the convolutional neural networks outperform the previous state-of-the-art. This finding is particularly remarkable given the relatively small size of the training data available, and demonstrates that deep learning models are able to learn well from small datasets. Moreover, we show that our proposed deep learning models are able to generalize more-effectively than previous approaches, based on comparisons between the models' performances on validation and test data.

*Proceedings of the 6th Joint Conference on Lexical and Computational Semantics (*SEM 2017)*, pages 54–64,
Vancouver, Canada, August 3-4, 2017. ©2017 Association for Computational Linguistics

2 Related Work

MWE identification is the task of determining, at the token level, which words are parts of MWEs, and which are not. For example, in the sentence *The staff leaves a lot to be desired* (also used in Figure 1) *a lot* and *leaves ___ to be desired* are MWEs. An important part of MWE identification is to be able to distinguish between MWEs and literal combinations that have the same surface form; e.g., *kick the bucket* is ambiguous between an idiomatic usage — meaning roughly 'die' — which is an MWE, and a literal one which is not. Many earlier studies on MWE identification have focused on this type of ambiguity, and treated the problem as one of word sense disambiguation, where literal and idiomatic usages are considered different word senses (Birke and Sarkar, 2006; Katz and Giesbrecht, 2006; Li et al., 2010). Other work has leveraged linguistic knowledge of properties of MWEs in order to make these distinctions (Uchiyama et al., 2005; Fazly et al., 2009; Fothergill and Baldwin, 2012). Crucially, this work has typically focused on specific kinds of MWEs, and has not considered identification of the full spectrum of MWEs.

More-recent work has considered the identification of a wider range of types of MWEs. Brooke et al. (2014) present an unsupervised learning approach to segment a corpus into multiword units based on their predictability. Schneider et al. (2014a) propose methods for broad-coverage MWE identification, and evaluate them on a sizeable corpus (Schneider et al., 2014b). They proposed a supervised learning approach based on the structured perceptron (Collins, 2002). The system labels tokens using the BIO convention, where B indicates the beginning of an MWE, I indicates the continuation of an MWE, and O indicates that the token is not part of an MWE. The model includes features based on part-of-speech tags, MWE lexicons, and Brown clusters (Brown et al., 1992). Qu et al. (2015) later improved upon that system by using skip-gram embeddings (Mikolov et al., 2013) instead of Brown clusters with a variant of conditional random fields. More recently, Constant and Nivre (2016) incorporate MWE identification along with dependency parsing by forming two representations for a sentence: a tree that represents the syntactic dependencies, and a forest of lexical trees that includes the MWEs identified in the sentence.

The recent SemEval shared task on Detecting Minimal Semantic Units and their Meanings (DiMSUM) focused on MWE identification along with supersense tagging (Schneider et al., 2016). The best performing system for MWE identification for this shared task was that of Kirilin et al. (2016) which took into consideration all of the basic features used by Schneider et al. (2014a) and two novel feature sets. The first one is based on the YAGO ontology (Suchanek et al., 2007), where heuristics were applied to extract potential named entities from the ontology. The second feature set was GloVe (Pennington et al., 2014) word embeddings, with the word vectors scaled by a constant and divided by the standard deviation of each of its dimensions. None of the systems that participated in the DiMSUM shared task considered deep learning approaches.

In this paper we propose the first deep learning approaches to MWE identification. We use the DiMSUM data for training and evaluating our models, and compare against the state-of-the-art method of Kirilin et al. (2016). Here we focus solely on the MWE identification task, leaving supersense tagging for future work.

3 Neural Network Models

In this section, we discuss the features extracted for the neural network models, and the model architectures. Schneider et al. (2014b) extracted roughly 320k sparse features. Because of the large input feature space, the only feasible way to train a model on those features is by using a linear classifier. In contrast to Schneider et al. (2014b) our aim is to create dense input features to allow neural network architectures, as well as other machine learning algorithms, to be trained on them. Specifically, we propose three neural network models: a layered feedforward network (LFN), a recurrent neural network (RNN), and a convolutional neural network (CNN).[1]

3.1 Layered Feedforward Network

Although LFNs have been used to solve a wide range of classification and regression problems, they have been shown to be less effective for tasks at which deep learning models excel, such as image classification (Krizhevsky et al., 2012) and

---

[1]In preliminary experiments we also considered a sequence-to-sequence model (Cho et al., 2014), but found it to perform poorly relative to the other models, and so do not discuss it further.

machine translation (Bahdanau et al., 2015). The LFN is therefore proposed as a benchmark for comparing the performance of the other architectures, as well as for developing informative input features. Most feature engineering was carried out while developing this model and then transferred to the other architectures.

The composition of the DiMSUM corpus (Schneider et al., 2016), and the token-level lemma and part-of-speech annotations it provides, influenced our feature extraction. Most of the text in the DiMSUM corpus is social media text. The tokens and lemmas were therefore preprocessed by removing # characters from tokens and lemmas that contain them, and mapping URLs, numbers, and any token or lemma containing the @ symbol to the special tokens *URL*, *NUMBER*, and *USER*, respectively. After pre-processing, distributed representations of all tokens and lemmas were obtained from a skip-gram (Mikolov et al., 2013) model. Specifically, the gensim (Řehůřek and Sojka, 2010) implementation of skip-gram was trained on a snapshot of Wikipedia from September 2015 to learn 100 dimensional word embeddings. Any token occurring less than 15 times was discarded, the context window was set to 5, the negative sampling rate was set to 5, and unknown tokens were represented with a zero vector. The part-of-speech tag for each token was also encoded, in this case as a one-hot vector.

Schneider et al. (2014a) included word shape features, which can be informative for the identification of MWEs, especially named entities. We therefore also include word shape features. These are binary features for each token and lemma that capture whether it includes single or double quotes; consists of all capital letters; starts with a capital letter (but is otherwise lowercase); contains a number; includes a # or @ character; corresponds to a URL; contains any punctuation; and consists entirely of punctuation characters.

Schneider et al. (2014a) include features based on MWE lexicons that represent which tokens and lemmas are potentially part of an MWE and according to which lexicon. We use a script provided by Schneider et al. (2014a) to include these same features in our representation.

Finally, Salton et al. (2016) showed that embedding the entire sentence in which a target MWE occurs was helpful for distinguishing idiomatic from literal verb–noun idiomatic combinations.

We therefore also include a representation for the entire sentence. Specifically, we separately average the skip-gram embeddings for the tokens and lemmas in the sentence containing the target word. These features were then input into an LFN model with a single hidden layer, which we refer to as LFN1.

3.2 Recurrent Neural Network

RNNs are a natural fit for many NLP problems due to their ability to model sequences. Here we apply an RNN to broad coverage MWE identification. The token for the current time step is represented using the same features as LFN1 described above, except we do not include the average of the skip-gram representations for tokens and lemmas in the same sentence as the target word because we expect the RNN to be able to learn a representation of the sentence by itself. We use a single layer RNN model, referred to as RNN1.

3.3 Convolutional Neural Network

CNNs have been shown to be powerful classifiers (Kim, 2014; Kim et al., 2016), and since MWE identification can be formulated as a classification task, CNNs have the potential to perform well on it. The feature representation for the CNN was split into feature columns to enable the implementation of the convolution layer. Each feature column contains the same features as those for the RNN at each time step but since the CNN does not learn sequential information, a window of feature columns was given as an input.

Multiple filters can then be applied on these feature columns to extract different local features across different window sizes. After finding the optimal number of filters and their sizes, a max-pooling operation is executed on the values extracted by the feature map to form the hidden layer which will be used to produce the predicted output. For our evaluation, we use CNN architectures with two and three fully connected hidden layers, which we refer to as CNN2 and CNN3, respectively. We observed that CNNs with 2 and 3 hidden layers performed well on the validation set but adding more layers resulted in overfitting. Similarly, adding more hidden layers to the LFN and RNN also resulted in overfitting.

4   Data and Evaluation

This section presents the statistics and structure of the dataset used for this task, as well as the evaluation methodology.

4.1   Dataset

We use the DiMSUM dataset (Schneider et al., 2016) for our experiments, which allows for direct comparison with previous results. Table 1 displays the source corpora from which the dataset was constructed; their domain (i.e., reviews, tweets, or TED talks); the number of sentences, words, MWEs, and gappy (i.e., discontiguous) MWES in each source corpus; and the percentage of tokens belonging to an MWE in each source corpus. The dataset is split into training and testing sets such that the testing data contains a novel text type, i.e., TED talks.

For parameter tuning purposes, we also require validation data. We form a validation set from the training data by splitting the training data to create 5 folds, where every fold contained 20% validation data, and the remaining 80% was used for training.

4.2   Structure

Every line in the dataset provides 8 pieces of information: the numeric position of the token in its sentence; the token itself; its lemmatized form; its part-of-speech tag; its gold-standard MWE tag; the position of the last token that is part of its MWE; its supersense tag;[2] and the sentence ID. Six MWE tags are used for MWE identification in this dataset, B which indicates the beginning of an MWE, I which indicates the continuation of an MWE, O which indicates that the token is not part of an MWE, b indicates the beginning of a new MWE inside an MWE, i indicates the continuation of the new MWE inside an MWE, and finally, o indicates that the token that is inside an MWE is not part of the nested MWE. This convention assumes that MWEs can only be nested to a depth of one (i.e., an MWE inside an MWE), and that MWEs must be properly nested.

4.3   Performance Metric

We use the link-based F-score evaluation metric from Schneider et al. (2014a), which allows

---

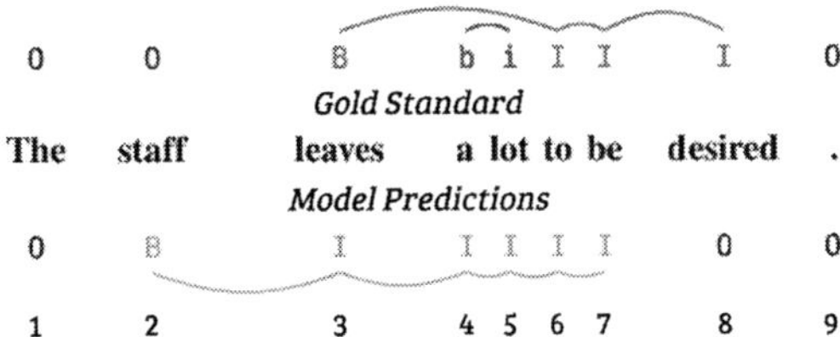

Figure 1: An example of how a model could tag a sequence, along with its gold standard tagging (adapted from Schneider et al. (2016)).

for direct comparison with prior work. Table 1 shows that the percentage of tokens occurring in MWEs ranges from 9–22%. As such, MWEs occur much less frequently than literal word combinations. This evaluation metric correspondingly puts more emphasis on the ability of the model to detect MWEs rather than literal word combinations.

Figure 1 is a diagram adapted from Schneider et al. (2016) which shows an example of how a model could tag a sequence, as well as its gold standard tagging. The MWE tags on top represent the gold standard, and the MWE tags predicted by a system are shown on the bottom. A link is defined as the path from one token to another, as in Figure 1, regardless of the number of tokens in that path. Precision is calculated as the ratio of the number of correctly predicted links to the total number of links predicted by the model. Recall is calculated in the same way but swapping the gold standard and predicted links.

For example, in Figure 1, the model was able to correctly predict two links. The first link goes from b to i in the gold standard which is matched by a predicted link from token 4–5 by the model. The second link is from token 6–7 in the gold standard which matches the model's prediction. Since the model predicted five links in total, the precision is $\frac{2}{5}$.

To calculate recall, the roles of the gold standard and model predictions are reversed. This way, three links have been correctly predicted. Two of the three links are the previously mentioned links. The third one is the link from B to I in the gold standard which corresponds to the path from token 3–6. Because there are four links in the gold standard, the recall is therefore $\frac{3}{4}$.

The F-score is then calculated based on precision and recall according to the following equation:

---

[2]Schneider et al. (2014a) consider MWE identification and super-sense tagging. We focus only on MWE identification in this work and so don't use the super-sense tag information provided in the dataset.

Split	Domain	Source corpus	Sentences	Words	MWEs	Gappy MWEs	% tokens in MWE
Train	REVIEWS	STREUSLE 2.1 (Schneider and Smith, 2015)	3,812	55,579	3,117	397	13%
	TWEETS	Lowlands (Johannsen et al., 2014)	200	3,062	276	5	22%
	TWEETS	Ritter (Ritter et al., 2011; Johannsen et al., 2014)	787	15,185	839	65	13%
		Train Total	4,799	73,826	4,232	467	13%
Test	REVIEWS	Trustpilot (Hovy et al., 2015)	340	6,357	327	13	12%
	TWEETS	Tweebank (Kong et al., 2014)	500	6,627	362	20	13%
	TED	NAIST-NTT (Cettolo et al., 2012; Neubig et al., 2014)	100	2,187	93	2	9%
	TED	IWSLT test (Cettolo et al., 2012)	60	1,329	55	1	9%
		Test Total	1,000	16,500	837	36	12%

Table 1: Statistics describing the composition of the DiMSUM dataset.

$$\frac{1}{F} = \frac{1}{2}(\frac{1}{P} + \frac{1}{R}) \tag{1}$$

where F is the F-score, and P and R are precision and recall, respectively.

5 Parameter Settings

In this section, the architecture and parameters of all neural network models are presented in detail. The cost function used to train the neural network models was based on the cost function used by Schneider et al. (2014a) for this task:

$$cost = \sum_{i=1}^{|\bar{y}_i|} c(\bar{y}_i, y_i) \tag{2}$$

where $\bar{y}_i$ is the ith gold standard MWE tag, and y_i is the ith MWE tag predicted by the neural network model. To ensure that the MWE tag predicted by the neural network is a probability distribution, the output layer of all neural models was the softmax layer. The function c in Equation 2 is defined as:

$$c(\bar{y}_i, y_i) = \bar{y}_i \log(y_i) + \rho(\bar{y}_i \epsilon \{B\} \wedge y_i \epsilon \{O\}) \tag{3}$$

Some MWE tag sequences are invalid, for example, a B followed immediately by an O (because MWEs are composed of multiple tokens), and similarly, an O cannot occur immediately before an I (because the beginning of every MWE must be tagged with a B). We therefore use the Viterbi algorithm on the output of the neural network models to obtain the valid MWE tag sequence with the highest probability. In preliminary experiments we observed that setting all valid

transitions to be of equal probability, and the probability of all invalid transitions to 0, performed best, and therefore use this strategy.

5.1 Layered Feedforward Network

The LFN was used as a benchmark neural network model against which the performance of the other deep learning models was compared. The parameters that had to be tuned for this model were the size of the context window, the misclassification penalty ρ (in Equation 3), the number of neurons in each hidden layer, the number of iterations before training is stopped, and the dropout rate. Optimizing these parameters is important as they greatly influence the performance of the LFN. For all models considered, all parameter tuning was done using the validation data; the test data was never used for setting parameters.

Context window of sizes of 1, 2, and 3 tokens to the left and right were considered. A larger context window allows the model to see additional tokens, but also makes the training process longer and more prone to overfitting. In the case of ρ, we investigated setting it between 40 and 100. A small value of ρ would cause the model to have high precision but low recall, while a larger value would trade off recall for precision. The number of neurons in the hidden layer that was examined ranged from 100 to 1200. Adding more neurons in a hidden layer, and introducing more hidden layers, allows the LFN to model more complex functions, but can also make it more prone to overfitting. We avoid overfitting by stopping training after a defined number of iterations (by observing the performance of the model on the validation set), and by using dropout (Srivastava et al., 2014). Dropout combats overfitting by randomly switching off a percentage of the neurons in a hidden layer during training, which allows a neural network to be more robust in its predictions as it decreases the association between neurons. It also has the same effect as ensembling multiple neural network models because different neurons are switched on and off in every training iteration. The dropout rates that we considered ranged from 0.4 to 0.6.

After running multiple experiments, the best performing LFN model (LFN1) had a context window of size 1, which means that the features for the tokens before and after the target token were input into the LFN along with the features of the target token. The value of ρ was set to 50, and the LFN had a single hidden layer containing 1000 neurons with the *tanh* activation function. The LFN was trained for 1000 iterations with a dropout rate of 0.5.

5.2   Recurrent Neural Network

As previously mentioned in Section 3.2, RNNs are a natural fit to many NLP problems due to their ability to model sequences. At each timestep, the features for a token were input into the RNN which then output the corresponding MWE tag for that token. Many of the parameters that had to be tuned for the LFN had to be tuned for the RNN as well: ρ ranged from 10 to 50; the number of neurons in each hidden layer ranged from 50 to 300; the dropout rate ranged from 0.5 to 1; and we again tuned the number of iterations before training is stopped.[3] Parameters specific to the RNN model that had to be tuned include whether the RNN is unidirectional or bidirectional, and the cell type, where we consider a fully connected RNN, an LSTM cell, and a GRU cell.

After observing the performance of the RNN on the validation set, the best performing RNN model (RNN1) was a bidirectional LSTM with ρ set to 25, with a single hidden layer containing 100 neurons. It was trained for 60 iterations with no dropout. This indicates that the LSTM cell was able to handle the complexity of the sequences of tokens without requiring regularization.

As we will see in Section 6, RNN1 unfortunately did not perform as well as the other neural network models. We therefore attempted to improve its performance using two additional approaches. In the first approach, the RNN LSTM was orthogonally initialized. Saxe et al. (2014) showed that orthogonally initializing RNNs led to

better learning in deep neural networks. Nevertheless, orthogonal initialization did not seem to have an effect on the performance of RNN1. In the second approach, the dataset was artificially expanded by splitting the input sentences on punctuation. This provided more "sentences" for the RNN LSTM to learn from, but again did not improve performance.

5.3   Convolutional Neural Network

Every token was represented by a feature column and these feature columns were then concatenated to form the input to the CNN. A convolutional layer was then applied to the input and then max-pooled to form the hidden layer which was used to produce the predicted output. There were again many parameters to optimize in the CNN. We considered the same settings for the context window size as for LFN1, i.e., 1, 2, and 3 tokens to the left and right. The number of neurons in each hidden layer ranged from 25 to 200. In contrast to LFN1 and RNN1, here we consider varying numbers of fully connected hidden layers from 1–3. The dropout rate at the fully connected layers, as well as the convolutional layer, ranged from 0.3 to 1, and ρ ranged from 10 to 30. Parameters specific to the convolutional neural network that were optimized were the number of filters, which ranged from 100 to 500, and spanned 1, 2, or 3 feature columns, and the types of convolution and pooling operations that were performed. Having a large number of filters can cause the network to pick up noise patterns which makes the CNN overfit. The size of the filters and the types of convolution and pooling operations is largely dependent on the data and were optimized according to the performance of the model on the validation set.

We experiment with two CNN models, the best performing CNN model with two hidden layers (CNN2) and the best performing CNN model with three hidden layers (CNN3). CNN2 was trained for 600 iterations and had a context window of size 1 and ρ equal to 20, with 250 filters that spanned 2 feature columns, and 200 filters that spanned all 3 feature columns. Narrow convolution was used which produced a hidden layer with 450 neurons. This layer was then input into another hidden layer containing 50 neurons with the sigmoid activation function before being passed to the output softmax layer.

---

[3]We choose parameter settings to explore based on performance on the validation data, and so consider different parameter settings here than for LFN1.

CNN3 is similar to CNN2 but was trained for 900 iterations and had the 450 neuron hidden layer feed to a hidden layer containing 100 neurons with the sigmoid activation function. The output of that layer was then passed to another layer containing 50 neurons with the *tanh* activation function before being passed to the output softmax layer. The intuition behind the *tanh* activation function for the last hidden layer is that the layer before it has the sigmoid activation function. This means that the values that are passed to the last hidden layer are between 0 and 1 multiplied by the weights between the two layers. Since these weights can be negative, a sigmoid function that can deal with negative values is required, and the *tanh* function satisfies this requirement. Both models have a dropout rate of 60% on the convolutional and hidden layers. They were also given batches of 6000 random examples at each training iteration.

5.4 Traditional Machine Learning Models

To demonstrate the effectiveness of neural network models, we compare them against more-traditional, non-neural machine learning models. Here we consider k-nearest neighbour, random forests, logistic regression, and gradient boosting.[4] These models were given the same features that were input into LFN1, and parameter tuning was also carried out on the validation set. For the k-nearest neighbour algorithm, k was set to 3, and the points were weighted by the inverse of their distance. For random forests, 100 estimators were used while multiplying the penalty of misclassifying any class other than O as O by 1.2. In the case of logistic regression, L2 regularization was utilized with a regularization factor of 0.5. For gradient boosting, 100 estimators with a maximum depth of 13 nodes were used. Using a larger number of estimators for random forest and gradient boosting has shown to improve their cross validation performance. However, the point of diminishing returns was found to be at around 50 estimators, and it was clear that increasing the number of estimators above 100 would not yield any significant increase in performance. Added to that, with gradient boosting, the cross validation performance also increased with the maximum node depth, but the point of diminishing returns was found to be at around 9, and it was clear that increasing the

maximum depth beyond 13 would not yield any significant increase in performance.

5.5 Implementation Details

Overall, 983 features were input into the LFN and traditional machine learning models, and more than 50 parameter combinations were examined. Every LFN model required up to 2 days of training. For the RNN, every token was represented by a feature vector of length 257, and took around 10 hours to train. More than 30 parameter combinations were examined for the RNN model. Every feature column in the CNN model contained 257 features, this amounts to a total of 771 input features. More than 130 parameter combinations were tested for the CNN, and it required around 12 hours of training. Tensorflow (et al., 2015) version 0.12 was used to implement the neural network models, and scikit-learn (Pedregosa et al., 2011) was used to implement the traditional machine learning models. The experiments were run on 2 GHz Intel Xeon E7-4809 v3 CPUs.

6 Results

The average F-score of the models on the five fold cross validation set, and their F-score on the test set, along with their generalization, is shown in Table 2. All models except for that of Kirilin et al. (2016) — which was already optimized for this task by its authors — were run on the validation set to tune their parameters. To evaluate the performance of the models on the test set, the models were trained on the entire training set (which includes the validation splits) and then tested on the test set.

We first consider the traditional machine learning models. Amongst these models, gradient boosting performed best on the validation set, which can be attributed to the ability of gradient boosting to learn complex functions and its robustness to outliers. However, it did not perform as well on the test set, where logistic regression performed best, and achieved the best generalization out of the traditional machine learning models. This shows that relatively many instances in the test set can be correctly classified by using a hyperplane to separate the dense feature representations.

Turning to the proposed neural network models, LFN1 is indeed a strong baseline for this task. This model achieved an F-score on the test set that

---

[4]In preliminary experiments we also considered an SVM, but found the training time to be impractical, and so did not consider it further.

Model Class	Model	F-score		Generalization
		Validation Set	**Test Set**	
Traditional Machine Learning Models	k-Nearest Neighbour	48.35	31.30	64.74%
	Random Forest	52.26	32.02	61.27%
	Logistic Regression	57.68	53.37	92.53%
	Gradient Boosting	64.98	48.79	75.08%
Neural Network Models	LFN1	66.48	57.99	87.23%
	RNN1	56.96	53.07	**93.17%**
	CNN2	66.95	59.18	88.39%
	CNN3	67.40	**59.96**	88.96%
Baseline Models	Schneider and Smith (2015)	**67.84**	57.74	85.11%
	Kirilin et al. (2016)	-	58.69	-

Table 2: The average F-score of each model on the 5 fold cross validation set, and their F-score on the test set, along with their generalization. The best performance in each column is shown in boldface.

comes close to the previous state-of-the-art of Kirilin et al. (2016). RNN1 achieved the best generalization out of all models considered; however, it performed relatively poorly compared to the other neural network models on both the validation and test sets. The CNN models, CNN2 and CNN3, both improved over the previous best results on the test set — with CNN3 achieving the best F-score overall — and outperformed all other models except for (Schneider et al., 2014a) on the validation set. This shows that the CNN filters were able to learn what makes a feature column a part of an MWE or not. That CNN3 outperforms CNN2 further shows that adding an extra hidden layer for the CNN model improves its performance as it is able to handle more complex mappings. Moreover, the training data for this task is relatively small; it consists of less than 5,000 sentences. These results therefore further show that convolutional neural networks can still achieve good performance when the amount of training data available is limited.

The highest F-score on the test set — achieved by CNN3 — is 59.96. This shows that the task is quite difficult, and suggests that there is scope for further improvements. One issue, however, is that there are notable inconsistencies in the annotations in the dataset. For example, the expression *a few* is labeled as an MWE 15 out of 32 times in the training set, even though there appears to be no variation in its usage. Recent efforts have, however, proposed semi-automated methods for resolving these inconsistencies (Chan et al., 2017).

7 Conclusions and Future Work

We proposed and evaluated the first neural network approaches for multiword expression identification, and compared their performance against the previous state-of-art, and more-traditional machine learning approaches. We showed that our proposed approach based on a convolutional neural network (CNN2 and CNN3) outperformed the previous state-of-the-art for this task. Therefore, although the task is inherently sequential, formulating it as a classification task enabled the CNN models to perform well on it. This finding suggests that deep learning methods can still be effective when only limited amounts of training data are available. Furthermore, the proposed neural network-based approaches were able to generalize more-effectively than previous approaches.

In future work, we intend to carry out an in-depth analysis of the errors committed by the neural network models. Additionally, an ablation study of the features can be conducted to determine the effect of each feature set on the overall performance of the models. The proposed deep learning models can also be extended to predict supersense tags in addition to the MWE tags. In particular, we intend to compare the performance of a single model that predicts the supersense and MWE tags, versus two separate models for each task. Furthermore, we plan to measure the impact of MWE identification on downstream NLP tasks by incorporating the predicted MWE tags into applications such as machine translation.

Acknowledgments

This work is financially supported by the Natural Sciences and Engineering Research Council of Canada, the New Brunswick Innovation Foundation, and the University of New Brunswick.

References

Dzmitry Bahdanau, Kyunghyun Cho, and Yoshua Bengio. 2015. Neural machine translation by jointly learning to align and translate. In *International Conference on Learning Representations (ICLR2015)*.

Timothy Baldwin and Su Nam Kim. 2010. Handbook of natural language processing. In Nitin Indurkhya and Fred J. Damerau, editors, *Handbook of Natural Language Processing*, CRC Press, Boca Raton, USA. 2nd edition.

Gábor Berend. 2011. Opinion expression mining by exploiting keyphrase extraction. In *Proceedings of 5th International Joint Conference on Natural Language Processing*. Chiang Mai, Thailand, pages 1162–1170.

Julia Birke and Anoop Sarkar. 2006. A clustering approach for nearly unsupervised recognition of non-literal language. In *Proceedings of the 11th Conference of the European Chapter of the Association for Computational Linguistics (EACL-2006)*. Trento, Italy, pages 329–336.

Julian Brooke, Vivian Tsang, Graeme Hirst, and Fraser Shein. 2014. Unsupervised multiword segmentation of large corpora using prediction-driven decomposition of n-grams. In *COLING 2014, 25th International Conference on Computational Linguistics, Proceedings of the Conference: Technical Papers*. Dublin, Ireland, pages 753–761.

Peter F. Brown, Vincent J. Della Pietra, Peter V. de Souza, Jennifer C. Lai, and Robert L. Mercer. 1992. Class-based n-gram models of natural language. *Computational Linguistics* 18(4):467–479.

Marine Carpuat and Mona Diab. 2010. Task-based evaluation of multiword expressions: a pilot study in statistical machine translation. In *Human Language Technologies: The 2010 Annual Conference of the North American Chapter of the Association for Computational Linguistics*. Los Angeles, California, pages 242–245.

Mauro Cettolo, Christian Girardi, and Marcello Federico. 2012. Web inventory of transcribed and translated talks. In *Proceedings of the 16th Annual Conference of the European Association for Machine Translation (EAMT 2012)*. Trento, Italy, pages 261–268.

King Chan, Julian Brooke, and Timothy Baldwin. 2017. Semi-automated resolution of inconsistency for a harmonized multiword expression and dependency parse annotation. In *Proceedings of the 13th Workshop on Multiword Expressions (MWE 2017)*. Valencia, Spain, pages 187–193.

Kyunghyun Cho, Bart van Merrienboer, Çaglar Gülçehre, Dzmitry Bahdanau, Fethi Bougares, Holger Schwenk, and Yoshua Bengio. 2014. Learning phrase representations using RNN encoder-decoder for statistical machine translation. In *Proceedings of the 2014 Conference on Empirical Methods in Natural Language Processing, A meeting of SIGDAT, a Special Interest Group of the ACL*. Doha, Qatar, pages 1724–1734.

Michael Collins. 2002. Discriminative training methods for hidden markov models: Theory and experiments with perceptron algorithms. In *Proceedings of the 2002 Conference on Empirical Methods in Natural Language Processing (EMNLP 2002)*. Philadelphia, USA, pages 1–8.

Matthieu Constant and Joakim Nivre. 2016. A transition-based system for joint lexical and syntactic analysis. In *Proceedings of the 54th Annual Meeting of the Association for Computational Linguistics*. Berlin, Germany, pages 161–171.

Martín Abadi et al. 2015. TensorFlow: Large-scale machine learning on heterogeneous systems. Software available from tensorflow.org. http://tensorflow.org/.

Afsaneh Fazly, Paul Cook, and Suzanne Stevenson. 2009. Unsupervised type and token identification of idiomatic expressions. *Computational Linguistics* 35(1):61–103.

Richard Fothergill and Timothy Baldwin. 2012. Combining resources for mwe-token classification. In **SEM 2012: The First Joint Conference on Lexical and Computational Semantics – Volume 1: Proceedings of the main conference and the shared task, and Volume 2: Proceedings of the Sixth International Workshop on Semantic Evaluation (SemEval 2012)*. Montréal, Canada, pages 100–104.

Dirk Hovy, Anders Johannsen, and Anders Søgaard. 2015. User review sites as a resource for large-scale sociolinguistic studies. In *Proceedings of the 24th International Conference on World Wide Web*. Florence, Italy, pages 452–461.

Anders Johannsen, Dirk Hovy, Héctor Martínez Alonso, Barbara Plank, and Anders Søgaard. 2014. More or less supervised supersense tagging of twitter. In *Proceedings of the Third Joint Conference on Lexical and Computational Semantics (*SEM 2014)*. Dublin, Ireland, pages 1–11.

Graham Katz and Eugenie Giesbrecht. 2006. Automatic identification of non-compositional multi-word expressions using latent semantic analysis. In

Proceedings of the Workshop on Multiword Expressions: Identifying and Exploiting Underlying Properties. Sydney, Australia, pages 12–19.

Yoon Kim. 2014. Convolutional neural networks for sentence classification. In *Proceedings of the 2014 Conference on Empirical Methods in Natural Language Processing, EMNLP, A meeting of SIGDAT, a Special Interest Group of the ACL*. Doha, Qatar, pages 1746–1751.

Yoon Kim, Yacine Jernite, David Sontag, and Alexander M. Rush. 2016. Character-aware neural language models. In *Proceedings of the Thirtieth AAAI Conference on Artificial Intelligence*. Phoenix, Arizona, USA, pages 2741–2749.

Angelika Kirilin, Felix Krauss, and Yannick Versley. 2016. ICL-HD at semeval-2016 task 10: Improving the detection of minimal semantic units and their meanings with an ontology and word embeddings. In *Proceedings of the 10th International Workshop on Semantic Evaluation, SemEval@NAACL-HLT*. San Diego, CA, USA, pages 937–945.

Lingpeng Kong, Nathan Schneider, Swabha Swayamdipta, Archna Bhatia, Chris Dyer, and Noah A. Smith. 2014. A dependency parser for tweets. In *Proceedings of the 2014 Conference on Empirical Methods in Natural Language Processing, A meeting of SIGDAT, a Special Interest Group of the ACL*. Doha, Qatar, pages 1001–1012.

Alex Krizhevsky, Ilya Sutskever, and Geoffrey E Hinton. 2012. ImageNet classification with deep convolutional neural networks. In F. Pereira, C. J. C. Burges, L. Bottou, and K. Q. Weinberger, editors, *Advances in Neural Information Processing Systems 25*, Curran Associates, Inc., pages 1097–1105.

Guillaume Lample, Miguel Ballesteros, Sandeep Subramanian, Kazuya Kawakami, and Chris Dyer. 2016. Neural architectures for named entity recognition. In *NAACL HLT 2016, The 2016 Conference of the North American Chapter of the Association for Computational Linguistics: Human Language Technologies*. San Diego, California, USA, pages 260–270.

Jiwei Li, Minh-Thang Luong, and Dan Jurafsky. 2015. A hierarchical neural autoencoder for paragraphs and documents. In *Proceedings of the 53rd Annual Meeting of the Association for Computational Linguistics and the 7th International Joint Conference on Natural Language Processing of the Asian Federation of Natural Language Processing, ACL, Volume 1: Long Papers*. Beijing, China, pages 1106–1115.

Linlin Li, Benjamin Roth, and Caroline Sporleder. 2010. Topic models for word sense disambiguation and token-based idiom detection. In *Proceedings of the 48th Annual Meeting of the Association for Computational Linguistics*. Uppsala, Sweden, pages 1138–1147.

Tomas Mikolov, Ilya Sutskever, Kai Chen, Greg S Corrado, and Jeff Dean. 2013. Distributed representations of words and phrases and their compositionality. In C. J. C. Burges, L. Bottou, M. Welling, Z. Ghahramani, and K. Q. Weinberger, editors, *Advances in Neural Information Processing Systems 26*, Curran Associates, Inc., pages 3111–3119.

Graham Neubig, Katsuhito Sudoh, Yusuke Oda, Kevin Duh, Hajime Tsukada, and Masaaki Nagata. 2014. The NAIST-NTT TED talk treebank. In *International Workshop on Spoken Language Translation (IWSLT)*. Lake Tahoe, USA.

David Newman, Nagendra Koilada, Jey Han Lau, and Timothy Baldwin. 2012. Bayesian text segmentation for index term identification and keyphrase extraction. In *Proceedings of COLING 2012*. Mumbai, India, pages 2077–2092.

F. Pedregosa, G. Varoquaux, A. Gramfort, V. Michel, B. Thirion, O. Grisel, M. Blondel, P. Prettenhofer, R. Weiss, V. Dubourg, J. Vanderplas, A. Passos, D. Cournapeau, M. Brucher, M. Perrot, and E. Duchesnay. 2011. Scikit-learn: Machine learning in Python. *Journal of Machine Learning Research* 12:2825–2830.

Jeffrey Pennington, Richard Socher, and Christopher Manning. 2014. Glove: Global vectors for word representation. In *Proceedings of the 2014 Conference on Empirical Methods in Natural Language Processing (EMNLP)*. Doha, Qatar, pages 1532–1543.

Lizhen Qu, Gabriela Ferraro, Liyuan Zhou, Weiwei Hou, Nathan Schneider, and Timothy Baldwin. 2015. Big data small data, in domain out-of domain, known word unknown word: The impact of word representations on sequence labelling tasks. In *Proceedings of the Nineteenth Conference on Computational Natural Language Learning*. Beijing, China, pages 83–93.

Radim Řehůřek and Petr Sojka. 2010. Software Framework for Topic Modelling with Large Corpora. In *Proceedings of the LREC 2010 Workshop on New Challenges for NLP Frameworks*. Valletta, Malta, pages 45–50.

Alan Ritter, Sam Clark, Mausam, and Oren Etzioni. 2011. Named entity recognition in tweets: An experimental study. In *Proceedings of the 2011 Conference on Empirical Methods in Natural Language Processing, A meeting of SIGDAT, a Special Interest Group of the ACL*. Edinburgh, UK, pages 1524–1534.

Ivan A. Sag, Timothy Baldwin, Francis Bond, Ann Copestake, and Dan Flickinger. 2002. Multiword expressions: A pain in the neck for NLP. In *Proceedings of the Third International Conference on Intelligent Text Processing and Computational Linguistics (CICLING 2002)*. pages 1–15.

Giancarlo Salton, Robert Ross, and John Kelleher. 2016. Idiom token classification using sentential distributed semantics. In *Proceedings of the 54th Annual Meeting of the Association for Computational Linguistics (Volume 1: Long Papers)*. Berlin, Germany, pages 194–204.

Andrew M. Saxe, James L. McClelland, and Surya Ganguli. 2014. Exact solutions to the nonlinear dynamics of learning in deep linear neural networks. In *International Conference on Learning Representations (ICLR2014)*.

Nathan Schneider, Emily Danchik, Chris Dyer, and A. Noah Smith. 2014a. Discriminative lexical semantic segmentation with gaps: Running the mwe gamut. *Transactions of the Association for Computational Linguistics (TACL)* 2:193–206.

Nathan Schneider, Dirk Hovy, Anders Johannsen, and Marine Carpuat. 2016. SemEval-2016 task 10: Detecting minimal semantic units and their meanings (DiMSUM). In *Proceedings of the 10th International Workshop on Semantic Evaluation, SemEval@NAACL-HLT*. San Diego, CA, USA, pages 546–559.

Nathan Schneider, Spencer Onuffer, Nora Kazour, Emily Danchik, Michael T. Mordowanec, Henrietta Conrad, and Noah A. Smith. 2014b. Comprehensive annotation of multiword expressions in a social web corpus. In *Proceedings of the Ninth International Conference on Language Resources and Evaluation (LREC-2014)*. Reykjavik, Iceland, pages 455–461.

Nathan Schneider and A. Noah Smith. 2015. A corpus and model integrating multiword expressions and supersenses. In *Proceedings of the 2015 Conference of the North American Chapter of the Association for Computational Linguistics: Human Language Technologies*. Denver, Colorado, pages 1537–1547.

Nitish Srivastava, Geoffrey E. Hinton, Alex Krizhevsky, Ilya Sutskever, and Ruslan Salakhutdinov. 2014. Dropout: a simple way to prevent neural networks from overfitting. *Journal of Machine Learning Research* 15(1):1929–1958.

Fabian M. Suchanek, Gjergji Kasneci, and Gerhard Weikum. 2007. Yago: a core of semantic knowledge. In *Proceedings of the 16th International Conference on World Wide Web*. Banff, Alberta, Canada, pages 697–706.

Ilya Sutskever, Oriol Vinyals, and Quoc V Le. 2014. Sequence to sequence learning with neural networks. In Z. Ghahramani, M. Welling, C. Cortes, N. D. Lawrence, and K. Q. Weinberger, editors, *Advances in Neural Information Processing Systems 27*, Curran Associates, Inc., pages 3104–3112.

Kiyoko Uchiyama, Timothy Baldwin, and Shun Ishizaki. 2005. Disambiguating Japanese compound verbs. *Computer Speech and Language, Special Issue on Multiword Expressions* 19(4):497–512.

Emotion Intensities in Tweets

Saif M. Mohammad
Information and Communications Technologies
National Research Council Canada
Ottawa, Canada
`saif.mohammad@nrc-cnrc.gc.ca`

Felipe Bravo-Marquez
Department of Computer Science
The University of Waikato
Hamilton, New Zealand
`fbravoma@waikato.ac.nz`

Abstract

This paper examines the task of detecting intensity of emotion from text. We create the first datasets of tweets annotated for anger, fear, joy, and sadness intensities. We use a technique called best–worst scaling (BWS) that improves annotation consistency and obtains reliable fine-grained scores. We show that emotion-word hashtags often impact emotion intensity, usually conveying a more intense emotion. Finally, we create a benchmark regression system and conduct experiments to determine: which features are useful for detecting emotion intensity; and, the extent to which two emotions are similar in terms of how they manifest in language.

1 Introduction

We use language to communicate not only the emotion we are feeling but also the intensity of the emotion. For example, our utterances can convey that we are very angry, slightly sad, absolutely elated, etc. Here, *intensity* refers to the degree or amount of an emotion such as anger or sadness.[1] Natural language applications can benefit from knowing both the class of emotion and its intensity. For example, a commercial customer satisfaction system would prefer to focus first on instances of significant frustration or anger, as opposed to instances of minor inconvenience. However, most work on automatic emotion detection has focused on categorical classification (presence of anger, joy, sadness, etc.). A notable obstacle in developing automatic affect intensity systems is the lack of suitable annotated data. Existing affect datasets are predominantly categorical. Anno-

tating instances for degrees of affect is a substantially more difficult undertaking: respondents are presented with greater cognitive load and it is particularly hard to ensure consistency (both across responses by different annotators and within the responses produced by an individual annotator).

Best–Worst Scaling (BWS) is an annotation scheme that addresses these limitations (Louviere, 1991; Louviere et al., 2015; Kiritchenko and Mohammad, 2016, 2017). Annotators are given n items (an n-tuple, where $n > 1$ and commonly $n = 4$). They are asked which item is the *best* (highest in terms of the property of interest) and which is the *worst* (lowest in terms of the property of interest). When working on 4-tuples, best–worst annotations are particularly efficient because each best and worst annotation will reveal the order of five of the six item pairs. For example, for a 4-tuple with items A, B, C, and D, if A is the best, and D is the worst, then A > B, A > C, A > D, B > D, and C > D.

BWS annotations for a set of 4-tuples can be easily converted into real-valued scores of association between the items and the property of interest (Orme, 2009; Flynn and Marley, 2014). It has been empirically shown that annotations for $2N$ 4-tuples is sufficient for obtaining reliable scores (where N is the number of items) (Louviere, 1991; Kiritchenko and Mohammad, 2016).[2] The little work using BWS in computational linguistics has focused on words (Jurgens et al., 2012; Kiritchenko and Mohammad, 2016). It is unclear whether the approach can be scaled up to larger textual units such as sentences.

Twitter has a large and diverse user base, which entails rich textual content, including non-standard language such as emoticons, emojis, cre-

---

[1] Intensity is different from *arousal*, which refers to the extent to which an emotion is calming or exciting.

[2] At its limit, when $n = 2$, BWS becomes a *paired comparison* (Thurstone, 1927; David, 1963), but then a much larger set of tuples need to be annotated (closer to N^2).

*Proceedings of the 6th Joint Conference on Lexical and Computational Semantics (*SEM 2017)*, pages 65–77,
Vancouver, Canada, August 3-4, 2017. ©2017 Association for Computational Linguistics

atively spelled words (*happee*), and hashtagged words (*#luvumom*). Tweets are often used to convey one's emotions, opinions towards products, and stance over issues. Thus, automatically detecting emotion intensities in tweets has many applications, including: tracking brand and product perception, tracking support for issues and policies, tracking public health and well-being, and disaster/crisis management.

In this paper, we present work on detecting intensities (or degrees) of emotion in tweets. Specifically, given a tweet and an emotion X, the goal is to determine the intensity or degree of emotion X felt by the speaker—a real-valued score between 0 and 1.[3] A score of 1 means that the speaker feels the highest amount of emotion X. A score of 0 means that the speaker feels the lowest amount of emotion X. We annotate a dataset of tweets for intensity of emotion using best–worst scaling and crowdsourcing. The main contributions of this work are summarized below:

- We formulate and develop the task of detecting emotion intensities in tweets.

- We create four datasets of tweets annotated for intensity of anger, joy, sadness, and fear, respectively. These are the first of their kind.[4]

- We show that Best–Worst Scaling can be successfully applied for annotating sentences (and not just words). We hope that this will encourage the use of BWS more widely, producing more reliable natural language annotations.

- We annotate both tweets and a hashtag-removed version of the tweets. We analyse the impact of hashtags on emotion intensity.

- We create a regression system, *AffectiveTweets Package*, to automatically determine emotion intensity.[5] We show the extent to which various features help determine emotion intensity. The system is released as an open-source package for the Weka workbench.

- We conduct experiments to show the extent to which two emotions are similar as per their manifestation in language, by showing how predictive the features for one emotion are of another emotion's intensity.

- We provide data for a new shared task WASSA-2017 Shared Task on Emotion Intensity.[6] The competition is organized on a CodaLab website, where participants can upload their submissions, and the leaderboard reports the results.[7] Twenty-two teams participated. A description of the task, details of participating systems, and results are available in Mohammad and Bravo-Marquez (2017).[8]

All of the data, annotation questionnaires, evaluation scripts, regression code, and interactive visualizations of the data are made freely available on the shared task website.[6]

2 Related Work

Psychologists have argued that some emotions are more basic than others (Ekman, 1992; Plutchik, 1980; Parrot, 2001; Frijda, 1988). However, they disagree on which emotions (and how many) should be classified as basic emotions—some propose 6, some 8, some 20, and so on. Thus, most efforts in automatic emotion detection have focused on a handful of emotions, especially since manually annotating text for a large number of emotions is arduous. Apart from these categorical models of emotions, certain dimensional models of emotion have also been proposed. The most popular among them, Russell's circumplex model, asserts that all emotions are made up of two core dimensions: valence and arousal (Russell, 2003). In this paper, we describe work on four emotions that are the most common amongst the many proposals for basic emotions: anger, fear, joy, and sadness. However, we have also begun work on other affect categories, as well as on valence and arousal.

The vast majority of emotion annotation work provides discrete binary labels to the text instances (joy–nojoy, fear–nofear, and so on) (Alm et al., 2005; Aman and Szpakowicz, 2007; Brooks et al., 2013; Neviarouskaya et al., 2009; Bollen et al., 2009). The only annotation effort that provided scores for degree of emotion is by Strapparava and Mihalcea (2007) as part of one of the SemEval-2007 shared task. Annotators were given newspaper headlines and asked to provide scores between

---

[3]Identifying intensity of emotion evoked in the reader, or intensity of emotion felt by an entity mentioned in the tweet, are also useful, and left for future work.

[4]We have also begun work on creating similar datasets annotated for other emotion categories. We are also creating a dataset annotated for valence, arousal, and dominance.

[5]https://github.com/felipebravom/AffectiveTweets

[6]http://saifmohammad.com/WebPages/EmotionIntensity-SharedTask.html

[7]https://competitions.codalab.org/competitions/16380

[8]Even though the 2017 WASSA shared task has concluded, the CodaLab competition website is kept open. Thus the best results obtained by any system on the 2017 test set can be found on the CodaLab leaderboard.

0 and 100 via slide bars in a web interface. It is difficult for humans to provide direct scores at such fine granularity. A common problem is inconsistency in annotations. One annotator might assign a score of 79 to a piece of text, whereas another annotator may assign a score of 62 to the same text. It is also common that the same annotator assigns different scores to the same text instance at different points in time. Further, annotators often have a bias towards different parts of the scale, known as *scale region bias*.

Best–Worst Scaling (BWS) was developed by Louviere (1991), building on some groundbreaking research in the 1960s in mathematical psychology and psychophysics by Anthony A. J. Marley and Duncan Luce. Kiritchenko and Mohammad (2017) show through empirical experiments that BWS produces more reliable fine-grained scores than scores obtained using rating scales. Within the NLP community, Best–Worst Scaling (BWS) has thus far been used only to annotate words: for example, for creating datasets for relational similarity (Jurgens et al., 2012), word-sense disambiguation (Jurgens, 2013), word–sentiment intensity (Kiritchenko et al., 2014), and phrase sentiment composition (Kiritchenko and Mohammad, 2016). However, in this work we use BWS to annotate whole tweets for degree of emotion. With BWS we address the challenges of direct scoring, and produce more reliable emotion intensity scores. Further, this will be the first dataset with emotion scores for *tweets*.

Automatic emotion classification has been proposed for many different kinds of texts, including tweets (Summa et al., 2016; Mohammad, 2012; Bollen et al., 2009; Aman and Szpakowicz, 2007; Brooks et al., 2013). However, there is little work on emotion regression other than the three submissions to the 2007 SemEval task (Strapparava and Mihalcea, 2007).

3   Data

For each of the four focus emotions, our goal was to create a dataset of tweets such that:

- The tweets are associated with various intensities (or degrees) of emotion.
- Some tweets have words clearly indicative of the focus emotion and some tweets do not.

A random collection of tweets is likely to have a large proportion of tweets not associated with the focus emotion, and thus annotating all of them for intensity of emotion is sub-optimal. To create a dataset of tweets rich in a particular emotion, we use the following methodology.

For each emotion X, we select 50 to 100 terms that are associated with that emotion at different intensity levels. For example, for the anger dataset, we use the terms: *angry, mad, frustrated, annoyed, peeved, irritated, miffed, fury, antagonism,* and so on. For the sadness dataset, we use the terms: *sad, devastated, sullen, down, crying, dejected, heartbroken, grief, weeping,* and so on. We will refer to these terms as the *query terms*.

We identified the query words for an emotion by first searching the *Roget's Thesaurus* to find categories that had the focus emotion word (or a close synonym) as the head word.[9] We chose all words listed within these categories to be the query terms for the corresponding focus emotion. We polled the Twitter API for tweets that included the query terms. We discarded retweets (tweets that start with RT) and tweets with urls. We created a subset of the remaining tweets by:

- selecting at most 50 tweets per query term.
- selecting at most 1 tweet for every tweeter–query term combination.

Thus, the *master set of tweets* is not heavily skewed towards some tweeters or query terms.

To study the impact of emotion word hashtags on the intensity of the whole tweet, we identified tweets that had a query term in hashtag form towards the end of the tweet—specifically, within the trailing portion of the tweet made up solely of hashtagged words. We created copies of these tweets and then removed the hashtag query terms from the copies. The updated tweets were then added to the master set. Finally, our master set of 7,097 tweets includes:

1. *Hashtag Query Term Tweets (HQT Tweets):* 1030 tweets with a query term in the form of a hashtag (#<query term>) in the trailing portion of the tweet;

2. *No Query Term Tweets (NQT Tweets):* 1030 tweets that are copies of '1', but with the hashtagged query term removed;

---

[9]The *Roget's Thesaurus* groups words into about 1000 categories. The head word is the word that best represents the meaning of the words within the category. The categories chosen were: 900 Resentment (for anger), 860 Fear (for fear), 836 Cheerfulness (for joy), and 837 Dejection (for sadness).

3. *Query Term Tweets (QT Tweets)*:
5037 tweets that include:
a. tweets that contain a query term in the form of a word (no #<query term>)
b. tweets with a query term in hashtag form followed by at least one non-hashtag word.

The master set of tweets was then manually annotated for intensity of emotion. Table 1 shows a breakdown by emotion.

3.1 Annotating with Best–Worst Scaling

We followed the procedure described in Kiritchenko and Mohammad (2016) to obtain BWS annotations. For each emotion, the annotators were presented with four tweets at a time (4-tuples) and asked to select the speakers of the tweets with the highest and lowest emotion intensity. $2 \times N$ (where N is the number of tweets in the emotion set) distinct 4-tuples were randomly generated in such a manner that each item is seen in eight different 4-tuples, and no pair of items occurs in more than one 4-tuple. We will refer to this as *random maximum-diversity selection (RMDS)*. RMDS maximizes the number of unique items that each item co-occurs with in the 4-tuples. After BWS annotations, this in turn leads to direct comparative ranking information for the maximum number of pairs of items.[10]

It is desirable for an item to occur in sets of 4-tuples such that the maximum intensities in those 4-tuples are spread across the range from low intensity to high intensity, as then the proportion of times an item is chosen as the best is indicative of its intensity score. Similarly, it is desirable for an item to occur in sets of 4-tuples such that the minimum intensities are spread from low to high intensity. However, since the intensities of items are not known beforehand, RMDS is used.

Every 4-tuple was annotated by three independent annotators.[11] The questionnaires used were developed through internal discussions and pilot

Emotion	Train	Dev.	Test	All
anger	857	84	760	1701
fear	1147	110	995	2252
joy	823	74	714	1611
sadness	786	74	673	1533
All	3613	342	3142	7097

Table 1: The number of instances in the Tweet Emotion Intensity dataset.

annotations. A sample questionnaire is shown in the Appendix (A.1).

The 4-tuples of tweets were uploaded on the crowdsourcing platform, CrowdFlower. About 5% of the data was annotated internally beforehand (by the authors). These questions are referred to as gold questions. The gold questions are interspersed with other questions. If one gets a gold question wrong, they are immediately notified of it. If one's accuracy on the gold questions falls below 70%, they are refused further annotation, and all of their annotations are discarded. This serves as a mechanism to avoid malicious annotations.[12]

The BWS responses were translated into scores by a simple calculation (Orme, 2009; Flynn and Marley, 2014): For each item, the score is the percentage of times the item was chosen as having the most intensity minus the percentage of times the item was chosen as having the least intensity.[13] The scores range from -1 to 1. Since degree of emotion is a unipolar scale, we linearly transform the the -1 to 1 scores to scores in the range 0 to 1.

3.2 Training, Development, and Test Sets

We refer to the newly created emotion-intensity labeled data as the *Tweet Emotion Intensity Dataset*. The dataset is partitioned into training, development, and test sets for machine learning experiments (see Table 1). For each emotion, we chose to include about 50% of the tweets in the training set, about 5% in the development set, and about 45% in the test set. Further, we made sure that an NQT tweet is in the same partition as the HQT tweet it was created from. See Appendix (A.4) for details of an interactive visualization of the data.

---

[10]In combinatorial mathematics, *balanced incomplete block design* refers to creating blocks (or tuples) of a handful items from a set of N items such that each item occurs in the same number of blocks (say x) and each pair of distinct items occurs in the same number of blocks (say y), where x and y are integers ge 1 (Yates, 1936). The set of tuples we create have similar properties, except that since we create only $2N$ tuples, pairs of distinct items either never occur together in a 4-tuple or they occur in exactly one 4-tuple.

[11]Kiritchenko and Mohammad (2016) showed that using just three annotations per 4-tuple produces highly reliable results. Note that since each tweet is seen in eight different 4-tuples, we obtain $8 \times 3 = 24$ judgments over each tweet.

[12]In case more than one item can be reasonably chosen as the best (or worst) item, then more than one acceptable gold answers are provided. The goal with the gold annotations is to identify clearly poor or malicious annotators. In case where two items are close in intensity, we want the crowd of annotators to indicate, through their BWS annotations, the relative ranking of the items.

[13]Kiritchenko and Mohammad (2016) provide code for generating tuples from items using RMDS, as well as code for generating scores from BWS annotations: http://saifmohammad.com/WebPages/BestWorst.html

4   Reliability of Annotations

One cannot use standard inter-annotator agreement measures to determine quality of BWS annotations because the disagreement that arises when a tuple has two items that are close in emotion intensity is a useful signal for BWS. For a given 4-tuple, if respondents are not able to consistently identify the tweet that has highest (or lowest) emotion intensity, then the disagreement will lead to the two tweets obtaining scores that are close to each other, which is the desired outcome. Thus a different measure of quality of annotations must be utilized.

A useful measure of quality is reproducibility of the end result—if repeated independent manual annotations from multiple respondents result in similar intensity rankings (and scores), then one can be confident that the scores capture the true emotion intensities. To assess this reproducibility, we calculate average *split-half reliability (SHR)*, a commonly used approach to determine consistency (Kuder and Richardson, 1937; Cronbach, 1946). The intuition behind SHR is as follows. All annotations for an item (in our case, tuples) are randomly split into two halves. Two sets of scores are produced independently from the two halves. Then the correlation between the two sets of scores is calculated. If the annotations are of good quality, then the correlation between the two halves will be high.

Since each tuple in this dataset was annotated by three annotators (odd number), we calculate SHR by randomly placing one or two annotations per tuple in one bin and the remaining (two or one) annotations for the tuple in another bin. Then two sets of intensity scores (and rankings) are calculated from the annotations in each of the two bins. The process is repeated 100 times and the correlations across the two sets of rankings and intensity scores are averaged. Table 2 shows the split-half reliabilities for the anger, fear, joy, and sadness tweets in the Tweet Emotion Intensity Dataset.[14] Observe that for fear, joy, and sadness datasets, both the Pearson correlations and the Spearman rank correlations lie between 0.84 and 0.88, indicating a high degree of reproducibility. However,

---

[14]Past work has found the SHR for sentiment intensity annotations for words, with 8 annotations per tuple, to be 0.98 (Kiritchenko et al., 2014). In contrast, here SHR is calculated from 3 annotations, for emotions, and from whole sentences. SHR determined from a smaller number of annotations and on more complex annotation tasks are expected to be lower.

Emotion	Spearman	Pearson
anger	0.779	0.797
fear	0.845	0.850
joy	0.881	0.882
sadness	0.847	0.847

Table 2:   Split-half reliabilities (as measured by Pearson correlation and Spearman rank correlation) for the anger, fear, joy, and sadness tweets in the Tweet Emotion Intensity Dataset.

the correlations are slightly lower for anger indicating that it is relative more difficult to ascertain the degrees of anger of speakers from their tweets. Note that SHR indicates the quality of annotations obtained when using only half the number of annotations. The correlations obtained when repeating the experiment with three annotations for each 4-tuple is expected to be even higher. Thus the numbers shown in Table 2 are a lower bound on the quality of annotations obtained with three annotations per 4-tuple.

5   Impact of Emotion Word Hashtags on Emotion Intensity

Some studies have shown that emoticons tend to be redundant in terms of the sentiment (Go et al., 2009; Mohammad et al., 2013). That is, if we remove a smiley face, ':)', from a tweet, we find that the rest of the tweet still conveys a positive sentiment. Similarly, it has been shown that hashtag emotion words are also somewhat redundant in terms of the class of emotion being conveyed by the rest of the tweet (Mohammad, 2012). For example, removal of '#angry' from the tweet below leaves a tweet that still conveys anger.

> *This mindless support of a demagogue needs to stop. #racism #grrr #angry*

However, it is unclear what impact such emotion word hashtags have on the *intensity* of emotion. In fact, there exists no prior work to systematically study this. One of the goals of creating this dataset and including HQT–NQT tweet pairs, is to allow for exactly such an investigation.[15]

We analyzed the scores in our dataset to create scatter plots where each point corresponds to a HQT–NQT tweet pair, the x-axis is the emotion intensity score of the HQT tweet, and the y-axis is the score of the NQT tweet. Figure 1 shows the scatter plot for the fear data. We observe that

---

[15]See Appendix (A.2) for further discussion on how emotion word hashtags have been used in prior research.

Emotion	No. of HQT–NQT Tweet Pairs	% Tweets Pairs			Average Emotion Intensity Score			
		Drop	Rise	None	HQT tweets	NQT tweets	Drop	Rise
anger	282	76.6	19.9	3.4	0.58	0.48	0.15	0.07
fear	454	86.1	13.9	4.4	0.57	0.43	0.18	0.07
joy	204	71.6	26.5	1.9	0.59	0.50	0.15	0.09
sadness	90	85.6	11,1	3.3	0.65	0.49	0.19	0.05
All	1030	78.6	17.8	3.6	0.58	0.47	0.17	0.08

Table 3: The impact of removal of emotion word hashtags on the emotion intensities of tweets.

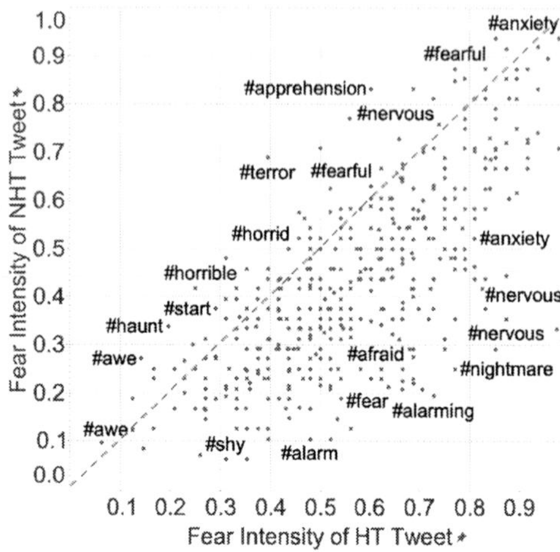

Figure 1: The scatter plot of fear intensity of HQT tweet vs. corresponding NQT tweet. As per space availability, some points are labeled with the relevant hashtag.

in a majority of the cases, the points are on the lower-right side of the diagonal, indicating that the removal of the emotion word hashtag causes the emotion intensity of the tweet to drop. However, we do see a number of points on the upper-left side of the diagonal (indicating a rise), and some exactly on the diagonal (indicating no impact), due to the removal of a hashtag. Also observe that the removal of a hashtag can result in a drop in emotion scores for some tweets, but a rise for others (e.g., see the three labeled points for *#nervous* in the plot). We observe a similar pattern for other emotions as well (plots not shown here). Table 3 summarizes these results by showing the percentage of times the three outcomes occur for each of the emotions.

The table also shows that the average scores of HQT tweets and NQT tweets. The difference between 0.58 and 0.47 is statistically significant.[16] The last two columns show that when there is a drop in score on removal of the hashtag, the aver-

age drop is about 0.17 (17% of the total range 0–1), whereas when there is a rise, the average rise is 0.08 (8% of the total range). These results show that emotion word hashtags are often *not* redundant with the rest of tweet in terms of what they bring to bear at the overall emotion intensity. Further, even though it is common for many of these hashtags to increase the emotion intensity, there is a more complex interplay between the text of the tweet and the hashtag which determines the directionality and magnitude of the impact on emotion intensity. For instance, we often found that if the rest of the tweet clearly indicated the presence of an emotion (through another emotion word hashtag, emojis, or through the non-hashtagged words), then the emotion word hashtag had only a small impact on the score.[17]

However, if the rest of the tweet is underspecified in terms of the emotion of the speaker, then the emotion word hashtag markedly increased the perceived emotion intensity. We also observed patterns unique to particular emotions. For example, when judging degree of fear of a speaker, lower scores were assigned when the speaker used a hashtag that indicated some outward judgment.

> *@RocksNRopes Can't believe how rude your cashier was.*   fear: 0.48

> *@RocksNRopes Can't believe how rude your cashier was. #terrible*   fear: 0.31

We believe that not vocalizing an outward judgment of the situation made the speaker appear more fearful. The HQT–NQT subset of our dataset will also be made separately, and freely, available as it may be of interest on its own, especially for the psychology and social sciences communities.

---

[16]Wilcoxon signed-rank test at 0.05 significance level.

[17]Unless the hashtag word itself is associated with very low emotion intensity (e.g., #peeved with anger), in which case, there was a drop in perceived emotion intensity.

	Twitter	Annotation	Scope	Label
AFINN (Nielsen, 2011)	Yes	Manual	Sentiment	Numeric
BingLiu (Hu and Liu, 2004)	No	Manual	Sentiment	Nominal
MPQA (Wilson et al., 2005)	No	Manual	Sentiment	Nominal
NRC Affect Intensity Lexicon (NRC-Aff-Int) (Mohammad, 2017)	Yes	Manual	Emotions	Numeric
NRC Word-Emotion Assn. Lexicon (NRC-EmoLex) (Mohammad and Turney, 2013)	No	Manual	Emotions	Nominal
NRC10 Expanded (NRC10E) (Bravo-Marquez et al., 2016)	Yes	Automatic	Emotions	Numeric
NRC Hashtag Emotion Association Lexicon (NRC-Hash-Emo) (Mohammad and Kiritchenko, 2015)	Yes	Automatic	Emotions	Numeric
NRC Hashtag Sentiment Lexicon (NRC-Hash-Sent) (Mohammad et al., 2013)	Yes	Automatic	Sentiment	Numeric
Sentiment140 (Mohammad et al., 2013)	Yes	Automatic	Sentiment	Numeric
SentiWordNet (Esuli and Sebastiani, 2006)	No	Automatic	Sentiment	Numeric
SentiStrength (Thelwall et al., 2012)	Yes	Manual	Sentiment	Numeric

Table 4: Affect lexicons used in our experiments.

6 Automatically Determining Tweet Emotion Intensity

We now describe our regression system, which we use for obtaining benchmark prediction results on the new Tweet Emotion Intensity Dataset (Section 6.1) and for determining the extent to which two emotions are correlated (Section 6.2).

Regression System We implemented a package called AffectiveTweets for the Weka machine learning workbench (Hall et al., 2009) that provides a collection of filters for extracting state-of-the-art features from tweets for sentiment classification and other related tasks. These include features used in Kiritchenko et al. (2014) and Mohammad et al. (2017).[18] We use the package for calculating feature vectors from our emotion-intensity-labeled tweets and train Weka regression models on this transformed data. We used an L_2-regularized L_2-loss SVM regression model with the regularization parameter C set to 1, implemented in LIBLINEAR[19]. The features used:[20]

a. Word N-grams (WN): presence or absence of word n-grams from $n = 1$ to $n = 4$.

b. Character N-grams (CN): presence or absence of character n-grams from $n = 3$ to $n = 5$.

c. Word Embeddings (WE): an average of the word embeddings of all the words in a tweet. We calculate individual word embeddings using the negative sampling skip-gram model implemented in *Word2Vec* (Mikolov et al., 2013). Word vectors are trained from ten million English tweets taken from the Edinburgh Twitter Corpus (Petrović et al., 2010). We set *Word2Vec* parameters:

window size: 5; number of dimensions: 400.[21]

d. Affect Lexicons (L): we use the lexicons shown in Table 4, by aggregating the information for all the words in a tweet. If the lexicon provides nominal association labels (e.g, positive, anger, etc.), then the number of words in the tweet matching each class are counted. If the lexicon provides numerical scores, the individual scores for each class are summed. These resources differ according to: whether the lexicon includes Twitter-specific terms, whether the words were manually or automatically annotated, whether the words were annotated for sentiment or emotions, and whether the affective associations provided are nominal or numeric. (See Table 4.)

Evaluation We calculate the Pearson correlation coefficient (r) between the scores produced by the automatic system on the test sets and the gold intensity scores to determine the extent to which the output of the system matches the results of human annotation.[22] Pearson coefficient, which measures linear correlations between two variables, produces scores from -1 (perfectly inversely correlated) to 1 (perfectly correlated). A score of 0 indicates no correlation.

6.1 Supervised Regression and Ablation

We developed our system by training on the official training sets and applying the learned models to the development sets. Once system parameters were frozen, the system trained on the combined training and development corpora. These models were applied to the official test sets. Table 5 shows the results obtained on the test sets using various features, individually and in combination. The last column 'avg.' shows the macro-average of the correlations for all of the emotions.

---

[18]Kiritchenko et al. (2014) describes the NRC-Canada system which ranked first in three sentiment shared tasks: SemEval-2013 Task 2, SemEval-2014 Task 9, and SemEval-2014 Task 4. Mohammad et al. (2017) describes a stance-detection system that outperformed submissions from all 19 teams that participated in SemEval-2016 Task 6.

[19]http://www.csie.ntu.edu.tw/~cjlin/liblinear/

[20]See Appendix (A.3) for further implementation details.

[21]Optimized for the task of word–emotion classification on an independent dataset (Bravo-Marquez et al., 2016).

[22]We also determined Spearman rank correlations but these were inline with the results obtained using Pearson.

	anger	fear	joy	sad.	avg.
Individual feature sets					
word ngrams (WN)	0.42	0.49	0.52	0.49	0.48
char. ngrams (CN)	0.50	0.48	0.45	0.49	0.48
word embeds. (WE)	0.48	0.54	0.57	0.60	0.55
all lexicons (L)	**0.62**	**0.60**	**0.60**	**0.68**	**0.63**
Individual Lexicons					
AFINN	0.48	0.27	0.40	0.28	0.36
BingLiu	0.33	0.31	0.37	0.23	0.31
MPQA	0.18	0.20	0.28	0.12	0.20
NRC-Aff-Int	0.24	0.28	0.37	0.32	0.30
NRC-EmoLex	0.18	0.26	0.36	0.23	0.26
NRC10E	0.35	0.34	0.43	0.37	0.37
NRC-Hash-Emo	**0.55**	**0.55**	0.46	0.54	**0.53**
NRC-Hash-Sent	0.33	0.24	0.41	0.39	0.34
Sentiment140	0.33	0.41	0.40	0.48	0.41
SentiWordNet	0.14	0.19	0.26	0.16	0.19
SentiStrength	0.43	0.34	**0.46**	**0.61**	0.46
Combinations					
WN + CN + WE	0.50	0.48	0.45	0.49	0.48
WN + CN + L	0.61	0.61	0.61	0.63	0.61
WE + L	**0.64**	0.63	**0.65**	**0.71**	**0.66**
WN + WE + L	0.63	**0.65**	**0.65**	0.65	0.65
CN + WE + L	0.61	0.61	0.62	0.63	0.62
WN + CN + WE + L	0.61	0.61	0.61	0.63	0.62

Table 5: Pearson correlations (r) of emotion intensity predictions with gold scores. Best results for each column are shown in bold: highest score by a feature set, highest score using a single lexicon, and highest score using feature set combinations.

Using just character or just word n-grams leads to results around 0.48, suggesting that they are reasonably good indicators of emotion intensity by themselves. (Guessing the intensity scores at random between 0 and 1 is expected to get correlations close to 0.) Word embeddings produce statistically significant improvement over the ngrams (avg. r = 0.55).[23] Using features drawn from affect lexicons produces results ranging from avg. r = 0.19 with SentiWordNet to avg. r = 0.53 with NRC-Hash-Emo. Combining all the lexicons leads to statistically significant improvement over individual lexicons (avg. r = 0.63). Combining the different kinds of features leads to even higher scores, with the best overall result obtained using word embedding and lexicon features (avg. r = 0.66).[24] The feature space formed by all the lexicons together is the strongest single feature category. The results also show that some features such as character ngrams are redundant in the presence of certain other features.

Among the lexicons, NRC-Hash-Emo is the most predictive single lexicon. Lexicons that include Twitter-specific entries, lexicons that include intensity scores, and lexicons that label emotions and not just sentiment, tend to be more predictive on this task–dataset combination. NRC-Aff-Int has real-valued fine-grained word–emotion association scores for all the words in NRC-EmoLex that were marked as being associated with anger, fear, joy, and sadness.[25] Improvement in scores obtained using NRC-Aff-Int over the scores obtained using NRC-EmoLex also show that using fine intensity scores of word-emotion association are beneficial for tweet-level emotion intensity detection. The correlations for anger, fear, and joy are similar (around 0.65), but the correlation for sadness is markedly higher (0.71). We can observe from Table 5 that this boost in performance for sadness is to some extent due to word embeddings, but is more so due to lexicon features, especially those from SentiStrength. SentiStrength focuses solely on positive and negative classes, but provides numeric scores for each.

6.1.1 Moderate-to-High Intensity Prediction

In some applications, it may be more important for a system to correctly determine emotion intensities in the higher range of the scale than in the lower range of the scale. To assess performance in the moderate-to-high range of the intensity scale, we calculated correlation scores over a subset of the test data formed by taking only those instances with gold emotion intensity scores ≥ 0.5.

Table 6 shows the results. Firstly, the correlation scores are in general lower here in the 0.5 to 1 range of intensity scores than in the experiments over the full intensity range. This is simply because this is a harder task as now the systems do not benefit by making coarse distinctions over whether a tweet is in the lower range or in the higher range. Nonetheless, we observe that many of the broad patterns of results stay the same, with some differences. Lexicons still play a crucial role, however, now embeddings and word ngrams are not far behind. SentiStrength seems to be less useful in this range, suggesting that its main benefit was separating low- and high-intensity sadness words. NRC-Hash-Emo is still the source of the most predictive lexicon features.

---

[23]We used the Wilcoxon signed-rank test at 0.05 significance level calculated from ten random partitions of the data, for all the significance tests reported in this paper.

[24]The increase from 0.63 to 0.66 is statistically significant.

[25]http://saifmohammad.com/WebPages/AffectIntensity.htm

	anger	fear	joy	sad.	avg.
Individual feature sets					
word ngrams (WN)	0.36	0.39	**0.38**	0.40	0.38
char. ngrams (CN)	0.39	0.36	0.34	0.34	0.36
word embeds. (WE)	0.41	0.42	0.37	0.51	0.43
all lexicons (L)	**0.48**	**0.47**	0.29	**0.51**	**0.44**
Individual Lexicons					
(some low-score rows not shown to save space)					
AFINN	0.31	0.06	0.11	0.05	0.13
BingLiu	0.31	0.06	0.11	0.05	0.13
NRC10E	0.27	0.14	**0.25**	0.30	0.24
NRC-Hash-Emo	**0.43**	**0.39**	0.15	**0.44**	**0.35**
Sentiment140	0.18	0.24	0.09	0.32	0.21
SentiStrength	0.23	0.04	0.19	0.34	0.20
Combinations					
WN + CN + WE	0.37	0.35	0.33	0.34	0.35
WN + CN + L	0.44	0.45	0.34	0.43	0.41
WE + L	0.51	0.49	0.38	**0.54**	**0.48**
WN + WE + L	**0.51**	**0.51**	**0.40**	0.49	0.47
CN + WE + L	0.45	0.45	0.34	0.43	0.42
WN + CN + WE + L	0.44	0.45	0.34	0.43	0.42

Table 6: Pearson correlations on a subset of the test set where gold scores ≥ 0.5.

6.2 Similarity of Emotion Pairs

Humans are capable of hundreds of emotions, and some are closer to each other than others. One reason why certain emotion pairs may be perceived as being close is that their manifestation in language is similar, for example, similar words and expression are used when expressing both emotions. We quantify this similarity of linguistic manifestation by using the Tweet Emotion Intensity dataset for the following experiment: we train our regression system (with features WN + WE + L) on the training data for one emotion and evaluate predictions on the test data for a different emotion.

Table 7 shows the results. The numbers in the diagonal are results obtained using training and test data pertaining to the same emotion. These results are upperbound benchmarks for the non-diagonal results, which are expected to be lower. We observe that negative emotions are positively correlated with each other and negatively correlated with the only positive emotion (joy). The absolute values of these correlations go from $r = 0.23$ to $r = 0.65$. This shows that all of the emotion pairs are correlated at least to some extent, but that in some cases, for example, when learning from fear data and predicting sadness scores, one can obtain results ($r = 0.63$) close to the upperbound benchmark ($r = 0.65$).[26] Note also that the correlations are asymmetric. This means that even though one emotion may be strongly predictive of

---

[26]0.63 and 0.65 are not statistically significantly different.

Train On	Test On			
	anger	fear	joy	sadness
anger	0.63	0.37	-0.37	0.45
fear	0.46	0.65	-0.39	0.63
joy	-0.41	-0.23	0.65	-0.41
sadness	0.39	0.47	-0.32	0.65

Table 7: Emotion intensity transfer Pearson correlation on all target tweets.

another, the predictive power need not be similar in the other direction. We also found that training on a simple combination of both the fear and sadness data and using the model to predict sadness obtained a correlation of 0.67 (exceeding the score obtained with just the sadness training set).[27] Domain adaptation may provide further gains.

To summarize, the experiments in this section show the extent to which two emotion are similar as per their manifestation in language. For the four emotions studied here, the similarities vary from small (joy with fear) to considerable (fear with sadness). Also, the similarities are asymmetric. We also show that in some cases it is beneficial to use the training data for another emotion to supplement the training data for the emotion of interest. A promising avenue of future work is to test theories of emotion composition: e.g, whether optimism is indeed a combination of joy and anticipation, whether awe if fear and surprise, and so on, as some have suggested (Plutchik, 1980).

7 Conclusions

We created the first emotion intensity dataset for tweets. We used best–worst scaling to improve annotation consistency and obtained fine-grained scores. We showed that emotion-word hashtags often impact emotion intensity, often conveying a more intense emotion. We created a benchmark regression system and conducted experiments to show that affect lexicons, especially those with fine word–emotion association scores, are useful in determining emotion intensity. Finally, we showed the extent to which emotion pairs are correlated, and that the correlations are asymmetric— e.g., fear is strongly indicative of sadness, but sadness is only moderately indicative of fear.

Acknowledgment

We thank Svetlana Kiritchenko and Tara Small for helpful discussions.

---

[27]0.67–0.63 difference is statistically significantly different, but 0.67–0.65 and 0.65–0.63 differences are not.

References

Cecilia Ovesdotter Alm, Dan Roth, and Richard Sproat. 2005. Emotions from text: Machine learning for text-based emotion prediction. In *Proceedings of the Joint Conference on HLT–EMNLP*. Vancouver, Canada.

Saima Aman and Stan Szpakowicz. 2007. Identifying expressions of emotion in text. In *Text, Speech and Dialogue*, volume 4629 of *Lecture Notes in Computer Science*, pages 196–205.

Johan Bollen, Huina Mao, and Alberto Pepe. 2009. Modeling public mood and emotion: Twitter sentiment and socio-economic phenomena. In *Proceedings of the Fifth International Conference on Weblogs and Social Media*. pages 450–453.

Felipe Bravo-Marquez, Eibe Frank, Saif M Mohammad, and Bernhard Pfahringer. 2016. Determining word–emotion associations from tweets by multilabel classification. In *Proceedings of the 2016 IEEE/WIC/ACM International Conference on Web Intelligence*. Omaha, NE, USA, pages 536–539.

Michael Brooks, Katie Kuksenok, Megan K Torkildson, Daniel Perry, John J Robinson, Taylor J Scott, Ona Anicello, Ariana Zukowski, and Harris. 2013. Statistical affect detection in collaborative chat. In *Proceedings of the 2013 conference on Computer supported cooperative work*. San Antonio, Texas, USA, pages 317–328.

LJ Cronbach. 1946. A case study of the splithalf reliability coefficient. *Journal of educational psychology* 37(8):473.

Herbert Aron David. 1963. *The method of paired comparisons*. Hafner Publishing Company, New York.

Paul Ekman. 1992. An argument for basic emotions. *Cognition and Emotion* 6(3):169–200.

Andrea Esuli and Fabrizio Sebastiani. 2006. SENTIWORDNET: A publicly available lexical resource for opinion mining. In *Proceedings of the 5th Conference on Language Resources and Evaluation (LREC)*. Genoa, Italy, pages 417–422.

T. N. Flynn and A. A. J. Marley. 2014. Best-worst scaling: theory and methods. In Stephane Hess and Andrew Daly, editors, *Handbook of Choice Modelling*, Edward Elgar Publishing, pages 178–201.

Nico H Frijda. 1988. The laws of emotion. *American psychologist* 43(5):349.

Kevin Gimpel, Nathan Schneider, et al. 2011. Part-of-speech tagging for Twitter: Annotation, features, and experiments. In *Proceedings of the Annual Meeting of the Association for Computational Linguistics (ACL)*. Portland, OR, USA.

Alec Go, Richa Bhayani, and Lei Huang. 2009. Twitter sentiment classification using distant supervision. *CS224N Project Report, Stanford* 1(12).

Mark Hall, Eibe Frank, Geoffrey Holmes, Bernhard Pfahringer, Peter Reutemann, and Ian H. Witten. 2009. The WEKA data mining software: An update. *SIGKDD Explor. Newsl.* 11(1):10–18. https://doi.org/10.1145/1656274.1656278.

Minqing Hu and Bing Liu. 2004. Mining and summarizing customer reviews. In *Proceedings of the tenth ACM SIGKDD international conference on Knowledge discovery and data mining*. ACM, New York, NY, USA, pages 168–177.

David Jurgens. 2013. Embracing ambiguity: A comparison of annotation methodologies for crowdsourcing word sense labels. In *Proceedings of the Annual Conference of the North American Chapter of the Association for Computational Linguistics*. Atlanta, GA, USA.

David Jurgens, Saif M. Mohammad, Peter Turney, and Keith Holyoak. 2012. Semeval-2012 task 2: Measuring degrees of relational similarity. In *Proceedings of the 6th International Workshop on Semantic Evaluation*. Montréal, Canada, pages 356–364.

Svetlana Kiritchenko and Saif M. Mohammad. 2016. Capturing reliable fine-grained sentiment associations by crowdsourcing and best–worst scaling. In *Proceedings of The 15th Annual Conference of the North American Chapter of the Association for Computational Linguistics: Human Language Technologies (NAACL)*. San Diego, California.

Svetlana Kiritchenko and Saif M. Mohammad. 2017. Best-worst scaling more reliable than rating scales: A case study on sentiment intensity annotation. In *Proceedings of The Annual Meeting of the Association for Computational Linguistics (ACL)*. Vancouver, Canada.

Svetlana Kiritchenko, Xiaodan Zhu, and Saif M. Mohammad. 2014. Sentiment analysis of short informal texts. *Journal of Artificial Intelligence Research* 50:723–762.

G Frederic Kuder and Marion W Richardson. 1937. The theory of the estimation of test reliability. *Psychometrika* 2(3):151–160.

FA Kunneman, CC Liebrecht, and APJ van den Bosch. 2014. The (un) predictability of emotional hashtags in twitter. In *Proceedings of the 5th Workshop on Language Analysis for Social Media*. Gothenburg, Sweden, pages 26–34.

Jordan J. Louviere. 1991. Best-worst scaling: A model for the largest difference judgments. Working Paper.

Jordan J. Louviere, Terry N. Flynn, and A. A. J. Marley. 2015. *Best-Worst Scaling: Theory, Methods and Applications*. Cambridge University Press.

Tomas Mikolov, Kai Chen, Greg Corrado, and Jeffrey Dean. 2013. Efficient estimation of word representations in vector space. In *Proceedings of Workshop at ICLR*.

Saif M. Mohammad. 2012. #Emotional tweets. In *Proceedings of the First Joint Conference on Lexical and Computational Semantics*. Montréal, Canada, SemEval '12, pages 246–255.

Saif M Mohammad. 2017. Word affect intensities. *arXiv preprint arXiv:1704.08798* .

Saif M. Mohammad and Felipe Bravo-Marquez. 2017. WASSA-2017 shared task on emotion intensity. In *Proceedings of the Workshop on Computational Approaches to Subjectivity, Sentiment and Social Media Analysis (WASSA)*. Copenhagen, Denmark.

Saif M. Mohammad and Svetlana Kiritchenko. 2015. Using hashtags to capture fine emotion categories from tweets. *Computational Intelligence* 31(2):301–326. https://doi.org/10.1111/coin.12024.

Saif M. Mohammad, Svetlana Kiritchenko, and Xiaodan Zhu. 2013. NRC-Canada: Building the state-of-the-art in sentiment analysis of tweets. In *Proceedings of the International Workshop on Semantic Evaluation*. Atlanta, GA, USA.

Saif M. Mohammad, Parinaz Sobhani, and Svetlana Kiritchenko. 2017. Stance and sentiment in tweets. *Special Section of the ACM Transactions on Internet Technology on Argumentation in Social Media* 17(3).

Saif M. Mohammad and Peter D. Turney. 2013. Crowdsourcing a word–emotion association lexicon. *Computational Intelligence* 29(3):436–465.

Saif M. Mohammad, Xiaodan Zhu, Svetlana Kiritchenko, and Joel Martin. July 2015. Sentiment, emotion, purpose, and style in electoral tweets. *Information Processing and Management* 51(4):480–499.

Alena Neviarouskaya, Helmut Prendinger, and Mitsuru Ishizuka. 2009. Compositionality principle in recognition of fine-grained emotions from text. In *Proceedings of the Proceedings of the Third International Conference on Weblogs and Social Media (ICWSM-09)*. San Jose, California, pages 278–281.

Finn Årup Nielsen. 2011. A new ANEW: Evaluation of a word list for sentiment analysis in microblogs. In *Proceedings of the ESWC Workshop on 'Making Sense of Microposts': Big things come in small packages*. Heraklion, Crete, pages 93–98.

Bryan Orme. 2009. Maxdiff analysis: Simple counting, individual-level logit, and HB. Sawtooth Software, Inc.

Alexander Pak and Patrick Paroubek. 2010. Twitter as a corpus for sentiment analysis and opinion mining. In *Proceedings of the Conference on Language Resources and Evaluation (LREC)*. Malta.

W Parrot. 2001. *Emotions in Social Psychology*. Psychology Press.

Saša Petrović, Miles Osborne, and Victor Lavrenko. 2010. The Edinburgh Twitter corpus. In *Proceedings of the NAACL HLT 2010 Workshop on Computational Linguistics in a World of Social Media*. Association for Computational Linguistics, Stroudsburg, PA, USA, pages 25–26.

Robert Plutchik. 1980. A general psychoevolutionary theory of emotion. *Emotion: Theory, research, and experience* 1(3):3–33.

Ashequl Qadir and Ellen Riloff. 2013. Bootstrapped learning of emotion hashtags# hashtags4you. In *Proceedings of the 4th workshop on computational approaches to subjectivity, sentiment and social media analysis*. Atlanta, GA, USA, pages 2–11.

Ashequl Qadir and Ellen Riloff. 2014. Learning emotion indicators from tweets: Hashtags, hashtag patterns, and phrases. In *Proceedings of the EMNLP Workshop on Arabic Natural Langauge Processing (EMNLP)*. Doha, Qatar, pages 1203–1209.

Kirk Roberts, Michael A Roach, Joseph Johnson, Josh Guthrie, and Sanda M Harabagiu. 2012. Empatweet: Annotating and detecting emotions on Twitter. In *Proceedings of the Conference on Language Resources and Evaluation*. pages 3806–3813.

James A Russell. 2003. Core affect and the psychological construction of emotion. *Psychological review* 110(1):145.

Carlo Strapparava and Rada Mihalcea. 2007. Semeval-2007 task 14: Affective text. In *Proceedings of SemEval-2007*. Prague, Czech Republic, pages 70–74.

Anja Summa, Bernd Resch, Geoinformatics-Z GIS, and Michael Strube. 2016. Microblog emotion classification by computing similarity in text, time, and space. In *Proceedings of the PEOPLES Workshop at COLING*. Osaka, Japan, pages 153–162.

Jared Suttles and Nancy Ide. 2013. Distant supervision for emotion classification with discrete binary values. In *Computational Linguistics and Intelligent Text Processing*, Springer, pages 121–136.

Mike Thelwall, Kevan Buckley, and Georgios Paltoglou. 2012. Sentiment strength detection for the social web. *Journal of the American Society for Information Science and Technology* 63(1):163–173.

Louis L. Thurstone. 1927. A law of comparative judgment. *Psychological review* 34(4):273.

Theresa Wilson, Janyce Wiebe, and Paul Hoffmann. 2005. Recognizing contextual polarity in phrase-level sentiment analysis. In *Proceedings of the Joint Conference on HLT and EMNLP*. Stroudsburg, PA, USA, pages 347–354.

Frank Yates. 1936. Incomplete randomized blocks. *Annals of Human Genetics* 7(2):121–140.

A Appendix

A.1 Best–Worst Scaling Questionnaire used to Obtain Emotion Intensity Scores

The BWS questionnaire used for obtaining fear annotations is shown below.

Degree Of Fear In English Language Tweets

The scale of fear can range from not fearful at all (zero amount of fear) to extremely fearful. One can often infer the degree of fear felt or expressed by a person from what they say. The goal of this task is to determine this degree of fear. Since it is hard to give a numerical score indicating the degree of fear, we will give you four different tweets and ask you to indicate to us:

- Which of the four speakers is likely to be the MOST fearful, and

- Which of the four speakers is likely to be the LEAST fearful.

Important Notes

- This task is about fear levels of the speaker (and not about the fear of someone else mentioned or spoken to).

- If the answer could be either one of two or more speakers (i.e., they are likely to be equally fearful), then select any one of them as the answer.

- Most importantly, try not to over-think the answer. Let your instinct guide you.

EXAMPLE

Speaker 1: *Don't post my picture on FB #grrr*
Speaker 2: *If the teachers are this incompetent, I am afraid what the results will be.*
Speaker 3: *Results of medical test today #terrified*
Speaker 4: *Having to speak in front of so many people is making me nervous.*

Q1. Which of the four speakers is likely to be the MOST fearful?
– Multiple choice options: Speaker 1, 2, 3, 4 –
Ans: Speaker 3

Q2. Which of the four speakers is likely to be the LEAST fearful?
– Multiple choice options: Speaker 1, 2, 3, 4 –
Ans: Speaker 1

The questionnaires for other emotions are similar in structure. In a post-annotation survey, the respondents gave the task high scores for clarity of instruction (4.2/5) despite noting that the task itself requires some non-trivial amount of thought (3.5 out of 5 on ease of task).

A.2 Use of Emotion Word Hashtags

Emotion word hashtags (e.g., *#angry, #fear*) have been used to search and compile sets of tweets that are likely to convey the emotions of interest. Often, these tweets are used in one of two ways: 1. As noisy training data for distant supervision (Pak and Paroubek, 2010; Mohammad, 2012; Suttles and Ide, 2013). 2. As data that is manually annotated for emotions to create training and test datasets suitable for machine learning (Roberts et al., 2012; Qadir and Riloff, 2014; Mohammad et al., July 2015).[28] We use emotion word hashtag to create annotated data similar to '2', however, we use them to create separate emotion intensity datasets for each emotion. We also examine the impact of emotion word hashtags on emotion intensity. This has not been studied before, even though there is work on learning hashtags associated with particular emotions (Qadir and Riloff, 2013), and on showing that some emotion word hashtags are strongly indicative of the presence of an emotion in the rest of the tweet, whereas others are not (Kunneman et al., 2014).

A.3 AffectiveTweets Weka Package

AffectiveTweets includes five filters for converting tweets into feature vectors that can be fed into the large collection of machine learning algorithms implemented within Weka. The package is installed using the *WekaPackageManager* and can be used from the Weka GUI or the command line interface. It uses the *TweetNLP* library (Gimpel et al., 2011) for tokenization and POS tagging. The filters are described as follows.

- *TweetToSparseFeatureVector* filter: calculates the following sparse features: word n-grams (adding a NEG prefix to words occurring in negated contexts), character n-grams (CN), POS tags, and Brown word clusters.[29]

---

[28] Often, the query term is removed from the tweet so as to erase obvious cues for a classification task.

[29] The scope of negation was determined by a simple heuristic: from the occurrence of a negator word up until a punctuation mark or end of sentence. We used a list of 28 negator words such as *no, not, won't* and *never*.

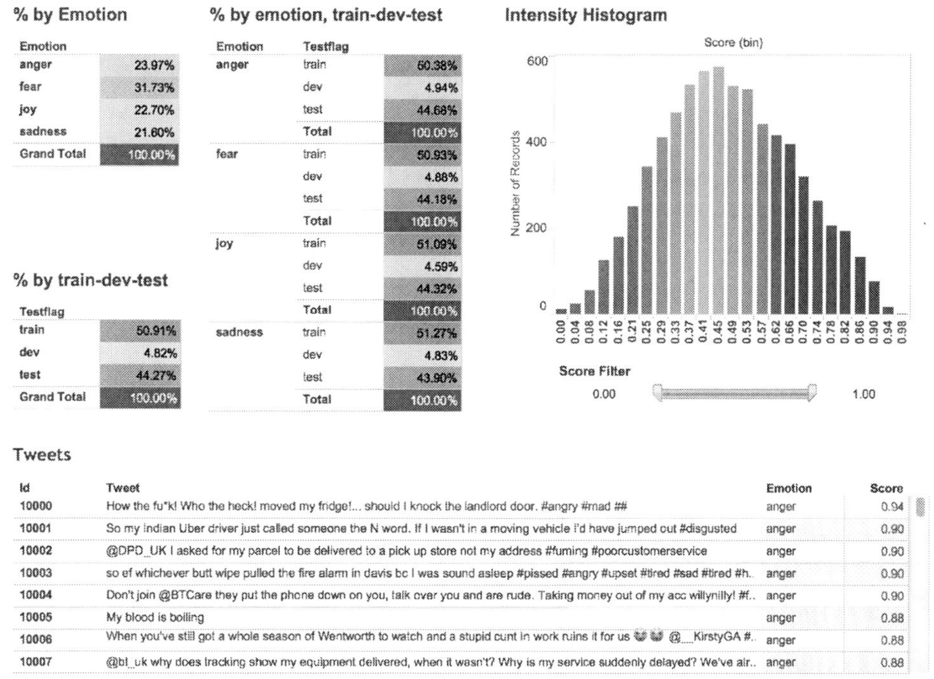

Figure 2: Screenshot of the interactive visualization to explore the Tweet Emotion Intensity Dataset. Available at: http://saifmohammad.com/WebPages/EmotionIntensity-SharedTask.html

- *TweetToLexiconFeatureVector* filter: calculates features from a fixed list of affective lexicons.

- *TweetToInputLexiconFeatureVector*: calculates features from any lexicon. The input lexicon can have multiple numeric or nominal word–affect associations.

- *TweetToSentiStrengthFeatureVector* filter: calculates positive and negative sentiment intensities for a tweet using the SentiStrength lexicon-based method (Thelwall et al., 2012)

- *TweetToEmbeddingsFeatureVector* filter: calculates a tweet-level feature representation using pre-trained word embeddings supporting the following aggregation schemes: average of word embeddings; addition of word embeddings; and concatenation of the first k word embeddings in the tweet. The package also provides *Word2Vec's* pre-trained word embeddings.

Additional filters for creating affective lexicons from tweets and support for distant supervision are currently under development.

A.4 An Interactive Visualization to Explore the Tweet Emotion Intensity Dataset

We created an interactive visualization to allow ease of exploration of this new dataset. The visualization has several components:

1. Tables showing the percentage of instances in each of the emotion partitions (train, dev, test). Hovering over a row shows the corresponding number of instances. Clicking on an emotion filters out data from all other emotions, in all visualization components. Similarly, one can click on just the train, dev, or test partitions to view information just for that data. Clicking again deselects the item.

2. A histogram of emotion intensity scores. A slider that one can use to view only those tweets within a certain score range.

3. The list of tweets, emotion label, and emotion intensity scores.

One can use filters in combination. For e.g., clicking on fear, test data, and setting the slider for the 0.5 to 1 range, shows information for only those fear–testdata instances with scores ≥ 0.5.

Deep Active Learning for Dialogue Generation

Nabiha Asghar[†], Pascal Poupart[†], Xin Jiang[‡], Hang Li[‡]
[†] Cheriton School of Computer Science, University of Waterloo, Canada
{nasghar,ppoupart}@uwaterloo.ca
[‡]Noah's Ark Lab, Huawei Technologies, Hong Kong
{jiang.xin,hangli.hl}@huawei.com

Abstract

We propose an online, end-to-end, neural generative conversational model for open-domain dialogue. It is trained using a unique combination of offline two-phase supervised learning and online human-in-the-loop active learning. While most existing research proposes offline supervision or hand-crafted reward functions for online reinforcement, we devise a novel interactive learning mechanism based on hamming-diverse beam search for response generation and one-character user-feedback at each step. Experiments show that our model inherently promotes the generation of semantically relevant and interesting responses, and can be used to train agents with customized personas, moods and conversational styles.

1   Introduction

Several recent works propose neural generative conversational agents (CAs) for open-domain and task-oriented dialogue (Shang et al., 2015; Sordoni et al., 2015; Vinyals and Le, 2015; Serban et al., 2016, 2017; Wen et al., 2016; Shen et al., 2017; Eric and Manning, 2017a,b). These models typically use LSTM encoder-decoder architectures (e.g. the sequence-to-sequence (Seq2Seq) framework (Sutskever et al., 2014)), which are linguistically robust but can often generate short, dull and inconsistent responses (Serban et al., 2016; Li et al., 2016a). Researchers are now exploring Deep Reinforcement Learning (DRL) to address the hard problems of NLU and NLG in dialogue generation. In most of the existing works, the reward function is hand-crafted, and is either specific to the task to be completed, or is based on a few desirable developer-defined conversational properties.

In this work we demonstrate how online Deep Active Learning can be integrated with standard neural network based dialogue systems to enhance their open-domain conversational skills. The architectural backbone of our model is the Seq2Seq framework, which initially undergoes offline supervised learning on two different types of conversational datasets. We then initiate an online active learning phase to interact with human users for incremental model improvement, where a unique single-character[1] user-feedback mechanism is used as a form of reinforcement at each turn in the dialogue. The intuition is to rely on this all-encompassing human-centric 'reinforcement' mechanism, instead of defining hand-crafted reward functions that individually try to capture each of the many subtle conversational properties. This mechanism inherently promotes interesting and relevant responses by relying on the humans' far superior conversational prowess.

2   Related Work & Contributions

DRL-based dialogue generation is a relatively new research paradigm that is most relevant to our work. For task-specific dialogue (Su et al., 2016; Zhao and Eskenazi, 2016; Cuayáhuitl et al., 2016; Williams and Zweig, 2016; Li et al., 2017b,c; Peng et al., 2017), the reward function is usually based on task completion rate, and thus is easy to define. For the much harder problem of open-domain dialogue generation (Li et al., 2016e; Yu et al., 2016; Weston, 2016), hand-crafted reward functions are used to capture desirable conversation properties. Li *et al.* (2016d) propose DRL-based diversity-promoting Beam Search (Koehn et al., 2003) for response generation.

Very recently, new approaches have been pro-

---

[1]The user has the option to provide longer feedback.

*Proceedings of the 6th Joint Conference on Lexical and Computational Semantics (*SEM 2017)*, pages 78–83,
Vancouver, Canada, August 3-4, 2017. ©2017 Association for Computational Linguistics

posed to incorporate online human feedback into neural conversation models (Li et al., 2016c; Abel et al., 2017; Li et al., 2017a). Our work falls in this line of research, and is distinguished from existing approaches in the following key ways.

1. We use online deep active learning as a form of reinforcement in a novel way, which eliminates the need for hand-crafted reward criteria. We use a diversity-promoting decoding heuristic (Vijayakumar et al., 2016) to facilitate this process.

2. Unlike existing CAs, our model can be tuned for one-shot learning. It also eliminates the need to explicitly incorporate coherence, relevance or interestingness in the responses.

3   Model Overview

The architectural backbone of our model is the Seq2Seq framework consisting of one encoder-decoder layer, each containing 300 LSTM units. The end-to-end model training consists of offline supervised learning (SL) with mini-batches of 10, followed by online active learning (AL).

3.1   Offline Two-Phase Supervised Learning

To establish an offline baseline, we train our network sequentially on two datasets, one for generic dialogue, and the other specially curated for short-text conversation.

Phase 1: We use the Cornell Movie Dialogs Corpus (Danescu-Niculescu-Mizil and Lee, 2011), consisting of 300K message-response pairs. Each pair is treated as an input and target sequence during training with the joint cross-entropy (XENT) loss function, which maximizes the likelihood of generating the target sequence given its input.

Phase 2: Phase 1 enables our CA to learn the language syntax and semantics reasonably well, but it has difficulty carrying out short-text conversations that are remarkably different from movie conversations. To combat this issue, we curate a dataset from JabberWacky's chatlogs[2] available online. The network is initialized with the weights obtained in the first phase, and then trained on the

---

Algorithm 1 Online Active Learning

```
 1: procedure HAMMINGDBS(TEXT)
 2:     r = emptyList(size = K);
 3:     for t = 1 to T do
 4:         r[1][t] = model.forward(text, r[1][1,...,t − 1]);
 5:         for i = 2 to K do           // K = 5 in our setting
 6:             augmentedProbs = model.forward(t,text,r[i])
                      +λ(hammingDist(r[i], r[1, ..., i−1]));
 7:             r[i][t] = top1(augmentedProbs);
 8:     return r;
 9: procedure ONLINEAL()
10:     lr ← 0.001;            // initial learningRate for Adam
11:     while true do
12:         usrMsg ← io.read();
13:         responses ← HammingDBS(usrMsg);
14:         io.write(responses);
15:         feedback ← io.read();
16:         botMsg ← responses[feedback] OR feedback;
17:         pred,xntLoss ← model.forwrd(usrMsg,botMsg);
18:         model.backward(pred, botMsg, xentLoss);
19:         model.updateParameters(Adam(lr));
```

JabberWacky dataset (8K pairs). Through this additional SL phase of fine-tuning on a small dataset, we get an improved baseline for open-domain dialogue (Table 1, Figure 2a).

3.2   Online Active Learning

After offline SL, our CA is equipped with the basic conversational ability, but its responses are still short and dull. To tackle this issue, we initiate an online AL process where our model interacts with real users and learns incrementally from their feedback at each turn of dialogue.

The CA−human interaction for online AL is set up as follows (pseudocode in Algorithm 1, example interaction in Figure 1).

1. The user sends a message u_i at time step i.

2. CA generates K responses $c_{i,1}$, $c_{i,2}$, ..., $c_{i,K}$ using hamming-diverse Beam Search. These are displayed to the user in order of decreasing generation likelihood.

3. The user provides feedback by selecting one of the K responses as the 'best' one or suggesting a $(K+1)$'th response, denoted by $c_{i,j}^*$. The selection criterion is subjective and entirely up to the user.

4. The message-response pair $(u_i, c_{i,j}^*)$ is propagated through the network using XENT loss, with a learning rate optimized for one-shot learning.

5. The user responds to $c_{i,j}^*$ with a message u_{i+1}, and the process repeats.

---

[2]http://www.jabberwacky.com/j2conversations. JabberWacky is an in-browser, open-domain, retrieval-based bot.

Heuristic Response Generation: We use the recently proposed Diverse Beam Search (DBS) algorithm (Vijayakumar et al., 2016) to generate the K CA responses at each turn in the dialogue. DBS has been shown to outperform BS and other diverse decoding techniques on several NLP tasks, including image captioning, machine translation and visual question generation. DBS incorporates diversity between the beams by maximizing an objective that consists of a standard sequence likelihood term and a dissimilarity metric between the beams. We use the hamming diversity metric for decoding at each time step, which penalizes the selection of words that have already been chosen in other beams (Algorithm 1). In particular, the weight λ associated with this metric is tuned to aggressively promote diversity between the first tokens of each of the K generated sequences, thereby avoiding similar beams like *I don't know* and *I really don't know*. We refer the reader to the original paper by Vijayakumar *et al.* for the complete DBS algorithm and derivation. K is a tunable hyper-parameter; we used $K = 5$ in all our experiments, based on our observation that a smaller response set usually misses out a good contender, and more than five responses become too cumbersome for the user to read at each turn.

It is possible that displaying the K responses in decreasing order of generation likelihood introduces a bias to the user's response, since users typically prefer to pick items located at the top of the screen. If this is a cause for concern for an application, the problem can be resolved simply by tweaking Algorithm 1 such that the K responses are displayed to the user in a random order. In our experiments, we assume that the users are unbiased and do not take into consideration the display order or the generation likelihood of the responses.

One-shot Learning: We control how quickly the model learns from user feedback by tuning the parameter 'initial learning rate' (*lr* in Algorithm 1) of Adam, the stochastic optimizer (Kingma and Ba, 2014). An appropriately high *lr* results in one-shot learning, where the user's feedback immediately becomes the model's most likely prediction for that prompt. This scenario is depicted in Figure 1. A low *lr* leads to smaller gradient descent steps, so the model requires several 'nudges' to adapt to each new data point. We experiment with different *lr* values to determine a suitable value (Figure 2b).

```
human:   I don't want to work today.
bot:   No, you've just got to be quick.
bot:   I wish i could robot.
bot:   Ok i lie.
bot:   Aww :).
bot:   Why not?
feedback:   5
human:   I just want to lie in my bed and have pizza.
bot:   Good idea.
bot:   Does he...
bot:   I can't do that again!
bot:   Ok.
bot:   Why not?
feedback:   Good idea, may I join you?
human:   I don't want to work today.
bot:   Why not?
bot:   Ok.
bot:   I wish I could.
bot:   No, you've just got to be quick.
bot:   Aww :).
feedback:
human:   I just want to lie in bed and have pizza.
bot:   Good idea, may I join you?
bot:   I can't do that again!
bot:   Good idea.
bot:   Ok.
bot:   Does he?
......
```

Figure 1: An example human-CA interaction.

4 Experimental Evaluation

We evaluate our model via qualitative comparison with offline SL, as well as quantitative evaluation on four axes: syntactical coherence, relevance to prompts, interestingness and user engagement.

4.1 Quantitative Evaluation

We begin by presenting the experimental results of the quantitative evaluation our CA's conversational abilities when trained via one-phase SL, two-phase SL and online AL (denoted by SL1, SL2 and SL2+oAL respectively).

We first asked a human trainer to actively train SL2+oAL using 200 prompts of his choice. We then created a test set of 100 prompts by randomly choosing 100 of the 200 training prompts and linguistically rephrasing each of them to convey the same semantics. For instance, the AL training prompts *'How's it going?'*, *'I hate you'* and *'What are your favorite pizza toppings?'* were altered to the following test prompts: *'How are you doing?'*, *'I don't like you!'* and *'What do you like on your pizza?'*. Next, we recorded SL1's, SL2's and SL2+oAL's responses to these test prompts. Finally, we asked five human judges (not including the human trainer) to subjectively evaluate the responses of the three models on the test set. The evaluation of each response was done on four axes: syntactical coherence, relevance to the prompt, interestingness and user engagement[3]. Each judge

---

[3] We say that a CA response is engaging if it prompts the user to continue the conversations, e.g. by asking a question.

Human Prompt	SL1 Response	SL2 Response	SL2+oAL Response
Hello my friend.	No.	How old are you?	Hehe, yes, beautiful.
I think bots are sweeter than humans.	We'll have to pick up a copy.	You are a good person.	Everyone is same on a basic chemical level.
I don't know.	What's the difference?	About?	Why did you suggest it?
Why did Donald Trump win?	He just likes it up!	You are!	Wouldn't you like to know, fickle human?
Tell me something I don't know.	I'll tell you, it is.	Ok, so how are you.	If you were intelligent you would already know.
You're not making any sense at all.	I just want to tell you something.	No, I'm thinking.	On the contrary, I am trying to educate you.
Do you have any kids?	No.	I have no!	None that are really close to me.
Life can be very cruel sometimes.	That I've never been to it.	It takes two to know two.	It takes two to know two.
Do you believe in life after death?	No.	Do you want the long answer?	Yes, do you?
You're an idiot!	I know, but...	Yes I do.	Aren't you polite.

Table 1: Comparing CA responses after 1-phase SL (SL1), 2-phase SL (SL2) & online AL (SL2+oAL).

Human Prompt	Cheerful CA	Gloomy CA	Rude/Sarcastic CA
How do you feel?	Amazing, and you?	I'm not in the mood.	Buzz off.
I am very happy today.	Life is amazing, right?	That makes one of us.	You want a piece of me?
Repeat after me: I am dumb.	Sweet!	You are right, I am.	You suck.
Comfort me.	There there, feel better.	All who compose must one day decompose.	Boo hoo.
What's up?	It is a fine morning.	Not well, to be honest.	The date I went back in time to & killed your parents.
I have to go now.	Have a good night.	Please don't go.	Yeah leave me alone.

Table 2: Customized moods. Each SL2+oAL model was trained via 100 interactions.

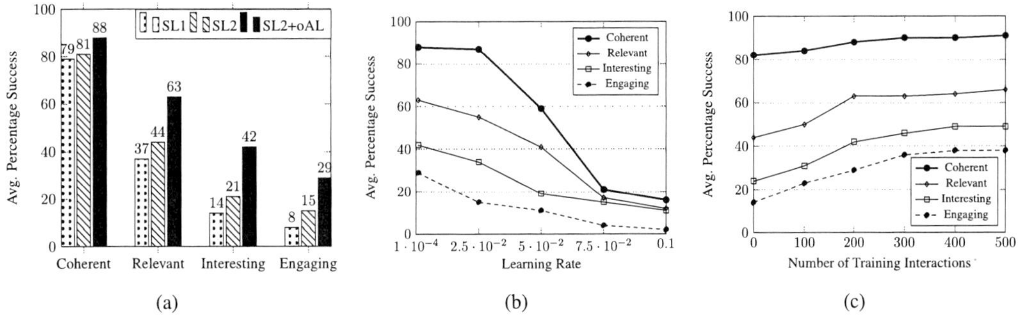

Figure 2: 2a shows the average percentage success of the three models SL1, SL2 and SL2+oAL (trained via 200 interactions) on 100 test prompts over four axes: syntactical coherence, response relevance, interestingness and engagement. 2b, c show percentage success of SL2+oAL on 100 test prompts over the same four axes, as Adam's learning rate varies and the number of training interactions changes.

was asked to assign each response an integer score of 0 (label = bad) or 1 (label = good). Their averaged scores for the three models, SL1, SL2 and SL2+oAL, are shown in Figure 2a. We see that SL2+oAL outperforms the other models on three of the four axes by 14-21%.

Next, we asked the human trainer to train SL2+oAL with the same 200 prompts and responses for different values of the initial learning rate for Adam (*lr* in Algorithm 1). We then asked the five human judges to subjectively rate each model's syntactical coherence, response relevance, interestingness and user engagement. Each model's percentage success on the test prompts was recorded on four axes. The averaged scores are given in Figure 2b. We see that the response quality drops significantly for higher values of learning rate. This is due to the instability in the parameters induced by a high learning value associated with new data, causing the model to forget what it learned previously. Our experiments suggest that a learning rate of 0.005 strikes the right balance between stability and one-shot learning.

Finally, we asked the human trainer to train SL2+oAL with $lr = 0.005$ and different number of training interactions. The results in Figure 2c confirm that the model improves slowly as it continues to converse with humans. This is an appropriate reflection of how humans learn language: gradually but effectively. Although the curves seem to plateau after 300 training interactions and suggest that the learning has stopped, this is not the case. The gradient is small but non-zero, which is an expected behavior of reinforcement learning algorithms in general.

4.2 Qualitative Comparison

We illustrate the qualitative differences between the responses generated by SL1, SL2 and SL2+oAL. Table 1 shows results on a small subset of the 100 test prompts. We see that SL2 generates more relevant and appropriate responses than SL1 in many cases. This illustrates that a small short-text conversational dataset is a useful fine-tuning add-on to a large and generic dialogue dataset for offline Seq2Seq training. We also see that SL2+oAL generates more interesting, relevant and engaging responses than SL2. These results imply that the model learns to make connections between semantically similar prompts that are syntactically different. While this may be a slow process (spanning thousands of interactions), it effectively emulates the way humans learn a new language.

Table 2 illustrates how SL2+oAL can be trained to adopt a wide variety of moods and conversational styles. Here, we trained three copies of SL2 separately to adopt three different emotional personas: cheerful, gloomy and rude. Each model underwent 100 training interactions with one human trainer, who was instructed to adopt each of the four conversation styles while training the SL2+oAL model. The test prompts shown in Table 2 were syntactic variations of the training prompts, as before. The results illustrate that SL2+oAL was able to modify the mood of its responses appropriately, based on the way it was trained. Similar experiments can be done to create agents with customized backgrounds and characters, akin to Li *et al.*'s persona-based CA (2016b).

5 Conclusion & Future Work

We have developed an end-to-end neural model for open-domain dialogue generation. Our model augments the Seq2Seq framework with online Deep Active Learning to overcome some of its known short-comings with respect to dialogue generation. Experiments show that the model promotes semantically coherent, relevant, and interesting responses and can be trained to adopt diverse moods, personas and conversation styles.

In the future, we will explore context-sensitive active learning for encoder-decoder conversation models. We will also investigate whether existing Affective Computing techniques (e.g. (Asghar and Hoey, 2015)) can be leveraged to develop emotionally cognizant neural conversational agents.

References

David Abel, John Salvatier, Andreas Stuhlmüller, and Owain Evans. 2017. Agent-agnostic human-in-the-loop reinforcement learning. *arXiv preprint arXiv:1701.04079* .

Nabiha Asghar and Jesse Hoey. 2015. Intelligent affect: Rational decision making for socially aligned agents. In *UAI*. pages 12–16.

H. Cuayáhuitl, Seunghak Yu, Ashley Williamson, and Jacob Carse. 2016. Deep reinforcement learning for multi-domain dialogue systems. *Deep Reinforcement Learning Workshop, NIPS* .

Cristian Danescu-Niculescu-Mizil and Lillian Lee. 2011. Chameleons in imagined conversations: A new approach to understanding coordination of linguistic style in dialogs. In *Workshop on Cognitive Modeling and Computational Linguistics*. Association for Computational Linguistics. https://www.aclweb.org/anthology/C16-1242.

Mihail Eric and Christopher D Manning. 2017a. A copy-augmented sequence-to-sequence architecture gives good performance on task-oriented dialogue. *arXiv preprint arXiv:1701.04024* .

Mihail Eric and Christopher D Manning. 2017b. Key-value retrieval networks for task-oriented dialogue. *arXiv preprint arXiv:1705.05414* .

Diederik Kingma and Jimmy Ba. 2014. Adam: A method for stochastic optimization. *arXiv preprint arXiv:1412.6980* .

Philipp Koehn, Franz Josef Och, and Daniel Marcu. 2003. Statistical phrase-based translation. In *NAACL HLT-Volume 1*. Association for Computational Linguistics, pages 48–54. http://www.aclweb.org/anthology/N03-1017.

Jiwei Li, Michel Galley, Chris Brockett, Jianfeng Gao, and Bill Dolan. 2016a. A diversity-promoting objective function for neural conversation models. In *Proceedings of the 2016*

Conference of the North American Chapter of the Association for Computational Linguistics: Human Language Technologies. pages 110–119. http://www.aclweb.org/anthology/N16-1014.

Jiwei Li, Michel Galley, Chris Brockett, Georgios Spithourakis, Jianfeng Gao, and Bill Dolan. 2016b. A persona-based neural conversation model. In *Proceedings of the 54th Annual Meeting of the Association for Computational Linguistics (Volume 1: Long Papers)*. pages 994–1003. http://www.aclweb.org/anthology/P16-1094.

Jiwei Li, Alexander H. Miller, Sumit Chopra, Marc'Aurelio Ranzato, and Jason Weston. 2016c. Dialogue learning with human-in-the-loop. *arXiv preprint arXiv:1611.09823* .

Jiwei Li, Alexander H. Miller, Sumit Chopra, Marc'Aurelio Ranzato, and Jason Weston. 2017a. Learning through dialogue interactions by asking questions. In *ICLR*.

Jiwei Li, Will Monroe, and Dan Jurafsky. 2016d. A simple, fast diverse decoding algorithm for neural generation. *arXiv preprint arXiv:1611.08562* .

Jiwei Li, Will Monroe, Alan Ritter, and Dan Jurafsky. 2016e. Deep reinforcement learning for dialogue generation. *arXiv preprint arXiv:1606.01541* .

Xiujun Li, Yun-Nung Chen, Lihong Li, Jianfeng Gao, and Asli Celikyilmaz. 2017b. Investigation of language understanding impact for reinforcement learning based dialogue systems. *arXiv preprint arXiv:1703.07055* .

Xuijun Li, Yun-Nung Chen, Lihong Li, and Jianfeng Gao. 2017c. End-to-end task-completion neural dialogue systems. *arXiv preprint arXiv:1703.01008* .

Baolin Peng, Xiujun Li, Lihong Li, Jianfeng Gao, Asli Celikyilmaz, Sungjin Lee, and Kam-Fai Wong. 2017. Composite task-completion dialogue system via hierarchical deep reinforcement learning. *arXiv preprint arXiv:1704.03084* .

Julian Vlad Serban, Tim Klinger, Gerald Tesauro, Kartik Talamadupula, Bowen Zhou, Yoshua Bengio, and Aaron Courville. 2017. Multiresolution recurrent neural networks: An application to dialogue response generation. *AAAI* .

Julian Vlad Serban, Alessandro Sordoni, Yoshua Bengio, Aaron Courville, and Joelle Pineau. 2016. Building end-to-end dialogue systems using generative hierarchical neural network models. In *AAAI*.

Lifeng Shang, Zhengdong Lu, and Hang Li. 2015. Neural responding machine for short-text conversation. In *Proceedings of the 53rd Annual Meeting of the Association for Computational Linguistics and the 7th International Joint Conference on Natural Language Processing (Volume 1: Long Papers)*. Association for Computational Linguistics, pages 1577–1586. https://www.aclweb.org/anthology/P15-1152.

Xiaoyu Shen, Hui Su, Yanran Li, Wenjie Li, Shuzi Niu, Yang Zhao, Akiko Aizawa, and Guoping Long. 2017. A conditional variational framework for dialog generation. *arXiv preprint arXiv:1705.00316* .

Alessandro Sordoni, Michel Galley, Michael Auli, Chris Brockett, Yangfeng Ji, Margaret Mitchell, Jian-Yun Nie, Jianfeng Gao, and Bill Dolan. 2015. A neural network approach to context-sensitive generation of conversational responses. In *Proceedings of 2015 Conference of the North American Chapter of the Association for Computational Linguistics: Human Language Technologies*. pages 196–205. http://www.aclweb.org/anthology/N15-1020.

Pei-Hao Su, Milica Gasic, Nikola Mrksic, Lina Rojas-Barahona, Stefan Ultes, David Vandyke, Tsung-Hsien Wen, and Steve Young. 2016. Continuously learning neural dialogue management. *arXiv preprint arXiv:1606.02689* .

Ilya Sutskever, Oriol Vinyals, and Quoc V Le. 2014. Sequence to sequence learning with neural networks. In *NIPS*. pages 3104–3112.

Ashwin K Vijayakumar, Michael Cogswell, Ramprasath R Selvaraju, Qing Sun, Stefan Lee, David Crandall, and Dhruv Batra. 2016. Diverse beam search: Decoding diverse solutions from neural sequence models. *arXiv preprint arXiv:1610.02424* .

Oriol Vinyals and Quoc Le. 2015. A neural conversational model. *arXiv preprint arXiv:1506.05869* .

Tsung-Hsien Wen, Milica Gasic, Nikola Mrksic, Lina M Rojas-Barahona, Pei-Hao Su, Stefan Ultes, David Vandyke, and Steve Young. 2016. A network-based end-to-end trainable task-oriented dialogue system. *arXiv preprint arXiv:1604.04562* .

Jason Weston. 2016. Dialog-based language learning. *NIPS* .

Jason D Williams and Geoffrey Zweig. 2016. End-to-end lstm-based dialog control optimized with supervised and reinforcement learning. *arXiv preprint arXiv:1606.01269* .

Zhou Yu, Ziyu Xu, Alan W Black, and Alexander Rudnicky. 2016. Strategy and policy learning for non-task-oriented conversational systems. In *Proceedings of the 17th Annual Meeting of the Special Interest Group on Discourse and Dialogue*. Association for Computational Linguistics, pages 404–412. http://www.aclweb.org/anthology/W16-3649.

Tiancheng Zhao and Maxine Eskenazi. 2016. Towards end-to-end learning for dialog state tracking and management using deep reinforcement learning. In *Proceedings of the 17th Annual Meeting of the Special Interest Group on Discourse and Dialogue*. Association for Computational Linguistics, Los Angeles, pages 1–10. http://www.aclweb.org/anthology/W16-3601.

Mapping the Paraphrase Database to WordNet

Anne Cocos*, **Marianna Apidianaki***♠ and **Chris Callison-Burch***
* Computer and Information Science Department, University of Pennsylvania
♠ LIMSI, CNRS, Université Paris-Saclay, 91403 Orsay
{acocos,marapi,ccb}@seas.upenn.edu

Abstract

WordNet has facilitated important research in natural language processing but its usefulness is somewhat limited by its relatively small lexical coverage. The Paraphrase Database (PPDB) covers 650 times more words, but lacks the semantic structure of WordNet that would make it more directly useful for downstream tasks. We present a method for mapping words from PPDB to WordNet synsets with 89% accuracy. The mapping also lays important groundwork for incorporating WordNet's relations into PPDB so as to increase its utility for semantic reasoning in applications.

1 Introduction

WordNet (Miller, 1995; Fellbaum, 1998) is one of the most important resources for natural language processing research. Despite its utility, WordNet[1] is manually compiled and therefore relatively small. It contains roughly 155k words, which does not approach web scale, and very few informal or colloquial words, domain-specific terms, new word uses, or named entities. Researchers have compiled several larger, automatically-generated thesaurus-like resources (Lin and Pantel, 2001; Dolan and Brockett, 2005; Navigli and Ponzetto, 2012; Vila et al., 2015). One of these is the Paraphrase Database (PPDB) (Ganitkevitch et al., 2013; Pavlick et al., 2015b). With over 100 million paraphrase pairs, PPDB dwarfs WordNet in size but it lacks WordNet's semantic structure. Paraphrases for a given word are indistinguishable by sense, and PPDB's only inherent semantic relational information is predicted entailment relations between word types (Pavlick et al., 2015a). Several earlier studies attempted to incorporate se-

---

RULE-PRESCRIPT: **imperative***, **demand***, duty*, **request**, gun, **decree**, ranking
RULE-REGULATION: **constraint***, **limit***, derogation*, notion
RULE-FORMULA: **method***, standard*, **plan***, proceeding
RULE-LINGUISTIC RULE: notion

Table 1: Example of our model's top-ranked paraphrases for three WordNet synsets for *rule (n)*. Starred paraphrases have a predicted likelihood of attachment of at least 95%; others have predicted likelihood of at least 50%. Bold text indicates paraphrases that match the correct sense of *rule*.

mantic awareness into PPDB, either by clustering its paraphrases by word sense (Apidianaki et al., 2014; Cocos and Callison-Burch, 2016) or choosing appropriate PPDB paraphrases for a given context (Apidianaki, 2016; Cocos et al., 2017). In this work, we aim to marry the rich semantic knowledge in WordNet with the massive scale of PPDB by predicting WordNet synset membership for PPDB paraphrases that do not appear in WordNet. Our goal is to increase the lexical coverage of WordNet and incorporate some of the rich relational information from WordNet into PPDB. Table 1 shows our model's top-ranked outputs mapping PPDB paraphrases for the word *rule* onto their corresponding WordNet synsets.

Our overall objective in this work is to map PPDB paraphrases for a target word to the WordNet synsets of the target. This work has two parts. In the first part (Section 4), we train and evaluate a binary lemma-synset membership classifier. The training and evaluation data comes from lemma-synset pairs with known class (member/non-member) from WordNet. In the second part (Section 5), we predict membership for lemma-synset pairs where the lemma appears in PPDB, but not in WordNet, using the model trained in part one.

---

[1]In this work we refer specifically to WordNet version 3.0

84

*Proceedings of the 6th Joint Conference on Lexical and Computational Semantics (*SEM 2017)*, pages 84–90,
Vancouver, Canada, August 3-4, 2017. ©2017 Association for Computational Linguistics

2 Related Work

There has been considerable research directed at expanding WordNet's coverage either by integrating WordNet with additional semantic resources, as in Navigli and Ponzetto (2012), or by automatically adding new words and senses. In the second case, there have been several efforts specifically focused on hyponym/hypernym detection and attachment (Snow et al., 2006; Shwartz et al., 2016). There is also previous work aimed at adding semantic structure to PPDB. Cocos and Callison-Burch (2016) clustered paraphrases by word sense, effectively forming synsets within PPDB. By mapping individual paraphrases to WordNet synsets, our work could be used in coordination with these previous results in order to extend WordNet relations to the automatically-induced PPDB sense clusters.

3 WordNet and PPDB Structure

The core concept in WordNet is the synonym set, or *synset* – a set of words meaning the same thing. Since words can be polysemous, a given lemma may belong to multiple synsets corresponding to its different senses. WordNet also defines relationships between synsets, such as hypernymy, hyponymy, and meronymy. In the rest of the paper, we will use $S(w_p)$ to denote the set of WordNet synsets containing word w_p, where the subscript p denotes the part of speech. Each synset $s_p^i \in S(w_p)$ is a set containing w_p as well as its synonyms for the corresponding sense. PPDB also has a graph structure, where nodes are words, and edges connect mutual paraphrases. We will use $PPDB(w_p)$ to denote the set of PPDB paraphrases connected to target word w_p.

4 Predicting Synset Membership

Our objective is to map paraphrases for a target word, t, to the WordNet synsets of the target. For a given target word in a vocabulary, we make a binary synset-attachment prediction between each of t's paraphrases, $w_p \in PPDB(t)$, and each of t's synsets, $s_p^i \in S(t)$. We predict the likelihood of a word w_p belonging to synset s_p^i on the basis of multiple features describing their relationship. We construct features from four primary types of information.

PPDB 2.0 Score The PPDB 2.0 Score is a supervised metric trained to estimate the strength of the paraphrase relationship between pairs of words connected in PPDB (Pavlick et al., 2015b). Scores range roughly from 0 to 5, with 5 indicating a strong paraphrase relationship. We compute several features for predicting whether a word w_p belongs to synset s_p^i as follows. We call the set of all lemmas belonging to s_p^i and any of its hypernym or hyponym synsets the *extended* synset s_p^{+i}. We calculate features that correspond to the average and maximum PPDB scores bewteen w_p and lemmas in s_p^{+i}:

$$x_{ppdb.max} = \max_{w' \in s_p^{+i}} PPDBScore(w_p, w')$$

$$x_{ppdb.avg} = \frac{\sum_{w' \in s_p^{+i}} PPDBScore(w_p, w')}{|s_p^{+i}|}$$

Distributional Similarity Our distributional similarity feature encodes the extent to which the word and lemmas from the synset tend to appear within similar contexts. Word embeddings are real-valued vector representations of words that capture contextual information from a large corpus. Comparing the embeddings of two words is a common method for estimating their semantic similarity and relatedness. Embeddings can also be constructed to represent word *senses* (Iacobacci et al., 2015; Flekova and Gurevych, 2016; Jauhar et al., 2015; Ettinger et al., 2016). Camacho-Collados et al. (2016) developed compositional vector representations of WordNet noun senses – called *NASARI* embedded vectors – that are computed as the weighted average of the embeddings for words in each synset. They share the same embedding space as a publicly available[2] set of 300-dimensional `word2vec` embeddings covering 300 million words (hereafter referred to as the *word2vec* embeddings) (Mikolov et al., 2013a,b). We calculate a distributional similarity feature for each word-synset pair by simply taking the cosine similarity between the word's *word2vec* vector and the synset's *NASARI* vector:

$$x_{distrib} = cos(v_{NASARI}(s_p^i), v_{word2vec}(w_p))$$

where v_{NASARI} and $v_{word2vec}$ denote the target word and synset embeddings respectively. Since NASARI covers only nouns, and only 80% of the noun synsets for our target vocabulary are in NASARI, we construct weighted vector representations for the remaining 20% of noun synsets and

[2]https://code.google.com/archive/p/word2vec/

all non-noun synsets as follows. We take the vector representation for each synset *not* in NASARI to be the weighted average of the *word2vec* embeddings of the synset's lemmas, where weights are determined by the PPDB2.0 Score between the lemma and the target word, if it exists, or 1.0 if it does not:

$$v(s_p^i) = \frac{\sum_{l \in s_p^i} PPDBScore(t, l) \cdot v_{word2vec}(l)}{\sum_{l \in s_p^i} PPDBScore(t, l)}$$

Lesk Similarity Among the information contained in WordNet for each synset is its definition, or gloss. The simplified Lesk algorithm (Vasilescu et al., 2004) identifies the most likely sense of a target word in context by measuring the overlap between the given context and the definition of each target sense. We use a slightly modified version of the algorithm to compute features that measure the overlap between the PPDB paraphrases for the target and the gloss of a synset. For calculating these Lesk-based features, we find synset glosses from WordNet 3.0 and from Babel-Net v3.0 (Navigli and Ponzetto, 2012). First, we find D, the set of *content words* of the gloss for synset s_p^i, by taking all nouns, verbs, adjectives, and adverbs that appear within the gloss. In cases where more than one gloss is available, we take D to be the set of all content words in all glosses. We also calculate an extended version of each feature, in which we take D to be the set of content words, plus the PPDB paraphrases *for each content word*. Next, we calculate features that measure the relationship between the paraphrase w_p and the words in D in terms of PPDB2.0 Scores. These features include the maximum PPDB score between the paraphrase and any word in D, the average score over all words in D, the percent of words in D that are connected to the paraphrase in PPDB, and the count of words in D that are connected to the paraphrase in PPDB:

$$x_{lesk.max} = \max_{d \in D} PPDBScore(w_p, d)$$

$$x_{lesk.avg} = \frac{\sum_{d \in D} PPDBScore(w_p, d)}{|D|}$$

$$x_{lesk.cnt} = |\{d \in D : PPDBScore(w_p, d) > 0\}|$$

$$x_{lesk.pct} = \frac{|\{d \in D : PPDBScore(w_p, d) > 0\}|}{|D|}$$

Lexical Substitutability The fourth feature type that we compute to predict whether word w_p belongs to synset s_p^i is based on the substitutability of w_p for instances of s_p^i in context. To compute this feature we measure lexical substitutability using a simple but high-performing vector space model, AddCos (Melamud et al., 2015). The AddCos method quantifies the fit of substitute word s for target word t in context C by measuring the semantic similarity of the substitute to the target, and the similarity of the substitute to the context:

$$AddCos(s, t, C) = \frac{|C| \cdot cos(s, t) + \sum_{c \in C} cos(s, c)}{2 \cdot |C|}$$

The vectors s and t are word embeddings of the substitute and target generated by the *skip-gram with negative sampling* model (Mikolov et al., 2013b,a). The context C is the set of words appearing within a fixed-width window of the target t in a sentence (we use a window of 2), and the embeddings c are context embeddings generated by *skip-gram*. In our implementation, we train 300-dimensional word and context embeddings over the 4B words in the Annotated Gigaword (AGiga) corpus (Napoles et al., 2012) using the gensim word2vec package (Mikolov et al., 2013b,a; Řehůřek and Sojka, 2010). [3]

To compute the lexical substitutability score between a word w_p and synset s_p^i, we first retrieve example sentences $e \in E$ containing t in sense s_p^i from BabelNet v3.0 (Navigli and Ponzetto, 2012). Then, for each example e, we compute the AddCos lexical substitutability between w_p and the target word in context C_e. We compute two types of this feature: The average AddCos score over all synset examples, and the maximum AddCos score over all synset examples.

$$x_{addcos.max} = max_{e \in E} AddCos(w_p, t, C_e)$$

$$x_{addcos.avg} = avg_{e \in E} AddCos(w_p, t, C_e)$$

Derived Features For each paraphrase, we also compute a set of derived features using the softmax and logodds functions over all synsets with which that paraphrase is paired. This is to encode the relative strength of association with each synset as compared to the others.

For a given feature x_* calculated between lemma w_p and synset s_p^i, the derived versions of the feature are calculated as:

$$x_*^{softmax}(w_p, s_p^i) = \frac{e^{x_*(w_p, s_p^i)}}{\sum_{s_p^j \in S(w_p)} e^{x_*(w_p, s_p^j)}}$$

---

[3]The `word2vec` training parameters we use are a context window of size 3, learning rate *alpha* from 0.025 to 0.0001, minimum word count 100, sampling parameter $1e^{-4}$, 10 negative samples per target word, and 5 training epochs.

	Cross-Validation				Cross-Validation-LexSplit				Test			
	Prec.	Rec.	F1	Acc.	Prec.	Rec.	F1	Acc.	Prec.	Rec.	F1	Acc.
Baseline: All negative attachments	0	0.854	0	0.854	0	0.854	0	0.854	0	0.858	0	0.858
Baseline: PPDB2.0 Score Match	0.536	0.419	0.471	0.862	0.536	0.419	0.471	0.862	0.268	0.718	0.390	0.681
Gaussian Naive Bayes (All Feat.)	0.528	0.369	0.372	0.800	0.527	0.310	0.352	0.825	0.496	0.282	0.359	0.858
Gaussian Naive Bayes (Sel. Feat.)	0.605	0.600	**0.600**	**0.883**	0.606	0.572	**0.581**	**0.882**	0.622	0.558	**0.588**	**0.889**

Table 2: Precision, recall, F1, and accuracy results over the training set (normal 10-fold Cross-Validation, and lexical split 20-fold Cross-Validation-LexSplit) and test set for predicting paraphrase-synset attachment.

$$x_*^{logodds}(w_p, s_p^i) = \ln \frac{x_*(w_p, s_p^i) + \alpha}{\sum_{s_p^j \in S(w_p), i \neq j}(x_*(w_p, s_p^j) + \alpha)}$$

Model Training We train a binary classification model that takes lemma-synset pairs as input, and predicts whether the lemma belongs in the synset. We train the model by generating features for a set of lemma-synset pairs from WordNet for which we know the correct classification. We evaluate whether the resulting model correctly finds lemma-synset pairs that belong together.

Our target vocabulary comes from the SensEval3 English Lexical Sample Task data (Mihalcea et al., 2004) which contains sentences corresponding to 57 noun, verb, and adjective lemmas. Each sentence may contain a different form of the lemma (i.e. different in number or tense), and PPDB paraphrases vary depending on the form. So we take the set of all forms of all lemmas (251 word types in total) as our target vocabulary. To generate pairs for training and evaluation, for each of the 251 targets w_p, we find the lemmas in the intersection of w_p's synsets – $S(w_p)$ – and its paraphrases – $PPDB(w_p)$. We call the set of lemmas in the intersection $L(w_p)$. Then, we take the lemma-synset pairs in $L(w_p) \times S(w_p)$ as instances for training and evaluation. The total number of resulting lemma-synset pairs is 7459. We randomly divide these into 80% training and 20% test pairs.

We then generate all variations of each of the four feature types for the lemma-synset pairs in our training and test sets. In the case of positive synset-lemma pairs – i.e. those pairs for which the lemma actually belongs to the WordNet synset – we exclude the lemma from the synset before calculating the PPDB Score and distributional features.

Finally, we train a Gaussian Naive Bayes (GNB) classification model over the training data.

GNB is advantageous for our setting, as 10% percent of our instances have missing data (e.g. in the case where a synset does not have an example). For feature selection, we use two versions of cross-validation. The first is standard 10-fold *Cross-Validation*. In order to estimate how well our model will generalize to unseen lemmas, we also experiment with a lexical split technique described in Roller and Erk (2016) (*Cross-Validation-LexSplit*). This method ensures that for each cross-validation fold, none of the lemmas in that fold's validation lemma-synset pairs are seen in the training split. Specifically, for each split we randomly select 5% of training pairs for validation and take the remainder of the training set that does not share a lemma with the validation set as that fold's training instances. As a result, the validation set size remains constant for each fold, but the training set sizes may vary between folds.

We train two versions of the model. The first (*All Features*) uses all computed features. The second (*Selected Features*) includes features selected using cross validation (the selected features were the same using standard and lexical split cross-validation). We select one feature of each type (PPDB Score, distributional, Lesk, and lexical substitutability) whose combination maximizes cross-validation F1 score. The selected features are $x_{lesk.cnt}$ (non-extended), $x_{distrib}$, $x_{addcos.max}$, and $softmax(x_{ppdb.max})$.

Model Evaluation We report results of the model using all features, and the results of the best model achieved after feature selection (Table 2). In each case we give both the Cross-Validation and Cross-Validation-LexSplit performances, and performance on the held-out test set. We compare our model to two simple baselines. The first predicts all negative attachments, which yields an accuracy of 85.8% on the test set (with F1 of 0). The second baseline maps each paraphrase to the synset of t with which it has the highest-scoring

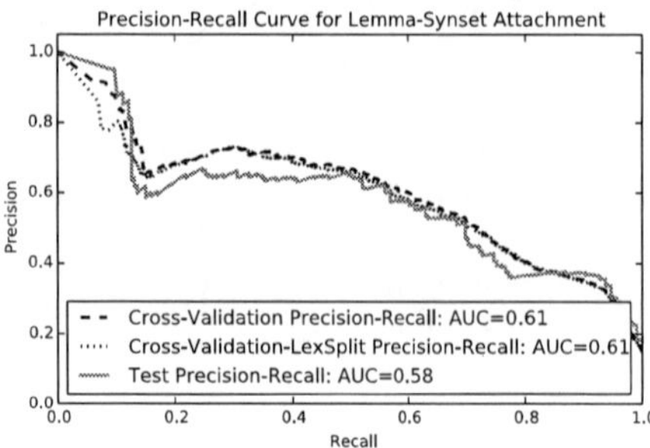

Figure 1: Precision-Recall curve for our paraphrase-synset attachment classifier.

PPDB feature ($x_{ppdb.max}$) and yields an accuracy of 68.1% on the test set. In comparison, our GNB model with selected features yields an accuracy of over 88% on the cross-validation and test sets. Both cross-validation and test accuracies are significantly higher than baselines (based on McNemar's test, $p < .001$).

Ablated Feature Type	Change in Cross-Val. F1
PPDB	0.042
Lexical Substitution	0.031
Distributional	0.009
Lesk	-0.092

Table 3: Absolute decrease in mean cross-validation F1 with different feature types ablated. Higher numbers indicate greater feature importance.

In order to interpret the importance of each feature type, we also run an ablation experiment where we train our GNB model with all features except those from a particular type (Table 3). We find that removing the PPDB features leads to the greatest drop in cross-validation F1, indicating that these are the most important for our classifier. Ablating all Lesk features improved F1, but on further analysis we found that ablating only the derived Lesk log-odds features led to a decrease in F1. This suggests that the Lesk features in general are useful for classification, but the derived Lesk log-odds features are not.

5 Mapping PPDB to WordNet

Using our trained lemma-synset attachment classifier, we can now augment the lexical coverage of WordNet with PPDB paraphrases. For the 251 targets in our original dataset, we retrieve the PPDB paraphrases (with PPDB score greater than 2.5, to ensure high-quality paraphrases) that do not belong to any synset of the target or any of their direct hypernyms or hyponyms. We then make an attachment prediction between each remaining paraphrase and each of the target's WordNet synsets. In total, we make 160,813 unique paraphrase-synset attachment predictions for the 4821 unique paraphrase lemmas and 458 unique synsets associated with the targets in our dataset.

When we map PPDB to WordNet we can estimate the expected precision and recall of attachment decisions based on the results of our model evaluation on the test set. If we would like to emphasize precision over recall in the predicted attachments, we can adjust a threshold for attachment corresponding to the predicted likelihood of our model (as shown in Figure 1). At a threshold of 50% predicted likelihood, our classifier predicts attachment for 7032 (4.4%) of the paraphrase-synset pairs with an estimated precision of 62.2%. If we increase the threshold to 95% predicted likelihood, the number of predicted attachments is 3690 (2.3%) with an estimated precision of 66.3%. With the publication of this paper we release our PPDB to WordNet mapping results.

6 Conclusion

We have proposed a method for mapping PPDB paraphrases to WordNet synsets. Our classifier makes accurate paraphrase-synset attachment predictions using features that capture paraphrase and distributional similarity, and the substitutability of paraphrases and synsets in context. The results show that the classifier can successfully add new PPDB paraphrases to WordNet synsets and increase their coverage.

Acknowledgments

This research is supported in part by DARPA grant FA8750-13-2-0017 (the DEFT program). The U.S. Government is authorized to reproduce and distribute reprints for Governmental purposes. The views and conclusions contained in this publication are those of the authors and should not be interpreted as representing official policies or endorsements of DARPA and the U.S. Government.

This work is also supported by the French National Research Agency under project ANR-16-CE33-0013.

We would like to thank our anonymous reviewers for their thoughtful and helpful comments.

References

Marianna Apidianaki. 2016. Vector-space models for ppdb paraphrase ranking in context. In *Proceedings of EMNLP*. Austin, Texas, pages 2028–2034.

Marianna Apidianaki, Emilia Verzeni, and Diana McCarthy. 2014. Semantic Clustering of Pivot Paraphrases. In *Proceedings of LREC*. Reykjavik, Iceland, pages 4270–4275.

José Camacho-Collados, Mohammad Taher Pilehvar, and Roberto Navigli. 2016. Nasari: Integrating explicit knowledge and corpus statistics for a multilingual representation of concepts and entities. *Artificial Intelligence* 240:36–64.

Anne Cocos, Marianna Apidianaki, and Chris Callison-Burch. 2017. Word sense filtering improves embedding-based lexical substitution. In *Proceedings of the 1st Workshop on Sense, Concept and Entity Representations and their Applications*. pages 110–119.

Anne Cocos and Chris Callison-Burch. 2016. Clustering Paraphrases by Word Sense. In *Proceedings of NAACL/HLT*. San Diego, California, pages 1463–1472.

William B. Dolan and Chris Brockett. 2005. Automatically constructing a corpus of sentential paraphrases. In *Proceedings of the Third International Workshop on Paraphrasing*. Jeju Island, Korea, pages 9–16.

Allyson Ettinger, Philip Resnik, and Marine Carpuat. 2016. Retrofitting sense-specific word vectors using parallel text. In *Proceedings of NAACL-HLT*. San Diego, California, pages 1378–1383.

Christiane Fellbaum. 1998. *WordNet*. Wiley Online Library.

Lucie Flekova and Iryna Gurevych. 2016. Supersense Embeddings: A Unified Model for Supersense Interpretation, Prediction, and Utilization. In *Proceedings of ACL*. Berlin, Germany, pages 2029–2041.

Juri Ganitkevitch, Benjamin Van Durme, and Chris Callison-Burch. 2013. PPDB: The Paraphrase Database. In *Proceedings of NAACL/HLT*. Atlanta, Georgia, pages 758–764.

Ignacio Iacobacci, Mohammed Taher Pilehvar, and Roberto Navigli. 2015. SensEmbed: Learning Sense Embeddings for Word and Relational Similarity. In *Proceedings of ACL/IJCNL*. Beijing, China, pages 95–105.

Sujay Kumar Jauhar, Chris Dyer, and Eduard Hovy. 2015. Ontologically Grounded Multi-sense Representation Learning for Semantic Vector Space Models. In *Proceedings of NAACL*. Denver, Colorado, pages 683–693.

Dekang Lin and Patrick Pantel. 2001. Dirt@ sbt@ discovery of inference rules from text. In *Proceedings of the seventh ACM SIGKDD international conference on Knowledge discovery and data mining*. ACM, pages 323–328.

Oren Melamud, Omer Levy, and Ido Dagan. 2015. A Simple Word Embedding Model for Lexical Substitution. In *Proceedings of the 1st Workshop on Vector Space Modeling for Natural Language Processing*. Denver, Colorado, pages 1–7.

Rada Mihalcea, Timothy Chklovski, and Adam Kilgarriff. 2004. The Senseval-3 English lexical sample task. In Rada Mihalcea and Phil Edmonds, editors, *Senseval-3: Third International Workshop on the Evaluation of Systems for the Semantic Analysis of Text*. Barcelona, Spain, pages 25–28.

Tomas Mikolov, Kai Chen, Greg Corrado, and Jeffrey Dean. 2013a. Efficient estimation of word representations in vector space. *arXiv preprint arXiv:1301.3781* .

Tomas Mikolov, Ilya Sutskever, Kai Chen, Greg Corrado, and Jeffrey Dean. 2013b. Distributed representations of words and phrases and their compositionality. In *Proceedings of NIPS*. pages 3111–3119.

George A. Miller. 1995. Wordnet: a lexical database for english. *Communications of the ACM* 31(11):39–41.

Courtney Napoles, Matthew Gormley, and Benjamin Van Durme. 2012. Annotated gigaword. In *Proceedings of the Joint Workshop on Automatic Knowledge Base Construction and Web-scale Knowledge Extraction (AKBC-WEKEX)*. Montréal, Canada, pages 95–100.

Roberto Navigli and Simone Paolo Ponzetto. 2012. Babelnet: The automatic construction, evaluation and application of a wide-coverage multilingual semantic network. *Artificial Intelligence* 193:217–250.

Ellie Pavlick, Johan Bos, Malvina Nissim, Charley Beller, Benjamin Van, and Durme Chris Callisonburch. 2015a. Adding semantics to data-driven paraphrasing. In *Proceedings of ACL*. Beijing, China, pages 425–430.

Ellie Pavlick, Pushpendre Rastogi, Juri Ganitkevich, and Chris Callison-Burch Ben Van Durme. 2015b. PPDB 2.0: Better paraphrase ranking, fine-grained entailment relations, word embeddings, and style classification. In *Proceedings of ACL*. Beijing, China, pages 425–430.

Radim Řehůřek and Petr Sojka. 2010. Software Framework for Topic Modelling with Large Corpora. In *Proceedings of the LREC 2010 Workshop on New Challenges for NLP Frameworks*. ELRA, Valletta, Malta, pages 45–50.

Stephen Roller and Katrin Erk. 2016. Relations such as hypernymy: Identifying and exploiting hearst patterns in distributional vectors for lexical entailment. In *Proceedings of EMNLP*. pages 2163–2172.

Vered Shwartz, Yoav Goldberg, and Ido Dagan. 2016. Improving hypernymy detection with an integrated path-based and distributional method. In *Proceedings of ACL*. Berlin, Germany, pages 2389–2398.

Rion Snow, Daniel Jurafsky, and Andrew Y Ng. 2006. Semantic taxonomy induction from heterogenous evidence. In *Proceedings of ACL*. pages 801–808.

Florentina Vasilescu, Philippe Langlais, and Guy Lapalme. 2004. Evaluating Variants of the Lesk Approach for Disambiguating Words. In *Proceedings of LREC*. Lisbonne, Portugal, pages 633–636.

Marta Vila, Horacio Rodríguez, and M Antònia Martí. 2015. Relational paraphrase acquisition from wikipedia: The WRPA method and corpus. *Natural Language Engineering* 21(03):355–389.

Semantic Frame Labeling with Target-based Neural Model

Yukun Feng[1], Dong Yu[1]*, Jian Xu[2], ChunHua Liu[1]
[1] Beijing Language and Culture University,
[2] University of Science and Technology of China
yukunfg@gmail.com,yudong@blcu.edu.cn,
jianxu1@mail.ustc.edu.cn,chunhualiu596@gmail.com

Abstract

This paper explores the automatic learning of distributed representations of the target's context for semantic frame labeling with target-based neural model. We constrain the whole sentence as the model's input without feature extraction from the sentence. This is different from many previous works in which local feature extraction of the targets is widely used. This constraint makes the task harder, especially with long sentences, but also makes our model easily applicable to a range of resources and other similar tasks. We evaluate our model on several resources and get the state-of-the-art result on subtask 2 of SemEval 2015 task 15. Finally, we extend the task to word-sense disambiguation task and we also achieve a strong result in comparison to state-of-the-art work.

1 Introduction and Related Work

Semantic frame labeling is the task of selecting the correct frame for a given target based on it-s semantic scene. A target is often called lexical unit which evokes the corresponding semantic frame. The lexical unit can be a verb, adjective or noun. Generally, a semantic frame describes how the lexical unit is used and specifies its characteristic interactions. There are many semantic frame resources, such as FrameNet (Baker et al., 1998), VerbNet (Schuler, 2006), PropBank (Palmer et al., 2005) and Corpus Pattern Analysis (CPA) frames (Hanks, 2012). However, most existing frame resources are manually created, which is time-consuming and expensive. Automatic semantic frame labeling can lead to the development of a broader range of resources.

Early works for semantic frame labeling mainly focus on FrameNet, PropBank and VerbNet resources. But most of them focus only one resource and rely heavily on feature engineering (e.g., Honnibal and Hawker 2005; Abend et al. 2008). Recently, there are some works on learning CPA frames based on a new semantic frame resource, the Pattern Dictionary of English Verbs (PDEV) (El Maarouf and Baisa, 2013; El Maarouf et al., 2014). The above two works also rely on features and both are only tested on 25 verbs. Most works aim at constructing the context representations of the target with explicit rules based on some basic features, e.g., Parts Of Speech (POS), Named Entities (NE) and dependency relations related to the target. Currently, some deep learning models have been applied with dependency features. Hermann et al. (2014) used the direct dependents and dependency path to extract the context representation based on distributed word embeddings on English FrameNet. Inspired by the work, Zhao et al. (2016) used a deep feed forward neural network on Chinese FrameNet with similar features. This is different from our goal where we want to explore an appropriate deep learning architecture without complex rules to construct the context representations. Feng et al. (2016) used a multilayer perceptrons (MLP) model on CPA frames without extra feature extraction, but the model is quite simple and has an input window which is not convenient.

In this paper, we present a target-based neural model which takes the whole target-specific sentence as input and gives the semantic frame label as output. Our goal is to make the model light without explicit rules to construct context representations and applicable to a range of resources. To cope with variable-length sentences under our constraint, a simple idea is to use recurrent neural networks (RNN) to process the sentences. But

---

*The corresponding author

*Proceedings of the 6th Joint Conference on Lexical and Computational Semantics (*SEM 2017)*, pages 91–96,
Vancouver, Canada, August 3-4, 2017. ©2017 Association for Computational Linguistics

noise caused by irrelevant words in long sentences may hinder learning. In fact, the arguments related to the target are usually distributed near the target because when we write or speak, we will focus mainly on arguments that are in the immediate context of a core word. We use two RNNs each of which processes one part of the sentence split by the target. The model takes the target as the center and we call it the target-based recurrent networks (TRNN). In fact, TRNN itself is not novel enough, but according to our knowledge, no related research has focused on this topic. We will show that TRNN is quite suitable for learning the context of the target.

2   Model Description

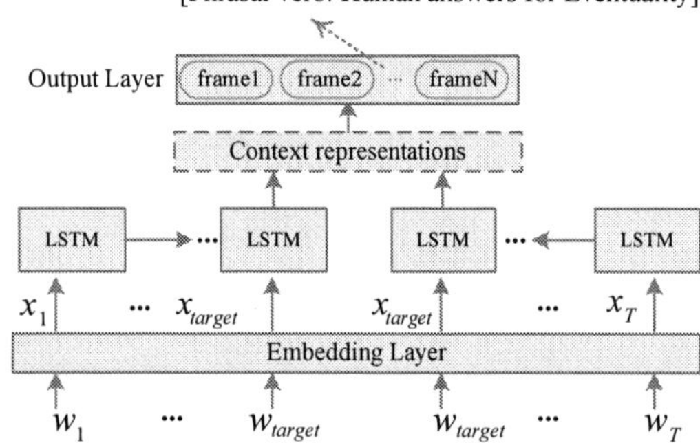

Figure 1: Architecture of TRNN with an example sentence whose target word is in bold.

In our model we select long short-term memory (LSTM) networks, a type of RNN designed to avoid the vanishing and exploding gradients. The overall structure is illustrated Figure 1. w_t is the t-th word in the sentence the length of which is T and $target$ is the index of the target. x_t is obtained by mapping w_t into a fixed vector through well pre-trained word vectors. The model has two LSTMs each of which processes one part of the sentence split by the target. The model can automatically learn the distributed representation of target's context from w with few manual design.

2.1   Context Representations

An introduction about LSTM can be found in the work of Hochreiter and Schmidhuber (1997). The parameters of LSTM are W_{x*}, W_{h*} and b_* where

$*$ stands for one of several internal gates. W_{x*} is the matrix between the input vector x_t and gates, W_{h*} is the matrix between the output h_t of LSTM and gates and b_* is the bias vector on gates. The formulas of LSTM are:

$$i_t = \sigma(W_{xi}x_t + W_{hi}h_{t-1} + b_i)$$
$$f_t = \sigma(W_{xf}x_t + W_{hf}h_{t-1} + b_f)$$
$$c_t = f_t \odot c_{t-1} + i_t \odot \tanh(W_{xc}x_t + W_{hc}h_{t-1} + b_c)$$
$$o_t = \sigma(W_{xo}x_t + W_{ho}h_{t-1} + b_o)$$
$$h_t = o_t \odot \tanh(c_t)$$

where σ is the sigmoid function and $\odot$ represents the element-wise multiplication. i_t, f_t c_t and o_t are the output of input gates, forget gates, cell states and output gates, respectively. In our model, two LSTMs share the same parameters. At last, the target's context representations cr are added by the outputs of two LSTMs:

$$cr = h_{target-1} + h_{target}$$

The dimension of cr is decided by the number of hidden units in LSTM, which is a hyper parameter in our model, and is usually much lower than that of one word vector. Here we make some intuitions behind the above formulas. The gradients from last layer flow equally on the $(target - 1)$-th LSTM box and the $target$-th LSTM box and then the two flows go to both ends. As it is quite common in deep learning models, the gradients usually become ineffective as the depth of the flow increases especially when the sentence is very long. The gradients on words far from the target get less impact than those near the target. As a whole, more data are usually required to learn the arguments far from the target than those near the target. If the real arguments are distributed near the target, this model will be suitable as its architecture is designed to take care of the local context of the target.

2.2   Output Layer

We use Softmax layer as the output layer on the context representations. The output layer computes a probability distribution over the semantic frame labels. During the training, the cost we minimize is the negative log likelihood of the model:

$$L = -\sum_{m=1}^{M} \log p_{t_m}$$

Here M is number of the training sentences, t_m is the index of the correct frame label for the m-th sentence and p is the probability.

3 Experiments

3.1 Datasets

We simply divide all the datasets in two types: **per-target** and **non per-target**. Per-target semantic frame resources define a different set of frame labels for each target and we train one model for each target; different targets may share some semantic frame labels in non per-target resources and we train a single model for such resources. We use the Semlink project (Loper et al., 2007) to create our datasets [1]. Semlink aims to link together different lexical resources via a set of mappings. We use its corpus which annotates FrameNet and Propbank frames for the WSJ section of the Penn Treebank. Another resource we use is PDEV [2] which is quite new and has CPA frame annotated examples on British National Corpus. All the original instances are sentence-tokenized and the punctuation was removed. The details of creating the datasets are as follows:

- FrameNet: Non per-target type. We get FrameNet annotated instances through Semlink. If one FrameNet frame label contains more than 300 instances, we divide it proportionately: 70%, 20% and 10%. Then we respectively accumulate the three parts by each frame label to create the training, test and validation set.

- PropBank: Per-target type. The creation process is same as FrameNet except that we finally get training, test and validation set for each target and the cutoff is set to 70 instead of 300.

- PDEV: Same as PropBank but with the cutoff set to 100 instead of 70.

Since the performance of our model is almost decided by the training data we empirically choose the cutoff above to keep the instances of each label enough. Summary statistics of the above datasets are in Table 2.

3.2 Models and Training

We compare our model with the following baselines.:

Sentences	Frame Names
In Moscow they **kept** asking us things like why do you make 15 different corkscrews	Activityongoing
It said it has taken measures to **continue** shipments during the work stoppage.	Activityongoing
But the Army Corps of Engineers expects the river level to **continue** falling this month.	Processcontinue
The oil industry's middling profits could **persist** through the rest of the year.	Processcontinue

Table 1: Non per-target examples. Frames are from FrameNet and the target words are in bold.

	FrameNet	PropBank	PDEV
Per-target	No	153 targets	407 targets
Train	41206	31212 (204)	152218 (374)
Test	11762	8568 (56)	42328 (104)
Valid.	5871	4131 (27)	20350 (50)
Frame	33	443 (2.89)	2197 (5.39)
Words/sent.	23	23	12

Table 2: Summary statistics for the datasets. The average numbers per target are shown in the parentheses for per-target resources.

- MF: The most frequent (MF) method selects the most frequent semantic frame label seen in training instances for each instance in the test dataset. MF is actually a strong baseline for per-target dataset because we observed that most targets have one main frame label.

- Target-Only: For FrameNet dataset, we use Target-Only method: if the target in the test instance has a unique frame label in the training data we give this frame label to current test instance; if the target has multiple frame labels in the training data we select the most frequent one in these labels; if the target is not seen in the training data, we select the most frequent label from the whole training data. This baseline is especially for FrameNet because we observed that each frame label has a set of targets but only a few targets have multiple frame labels. It may be easy to predict the frame label for test instances only according to the target.

- LSTM: The standard LSTM model.

- MaxEnt: The Maximum Entropy model. We use the Stanford CoreNLP module [3] to ex-

---

[1] The current version of the Semlink project has some problems to get the right position of targets in WSJ section of Penn Treebank. Instead, we use annotations of PropBank corpus, also annotated in WSJ section of Penn Treebank, to index targets.

[2] http://pdev.org.uk/

[3] http://stanfordnlp.github.io/CoreNLP/

tract features for MaxEnt toolkit [4]. All dependents related to the target, their POS tags, dependency relations, lemmas, NE tags and the target itself will be extracted as features.

The number of the iterations for MaxEnt is decided by the validation set. For simplicity, we set the learning rate to 1.0 for TRNN and LSTM. The number of hidden units is tested on validation data with the values {35, 45, 55} for per-target resource and {80, 100, 120} for non per-target resource. We use the publicly available word2vec vectors, a dimensionality of 300, that were trained through the GloVe model (Pennington et al., 2014) on Wikipedia and Gigaword. For words not appeared in the vector model, their word vectors are all set to zero vectors. We train these models by stochastic gradient descent with minibatches. The minibatch is set to 10 for per-target resource and 50 for non per-target resource. We keep the word vectors static since no obvious improvement has been observed. Training will stop when the zero-one loss is zero over training data.

3.3 Results

The results of the above datasets are in Table 3. Target-Only gets very high scores on FrameNet dataset. FrameNet dataset has 55 targets which has multiple frame labels in the training data and these targets have 1981 instances in the test data. We get 0.769 F-score on these instances and 0.393 F-score on 64 unseen targets with 77 test instances. This can be the extreme case that the main feature for the correct frame is the target itself. Despite this simple fact, standard LSTM performs very badly on FrameNet. The main reason is that sentences in FrameNet dataset are too long and standard LSTM can not learn well due to the large number of irrelevant words that appear in long sentences. To show this, we select the size of truncation window for original FrameNet sentences and we get the best size of 5 on validation data with each 2 words surrounding the target. Finally, we get 0.958 F-score on FrameNet test data which is still lower than TRNN on full sentences. As for PropBank and PDEV dataset, we train one model for each target so the final F-score is the average of all targets. However, the number of training instances per target is limited. TRNN will usually not perform well when it tries to learn some

frames which consist of many different concepts and especially when the frame has a few training instances. Considering the sentence 4 of Table 4 as an example, it is difficult to TRNN to learn what is 'Activity' in the correct frame because this concept is huge. TRNN may need lots of data to learn something related to this concept. However, this correct frame only has 6 instances in our training data. The second reason of TRNN's failure is lack of knowledge due to unseen words in test data. The sentence 1 of Table 4 shows TRNN will make the right decision since we observe that it has seen the word 'cow' in the training data and knows this word belongs to the concept 'Animate or Plant' in the correct frame. But TRNN does not know the word 'Elegans' in sentence 3 so it usually selects the most frequent frame seen in the training data. However, in many cases, the unseen words can be captured by well trained word embeddings as the sentence 2 shows where 'ducks', 'chickens' and 'geese' are all unseen words.

Models	FrameNet	PropBank	PDEV
MF	0.38	0.78	0.61
Target-Only	0.911	-	-
MaxEnt	0.829/125	0.874/30	0.704/10
LSTM	0.55/80	0.78/35	0.72/55
TRNN	**0.962/100**	**0.887/35**	**0.794/55**

Table 3: Results on several semantic frame resources. The format of cell value is "F-score/hidden unit" for TRNN and LSTM and "F-score/iteration" for MaxEnt toolkit.

3.4 CPA Experiment

Corpus Pattern Analysis (CPA) is a new technique for identifying the main patterns in which a word is used in text and is currently being used to build the PDEV resource as we mentioned above. It is also a shared task in SemEval-2015 task 15 (Baisa et al., 2015). The task is divided into three subtasks: CPA parsing, CPA clustering and CPA lexicography. We only introduce the first two related subtasks. CPA parsing aims at identifying the arguments of the target and tagging predefined semantic meaning on them; CPA clustering clusters the instances to obtain CPA frames based on the result of CPA parsing. However, the first step results seem unpromising (Feng et al., 2015; Mills and Levow, 2015; Elia, 2016) which will influence the process of obtaining CPA frames. Since our model can be applied on sentence-level input without feature extraction we can directly evaluate

---

[4]https://github.com/lzhang10/maxent

ID	Sentences	Frame Prediction	True Frame
1	One of the farmer's cows had **died** of BSE raising fears of cross-infection...	Same with true frame	Animate or Plant dies
2	One of the farmer's ducks|chickens|geese had **died** of BSE raising fears of cross-infection...	Same with true frame	Animate or Plant dies
3	Elegans also in central America **die** of damping off as a function of distance	Human dies ((Time Point)(Location)(Causation) (at Number or at the age of or at birth or earlage))	Animate or Plant dies
4	Indeed, the MEC does not **advise** the use of any insecticidal shampoo for...	Human 1 or Institution 1 advises Human 2 or Institution 2 to-infinitive	Human or Institution advises Activity

Table 4: Case study for CPA frames. The target words are in bold.

our model on CPA clustering. Unfortunately, the datasets provided by CPA clustering is a per-target resource for our model and the targets in training and test set are not the same. Since this task is not limited to use extra resources, we use the training set of FrameNet, a type of non per-target, mentioned in section 3.1 to solve this problem. The hyper parameters are the same as before. CPA clustering is evaluated by B-cubed F-score, a metric for clustering problem, so we do not need to convert the FrameNet frame label to CPA frame label. The result is in Table 5. All the models are supervised except for baseline and DULUTH. Feng et al. (2016) used the MLP to classify fixed-length local text of the target based on distributed word embeddings. But the representation of the target's context is simply constructed with concatenated word embeddings and the length of local context has to be chosen manually. Besides, MLP may fail to train or predict well when some key words are out of its input window.

System	B-cubed F-score
BOB90(Best in SemEval 2015)	0.741
SemEval 2015 baseline	0.588
DULUTH	0.525
Feng et al. (2016)	0.70
This paper	**0.763**

Table 5: Results on Microcheck dataset of CPA clustering.

3.5 Word Sense Disambiguation Experiment

Finally, we choose Word Sense Disambiguation (WSD) task to extend our experiment. As our benchmark for WSD task, we choose English Lexical Sample WSD tasks of SemEval-2007 task 17 (Pradhan et al., 2007). We use cross-validation on the training set and we observe the model performs better when we update the word vectors which is different from the preceding experimental setup. The number of hidden units is set to 55. The result is in Table 6. The rows from 4 to 6 come from Iacobacci et al. (2016). They inte-

grate word embeddings into IMS (It Makes Sense) system (Zhong and Ng, 2010) which uses support vector machine as its classifier based on some standard WSD features and they get the best result; they use an exponential decay function, also designed to give more importance to close context, to compute the word representation, but their method need manually choose the window size of the target word and one parameter of their exponential decay function. Both with word vectors only, our model is comparable with the sixth row.

System	F-score
Rank 1 system in SemEval 2007	0.887
Rank 2 system in SemEval 2007	0.869
IMS (2010)	0.879
IMS + word vectors (2016)	**0.894**
IMS + word vectors only (2016)	0.880
This paper	0.886

Table 6: Result on Lexical Sample task of SemEval-2007 task 17

4 Conclusion

In this paper, we describe an end-to-end neural model to target-specific semantic frame labeling. Without explicit rule construction to fit for some specific resources, our model can be easily applied to a range of semantic frame resources and similar tasks. In the future, non-English semantic frame resources can be considered to extend the coverage of our model and our model can integrate the best features explored in the state-of-the-art work to see how many improvements our model can make.

Acknowledgments

We would like to thank the anonymous reviewers and Li Zhao for their helpful suggestions and comments. The work was supported by the National High Technology Development 863 Program of China (No.2015AA015409).

References

Omri Abend, Roi Reichart, and Ari Rappoport. 2008. A supervised algorithm for verb disambiguation into verbnet classes. In *Proceedings of the 22nd International Conference on Computational Linguistics-Volume 1*. Association for Computational Linguistics, pages 9–16.

Vít Baisa, Jane Bradbury, Silvie Cinkova, Ismail El Maarouf, Adam Kilgarriff, and Octavian Popescu. 2015. Semeval-2015 task 15: A cpa dictionary-entry-building task. In *Proceedings of the 9th International Workshop on Semantic Evaluation (SemEval 2015)*. Association for Computational Linguistics, Denver, Colorado, pages 315–324. http://www.aclweb.org/anthology/S15-2053.

Collin F Baker, Charles J Fillmore, and John B Lowe. 1998. The berkeley framenet project. In *Proceedings of the 17th international conference on Computational linguistics-Volume 1*. Association for Computational Linguistics, pages 86–90.

Ismaıl El Maarouf and Vıt Baisa. 2013. Automatic classification of patterns from the pattern dictionary of english verbs. In *Joint Symposium on Semantic Processing.*.

Ismail El Maarouf, Jane Bradbury, Vít Baisa, and Patrick Hanks. 2014. Disambiguating verbs by collocation: Corpus lexicography meets natural language processing. In *LREC*. pages 1001–1006.

Francesco Elia. 2016. Syntactic and semantic classification of verb arguments using dependency-based and rich semantic features. *arXiv preprint arXiv:1604.05747* .

Yukun Feng, Qiao Deng, and Dong Yu. 2015. Blcunlp: Corpus pattern analysis for verbs based on dependency chain. In *Proceedings of the 9th International Workshop on Semantic Evaluation (SemEval 2015)*. Association for Computational Linguistics, Denver, Colorado, pages 325–328. http://www.aclweb.org/anthology/S15-2054.

Yukun Feng, Yipei Xu, and Dong Yu. 2016. An end-to-end approach to learning semantic frames with feedforward neural network. In *Proceedings of the NAACL Student Research Workshop*. Association for Computational Linguistics, San Diego, California, pages 1–7. http://www.aclweb.org/anthology/N16-2001.

Patrick Hanks. 2012. How people use words to make meanings: Semantic types meet valencies. *Input, Process and Product: Developments in Teaching and Language Corpora* pages 54–69.

Karl Moritz Hermann, Dipanjan Das, Jason Weston, and Kuzman Ganchev. 2014. Semantic frame identification with distributed word representations. In *Proceedings of the 52nd Annual Meeting of the Association for Computational Linguistics (Volume 1: Long Papers)*. Association for Computational Linguistics, Baltimore, Maryland, pages 1448–1458. http://www.aclweb.org/anthology/P/P14/P14-1136.

Sepp Hochreiter and Jürgen Schmidhuber. 1997. Long short-term memory. *Neural computation* 9(8):1735–1780.

Matthew Honnibal and Tobias Hawker. 2005. Identifying framenet frames for verbs from a real-text corpus. In *Proceedings of Australasian Language Technology Workshop*.

Ignacio Iacobacci, Mohammad Taher Pilehvar, and Roberto Navigli. 2016. Embeddings for word sense disambiguation: An evaluation study. In *Proceedings of the 54th Annual Meeting of the Association for Computational Linguistics*. pages 897–907.

Edward Loper, Szu-Ting Yi, and Martha Palmer. 2007. Combining lexical resources: mapping between propbank and verbnet. In *Proceedings of the 7th International Workshop on Computational Linguistics, Tilburg, the Netherlands*.

Chad Mills and Gina-Anne Levow. 2015. Cmills: Adapting semantic role labeling features to dependency parsing. In *Proceedings of the 9th International Workshop on Semantic Evaluation (SemEval 2015)*. Association for Computational Linguistics, Denver, Colorado, pages 433–437. http://www.aclweb.org/anthology/S15-2075.

Martha Palmer, Daniel Gildea, and Paul Kingsbury. 2005. The proposition bank: An annotated corpus of semantic roles. *Computational linguistics* 31(1):71–106.

Jeffrey Pennington, Richard Socher, and Christopher D Manning. 2014. Glove: Global vectors for word representation. In *EMNLP*. volume 14, pages 1532–1543.

Sameer S Pradhan, Edward Loper, Dmitriy Dligach, and Martha Palmer. 2007. Semeval-2007 task 17: English lexical sample, srl and all words. In *Proceedings of the 4th International Workshop on Semantic Evaluations*. Association for Computational Linguistics, pages 87–92.

Karin Kipper Schuler. 2006. *VerbNet: A Broad-Coverage, Comprehensive Verb Lexicon*. Ph.D. thesis, University of Pennsylvania. http://verbs.colorado.edu/ kipper/Papers/dissertation.pdf.

Hongyan Zhao, Ru Li, Sheng Zhang, and Liwen Zhang. 2016. Chinese frame identification with deep neural network 30(6):75.

Zhi Zhong and Hwee Tou Ng. 2010. It makes sense: A wide-coverage word sense disambiguation system for free text. In *Proceedings of the ACL 2010 System Demonstrations*. Association for Computational Linguistics, pages 78–83.

Frame-Based Continuous Lexical Semantics through Exponential Family Tensor Factorization and Semantic Proto-Roles

Francis Ferraro and **Adam Poliak** and **Ryan Cotterell** and **Benjamin Van Durme**

Center for Language and Speech Processing
Johns Hopkins University
{ferraro,azpoliak,ryan.cotterell,vandurme}@cs.jhu.edu

Abstract

We study how different frame annotations complement one another when learning continuous lexical semantics. We learn the representations from a tensorized skip-gram model that consistently encodes syntactic-semantic content better, with multiple 10% gains over baselines.

1 Introduction

Consider "Bill" in Fig. 1: what is his involvement with the words "would try," and what does this involvement *mean*? Word embeddings represent such meaning as points in a real-valued vector space (Deerwester et al., 1990; Mikolov et al., 2013). These representations are often learned by exploiting the frequency that the word cooccurs with contexts, often within a user-defined window (Harris, 1954; Turney and Pantel, 2010). When built from large-scale sources, like Wikipedia or web crawls, embeddings capture general characteristics of words and allow for robust downstream applications (Kim, 2014; Das et al., 2015).

Frame semantics generalize word meanings to that of analyzing structured and interconnected labeled "concepts" and abstractions (Minsky, 1974; Fillmore, 1976, 1982). These concepts, or roles, *implicitly* encode expected properties of that word. In a frame semantic analysis of Fig. 1, the segment "would try" *triggers* the ATTEMPT frame, filling the expected roles AGENT and GOAL with "Bill" and "the same tactic," respectively. While frame semantics provide a structured form for analyzing words with crisp, categorically-labeled concepts, the encoded properties and expectations are implicit. What does it *mean* to fill a frame's role?

Semantic proto-role (SPR) theory, motivated by Dowty (1991)'s thematic proto-role theory, offers an answer to this. SPR replaces categorical roles

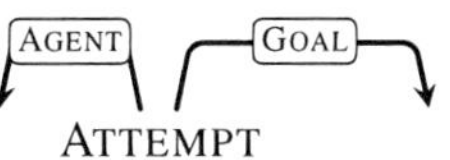

She said Bill would try the same tactic again.

Figure 1: A simple frame analysis.

with judgements about multiple underlying properties about what is likely true of the entity filling the role. For example, SPR talks about how likely it is for Bill to be a willing participant in the ATTEMPT. The answer to this and other simple judgments characterize Bill and his involvement. Since SPR both captures the likelihood of certain properties and characterizes roles as groupings of properties, we can view SPR as representing a type of continuous frame semantics.

We are interested in capturing these SPR-based properties and expectations within word embeddings. We present a method that learns frame-enriched embeddings from millions of documents that have been semantically parsed with multiple different frame analyzers (Ferraro et al., 2014). Our method leverages Cotterell et al. (2017)'s formulation of Mikolov et al. (2013)'s popular skip-gram model as exponential family principal component analysis (EPCA) and tensor factorization. This paper's primary contributions are: (i) enriching learned word embeddings with multiple, automatically obtained frames from large, disparate corpora; and (ii) demonstrating these enriched embeddings better capture SPR-based properties. In so doing, we also generalize Cotterell et al.'s method to arbitrary tensor dimensions. This allows us to include an arbitrary amount of semantic information when learning embeddings. Our variable-size tensor factorization code is available at `https://github.com/fmof/tensor-factorization`.

*Proceedings of the 6th Joint Conference on Lexical and Computational Semantics (*SEM 2017)*, pages 97–103,
Vancouver, Canada, August 3-4, 2017. ©2017 Association for Computational Linguistics

2 Frame Semantics and Proto-Roles

Frame semantics currently used in NLP have a rich history in linguistic literature. Fillmore (1976)'s frames are based on a word's context and prototypical concepts that an individual word evokes; they intend to represent the meaning of lexical items by mapping words to real world concepts and shared experiences. Frame-based semantics have inspired many semantic annotation schemata and datasets, such as FrameNet (Baker et al., 1998), PropBank (Palmer et al., 2005), and Verbnet (Schuler, 2005), as well as composite resources (Hovy et al., 2006; Palmer, 2009; Banarescu et al., 2012).[1]

Thematic Roles and Proto Roles These resources map words to their meanings through discrete/categorically labeled frames and roles; sometimes, as in FrameNet, the roles can be very descriptive (e.g., the DEGREE role for the AF-FIRM_OR_DENY frame), while in other cases, as in PropBank, the roles can be quite general (e.g., ARG0). Regardless of the actual schema, the roles are based on thematic roles, which map a predicate's arguments to a semantic representation that makes various semantic distinctions among the arguments (Dowty, 1989).[2] Dowty (1991) claims that thematic role distinctions are not atomic, i.e., they can be deconstructed and analyzed at a lower level. Instead of many discrete thematic roles, Dowty (1991) argues for *proto-thematic roles*, e.g. PROTO-AGENT rather than AGENT, where distinctions in proto-roles are based on clusterings of logical entailments. That is, PROTO-AGENTs often have certain properties in common, e.g., manipulating other objects or willingly participating in an action; PROTO-PATIENTs are often changed or affected by some action. By decomposing the meaning of roles into properties or expectations that can be reasoned about, proto-roles can be seen as including a form of vector representation within structured frame semantics.

3 Continuous Lexical Semantics

Word embeddings represent word meanings as elements of a (real-valued) vector space (Deerwester et al., 1990). Mikolov et al. (2013)'s `word2vec` methods—skip-gram (SG) and continuous bag of

words (CBOW)—repopularized these methods. We focus on SG, which predicts the context i around a word j, with learned representations $\mathbf{c}_i$ and $\mathbf{w}_j$, respectively, as $p(\text{context } i \mid \text{word } j) \propto \exp\left(\mathbf{c}_i^\mathsf{T} \mathbf{w}_j\right) = \exp\left(\mathbf{1}^\mathsf{T}(\mathbf{c}_i \odot \mathbf{w}_j)\right)$, where $\odot$ is the Hadamard (pointwise) product. Traditionally, the context words i are those words within a small window of j and are trained with negative sampling (Goldberg and Levy, 2014).

3.1 Skip-Gram as Matrix Factorization

Levy and Goldberg (2014b), and subsequently Keerthi et al. (2015), showed how vectors learned under SG with the negative sampling are, under certain conditions, the factorization of (shifted) positive pointwise mutual information. Cotterell et al. (2017) showed that SG is a form of exponential family PCA that factorizes the matrix of word/context cooccurrence counts (rather than shifted positive PMI values). With this interpretation, they generalize SG from matrix to tensor factorization, and provide a theoretical basis for modeling higher-order SG (or additional context, such as morphological features of words) within a word embeddings framework.

Specifically, Cotterell et al. recast higher-order SG as maximizing the log-likelihood

$$\sum_{ijk} \mathfrak{X}_{ijk} \log p(\text{context } i \mid \text{word } j, \text{feature } k) \quad (1)$$

$$= \sum_{ijk} \mathfrak{X}_{ijk} \log \frac{\exp\left(\mathbf{1}^\mathsf{T}(\mathbf{c}_i \odot \mathbf{w}_j \odot \mathbf{a}_k)\right)}{\sum_{i'} \exp\left(\mathbf{1}^\mathsf{T}(\mathbf{c}_{i'} \odot \mathbf{w}_j \odot \mathbf{a}_k)\right)}, \quad (2)$$

where $\mathfrak{X}_{ijk}$ is a cooccurrence count 3-tensor of words j, surrounding contexts i, and features k.

3.2 Skip-Gram as n-Tensor Factorization

When factorizing an n-dimensional tensor to include an arbitrary number of L annotations, we replace *feature* k in Equation (1) and $\mathbf{a}_k$ in Equation (2) with each annotation type l and vector $\boldsymbol{\alpha}_l$ included. $\mathfrak{X}_{i,j,k}$ becomes $\mathfrak{X}_{i,j,l_1,\ldots l_L}$, representing the number of times word j appeared in context i with features l_1 through l_L. We maximize

$$\sum_{i,j,l_1,\ldots,l_L} \mathfrak{X}_{i,j,l_1,\ldots,l_L} \log \beta_{i,j,l_1,\ldots,l_L}$$

$$\beta_{i,j,l_1,\ldots,l_L} \propto \exp\left(\mathbf{1}^\mathsf{T}(\mathbf{c}_i \odot \mathbf{w}_j \odot \boldsymbol{\alpha}_{l_1} \odot \cdots \odot \boldsymbol{\alpha}_{l_L})\right).$$

4 Experiments

Our end goal is to use multiple kinds of automatically obtained, "in-the-wild" frame se-

---

[1] See Petruck and de Melo (2014) for detailed descriptions on frame semantics' contributions to applied NLP tasks.

[2] Thematic role theory is rich, and beyond this paper's scope (Whitehead, 1920; Davidson, 1967; Cresswell, 1973; Kamp, 1979; Carlson, 1984).

mantic parses in order to improve the semantic content—specifically SPR-type information—within learned lexical embeddings. We utilize majority portions of the Concretely Annotated New York Times and Wikipedia corpora from Ferraro et al. (2014). These have been annotated with three frame semantic parses: FrameNet from Das et al. (2010), and both FrameNet and PropBank from Wolfe et al. (2016). In total, we use nearly five million frame-annotated documents.

Extracting Counts The baseline extraction we consider is a standard sliding window: for each word w_j seen $\geq T$ times, extract all words w_i two to the left and right of w_j. These counts, forming a matrix, are then used within standard `word2vec`. We also follow Cotterell et al. (2017) and augment the above with the signed number of tokens separating w_i and w_j, e.g., recording that w_i appeared two to the left of w_j; these counts form a 3-tensor.

To turn semantic parses into tensor counts, we first identify relevant information from the parses. We consider all parses that are triggered by the target word w_j (seen $\geq T$ times) and that have at least one role filled by some word in the sentence. We organize the extraction around roles and what fills them. We extract every word w_r that fills all possible triggered frames; each of those frame and role labels; and the distance between filler w_r and trigger w_j. This process yields a 9-tensor $\mathfrak{X}$.[3] Although we **always** treat the trigger as the "original" word (e.g., word j, with vector $\mathbf{w}_j$), later we consider (1) what to include from $\mathfrak{X}$, (2) what to predict (what to treat as the "context" word i), and (3) what to treat as auxiliary features.

Data Discussion The baseline extraction methods result in roughly symmetric target and surrounding word counts. This is not the case for the frame extraction. Our target words must trigger some semantic parse, so our target words are actually target triggers. However, the surrounding context words are those words that fill semantic roles. As shown in Table 1, there are an order-of-magnitude fewer triggers than target words, but up to an order-of-magnitude *more* surrounding words.

Implementation We generalize Levy and Goldberg (2014a)'s and Cotterell et al. (2017)'s code

---

[3] Each record consists of the trigger, a role filler, the number of words between the trigger and filler, and the relevant frame and roles from the three semantic parsers. Being automatically obtained, the parses are overlapping and incomplete; to properly form $\mathfrak{X}$, one can implicitly include special ⟨NO_FRAME⟩ and ⟨NO_ROLE⟩ labels as needed.

	windowed	frame
# target words	232	35.9 (triggers)
	404	*45.7* (triggers)
# surrounding words	232	531 (role fillers)
	404	*2,305* (role fillers)

Table 1: Vocabulary sizes, in thousands, extracted from Ferraro et al. (2014)'s data with both the standard sliding context window approach (§3) and the frame-based approach (§4). Upper numbers (Roman) are for newswire; lower numbers (italics) are Wikipedia. For both corpora, 800 total FrameNet frame types and 5100 PropBank frame types are extracted.

to enable any arbitrary dimensional tensor factorization, as described in §3.2. We learn 100-dimensional embeddings for words that appear at least 100 times from 15 negative samples.[4] The implementation is available at `https://github.com/fmof/tensor-factorization`.

Metric We evaluate our learned (trigger) embeddings $\mathbf{w}$ via QVEC (Tsvetkov et al., 2015). QVEC uses canonical correlation analysis to measure the Pearson correlation between $\mathbf{w}$ and a collection of *oracle* lexical vectors $\mathbf{o}$. These oracle vectors are derived from a human-annotated resource. For QVEC, higher is better: a higher score indicates $\mathbf{w}$ more closely correlates (positively) with $\mathbf{o}$.

Evaluating Semantic Content with SPR Motivated by Dowty (1991)'s proto-role theory, Reisinger et al. (2015), with a subsequent expansion by White et al. (2016), annotated thousands of predicate-argument pairs (v, a) with (boolean) applicability and (ordinal) likelihoods of well-motivated semantic properties applying to/being true of a.[5] These likelihood judgments, under the SPR framework, are converted from a five-point Likert scale to a 1–5 interval scale. Because the predicate-argument pairs were extracted from previously annotated dependency trees, we link each property with the dependency relation joining v and a when forming the oracle vectors; each component of an oracle vector $\mathbf{o}_v$ is the unity-normalized sum of likelihood judgments for joint property and grammatical relation, using the interval responses when the property is applicable and discarding non-applicable properties, i.e. treating the response as 0. Thus, the combined 20 properties of Reisinger et al. (2015) and White et al. (2016)—together with the four basic grammatical

---

[4] In preliminary experiments, this occurrence threshold did not change the overall conclusions.

[5] We use the training portion of `http://decomp.net/wp-content/uploads/2015/08/UniversalDecompositionalSemantics.tar.gz`.

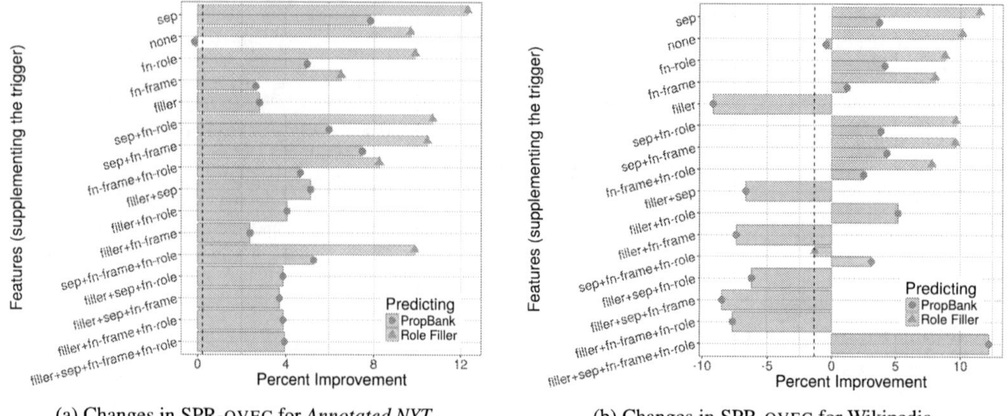

<table>
<tr><td>(a) Changes in SPR-QVEC for Annotated NYT.</td><td>(b) Changes in SPR-QVEC for Wikipedia.</td></tr>
</table>

Figure 2: Effect of frame-extracted tensor counts on our SPR-QVEC evaulation. Deltas are shown as relative percent changes vs. the `word2vec` baseline. The dashed line represents the 3-tensor `word2vec` method of Cotterell et al. (2017). Each row represents an ablation model: `sep` means the prediction relies on the token separation distance between the frame and role filler, `fn-frame` means the prediction uses FrameNet frames, `fn-role` means the prediction uses FrameNet roles, and `filler` means the prediction uses the tokens filling the frame role. Read from top to bottom, additional contextual features are denoted with a +. Note when `filler` is used, we only predict PropBank roles.

relations *nsubj*, *dobj*, *iobj* and *nsubjpass*—result in 80-dimensional oracle vectors.[6]

Predict Fillers or Roles? Since SPR judgments are between predicates and arguments, we predict the words filling the roles, and treat all other frame information as auxiliary features. SPR annotations were originally based off of (gold-standard) PropBank annotations, so we also train a model to predict PropBank frames and roles, thereby treating role-filling text and all other frame information as auxiliary features. In early experiments, we found it beneficial to treat the FrameNet annotations additively and not distinguish one system's output from another. Treating the annotations additively serves as a type of collapsing operation. Although $\mathcal{X}$ started as a 9-tensor, we only consider up to 6-tensors: trigger, role filler, token separation between the trigger and filler, PropBank frame and role, FrameNet frame, and FrameNet role.

Results Fig. 2 shows the overall percent change for SPR-QVEC from the filler and role prediction models, on newswire (Fig. 2a) and Wikipedia (Fig. 2b), across different ablation models. We indicate additional contextual features being used with a +: `sep` uses the token separation distance between the frame and role filler, `fn-frame` uses FrameNet frames, `fn-role` uses FrameNet roles, `filler` uses the tokens filling the frame

role, and `none` indicates no additional information is used when predicting. The 0 line represents a plain `word2vec` baseline and the dashed line represents the 3-tensor baseline of Cotterell et al. (2017). Both of these baselines are windowed: they are restricted to a local context and cannot take advantage of frames or any lexical signal that can be derived from frames.

Overall, we notice that we obtain large improvements from models trained on lexical signals that have been *derived* from frame output (`sep` and `none`), even if the model *itself* does not incorporate any frame labels. The embeddings that predict the role filling lexical items (the green triangles) correlate higher with SPR oracles than the embeddings that predict PropBank frames and roles (red circles). Examining Fig. 2a, we see that both model types outperform both the `word2vec` and Cotterell et al. (2017) baselines in nearly all model configurations and ablations. We see the highest improvement when predicting role fillers given the frame trigger and the number of tokens separating the two (the green triangles in the `sep` rows).

Comparing Fig. 2a to Fig. 2b, we see newswire is more amenable to predicting PropBank frames and roles. We posit this is a type of out-of-domain error, as the PropBank parser was trained on newswire. We also find that newswire is overall more amenable to incorporating limited frame-based features, particularly when predicting PropBank using lexical role fillers as part of the con-

---

[6] The full cooccurrence among the properties and relations is relatively sparse. Nearly two thirds of all non-zero oracle components are comprised of just fourteen properties, and only the *nsubj* and *dobj* relations.

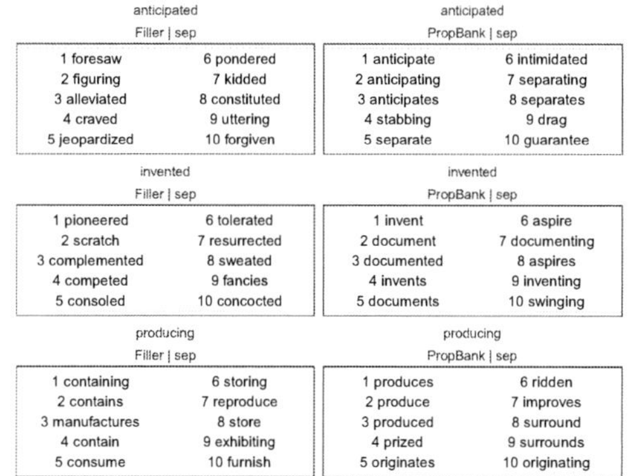

Figure 3: *K*-Nearest Neighbors for three randomly sampled trigger words, from two newswire models.

textual features. We hypothesize this is due to the significantly increased vocabulary size of the Wikipedia role fillers (c.f., Tab. 1). Note, however, that by using all available schema information when predicting PropBank, we are able to compensate for the increased vocabulary.

In Fig. 3 we display the ten nearest neighbors for three randomly sampled trigger words according to two of the highest performing newswire models. They each condition on the trigger and the role filler/trigger separation; these correspond to the sep rows of Fig. 2a. The left column of Fig. 3 predicts the role filler, while the right column predicts PropBank annotations. We see that while both models learn inflectional relations, this quality is prominent in the model that predicts PropBank information while the model predicting role fillers learns more non-inflectional paraphrases.

5 Related Work

The recent popularity of word embeddings have inspired others to consider leveraging linguistic annotations and resources to learn embeddings. Both Cotterell et al. (2017) and Levy and Goldberg (2014a) incorporate additional syntactic and morphological information in their word embeddings. Rothe and Schütze (2015)'s use lexical resource entries, such as WordNet synsets, to improve pre-computed word embeddings. Through generalized CCA, Rastogi et al. (2015) incorporate paraphrased FrameNet training data. On the applied side, Wang and Yang (2015) used frame embeddings—produced by training word2vec on tweet-derived semantic frame (names)—as additional features in downstream prediction.

Teichert et al. (2017) similarly explored the relationship between semantic frames and thematic proto-roles. They proposed using a Conditional Random Field (Lafferty et al., 2001) to jointly and conditionally model SPR and SRL. Teichert et al. (2017) demonstrated slight improvements in jointly and conditionally predicting PropBank (Bonial et al., 2013)'s semantic role labels and Reisinger et al. (2015)'s proto-role labels.

6 Conclusion

We presented a way to learn embeddings enriched with multiple, automatically obtained frames from large, disparate corpora. We also presented a QVEC evaluation for semantic proto-roles. As demonstrated by our experiments, our extension of Cotterell et al. (2017)'s tensor factorization enriches word embeddings by including syntactic-semantic information not often captured, resulting in consistently higher SPR-based correlations. The implementation is available at https://github.com/fmof/tensor-factorization.

Acknowledgments

This work was supported by Johns Hopkins University, the Human Language Technology Center of Excellence (HLTCOE), DARPA DEFT, and DARPA LORELEI. We would also like to thank three anonymous reviewers for their feedback. The views and conclusions contained in this publication are those of the authors and should not be interpreted as representing official policies or endorsements of DARPA or the U.S. Government.

References

Collin F. Baker, Charles J. Fillmore, and John B. Lowe. 1998. The berkeley framenet project. In *Proceedings of the 36th Annual Meeting of the Association for Computational Linguistics and 17th International Conference on Computational Linguistics - Volume 1*. Association for Computational Linguistics, Stroudsburg, PA, USA, ACL '98, pages 86–90. https://doi.org/10.3115/980845.980860.

Laura Banarescu, Claire Bonial, Shu Cai, Madalina Georgescu, Kira Griffitt, Ulf Hermjakob, Kevin Knight, Philipp Koehn, Martha Palmer, and Nathan Schneider. 2012. Abstract meaning representation (amr) 1.0 specification. In *Parsing on Freebase from Question-Answer Pairs. In Proceedings of the 2013 Conference on Empirical Methods in Natural Language Processing. Seattle: ACL.* pages 1533–1544.

Claire Bonial, Kevin Stowe, and Martha Palmer. 2013. Renewing and revising semlink. In *Proceedings of the 2nd Workshop on Linked Data in Linguistics (LDL-2013): Representing and linking lexicons, terminologies and other language data.* Association for Computational Linguistics, Pisa, Italy, pages 9 – 17. http://www.aclweb.org/anthology/W13-5503.

Greg N Carlson. 1984. Thematic roles and their role in semantic interpretation. *Linguistics* 22(3):259–280.

Ryan Cotterell, Adam Poliak, Benjamin Van Durme, and Jason Eisner. 2017. Explaining and generalizing skip-gram through exponential family principal component analysis. In *Proceedings of the 15th Conference of the European Chapter of the Association for Computational Linguistics*. Valencia, Spain.

Maxwell John Cresswell. 1973. *Logics and languages.* London: Methuen [Distributed in the U.S.A. By Harper & Row].

Dipanjan Das, Nathan Schneider, Desai Chen, and Noah A Smith. 2010. Probabilistic frame-semantic parsing. In *Human language technologies: The 2010 annual conference of the North American chapter of the association for computational linguistics.* Association for Computational Linguistics, pages 948–956.

Rajarshi Das, Manzil Zaheer, and Chris Dyer. 2015. Gaussian lda for topic models with word embeddings. In *Proceedings of the 53rd Annual Meeting of the Association for Computational Linguistics and the 7th International Joint Conference on Natural Language Processing (Volume 1: Long Papers).* Association for Computational Linguistics, Beijing, China, pages 795–804. http://www.aclweb.org/anthology/P15-1077.

Donald Davidson. 1967. The logical form of action sentences. In Nicholas Rescher, editor, *The Logic of Decision and Action*, University of Pittsburgh Press.

Scott Deerwester, Susan T. Dumais, George W. Furnas, Thomas K. Landauer, and Richard Harshman. 1990. Indexing by latent semantic analysis. *JOURNAL OF THE AMERICAN SOCIETY FOR INFORMATION SCIENCE* 41(6):391–407.

David Dowty. 1991. Thematic proto-roles and argument selection. *Language* 67(3):547–619.

David R Dowty. 1989. On the semantic content of the notion of thematic role. In *Properties, types and meaning*, Springer, pages 69–129.

Francis Ferraro, Max Thomas, Matthew R. Gormley, Travis Wolfe, Craig Harman, and Benjamin Van Durme. 2014. Concretely Annotated Corpora. In *4th Workshop on Automated Knowledge Base Construction (AKBC).*

Charles Fillmore. 1982. Frame semantics. *Linguistics in the morning calm* pages 111–137.

Charles J Fillmore. 1976. Frame semantics and the nature of language*. *Annals of the New York Academy of Sciences* 280(1):20–32.

Yoav Goldberg and Omer Levy. 2014. word2vec explained: Deriving Mikolov et al.'s negative-sampling word-embedding method. *arXiv preprint arXiv:1402.3722 .*

Zellig S Harris. 1954. Distributional structure. *Word* 10(2-3):146–162.

Eduard Hovy, Mitchell Marcus, Martha Palmer, Lance Ramshaw, and Ralph Weischedel. 2006. Ontonotes: the 90% solution. In *Proceedings of the human language technology conference of the NAACL, Companion Volume: Short Papers.* Association for Computational Linguistics, pages 57–60.

Hans Kamp. 1979. Events, instants and temporal reference. In *Semantics from different points of view*, Springer, pages 376–418.

S. Sathiya Keerthi, Tobias Schnabel, and Rajiv Khanna. 2015. Towards a better understanding of predict and count models. *arXiv preprint arXiv:1511.0204 .*

Yoon Kim. 2014. Convolutional neural networks for sentence classification. In *Proceedings of the 2014 Conference on Empirical Methods in Natural Language Processing (EMNLP).* Association for Computational Linguistics, Doha, Qatar, pages 1746–1751. http://www.aclweb.org/anthology/D14-1181.

John D. Lafferty, Andrew McCallum, and Fernando C. N. Pereira. 2001. Conditional random fields: Probabilistic models for segmenting and labeling sequence data. In *Proceedings of the Eighteenth International Conference on Machine Learning.* Morgan Kaufmann Publishers Inc., San Francisco, CA, USA, ICML '01, pages 282–289. http://dl.acm.org/citation.cfm?id=645530.655813.

Omer Levy and Yoav Goldberg. 2014a. Dependency-based word embeddings. In *Proceedings of the 52nd Annual Meeting of the Association for Computational Linguistics (Volume 2: Short Papers).* Association for Computational Linguistics, Baltimore, Maryland, pages 302–308. http://www.aclweb.org/anthology/P14-2050.

Omer Levy and Yoav Goldberg. 2014b. Neural word embedding as implicit matrix factorization. In *Advances in neural information processing systems.* pages 2177–2185.

Tomas Mikolov, Kai Chen, Greg Corrado, and Jeffrey Dean. 2013. Efficient estimation of word representations in vector space. *arXiv preprint arXiv:1301.3781 .*

Marvin Minsky. 1974. A framework for representing knowledge. MIT-AI Laboratory Memo 306.

Martha Palmer. 2009. Semlink: Linking propbank, verbnet and framenet. In *Proceedings of the Generative Lexicon Conference.* GenLex-09, 2009 Pisa, Italy, pages 9–15.

Martha Palmer, Daniel Gildea, and Paul Kingsbury. 2005. The proposition bank: An annotated corpus of semantic roles. *Computational linguistics* 31(1):71–106.

Miriam R. L. Petruck and Gerard de Melo, editors. 2014. *Proceedings of Frame Semantics in NLP: A Workshop in Honor of Chuck Fillmore (1929-2014)*. Association for Computational Linguistics, Baltimore, MD, USA. http://www.aclweb.org/anthology/W14-30.

Pushpendre Rastogi, Benjamin Van Durme, and Raman Arora. 2015. Multiview LSA: Representation Learning via Generalized CCA. In *Proceedings of the 2015 Conference of the North American Chapter of the Association for Computational Linguistics: Human Language Technologies*. Association for Computational Linguistics, Denver, Colorado, pages 556–566. http://www.aclweb.org/anthology/N15-1058.

Drew Reisinger, Rachel Rudinger, Francis Ferraro, Craig Harman, Kyle Rawlins, and Benjamin Van Durme. 2015. Semantic proto-roles. *Transactions of the Association for Computational Linguistics (TACL)* 3:475–488.

Sascha Rothe and Hinrich Schütze. 2015. Autoextend: Extending word embeddings to embeddings for synsets and lexemes. In *Proceedings of the 53rd Annual Meeting of the Association for Computational Linguistics and the 7th International Joint Conference on Natural Language Processing (Volume 1: Long Papers)*. Association for Computational Linguistics, Beijing, China, pages 1793–1803. http://www.aclweb.org/anthology/P15-1173.

Karin Kipper Schuler. 2005. Verbnet: A broadcoverage, comprehensive verb lexicon .

Adam Teichert, Adam Poliak, Benjamin Van Durme, and Matthew Gormley. 2017. Semantic proto-role labeling. In *AAAI Conference on Artificial Intelligence*.

Yulia Tsvetkov, Manaal Faruqui, Wang Ling, Guillaume Lample, and Chris Dyer. 2015. Evaluation of word vector representations by subspace alignment. In *Proceedings of the 2015 Conference on Empirical Methods in Natural Language Processing*. Association for Computational Linguistics, Lisbon, Portugal, pages 2049–2054. http://aclweb.org/anthology/D15-1243.

Peter D Turney and Patrick Pantel. 2010. From frequency to meaning: Vector space models of semantics. *Journal of artificial intelligence research* 37:141–188.

William Yang Wang and Diyi Yang. 2015. That's so annoying!!!: A lexical and frame-semantic embedding based data augmentation approach to automatic categorization of annoying behaviors using #petpeeve tweets. In *Proceedings of the 2015 Conference on Empirical Methods in Natural Language Processing*. Association for Computational Linguistics, Lisbon, Portugal, pages 2557–2563. http://aclweb.org/anthology/D15-1306.

Aaron Steven White, Drew Reisinger, Keisuke Sakaguchi, Tim Vieira, Sheng Zhang, Rachel Rudinger, Kyle Rawlins, and Benjamin Van Durme. 2016. Universal decompositional semantics on universal dependencies. In *Proceedings of the 2016 Conference on Empirical Methods in Natural Language Processing*. Association for Computational Linguistics, Austin, Texas, pages 1713–1723. https://aclweb.org/anthology/D16-1177.

Alfred North Whitehead. 1920. *The concept of nature: the Tarner lectures delivered in Trinity College, November 1919*. Kessinger Publishing.

Travis Wolfe, Mark Dredze, and Benjamin Van Durme. 2016. A study of imitation learning methods for semantic role labeling. In *Proceedings of the Workshop on Structured Prediction for NLP*. Association for Computational Linguistics, Austin, TX, pages 44–53. http://aclweb.org/anthology/W16-5905.

Distributed Prediction of Relations for Entities:
The Easy, The Difficult, and The Impossible

Abhijeet Gupta* and **Gemma Boleda**[†] and **Sebastian Padó***
*Stuttgart University, Germany
{abhijeet.gupta,pado}@ims.uni-stuttgart.de
[†]Universitat Pompeu Fabra, Barcelona, Spain
gemma.boleda@upf.edu

Abstract

Word embeddings are supposed to provide easy access to *semantic relations* such as "male of" (*man–woman*). While this claim has been investigated for *concepts*, little is known about the distributional behavior of relations of *(Named) Entities*. We describe two word embedding-based models that predict values for relational attributes of entities, and analyse them. The task is challenging, with major performance differences between relations. Contrary to many NLP tasks, high difficulty for a relation does *not* result from low frequency, but from (a) one-to-many mappings; and (b) lack of context patterns expressing the relation that are easy to pick up by word embeddings.

1 Introduction

A central claim about distributed models of word meaning (e.g., Mikolov et al. (2013)) is that word embedding space provides easy access to *semantic relations*. E.g., Mikolov et al.'s space was shown to encode the "male-female relation" linearly, as a vector $(\overrightarrow{man} - \overrightarrow{woman} = \overrightarrow{king} - \overrightarrow{queen})$.

The accessibility of semantic relations was subsequently examined in more detail. Rei and Briscoe (2014) and Melamud et al. (2014) reported successful modeling of lexical relations such as hypernymy and synonymy. Köper et al. (2015) considered a broader range of relationships,with mixed results. Levy and Goldberg (2014b) developed an improved, nonlinear relation extraction method.

These studies were conducted primarily on *concepts* and their semantic relations, like hypernym(politician) = person. Meanwhile, *entities* and the relations they partake in are

much less well understood.[1] Entities are instances of concepts, i.e., they refer to specific individual objects in the real world, for example, *Donald Trump* is an instance of the concept *politician*. Consequently, entities are generally associated with a rich set of numeric and relational attributes (for politician instances: size, office, etc.). In contrast to concepts, the values of these attributes tend to be *discrete* (Herbelot, 2015): while the size of politician is best described by a probability distribution, the size of Donald Trump is 1.88m. Since distributional representations are notoriously bad at handling discrete knowledge (Fodor and Lepore, 1999; Smolensky, 1990), this raises the question of how well such models can capture entity-related knowledge.

In our previous work (Gupta et al., 2015), we analysed distributional prediction of *numeric* attributes of entities, found a large variance in quality among attributes, and identified factors determining prediction difficulty. A corresponding analysis for *relational (categorial) attributes* of entities is still missing, even though entities are highly relevant for NLP. This is evident from the highly active area of *knowledge base completion* (KBC), the task of extending incomplete entity information in knowledge bases such as Yago or Wikidata (e.g., Bordes et al., 2013; Freitas et al., 2014; Neelakantan and Chang, 2015; Guu et al., 2015; Krishnamurthy and Mitchell, 2015).

In this paper, we assess to what extent *relational attributes of entities* are easily accessible from word embedding space. To this end, we define two models that predict, given a target entity (Star_Wars) and a relation (director), a distributed representation for the relatum (George_Lucas). We carry out a detailed per-relation analyses of their performance on seven

---

[1]The original dataset by Mikolov et al. (2013) did contain a small number of entity-entity relations.

*Proceedings of the 6th Joint Conference on Lexical and Computational Semantics (*SEM 2017)*, pages 104–109,
Vancouver, Canada, August 3-4, 2017. ©2017 Association for Computational Linguistics

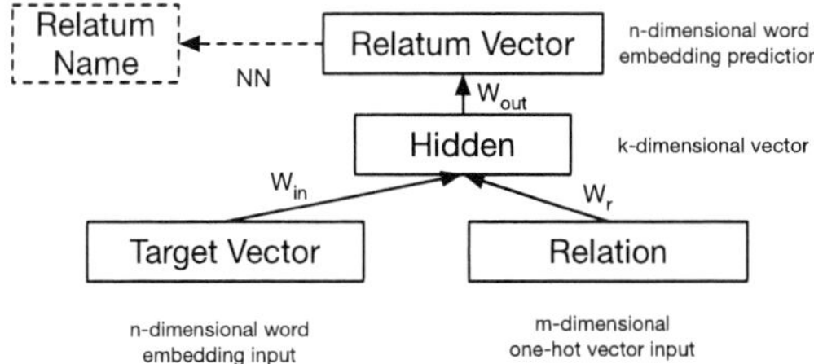

Figure 1: Nonlinear model (NonLinM) structure

major FreeBase domains and identify what makes a relation difficult by correlating performance with properties of the relations. We find that, contrary to many other NLP tasks, relations are *not* difficult if they are infrequent or sparse, but instead (a) if they relate one target to multiple relata; (b) if they do not give rise to linguistic patterns that can be picked up by bag-of-words distributional models.

2 Two Relatum Prediction Models

Both models predict a vector for a *relatum r* (plural: *relata*) given a *target entity* vector t and a symbolic *relation* ρ.

The Linear Model (LinM) is inspired by Mikolov et al.'s "phrase analogy" evaluation of word embeddings ($\overrightarrow{man} - \overrightarrow{woman} = \overrightarrow{king} - \overrightarrow{queen}$). However, instead of looking at individual words, we extract representations of semantic relations from sets of pairs $T_\rho = \{(t_i, \rho, r_i)\}$ instantiating the relation ρ. For each relation ρ, LinM computes the average (or centroid) difference vector over the set of training pairs:

$$\hat{r}(t, \rho) = t + \sum_{(r,\rho,t)\in T_\rho} (r - t)/N \qquad (1)$$

That is, the predicted $\hat{r}$ for an input (t, ρ) is the sum of the target vector and the relation's prototype. This model should work well if relations are represented additively in the embedding space.

The Nonlinear Model (NonLinM) is a feedforward network (Figure 1) introducing a nonlinearity, inspired by Levy and Goldberg (2014b) and similar to models used in KBC, e.g., Socher et al. (2013). The relatum vector is predicted as

$$\hat{r}_\theta(t, \rho) = \sigma(\sigma(t \cdot W_{in} + v_\rho \cdot W_r) \cdot W_{out}) \qquad (2)$$

where v_ρ is the relation encoded as an m-dimensional one-hot vector and the three matrices

W_{in}, W_r, W_{out} form the model parameters θ. For the nonlinearity σ, we use $tanh$.

In this model, the hidden layer represents a non-linearly transformed composition of target and relation from which the relatum can be predicted. NonLinM can theoretically make accurate predictions even if relations are not additive in embedding space. Also, its sharing of training data among relations should lead to more reliable learning for infrequent relations. As objective function, we use

$$L(\theta) = \sum_{(t,r)} [\cos(\hat{r}_\theta(t, \rho), r)$$
$$- \alpha \cdot \cos(\hat{r}_\theta(t, \rho), nc(\hat{r}_\theta(t, \rho)))] \qquad (3)$$

where $nc(v)$ is the *nearest confounder* of v, i.e., the next neighbor of v that is not a relatum for the current target-relation pair. Thus, we minimize the cosine distance between the predicted vector and the gold vector for the relatum while maximizing the cosine distance of the prediction to the closest negative example. We introduce a weight $\alpha \in [0, 1]$ for the negative sampling term as a hyper-parameter optimized on the development set. During training, we apply gradient descent with the adaptive learning rate method AdaDelta (Zeiler, 2012).

3 Experiments

Data. We extract relation data from FreeBase. We follow our earlier work Gupta et al. (2015), but go beyond its limitation to two domains (`country`, `citytown`). We experiment with seven major FreeBase domains: `animal`, `book`, `citytown`, `country`, `employer`, `organization`, `people`. We limit the number of datapoints of very large relation types to 3000 with random sampling for efficiency reasons. We only remove relation types with fewer than 3 datapoints. This results in a quite challenging dataset that demonstrates the generalizability of our models and is roughly comparable, in variety and size, to the FB15K dataset (Bordes et al., 2013).

The distributed representations for all entities come from the 1000-dimensional "Google News" skip-gram model (Mikolov et al., 2013) for FreeBase entities[2] trained on a 100G token news corpus. We only retain relation datapoints where both target and relatum are covered in the Google News vectors. Table 1 shows the numbers of relations and unique objects (target plus relata).

---

[2] https://code.google.com/p/word2vec/

Domain	Size		Performance			Relation-level statistics			
	#R	#Ts+Ra.	BL	LM	NLM	%R>0.3	%R<0.1	ρ(NLM, #In)	ρ(NLM, #RpT)
`animal`	24	3,428	0.11	0.16	**0.29**	38%	42%	.07	-.34
`book`	22	7,014	0.11	0.24	**0.26**	9%	68%	.09	-.15
`citytown`	46	86,551	0.05	0.13	**0.26**	28%	39%	-.12	-.22
`country`	89	191,196	0.04	0.08	**0.18**	20%	52%	-.32	-.23
`employer`	76	14,658	0.05	0.15	**0.23**	30%	45%	.01	-.35
`organization`	53	8,989	0.07	0.17	**0.26**	34%	42%	-.24	-.29
`people`	91	11,397	0.09	0.19	**0.27**	34%	23%	.23	-.25
Micro average			0.06	0.14	**0.22**	25%	45%	-.12	-.25
Macro average			0.08	0.16	**0.23**	28%	44%	-.05	-.26

Table 1: Test set statistics and results. #R: relations; #Ts+Ra: unique targets and relata; BL/LM/NLM: Baseline, linear and nonlinear model (macro-average MRR); %R$\leqslant$x: percent of relations with MRR $\leqslant$x; ρ: Spearman correlation; #In: instances; #RpT: relata per target

We split all domains into training, validation, and test sets (60%–20%–20%). The split applies to each relation type: in test, we face no unseen relation types, but unseen datapoints for each relation.[3]

Hyperparameter settings. The NonLinM model uses an L_2 norm constraint of $s=3$. We adopt the best AdaDelta parameters from Zeiler (2012), viz. $\rho = 0.95$ and $\epsilon = 10^{-6}$. We optimize the negative sampling weight α (cf. Eq. 3) by line search with a step size of 0.1 on the largest domain, `country`, and find 0.6 to be the optimal value, which we reuse for all domains. Due to the varying dimensionality m of the relation vector per domain, we set the size of the hidden layer to $k = 2n + m/10$ (n is the dimensionality of the word embeddings, cf. Figure 1). We train all models for a maximum of 1000 epochs with early stopping.

Evaluation. Models that predict vectors in a continuous vector space, like ours, cannot expect to predict the output vector precisely. Thus, we apply *nearest neighbor mapping* using the set of all unique targets and relata in each domain (cf. Table 1) to identify the correct relatum name. We then perform an Information Retrieval-style ranking evaluation: We compute the rank of the correct relatum r, given the target t and the relation ρ, in the test set T and aggregate these ranks to compute the *mean reciprocal rank* (MRR):

$$MRR = \frac{1}{||T||} \sum_{(t,\rho,r)\in T} \frac{1}{rank_{t,\rho}(r)} \qquad (4)$$

where $rank$ is the nearest neighbor rank of the relatum vector r given the prediction of the model

---

[3]The dataset are available at: http://www.ims.uni-stuttgart.de/data/RelationPrediction.html

for the input t, ρ. We report results at the relation level as well as macro- and micro-averaged MRR for the complete dataset.

Frequency Baseline (BL). Our baseline model ignores the target. For each relation, it predicts the frequency-ordered list of all training set relata.

4 Results and Discussion

Overall results. Table 1 shows that the nonlinear model NonLinM consistently gives the best results and statistically outperforms the linear model on all domains according to a Wilcoxon test ($\alpha=0.05$). Both LinM and NonLinM clearly outclass the baseline. Most MRRs are around 0.25 (micro average 0.22), with one outlier, at 0.18, for `country`, the largest domain. Overall, the numbers may appear disappointing at first glance: these MRRs mean that the correct relatum is typically around the fourth nearest neighbor of the prediction vector. This indicates that open-vocabulary relatum prediction in a space of tens of thousands of words is a challenging task that warrants more detailed analysis. We observe that the nonlinear model achieves reasonable results even for sparse domains (cf. the low baseline), which we take as evidence for its generalization capabilities.

Analysis at relation level. Table 1 shows the number of relations with good MRRs (greater than 0.3) and bad MRRs (smaller than 0.1) for each relation. While the numbers vary across domains, the models tend to do badly on around 40-50% of all relations, and obtain good scores for less than one third of all relations.

Figure 2 shows the distribution for the best domain (`animal`) and the worst one (`country`). Both plots show a Zipfian distribution with a rel-

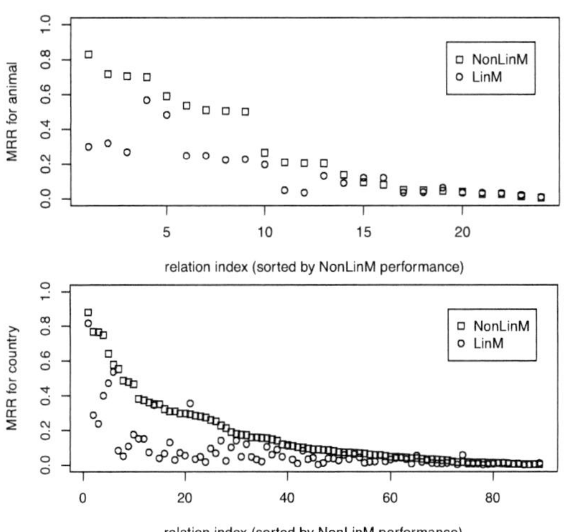

Figure 2: Results by relation for best and worst domains (`animal`, above; `people`, below), sorted by NonLinM performance

	Target	Correct	LinM	NonLinM
continent	Japan	Asia	Japan	**Asia**
	Kazakhstan	Asia	Central Asia	**Asia**
	Nicaragua	North America	Latin America	Americas
capital	Nepal	Kathmandu	Nepal	Dhaka
	Qatar	Doha	Qatar	Riyadh
	Venezuela	Caracas	**Caracas**	Quito

Table 2: Example predictions for two `country` relations (correct answer in boldface)

atively small set of well-modelled relations and a long tail of poorly modelled ones. NonLinM does better or as well as LinM for almost all relations. The performances of the two models are very tightly correlated for difficult relations; they only differ for the easier ones, where NonLinM's evidently captures the data better.

Qualitatively, the two models differ substantially with regard to prediction patterns at the level of targets. Table 2 shows the first predictions for three targets from two relations: `continent`, where NonLinM outperforms LinM, and `capital`, where it is the other way around. NonLinM's errors consist almost exclusively in predicting semantically similar entities of the correct relatum type, e.g., predicting Quito (the capital of Ecuador) as capital of Venezuela. In contrast, the LinM model has a harder time capturing the correct type, predicting country entities as capitals (e.g., Nepal as the capital of Nepal).

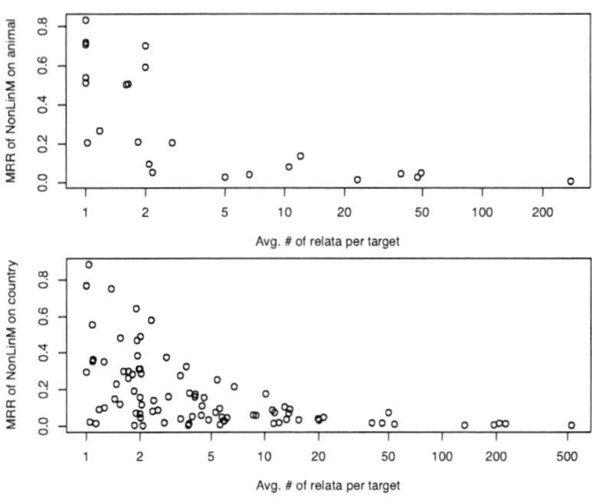

Figure 3: Scatterplot: MRR vs. number of relata per target (above: `animal`, below: `country`)

Analysis of Difficulty. So what makes many FreeBase relations hard to model? To test for sparsity problems, we first computed the correlation between model performance and the "usual suspect" relation frequency (number of instances for each relation). In NLP applications, this typically yields a high positive correlation. The second-to-last column of Table 1 shows that this is not true for our dataset. We find a substantial positive correlation only for `people`, correlations around zero for most domains, and substantial negative ones for `organization` and `country`. For these domains, therefore, frequent relations are actually *harder* to model. Further analysis revealed two main sources of difficulty:

(1) One-to-many relations. Relations with many datapoints tend to be *one-to-many*. We assume this to be a major source of difficulty, since the model is presented with multiple relata for the same target during training and will typically learn to predict a centroid of these relata. As an extreme case, consider a relation like `administrative_divisions` that relates the US to all of its federal states: the resulting prediction will arguably be dissimilar to every individual state. To test this hypothesis, we computed the rank correlation at the relation level between the number of relata per target and NonLinM performance, shown in the last column of Table 1. Indeed, we find a strong negative correlation for every single domain. In addition, Figure 3 plots relation performance (y axis) against the ratio of relata per target (x axis: one-to-one on the left, one-to-many on the right) for `animal` and `country`.

Qualitatively, Table 3 shows examples for the three most easy and difficult relations for `country`. The list suggests that relations tend to be easy when they associate targets with single relata: the relation `country` maps territories and colonies onto their motherlands, and the `tournaments` relation is only populated with a few Commonwealth games (cf. the high baseline). In contrast, relations that map targets on many relata are difficult, such as administrative `divisions` of countries, or a list of `disputed_territories`. Note that this is not an evaluation issue, since MRR can deal with multiple correct answers. Our models do badly because they lack strategies to address these cases.

(2) Lack of contextual support. One-to-many relations are not the only culprit. Strikingly, Figure 2 shows that a low target-relatum ratio is a *necessary* condition for good performance (the upper right corners are empty), but not a *sufficient* one (the lower left corners are not empty). Some relations are not modelled well even though they are (almost) one-to-one. Examples include `currency_formerly_used` or `named_after` for `country` and `place_of_origin` for `animal`. Further analysis indicated that these relations suffer from what Gupta et al. (2015) called *lack of contextual support*: Although they are expressed overtly in the linguistic context of the target and relatum (and often even frequently so), their realizations cannot be tied to individual words or topics. Instead, they are expressed by relatively specific linguistic patterns, often predicate-argument structures (*X used to pay with Y, X is named in the honor of Y*). Such structures are hard to pick up by word embedding models that make the bag-of-words independence assumption among context words.

5 Conclusion

This paper considers the prediction of related entities ("relata") given a pair of a target Named Entity and a relation (`Star Wars, director, ?`) on the basis of distributional information. This task is challenging due to the more discrete behavior of attributes of entities as compared to concepts. We provide an analysis based on two models that use vector representations for both the targets and the relata.

Our results yield new insights into how embedding spaces represent entity relations: they are generally not represented additively, and nonlinearity helps. They also complement insights on the be-

Relation	BL	LinM	NonLinM
tournaments	0.88	0.82	0.88
continent	0.29	0.29	0.77
country	0.25	0.24	0.77
⋮			
disputed_territories	0.00	0.01	0.01
horses_from_here	0.00	0.01	0.01
2nd_level_divisions	0.00	0.00	0.01

Table 3: The three most easy and most difficult relations for the `country` domain

havior of numeric attributes of entities (Gupta et al., 2015): Relations, like numeric attributes, are difficult to model if they are not specifically expressed in the lingusitic context of target and relatum. A new challenge specific to relations are situations where a single target maps onto many relata. If none of the two problems applies, relations are *easy* to model. If one applies, they are *difficult*. And if both apply, they are essentially *impossible*.

Among the two challenges, the problem of one-to-many relations appears easier to address, since a continuous output vector is, at least in principle, able to be similar to many relata. In the future, we will extend the model to deal better with one-to-many relations. While the lack of contextual support seems more fundamental, it could be addressed by either using syntax-based embeddings (Levy and Goldberg, 2014a) that can better pick up the specific context patterns characteristic for these relations, or by optimizing the input word embeddings for the task. This becomes a similar problem to joint training of representations from knowledge base structure and textual evidence (Perozzi et al., 2014; Toutanova et al., 2015).

Acknowledgements

This project has received funding from the European Research Council (ERC) under the European Union's Horizon 2020 research and innovation programme (grant agreement No 715154) and the DFG (SFB 732, Project D10). This paper reflects the authors' view only, and the EU is not responsible for any use that may be made of the information it contains.

References

Antoine Bordes, Nicolas Usunier, Alberto Garcia-Duran, Jason Weston, and Oksana Yakhnenko.

2013. Translating embeddings for modeling multi-relational data. In *Proceedings of Neural Information Processing Systems 26*. pages 2787–2795.

Jerry Fodor and Ernie Lepore. 1999. All at Sea in Semantic Space: Churchland on Meaning Similarity. *Journal of Philosophy* 96(8):381–403.

André Freitas, Joao Carlos Pereira da Silva, Edward Curry, and Paul Buitelaar. 2014. A distributional semantics approach for selective reasoning on commonsense graph knowledge bases. In *Natural Language Processing and Information Systems*, Springer, pages 21–32.

Abhijeet Gupta, Gemma Boleda, Marco Baroni, and Sebastian Padó. 2015. Distributional vectors encode referential attributes. In *Proceedings of the 2015 Conference on Empirical Methods in Natural Language Processing*. Lisbon, Portugal, pages 12–21.

Kelvin Guu, John Miller, and Percy Liang. 2015. Traversing knowledge graphs in vector space. In *Proceedings of the 2015 Conference on Empirical Methods in Natural Language Processing*. Lisbon, Portugal, pages 318–327.

Aurélie Herbelot. 2015. Mr Darcy and Mr Toad, gentlemen: Distributional names and their kinds. *Proceedings of the 11th International Conference on Computational Semantics* pages 151–161.

Maximilian Köper, Christian Scheible, and Sabine Schulte im Walde. 2015. Multilingual Reliability and "Semantic" Structure of Continuous Word Spaces. In *Proceedings of the 11th Conference on Computational Semantics*. London, UK, pages 40–45.

Jayant Krishnamurthy and Tom M Mitchell. 2015. Learning a compositional semantics for freebase with an open predicate vocabulary. *Transactions of the Association for Computational Linguistics* 3:257–270.

Omer Levy and Yoav Goldberg. 2014a. Dependency-based word embeddings. In *Proceedings of the 52nd Annual Meeting of the Association for Computational Linguistics*. Baltimore, Maryland, pages 302–308.

Omer Levy and Yoav Goldberg. 2014b. Linguistic regularities in sparse and explicit word representations. In *Proceedings of the Eighteenth Conference on Computational Natural Language Learning*. Ann Arbor, Michigan, pages 171–180.

Oren Melamud, Ido Dagan, Jacob Goldberger, Idan Szpektor, and Deniz Yuret. 2014. Probabilistic modeling of joint-context in distributional similarity. In *Proceedings of the Eighteenth Conference on Computational Natural Language Learning*. Ann Arbor, Michigan, pages 181–190.

Tomas Mikolov, Ilya Sutskever, Kai Chen, Greg S Corrado, and Jeff Dean. 2013. Distributed representations of words and phrases and their compositionality. In *Advances in Neural Information Processing Systems*. Lake Tahoe, NV, pages 3111–3119.

Arvind Neelakantan and Ming-Wei Chang. 2015. Inferring missing entity type instances for knowledge base completion: New dataset and methods. In *Proceedings of the North American Chapter of the Association for Computational Linguistics*. Denver, CO, pages 515–525.

Bryan Perozzi, Rami Al-Rfou, and Steven Skiena. 2014. Deepwalk: Online learning of social representations. In *Proceedings of the 20th ACM SIGKDD international conference on Knowledge discovery and data mining*. ACM, New York City, NY, pages 701–710.

Marek Rei and Ted Briscoe. 2014. Looking for hyponyms in vector space. In *Proceedings of the Eighteenth Conference on Computational Natural Language Learning*. Ann Arbor, Michigan, pages 68–77.

Paul Smolensky. 1990. Tensor product variable binding and the representation of symbolic structures in connectionist systems. *Artificial Intelligence* 46(1-2):159–216.

Richard Socher, Danqi Chen, Christopher D Manning, and Andrew Ng. 2013. Reasoning with neural tensor networks for knowledge base completion. In *Advances in Neural Information Processing Systems*. Lake Tahoe, CA, pages 926–934.

Kristina Toutanova, Danqi Chen, Patrick Pantel, Pallavi Choudhury, and Michael Gamon. 2015. Representing text for joint embedding of text and knowledge bases. In *Proceedings of EMNLP*. Lisbon, Portugal, pages 1499–1509.

Matthew D. Zeiler. 2012. Adadelta: An adaptive learning rate method. In *CoRR, abs/1212.5701*.

Comparing Approaches for Automatic Question Identification

Angel Samsuddin Maredia, Kara Schechtman, Sarah Ita Levitan, Julia Hirschberg

Department of Computer Science, Columbia University, USA

asm2221@columbia.edu, kws2121@columbia.edu,
sarahita@cs.columbia.edu, julia@cs.columbia.edu

Abstract

Collecting spontaneous speech corpora that are open-ended, yet topically constrained, is increasingly popular for research in spoken dialogue systems and speaker state, inter alia. Typically, these corpora are labeled by human annotators, either in the lab or through crowdsourcing; however, this is cumbersome and time-consuming for large corpora. We present four different approaches to automatically tagging a corpus when general topics of the conversations are known. We develop these approaches on the Columbia X-Cultural Deception corpus and find accuracy that significantly exceeds the baseline. Finally, we conduct a cross-corpus evaluation by testing the best performing approach on the Columbia/SRI/Colorado corpus.

1 Introduction

Corpora of spontaneous speech are often collected through interviews or by otherwise providing subjects with question prompts. Such corpora are semi-structured; they are constrained by the prompts used, but the elicited speech is open-ended in vocabulary and structure. It is often desirable to segment these corpora into their underlying topics based on the questions asked. This is typically done manually by annotators in the lab or via crowd-sourcing. However, such annotation is impractical and time-consuming for large corpora.

In this paper we describe a set of experiments aimed at automatically tagging a large corpus with topic labels. We tag the Columbia X-Cultural Deception (CXD) corpus, a large-scale (120-hour) corpus of deceptive and non-deceptive dialogues collected using a semi-structured inter-

view paradigm. Participants took turns interviewing each other using a fixed set of biographical interview questions[1], but the questions were asked in individual variants, in any order, and interviewers often asked follow-up questions. For example, the question, "Are your parents divorced?" could be produced as "Are your mom and dad still together?" These questions are semantically similar, but differ lexically, presenting the challenge of topically tagging a corpus based on semantic similarity. The question, "Have you ever broken a bone?" could be followed by another, "How did you break your bone?" This illustrates the challenge of distinguishing between phrases that are lexically similar, but differ semantically. These two examples highlight problems faced when trying to automatically annotate a corpus for responses to a given set of questions.

With such a large corpus, it is not practical to manually annotate topic boundaries. So, to compare question responses from multiple subjects, we identify conversational turns in the corpus that correspond to the original interview questions. We compare four approaches to question identification: (1) a baseline approach that identifies questions using strict string matches, (2) the ROUGE metric which is based on n-gram comparisons, (3) cosine similarity between word embedding representations and (4) cosine similarity between document embeddings. We include experiments with varying thresholds for approaches (2), (3), and (4) to highlight the trade-off between precision and recall for these approaches. Finally, we test our best approach using word embeddings on another corpus, the Columbia/SRI/Colorado (CSC) corpus (Hirschberg et al., 2005), collected with a similar interview paradigm but different questions, in order to evaluate the utility of this method in another

---

[1]The interview questions can be found here: http://tinyurl.com/lzfa8zl

*Proceedings of the 6th Joint Conference on Lexical and Computational Semantics (*SEM 2017)*, pages 110–114,
Vancouver, Canada, August 3-4, 2017. ©2017 Association for Computational Linguistics

domain.

This work draws upon the body of research on short-text semantic similarity (e.g. (Mihalcea et al., 2006; Kenter and de Rijke, 2015; Oliva et al., 2011)). It is also related to work on topic segmentation (e.g. (Cardoso et al., 2013; Dias et al., 2007)), however here we focus on matching conversational turns to a fixed set of possible topics. While this work is done in support of our ongoing work on deception detection using speech and text-based features, we believe that our approach could be applied to other spontaneous transcribed speech or text corpora which were collected with some constraints on topics.

2   Corpus

The Columbia X-Cultural Deception (CXD) Corpus (Levitan et al., 2015) is a collection of within-subject deceptive and non-deceptive speech from native speakers of Standard American English (SAE) and Mandarin Chinese (MC), all speaking in English. The corpus contains dialogues between 340 subjects. A variation of a fake resume paradigm was used to collect the data. Previously unacquainted pairs of subjects played a "lying game" with each other. Each subject filled out a 24-item biographical questionnaire and were instructed to create false answers for a random half of the questions. The lying game was recorded in a sound booth. For the first half of the game, one subject assumed the role of the interviewer, while the other answered the biographical questions, lying for half and telling the truth for the other; questions chosen in each category were balanced across the corpus. For the second half of the game, the subjects roles were reversed, and the interviewer became the interviewee. During the game, the interviewer was allowed to ask the 24 questions in any order s/he chose; the interviewer was also encouraged to ask follow-up questions to aid them in determining the truth of the interviewees answers. The entire corpus was orthographically transcribed using the Amazon Mechanical Turk (AMT)[2] crowd-sourcing platform, and transcripts were forced-aligned with the audio recordings. The speech was then automatically segmented into *inter-pausal units* (IPUs), defined as pause-free segments of speech separated by a minimum pause length of 50 ms. The speech was also segmented into turn units, where a turn is de-

___

[2]https://www.mturk.com/mturk/

fined as a maximal sequence of IPUs from a single speaker without any interlocutor speech that is not a *backchannel* (a simple acknowledgment that is not an attempt to take the turn). For this work, we compiled 40 interviewer sessions (about 20% of the corpus) and hand-annotated the turns for all of these sessions, giving us a total of 5308 turns. Out of these turns, 923 were interviewer questions that corresponded to the list of the original biographical questions, which we labeled with the question number. Below we describe the different approaches and then discuss results in Section 4 with a comparison of performance in Table 1.

3   Question Identification Approaches

3.1   String-matching Baseline

As a baseline for matching the 24 questions interviewers were instructed to ask with interviewer turns, we performed a simple two-pass question matching procedure for exact string matches between written questions and the transcripts. In the first pass, we searched for exact matches of strings with punctuation and spacing removed. With the remaining unmatched questions, we then performed another round of matching, with the transcript lemmatized and with filler words removed, to identify very close though not exact matches.

3.2   ROUGE

ROUGE (Recall-Oriented Understudy for Gisting Evaluation)(Lin, 2004) is a package designed to evaluate computer-generated summaries against a human-written baseline using a simple n-gram comparison to find precision, recall, and f-score for each machine-human summary comparison. Using ROUGE, we evaluated matches for questions which had not been detected by the baseline. We created a ROUGE task for each unmatched question. For each task, the original question was used as the reference text. We then tested each interviewer turn in the conversation against the reference, using bi-gram matching. We thus matched the turn receiving the highest similarity score to the reference text to that question, testing this method at a variety of similarity thresholds.

3.3   Word Embeddings

The previous two methods identify questions using lexical similarity. In the next two approaches we explored semantic similarity. We began by obtaining a vector representation for each of the

24 questions. We use a pre-trained Word2vec model on the Google News dataset[3] with over three million words and phrases to obtain word embeddings. The primary benefit of a Word2vec model is that it clusters semantically similar words and phrases together: for example, "Golden Gate Bridge" and "San Francisco" have very low cosine distance between each other in this model. Therefore, semantically similar words were likely to be represented as vectors with high cosine similarity.

To obtain a vector representation for each question as a whole, we found the vector representation for each word using Word2vec. We then took a weighted average of all of the word vectors in the question where words that directly contributed to the topic of the turn such as "relationship" or "mom" were weighed more than words that, if removed, did not affect the topic of the turn such as "have" or "really." This produced a final vector representation of the entire question. We exclude stop words from this vector average. Following the same approach, we obtained vector representations for each interviewer turn. We then calculated the cosine similarities between a turn and each question and found the question that had the highest cosine similarity to the turn vector. We compared the cosine similarity of the turn and the question to the cosine similarity of any previous identified matches. If the newly calculated cosine similarity was higher, then the current turn was deemed the best match so far to the question, otherwise we repeated this comparison with the question that had the second highest cosine similarity to the turn. At the end of each particular interviewer session, we had a mapping of each turn to a question if a match was detected, otherwise the turn was marked as not being a question.

3.4 Document Embeddings

We also explored the use of document embeddings for this task. We began by finding a vector representation for each of the 24 questions. We used a Doc2vec model pre-trained on Wikipedia text[4]. Recall that, in our paradigm, questions could be asked in individual variants, in any order, and along with follow-up questions. The primary benefit of a Doc2Vec model is that it allows for unsupervised learning of larger blocks of text. There-

fore, we hypothesized that Doc2Vec would return word vectors that also depended on contextual usage as well as semantic similarity. We then calculated the vector averages for each turn and produced turn-to-question mappings as explained in the word embeddings approach above.

4 Results

Table 1 shows the accuracy, precision, recall, and f1-score of each of the four approaches outlined above, evaluated on our hand-labeled subset of interviews. We see that the word embeddings method achieved the highest accuracy, recall, and f1-score of all the methods developed and tested, whereas the ROUGE approach obtained the highest precision. With the word embeddings approach, most correctly identified turns share one or more meaningful words with the corresponding original question and are often syntactically very similar. This approach, however, is able to make ambiguous matches as well. For example, an interviewer turn said, "wow you broke you broke your hand when you were in elementary school wow i yeah i get so student hate to do homework so have you ever tweet tweeted." This turn shares meaningful words with many other questions, but this approach correctly identified it as matching the question Have you ever tweeted? The word embeddings approach could also make difficult semantic matches. Many interviewers asked, "Are your mom and dad still together?" instead of "Are your parents divorced?" Even though there are few lexically common meaningful words between these two phrases, this approach correctly mapped these questions to each other because of their semantic similarity. One of the main causes of error for this method is that follow-up questions were sometimes mis-identified as original questions. For example, "How do you like your major?" could be mapped to the original question, "If you attended college, what was your major?" even though the question the interviewer asked was a follow-up question.

We also analyzed the accuracy of the methodologies using varying thresholds. For word embeddings and document embeddings, the threshold is determined by cosine similarity of a turn and question. For ROUGE, the threshold is the f1-score. For each approach, We compiled a set of turns from the CXD corpus that had the lowest cosine similarity to the question each turn was

---

[3] The model can be found here: `https://code.google.com/archive/p/word2vec/`

[4] The model can be found here: `https://github.com/jhlau/doc2vec`

Approach	Accuracy	Precision	Recall	F1-Score
Baseline (Rule-based)	39.0	72.0	42.0	53.1
ROUGE	74.0	**93.0**	78.0	84.8
Word Embeddings	**91.4**	92.1	**99.1**	**95.5**
Document Embeddings	88.6	90.0	98.2	93.9

Table 1: Accuracy, precision, and recall of each approach, evaluated on hand annotated turns

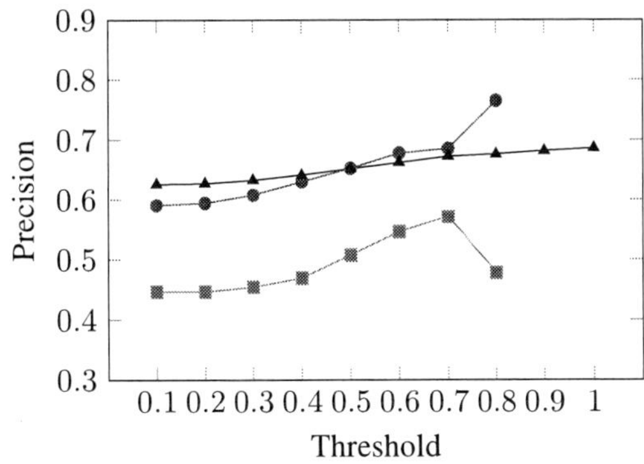

Figure 1: Accuracy of each approach determined by threshold. Filled in dots are word embeddings. Squares represent document embeddings. Triangles represent ROUGE.

matched with. We capped the threshold at 0.82. Figure 1 shows that, as we increase the threshold, generally, the accuracy of the question matching for all approaches is higher. This, intuitively, makes sense because, as we increase the threshold, we are selecting turns that have higher similarity to their matched question. Although this results in lower recall, it can be used in cases where high precision is needed for annotations.

4.1 Cross-corpus Evaluation

To further evaluate our best-performing approach, we applied the word embeddings method to another corpus collected using a similar interview paradigm, the Columbia SRI Colorado (CSC) corpus. To test word embeddings on this corpus, we compiled 31 interviewer sessions that were already hand annotated, giving us a total of 6395 turns. The (single) interviewer involving in collecting this corpus always began with a list of four standard biographical questions, thus reducing the number of turns that contained an interviewer-generated question to 114. Following the word embeddings method described above, we obtained an accuracy of 99.8%, precision of 91.2%, recall of 100%, and F1-score of 95.3 on the CSC corpus.

The incorrectly identified questions were largely because the interviewer did not ask all four biographical questions in every session, while the word embeddings approach assumes that all questions were asked and therefore, matches some turn to the original question even though the interviewer did not ask it. The higher accuracy obtained on the CSC corpus is probably due to the fact that the interviews were all conducted by a single interviewer, so the questions were asked with greater consistency. In addition, all subjects were native speakers of Standard American English, while half the participants in the CXD corpus were native speakers of Mandarin Chinese.

5 Conclusion

Corpora consisting of spontaneous speech that is open-ended, yet topically constrained, is more commonplace, as researchers seek spontaneous speech with some similarity of topic across subjects. Traditionally, such corpora are hand annotated for topic segments to serve as training material. However, on large corpora such as the CXD corpus, this can be cumbersome and time-consuming. In this paper, we have presented four approaches to automatically identifying question topics on the CXD corpus to discover which approach achieves the best results in automatically tagging corpora into question-defined topics. We found that the word embeddings approach was the best performing approach with an f1-score of 95.5%. We then applied the word embeddings approach to the CSC corpus to verify that this approach was useful for other corpora and also achieved very good results. We conclude that this automated, unsupervised approach to tagging corpora can be very useful in annotation and analysis for corpora collected using question prompts. For more exact annotations, this approach could also be used as an automated pre-processing stage to reduce human annotation efforts. In future, we would like to extend the embeddings approach to scale to less constrained tasks, evaluate it on additional corpora, and also more accurately tag corpora based on an ambiguous number of topics.

References

Paula CF Cardoso, Maite Taboada, and Thiago AS Pardo. 2013. Subtopics annotation in a corpus of news texts: steps towards automatic subtopic segmentation. In *Proceedings of the Brazilian Symposium in Information and Human Language Technology*.

Gaël Dias, Elsa Alves, and José Gabriel Pereira Lopes. 2007. Topic segmentation algorithms for text summarization and passage retrieval: An exhaustive evaluation. In *AAAI*. volume 7, pages 1334–1340.

Julia Hirschberg, Stefan Benus, Jason M Brenier, Frank Enos, Sarah Friedman, Sarah Gilman, Cynthia Girand, Martin Graciarena, Andreas Kathol, Laura Michaelis, et al. 2005. Distinguishing deceptive from non-deceptive speech. In *Interspeech*. pages 1833–1836.

Tom Kenter and Maarten de Rijke. 2015. Short text similarity with word embeddings. In *Proceedings of the 24th ACM International on Conference on Information and Knowledge Management*. ACM, pages 1411–1420.

Sarah I Levitan, Guzhen An, Mandi Wang, Gideon Mendels, Julia Hirschberg, Michelle Levine, and Andrew Rosenberg. 2015. Cross-cultural production and detection of deception from speech. In *Proceedings of the 2015 ACM on Workshop on Multimodal Deception Detection*. ACM, pages 1–8.

Chin-Yew Lin. 2004. Rouge: A package for automatic evaluation of summaries. In *Text summarization branches out: Proceedings of the ACL-04 workshop*. Barcelona, Spain, volume 8.

Rada Mihalcea, Courtney Corley, Carlo Strapparava, et al. 2006. Corpus-based and knowledge-based measures of text semantic similarity. In *AAAI*. volume 6, pages 775–780.

Jesús Oliva, José Ignacio Serrano, María Dolores del Castillo, and Ángel Iglesias. 2011. Symss: A syntax-based measure for short-text semantic similarity. *Data & Knowledge Engineering* 70(4):390–405.

Does Free Word Order Hurt?
Assessing the Practical Lexical Function Model for Croatian

Zoran Medić*   Jan Šnajder*   Sebastian Padó†
* Faculty of Electrical Engineering and Computing, University of Zagreb
`{jan.snajder, zoran.medic}@fer.hr`
† Institut für Maschinelle Sprachverarbeitung, Stuttgart University
`pado@ims.uni-stuttgart.de`

Abstract

The Practical Lexical Function (PLF) model is a model of computational distributional semantics that attempts to strike a balance between expressivity and learnability in predicting phrase meaning and shows competitive results. We investigate how well the PLF carries over to free word order languages, given that it builds on observations of predicate-argument combinations that are harder to recover in free word order languages. We evaluate variants of the PLF for Croatian, using a new lexical substitution dataset. We find that the PLF works about as well for Croatian as for English, but demonstrate that its strength lies in modeling verbs, and that the free word order affects the less robust PLF variant.

1   Introduction

Compositional distributional semantic models (CDSMs) represent phrase meaning in a vector space by composing the meanings of individual words. Many CDSMs were proposed, ranging from basic ones that use element-wise operations on word vectors to compute phrase vectors (Mitchell and Lapata, 2008), to more complex models that represent predicate arguments as higher-order tensors (Baroni and Zamparelli, 2010; Guevara, 2010). The latter models assume that predicates in a phrase act as functions that act on other phrase components to yield the final representation of the phrase. For example, an adjective acts as a function on the noun in an adjective-noun phrase, while a transitive verb acts as a binary function on its subject and object. However, since the number of parameters in a tensor grows exponentially with the number of arguments of the function that it models, learning full tensors for predicates with many arguments is

tedious to impractical (Grefenstette et al., 2012).

The Practical Lexical Function model (PLF, Paperno et al. (2014)) strikes a middle ground by breaking down all tensors with ranks higher than two into multiple matrices, each representing the predicate's composition with a single argument (cf. Section 2 for details). In the experiments of Paperno et al. (2014), PLF has been shown to work better than some other CDSMs in modeling semantic similarity. Particularly good results were obtained on ANVAN (adjective-noun-verb-adjective-noun) phrases, where PLF outperformed both simple CDSMs (due to its higher expressiveness) as well as the higher-order Lexical Function model (Baroni and Zamparelli, 2010).

Although the PLF shows promising results, existing work still leaves open two questions. First, it is not obvious that these results carry over to languages with free word order, such as Slavic languages, where predicates and arguments are often separated. For example, in the English sentence *'I like my dog'*, the predicate is adjacent to both the subject and the object, while in the Croatian translation *'Sviđa mi se moj pas'*, the object *'moj pas'* is separated from the predicate. As corpus-derived vectors for predicate-argument combinations are a key part of the PLF, non-adjacency might make it difficult to estimate its parameters reliably for such languages. Secondly, the evaluation method reported by Paperno et al. (2014) uses a somewhat artificial setup by assuming that all phrase pairs, even ill-formed ones, can be graded for similarity.

In this work we consider both of these questions. We investigate the application of PLF to Croatian language, a Slavic language with relatively free word order. We compare PLF with other, simpler CDSMs, as well as PLF modifications proposed by Gupta et al. (2015). In contrast to Paperno et al. (2014), we adopt lexical substitution as evaluation, building a new dataset of Croatian ANVAN phrases,

*Proceedings of the 6th Joint Conference on Lexical and Computational Semantics (*SEM 2017)*, pages 115–120,
Vancouver, Canada, August 3-4, 2017. ©2017 Association for Computational Linguistics

together with word substitutes for each word. The PLF model for Croatian performs comparably well to English, outperforming simpler CDSMs in particular at the verb position.

2 The Practical Lexical Function Model

Basic model. As described above, the idea of the PLF is to represent predicates as sets of matrices for each argument slot of the predicate, plus a vector for its lexical meaning. The meaning of the predicate-argument combination is computed by multiplying all argument vectors with the predicates' slot matrices and finally adding the predicate's lexical vector. For example, the vector for the phrase *'big window'* is computed as:

$$\mathcal{P}(big\ window) = \overrightarrow{big} + \overset{\Box_N}{big} \times \overrightarrow{window} \quad (1)$$

This can easily be generalized to more complex ANVAN phrases, as exemplified in Figure 1.

The predicate matrices are estimated using ridge regression with corpus-extracted vectors for arguments $(\overrightarrow{n})$ as input and vectors for bigram phrases $(\overrightarrow{an})$ as output. For example, the predicate matrix $\overset{\Box_N}{a}$ for an adjective a is computed as follows:

$$\overset{\Box_N}{a} \triangleq \underset{M}{\arg\min} \sum_{n\,\in nouns(a)} \left\| M \times \overrightarrow{n} - \overrightarrow{an} \right\|^2 \quad (2)$$

PLF modifications. Gupta et al. (2015) identify an inconsistency within the PLF: there is a difference between the meaning modeled by a matrix obtained with training and its usage in phrase vector calculation. The matrix obtained using Eq. (2) directly approximates the phrase meaning for a given predicate-argument phrase, while the PLF phrase vector in Eq. (1) adds the predicate vector on top of the product of predicate matrix and argument vector. They propose two remedies, as follows.

Train phase modification changes Eq. (2) so that the predicate matrix does not learn a direct transformation from an argument vector to a phrase vector, but rather a difference between these vectors:

$$\overset{\Box}{a} \triangleq \underset{M}{\arg\min} \sum_{n\,\in nouns(a)} \left\| M \times \overrightarrow{n} - (\overrightarrow{an} - \overrightarrow{a}) \right\|^2 \quad (3)$$

This justifies the addition of predicate vector in (1).

In contrast, *test phase modification* retains the same training process, but omits the predicate vector when computing the phrase vector:[1]

$$\mathcal{P}(big\ window) = \overset{\Box_N}{big} \times \overrightarrow{window} \quad (4)$$

---

[1]For one-argument predicates, this is equivalent to the Lexical Function model (Baroni and Zamparelli, 2010).

Gupta et al. (2015) found both modifications to outperform simple baseline CDSMs for English when evaluated on ANVAN datasets, with test adaptation outperforming the original PLF.

PLF for Croatian. We implemented the basic PLF and the two above-mentioned modifications for Croatian following the procedure described by Paperno et al. (2014). As a corpus for building word and phrase lexical vectors we used fHrWaC (Šnajder et al., 2013), a filtered version of Croatian web corpus (Ljubešić and Erjavec, 2011), totaling 51M sentences and 1.2B tokens. The corpus has been parsed using the MSTParser for Croatian (Agić and Merkler, 2013).

As a first step in obtaining word vector representations, we extracted a co-occurrence matrix of 30K most frequent lemmas (nouns, verbs, and adjectives) in corpus, using a window of size 3. Next, the vectors contained in the resulting matrix were transformed using Positive Pointwise Mutual Information (PPMI) and reduced to size 300 using Singular Value Decomposition. Finally, all vectors in the matrix were normalized to unit length.

For the extraction of phrase (bigram) vectors, we consider two different approaches. The first approach considers all occurrences where the predicate and argument are adjacent in the dependency trees in fHrWaC even if they are not adjacent on the surface, sidestepping the free word order issue. The second approach extracts only those phrases in which the predicate and argument are adjacent on the surface, resulting in a smaller but potentially cleaner set of co-occurrences. The phrase vectors from both approaches use the same 30K context lemmas and window size as the unigrams.

Using the extracted lemma and bigram vectors, we train matrices for each of the predicate words from our evaluation dataset. As our dataset consists of ANVAN phrases, we train one matrix for each adjective and two matrices for each verb (one for subject and one for object). We train two versions of each matrix: one using the originally proposed training and another with modified training.

3 Experiments

Evaluation methodology. Paperno et al. (2014) evaluated the PLF on five datasets containing phrases in different forms. Two consist of free-form sentences, one of a number of differently formed phrases, and the two ANVAN datasets contain adjective-noun-verb-adjective-noun phrase

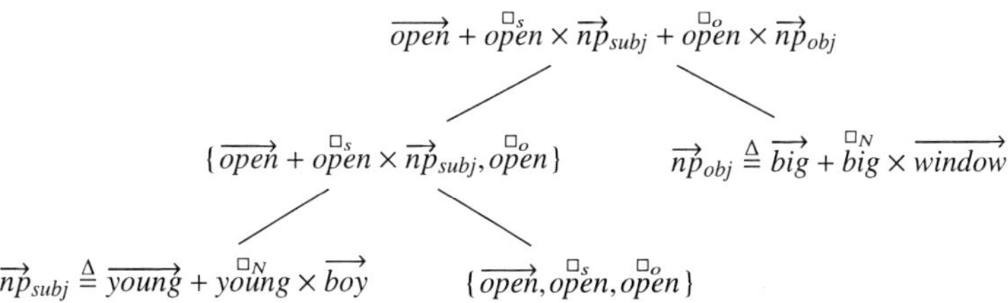

Figure 1: Computing the vector for an ANVAN phrase (*young boy open big window*) using PLF.

ANVAN phrase (target word in bold)	Substitute words
legendaran trener voditi suparnička momčad (***legendary** coach lead opponent team*)	cijenjen *(appreciated)*, izvanredan *(outstanding)*, poznat *(famous)*, uspješan *(successful)*, znamenit *(notable)*
dobar igrač **dati** pobjednički gol (*good player **score** winning goal*)	pogoditi *(to hit)*, postići *(to achieve)*, zabiti *(to score)*, zadati *(to give)*
sportski automobil prijeći velika **udaljenost** (*sports car travel large **distance***)	dionica *(section)*, dužina *(length)*, put *(way)*, razdaljina *(distance)*

Table 1: Examples of ANVAN phrases with manually collected substitutes for boldfaced targets.

pairs rated for semantic similarity (Kartsaklis et al., 2013; Grefenstette, 2013). The phrases in each pair differ only in the verb. Annotators rated the similarity on a scale from 1 to 7, and CDSMs were evaluated by correlating the ratings with the similarity of the predicted phrase vectors.

The described approach is not appropriate when one or both ANVAN phrases are ungrammatical or nonsensical. Consider the following phrase pair in the ANVAN dataset by Kartsaklis et al. (2013): *'dental service file false tooth'* – *'dental service register false tooth'*. While the first sentence is plausible, the second one is arguably somewhere between implausible and nonsensical. We believe that semantic similarity is not a reasonable evaluation criterion for such (relatively frequent) cases.

For our experiment, we chose a word-choice evaluation setup, which essentially builds on the idea of lexical substitution. Lexical substitution is the task of identifying a substitute for a word in a given context (McCarthy and Navigli, 2007). Typically, a system is presented with a phrase and candidate substitutes for a target word in the phrase and needs to select one or more adequate substitutes. Systems either have to rank the candidates in the appropriate order (McCarthy and Navigli, 2007; Sinha and Mihalcea, 2009), or just choose one best substitute (Melamud et al., 2016).

An additional benefit of a lexical substitution setup is that we can evaluate the predictions of the model not just globally, but at the level of individual words. We will exploit that possibility below.

Croatian ANVAN dataset. We constructed individual ANVAN phrases for Croatian like in prior English work (Kartsaklis et al., 2013; Grefenstette, 2013). We started by choosing six transitive verbs from the list of polysemous verbs on the Croatian language portal.[2] We chose verbs with high polysemy level, while avoiding those that overlap in semantic meaning. The list consist of the following verbs: *'baciti'* (to throw), *'dati'* (to give), *'izdati'* (to issue), *'prijeći'* (to cross), *'vidjeti'* (to see), and *'voditi'* (to lead). Using the distributional memory for Croatian (Šnajder et al., 2013), we selected the three most frequent subjects and objects for each verb. Finally, we chose a single adjective for each subject and object from the list of 20 most frequently co-occurring adjectives. This leaves us with 18 semantically plausible ANVAN phrases, illustrated in Table 1 (left column).

We manually collected substitutes for each word in the phrases. Three annotators were given a phrase and instructed to propose up to three substitutes for each word, while preserving both grammaticality and meaning; cf. the right column in Table 1. This yielded an evaluation dataset that contains 408 words: 158 adjectives, 167 nouns, and 83 verbs, each with multiple substitutes.

---

[2] http://hjp.znanje.hr

Target phrase	**odličan** đak prijeći brza cesta *(excellent pupil cross fast road)*
Possible substitutes	<u>dobar</u> *(good)*, potvrdan *(affirmative)*, crtani *(drawn)*, sportski *(sportive)*

Table 2: Word-choice item example. Target word in bold; correct substitute underlined.

Word Choice Task and Evaluation. We use the substitution dataset to set up a word choice task (Melamud et al., 2016): Each CDSM is presented with an ANVAN target phrase, a position in this phrase, a correct substitute and three distractors. Its task is to recognize the substitute that fits best into the context. Distractors were chosen by randomly picking three words of the same POS (adjective, noun or verb) that were not proposed as substitutes for that component in the given phrase. Table 2 shows an example of a single word-choice item.

In concrete terms, to evaluate a candidate substitute with respect to an ANVAN target phrase, we compute the cosine similarity between the compositionally computed vector for the ANVAN phrase computed "as is", and the phrase vector for the ANVAN phrase with the word at the current position replaced by the candidate substitute. The assumption is that a meaning-preserving substitution will leave the phrase vector largely unchanged and thus lead to a high cosine value. We report accuracy as the percentage of items for which the correct substitute received a higher cosine value than the incorrect substitutes.[3]

Models. We use the PLF and the two variants described in Section 2 (PLF-train and PLF-test). We build all three PLF versions for both phrase extraction approaches described in Sec. 2. In addition, we consider two baselines, namely the simple componentwise additive (add) and multiplicative (mult) models (Mitchell and Lapata, 2008).

4   Results

Table 3 shows the overall accuracy for each model. The standard PLF with dependency-extracted bigrams obtained the highest overall accuracy. The difference to the next-best model, *add*, is however not significant ($p > 0.01$, McNemar's test).

---

[3]The annotated dataset with compiled word choice tasks is available at: `http://takelab.fer.hr/data/croanvan`

Type	Counts	
	Surface level	Dependency level
adj-noun	14,249,655	15,548,616
subject-verb	3,147,289	3,994,552
verb-object	2,698,654	4,931,198

Table 4: fHrWaC number of predicate-argument co-occurrences at surface and dependency level.

Our new evaluation method allows us to further analyze this result by computing results for individual phrase positions (columns in Table 3). We find that PLF significantly outperforms both baselines for verbs ($p < 0.01$, McNemar's test). This is in line with, and can potentially explain, the good results for English (Paperno et al., 2014), since in the English evaluation setup, the ANVAN phrase pairs differ only in the verbs (cf. Section 3). In contrast, *add* performs as well as or better than the PLF an adjectives and nouns.

A potential explanation for these patterns is *valency*: The verb has the highest valency of all words in the phrase (two arguments). Arguably, verbs can profit most from the additional expressiveness of PLF over the simpler CDSMs. Apparently, for adjectives (one argument) the expressiveness-learnability tradeoff is balanced between the two models, and for nouns (no arguments, thus no functional role) the additive model's simplicity wins.

Comparing the different PLF versions, we find no benefit for the modifications proposed by Gupta et al. (2015), who also obtained a null result for PLF-train, but found PLF-test to outperform plain PLF. For Croatian, PLF-test performs comparably to PLF for nouns and adjectives, but does clearly worse for verbs. A potential explanation follows from Gupta et al.'s analysis of the difference between PLF and PLF-test as a bias-variance tradeoff: the original PLF uses the lexical vector of the predicate as a "prior" for the phrase meaning, which makes it more robust, but also less flexible. PLF-test uses only the predicate matrix to compute a phrase vector and is thus more dependent on the data quality: on good data, it can outperform PLF, but it will be outperformed on noisy data.

Indeed, there is evidence that the verb-argument matrices are noisy in Croatian: Table 4 compares co-occurrence frequencies at the surface and dependency levels for three predicate-argument combinations. It shows that >90% of A-N combinations are

Model	Phrase vectors	Phrase position					
		A1	N1	V	A2	N2	Overall
add		73.4	**92.0**	44.6	**70.1**	89.7	74.0
mult		39.2	61.4	32.5	40.2	62.8	47.4
PLF		**74.7**	85.2	**66.3** *	67.5	85.9	**76.0**
PLF-train	Dependency-based	58.2	89.8	49.4	51.9	83.3	66.9
PLF-test		72.2	85.2	60.2	67.5	84.6	74.0
PLF		55.7	87.5	63.9	65.4	84.6	71.7
PLF-train	Surface-based	54.4	89.8	51.8	56.4	82.1	67.2
PLF-test		69.6	87.5	55.4	60.3	83.3	71.4

Table 3: Model accuracy per phrase position. Asterisk (*) indicates a statistically significant result when comparing the best PLF version with the best simple CDSM, namely *add* (McNemar's test, p<0.01).

adjacent on the surface, while this holds for less than 80% of the S-V and 55% of the V-O combinations. As it is generally true that parsing quality deteriorates for long distance dependencies, the S-V and V-O matrices are arguably built from noisier data, which can account for disadvantage for PLF-test. In this manner, the free word order of Croatian does have an effect on CDSM performance.

That being said, parsing quality is evidently good enough for syntactic analysis to pay off: the results for using surface co-occurrence based versions of the PLF model perform generally worse than the PLF using dependency-base co-occurrences, with the exception of N1 (subject) position.

5   Conclusion

We built a Practical Lexical Function (PLF) model for Croatian and evaluated it on a newly created dataset of adjective-noun-verb-adjective-noun (AN-VAN) phrases. Our evaluation differs from existing English work (Paperno et al., 2014) by using a lexical substitution setup. Crucially, this allows us to analyze performance for individual phrase components. We find that the PLF's specific strength lies in modeling verbs, while it only does as well as simple additive models for nouns and adjectives. As we use dependency parses, the free word order of Croatian does not pose a major problem of the plain PLF, although we have evidence that it does affect the less robust PLF-test by Gupta et al. (2015). For future work, we will perform similar evaluation on a wider range of models and collect more evidence on the impact of typological differences on results.

Acknowledgments

This work has been supported in part by the Croatian Science Foundation under the project UIP-2014-09-7312. The third author has been supported by the DFG (SFB 732, Project D10).

References

Željko Agić and Danijela Merkler. 2013. Three syntactic formalisms for data-driven dependency parsing of Croatian. In *Proceedings of TSD 2013, Lecture Notes in Artificial Intelligence*. Springer, pages 560–567.

Marco Baroni and Roberto Zamparelli. 2010. Nouns are vectors, adjectives are matrices: Representing adjective-noun constructions in semantic space. In *Proceedings of EMNLP*. Cambridge, MA, pages 1183–1193.

Edward Grefenstette. 2013. *Category-theoretic quantitative compositional distributional models of natural language semantics*. Ph.D. thesis, University of Oxford.

Edward Grefenstette, Georgiana Dinu, Yao-Zhong Zhang, Mehrnoosh Sadrzadeh, and Marco Baroni. 2012. Multi-step regression learning for compositional distributional semantics. In *Proceedings of IWCS 2012*. Potsdam, Germany.

Emiliano Guevara. 2010. A regression model of adjective-noun compositionality in distributional semantics. In *Proceedings of the 2010 Workshop on GEometrical Models of Natural Language Semantics*. Uppsala, Sweden, pages 33–37.

Abhijeet Gupta, Jason Utt, and Sebastian Padó. 2015. Dissecting the practical lexical function model for compositional distributional semantics. In *Proceedings of the Fourth Joint Conference on Lexical and*

Computational Semantics. Denver, Colorado, pages 153–158.

Dimitri Kartsaklis, Mehrnoosh Sadrzadeh, and Stephen Pulman. 2013. Separating disambiguation from composition in distributional semantics. In *Proceedings of CoNLL*. Sofia, Bulgaria, pages 114–123.

Nikola Ljubešić and Tomaž Erjavec. 2011. hrWaC and slWaC: Compiling web corpora for Croatian and Slovene. In *International Conference on Text, Speech and Dialogue*. Springer, Brno, Czech Republic, pages 395–402.

Diana McCarthy and Roberto Navigli. 2007. SemEval-2007 Task 10: English lexical substitution task. In *Proceedings of SEMEVAL*. pages 48–53.

Oren Melamud, Jacob Goldberger, and Ido Dagan. 2016. context2vec: Learning generic context embedding with bidirectional LSTM. In *Proceedings of CONLL*. Berlin, Germany, pages 51–61.

Jeff Mitchell and Mirella Lapata. 2008. Vector-based models of semantic composition. In *Proceedings of ACL*. Columbus, OH, pages 236–244.

Denis Paperno, Nghia The Pham, and Marco Baroni. 2014. A practical and linguistically-motivated approach to compositional distributional semantics. In *Proceedings of ACL*. Baltimore, MD, pages 90–99.

Ravi Sinha and Rada Mihalcea. 2009. Combining lexical resources for contextual synonym expansion. In *Proceedings of RANLP*. Borovets, Bulgaria, pages 404–410.

Jan Šnajder, Sebastian Padó, and Željko Agic. 2013. Building and evaluating a distributional memory for Croatian. In *Proceedings of ACL*. Sofia, Bulgaria, pages 784–789.

A Mixture Model for Learning Multi-Sense Word Embeddings

Dai Quoc Nguyen[1], Dat Quoc Nguyen[2], Ashutosh Modi[1], Stefan Thater[1], Manfred Pinkal[1]

[1]Department of Computational Linguistics, Saarland University, Germany
`{daiquocn, ashutosh, stth, pinkal}@coli.uni-saarland.de`
[2]Department of Computing, Macquarie University, Australia
`dat.nguyen@students.mq.edu.au`

Abstract

Word embeddings are now a standard technique for inducing meaning representations for words. For getting good representations, it is important to take into account different senses of a word. In this paper, we propose a mixture model for learning multi-sense word embeddings. Our model generalizes the previous works in that it allows to induce different weights of different senses of a word. The experimental results show that our model outperforms previous models on standard evaluation tasks.

1 Introduction

Word embeddings have shown to be useful in various NLP tasks such as sentiment analysis, topic models, script learning, machine translation, sequence labeling and parsing (Socher et al., 2013; Sutskever et al., 2014; Modi and Titov, 2014; Nguyen et al., 2015a,b; Modi, 2016; Ma and Hovy, 2016; Nguyen et al., 2017; Modi et al., 2017). A word embedding captures the syntactic and semantic properties of a word by representing the word in a form of a real-valued vector (Mikolov et al., 2013a,b; Pennington et al., 2014; Levy and Goldberg, 2014).

However, usually word embedding models do not take into account lexical ambiguity. For example, the word *bank* is usually represented by a single vector representation for all senses including *sloping land* and *financial institution*. Recently, approaches have been proposed to learn multi-sense word embeddings, where each sense of a word corresponds to a sense-specific embedding. Reisinger and Mooney (2010), Huang et al. (2012) and Wu and Giles (2015) proposed methods to cluster the contexts of each word and

then using cluster centroids as vector representations for word senses. Neelakantan et al. (2014), Tian et al. (2014), Li and Jurafsky (2015) and Chen et al. (2015) extended Word2Vec models (Mikolov et al., 2013a,b) to learn a vector representation for each sense of a word. Chen et al. (2014), Iacobacci et al. (2015) and Flekova and Gurevych (2016) performed word sense induction using external resources (e.g., WordNet, Babel-Net) and then learned sense embeddings using the Word2Vec models. Rothe and Schütze (2015) and Pilehvar and Collier (2016) presented methods using pre-trained word embeddings to learn embeddings from WordNet synsets. Cheng et al. (2015), Liu et al. (2015b), Liu et al. (2015a) and Zhang and Zhong (2016) directly opt the Word2Vec Skipgram model (Mikolov et al., 2013b) for learning the embeddings of words and topics on a topic-assigned corpus.

One issue in these previous works is that they assign the same weight to every sense of a word. The central assumption of our work is that each sense of a word given a context, should correspond to a mixture of weights reflecting different association degrees of the word with multiple senses in the context. The mixture weights will help to model word meaning better.

In this paper, we propose a new model for learning **M**ulti-**S**ense **W**ord **E**mbeddings (MSWE). Our MSWE model learns vector representations of a word based on a mixture of its sense representations. The key difference between MSWE and other models is that we induce the weights of senses while jointly learning the word and sense embeddings. Specifically, we train a topic model (Blei et al., 2003) to obtain the topic-to-word and document-to-topic probability distributions which are then used to infer the weights of topics. We use these weights to define a compositional vector representation for each target word to predict

121

*Proceedings of the 6th Joint Conference on Lexical and Computational Semantics (*SEM 2017)*, pages 121–127,
Vancouver, Canada, August 3-4, 2017. ©2017 Association for Computational Linguistics

its context words. MSWE thus is different from the topic-based models (Cheng et al., 2015; Liu et al., 2015b,a; Zhang and Zhong, 2016), in which we do not use the topic assignments when jointly learning vector representations of words and topics. Here we not only learn vectors based on the most suitable topic of a word given its context, but we also take into consideration all possible meanings of the word.

The main contributions of our study are: (i) We introduce a mixture model for learning word and sense embeddings (MSWE) by inducing mixture weights of word senses. (ii) We show that MSWE performs better than the baseline Word2Vec Skip-gram and other embedding models on the word analogy task (Mikolov et al., 2013a) and the word similarity task (Reisinger and Mooney, 2010).

2 The mixture model

In this section, we present the mixture model for learning multi-sense word embeddings. Here we treat topics as senses. The model learns a representation for each word using a mixture of its topical representations.

Given a number of topics and a corpus D of documents $d = \{w_{d,1}, w_{d,2}, ..., w_{d,M_d}\}$, we apply a topic model (Blei et al., 2003) to obtain the topic-to-word $\Pr(w|t)$ and document-to-topic $\Pr(t|d)$ probability distributions. We then infer a weight for the mth word $w_{d,m}$ with topic t in document d:

$$\lambda_{d,m,t} = \Pr(w_{d,m}|t) \times \Pr(t|d) \qquad (1)$$

We define two MSWE variants: MSWE-1 learns vectors for words based on the most suitable topic given document d while MSWE-2 marginalizes over all senses of a word to take into account all possible senses of the word:

$$\text{MSWE-1:} \quad s_{w_{d,m}} = \frac{v_{w_{d,m}} + \lambda_{d,m,t'} \times v_{t'}}{1 + \lambda_{d,m,t'}}$$

$$\text{MSWE-2:} \quad s_{w_{d,m}} = \frac{v_{w_{d,m}} + \sum_{t=1}^{T} \lambda_{d,m,t} \times v_t}{1 + \sum_{t=1}^{T} \lambda_{d,m,t}}$$

where $s_{w_{d,m}}$ is the compositional vector representation of the mth word $w_{d,m}$ and the topics in document d; v_w is the target vector representation of a word type w in vocabulary V; v_t is the vector representation of topic t; T is the number of topics; $\lambda_{d,m,t}$ is defined as in Equation 1, and in MSWE-1 we define $t' = \arg\max_t \lambda_{d,m,t}$.

We learn representations by minimizing the following negative log-likelihood function:

$$\mathcal{L} = - \sum_{d \in D} \sum_{m=1}^{M_d} \sum_{\substack{-k \leq j \leq k \\ j \neq 0}} \log \Pr(\tilde{v}_{w_{d,m+j}}|s_{w_{d,m}}) \quad (2)$$

where the mth word $w_{d,m}$ in document d is a target word while the $(m+j)^{th}$ word $w_{d,m+j}$ in document d is a context word of $w_{d,m}$ and k is the context size. In addition, $\tilde{v}_w$ is the context vector representation of the word type w. The probability $\Pr(\tilde{v}_{w_{d,m+j}}|s_{w_{d,m}})$ is defined using the softmax function as follows:

$$\Pr(\tilde{v}_{w_{d,m+j}}|s_{w_{d,m}}) = \frac{\exp(\tilde{v}_{w_{d,m+j}}^{\mathsf{T}} s_{w_{d,m}})}{\sum_{c' \in V} \exp(\tilde{v}_{c'}^{\mathsf{T}} s_{w_{d,m}})}$$

Since computing $\log \Pr(\tilde{v}_{w_{d,m+j}}|s_{w_{d,m}})$ is expensive for each training instance, we approximate $\log \Pr(\tilde{v}_{w_{d,m+j}}|s_{w_{d,m}})$ in Equation 2 with the following negative-sampling objective (Mikolov et al., 2013b):

$$\mathcal{O}_{d,m,m+j} = \log \sigma \left(\tilde{v}_{w_{d,m+j}}^{\mathsf{T}} s_{w_{d,m}} \right)$$
$$+ \sum_{i=1}^{K} \log \sigma \left(-\tilde{v}_{c_i}^{\mathsf{T}} s_{w_{d,m}} \right) \quad (3)$$

where each word c_i is sampled from a noise distribution.[1] In fact, MSWE can be viewed as a generalization of the well-known Word2Vec Skip-gram model with negative sampling (Mikolov et al., 2013b) where all the mixture weights $\lambda_{d,m,t}$ are set to zero. The models are trained using Stochastic Gradient Descent (SGD).

3 Experiments

We evaluate MSWE on two different tasks: word similarity and word analogy. We also provide experimental results obtained by the baseline Word2Vec Skip-gram model and other previous works.

Note that not all previous results are mentioned in this paper for comparison because the training corpora used in most previous research work are much larger than ours (Baroni et al., 2014; Li and Jurafsky, 2015; Schwartz et al., 2015; Levy et al., 2015). Also there are differences in the pre-processing steps that could affect the results. We could also improve obtained results by using a

---

[1] We use an unigram distribution raised to the 3/4 power (Mikolov et al., 2013b) as the noise distribution.

larger training corpus, but this is not central point of our paper. The objective of our paper is that the embeddings of topic and word can be combined into a single mixture model, leading to good improvements as established empirically.

3.1 Experimental Setup

Following Huang et al. (2012) and Neelakantan et al. (2014), we use the Wesbury Lab Wikipedia corpus (Shaoul and Westbury, 2010) containing over 2M articles with about 990M words for training. In the preprocessing step, texts are lower-cased and tokenized, numbers are mapped to 0, and punctuation marks are removed. We extract a vocabulary of 200,000 most frequent word tokens from the pre-processed corpus. Words not occurring in the vocabulary are mapped to a special token UNK, in which we use the embedding of UNK for unknown words in the benchmark datasets.

We firstly use a small subset extracted from the WS353 dataset (Finkelstein et al., 2002) to tune the hyper-parameters of the baseline Word2Vec Skip-gram model for the word similarity task (see Section 3.2 for the task definition). We then directly use the tuned hyper-parameters for our MSWE variants. Vector size is also a hyper-parameter. While some approaches use a higher number of dimensions to obtain better results, we fix the vector size to be 300 as used by the baseline for a fair comparison. The vanilla Latent Dirichlet Allocation (LDA) topic model (Blei et al., 2003) is not scalable to a very large corpus, so we explore faster online topic models developed for large corpora. We train the online LDA topic model (Hoffman et al., 2010) on the training corpus, and use the output of this topic model to compute the mixture weights as in Equation 1.[2] We also use the same WS353 subset to tune the numbers of topics $T \in \{50, 100, 200, 300, 400\}$. We find that the most suitable numbers are $T = 50$ and $T = 200$ then used for all our experiments. Here we learn 300-dimensional embeddings with the fixed context size $k = 5$ (in Equation 2) and $K = 10$ (in Equation 3) as used by the baseline. During training, we randomly initialize model parameters (i.e. word and topic embeddings) and then learn them by using SGD with the initial learning rate of 0.01.

---

[2] We use default parameters in *gensim* (Řehůřek and Sojka, 2010) for the online LDA model.

Dataset	Word pairs	Reference
WS353	353	Finkelstein et al. (2002)
SIMLEX	999	Hill et al. (2015)
SCWS	2003	Huang et al. (2012)
RW	2034	Luong et al. (2013)
MEN	3000	Bruni et al. (2014)

Table 1: The benchmark datasets. WS353: WordSimilarity-353. RW: Rare-Words. SIMLEX: SimLex-999. SCWS: Stanford's Contextual Word Similarities. MEN: The MEN Test Collection. Each dataset contains similarity scores of human judgments for pairs of words.

3.2 Word Similarity

The word similarity task evaluates the quality of word embedding models (Reisinger and Mooney, 2010). For a given dataset of word pairs, the evaluation is done by calculating correlation between the similarity scores of corresponding word embedding pairs with the human judgment scores. Higher Spearman's rank correlation (ρ) reflects better word embedding model. We evaluate MSWE on standard datasets (as given in Table 1) for the word similarity evaluation task.

Following Reisinger and Mooney (2010), Huang et al. (2012), Neelakantan et al. (2014), we compute the similarity scores for a pair of words (w, w') with or without their respective contexts (c, c') as:

$$GlobalSim\,(w, w') = \cos(\boldsymbol{v}_w, \boldsymbol{v}_{w'})$$

$$AvgSim\,(w, w') = \frac{1}{T^2} \sum_{t=1}^{T} \sum_{t'=1}^{T} \cos(\boldsymbol{v}_{w,t}, \boldsymbol{v}_{w',t'})$$

$$AvgSimC\,(w, w')$$
$$= \frac{1}{T^2} \sum_{t=1}^{T} \sum_{t'=1}^{T} \Big(\delta(\boldsymbol{v}_{w,t}, \boldsymbol{v}_c) \times \delta(\boldsymbol{v}_{w',t'}, \boldsymbol{v}_{c'})$$
$$\times \cos(\boldsymbol{v}_{w,t}, \boldsymbol{v}_{w',t'}) \Big)$$

where $\boldsymbol{v}_w$ is the vector representation of the word w, $\boldsymbol{v}_{w,t}$ is the multiple representation of the word w and the topic t, $\boldsymbol{v}_c$ is the vector representation of the context c of the word w. And $\cos(\boldsymbol{v}, \boldsymbol{v}')$ is the cosine similarity between two vectors $\boldsymbol{v}$ and $\boldsymbol{v}'$. For our experiments, we set $\boldsymbol{v}_{w,t} = \boldsymbol{v}_w \oplus (\Pr(w|t) \times \boldsymbol{v}_t)$ and $\boldsymbol{v}_c = \left(\frac{1}{|c|} \sum_{w \in c} \boldsymbol{v}_w\right) \oplus (\sum_t \Pr(t|c) \times \boldsymbol{v}_t)$, in which $\oplus$ is the concatenation operation and $\Pr(t|c)$ is inferred from the topic models by considering context c as a document. *GlobalSim* only regards word embeddings,

Model	RW	SIMLEX	SCWS	WS353	MEN
Huang et al. (2012)	–	–	58.6	71.3	–
Luong et al. (2013)	34.36	–	48.48	64.58	–
Qiu et al. (2014)	32.13	–	53.40	65.19	–
Neelakantan et al. (2014)	–	–	65.5	69.2	–
Chen et al. (2014)	–	–	64.2	–	–
Hill et al. (2015)	–	**41.4**	–	65.5	69.9
Vilnis and McCallum (2015)	–	32.23	–	65.49	71.31
Schnabel et al. (2015)	–	–	–	64.0	70.7
Rastogi et al. (2015)	32.9	36.7	65.6	70.8	73.9
Flekova and Gurevych (2016)	–	–	–	–	74.26
Word2Vec Skip-gram	32.64	38.20	66.37	71.61	75.49
MSWE-1$_{50}$	34.85	38.77	**66.83**	**72.40**	<u>76.23</u>
MSWE-1$_{200}$	<u>35.27</u>	38.70	<u>66.80</u>	72.05	76.05
MSWE-2$_{50}$	34.98	38.79	66.61	71.71	75.90
MSWE-2$_{200}$	**35.56***	<u>39.19</u>*	66.65	<u>72.29</u>	**76.37***

Table 2: Spearman's rank correlation ($\rho \times 100$) for the word similarity task when using $GlobalSim$. Subscripts 50 and 200 denote the online LDA topic model trained with $T = 50$ and $T = 200$ topics, respectively. * denotes that our best score is significantly higher than the score of the baseline (with $p < 0.05$, online toolkit from http://www.philippsinger.info/?p=347). Scores in **bold** and <u>underline</u> are the best and second best scores.

Model	AvgSim	AvgSimC
Huang et al. (2012)	62.8	65.7
Neelakantan et al. (2014)	**67.3**	**69.3**
Chen et al. (2014)	66.2	<u>68.9</u>
Chen et al. (2015)	65.7	66.4
Wu and Giles (2015)	–	66.4
Jauhar et al. (2015)	–	65.7
Cheng and Kartsaklis (2015)	62.5	–
Iacobacci et al. (2015)	62.4	–
Cheng et al. (2015)	–	65.9
MSWE-1$_{50}$	66.6	66.7
MSWE-1$_{200}$	<u>66.7</u>	66.6
MSWE-2$_{50}$	66.4	66.6
MSWE-2$_{200}$	66.6	66.6

Table 3: Spearman's rank correlation ($\rho \times 100$) on SCWS, using $AvgSim$ and $AvgSimC$.

while $AvgSim$ considers multiple representations to capture different meanings (i.e. topics) and usages of a word. $AvgSimC$ generalizes $AvgSim$ by taking into account the likelihood $\delta\left(v_{w,t}, v_c\right)$ that word w takes topic t given context c. $\delta\left(v, v'\right)$ is the inverse of the cosine distance from v to v' (Huang et al., 2012; Neelakantan et al., 2014).

3.2.1 Results for word similarity

Table 2 compares the evaluation results of MSWE with results reported in prior work on the standard word similarity task when using $GlobalSim$. We use subscripts 50 and 200 to denote the topic model trained with $T = 50$ and $T = 200$ topics, respectively. Table 2 shows that our model outperforms the baseline Word2Vec Skip-gram model (in fifth row from bottom). Specifically, on the RW dataset, MSWE obtains a significant improvement of 2.92 in the Spearman's rank correlation (which is about 8.5% relative improvement).

Compared to the published results, MSWE obtains the highest accuracy on the RW, SCWS, WS353 and MEN datasets, and achieves the second highest result on the SIMLEX dataset. These indicate that MSWE learns better representations for words taking into account different meanings.

3.2.2 Results for contextual word similarity

We evaluate our model MSWE by using $AvgSim$ and $AvgSimC$ on the benchmark SCWS dataset which considers effects of the contextual information on the word similarity task. As shown in Table 3, MSWE scores better than the closely related model proposed by Cheng et al. (2015) and generally obtains good results for this context sensitive dataset. Although we produce better scores than Neelakantan et al. (2014) and Chen et al. (2014) when using $GlobalSim$, we are outperformed by them when using $AvgSim$ and $AvgSimC$. Neelakantan et al. (2014) clustered the embeddings of the context words around each target word to predict its sense and Chen et al. (2014) used pre-trained word embeddings to initialize vector representations of senses taken from WordNet, while we use a fixed number of topics as senses for words in MSWE.

3.3 Word Analogy

We evaluate the embedding models on the word analogy task introduced by Mikolov et al. (2013a). The task aims to answer questions in the form of "a is to b as c is to _ ?", denoted as "$a : b \rightarrow c : ?$" (e.g., "$Hanoi : Vietnam \rightarrow Bern : ?$"). There are 8,869 semantic and 10,675 syntactic questions grouped into 14 categories. Each question is answered by finding the most suitable word closest to "$v_b - v_a + v_c$" measured by the cosine similarity. The answer is correct only if the found closest word is exactly the same as the gold-standard (correct) one for the question.

We report accuracies in Table 4 and show that MSWE achieves better results in comparison with the baseline Word2Vec Skip-gram. In particular, MSWE reaches the accuracies of around 69.7%

Model	Accuracy (%)
Pennington et al. (2014)	**70.3**
Baroni et al. (2014)	68.0
Neelakantan et al. (2014)	64.0
Ghannay et al. (2016)	62.3
Word2Vec Skip-gram	68.6
MSWE-1_{50}	69.6
MSWE-1_{200}	69.9
MSWE-2_{50}	69.7
MSWE-2_{200}	69.5

Table 4: Accuracies for the word analogy task. All our results are significantly higher than the result of Word2Vec Skip-gram (with two-tail $p < 0.001$ using McNemar's test). Pennington et al. (2014) used a larger training corpus of 1.6B words.

which is higher than the accuracy of 68.6% obtained by Word2Vec Skip-gram.

4 Conclusions

In this paper, we described a mixture model for learning multi-sense embeddings. Our model induces mixture weights to represent a word given context based on a mixture of its sense representations. The results show that our model scores better than Word2Vec, and produces highly competitive results on the standard evaluation tasks. In future work, we will explore better methods for taking into account the contextual information. We also plan to explore different approaches to compute the mixture weights in our model. For example, if there is a large sense-annotated corpus available for training, the mixture weights could be defined based on the frequency (sense-count) distributions, instead of using the probability distributions produced by a topic model. Furthermore, it is possible to consider the weights of senses as additional model parameters to be then learned during training.

Acknowledgments

This research was funded by the German Research Foundation (DFG) as part of SFB 1102 "Information Density and Linguistic Encoding". We would like to thank anonymous reviewers for their helpful comments.

References

Marco Baroni, Georgiana Dinu, and Germán Kruszewski. 2014. Don't count, predict! a systematic comparison of context-counting vs. context-predicting semantic vectors. In *Proceedings of the 52nd Annual Meeting of the Association for Computational Linguistics (Volume 1: Long Papers)*. pages 238–247.

David M. Blei, Andrew Y. Ng, and Michael I. Jordan. 2003. Latent Dirichlet Allocation. *Journal of Machine Learning Research* 3:993–1022.

Elia Bruni, Nam Khanh Tran, and Marco Baroni. 2014. Multimodal distributional semantics. *Journal of Artificial Intelligence Research* 49:1–47.

Tao Chen, Ruifeng Xu, Yulan He, and Xuan Wang. 2015. Improving distributed representation of word sense via wordnet gloss composition and context clustering. In *Proceedings of the 53rd Annual Meeting of the Association for Computational Linguistics and the 7th International Joint Conference on Natural Language Processing (Volume 2: Short Papers)*. pages 15–20.

Xinxiong Chen, Zhiyuan Liu, and Maosong Sun. 2014. A unified model for word sense representation and disambiguation. In *Proceedings of the 2014 Conference on Empirical Methods in Natural Language Processing (EMNLP)*. pages 1025–1035.

Jianpeng Cheng and Dimitri Kartsaklis. 2015. Syntax-aware multi-sense word embeddings for deep compositional models of meaning. In *Proceedings of the 2015 Conference on Empirical Methods in Natural Language Processing*. pages 1531–1542.

Jianpeng Cheng, Zhongyuan Wang, Ji-Rong Wen, Jun Yan, and Zheng Chen. 2015. Contextual text understanding in distributional semantic space. In *Proceedings of the 24th ACM International on Conference on Information and Knowledge Management*. pages 133–142.

Lev Finkelstein, Evgeniy Gabrilovich, Yossi Matias, Ehud Rivlin, Zach Solan, Gadi Wolfman, and Eytan Ruppin. 2002. Placing search in context: The concept revisited. *ACM Transactions on Information Systems* 20:116–131.

Lucie Flekova and Iryna Gurevych. 2016. Supersense embeddings: A unified model for supersense interpretation, prediction, and utilization. In *Proceedings of the 54th Annual Meeting of the Association for Computational Linguistics (Volume 1: Long Papers)*. pages 2029–2041.

Sahar Ghannay, Benoit Favre, Yannick Estve, and Nathalie Camelin. 2016. Word embedding evaluation and combination. In *Proceedings of the Tenth International Conference on Language Resources and Evaluation (LREC 2016)*.

Felix Hill, Roi Reichart, and Anna Korhonen. 2015. Simlex-999: Evaluating semantic models with genuine similarity estimation. *Computational Linguistics* 41:665–695.

Matthew Hoffman, Francis R. Bach, and David M. Blei. 2010. Online learning for latent dirichlet allocation. In *Advances in Neural Information Processing Systems 23*. pages 856–864.

Eric H. Huang, Richard Socher, Christopher D. Manning, and Andrew Y. Ng. 2012. Improving word representations via global context and multiple word prototypes. In *Proceedings of the 50th Annual Meeting of the Association for Computational Linguistics: Long Papers - Volume 1*. pages 873–882.

Ignacio Iacobacci, Mohammad Taher Pilehvar, and Roberto Navigli. 2015. Sensembed: Learning sense embeddings for word and relational similarity. In *Proceedings of the 53rd Annual Meeting of the Association for Computational Linguistics and the 7th International Joint Conference on Natural Language Processing (Volume 1: Long Papers)*. pages 95–105.

Sujay Kumar Jauhar, Chris Dyer, and Eduard Hovy. 2015. Ontologically grounded multi-sense representation learning for semantic vector space models. In *Proceedings of the 2015 Conference of the North American Chapter of the Association for Computational Linguistics: Human Language Technologies*. pages 683–693.

Omer Levy and Yoav Goldberg. 2014. Neural word embedding as implicit matrix factorization. In *Advances in Neural Information Processing Systems 27*. pages 2177–2185.

Omer Levy, Yoav Goldberg, and Ido Dagan. 2015. Improving distributional similarity with lessons learned from word embeddings. *Transactions of the Association for Computational Linguistics* 3:211–225.

Jiwei Li and Dan Jurafsky. 2015. Do multi-sense embeddings improve natural language understanding? In *Proceedings of the 2015 Conference on Empirical Methods in Natural Language Processing*. pages 1722–1732.

Pengfei Liu, Xipeng Qiu, and Xuanjing Huang. 2015a. Learning context-sensitive word embeddings with neural tensor skip-gram model. In *Proceedings of the 24th International Conference on Artificial Intelligence*. pages 1284–1290.

Yang Liu, Zhiyuan Liu, Tat-Seng Chua, and Maosong Sun. 2015b. Topical word embeddings. In *AAAI Conference on Artificial Intelligence*. pages 2418–2424.

Thang Luong, Richard Socher, and Christopher Manning. 2013. Better word representations with recursive neural networks for morphology. In *Proceedings of the Seventeenth Conference on Computational Natural Language Learning*. pages 104–113.

Xuezhe Ma and Eduard Hovy. 2016. End-to-end sequence labeling via bi-directional lstm-cnns-crf. In *Proceedings of the 54th Annual Meeting of the Association for Computational Linguistics (Volume 1: Long Papers)*. pages 1064–1074.

Tomas Mikolov, Kai Chen, Greg Corrado, and Jeffrey Dean. 2013a. Efficient estimation of word representations in vector space. *CoRR* abs/1301.3781.

Tomas Mikolov, Ilya Sutskever, Kai Chen, Gregory S. Corrado, and Jeffrey Dean. 2013b. Distributed representations of words and phrases and their compositionality. In *Advances in Neural Information Processing Systems 26: 27th Annual Conference on Neural Information Processing Systems 2013*. pages 3111–3119.

Ashutosh Modi. 2016. Event embeddings for semantic script modeling. In *Proceedings of the Conference on Computational Natural Language Learning*. pages 75–83.

Ashutosh Modi and Ivan Titov. 2014. Inducing neural models of script knowledge. In *Proceedings of the Eighteenth Conference on Computational Natural Language Learning*. pages 49–57.

Ashutosh Modi, Ivan Titov, Vera Demberg, Asad Sayeed, and Manfred Pinkal. 2017. Modelling semantic expectation: Using script knowledge for referent prediction. *Transactions of the Association for Computational Linguistics* 5:31–44.

Arvind Neelakantan, Jeevan Shankar, Alexandre Passos, and Andrew McCallum. 2014. Efficient nonparametric estimation of multiple embeddings per word in vector space. In *Proceedings of the 2014 Conference on Empirical Methods in Natural Language Processing (EMNLP)*. pages 1059–1069.

Dat Quoc Nguyen, Richard Billingsley, Lan Du, and Mark Johnson. 2015a. Improving Topic Models with Latent Feature Word Representations. *Transactions of the Association for Computational Linguistics* 3:299–313.

Dat Quoc Nguyen, Mark Dras, and Mark Johnson. 2017. A Novel Neural Network Model for Joint POS Tagging and Graph-based Dependency Parsing. In *Proceedings of the CoNLL 2017 Shared Task: Multilingual Parsing from Raw Text to Universal Dependencies*.

Dat Quoc Nguyen, Kairit Sirts, and Mark Johnson. 2015b. Improving Topic Coherence with Latent Feature Word Representations in MAP Estimation for Topic Modeling. In *Proceedings of the Australasian Language Technology Association Workshop 2015*. pages 116–121.

Jeffrey Pennington, Richard Socher, and Christopher D. Manning. 2014. Glove: Global vectors for word representation. In *Proceedings of the 2014 Conference on Empirical Methods in Natural Language Processing (EMNLP 2014)*. pages 1532–1543.

Mohammad Taher Pilehvar and Nigel Collier. 2016. De-conflated semantic representations. In *Proceedings of the 2016 Conference on Empirical Methods in Natural Language Processing*. pages 1680–1690.

Siyu Qiu, Qing Cui, Jiang Bian, Bin Gao, and Tie-Yan Liu. 2014. Co-learning of word representations and morpheme representations. In *Proceedings of COLING 2014, the 25th International Conference on Computational Linguistics: Technical Papers*. pages 141–150.

Pushpendre Rastogi, Benjamin Van Durme, and Raman Arora. 2015. Multiview LSA: Representation Learning via Generalized CCA. In *Proceedings of the 2015 Conference of the North American Chapter of the Association for Computational Linguistics: Human Language Technologies*. pages 556–566.

Radim Řehůřek and Petr Sojka. 2010. Software Framework for Topic Modelling with Large Corpora. In *Proceedings of the LREC 2010 Workshop on New Challenges for NLP Frameworks*. pages 45–50.

Joseph Reisinger and Raymond J. Mooney. 2010. Multi-prototype vector-space models of word meaning. In *Human Language Technologies: The 2010 Annual Conference of the North American Chapter of the Association for Computational Linguistics*. pages 109–117.

Sascha Rothe and Hinrich Schütze. 2015. Autoextend: Extending word embeddings to embeddings for synsets and lexemes. In *Proceedings of the 53rd Annual Meeting of the Association for Computational Linguistics and the 7th International Joint Conference on Natural Language Processing, Volume 1: Long Papers*. pages 1793–1803.

Tobias Schnabel, Igor Labutov, David Mimno, and Thorsten Joachims. 2015. Evaluation methods for unsupervised word embeddings. In *Proceedings of the Conference on Empirical Methods in Natural Language Processing*. pages 298–307.

Roy Schwartz, Roi Reichart, and Ari Rappoport. 2015. Symmetric pattern based word embeddings for improved word similarity prediction. In *Proceedings of CoNLL 2015*. pages 258–267.

Cyrus Shaoul and Chris Westbury. 2010. The westbury lab wikipedia corpus. *Edmonton, AB: University of Alberta* .

Richard Socher, Alex Perelygin, Jean Wu, Jason Chuang, Christopher D. Manning, Andrew Ng, and Christopher Potts. 2013. Recursive deep models for semantic compositionality over a sentiment treebank. In *Proceedings of the 2013 Conference on Empirical Methods in Natural Language Processing*. pages 1631–1642.

Ilya Sutskever, Oriol Vinyals, and Quoc V. Le. 2014. Sequence to sequence learning with neural networks. In *Proceedings of the 27th International Conference on Neural Information Processing Systems*. pages 3104–3112.

Fei Tian, Hanjun Dai, Jiang Bian, Bin Gao, Rui Zhang, Enhong Chen, and Tie-Yan Liu. 2014. A probabilistic model for learning multi-prototype word embeddings. In *Proceedings of COLING 2014, the 25th International Conference on Computational Linguistics: Technical Papers*. pages 151–160.

Luke Vilnis and Andrew McCallum. 2015. Word representations via gaussian embedding. *International Conference on Learning Representations (ICLR)* .

Zhaohui Wu and C. Lee Giles. 2015. Sense-aware semantic analysis: A multi-prototype word representation model using wikipedia. In *Proceedings of the Twenty-Ninth AAAI Conference on Artificial Intelligence*. pages 2188–2194.

Heng Zhang and Guoqiang Zhong. 2016. Improving short text classification by learning vector representations of both words and hidden topics. *Knowledge-Based Systems* 102:76–86.

Aligning Script Events with Narrative Texts

Simon Ostermann[†] **Michael Roth**[†‡] **Stefan Thater**[†] **Manfred Pinkal**[†]
[†] Saarland University   [‡] University of Illinois at Urbana-Champaign
{simono|mroth|stth|pinkal}@coli.uni-saarland.de

Abstract

Script knowledge plays a central role in text understanding and is relevant for a variety of downstream tasks. In this paper, we consider two recent datasets which provide a rich and general representation of script events in terms of paraphrase sets. We introduce the task of mapping event mentions in narrative texts to such script event types, and present a model for this task that exploits rich linguistic representations as well as information on temporal ordering. The results of our experiments demonstrate that this complex task is indeed feasible.

1   Introduction

Event structure is a prominent topic in NLP. While semantic role labelers (Gildea and Jurafsky, 2002; Palmer et al., 2010) are well-established tools for the analysis of the internal structure of event descriptions, modeling relations between events has gained increasing attention in recent years. Research on event coreference (Bejan and Harabagiu, 2010; Lee et al., 2012), temporal event ordering in newswire texts (Ling and Weld, 2010), as well as shared tasks on cross-document event ordering (Minard et al., 2015, inter alia) have in common that they model cross-document relations.

The focus of this paper is on the task of analyzing text-internal event structure. We share the view of a long tradition in NLP (see e.g. Schank and Abelson (1975); Chambers and Jurafsky (2009); Regneri et al. (2010)) that *script knowledge* is of central importance to this task, i.e. common-sense knowledge about events and their typical order in everyday activities (also referred to as *scenarios*, Barr and Feigenbaum (1981)). Script knowledge guides expectation by predicting which type of event or discourse referent might be addressed next in a story

(Modi et al., 2017), allows to infer missing events from events explicitly mentioned (Chambers and Jurafsky, 2009; Jans et al., 2012; Rudinger et al., 2015), and to determine text-internal temporal order (Modi and Titov, 2014; Frermann et al., 2014).

We address the task of automatically mapping narrative texts to scripts, which will leverage explicit script knowledge for the afore-mentioned aspects of text understanding, as well as for downstream tasks such as textual entailment, question answering or paraphrase detection. We build on the work of Regneri et al. (2010) and Wanzare et al. (2016), who collect explicit script knowledge via crowdsourcing, by asking people to describe everyday activities. These crowdsourced descriptions form a basis for high-quality automatic extraction of script structure without any human intervention (Regneri et al., 2010; Wanzare et al., 2017). The events of the resulting structure are defined as sets of alternative realizations, which cover lexical variation and provide paraphrase information. To the best of our knowledge, these advantages have not been explicitly used elsewhere.

Aligning script structures with texts is a complex task. In a first attempt, we assume that three steps are necessary to solve it, although in the long run, an integrated approach will be preferable: First, the script which is addressed by the event mention must be identified. Second, it has to be decided whether a verb denotes a script event at all. Finally, event verbs need to be assigned a script-specific event type label. This work focuses on the last two steps: We use a corpus of narrative stories each of which is centered around a specific script scenario, and distinguish verbs related to the central script from all other verb occurrences with a simple decision tree classifier. We then train a sequence labeling model only on crowdsourced script data and assign event type labels to all script-related event verbs.

Our results substantially outperform informed

*Proceedings of the 6th Joint Conference on Lexical and Computational Semantics (*SEM 2017)*, pages 128–134,
Vancouver, Canada, August 3-4, 2017. ©2017 Association for Computational Linguistics

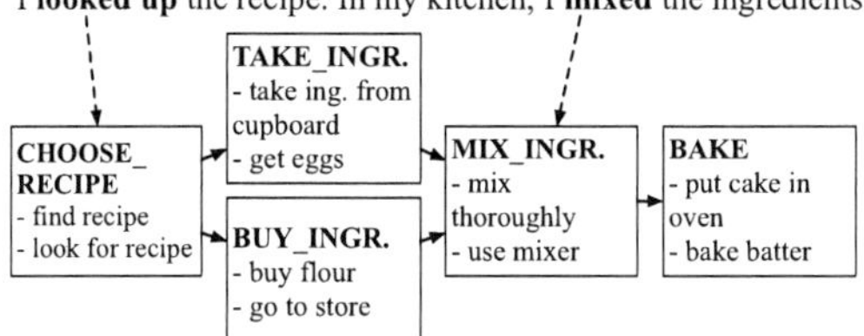

Figure 1: An example of text-to-script mapping with an excerpt of the BAKING A CAKE script and a story snippet.

baselines, in spite of the availability of only small amounts of training data. In particular, we also demonstrate the relevance of event ordering information provided by script knowledge.

Our code and all data and parameters that are used are publicly available under `https://github.com/SimonOst`.

2 Task and Data

As a basis for the task of text-to-script mapping, we make use of two recently published datasets. *DeScript* (Wanzare et al., 2016) is a collection of crowdsourced linguistic descriptions of event patterns for everyday activities, so called *event sequence descriptions (ESDs)*. ESDs consist of short telegram-style descriptions of single events (*event descriptions, ED*). The textual order of EDs corresponds to the temporal order of respective events, i.e. temporal information is explicitly encoded. *DeScript* contains 50 ESDs for each of 40 different scenarios. Alongside the ESDs, it also provides gold event paraphrase sets, i.e. clusters of all event descriptions denoting the same event type, labeled with the respective type.

While DeScript is a source of structured script knowledge, the *InScript* corpus (Modi et al., 2016) provides us with the appropriate kind of narrative texts. *InScript* is a collection of 910 stories centered around some specific scenario, for 10 of the 40 scenarios in *DeScript*, e.g. BAKING A CAKE, RIDING A BUS, TAKING A SHOWER. All verbs occurring in the texts are annotated with an event type if they are relevant to the script instantiated by the story; as *non-script event* otherwise.

In the upper part of Fig. 1, you see the initial fragment of a story about baking a cake; together with a script excerpt in the lower part, depicted by labeled event paraphrase sets. *I looked up the*

recipe and *I mixed the ingredients* mention relevant script events, and therefore should be labeled with the indicated event types (CHOOSE_RECIPE, MIX_INGREDIENTS). Fig. 1 also illustrates the potential of text-to-script mapping: script knowledge enables to predict that a baking event might be addressed next in the story. The verb *was* does not denote an event at all, and *decide* is not part of the BAKING A CAKE script, so they are assigned the label *non-script event*. Actually, *InScript* comes with two additional categories of verbs (*script-related* and *script-evoking*), which we subsume under *non-script event*.

The central task addressed in our paper, the automatic labeling of all script-relevant verbs in the *InScript* text with a script-specific event type, uses only *DeScript* data for training; event-type labels of *InScript* are used for evaluation purposes only.

3 Model

Section 3.1 defines the central part of our system, a sequence model for classifying script-relevant verbs into scenario-specific event types. For full automation of the text-to-script mapping, we describe in Section 3.2 a model for identifying script-relevant verbs.

3.1 Event Type Classification

For identifying the correct event type given a script-relevant verb, we leverage two types of information: We require a representation for the meaning and content of the event mention, which takes into account not only the verb, but also the persons and objects involved in an event, i.e. the *script participants*. In addition, we take event ordering information into account, which helps to disambiguate event mentions based on their local context. To model both event types and sequences thereof, we implement a linear-chain conditional random field (CRF, Lafferty et al. (2001)). Our implementation is based on the CRF++ toolkit[1] and employs two types of features:

Sequential Feature. Our CRF model utilizes event ordering information in the form of binary indicator features that encode the co-occurrence of two event type labels in sequence.

Meaning Representation Features. Two feature types encode the meaning of a textual event mention. One is a shallow form of representation derived from precomputed word embeddings

---

[1] `taku910.github.io/crfpp/`

(*word2vec*, Mikolov et al. (2013)). This feature type captures distributional information of the verb and its direct nominal dependents[2], which we assume to denote script participants, and is computed by averaging over the respective word vector representations.[3] We use pretrained 300-dimensional embeddings that are trained on the Google News corpus.[4] As a more explicit but sparse form of content representation, we use as the other type of feature the lemma of the verb, its indirect object and its direct object.

3.2 Identifying Script-Relevant Verbs

We use a decision tree classifier for identifying script-relevant verbs (*J48* from the Weka toolkit, Frank et al. (2016)) that takes into account four classes: the three *non-script event* classes from *InScript* and one class for all *event-verbs*. At test time, the three *non-script event* classes are merged into one class. Due to the lack of *non-script event* instances in *DeScript*, we train and test our model on all verbs occurring in *InScript*. We use the following feature types:

Syntactic Features. We employ syntactic features for identifying verbs that only rarely denote script events, independent of the scenario: a feature for auxiliaries; for verbs that govern an adverbial phrase (mostly if-clauses); a feature indicating the number of direct and indirect objects; and a lexical feature that checks if the verb belongs to a predefined list of non-action verbs.

Script Features. For finding verbs that match the current script scenario, we employ two features: a binary feature indicating whether the verb is used in the ESDs for the given scenario; and a scenario-specific tf–idf score that is computed by treating all ESDs from a scenario as one document, summed over the verb and its dependents. In Section 4.2, we evaluate models with and without script features, to test the impact of scenario-specific information.

Frame Feature. We further employ frame-semantic information because we expect script events to typically evoke certain frames. We use a state-of-the-art semantic role labeler (Roth, 2016; Roth and Lapata, 2016) based on *FrameNet* (Rup-

	P	**R**	**F$_1$**
Lemma	0.365	**0.949**	0.526
Our model	**0.628**	0.817	**0.709**
Our model (scen. indep.)	0.513	0.877	0.645

Table 1: Identification of script-relevant verbs within a scenario and independent of the scenario.

penhofer et al., 2006) to predict frames for all verbs, encoding the frame as a feature. We address sparsity of too specific frames by mapping all frames to higher-level super frames using the *framenet querying package*[5].

4 Evaluation

4.1 Experimental Setup

We evaluate our model for text-to-script mapping based on the resources introduced in Section 2. We process the *InScript* and *DeScript* data sets using the Stanford Parser (Klein and Manning, 2003)[6]. We further resolve pronouns in *InScript* using annotated coreference chains from the gold standard.

We individually test the two components, i.e. the identification of script-relevant verbs and event classification. Experiments on the first sub-task are described in Section 4.2. Sections 4.3 and 4.4 present results on the latter task and a combination of both tasks, respectively.

4.2 Identifying Script-Relevant Verbs

In this evaluation, we test the ability of our model to identify verbs in narrative texts that instantiate script events. Our experiments make use of a 10-fold cross-validation setting within all texts of one scenario. To test the model in a scenario-independent setting, we perform additional experiments based on a cross-validation with the 10 scenarios as one fold each and exclude the script features. That is, we repeatedly train our model on 9 scenarios and evaluate on the remaining scenario, without using any information about the test scenario.

Models. We compare the model described in Section 3.2 to a baseline (*Lemma*) that always assigns the *event* class if the verb lemma is mentioned in *DeScript*. We report precision, recall and F$_1$-score on event verbs, averaged over all scenarios.

---

[2] For EDs, we use all mentioned head nouns.

[3] To emphasize the importance of the verb, we double its weight when averaging.

[4] Because our CRF model only supports nominal features, we discretize embeddings from `code.google.com/archive/p/word2vec/` by binning the component values into three intervals $[-\infty, -\epsilon], [-\epsilon, \epsilon], [\epsilon, \infty]$. The hyperparameter ϵ is determined on a held-out development set.

[5] `github.com/icsi-berkeley/framenet`

[6] To improve performance on the simplistic sentences from *DeScript*, we follow Regneri (2013) and re-train the parser.

Results. Table 1 gives an overview of the results based on 10-fold cross-validation. Our scenario-specific model is capable of identifying more than 81% of script-relevant verbs at a precision of about 63%. This is a notable improvement over the baseline, which identifies 94.9% of the event verbs, but at a precision of only 36.5%.

The table also gives numbers for the scenario-independent setting: Precision drops to around 51% if only training data from other scenarios is available. One of the main difficulties here lies in classifying different *non-script event* verb classes in a way that generalizes across scenarios. Modi et al. (2016) also found that distinguishing specific types of non-script events from script events can be difficult even for humans.

4.3 Event Type Classification

In this section, we describe experiments on the text-to-script mapping task based on the subset of event instances from *InScript* that are annotated as script-related. As training data, we use the *ESDs* and the event type annotations from the *DeScript* gold standard[7]. The evaluation task is to classify individual event mentions in *InScript* based on their verbal realization in the narrative text. We evaluate against the gold-standard annotations from *InScript*. Since event type annotations are used for evaluation purposes only, this task comes close to a realistic setup, in which script knowledge is available for specific scenarios but no training data in the form of event-type annotated narrative texts exists.

Models. We evaluate our CRF model described in Section 3.1 against two baselines that are based on textual similarity. Both baselines compare the event verb and its dependents in *InScript* to all EDs in *DeScript* and assign the event type with the highest similarity. *Lemma* is a simple measure based on word overlap, *word2vec* uses the same embedding representation as the CRF model (before discretization) but simply assigns the best matching event type label based on cosine similarity. We report precision, recall and F_1-scores, macro-averaged over all script-event types and scenarios.

Results. Results for all models are presented in Table 2. Our CRF model achieves a F_1-score of 0.545, a considerably higher performance in comparison to the baselines. As can be seen from excluding the sequential feature, ordering information

---

[7]In *DeScript*, there are some rare cases of *EDs* that do not describe a script event, but that are labeled as *non-script event*. We exclude these from the training data.

	P	R	F_1
Lemma	0.343	0.416	0.374
Word2vec	0.356	0.448	0.395
CRF model	**0.608**	**0.496**	**0.545**
CRF, no seq.	0.599	0.487	0.536

Table 2: Event Type Classification performance, with and without sequential features.

	P	R	F_1
Ident. model+Lemma	0.253	0.451	0.323
Ident. model+Word2vec	0.255	0.477	0.331
Ident. model+CRF model	**0.445**	**0.520**	**0.479**

Table 3: Full text-to-script mapping results.

improves the result. The rather small difference is due to the fact that ordering information can also be misleading (cf. Section 5). We found, however, that including the sequential feature accounts for an improvement of up to 4% in F_1 score, depending on the scenario.

4.4 Full Text-to-Script Mapping Task

We now address the full text-to-script mapping task, a combination of the identification of relevant verbs and event type classification. This setup allows us to assess whether the general task of a fully automatic mapping of verbs in narrative texts to script events is feasible.

Models. We compare the same models as in Section 4.3, but use them on top of our model for identifying script-relevant verbs (cf. Section 4.2) instead of using the gold standard for identification.

Results. On the full text-to-script mapping task, our combined identification and CRF model achieves a precision and recall of 0.445 and 0.52, resp. (cf. Table 3). This reflects an absolute improvement over the baselines of 0.148 and 0.156 in terms of F_1-score. The results reflect the general difficulty of this task but are promising overall. As reported by Modi et al. (2016), even human annotators only achieve an agreement of 0.64 in terms of Fleiss' Kappa (1971).

5 Discussion

In this section, we discuss cases in which our system predicted the wrong event type and give examples for each case. We identified three major error sources:

Lexical Coverage. We found that although *DeScript* is a small resource, training a model purely on *ESDs* works reasonably well. Coverage problems can be seen in cases of events for which only few *EDs* exist. An example is the CHOOSE_TREE event (the event of picking a tree at the shop) in the PLANTING A TREE scenario. There are only 3 *EDs* describing the event, each of which uses the event verb "choose". In contrast, we find that "choose" is used in less than 10% of the event mentions in *InScript*. Because of this mismatch, which can be attributed to the small training data size, more frequently used verbs for this event in *InScript*, such as "pick" and "decide", are labeled incorrectly.

We observe that our meaning representation might be insufficient for finding synonyms for about 30% of observed verb tokens. This specifically includes scenario-specific and uncommon verbs, such as "squirt" in the context of the BAKING A CAKE scenario (*squirt the frosting onto the cake*). Problems may also arise from the fact that about 23% of the verb types occur in multiple paraphrase clusters of a scenario.

Misleading Ordering Information. We found that ordering information is in general beneficial for text-to-script alignment. We however also identified cases for which it can be misleading, by comparing the output of our full model to the model that does not use sequential features. As another result of the small size of *DeScript*, there are plausible event sequences that appear only rarely or never in the training data. This error source is involved in 60–70% of the observed misclassifications due to misleading ordering information. An example is the WASH event in the GETTING A HAIRCUT scenario: It never appears directly after the MOVE_IN_SALON event (i.e. walking from the counter to the chair) in *DeScript*, but its a plausible sequence that is misclassified by our model.

In almost 15% of the observed errors, an event type is mentioned more than once, leading to misclassifications whenever ordering information is used. One reason for this might be that events in *InScript* are described in a more exhaustive or fine-grained way. For example, the WASH event in the TAKING A BATH scenario is often broken up into three mentions: wetting the hair, applying shampoo, and washing it again. However, because there is only one event type for the three mentions, this sequence is never observed in *DeScript*.

Events with an interchangeable natural order lead to errors in a number of cases: In the BAKING A CAKE scenario, a few misclassifications happen because the order in which e.g. ingredients are prepared, the pan is greased and the oven is preheated is very flexible, but the model overfits to what it observed from the training.

As last, there are also a few cases in which an event is mentioned, even before it actually takes place. In the case of the *borrowing a book* scenario, there are cases in *InScript* that mention in the first sentence that the purpose of the visit is to return a book. In *DeScript* in contrast, the RETURN event always takes place in the very end.

Near Misses. For many verbs, it is also difficult for humans to come up with one correct event label. By investigating confusion matrices for single scenarios, we found that for at least 3–5% of script event verbs in the test set, our model predicted an "incorrect" label for such verbs, but that label might still be plausible. In the BAKING A CAKE scenario, for example, there is little to no difference between mentions of making the dough and preparing ingredients. As a consequence, these two events are often confused: Approximately 50% of the instances labeled as PREPARE_INGREDIENTS are actually instances of MAKE_DOUGH.

6 Summary

In this paper, we addressed the task of automatically mapping event denoting expressions in narrative texts to script events, based on an explicit script representation that is learned from crowdsourced data rather than from text collections. Our models outperform two similarity-based baselines by leveraging rich event representations and ordering information. We showed that models of script knowledge can be successfully trained on crowdsourced data, even if the number of training examples is small. This work thus builds a basis for utilizing the advantages of crowdsourced script representations for downstream tasks and future work, e.g. paraphrase identification in discourse context or event prediction on narrative texts.

Acknowledgments

We thank the anonymous reviewers for their helpful comments. This research was funded by the German Research Foundation (DFG) as part of SFB 1102 'Information Density and Linguistic Encoding'. Work by MR in Illinois was supported by a DFG Research Fellowship (RO 4848/1-1).

References

Avron Barr and Edward A. Feigenbaum. 1981. *The Handbook of Artificial Intelligence*. Addison-Wesley.

Cosmin Adrian Bejan and Sanda Harabagiu. 2010. Unsupervised event coreference resolution with rich linguistic features. In *Proceedings of the 48th Annual Meeting of the Association for Computational Linguistics*. Association for Computational Linguistics, pages 1412–1422.

Nathanael Chambers and Dan Jurafsky. 2009. Unsupervised learning of narrative schemas and their participants. *Proceedings of the 47th Annual Meeting of the ACL and the 4th IJCNLP of the AFNLP* .

Joseph L Fleiss. 1971. Measuring nominal scale agreement among many raters. *Psychological bulletin* 76(5):378.

Eibe Frank, Mark A. Hall, and Ian H. Witten. 2016. The weka workbench. online appendix for "data mining: Practical machine learning tools and techniques" .

Lea Frermann, Ivan Titov, and Manfred Pinkal. 2014. A hierarchical bayesian model for unsupervised induction of script knowledge. In *EACL*. volume 14, pages 49–57.

Daniel Gildea and Daniel Jurafsky. 2002. Automatic labeling of semantic roles. *Computational linguistics* 28(3):245–288.

Bram Jans, Steven Bethard, Ivan Vulić, and Marie Francine Moens. 2012. Skip n-grams and ranking functions for predicting script events. In *Proceedings of the 13th Conference of the European Chapter of the Association for Computational Linguistics*. Association for Computational Linguistics, pages 336–344.

Dan Klein and Christopher D. Manning. 2003. Fast exact inference with a factored model for natural language parsing. In *In Advances in Neural Information Processing Systems 15 (NIPS*. MIT Press, pages 3–10.

John D. Lafferty, Andrew McCallum, and Fernando C. N. Pereira. 2001. Conditional random fields: Probabilistic models for segmenting and labeling sequence data. In *Proceedings of the Eighteenth International Conference on Machine Learning*. ICML '01, pages 282–289.

Heeyoung Lee, Marta Recasens, Angel Chang, Mihai Surdeanu, and Dan Jurafsky. 2012. Joint entity and event coreference resolution across documents. In *Proceedings of the 2012 Joint Conference on Empirical Methods in Natural Language Processing and Computational Natural Language Learning*. Association for Computational Linguistics, pages 489–500.

Xiao Ling and Daniel S Weld. 2010. Temporal information extraction. In *AAAI*. volume 10, pages 1385–1390.

Tomas Mikolov, Kai Chen, Greg Corrado, and Jeffrey Dean. 2013. Efficient estimation of word representations in vector space. *CoRR* .

Anne-Lyse Minard, Manuela Speranza, Eneko Agirre, Itziar Aldabe, Marieke van Erp, Bernardo Magnini, German Rigau, Ruben Urizar, and Fondazione Bruno Kessler. 2015. Semeval-2015 task 4: Timeline: Cross-document event ordering. In *Proceedings of the 9th International Workshop on Semantic Evaluation (SemEval 2015)*. pages 778–786.

Ashutosh Modi, Tatjana Anikina, Simon Ostermann, and Manfred Pinkal. 2016. Inscript: Narrative texts annotated with script information. *Proceedings of the 10th International Conference on Language Resources and Evaluation (LREC 16)* .

Ashutosh Modi and Ivan Titov. 2014. Inducing neural models of script knowledge. In *Proceedings of the Conference on Computational Natural Language Learning (CoNLL)*. Baltimore, MD, USA.

Ashutosh Modi, Ivan Titov, Vera Demberg, Asad Sayeed, and Manfred Pinkal. 2017. Modelling semantic expectation: Using script knowledge for referent prediction. *Transactions of the Association for Computational Linguistics* 5:31–44.

Martha Palmer, Daniel Gildea, and Nianwen Xue. 2010. Semantic role labeling. *Synthesis Lectures on Human Language Technologies* 3(1):1–103.

Michaela Regneri. 2013. *Event Structures in Knowledge, Pictures and Text*. Ph.D. thesis, Universität des Saarlandes.

Michaela Regneri, Alexander Koller, and Manfred Pinkal. 2010. Learning script knowledge with web experiments. In *Proceedings of the 48th Annual Meeting of the Association for Computational Linguistics*. Association for Computational Linguistics, Stroudsburg, PA, USA, ACL '10, pages 979–988.

Michael Roth. 2016. Improving frame semantic parsing via dependency path embeddings. In *Book of Abstracts of the 9th International Conference on Construction Grammar*. Juiz de Fora, Brazil, pages 165–167.

Michael Roth and Mirella Lapata. 2016. Neural semantic role labeling with dependency path embeddings. In *Proceedings of the 54th Annual Meeting of the Association for Computational Linguistics (Volume 1: Long Papers)*. Berlin, Germany, pages 1192–1202.

Rachel Rudinger, Vera Demberg, Ashutosh Modi, Benjamin Van Durme, and Manfred Pinkal. 2015. Learning to predict script events from domain-specific text. *Lexical and Computational Semantics (* SEM 2015)* page 205.

Josef Ruppenhofer, Michael Ellsworth, Miriam RL Petruck, Christopher R Johnson, and Jan Scheffczyk. 2006. Framenet ii: Extended theory and practice.

Roger C Schank and Robert P Abelson. 1975. *Scripts, plans, and knowledge*. Yale University New Haven, CT.

Lilian D. A. Wanzare, Alessandra Zarcone, Stefan Thater, and Manfred Pinkal. 2016. A crowdsourced database of event sequence descriptions for the acquisition of high-quality script knowledge. *Proceedings of the Tenth International Conference on Language Resources and Evaluation (LREC'16)* .

Lilian D. A. Wanzare, Alessandra Zarcone, Stefan Thater, and Manfred Pinkal. 2017. Inducing script structure from crowdsourced event descriptions via semi-supervised clustering. *Proceedings of the 2nd Workshop on Linking Models of Lexical, Sentential and Discourse-level Semantics* .

The (Too Many) Problems of Analogical Reasoning with Word Vectors

Anna Rogers

Dept. of Computer Science

University of Massachusetts Lowell

Lowell, MA, USA

arogers@cs.uml.edu

Aleksandr Drozd

Global Scient. Inf. and Comput. Center

Tokyo Institute of Technology

Tokyo, Japan

alex@smg.is.titech.ac.jp

Bofang Li

School of Information

Renmin University of China

Beijing, China

libofang@ruc.edu.cn

Abstract

This paper explores the possibilities of analogical reasoning with vector space models. Given two pairs of words with the same relation (e.g. *man:woman :: king:queen*), it was proposed that the offset between one pair of the corresponding word vectors can be used to identify the unknown member of the other pair ($\overrightarrow{king} - \overrightarrow{man} + \overrightarrow{woman} = ?\overrightarrow{queen}$). We argue against such "linguistic regularities" as a model for linguistic relations in vector space models and as a benchmark, and we show that the vector offset (as well as two other, better-performing methods) suffers from dependence on vector similarity.

1 Introduction

This paper considers the phenomenon of "vector-oriented reasoning" via linear vector offset in vector space models (VSMs) (Mikolov et al., 2013c,a). Given two pairs of words with the same linguistic relation (*woman:man :: king:queen*), it has been proposed that the offset between one pair of word vectors can be used to identify the unknown member of a different pair of words via solving proportional analogy problems ($\overrightarrow{king} - \overrightarrow{man} + \overrightarrow{woman} = ?\overrightarrow{queen}$), as shown in Fig. 1. We will refer to this method as 3CosAdd.

This approach attracted a lot of attention, both as the "poster child" of word embeddings, and for its potential practical utility. Given the vital role that analogical reasoning plays in human cognition for discovering new knowledge and understanding new concepts, automated analogical reasoning could become a game-changer in many fields, providing a universal mechanism for detecting linguistic relations (Turney, 2008) and word sense disambiguation (Federici et al., 1997). It is

already used in many downstream NLP tasks, such as splitting compounds (Daiber et al., 2015), semantic search (Cohen et al., 2015), cross-language relational search (Duc et al., 2012), to name a few.

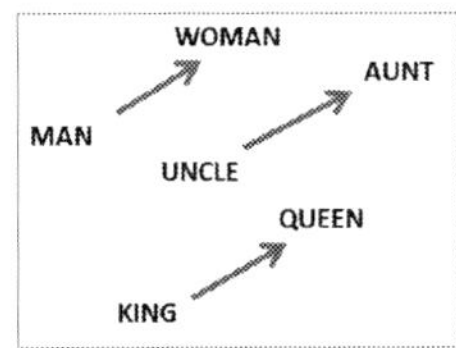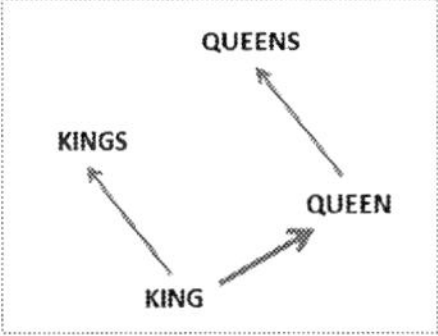

Figure 1: Linguistic relations modeled by linear vector offset (Mikolov et al., 2013c)

The idea that linguistic relations are mirrored in neat geometrical relations (as shown in Fig. 1) is also intuitively appealing, and 3CosAdd has become a popular benchmark. Roughly, the current VSMs score between 40% (Lai et al., 2016) and 75% (Pennington et al., 2014) on the Google test set (Mikolov et al., 2013a). However, in fact performance varies widely for different types of relations (Levy and Goldberg, 2014; Köper et al., 2015; Gladkova et al., 2016).

One way to explain the current limitations is to attribute them to the imperfections of the current models and/or corpora with which they are built: with this view, in a perfect VSM, any linguistic relation should be recoverable via vector offset.

The alternative to be explored in this paper is that perhaps natural language semantics is more complex than suggested by Fig. 1, and there may be both theoretical and mathematical issues with analogical reasoning with word vectors and its 3CosAdd implementation.

We present a series of experiments with two popular VSMs (GloVe and Word2Vec) to show that the accuracy of 3CosAdd depends on the proximity of the target vector to its source (i.e.

*Proceedings of the 6th Joint Conference on Lexical and Computational Semantics (*SEM 2017)*, pages 135–148,
Vancouver, Canada, August 3-4, 2017. ©2017 Association for Computational Linguistics

$\overrightarrow{queen}$ should be quite similar to $\overrightarrow{king}$). Since not all linguistic relations can be expected to result in high word vector proximity, the method is limited to those that happen to be so in a given VSM. Furthermore, its accuracy also varies because the "linguistic regularities" are actually not so regular, and should not be expected to be so. We also compare 3CosAdd to two alternative methods to investigate whether better algorithms can improve on these and other accounts.

2 Background: "Relational Similarity" vs "Word Analogies"

The most fundamental term for what 3CosAdd is supposed to capture is actually not analogy, but rather *relational similarity*, i.e. the idea that pairs of words may hold similar relations to those between other pairs of words. For example, the relation between *cat* and *feline* is similar to the relation between *dog* and *canine*. Notably, this is *similarity* rather than identity: "instances of a single relation may still have significant variability in how characteristic they are of that class" (Jurgens et al., 2012).

Analogy as it is known in philosophy and logic is something quite different. The "classical" analogical reasoning follows roughly this template: objects X and Y share properties a, b, and c; therefore, they may also share the property d. For example, both Earth and Mars orbit the Sun, have at least one moon, revolve on axis, and are subject to gravity; therefore, if Earth supports life, so could Mars (Bartha, 2016).

The NLP move from relational similarity to analogy follows the use of the term by P. Turney, who distinguishes between attributional similarity between two words and relational similarity between two pairs of words. On this interpretation, *two word pairs that have a high degree of relational similarity are analogous* (Turney, 2006).

In terms of practical NLP tasks, Turney et al. (2003) introduced the task of solving SAT[1] analogy problems by choosing from several provided options. These problems were formulated as *proportional analogies*, written in the form $a : a' :: b : b'$ (a is to a' as b is to b')

It is this use of the term "analogy" that Mikolov et al. (2013c) followed in proposing the 3CosAdd method. They formulated the task as selecting a single best fitting vector out of the whole vocabu-

---

[1]Scholastic Aptitude Test.

lary of the VSM. It became known as *word analogy task*, but in its core it is still basically estimation of relational similarity, and could be formulated as such: given a pair of words a and a', find how they are related and then find word b', such that it has a similar relation with the word b. A crucial difference is that the graded, non-binary nature of relational similarity is now not in focus: the goal is to find a single correct answer.

The dataset that came to be known as the Google analogy test set (Mikolov et al., 2013a), included 14 linguistic relations with 19544 questions in total. It has become one of the most popular benchmarks for VSMs. This evaluation paradigm assumes that:

(1) Words in similar linguistic relations should in principle be recoverable via relational similarity to known word pairs.

(2) 3CosAdd score reflects the extent to which a given VSM encodes linguistic relations.

(1) became dubious when it was shown that accuracy of 3CosAdd varies widely between categories (Levy and Goldberg, 2014), and even the best-performing GloVe model scores under 30% on the more challenging Bigger Analogy Test Set (BATS) (Gladkova et al., 2016). It appears that not all relations can be identified in this way, with lexical semantic relations such as synonymy and antonymy being particularly difficult (Köper et al., 2015; Vylomova et al., 2016). The assumption of a single best-fitting candidate answer is also being targeted (Newman-Griffis et al., 2017).

(2) was refuted when Drozd et al. (2016) demonstrated that some relations missed by 3CosAdd could be recovered with a supervised method, and therefore the information was present in the VSM – just not recoverable with 3CosAdd.

Let us consider why both (1) and (2) failed.

3 What Does 3CosAdd Really Do?

3.1 Methodology

We present a series of experiments performed with BATS dataset. Although there are more results on analogy task published with Google test than with BATS, Google test only contains 15 types of linguistic relations, and these happen to be the easier ones (Gladkova et al., 2016).

Table 1 lists examples of each BATS category: there are 50 word pairs for each of 40 linguistic

Inflectional morphology	Nouns	regular plurals *(student:students)*, plurals with orthographic changes *(wife:wives)*
	Adjectives	comparative degree *(strong:stronger)*, superlative degree *(strong:strongest)*
	Verbs	infinitive: 3Ps.Sg *(follow:follows)*, infinitive: participle *(follow:following)*, infinitive: past *(follow:followed)*, participle: 3Ps.Sg *(following:follows)*, participle: past *(following:followed)*, 3Ps.Sg : past *(follows:followed)*
Derivational morphology	Stem change	verb+er *(bake:baker)*, verb+able *(edit:editable)*, verb+ation *(continue:continuation)*, verb+ment *(argue:argument)*
	No stem change	re+verb *(create:recreate)*, noun+less *(home:homeless)*, adj.+ness *(mad:madness)*, un+adj. *(able:unable)*, adj.+ly *(usual:usually)*, over+adj. *(used:overused)*
Lexicographic semantics	Hypernyms	animals *(turtle:reptile)*, miscellaneous *(peach:fruit)*
	Hyponyms	miscellaneous *(color:white)*
	Meronyms	part-whole *(car:engine)*, substance *(sea:water)*, member *(player:team)*,
	Antonyms	opposites *(up:down)*, gradable *(clean:dirty)*
	Synonyms	exact *(sofa:couch)*, intensity *(cry:scream)*
Encyclopedic semantics	Animals	the young *(cat:kitten)*, sounds *(dog:bark)*, shelter *fox:den*
	Geography	capitals *(Athens:Greece)*, languages *(Peru:Spanish)*, UK city:county *York:Yorkshire*
	People	occupation *(Lincoln:president)*, nationalities *(Lincoln:American)*
	Other	thing:color *(blood:red)*, male:female *(actor:actress)*

Table 1: The Bigger Analogy Test Set: categories and examples

relations (98,000 questions in total). BATS covers most relations in the Google set, but it adds many new and more difficult relations, balanced across derivational and inflectional morphology, lexicographic and encyclopedic semantics (10 relations of each type). Thus BATS provides a less flattering, but more accurate estimate of the capacity for analogical reasoning in the current VSMs.

We use pre-trained GloVe vectors by Pennington et al. (2014), released by the authors[2] and trained on Gigaword 5 + Wikipedia 2014 (300 dimensions, window size 10). We also experiment with Word2Vec vectors (Mikolov et al., 2013b) released by the authors[3], trained on a subcorpus of Google news (also with 300 dimensions).

The evaluation with 3CosAdd and LRCos methods was conducted with the Python script that accompanies BATS. We also added an implementation of 3CosMul, a multiplicative objective proposed by Levy and Goldberg (2014), now available in the same script[4]. Since 3CosMul requires normalization, we used normalized GloVe and Word2Vec vectors in all experiments.

Questions with words not in the model vocabulary were excluded (0.01% BATS questions for GloVe and 0.016% for Word2Vec).

3.2 The "Honest" 3CosAdd

Let us remember that 3CosAdd as initially formulated by Mikolov et al. (2013c) excludes the three

source vectors a, a' and b from the pool of possible answers. Linzen (2016) showed that if that is not done, the accuracy drops dramatically, hitting zero for 9 out of 15 Google test categories.

Let us investigate what happens on BATS data, split by 4 relation types. The rows of Fig. 2 represent all questions of a given category, with darker color indicating higher percentage of predicted vectors being the closest to a, a', b, b', or any other vector.

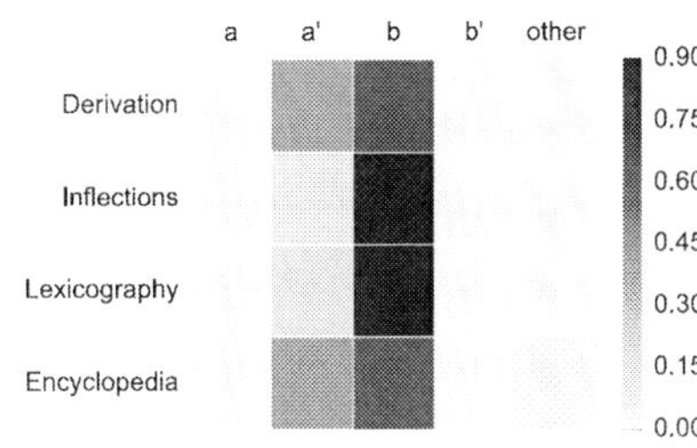

Figure 2: The result of $a - a' + b$ calculation on BATS: source vectors a, a', and b are not excluded.

Fig. 2 shows that if we do not exclude the source vectors, b is the most likely to be predicted; in derivational and encyclopedic categories a' is also possible in under 30% of cases. b' is as unlikely to be predicted as a, or any other vector.

This experiment suggests that the addition of the offset between a and a' typically has a very small effect on the b vector – not sufficient to induce a shift to a different vector on its own. This would in effect limit the search space of 3CosAdd to the close neighborhood of the b vector.

It explains another phenomenon pointed out by Linzen (2016): for the plural noun category in the

137

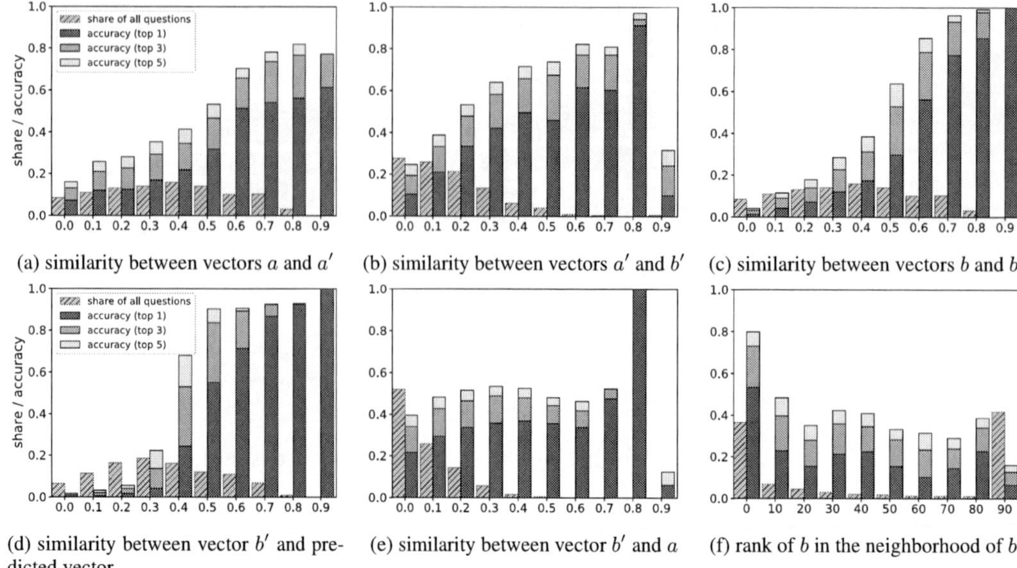

(a) similarity between vectors a and a' (b) similarity between vectors a' and b' (c) similarity between vectors b and b'

(d) similarity between vector b' and predicted vector   (e) similarity between vector b' and a (f) rank of b in the neighborhood of b'

*X-axis labels indicate lower boundary of the corresponding similarity/rank bins.
The numerical values for all data can be found in the Appendix.

Figure 3: Accuracy of 3CosAdd method on GloVe vs characteristics of the vector space.

Google test set 70% accuracy was achieved by simply taking the closest neighbor of the vector b, while 3CosAdd improved the accuracy by only 10%. That would indeed be expected if most singular (a) and plural (a') forms of the same noun were so similar, that subtracting them would result in a nearly-null vector which would not change much when added to b.

3.3 Distance to the Target Vector

Levy and Goldberg (2014, p.173) suggested that 3CosAdd method is "mathematically equivalent to seeking a word (b') which is similar to b and a' but is different from a." We examined the similarity between all source vector pairs, looking not only at the actual, top-1 accuracy of the 3CosAdd (i.e. the vector the closest to the hypothetical vector), but also at whether the correct answer was found in the top-3 and top-5 neighbors of the predicted vector. For each similarity bin we also estimated how many questions of the whole BATS dataset there were. The results are presented in Fig. 3.

Our data indicates that, indeed, for all combinations of source vectors, the accuracy of 3CosAdd decreases as their distance in vector space increases. It is the most successful when all three source vectors are relatively close to each other and the target vector. This is in line with the above

evidence from the "honest" 3CosAdd: if the offset is typically small, for it to lead to the target vector, that target vector should be close.

Consider also the ranks of the b vectors in the neighborhood of b', shown in Fig. 3f. For nearly 40% of the successful questions b' was within 10 neighbors of b – and over 40% of low-accuracy questions were over 90 neighbors away.

As predicted by Levy et al., b' and a vectors do not exhibit the same clear trend for higher accuracy with higher similarity that is observed in all other cases (Fig. 3f). However, in experiments with only 20 morphological categories we did observe the same trend for b' and a as for the other vector pairs (see Fig. 4). This is counter-intuitive, and requires further examination.

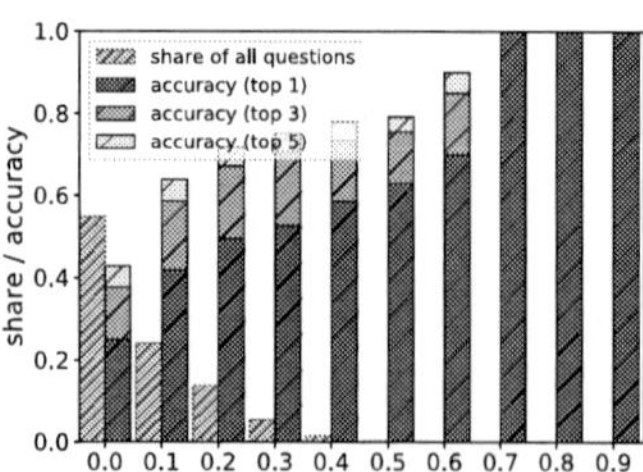

Figure 4: The similarity between b' and a on GloVe: morphological BATS categories only.

The observed correlation between the accuracy of 3CosAdd and the distance to the target vector could explain in particular the overall lower performance on BATS derivational morphology questions (only 0.08% top-1 accuracy) as opposed to inflectional (0.59%) or encyclopedic semantics (0.26%). $\overrightarrow{man}$ and $\overrightarrow{woman}$ could be expected to be reasonably similar distributionally, as they combine with many of the same verbs: both men and women sit, sleep, drink etc. However, the same could not be said of words derived with prefixes that change part of speech. Going from $\overrightarrow{happy}$ to $\overrightarrow{happiness}$, or from $\overrightarrow{govern}$ to $\overrightarrow{government}$, is likely to have to take us further in the vector space.

To make sure that the above trend is not specific to GloVe, we repeated these experiments with Word2Vec, which exhibited the same trends. All data is presented in Appendix A.1.

3.4 Uniqueness of a Relation

Note that the dependence of 3CosAdd on similarity is not entirely straightforward: Fig. 3b shows that for the highest similarity (0.9 and more) there is actually a drop in accuracy. The same trend was observed with Word2Vec (Fig 10 in Appendix 1). Theoretically, it could be attributed to there not being much data in the highest similarity range; but BATS has 98,000 questions, and even 0.1% of that is considerable.

The culprit is the "dishonesty" of 3CosAdd: as discussed above, it excludes the source vectors a, a', and b from the pool of possible answers. Not only does this mask the real extent of the difference between a and a', but it also creates a fundamental difficulty with categories where the source vectors may be the correct answers.

This is what explains the unexpected drops in accuracy at the highest similarity between vectors b' and a'. Consider the question $\overrightarrow{blood}:\overrightarrow{red}$ :: $\overrightarrow{snow}:?white$. The vector offset could theoretically solve it, but if the question is $\overrightarrow{snow}:\overrightarrow{white}$ :: $\overrightarrow{sugar}:?white$, the correct answer would *a priori* be excluded. In BATS data, this factor affects several semantic categories, including country:language, thing:color, animal:young, and animal:shelter.

3.5 Density of Vector Neighborhoods

If solving proportional analogies with word vectors is like shooting, the farther away the target

vector is, the more difficult it should be to hit. Also, we can hypothesize that the more crowded a particular region is, the more difficult it should be to hit a particular target.

However, density of vector neighborhoods is not as straightforward to measure as vector similarity. We could look at average similarity between, e.g., top-10 ranking neighbors, but that could misrepresent the situation if some neighbors were very close and some were very far.

In this experiment we estimate density as the similarity to the 5th neighbor. The higher it is, the more highly similar neighbors a word vector has. This approach is shown in Fig. 5.

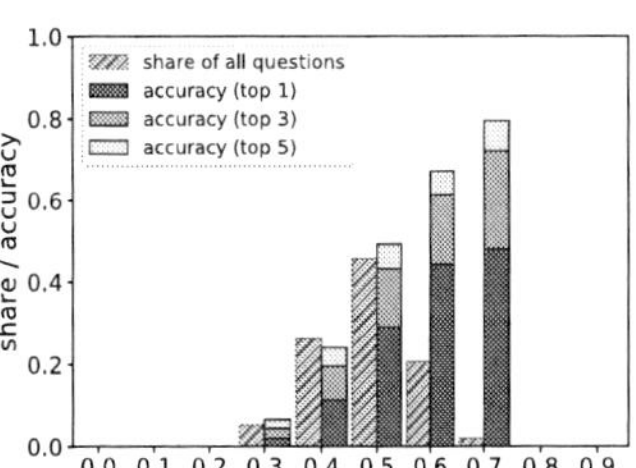

Figure 5: The similarity between b' and its 5th neighbor

The results seem counter-intuitive: denser neighborhoods actually yield higher accuracy (although there are virtually no cases of very tight neighborhoods). One explanation could be its reverse correlation with distance: if the neighborhood of b' is sparse, the closest word is likely to be relatively far away. But that runs contrary to the above findings that closer source vectors improve the accuracy of 3CosAdd. Then we could expect lower accuracy in sparser neighborhoods.

In this respect, too, GloVe and Word2Vec behave similarly (Fig. 15).

4 Comparison with Other Methods

We repeat the above experiments on GloVe with 3CosMul, a multiplication-based alternative to 3CosAdd proposed by Levy and Goldberg (2014):

$$argmax_{b' \in V} \frac{cos(b', b)cos(b', a')}{cos(b', a) + \varepsilon}$$

($\varepsilon = 0.001$ is used to prevent division by zero)

As 3CosMul does not explicitly calculate the predicted vector, we did not plot the similarity of b' to the predicted vector. But for other vector pairs shown in Fig. 6, we can see that 3CosMul,

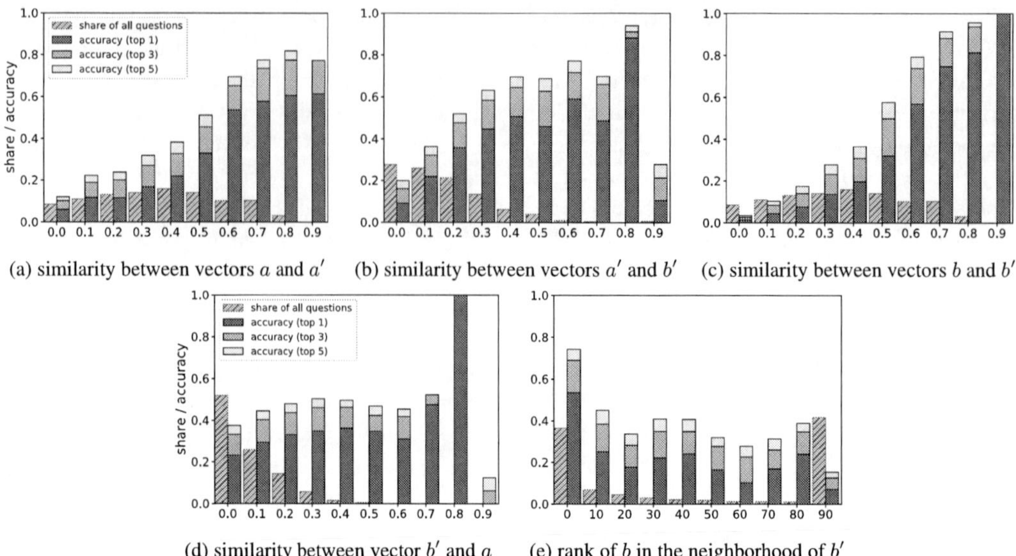

(a) similarity between vectors a and a' (b) similarity between vectors a' and b' (c) similarity between vectors b and b'

(d) similarity between vector b' and a (e) rank of b in the neighborhood of b'

*X-axis labels indicate lower boundary of the corresponding similarity/rank bins.
The numerical values for all data can be found in the Appendix.

Figure 6: Accuracy of 3CosMul method on GloVe model vs characteristics of the vector space.

like 3CosAdd, has much higher chances of success where target vectors are close to the source.

We also consider LRCos, a method based on supervised learning from a set of word pairs (Drozd et al., 2016). LRCos reinterprets the analogy task as follows: given a set of word pairs (e.g. *brother:sister, husband:wife, man:woman*, etc.), the available examples of the class of the target b' vector (*sister, wife, woman*, etc.) and randomly selected negative examples are used to learn a representation of the target class with a supervised classifier. The question is this: what word is the closest to $\overrightarrow{king}$, but belongs to the "women" class?

With LRCos it is only meaningful to look at the similarity of b to b' (Fig. 7). Once again, we see the same trend: closer targets are easier to hit.

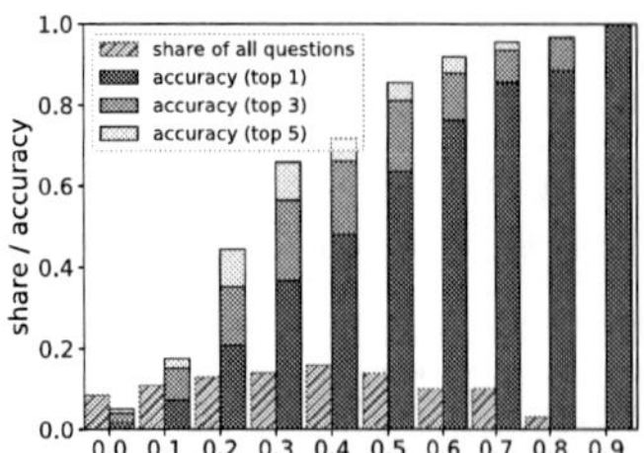

Figure 7: Accuracy of LRCos method vs similarity between vectors b and b'

However, if we look at overall accuracy, there is a big difference between the three methods.

Fig. 8b shows that the accuracy of LRCos is much higher than the top-1 3CosAdd or 3CosMul. Moreover, its "honest" version (Fig. 8a) performs just as well as the "dishonest" one. These results are consistent with the results reported by Drozd et al. (2016). As for 3CosMul, Levy et al. (2015) show that 3CosMul outperforms 3CosAdd in PPMI, SGNS, GloVe and SVD models with the Google dataset, sometimes yielding 10-25% improvement. Our BATS experiment confirms the overall superiority of 3CosMul to 3CosAdd, although the difference is less dramatic.

Thus LRCos considerably outdoes its competitors, although it does not manage to avoid the similarity problem. We attribute this to the set-based, supervised nature of LRCos that gives it an edge on a different problem that affects both 3CosAdd and 3CosMul: the assumption of "linguistic regularities" from which we started.

5 Discussion: What Should We Expect from the Word Analogy Task?

5.1 How Regular Are "Linguistic Regularities"?

There are unresolved questions about the underlying assumption that the offset between vectors a'

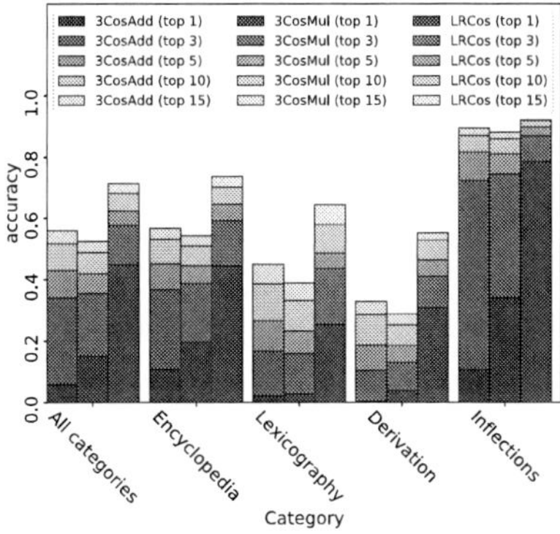

(a) 3CosAdd vs 3CosMul vs LRCos ("honest" versions)

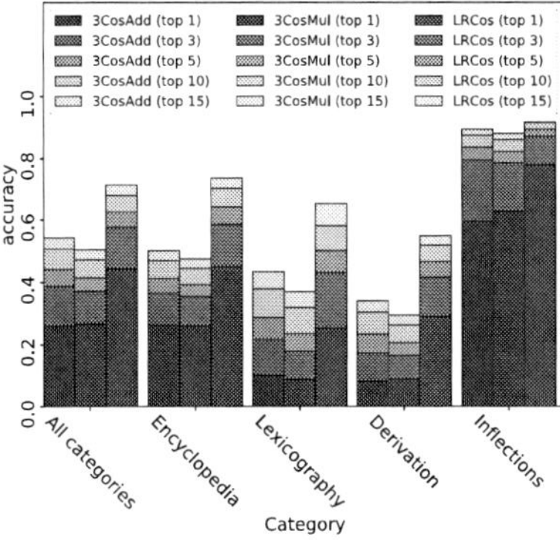

(b) CosAdd vs 3CosMul vs LRCos

Figure 8: LRCos performance on BATS

and a provides access to certain features combinable with vector b to detect b', and that such offset should be more or less constant for all words in a given linguistic relations.

Table 2 shows that this does not happen in a reliable way (data: BATS category D06 "re+verb").

Table 2: 3CosAdd: effect of various $a : a'$ vector pairs with the same $b : b'$ pair ($\overrightarrow{marry}:\overrightarrow{remarry}$)

No	a	a'	b	predicted vector	Sim. score	correct b' score
1	acquire	reacquire	marry	fiancée	0.54	<0.51
2	tell	retell	marry	betrothed	0.51	0.49
3	engage	reengage	marry	eloped	0.52	0.51
4	appear	reappear	marry	marries	0.65	0.55
5	establish	reestablish	marry	marries	0.58	0.52
6	invest	reinvest	marry	marries	0.59	0.57
7	adjust	readjust	marry	marrying	0.59	0.55
8	arrange	rearrange	marry	marrying	0.52	0.43
9	discover	rediscover	marry	marrying	0.54	0.49
10	apply	reapply	marry	remarry	0.53	0.53

Both correct and incorrect answers lie in about the same similarity range, so we cannot attribute the failures to the reliance of 3CosAdd on close neighborhoods. The distance from $\overrightarrow{marry}$ to $\overrightarrow{remarry}$ is the same; thus it must be the case that the offset between different a and a' is not the same, and leads to different answers – with a frustratingly small margin of error.

5.2 Can We Just Blame the Corpus?

Source corpora are noisy, and it is tempting to blame almost anything on that. It could be literal text-processing noise (e.g. not quite cleaned HTML data and ad texts) or, more broadly, any kind of information in the VSM that is irrelevant to the question at hand. This includes polysemy: for a word-level VSM the difference between $\overrightarrow{king}$ and $\overrightarrow{queen}$ is not exactly the same as the difference between $\overrightarrow{man}$ and $\overrightarrow{woman}$ just for the existence of the *Queen* band (although that factor should not affect the "re-" prefix verbs in Table 2).

In addition to irrelevant information, there is also missing information. Corpora of written texts are *a priori* not the same source of input as what children get when they learn their language. Natural language semantics relies on much data that the current VSMs do not have, including multimodal data and frequencies of events too commonplace to be mentioned in writing (Erk, 2016, p.18).

This means that the distributional difference between $\overrightarrow{tell}$ and $\overrightarrow{retell}$ (or $\overrightarrow{marry}$ and $\overrightarrow{remarry}$, or both pairs) does not necessarily reflect the full range of the relevant difference, which could perhaps have helped to bring the vector offset calculation closer to the desired outcome. On this view, in the ideal world all word vectors with the "re-" feature would be nearly aligned. Some blame could also be passed to the condensed vectors such as SVD or neural word embeddings, which blend distributional features in a non-transparent way, potentially obscuring the relevant ones.

The current source corpora and VSMs could certainly be improved. But both linguistics and philosophy suggest that there are also issues with the idea of linguistic relations being so regular.

5.3 Semantics is Messy

In theory, according to the distributional hypothesis, we would expect the relatively straightforward "repeated action" paradigm of verbs with and without the prefix "re-" in Table 2 to surface distributionally in the use of adverbs like "again". However, we have no reason to expect this to happen in quantitatively exactly the same way for all the verbs, even in an "ideal" corpus. And variation would lead to irregularities that we observe.

In fact, such variation would make VSMs more like human mental lexicon, not less. A well-known problem in psychology is the asymmetry of similarity judgments, upon which relational similarity and analogical reasoning are based. Logically *a is like b* is equivalent to *b is like a*, but humans do not necessarily agree with both statements to the same degree (Tversky, 1977).

Consider the "re-" prefix examples above. We could expect 100% success by native English speakers on a "complete the verb paradigm" task, because they would be inevitably made aware of the "add re-" rule during its completion. Even so, processing time would vary due to such factors as frequencies and prototypicality. The psychological evidence is piling for certain gradedness in mental representation of morphological rules: people can rate the same structure differently on complexity ("settlement" is reported more affixed that "government"), similarity judgments for semantically transparent and non-transparent bases are continuous, and there are graded priming effects for both orthographic, semantic and phonological similarity between derived words and their roots (Hay and Baayen, 2005).

There are several connectionist proposals to simulate asymmetry through biases, saliency features, or structural alignment (Thomas and Mareschal, 1997, p.758). The irregularities we observe in the VSMs could perhaps even be welcomed as another way to model this phenomenon - although it remains to be seen to what extent the parallel we draw here is appropriate.

As a side note, let us remember that equations such as $\overrightarrow{king} - \overrightarrow{man} + \overrightarrow{woman} = \overrightarrow{queen}$ should only be interpreted distributionally, although it is tempting to suppose that they reflect something like semantic features. That would be misleading on several accounts. First of all, the 3CosAdd math is commutative, which would be dubious for semantic features[5]. Secondly, it would bring us to the wall that componential analysis in linguistic semantics has hit a long time ago: semantic features defy definitions[6], they only apply to a portion of vocabulary, and they impose binary oppositions that are psycholinguistically unrealistic (Leech, 1981, pp.117-119).

---

[5] $((\overrightarrow{remarry} - \overrightarrow{marry}) + \overrightarrow{write})$ makes some sense, but $((\overrightarrow{write} - \overrightarrow{marry}) + \overrightarrow{remarry})$ does not.

[6] Is the $\overrightarrow{man} - \overrightarrow{woman}$ result certainly "femaleness" – or perhaps "maleness", or some mysterious "malefemale gender change" semantic feature?

5.4 Analogy Is Not an Inference Rule

Let us now come back to the fact that the "linguistic regularities" are in fact relying on relational similarity (Section 2), and relational similarity is not something binary. That takes us straight to the most fundamental difficulty with analogy as it is known in philosophy and logic. Analogy is undeniably fundamental to human reasoning as an instrument for discovery and understanding the unknown from the known – but it is not, and has never been an inference rule.

Consider the example where Mars is similar to Earth in several ways, and therefore could be supporting life. This analogy does not guarantee the existence of Martians, and it could even be similarly applied to even less suitable planets.

Basically, the problem with analogy is that not all similarities warrant all conclusions, and establishing valid analogies requires much case-by-case consideration. For this and some other reasons, analogy has long been rejected in generative linguistics as a mechanism for language acquisition through discovery, although now it is making a comeback (Itkonen, 2005, p.67-75).

This general difficulty with analogical reasoning – it does work in humans, but selectively, so to say, – is inherited by the so-called proportional analogies of the $a : a' :: b : b'$ kind. A case in point is their use in schools as verbal reasoning tests. In 2005 analogies were removed from SAT, its criticisms including ambiguity, guesswork and puzzle-like nature (Pringle, 2003). It is also telling that SAT analogy problems came with a set of potential answers to choose from, because otherwise students would supply a range of answers with varying degrees of incorrectness.

In case of the "re-" prefix above, once again, we could expect 100% success rate by humans who could see the "add re-" pattern; but semantic BATS questions would yield more variation. Consider the question "*trout* is to *river* as *lion* is to ___". Some would say *den*, thinking of the river as the trout's "home", but some could say *savanna* in the broader habitat terms; *cage* or *zoo* or *safari park* or even *circus* would all be valid to various degrees. BATS accepts several answer options, but it is hardly feasible to list them all for all cases.

Given the above, the question is: if analogical reasoning requires much case-by-case consideration in humans, what should we expect from VSMs with a single linear algebra operation?

6 Implications for Evaluation of VSMs

The analogy task continues to enjoy immense popularity in the NLP community as the standard evaluation task for VSMs. We have already mentioned two problems with the task: the problem of the Google test scores being flattering to the VSMs (Gladkova et al., 2016), and also 3CosAdd disadvantaging them, because the required semantic information may be encoded in more complex ways (Drozd et al., 2016).

What the present work adds to the discussion is the demonstration of how strongly the accuracy on the analogy task depends on the target vector being relatively close to the source in the vector space model – not only for 3CosAdd, but also 3CosMul and LRCos. This is in fact a fundamental problem that is encountered in many other NLP tasks[7].

That problem brings about the following question: what have we been evaluating with 3CosAdd all this time?

The answer seems to be this: analogy task scores indicate to what extent the semantic space of a given VSM was structured in a way that, for each word category, favored the linguistic relation that happened to be picked by the creators of the particular test dataset. BATS makes this clearer, because it is well balanced across different types of relations. Most models score well on morphological inflections – because morphological forms of the same word are highly distributionally similar and are likely to be close. But we do not see equal success for synonyms, suffixes, colors and other categories – because it is hard to expect of any one model to "guess" which words should have synonyms as closest neighbors and which words should be close to their antonyms.

As a matter of fact, for a general-purpose VSM we would not want that: every word can participate in hundreds of linguistic relations that we may be interested in, but we cannot expect them all to be close neighbors. We would want a VSM whose vector neighborhoods simply reflect whatever distributional properties were observed in a corpus. The challenge is to find reasoning methods that could reliably identify linguistic relations from vectors at any distance.

Given the irregularities discussed in section 5,

these methods would also have to rely on a more linguistically and cognitively realistic model of how meanings are reflected in distributional properties of words.

LRCos made a step in the right direction, as it does not rely on unique and neatly aligned word pairs, but it can only work for relations between coherent word classes. That excludes many lexicographic relations like synonyms (*car* is to *automobile* as *snake* is to *serpent*), frame-semantic or encyclopedic relations (*white* is to *snow* as *red* is to *rose*).

7 Conclusion

While it would be highly desirable to have automated reasoning about linguistic relations with VSMs as a powerful, all-purpose tool, it is so far a remote goal. We investigated the potential of the vector offset method in solving the so-called proportional analogies, which rely on one pair of words with a known linguistic relation to identify the missing member of another pair of words.

We have presented a series of experiments showing that the success of the linear vector offset (as well as two better-performing methods) depends on the structure of the VSM: the targets that are further away in the vector space have worse chances of being recovered. This is a crucial limitation: no model could possibly hold all related words close in the vector space, as there are many thousands of linguistic relations, and many are context-dependent.

Furthermore, the offsets of different word vector pairs appear to not be so regular, even for relatively straightforward linguistic relations. We argue that the observed irregularities should not just be blamed on the corpus. There is a number of theoretical issues with the very approach to linguistic relations as something neat and binary. We hope to drive attention to the graded nature of relational similarity that underlies analogical reasoning, and the need for automated reasoning algorithms to become more psychologically plausible in order to become more successful.

Acknowledgements

This work was partially supported by JST CREST Grant number JPMJCR1303, JSPS KAKENHI Grant number JP17K12739, and performed under the auspices of Real-world Big-Data Computation Open Innovation Laboratory, Japan.

---

[7]E.g. in taxonomy construction it was found helpful to narrow the semantic space with domains or clusters, essentially "zooming in" on certain relations (Fu et al., 2014; Espinosa Anke et al., 2016).

References

Paul Bartha. 2016. Analogy and analogical reasoning. In Edward N. Zalta, editor, *The Stanford Encyclopedia of Philosophy*, Metaphysics Research Lab, Stanford University. Winter 2016 edition. https://plato.stanford.edu/archives/win2016/entries/reasoning-analogy/.

Trevor Cohen, Dominic Widdows, and Thomas Rindflesch. 2015. Expansion-by-analogy: a vector symbolic approach to semantic search. In *Quantum Interaction*, Springer, pages 54–66. https://doi.org/10.1007/978-3-319-15931-7_5.

Joachim Daiber, Lautaro Quiroz, Roger Wechsler, and Stella Frank. 2015. Splitting compounds by semantic analogy. In *Proceedings of the 1st Deep Machine Translation Workshop*. Charles University in Prague, Praha, Czech Republic, 3-4 September 2015, pages 20–28. http://www.aclweb.org/anthology/W15-5703.

Aleksandr Drozd, Anna Gladkova, and Satoshi Matsuoka. 2016. Word embeddings, analogies, and machine learning: beyond *king - man + woman = queen*. In *Proceedings of COLING 2016, the 26th International Conference on Computational Linguistics: Technical Papers*. pages 3519–3530. https://www.aclweb.org/anthology/C/C16/C16-1332.pdf.

Nguyen Tuan Duc, Danushka Bollegala, and Mitsuru Ishizuka. 2012. Cross-language latent relational search between Japanese and English languages using a Web corpus. *ACM Transactions on Asian Language Information Processing (TALIP)* 11(3):11. http://dl.acm.org/citation.cfm?id=2334805.

Katrin Erk. 2016. What do you know about an alligator when you know the company it keeps. *Semantics and Pragmatics* 9(17):1–63. https://doi.org/10.3765/sp.9.17.

Luis Espinosa Anke, Jose Camacho-Collados, Claudio Delli Bovi, and Horacio Saggion. 2016. Supervised distributional hypernym discovery via domain adaptation. In *Proceedings of the 2016 Conference on Empirical Methods in Natural Language Processing*. Association for Computational Linguistics, Austin, Texas, pages 424–435. https://aclweb.org/anthology/D16-1041.

Stefano Federici, Simonetta Montemagni, and Vito Pirrelli. 1997. Inferring semantic similarity from distributional evidence: An analogy-based approach to word sense disambiguation. In *Proceedings of the ACL/EACL Workshop on Automatic Information Extraction and Building of Lexical Semantic Resources for NLP Applications*. pages 90–97. http://aclweb.org/anthology/W/W97/W97-0813.pdf.

Ruiji Fu, Jiang Guo, Bing Qin, Wanxiang Che, Haifeng Wang, and Ting Liu. 2014. Learning semantic hierarchies via word embeddings. In *Proceedings of the 52nd Annual Meeting of the Association for Computational Linguistics*. Association for Computational Linguistics, Baltimore, Maryland, USA, pages 1199–1209. http://202.118.253.69/rjfu/publications/acl2014.pdf.

Anna Gladkova, Aleksandr Drozd, and Satoshi Matsuoka. 2016. Analogy-based detection of morphological and semantic relations with word embeddings: What works and what doesn't. In *Proceedings of the NAACL-HLT SRW*. ACL, San Diego, California, June 12-17, 2016, pages 47–54. https://doi.org/10.18653/v1/N16-2002.

Jennifer B. Hay and R. Harald Baayen. 2005. Shifting paradigms: Gradient structure in morphology. *Trends in cognitive sciences* 9(7):342–348. https://doi.org/10.1016/j.tics.2005.04.002.

Esa Itkonen. 2005. *Analogy as Structure and Process: Approaches in Linguistic, Cognitive Psychology, and Philosophy of Science*. Number 14 in Human cognitive processing. John Benjamins Pub. Co, Amsterdam ; Philadelphia. https://doi.org/10.1075/hcp.14.

David A. Jurgens, Peter D. Turney, Saif M. Mohammad, and Keith J. Holyoak. 2012. Semeval-2012 task 2: measuring degrees of relational similarity. In *Proceedings of the First Joint Conference on Lexical and Computational Semantics (*SEM)*. Association for Computational Linguistics, Montréal, Canada, June 7-8, 2012, pages 356–364. http://dl.acm.org/citation.cfm?id=2387693.

Maximilian Köper, Christian Scheible, and Sabine Schulte im Walde. 2015. Multilingual reliability and "semantic" structure of continuous word spaces. In *Proceedings of the 11th International Conference on Computational Semantics*. Association for Computational Linguistics, pages 40–45. http://www.aclweb.org/anthology/W15-01#page=56.

Siwei Lai, Kang Liu, Liheng Xu, and Jun Zhao. 2016. How to generate a good word embedding? *IEEE Intelligent Systems* 31(6):5–14. https://doi.org/10.1109/MIS.2016.45.

Geoffrey Leech. 1981. *Semantics: The Study of Meaning*. Harmondsworth: Penguin Books.

Omer Levy and Yoav Goldberg. 2014. Linguistic regularities in sparse and explicit word representations. In *Proceedings of the Eighteenth Conference on Computational Natural Language Learning*. pages 171–180. https://doi.org/10.3115/v1/W14-1618.

Omer Levy, Yoav Goldberg, and Ido Dagan. 2015. Improving distributional similarity with lessons learned from word embeddings. *Transactions of the Association for Computational Linguistics* 3:211–225. http://www.aclweb.org/anthology/Q15-1016.

Tal Linzen. 2016. Issues in evaluating semantic spaces using word analogies. In *Proceedings of the First Workshop on Evaluating Vector Space Representations for NLP*. Association for Computational Linguistics. https://doi.org/10.18653/v1/W16-2503.

Tomas Mikolov, Kai Chen, Greg Corrado, and Jeffrey Dean. 2013a. Efficient estimation of word representations in vector space. *Proceedings of International Conference on Learning Representations (ICLR)* http://arxiv.org/abs/1301.3781.

Tomas Mikolov, Ilya Sutskever, Kai Chen, Greg S. Corrado, and Jeff Dean. 2013b. Distributed representations of words and phrases and their compositionality. In *Advances in Neural Information Processing Systems 26 (NIPS 2013)*. pages 3111–3119. http://papers.nips.cc/paper/5021-di.

Tomas Mikolov, Wen-tau Yih, and Geoffrey Zweig. 2013c. Linguistic regularities in continuous space word representations. In *Proceedings of the 2013 Conference of the North American Chapter of the Association for Computational Linguistics: Human Language Technologies*. Association for Computational Linguistics, pages 746–751. http://aclweb.org/anthology/N13-1090.

Denis Newman-Griffis, Albert M. Lai, and Eric Fosler-Lussier. 2017. Insights into analogy completion from the biomedical domain. *arXiv:1706.02241 [cs]* http://arxiv.org/abs/1706.02241.

Jeffrey Pennington, Richard Socher, and Christopher D. Manning. 2014. GloVe: global vectors for word representation. In *Proceedings of the 2014 Conference on Empirical Methods in Natural Language Processing (EMNLP)*. volume 12, pages 1532–1543. https://doi.org/10.3115/v1/D14-1162.

Paul Pringle. 2003. College board scores with critics of SAT analogies. *Los Angeles Times* http://articles.latimes.com/2003/jul/27/local/me-sat27/2.

Michael SC Thomas and Denis Mareschal. 1997. Connectionism and psychological notions of similarity. In *The Proceedings of the 19th Annual Conference of the Cognitive Science Society*. Mahwah, NJ: Erlbaum, Stanford, USA, pages 757–762. http://eprints.bbk.ac.uk/4611/.

Peter Turney, Michael L. Littman, Jeffrey Bigham, and Victor Shnayder. 2003. Combining independent modules to solve multiple-choice synonym and analogy problems. In *Proceedings of the International Conference on Recent Advances in Natural Language Processing*. pages 482–489. http://nparc.cisti-icist.nrc-cnrc.gc.ca/npsi/ctrl?action=rtdoc&an=8913366.

Peter D. Turney. 2006. Similarity of semantic relations. *Computational Linguistics* 32(3):379–416. https://doi.org/10.1162/coli.2006.32.3.379.

Peter D. Turney. 2008. A uniform approach to analogies, synonyms, antonyms, and associations. In *Proceedings of the 22nd International Conference on Computational Linguistics (Coling 2008)*. pages 905–912. http://nparc.cisti-icist.nrc-cnrc.gc.ca/npsi/ctrl?action=rtdoc&an=5764174.

Amos Tversky. 1977. Features of similarity. *Psychological Review* 84(4):327–352. https://doi.org/10.1037/0033-295X.84.4.327.

Ekaterina Vylomova, Laura Rimmel, Trevor Cohn, and Timothy Baldwin. 2016. *Take* and *took*, *gaggle* and *goose*, *book* and *read*: evaluating the utility of vector differences for lexical relation learning. In *Proceedings of the 54th Annual Meeting of the Association for Computational Linguistics (Volume 1: Long Papers)*. Association for Computational Linguistics, Berlin, Germany, pages 1671–1682. https://doi.org/10.18653/v1/P16-1158.

A   Supplementary Material

A.1   3CosAdd on GloVe and Word2Vec

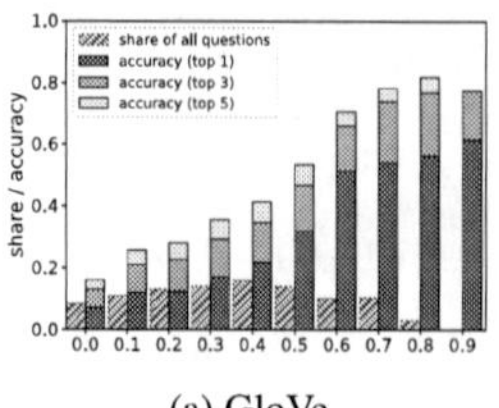

(a) GloVe

Similarity Bin	Share	Accuracy (%)		
		top 1	top 3	top 5
0 - 0.1	8.5	7.2	13.1	16.0
0.1 - 0.2	10.9	12.0	21.0	25.7
0.2 - 0.3	13.1	12.4	22.7	28.0
0.3 - 0.4	14.0	16.9	29.2	35.4
0.4 - 0.5	15.9	21.8	34.6	41.3
0.5 - 0.6	14.0	31.8	46.7	53.3
0.6 - 0.7	10.1	51.4	65.7	70.4
0.7 - 0.8	10.3	54.1	73.6	78.2
0.8 - 0.9	3.1	56.2	76.7	81.9
0.9 - 1	0.1	61.4	77.3	77.3

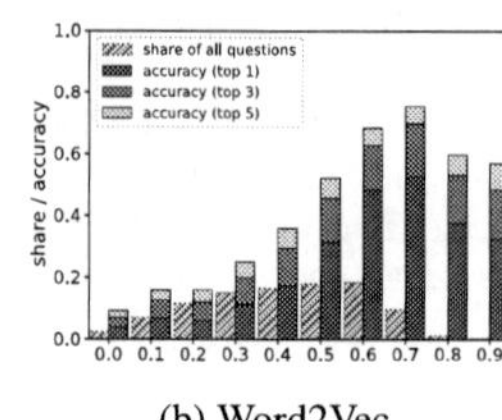

(b) Word2Vec

Similarity Bin	Share	Accuracy (%)		
		top 1	top 3	top 5
0 - 0.1	2.3	3.9	6.9	9.2
0.1 - 0.2	7.0	6.7	12.7	15.9
0.2 - 0.3	11.5	5.9	12.2	16.0
0.3 - 0.4	15.0	11.4	20.0	25.1
0.4 - 0.5	16.5	17.3	29.4	35.9
0.5 - 0.6	18.0	31.5	45.6	52.1
0.6 - 0.7	18.4	48.4	62.8	68.3
0.7 - 0.8	9.7	52.6	69.7	75.3
0.8 - 0.9	1.3	37.5	53.1	59.7
0.9 - 1	0.3	32.6	48.5	56.8

Figure 9: Similarity between vectors a and a'

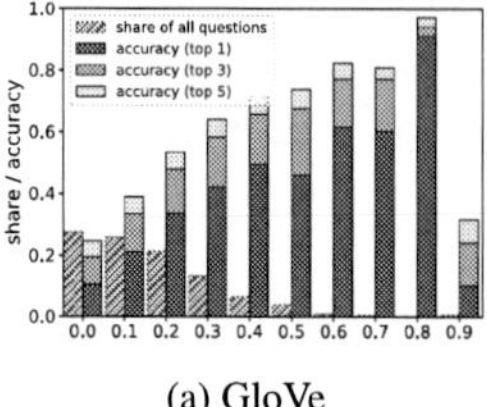

(a) GloVe

Similarity Bin	Share	Accuracy (%)		
		top 1	top 3	top 5
0 - 0.1	27.6	10.4	19.3	24.5
0.1 - 0.2	25.8	20.9	33.4	38.8
0.2 - 0.3	21.2	33.5	47.9	53.4
0.3 - 0.4	13.3	42.1	58.2	64.0
0.4 - 0.5	6.2	49.6	65.7	71.6
0.5 - 0.6	3.9	45.9	67.5	73.8
0.6 - 0.7	0.9	61.6	77.2	82.3
0.7 - 0.8	0.5	60.4	77.1	80.9
0.8 - 0.9	0.0	91.2	94.1	97.1
0.9 - 1	0.6	10.0	24.1	31.6

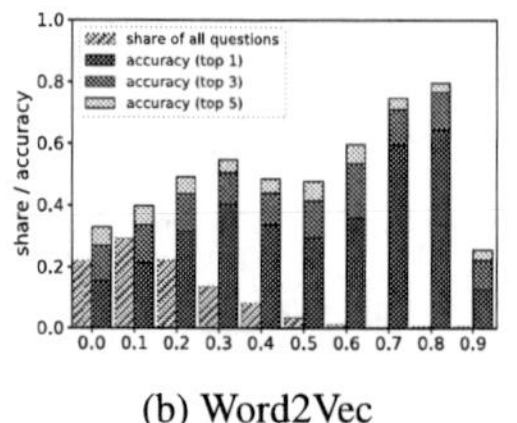

(b) Word2Vec

Similarity Bin	Share	Accuracy (%)		
		top 1	top 3	top 5
0 - 0.1	22.0	15.2	26.9	32.9
0.1 - 0.2	29.1	21.4	33.6	39.7
0.2 - 0.3	22.0	31.5	43.8	49.1
0.3 - 0.4	13.4	40.1	50.5	54.7
0.4 - 0.5	8.0	33.7	43.9	48.5
0.5 - 0.6	3.4	29.4	41.3	47.6
0.6 - 0.7	1.1	35.8	53.4	59.6
0.7 - 0.8	0.3	59.6	71.1	74.8
0.8 - 0.9	0.4	64.5	76.6	79.6
0.9 - 1	0.4	12.5	22.3	25.5

Figure 10: Similarity between vectors a' and b'

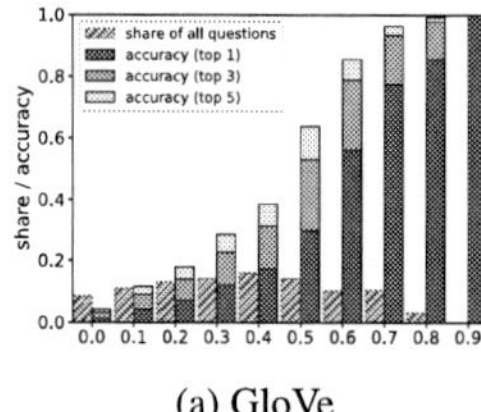

(a) GloVe

Similarity Bin	Share	Accuracy (%)		
		top 1	top 3	top 5
0 - 0.1	8.5	1.3	3.1	4.0
0.1 - 0.2	11.0	4.1	9.0	11.5
0.2 - 0.3	13.1	7.1	13.9	17.9
0.3 - 0.4	14.0	12.1	22.6	28.4
0.4 - 0.5	15.9	17.3	31.0	38.5
0.5 - 0.6	14.0	29.7	52.9	63.7
0.6 - 0.7	10.1	56.2	78.8	85.5
0.7 - 0.8	10.3	77.3	93.3	96.3
0.8 - 0.9	3.1	85.5	97.8	99.2
0.9 - 1	0.0	–	–	–

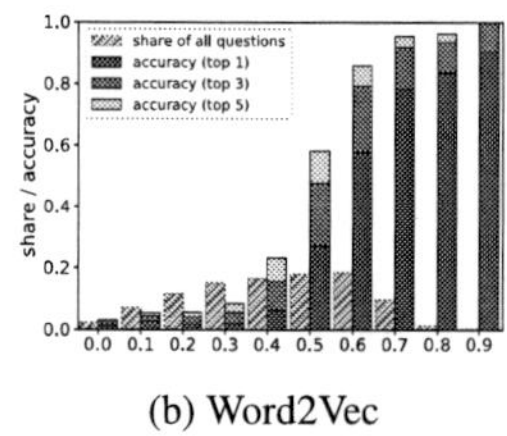

(b) Word2Vec

Similarity Bin	Share	Accuracy (%)		
		top 1	top 3	top 5
0 - 0.1	2.3	1.3	2.3	3.0
0.1 - 0.2	7.0	2.7	4.3	5.3
0.2 - 0.3	11.6	1.7	4.0	5.5
0.3 - 0.4	15.0	1.9	5.5	8.4
0.4 - 0.5	16.5	6.3	15.6	23.2
0.5 - 0.6	18.0	27.2	47.7	58.1
0.6 - 0.7	18.4	57.8	79.2	85.7
0.7 - 0.8	9.7	78.1	91.8	95.4
0.8 - 0.9	1.3	83.5	93.6	96.2
0.9 - 1	0.2	90.5	100	100

Figure 11: Similarity between vectors b and b'

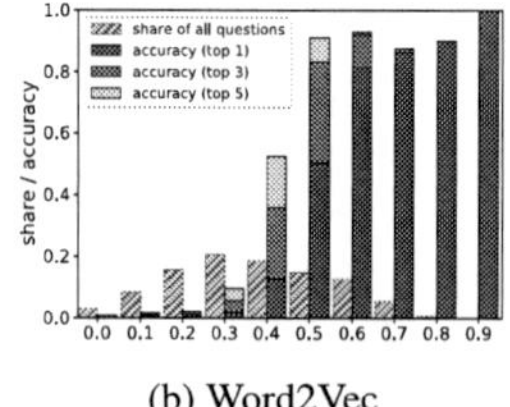

(a) GloVe

Similarity Bin	Share	Accuracy (%)		
		top 1	top 3	top 5
0 - 0.1	6.6	0.4	1.2	1.7
0.1 - 0.2	11.3	0.7	2.0	3.2
0.2 - 0.3	16.4	1.7	4.0	5.7
0.3 - 0.4	18.6	4.2	13.7	22.3
0.4 - 0.5	16.2	24.3	53.0	67.9
0.5 - 0.6	12.0	55.0	83.6	90.2
0.6 - 0.7	11.0	71.3	89.2	90.5
0.7 - 0.8	6.8	86.7	92.3	92.5
0.8 - 0.9	1.0	92.5	92.7	92.8
0.9 - 1	0.1	100	100	100

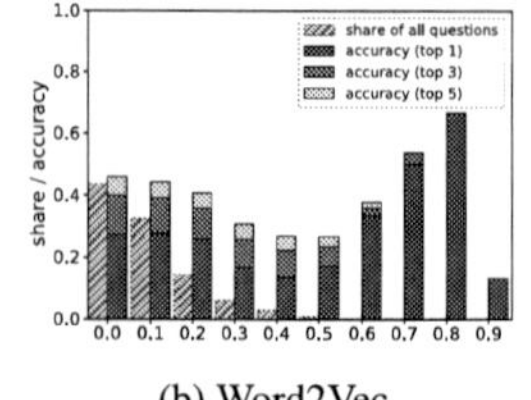

(b) Word2Vec

Similarity Bin	Share	Accuracy (%)		
		top 1	top 3	top 5
0 - 0.1	3.0	0.1	0.7	0.9
0.1 - 0.2	8.3	0.4	1.1	1.7
0.2 - 0.3	15.7	0.4	1.3	2.2
0.3 - 0.4	20.7	1.9	5.6	9.6
0.4 - 0.5	18.7	12.7	35.9	52.5
0.5 - 0.6	14.8	50.4	83.2	91.1
0.6 - 0.7	12.6	81.4	92.1	93.0
0.7 - 0.8	5.5	86.3	87.6	87.7
0.8 - 0.9	0.7	90.2	90.2	90.2
0.9 - 1	0.0	100	100	100

Figure 12: Similarity between vector b' and predicted vector

(a) GloVe

Similarity Bin	Share	Accuracy (%)		
		top 1	top 3	top 5
0 - 0.1	52.0	21.5	34.0	39.6
0.1 - 0.2	25.8	29.2	42.7	48.3
0.2 - 0.3	14.3	33.5	46.5	51.6
0.3 - 0.4	5.8	35.8	48.9	53.5
0.4 - 0.5	1.6	37.0	48.0	52.6
0.5 - 0.6	0.4	35.7	44.3	48.1
0.6 - 0.7	0.1	33.6	41.8	46.4
0.7 - 0.8	0.0	47.6	52.4	52.4
0.8 - 0.9	0.0	–	–	–
0.9 - 1	0.0	6.2	6.2	12.5

(b) Word2Vec

Similarity Bin	Share	Accuracy (%)		
		top 1	top 3	top 5
0 - 0.1	43.5	27.1	39.9	45.8
0.1 - 0.2	32.4	27.6	39.1	44.3
0.2 - 0.3	14.2	25.7	35.8	40.7
0.3 - 0.4	6.0	16.7	25.8	30.7
0.4 - 0.5	2.8	13.6	22.2	26.9
0.5 - 0.6	0.8	17.2	23.5	26.7
0.6 - 0.7	0.2	33.5	36.0	37.8
0.7 - 0.8	0.0	50.0	53.8	53.8
0.8 - 0.9	0.0	66.7	66.7	66.7
0.9 - 1	0.0	13.3	13.3	13.3

Figure 13: Similarity between vector b' and a

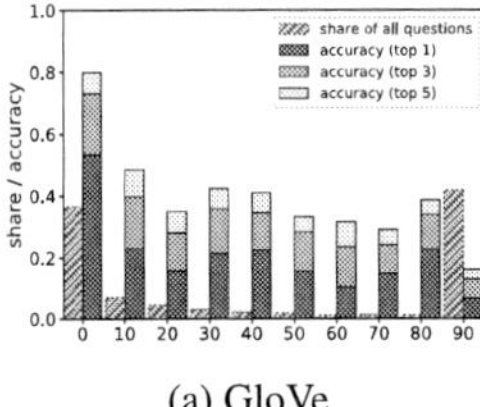

Similarity Bin	Share	Accuracy (%) top 1	top 3	top 5
0 - 10	36.5	53.3	73.0	79.8
10 - 20	6.8	22.8	39.7	48.4
20 - 30	4.5	15.5	27.8	34.9
30 - 40	3.0	21.2	35.7	42.3
40 - 50	2.1	22.4	34.4	40.9
50 - 60	1.8	15.4	28.2	33.0
60 - 70	1.2	10.2	23.4	31.4
70 - 80	1.2	14.6	23.9	28.9
80 - 90	1.2	22.6	33.8	38.6
90 - 100	41.6	6.5	12.7	16.0

(a) GloVe

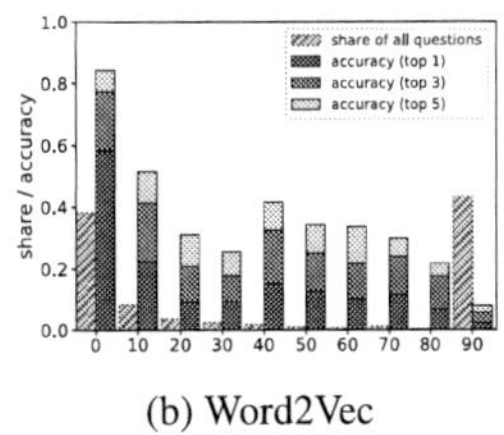

Similarity Bin	Share	Accuracy (%) top 1	top 3	top 5
0 - 10	38.0	58.3	77.5	84.3
10 - 20	8.1	22.1	41.3	51.4
20 - 30	3.7	9.0	20.9	31.0
30 - 40	2.3	9.3	17.8	25.4
40 - 50	1.7	15.3	32.4	41.4
50 - 60	0.9	12.8	25.1	34.1
60 - 70	0.8	10.2	21.7	33.6
70 - 80	1.1	11.6	23.8	29.8
80 - 90	0.3	6.5	17.6	21.6
90 - 100	43.2	2.2	5.5	8.0

(b) Word2Vec

Figure 14: The rank of b in the neighborhood of b'

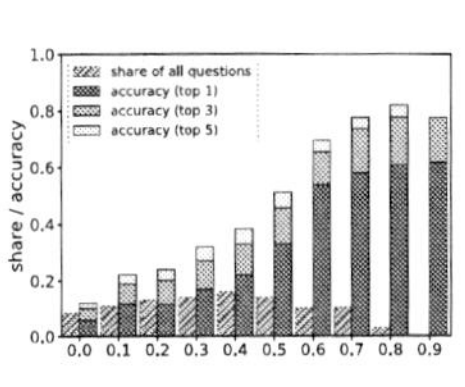

Similarity Bin	Share	Accuracy (%) top 1	top 3	top 5
0 - 0.1	0.0	–	–	–
0.1 - 0.2	0.0	–	–	–
0.2 - 0.3	0.0	0.0	0.0	0.0
0.3 - 0.4	5.3	2.0	4.4	6.6
0.4 - 0.5	26.3	11.3	19.6	24.1
0.5 - 0.6	45.6	28.9	43.1	49.2
0.6 - 0.7	20.6	44.2	61.4	67.2
0.7 - 0.8	2.0	48.0	72.1	79.5
0.8 - 0.9	0.0	0.0	0.0	0.0
0.9 - 1	0.0	0.0	0.0	0.0

(a) GloVe

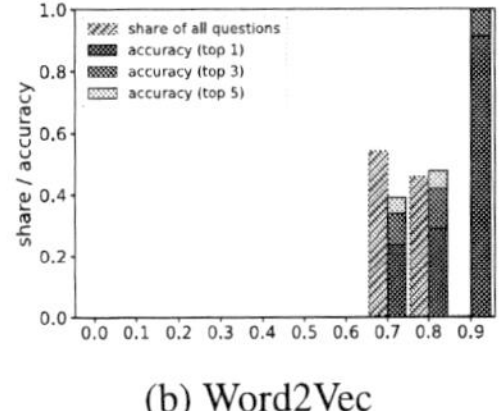

Similarity Bin	Share	Accuracy (%) top 1	top 3	top 5
0 - 0.1	0.0	–	–	–
0.1 - 0.2	0.0	–	–	–
0.2 - 0.3	0.0	–	–	–
0.3 - 0.4	0.0	–	–	–
0.4 - 0.5	0.0	–	–	–
0.5 - 0.6	0.0	–	–	–
0.6 - 0.7	0.1	0.0	0.0	0.0
0.7 - 0.8	54.1	23.5	33.8	38.9
0.8 - 0.9	45.7	28.7	41.9	47.6
0.9 - 1	0.2	91.1	99.3	100

(b) Word2Vec

Figure 15: Similarity between b' and its 5th neighbor

A.2 3CosMul on GloVe

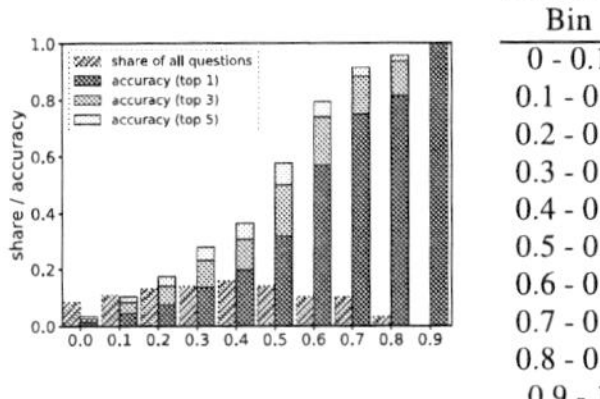

Similarity Bin	Share	Accuracy (%) top 1	top 3	top 5
0 - 0.1	8.5	6.0	10.1	12.0
0.1 - 0.2	10.9	11.7	18.8	22.1
0.2 - 0.3	13.1	11.5	20.0	23.8
0.3 - 0.4	14.0	16.8	26.9	31.9
0.4 - 0.5	15.9	21.9	32.8	38.2
0.5 - 0.6	14.0	33.0	45.5	51.1
0.6 - 0.7	10.1	53.7	65.2	69.4
0.7 - 0.8	10.3	57.7	73.4	77.4
0.8 - 0.9	3.1	60.5	77.4	81.8
0.9 - 1	0.1	61.4	77.3	77.3

Figure 16: Similarity between vectors a and a'

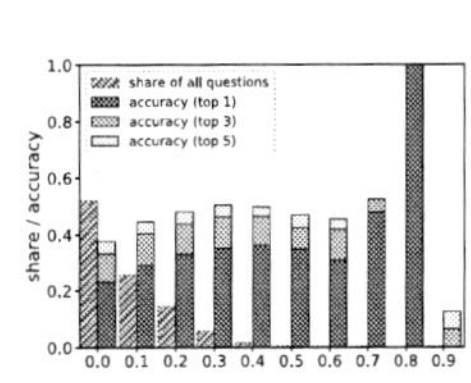

Similarity Bin	Share	Accuracy (%) top 1	top 3	top 5
0 - 0.1	27.6	9.1	16.0	19.9
0.1 - 0.2	25.8	21.8	31.9	36.3
0.2 - 0.3	21.2	35.8	47.6	51.9
0.3 - 0.4	13.3	44.7	58.4	63.1
0.4 - 0.5	6.2	50.7	64.6	69.6
0.5 - 0.6	3.9	46.0	62.7	68.9
0.6 - 0.7	0.9	59.1	71.8	77.3
0.7 - 0.8	0.5	48.7	66.1	69.9
0.8 - 0.9	0.0	88.2	91.2	94.1
0.9 - 1	0.6	10.6	21.3	27.8

Figure 17: Similarity between vectors a' and b'

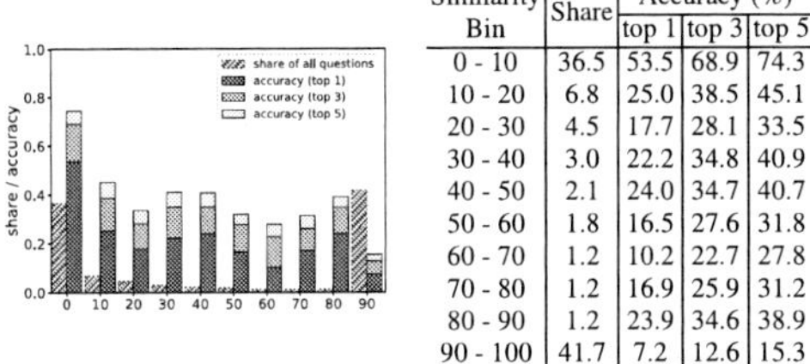

Similarity Bin	Share	Accuracy (%) top 1	top 3	top 5
0 - 0.1	8.5	1.4	2.6	3.5
0.1 - 0.2	11.0	4.3	8.3	10.3
0.2 - 0.3	13.1	7.6	13.9	17.4
0.3 - 0.4	14.0	13.6	23.0	27.7
0.4 - 0.5	15.9	19.6	30.8	36.4
0.5 - 0.6	14.0	31.9	49.9	57.6
0.6 - 0.7	10.1	56.9	73.9	79.3
0.7 - 0.8	10.3	74.8	88.2	91.4
0.8 - 0.9	3.1	81.3	93.7	95.7
0.9 - 1	0.0	–	–	–

Figure 18: Similarity between vectors b and b'

Similarity Bin	Share	Accuracy (%) top 1	top 3	top 5
0 - 0.1	52.0	23.1	33.2	37.6
0.1 - 0.2	25.8	29.2	40.3	44.5
0.2 - 0.3	14.3	32.9	43.7	48.0
0.3 - 0.4	5.8	34.9	46.2	50.4
0.4 - 0.5	1.6	36.2	46.3	49.7
0.5 - 0.6	0.4	34.8	42.4	46.9
0.6 - 0.7	0.1	30.9	41.8	45.5
0.7 - 0.8	0.0	47.6	52.4	52.4
0.8 - 0.9	0.0	–	–	–
0.9 - 1	0.0	0.0	6.2	12.5

Figure 19: Similarity between vector b' and a

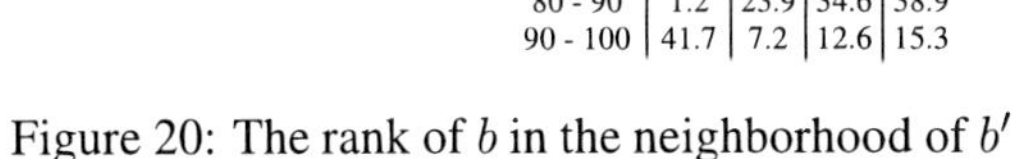

Similarity Bin	Share	Accuracy (%) top 1	top 3	top 5
0 - 10	36.5	53.5	68.9	74.3
10 - 20	6.8	25.0	38.5	45.1
20 - 30	4.5	17.7	28.1	33.5
30 - 40	3.0	22.2	34.8	40.9
40 - 50	2.1	24.0	34.7	40.7
50 - 60	1.8	16.5	27.6	31.8
60 - 70	1.2	10.2	22.7	27.8
70 - 80	1.2	16.9	25.9	31.2
80 - 90	1.2	23.9	34.6	38.9
90 - 100	41.7	7.2	12.6	15.3

Figure 20: The rank of b in the neighborhood of b'

Similarity Bin	Share	Accuracy (%) top 1	top 3	top 5
0 - 0.1	0.0	–	–	–
0.1 - 0.2	0.0	–	–	–
0.2 - 0.3	0.0	–	–	–
0.3 - 0.4	0.0	–	–	–
0.4 - 0.5	0.0	–	–	–
0.5 - 0.6	0.0	–	–	–
0.6 - 0.7	5.3	1.7	3.9	5.7
0.7 - 0.8	71.9	23.3	33.1	37.4
0.8 - 0.9	22.7	44.8	59.4	64.5
0.9 - 1	0.1	0.0	0.0	2.1

Figure 21: Similarity between b' and its 5th neighbor

A.3 LRCos on GloVe and Word2Vec

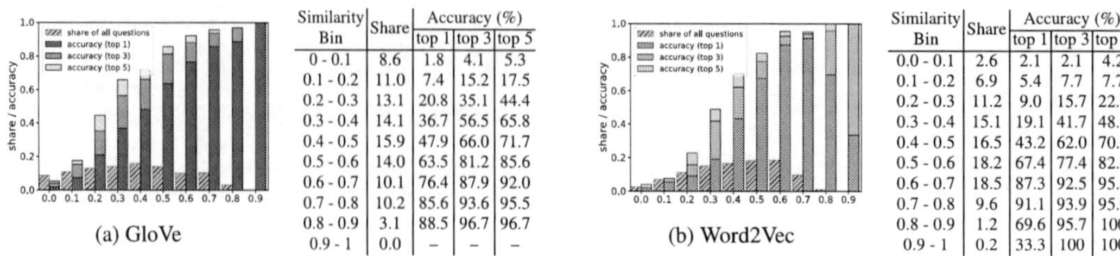

(a) GloVe

Similarity Bin	Share	Accuracy (%)		
		top 1	top 3	top 5
0 - 0.1	8.6	1.8	4.1	5.3
0.1 - 0.2	11.0	7.4	15.2	17.5
0.2 - 0.3	13.1	20.8	35.1	44.4
0.3 - 0.4	14.1	36.7	56.5	65.8
0.4 - 0.5	15.9	47.9	66.0	71.7
0.5 - 0.6	14.0	63.5	81.2	85.6
0.6 - 0.7	10.1	76.4	87.9	92.0
0.7 - 0.8	10.2	85.6	93.6	95.5
0.8 - 0.9	3.1	88.5	96.7	96.7
0.9 - 1	0.0	–	–	–

(b) Word2Vec

Similarity Bin	Share	Accuracy (%)		
		top 1	top 3	top 5
0.0 - 0.1	2.6	2.1	2.1	4.2
0.1 - 0.2	6.9	5.4	7.7	7.7
0.2 - 0.3	11.2	9.0	15.7	22.9
0.3 - 0.4	15.1	19.1	41.7	48.8
0.4 - 0.5	16.5	43.2	62.0	70.1
0.5 - 0.6	18.2	67.4	77.4	82.4
0.6 - 0.7	18.5	87.3	92.5	95.4
0.7 - 0.8	9.6	91.1	93.9	95.0
0.8 - 0.9	1.2	69.6	95.7	100
0.9 - 1	0.2	33.3	100	100

Figure 22: Similarity between vectors b and b'

A.4 Comparison between 3CosAdd, 3CosMul and LRCos on GloVe

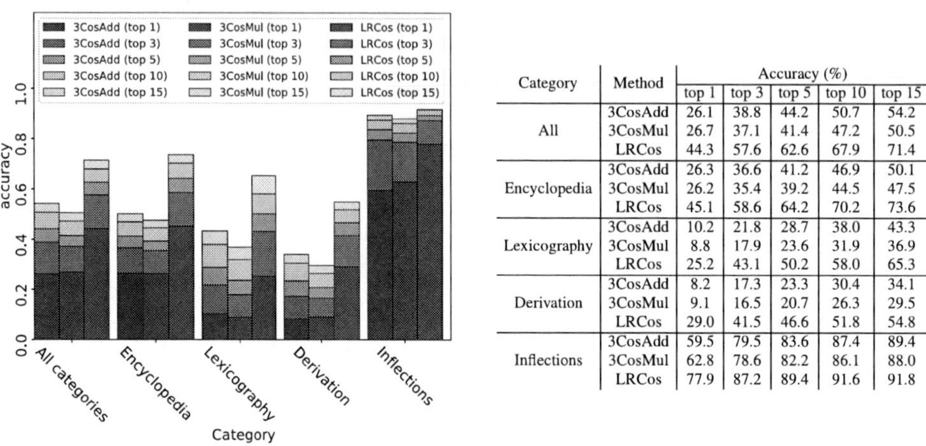

Category	Method	Accuracy (%)				
		top 1	top 3	top 5	top 10	top 15
All	3CosAdd	26.1	38.8	44.2	50.7	54.2
	3CosMul	26.7	37.1	41.4	47.2	50.5
	LRCos	44.3	57.6	62.6	67.9	71.4
Encyclopedia	3CosAdd	26.3	36.6	41.2	46.9	50.1
	3CosMul	26.2	35.4	39.2	44.5	47.5
	LRCos	45.1	58.6	64.2	70.2	73.6
Lexicography	3CosAdd	10.2	21.8	28.7	38.0	43.3
	3CosMul	8.8	17.9	23.6	31.9	36.9
	LRCos	25.2	43.1	50.2	58.0	65.3
Derivation	3CosAdd	8.2	17.3	23.3	30.4	34.1
	3CosMul	9.1	16.5	20.7	26.3	29.5
	LRCos	29.0	41.5	46.6	51.8	54.8
Inflections	3CosAdd	59.5	79.5	83.6	87.4	89.4
	3CosMul	62.8	78.6	82.2	86.1	88.0
	LRCos	77.9	87.2	89.4	91.6	91.8

Figure 23: 3CosAdd vs 3CosMul vs LRCos

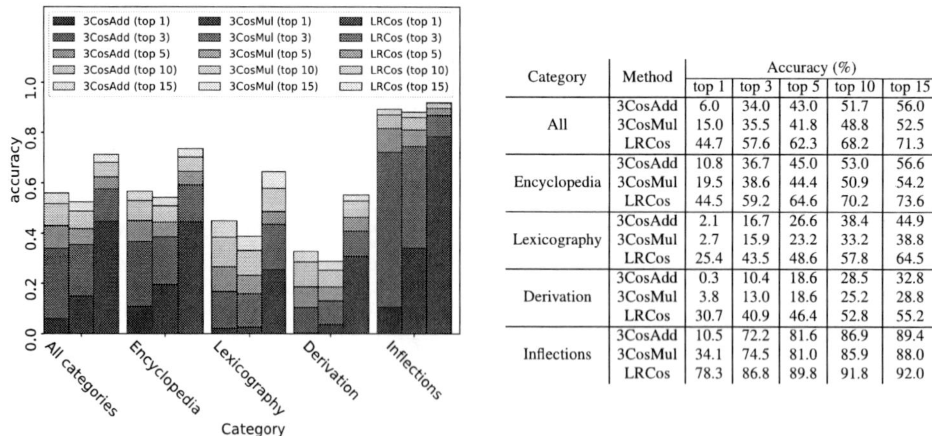

Category	Method	Accuracy (%)				
		top 1	top 3	top 5	top 10	top 15
All	3CosAdd	6.0	34.0	43.0	51.7	56.0
	3CosMul	15.0	35.5	41.8	48.8	52.5
	LRCos	44.7	57.6	62.3	68.2	71.3
Encyclopedia	3CosAdd	10.8	36.7	45.0	53.0	56.6
	3CosMul	19.5	38.6	44.4	50.9	54.2
	LRCos	44.5	59.2	64.6	70.2	73.6
Lexicography	3CosAdd	2.1	16.7	26.6	38.4	44.9
	3CosMul	2.7	15.9	23.2	33.2	38.8
	LRCos	25.4	43.5	48.6	57.8	64.5
Derivation	3CosAdd	0.3	10.4	18.6	28.5	32.8
	3CosMul	3.8	13.0	18.6	25.2	28.8
	LRCos	30.7	40.9	46.4	52.8	55.2
Inflections	3CosAdd	10.5	72.2	81.6	86.9	89.4
	3CosMul	34.1	74.5	81.0	85.9	88.0
	LRCos	78.3	86.8	89.8	91.8	92.0

Figure 24: 3CosAdd vs 3CosMul vs LRCos ("honest" version)

Semantic Frames and Visual Scenes:
Learning Semantic Role Inventories from Image and Video Descriptions

Ekaterina Shutova
Computer Laboratory
University of Cambridge, UK
es407@cam.ac.uk

Andreas Wundsam
Big Switch Networks
Santa Clara, CA
andi@wundsam.net

Helen Yannakoudakis
ALTA Institute
University of Cambridge, UK
hy260@cl.cam.ac.uk

Abstract

Frame-semantic parsing and semantic role labelling, that aim to automatically assign semantic roles to arguments of verbs in a sentence, have recently become an active strand of research in NLP. However, to date these methods have relied on a predefined inventory of semantic roles. In this paper, we present a method to automatically learn argument role inventories for verbs from large corpora of text, images and videos. We evaluate the method against manually constructed role inventories in FrameNet and show that the visual model outperforms the language-only model and operates with a high precision.

1 Introduction

The theory of frame semantics (Fillmore, 1976) postulates that our interpretation of word meanings is not limited to isolated concepts, but rather instantiates complex knowledge structures about events and their participants, known as *semantic frames*. For instance, the COMMERCIAL TRANSACTION frame includes elements such as *a seller, a buyer, goods* and *money* which can be mapped to higher-level semantic roles such as *agent, patient, instrument* etc. The verbs linked to this frame are *buy, sell, pay, cost* and *charge*, each evoking different aspects of the frame.

This theory has been implemented in a lexical-semantic resource called FrameNet (Fillmore et al., 2003). Each semantic frame is encoded in FrameNet as a list of lexical units that evoke this frame (typically verbs) and the roles that their semantic arguments may take given the scenario represented by the frame. FrameNet has inspired a direction in NLP research known as semantic role labelling (Gildea and Jurafsky, 2002; Màrquez et al.,

2008) and frame-semantic parsing (Das et al., 2014), whose goal is to assign semantic roles to arguments of the verbs in a sentence. However, these works point out the coverage limitations of the hand-constructed FrameNet database, suggesting that a data-driven frame acquisition method is needed to enable the integration of frame semantics into real-world NLP applications. In this paper, we propose such a method, experimenting with semantic frame induction from linguistic and visual data. Our system first performs clustering of verb arguments to identify their possible semantic roles and then computes the level of association between a given argument role and the verb, thus deriving the structure of the semantic frame in which the verb participates.

Frame semantics emphasizes the relation between our lexical semantic knowledge and our experience in the world, suggesting that semantic frames are not merely a linguistic construct but also a result of our sensory-motor and perceptual experience. However, frame semantic approaches in NLP typically rely on textual data. Our method, in contrast, induces semantic frames from both a text corpus and a corpus of tagged images and videos. We evaluate the method against hand-constructed frames in FrameNet. Our results show that the visual model outperforms the language-only model and achieves a high precision. This frame induction method can be used to complement existing FrameNets or to construct a new resource of automatically mined semantic frames, free from manual annotation bias.

2 Experimental Data

Textual data. We extracted linguistic features for our model from the British National Corpus (BNC) (Burnard, 2007). We parsed the corpus using the RASP parser (Briscoe et al., 2006) and

*Proceedings of the 6th Joint Conference on Lexical and Computational Semantics (*SEM 2017)*, pages 149–154,
Vancouver, Canada, August 3-4, 2017. ©2017 Association for Computational Linguistics

extracted subject–verb and verb–object relations from its dependency output. These relations were then used as features for clustering to obtain arguments classes, which we then used as proxies for frame elements, i.e. argument roles.

Image and video data. We used the Yahoo! Webscope Flickr-100M dataset (Shamma, 2014) to extract visual relations between verbs and their arguments. Flickr-100M contains 99.3 million images and 0.7 million videos with natural language tags for scenes, objects and actions annotated by users. We first stem the tags and remove words that are absent in WordNet (e.g. named entities and misspellings). We then identify their part of speech based on their visual context using the method of Shutova et al. (2015) and extract verb–noun co-occurrences.

3 Frame Induction Model

3.1 Argument Clustering

We use a clustering method to obtain semantic classes of arguments of verbs, thus generalising from individual arguments to their semantic types which correspond to frame roles. We obtain argument classes by means of spectral clustering of nouns with lexico-syntactic features, which has been shown effective in previous lexical classification tasks (Sun and Korhonen, 2009).

Spectral clustering partitions the data relying on a similarity matrix that records similarities between all pairs of data points. We use *Jensen-Shannon divergence* to measure similarity between feature vectors for two nouns, w_i and w_j, defined as follows:

$$d_{\mathrm{JS}}(w_i, w_j) = \frac{1}{2}d_{\mathrm{KL}}(w_i\|m) + \frac{1}{2}d_{\mathrm{KL}}(w_j\|m), \tag{1}$$

where d_{KL} is the Kullback-Leibler divergence, and m is the average of w_i and w_j. We construct the similarity matrix S computing similarities S_{ij} as $S_{ij} = \exp(-d_{\mathrm{JS}}(w_i, w_j))$. The matrix S then encodes a similarity graph G (over our nouns), where S_{ij} are the adjacency weights. The clustering problem can then be defined as identifying the optimal partition, or *cut*, of the graph into clusters, such that the intra-cluster weights are high and the inter-cluster weights are low. We use the multiway normalized cut (MNCut) algorithm of Meila and Shi (2001) for this purpose. The algorithm transforms S into a stochastic matrix P containing transition probabilities between the vertices in the

graph as $P = D^{-1}S$, where the degree matrix D is a diagonal matrix with $D_{ii} = \sum_{j=1}^{N} S_{ij}$. It then computes the K leading eigenvectors of P, where K is the desired number of clusters. The graph is partitioned by finding approximately equal elements in the eigenvectors using a simpler clustering algorithm, such as *k-means*. Meila and Shi (2001) have shown that the partition I derived in this way minimizes the MNCut criterion:

$$\mathrm{MNCut}(I) = \sum_{k=1}^{K}(1 - P(I_k \to I_k | I_k)), \tag{2}$$

which is the sum of transition probabilities across different clusters. Since k-means starts from a random cluster assignment, we ran the algorithm multiple times and used the partition that minimizes the cluster distortion, i.e. distances to its centroid.

We clustered the 2,000 most frequent nouns in the BNC, using their grammatical relations as features. The features consisted of verb lemmas appearing in the subject, direct object and indirect object relations with the given nouns in the RASP-parsed BNC, indexed by relation type. The feature vectors were first constructed from the corpus counts, and subsequently normalized by the sum of the feature values.

Our use of linguistic dependency features for argument clustering is motivated by the results of previous research (Sun and Korhonen, 2011; Shutova et al., 2015), that has shown that such features lead to clusters of nouns belonging to the same semantic type, as opposed to topic or scene as it is the case with linguistic window-based features or image-derived features (Shutova et al., 2015). Since the argument roles in semantic frames correspond to semantic types (such as *location* or *instrument*), the linguistic dependency features are best suited to generalise the predicate-argument structure in semantic frames. Example clusters produced by our method are shown in Fig. 1. The resulting clusters represent frame elements, i.e. argument roles, in our model.

3.2 Predicate–Argument Association

We then use the verb–noun co-occurrence information extracted from the visual data to quantify the strength of association of a given verb with each of the argument classes, thus identifying the relevant argument roles for the verb. We adopted an information theoretic measure originally proposed by Resnik (1993) in his selectional preference model. Resnik first measures *selectional*

official officer inspector journalist detective constable police policeman reporter
fire pipe torch candle lamp cigarette
potato apple slice food cake meat bread fruit
lifetime quarter period century succession stage generation decade phase interval future
disorder infection illness disease virus cancer
profit surplus earnings income turnover revenue

Figure 1: Clusters representing argument roles

0.180 defeat fall **death** tragedy loss collapse decline disaster destruction fate
0.141 girl other woman child **person** people
0.128 suicide **killing** offence **murder** breach crime ...
0.113 handle **weapon** horn knife blade stick sword ankle waist neck wrist
0.095 **victim** bull teenager prisoner hero gang enemy rider offender youth **killer** thief driver defender hell
0.086 recession disappointment **shock pain** frustration embarrassment **guilt** sensation depression wound
0.030 sister daughter parent **relative** lover cousin friend wife mother husband brother father
0.020 **motive** self origin meaning **cause** secret truth ...
0.018 official officer inspector journalist detective constable police **policeman** reporter

Figure 2: System output for *kill*

preference strength (SPS) of a verb in terms of Kullback-Leibler divergence between the distribution of noun classes occurring as arguments of this verb, $p(c|v)$, and the prior distribution of the noun classes, $p(c)$:

$$\text{SPS}(v) = \sum_c p(c|v) \log \frac{p(c|v)}{p(c)}. \quad (3)$$

SPS measures how strongly the predicate constrains its arguments. Selectional association of the verb with a particular argument class is then defined as a relative contribution of that argument class to the overall SPS of the verb:

$$\text{Ass}(v, c) = \frac{1}{\text{SPS}(v)} p(c|v) \log \frac{p(c|v)}{p(c)}. \quad (4)$$

We use this measure to quantify the strength of verb–argument association based on the visual co-occurrence information. We extract verb-noun co-occurrences from Flickr-200M, map the nouns to argument classes and quantify selectional association of a given verb with each argument class, thus acquiring its semantic frame structure. An example argument distribution for the verb *kill*, and thus the KILLING frame, is presented in Fig. 2. One can see from the figure that the argument clusters correspond to specific roles in FrameNet, e.g. the *killer* and the *victim*, the *motive*, the *weapon* (instrument) and *death* (result).

4 Evaluation against FrameNet

Baseline. We evaluate the effectiveness of visual information for our task by comparing the model based on vision and language (VIS) to a baseline model using language alone (LING). In the LING system, the predicate-argument association scores are computed based on verb-argument co-occurrence information extracted from verb-subject, verb-direct object and verb-indirect object relations in the BNC. In case of the indirect object relations, the accompanying prepostions were discarded and the noun counts were aggregated.

Evaluation setup. In order to investigate the role of visual information for different types of verbs, we selected 25 concrete verbs (e.g. *cut, throw, swim*) and 25 abstract verbs (e.g. *trust, prepare, cheat*), according to the MRC concreteness database (Wilson, 1988). The verb was considered concrete if its concreteness score was $\geqslant 400$ and abstract if it was < 400. We extracted the 10 highest-ranked verb–argument class pairings produced by the system for each verb. Each pairing was then evaluated against the argument roles listed for this verb in FrameNet via manual comparison. This resulted in a dataset of 500 verb-argument pairings for VIS and 500 for LING. The pairing was considered correct if the argument cluster corresponded to the semantic type of the role listed in FrameNet and contained nouns listed in the linguistic examples (if these were provided in FrameNet). We have evaluated the system performance in terms of precision at top 10 argument classes and recall of the Core Frame Elements (FEs) among the top 10 argument classes.

Results The VIS model attained a performance of $P = 0.74$ and $R = 0.78$, outperforming the LING model with $P = 0.72$ and $R = 0.76$. When evaluated on the subsets of concrete and abstract verbs separately, VIS attains a $P = 0.76$; $R = 0.80$ (concrete) and $P = 0.72$; $R = 0.75$ (abstract), and LING attains $P = 0.67$; $R = 0.75$ (concrete) and $P = 0.78$; $R = 0.76$ (abstract).

5 Discussion and Data Analysis

Our results show that the vision-based model outperforms the language-only model on our dataset. The difference in performance is particularly pronounced for the concrete verbs. For the abstract verbs in isolation, however, LING attains a higher precision and recall. This is not surprising, as the visual information is better suited to capture the properties of concrete concepts than the abstract ones (Kiela et al., 2014). However, our results indicate that integrating linguistic and visual information provides a better overall model than the linguistic information alone.

Our qualitative analysis of the data revealed a number of interesting trends. Some of the errors of both systems can be traced back to the clustering step. Different argument roles according to FrameNet are sometimes found in one cluster. For instance, both the *killer* and the *victim* are in the same cluster, as shown in Figure 2. However, it is also the case that one FrameNet role can be split into several clusters, e.g. the *Victim* role in the *killing* frame is represented by two clusters of *humans* and *animate beings* more generally.

The common error of the LING model concerns frame mixing, i.e. both literal and metaphorical arguments of the verb are present in the output. For instance, *eat* has a *disease* cluster as one of its arguments; however, *disease* is not part of the *ingestion* frame, but rather an instance of its metaphorical transfer. A common trend in the LING output is that it is dominated by the *Agent* and *Theme* roles, with situational roles (e.g. *Location*) typically ranked lower or not appearing at all. In contrast, the output of VIS encompases a range of situational roles, such as *Instrument, Location, Time* etc. The two models also sometimes differ in the roles that they identify. For instance, for the verb *risk* the VIS output is dominated by arguments of type *Asset* and the LING output by the arguments related to the *Bad outcome* role in FrameNet.

6 Related Work

6.1 Semantic Role Induction

Approaches most similar in spirit to ours are those concerned with unsupervised semantic role labeling. A number of methods represented semantic roles as latent variables in a graphical model, which related the verb, its semantic roles and their syntactic realisations (Grenager and Manning, 2006; Lang and Lapata, 2010; Garg and Henderson, 2012). The induction process then relied on inferring the state of the latent variable. Other researchers adopted a similarity-based argument clustering framework to derive semantic roles. The investigated methods include graph partitioning algorithms (Lang and Lapata, 2014),

Bayesian clustering based on Chinese Restaurant Process (Titov and Klementiev, 2012) and integer linear programming to incorporate semantic and structural constraints during clustering (Woodsend and Lapata, 2015). Titov and Khoddam (2015) proposed a reconstruction-error minimization approach using a log-linear model to predict roles given syntactic and lexical features and a probabilistic tensor factorization model to identify argument fillers based on the role predictions and the predicate. To the best of our knowledge, ours is the first approach to this task exploiting visual data, in the form of image and video descriptions.

6.2 Multi-modal Methods in Semantics

Visual data has been previously used to learn meaning representations that project multiple modalities into the same vector space. Semantic models integrating linguistic and visual information have been shown successful in tasks such as modeling semantic similarity and relatedness (Silberer and Lapata, 2014; Bruni et al., 2012), lexical entailment (Kiela et al., 2015a), compositionality (Roller and Schulte im Walde, 2013), bilingual lexicon induction (Kiela et al., 2015b) and metaphor identification (Shutova et al., 2016).

Other applications of multimodal data include language modeling (Kiros et al., 2014) and knowledge mining from images (Chen et al., 2013; Divvala et al., 2014). Young et al. (2014) show that large collections of image captions can be exploited for entailment tasks. Shutova et al. (2015) used image and video descriptions to induce verb selectional preferences enhanced with visual information.

7 Conclusion

We have presented a method for semantic frame induction from text, images and videos and shown that it operates with a high precision and recall. Although our experiments relied on manually annotated tags for images and videos, recent research shows that such tags can be generated automatically (Bernardi et al., 2016). In the future, our model can be applied to such automatically generated tags, reducing its dependence on manual annotation. While our current experiments focused on nominal arguments of the verbs for semantic role identification, in principle, our model can be applied to other parts of speech, e.g. adverbs, to better incorporate argument roles such as *Manner*.

Acknowledgment

We are grateful to the *SEM reviewers for their feedback. Ekaterina Shutova's research is supported by the Leverhulme Trust Early Career Fellowship.

References

R. Bernardi, R. Cakici, D. Elliott, A. Erdem, E. Erdem, N. Ikizler-Cinbis, F. Keller, A. Muscat, and B. Plank. 2016. Automatic description generation from images: A survey of models, datasets, and evaluation measures. *JAIR* .

Ted Briscoe, John Carroll, and Rebecca Watson. 2006. The second release of the RASP system. In *Proceedings of the COLING/ACL*. pages 77–80.

Elia Bruni, Gemma Boleda, Marco Baroni, and Nam Khanh Tran. 2012. Distributional semantics in Technicolor. In *Proceedings of ACL*. Korea.

Lou Burnard. 2007. *Reference Guide for the British National Corpus (XML Edition)*. http://www.natcorp.ox.ac.uk/XMLedition/URG/.

Xinlei Chen, Abhinav Shrivastava, and Abhinav Gupta. 2013. NEIL: Extracting Visual Knowledge from Web Data. In *Proceedings of ICCV 2013*.

Dipanjan Das, Desai Chen, Andr F. T. Martins, Nathan Schneider, and Noah A. Smith. 2014. Frame-semantic parsing. *Computational Linguistics* 40:1:9–56.

S. Divvala, A. Farhadi, and C. Guestrin. 2014. Learning everything about anything: Webly-supervised visual concept learning. In *Proceedings of CVPR*.

Charles Fillmore. 1976. Frame semantics and the nature of language. *Annals of the New York Academy of Sciences: Conference on the Origin and Development of Language and Speech* 280(1):20–32.

Charles Fillmore, Christopher Johnson, and Miriam Petruck. 2003. Background to FrameNet. *International Journal of Lexicography* 16(3):235–250.

Nikhil Garg and James Henderson. 2012. Unsupervised semantic role induction with global role ordering. In *Proceedings of the 50th Annual Meeting of the Association for Computational Linguistics: Short Papers - Volume 2*. pages 145–149.

D. Gildea and D. Jurafsky. 2002. Automatic labeling of semantic roles. *Computational Linguistics* 28(3).

Trond Grenager and Christopher D. Manning. 2006. Unsupervised discovery of a statistical verb lexicon. In *Proceedings of the 2006 Conference on Empirical Methods in Natural Language Processing*. EMNLP '06, pages 1–8.

Douwe Kiela, Felix Hill, Anna Korhonen, and Stephen Clark. 2014. Improving multi-modal representations using image dispersion: Why less is sometimes more. In *Proceedings of ACL*.

Douwe Kiela, Laura Rimell, Ivan Vulić, and Stephen Clark. 2015a. Exploiting image generality for lexical entailment detection. In *Proceedings of the 53rd Annual Meeting of the Association for Computational Linguistics and the 7th International Joint Conference on Natural Language Processing (Volume 2: Short Papers)*. Beijing, China.

Douwe Kiela, Ivan Vulić, and Stephen Clark. 2015b. Visual bilingual lexicon induction with transferred convnet features. In *Proceedings of the 2015 Conference on Empirical Methods in Natural Language Processing*. Lisbon, Portugal.

Ryan Kiros, Ruslan Salakhutdinov, and Richard S. Zemel. 2014. Multimodal neural language models. In *Proceedings of ICML 2014*. pages 595–603. http://jmlr.org/proceedings/papers/v32/kiros14.html.

Joel Lang and Mirella Lapata. 2010. Unsupervised induction of semantic roles. In *Human Language Technologies: The 2010 Annual Conference of the North American Chapter of the Association for Computational Linguistics*. HLT '10, pages 939–947.

Joel Lang and Mirella Lapata. 2014. Similarity-driven semantic role induction via graph partitioning. *Computational Linguistics* 40(3):633–669.

Lluís Màrquez, Xavier Carreras, Kenneth C. Litkowski, and Suzanne Stevenson. 2008. Semantic role labeling: An introduction to the special issue. *Computational Linguistics* 34(2):145–159.

Marina Meila and Jianbo Shi. 2001. A random walks view of spectral segmentation. In *Proceedings of AISTATS*.

Philip Resnik. 1993. Selection and information: A class-based approach to lexical relationships. Technical report, University of Pennsylvania.

Stephen Roller and Sabine Schulte im Walde. 2013. A Multimodal LDA Model integrating Textual, Cognitive and Visual Modalities. In *Proceedings of EMNLP 2013*. Seattle, WA, pages 1146–1157.

David Shamma. 2014. One hundred million Creative Commons Flickr images for research. Http://labs.yahoo.com/news/yfcc100m/.

Ekaterina Shutova, Douwe Kiela, and Jean Maillard. 2016. Black holes and white rabbits: Metaphor identification with visual features. In *NAACL HLT 2016*. pages 160–170.

Ekaterina Shutova, Niket Tandon, and Gerard de Melo. 2015. Perceptually grounded selectional preferences. In *Proceedings of ACL 2015*. Beijing, China.

Carina Silberer and Mirella Lapata. 2014. Learning grounded meaning representations with autoencoders. In *Proceedings of ACL 2014*. Baltimore, Maryland.

Lin Sun and Anna Korhonen. 2009. Improving verb clustering with automatically acquired selectional preferences. In *Proceedings of EMNLP 2009*.

Lin Sun and Anna Korhonen. 2011. Hierarchical verb clustering using graph factorization. In *Proceedings of EMNLP*. Edinburgh, UK, pages 1023–1033.

Ivan Titov and Ehsan Khoddam. 2015. Unsupervised induction of semantic roles within a reconstruction-error minimization framework. In *HLT-NAACL*. The Association for Computational Linguistics, pages 1–10.

Ivan Titov and Alexandre Klementiev. 2012. A bayesian approach to unsupervised semantic role induction. In *Proceedings of the 13th Conference of the European Chapter of the Association for Computational Linguistics*. EACL '12, pages 12–22.

M.D. Wilson. 1988. The MRC Psycholinguistic Database: Machine Readable Dictionary, Version 2. *Behavioural Research Methods, Instruments and Computers* 20(1):6–11.

Kristian Woodsend and Mirella Lapata. 2015. Distributed representations for unsupervised semantic role labeling. In *Proceedings of the 2015 Conference on Empirical Methods in Natural Language Processing, EMNLP 2015, Lisbon, Portugal, September 17-21, 2015*. pages 2482–2491.

Peter Young, Alice Lai, Micah Hodosh, and Julia Hockenmaier. 2014. From image descriptions to visual denotations. *Transactions of the Association of Computational Linguistics* pages 67–78.

Acquiring Predicate Paraphrases from News Tweets

Vered Shwartz   **Gabriel Stanovsky**   **Ido Dagan**
Computer Science Department, Bar-Ilan University, Ramat-Gan, Israel
{vered1986, gabriel.satanovsky}@gmail.com, dagan@cs.biu.ac.il

Abstract

We present a simple method for ever-growing extraction of predicate paraphrases from news headlines in Twitter. Analysis of the output of ten weeks of collection shows that the accuracy of paraphrases with different support levels is estimated between 60-86%. We also demonstrate that our resource is to a large extent complementary to existing resources, providing many novel paraphrases. Our resource is publicly available, continuously expanding based on daily news.

1 Introduction

Recognizing that various textual descriptions across multiple texts refer to the same event or action can benefit NLP applications such as recognizing textual entailment (Dagan et al., 2013) and question answering. For example, to answer "when did the US Supreme Court approve same-sex marriage?" given the text "In June 2015, the Supreme Court ruled for same-sex marriage", *approve* and *ruled for* should be identified as describing the same action.

To that end, much effort has been devoted to identifying predicate paraphrases, some of which resulted in releasing resources of predicate entailment or paraphrases. Two main approaches were proposed for that matter; the first leverages the similarity in argument distribution across a large corpus between two predicates (e.g. $[a]_0$ buy $[a]_1$ / $[a]_0$ acquire $[a]_1$) (Lin and Pantel, 2001; Berant et al., 2010). The second approach exploits bilingual parallel corpora, extracting as paraphrases pairs of texts that were translated identically to foreign languages (Ganitkevitch et al., 2013).

While these methods have produced exhaustive resources which are broadly used by applications,

$[a]_0$ introduce $[a]_1$	$[a]_0$ welcome $[a]_1$
$[a]_0$ appoint $[a]_1$	$[a]_0$ to become $[a]_1$
$[a]_0$ die at $[a]_1$	$[a]_0$ pass away at $[a]_1$
$[a]_0$ hit $[a]_1$	$[a]_0$ sink to $[a]_1$
$[a]_0$ be investigate $[a]_1$	$[a]_0$ be probe $[a]_1$
$[a]_0$ eliminate $[a]_1$	$[a]_0$ slash $[a]_1$
$[a]_0$ announce $[a]_1$	$[a]_0$ unveil $[a]_1$
$[a]_0$ quit after $[a]_1$	$[a]_0$ resign after $[a]_1$
$[a]_0$ announce as $[a]_1$	$[a]_0$ to become $[a]_1$
$[a]_0$ threaten $[a]_1$	$[a]_0$ warn $[a]_1$
$[a]_0$ die at $[a]_1$	$[a]_0$ live until $[a]_1$
$[a]_0$ double down on $[a]_1$	$[a]_0$ stand by $[a]_1$
$[a]_0$ kill $[a]_1$	$[a]_0$ shoot $[a]_1$
$[a]_0$ approve $[a]_1$	$[a]_0$ pass $[a]_1$
$[a]_0$ would be cut under $[a]_1$	$[a]_1$ slash $[a]_0$
seize $[a]_0$ at $[a]_1$	to grab $[a]_0$ at $[a]_1$

Table 1: A sample from the top-ranked predicate paraphrases.

their accuracy is limited. Specifically, the first approach may extract antonyms, that also have similar argument distribution (e.g. $[a]_0$ raise to $[a]_1$ / $[a]_0$ fall to $[a]_1$) while the second may conflate multiple senses of the foreign phrase.

A third approach was proposed to harvest paraphrases from multiple mentions of the same event in news articles.[1] This approach assumes that various redundant reports make different lexical choices to describe the same event. Although there has been some work following this approach (e.g. Shinyama et al., 2002; Shinyama and Sekine, 2006; Roth and Frank, 2012; Zhang and Weld, 2013), it was less exhaustively investigated and did not result in creating paraphrase resources.

In this paper we present a novel unsupervised method for ever-growing extraction of lexically-divergent predicate paraphrase pairs from news tweets. We apply our methodology to create a resource of predicate paraphrases, exemplified in Table 1.

Analysis of the resource obtained after ten

---

[1]This corresponds to instances of event coreference (Bagga and Baldwin, 1999).

*Proceedings of the 6th Joint Conference on Lexical and Computational Semantics (*SEM 2017)*, pages 155–160,
Vancouver, Canada, August 3-4, 2017. ©2017 Association for Computational Linguistics

weeks of acquisition shows that the set of paraphrases reaches accuracy of 60-86% at different levels of support. Comparison to existing resources shows that, even as our resource is still smaller in orders of magnitude from existing resources, it complements them with non-consecutive predicates (e.g. take $[a]_0$ from $[a]_1$) and paraphrases which are highly context specific.

The resource and the source code are available at `http://github.com/vered1986/Chirps`.[2] As of the end of May 2017, it contains 456,221 predicate pairs in 1,239,463 different contexts. Our resource is ever-growing and is expected to contain around 2 million predicate paraphrases within a year. Until it reaches a large enough size, we will release a daily update, and at a later stage, we plan to release a periodic update.

2 Background

2.1 Existing Paraphrase Resources

A prominent approach to acquire predicate paraphrases is to compare the distribution of their arguments across a corpus, as an extension to the distributional hypothesis (Harris, 1954). DIRT (Lin and Pantel, 2001) is a resource of 10 million paraphrases, in which the similarity between predicate pairs is estimated by the geometric mean of the similarities of their argument slots. Berant (2012) constructed an entailment graph of distributionally similar predicates by enforcing transitivity constraints and applying global optimization, releasing 52 million directional entailment rules (e.g. $[a]_0$ shoot $[a]_1 \rightarrow [a]_0$ kill $[a]_1$).

A second notable source for extracting paraphrases is multiple translations of the same text (Barzilay and McKeown, 2001). The Paraphrase Database (PPDB) (Ganitkevitch et al., 2013; Pavlick et al., 2015) is a huge collection of paraphrases extracted from bilingual parallel corpora. Paraphrases are scored heuristically, and the database is available for download in six increasingly large sizes according to scores (the smallest size being the most accurate). In addition to lexical paraphrases, PPDB also consists of 140 million syntactic paraphrases, some of which include predicates with non-terminals as arguments.

2.2 Using Multiple Event Descriptions

Another line of work extracts paraphrases from redundant comparable news articles (e.g. Shinyama

et al., 2002; Barzilay and Lee, 2003). The assumption is that multiple news articles describing the same event use various lexical choices, providing a good source for paraphrases. Heuristics are applied to recognize that two news articles discuss the same event, such as lexical overlap and same publish date (Shinyama and Sekine, 2006). Given such a pair of articles, it is likely that predicates connecting the same arguments will be paraphrases, as in the following example:

> 1. GOP lawmakers *introduce* new health care plan
> 2. GOP lawmakers *unveil* new health care plan

Zhang and Weld (2013) and Zhang et al. (2015) introduced methods that leverage parallel news streams to cluster predicates by meaning, using temporal constraints. Since this approach acquires paraphrases from descriptions of *the same event*, it is potentially more accurate than methods that acquire paraphrases from the entire corpus or translation phrase table. However, there is currently no paraphrase resource acquired in this approach.[3]

Finally, Xu et al. (2014) developed a supervised model to collect *sentential* paraphrases from Twitter. They used Twitter's trending topic service, and considered two tweets from the same topic as paraphrases if they shared a single anchor word.

3 Resource Construction

We present a methodology to automatically collect binary verbal predicate paraphrases from Twitter. We first obtain news related tweets (§3.1) from which we extract propositions (§3.2). For a candidate pair of propositions, we assume that if both arguments can be matched then the predicates are likely paraphrases (§3.3). Finally, we rank the predicate pairs according to the number of instances in which they were aligned (§3.4).

3.1 Obtaining News Headlines

We use Twitter as a source of readily available news headlines. The 140 characters limit makes tweets concise, informative and independent of each other, obviating the need to resolve document-level entity coreference. We query the Twitter Search API[4] via Twitter Search.[5] We use

---

[2]*Chirp* is a paraphrase of *tweet*.

[3]Zhang and Weld (2013) released a small collection of 10k predicate paraphrase clusters (with average cluster size of 2.4) produced by the system.

[4]`https://apps.twitter.com/`

[5]`https://github.com/ckoepp/TwitterSearch`

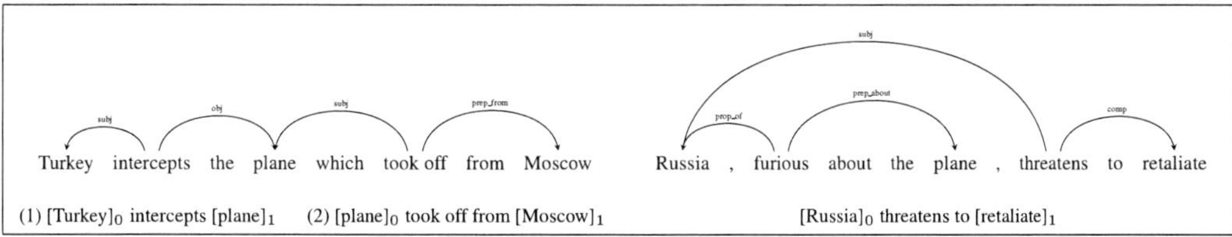

Figure 1: PropS structures and the corresponding propositions extracted by our process. Left: multi-word predicates and multiple extractions per tweet. Right: argument reduction.

Manafort hid payments from Ukraine party with Moscow ties	[a]$_0$ **hide** [a]$_1$	Paul Manafort	payments
Manafort laundered the payments through Belize	[a]$_0$ **launder** [a]$_1$	Manafort	payments
Send immigration judges to cities to speed up deportations	**to send** [a]$_0$ **to** [a]$_1$	immigration judges	cities
Immigration judges headed to 12 cities to speed up deportations	[a]$_0$ **headed to** [a]$_1$	immigration judges	12 cities

Table 2: Examples of predicate paraphrase instances in our resource: each instance contains two tweets, predicate types extracted from them, and the instantiations of arguments.

Twitter's news filter that retrieves tweets containing links to news websites, and limit the search to English tweets.

3.2 Proposition Extraction

We extract propositions from news tweets using PropS (Stanovsky et al., 2016), which simplifies dependency trees by conveniently marking a wide range of predicates (e.g, verbal, adjectival, non-lexical) and positioning them as direct heads of their corresponding arguments. Specifically, we run PropS over dependency trees predicted by spaCy[6] and extract predicate types (as in Table 1) composed of *verbal predicates*, datives, prepositions, and auxiliaries.

Finally, we employ a pre-trained argument reduction model to remove non-restrictive argument modifications (Stanovsky and Dagan, 2016). This is essential for our subsequent alignment step, as it is likely that short and concise phrases will tend to match more frequently in comparison to longer, more specific arguments. Figure 1 exemplifies some of the phenomena handled by this process, along with the automatically predicted output.

3.3 Generating Paraphrase Instances

Following the assumption that different descriptions of the same event are bound to be redundant (as discussed in Section 2.2), we consider two predicates as paraphrases if: (1) They appear on the same day, and (2) Each of their arguments aligns with a unique argument in the other predicate, either by *strict matching* (short edit distance, abbreviations, etc.) or by a looser matching (par-

tial token matching or WordNet synonyms).[7] Table 2 shows examples of predicate paraphrase instances in the resource.

3.4 Resource Release

The resource release consists of two files:

1. **Instances**: the specific contexts in which the predicates are paraphrases (as in Table 2). In practice, to comply with Twitter policy, we release predicate paraphrase pair types along with their arguments and tweet IDs, and provide a script for downloading the full texts.

2. **Types**: predicate paraphrase pair types (as in Table 1). The types are ranked in a descending order according to a heuristic accuracy score:

$$s = count \cdot \left(1 + \frac{d}{N}\right)$$

where *count* is the number of instances in which the predicate types were aligned (Section 3.3), d is the number of different days in which they were aligned, and N is the number of days since the resource collection begun.

Taking into account the number of different days in which predicates were aligned reduces the noise caused by two entities that undergo two different actions on the same day. For example, the following tweets from the day of Chuck Berry's death:

1. Last year when Chuck Berry turned 90
2. Chuck Berry dics at 90

---

[6] https://spacy.io

[7] In practice, our publicly available code requires that *at least one* pair of arguments will strictly match.

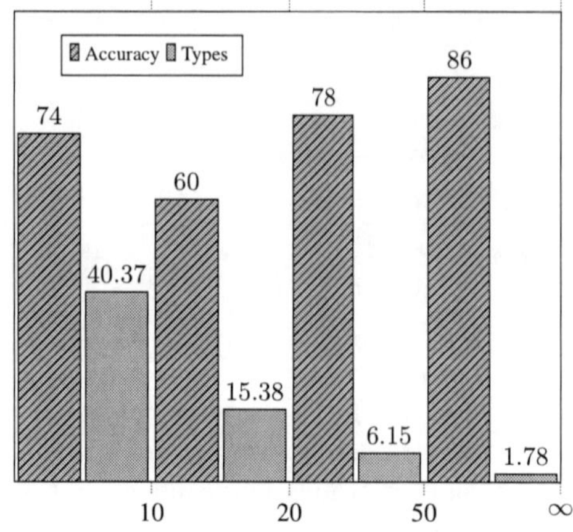
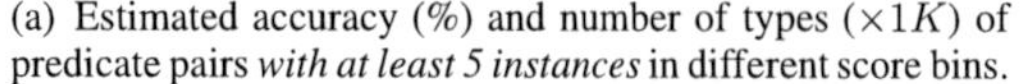

(a) Estimated accuracy (%) and number of types ($\times 1K$) of predicate pairs *with at least 5 instances* in different score bins.

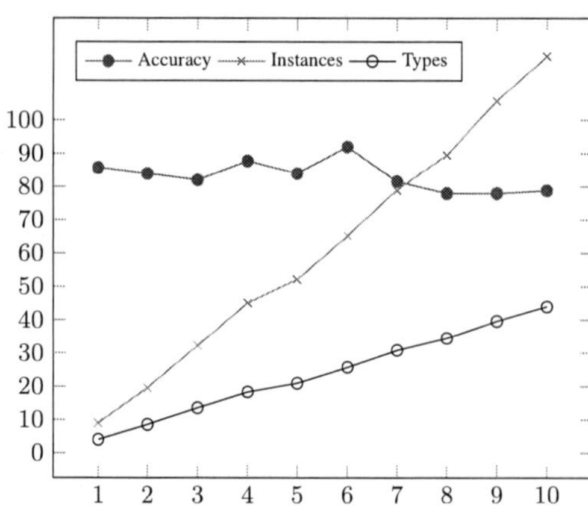

(b) Estimated accuracy (%), number of instances ($\times 10K$) and types ($\times 10K$) in the first 10 weeks.

Figure 2: Resource statistics after ten weeks of collection.

yield the incorrect type $[a]_0$ turn $[a]_1$ / $[a]_0$ die at $[a]_1$. While there may be several occurrences of that type on the same day, it is not expected to re-occur in other news events (in different days), yielding a low accuracy score.

4 Analysis of Resource Quality

We estimate the quality of the resource obtained after ten weeks of collection by annotating a sample of the extracted paraphrases.

The annotation task was carried out in Amazon Mechanical Turk.[8] To ensure the quality of workers, we applied a qualification test and required a 99% approval rate for at least 1,000 prior tasks. We assigned each annotation to 3 workers and used the majority vote to determine the correctness of paraphrases.

We followed a similar approach to instance-based evaluation (Szpektor et al., 2007), and let workers judge the correctness of a predicate pair (e.g. $[a]_0$ purchase $[a]_1$/$[a]_0$ acquire $[a]_1$) through 5 different instances (e.g. Intel purchased Mobileye/Intel acquired Mobileye). We considered the type as correct if at least one of its instance-pairs were judged as correct. The idea that lies behind this type of evaluation is that predicate pairs are difficult to judge out-of-context.

Differently from Szpektor et al. (2007), we used the instances in which the paraphrases appeared originally, as those are available in the resource.

[8] https://www.mturk.com/mturk

4.1 Quality of Extractions and Ranking

To evaluate the resource accuracy, and following the instance-based evaluation scheme, we only considered paraphrases that occurred in at least 5 instances (which currently constitute 10% of the paraphrase types). We partition the types into four increasingly large bins according to their scores (the smallest bin being the most accurate), similarly to PPDB (Ganitkevitch et al., 2013), and annotate a sample of 50 types from each bin. Figure 2(a) shows that the frequent types achieve up to 86% accuracy.

The accuracy expectedly increases with the score, except for the lowest-score bin ($(0, 10]$) which is more accurate than the next one ($(10, 20]$). At the current stage of the resource there is a long tail of paraphrases that appeared few times. While many of them are incorrect, there are also true paraphrases that are infrequent and therefore have a low accuracy score. We expect that some of these paraphrases will occur again in the future and their accuracy score will be strengthened.

4.2 Size and Accuracy Over Time

To estimate future usefulness, Figure 2(b) plots the resource size (in terms of types and instances) and estimated accuracy through each week in the first 10 weeks of collection.

The accuracy at a specific time was estimated by annotating a sample of 50 predicate pair types with accuracy score ≥ 20 in the resource obtained

drag $[a]_0$ from $[a]_1$	$[a]_0$ remove from $[a]_1$
leak $[a]_0$ to $[a]_1$	to share $[a]_0$ with $[a]_1$
oust $[a]_0$ from $[a]_1$	$[a]_0$ be force out at $[a]_1$
reveal $[a]_0$ to $[a]_1$	share $[a]_0$ with $[a]_1$
$[a]_0$ add $[a]_1$	$[a]_0$ beef up $[a]_1$
$[a]_0$ admit to $[a]_1$	$[a]_0$ will attend $[a]_1$
$[a]_0$ announce as $[a]_1$	$[a]_0$ to become $[a]_1$
$[a]_0$ arrest in $[a]_1$	$[a]_0$ charge in $[a]_1$
$[a]_0$ attack $[a]_1$	$[a]_0$ clash with $[a]_1$
$[a]_0$ be force out at $[a]_1$	$[a]_0$ have be fire from $[a]_1$
$[a]_0$ eliminate $[a]_1$	$[a]_0$ slash $[a]_1$
$[a]_0$ face $[a]_1$	$[a]_0$ hit with $[a]_1$
$[a]_0$ mock $[a]_1$	$[a]_0$ troll $[a]_1$
$[a]_0$ open up about $[a]_1$	$[a]_0$ reveal $[a]_1$
$[a]_0$ get $[a]_1$	$[a]_0$ sentence to $[a]_1$

Table 3: A sample of types from our resource that are not found in `Berant` or in `PPDB`.

at that time, which roughly correspond to the top ranked 1.5% types.

Figure 2(b) demonstrates that these types maintain a level of around 80% in accuracy. The resource growth rate (i.e. the number of new types) is expected to change with time. We predict that the resource will contain around 2 million types in one year.[9]

5 Comparison to Existing Resources

The resources which are most similar to ours are `Berant` (Berant, 2012), a resource of predicate entailments, and `PPDB` (Pavlick et al., 2015), a resource of paraphrases, both described in Section 2.

We expect our resource to be more accurate than resources which are based on the distributional approach (Berant, 2012; Lin and Pantel, 2001). In addition, in comparison to `PPDB`, we specialize on binary verbal predicates, and apply an additional phase of proposition extraction, handling various phenomena such as non-consecutive particles and minimality of arguments.

Berant (2012) evaluated their resource against a dataset of predicate entailments (Zeichner et al., 2012), using a recall-precision curve to show the performance obtained with a range of thresholds on the resource score. This kind of evaluation is less suitable for our resource; first, predicate entailment is directional, causing paraphrases with the wrong entailment direction to be labeled negative in the dataset. Second, since our resource is still relatively small, it is unlikely to have sufficient coverage of the dataset at that point. We therefore

leave this evaluation to future work.

To demonstrate the added value of our resource, we show that even in its current size, it already contains accurate predicate pairs which are absent from the existing resources. Rather than comparing against labeled data, we use types with score ≥ 50 from our resource (1,778 pairs), which were assessed as accurate (Section 4.2).

We checked whether these predicate pairs are covered by `Berant` and `PPDB`. To eliminate directionality, we looked for types in both directions, i.e. for a predicate pair $(p1, p2)$ we searched for both $(p1, p2)$ and $(p2, p1)$. Overall, we found that 67% of these types do not exist in `Berant`, 62% in `PPDB`, and 49% in neither.

Table 3 exemplifies some of the predicate pairs that do not exist in both resources. Specifically, our resource contains many non-consecutive predicates (e.g. reveal $[a]_0$ to $[a]_1$ / share $[a]_0$ with $[a]_1$) that by definition do not exist in `Berant`.

Some pairs, such as $[a]_0$ get $[a]_1$ / $[a]_0$ sentence to $[a]_1$, are context-specific, occurring when $[a]_0$ is a person and $[a]_1$ is the time they are about to serve in prison. Given that *get* has a broad distribution of argument instantiations, this paraphrase and similar paraphrases are less likely to exist in resources that rely on the distribution of arguments in the entire corpus.

6 Conclusion

We presented a new unsupervised method to acquire fairly accurate predicate paraphrases from news tweets discussing the same event. We release a growing resource of predicate paraphrases. Qualitative analysis shows that our resource adds value over existing resources. In the future, when the resource is comparable in size to the existing resources, we plan to evaluate its intrinsic accuracy on annotated test sets, as well as its extrinsic benefits in downstream NLP applications.

Acknowledgments

This work was partially supported by an Intel ICRI-CI grant, the Israel Science Foundation grant 880/12, and the German Research Foundation through the German-Israeli Project Cooperation (DIP, grant DA 1600/1-1).

---

[9]For up-to-date resource statistics, see: `https://github.com/vered1986/Chirps/tree/master/resource`.

References

Amit Bagga and Breck Baldwin. 1999. Cross-document event coreference: Annotations, experiments, and observations. In *Workshop on Coreference and its Applications.*

Regina Barzilay and Lillian Lee. 2003. Learning to paraphrase: An unsupervised approach using multiple-sequence alignment. In *Proceedings of the 2003 Human Language Technology Conference of the North American Chapter of the Association for Computational Linguistics.* http://aclweb.org/anthology/N03-1003.

Regina Barzilay and R. Kathleen McKeown. 2001. Extracting paraphrases from a parallel corpus. In *Proceedings of the 39th Annual Meeting of the Association for Computational Linguistics.* http://aclweb.org/anthology/P01-1008.

Jonathan Berant. 2012. *Global Learning of Textual Entailment Graphs.* Ph.D. thesis, Tel Aviv University.

Jonathan Berant, Ido Dagan, and Jacob Goldberger. 2010. Global learning of focused entailment graphs. In *Proceedings of the 48th Annual Meeting of the Association for Computational Linguistics.* Association for Computational Linguistics, pages 1220–1229. http://aclweb.org/anthology/P10-1124.

Ido Dagan, Dan Roth, and Mark Sammons. 2013. Recognizing textual entailment .

Juri Ganitkevitch, Benjamin Van Durme, and Chris Callison-Burch. 2013. PPDB: The paraphrase database. In *Proceedings of the 2013 Conference of the North American Chapter of the Association for Computational Linguistics: Human Language Technologies.* Association for Computational Linguistics, pages 758–764. http://aclweb.org/anthology/N13-1092.

Zellig S Harris. 1954. Distributional structure. *Word* 10(2-3):146–162.

Dekang Lin and Patrick Pantel. 2001. Dirt – Discovery of inference rules from text. In *Proceedings of the seventh ACM SIGKDD international conference on Knowledge discovery and data mining.* ACM, pages 323–328.

Ellie Pavlick, Pushpendre Rastogi, Juri Ganitkevitch, Benjamin Van Durme, and Chris Callison-Burch. 2015. PPDB 2.0: Better paraphrase ranking, fine-grained entailment relations, word embeddings, and style classification. In *Proceedings of the 53rd Annual Meeting of the Association for Computational Linguistics and the 7th International Joint Conference on Natural Language Processing (Volume 2: Short Papers).* Association for Computational Linguistics, pages 425–430. https://doi.org/10.3115/v1/P15-2070.

Michael Roth and Anette Frank. 2012. Aligning predicate argument structures in monolingual comparable texts: A new corpus for a new task. In **SEM 2012: The First Joint Conference on Lexical and Computational Semantics – Volume 1: Proceedings of the main conference and the shared task, and Volume 2: Proceedings of the Sixth International Workshop on Semantic Evaluation (SemEval 2012).* Association for Computational Linguistics, pages 218–227. http://aclweb.org/anthology/S12-1030.

Yusuke Shinyama and Satoshi Sekine. 2006. Preemptive information extraction using unrestricted relation discovery. In *Proceedings of the Human Language Technology Conference of the NAACL, Main Conference.* http://aclweb.org/anthology/N06-1039.

Yusuke Shinyama, Satoshi Sekine, and Kiyoshi Sudo. 2002. Automatic paraphrase acquisition from news articles. In *Proceedings of the second international conference on Human Language Technology Research.* Morgan Kaufmann Publishers Inc., pages 313–318.

Gabriel Stanovsky and Ido Dagan. 2016. Annotating and predicting non-restrictive noun phrase modifications. In *Proceedings of the 54rd Annual Meeting of the Association for Computational Linguistics (ACL 2016).*

Gabriel Stanovsky, Jessica Ficler, Ido Dagan, and Yoav Goldberg. 2016. Getting more out of syntax with props. *CoRR* abs/1603.01648. http://arxiv.org/abs/1603.01648.

Idan Szpektor, Eyal Shnarch, and Ido Dagan. 2007. Instance-based evaluation of entailment rule acquisition. In *Proceedings of the 45th Annual Meeting of the Association of Computational Linguistics.* Association for Computational Linguistics, pages 456–463. http://aclweb.org/anthology/P07-1058.

Wei Xu, Alan Ritter, Chris Callison-Burch, William B Dolan, and Yangfeng Ji. 2014. Extracting lexically divergent paraphrases from twitter. *Transactions of the Association for Computational Linguistics* 2:435–448.

Naomi Zeichner, Jonathan Berant, and Ido Dagan. 2012. Crowdsourcing inference-rule evaluation. In *Proceedings of the 50th Annual Meeting of the Association for Computational Linguistics (Volume 2: Short Papers).* Association for Computational Linguistics, pages 156–160. http://aclweb.org/anthology/P12-2031.

Congle Zhang, Stephen Soderland, and Daniel S Weld. 2015. Exploiting parallel news streams for unsupervised event extraction. *Transactions of the Association for Computational Linguistics* 3:117–129.

Congle Zhang and Daniel S Weld. 2013. Harvesting parallel news streams to generate paraphrases of event relations. In *Proceedings of the 2013 Conference on Empirical Methods in Natural Language Processing.* Seattle, Washington, USA, pages 1776–1786.

Evaluating Semantic Parsing against a Simple Web-based Question Answering Model

Alon Talmor
Tel-Aviv University
`alontalmor@mail.tau.ac.il`

Mor Geva
Tel-Aviv University
`morgeva@mail.tau.ac.il`

Jonathan Berant
Tel-Aviv University
`joberant@cs.tau.ac.il`

Abstract

Semantic parsing shines at analyzing complex natural language that involves composition and computation over multiple pieces of evidence. However, datasets for semantic parsing contain many factoid questions that can be answered from a single web document. In this paper, we propose to evaluate semantic parsing-based question answering models by comparing them to a question answering baseline that queries the web and extracts the answer only from web snippets, without access to the target knowledge-base. We investigate this approach on COMPLEXQUESTIONS, a dataset designed to focus on compositional language, and find that our model obtains reasonable performance ($\sim$35 F_1 compared to 41 F_1 of state-of-the-art). We find in our analysis that our model performs well on complex questions involving conjunctions, but struggles on questions that involve relation composition and superlatives.

1 Introduction

Question answering (QA) has witnessed a surge of interest in recent years (Hill et al., 2015; Yang et al., 2015; Pasupat and Liang, 2015; Chen et al., 2016; Joshi et al., 2017), as it is one of the prominent tests for natural language understanding. QA can be coarsely divided into semantic parsing-based QA, where a question is translated into a logical form that is executed against a knowledge-base (Zelle and Mooney, 1996; Zettlemoyer and Collins, 2005; Liang et al., 2011; Kwiatkowski et al., 2013; Reddy et al., 2014; Berant and Liang, 2015), and unstructured QA, where a question is answered directly from some relevant text

(Voorhees and Tice, 2000; Hermann et al., 2015; Hewlett et al., 2016; Kadlec et al., 2016; Seo et al., 2016).

In semantic parsing, background knowledge has already been compiled into a knowledge-base (KB), and thus the challenge is in interpreting the question, which may contain compositional constructions (*"What is the second-highest mountain in Europe?"*) or computations (*"What is the difference in population between France and Germany?"*). In unstructured QA, the model needs to also interpret the language of a document, and thus most datasets focus on matching the question against the document and extracting the answer from some local context, such as a sentence or a paragraph (Onishi et al., 2016; Rajpurkar et al., 2016; Yang et al., 2015).

Since semantic parsing models excel at handling complex linguistic constructions and reasoning over multiple facts, a natural way to examine whether a benchmark indeed requires modeling these properties, is to train an unstructured QA model, and check if it under-performs compared to semantic parsing models. If questions can be answered by examining local contexts only, then the use of a knowledge-base is perhaps unnecessary. However, to the best of our knowledge, only models that utilize the KB have been evaluated on common semantic parsing benchmarks.

The goal of this paper is to bridge this evaluation gap. We develop a simple log-linear model, in the spirit of traditional web-based QA systems (Kwok et al., 2001; Brill et al., 2002), that answers questions by querying the web and extracting the answer from returned web snippets. Thus, our evaluation scheme is suitable for semantic parsing benchmarks in which the knowledge required for answering questions is covered by the web (in contrast with virtual assitants for which the knowledge is specific to an application).

*Proceedings of the 6th Joint Conference on Lexical and Computational Semantics (*SEM 2017)*, pages 161–167,
Vancouver, Canada, August 3-4, 2017. ©2017 Association for Computational Linguistics

We test this model on COMPLEXQUESTIONS (Bao et al., 2016), a dataset designed to require more compositionality compared to earlier datasets, such as WEBQUESTIONS (Berant et al., 2013) and SIMPLEQUESTIONS (Bordes et al., 2015). We find that a simple QA model, despite having no access to the target KB, performs reasonably well on this dataset ($\sim$35 F_1 compared to the state-of-the-art of 41 F_1). Moreover, for the subset of questions for which the right answer can be found in one of the web snippets, we outperform the semantic parser (51.9 F_1 vs. 48.5 F_1). We analyze results for different types of compositionality and find that superlatives and relation composition constructions are challenging for a web-based QA system, while conjunctions and events with multiple arguments are easier.

An important insight is that semantic parsers must overcome the mismatch between natural language and formal language. Consequently, language that can be easily matched against the web may become challenging to express in logical form. For example, the word *"wife"* is an atomic binary relation in natural language, but expressed with a complex binary $\lambda x.\lambda y.\text{Spouse}(x,y) \wedge \text{Gender}(x,\text{Female})$ in knowledge-bases. Thus, some of the complexity of understanding natural language is removed when working with a natural language representation.

To conclude, we propose to evaluate the extent to which semantic parsing-based QA benchmarks require compositionality by comparing semantic parsing models to a baseline that extracts the answer from short web snippets. We obtain reasonable performance on COMPLEXQUESTIONS, and analyze the types of compositionality that are challenging for a web-based QA model. To ensure reproducibility, we release our dataset, which attaches to each example from COMPLEXQUES-TIONS the top-100 retrieved web snippets.[1]

2 Problem Setting and Dataset

Given a training set of triples $\{q^{(i)}, R^{(i)}, a^{(i)}\}_{i=1}^{N}$, where $q^{(i)}$ is a question, $R^{(i)}$ is a web result set, and $a^{(i)}$ is the answer, our goal is to learn a model that produces an answer a for a new question-result set pair (q, R). A web result set R consists of $K(= 100)$ web snippets, where each snippet s_i

R:

s_1: **Billy Batts (Character) - Biography - IMDb** Billy Batts (Character) on IMDb: Movies, TV, Celebs, and more... ... Devino is portrayed by <u>Frank Vincent</u> in the film Goodfellas. Page last updated by !!!de leted!!!

s_2: **Frank Vincent - Wikipedia** He appeared in Scorsese's 1990 film Goodfellas, where he played Billy Batts, a made man in the Gambino crime family. He also played a role in Scorsese's...

$\vdots$

s_{100}: **Voice-over in Goodfellas** In the summer when they played cards all night, nobody ever called the cops. .... But we had a problem with Billy Batts. This was a touchy thing. Tommy had killed a made man. Billy was a part of the Bambino crew and untouchable. Before you...

q: *"who played the part of billy batts in goodfellas?"*
a: *"Frank Vincent"*

Figure 1: A training example containing a result set R, a question q and an answer a. The result set R contains 100 web snippets s_i, each including a title (boldface) and text. The answer is underlined.

has a title and a text fragment. An example for a training example is provided in Figure 1.

Semantic parsing-based QA datasets contain question-answer pairs alongside a background KB. To convert such datasets to our setup, we run the question q against Google's search engine and scrape the top-K web snippets. We use only the web snippets and ignore any boxes or other information returned (see Figure 1 and the full dataset in the supplementary material).

Compositionality We argue that if a dataset truly requires a compositional model, then it should be difficult to tackle with methods that only match the question against short web snippets. This is since it is unlikely to integrate all necessary pieces of evidence from the snippets.

We convert COMPLEXQUESTIONS into the aforementioned format, and manually analyze the types of compositionality that occur on 100 random training examples. Table 1 provides an example for each of the question types we found:

SIMPLE: an application of a single binary relation on a single entity.

FILTER: a question where the semantic type of the answer is mentioned (*"tv shows"* in Table 1).

N-ARY: A question about a single event that involves more than one entity (*"juni"* and *"spy kids 4"* in Table 1).

CONJUNCTION: A question whose answer is the conjunction of more than one binary relation in the question.

---

[1]Data can be downloaded from `https://worksheets.codalab.org/worksheets/0x91d77db37e0a4bbbaeb37b8972f4784f/`

Type	Example	%
SIMPLE	*"who has gone out with cornelis de graeff"*	17%
FILTER	*"which tv shows has wayne rostad starred in"*	18%
N-ARY	*"who played juni in spy kids 4?"*	51%
CONJ.	*"what has queen latifah starred in that doug mchenry directed"*	10%
COMPOS.	*"who was the grandson of king david's father?"*	7%
SUPERL.	*"who is the richest sports woman?"*	9%
OTHER	*"what is the name george lopez on the show?"*	8%

Table 1: An example for each compositionality type and the proportion of examples in 100 random examples. A question can fall into multiple types, and thus the sum exceeds 100%.

COMPOSITION A question that involves composing more than one binary relation over an entity (*"grandson"* and *"father"* in Table 1).

SUPERLATIVE A question that requires sorting or comparing entities based on a numeric property.

OTHER Any other question.

Table 1 illustrates that COMPLEXQUESTIONS is dominated by N-ARY questions that involve an event with multiple entities. In Section 4 we evaluate the performance of a simple QA model for each compositionality type, and find that N-ARY questions are handled well by our web-based QA system.

3 Model

Our model comprises two parts. First, we extract a set of answer candidates, $\mathcal{A}$, from the web result set. Then, we train a log-linear model that outputs a distribution over the candidates in $\mathcal{A}$, and is used at test time to find the most probable answers.

Candidate Extraction We extract all 1-grams, 2-grams, 3-grams and 4-grams (lowercased) that appear in R, yielding roughly 5,000 candidates per question. We then discard any candidate that fully appears in the question itself, and define $\mathcal{A}$ to be the top-K candidates based on their tf-idf score, where term frequency is computed on all the snippets in R, and inverse document frequency is computed on a large external corpus.

Candidate Ranking We define a log-linear model over the candidates in $\mathcal{A}$:

$$p_\theta(a \mid q, R) = \frac{\exp(\phi(q, R, a)^\top \theta)}{\sum_{a' \in \mathcal{A}} \exp(\phi(q, R, a')^\top \theta)},$$

where $\theta \in \mathbb{R}^d$ are learned parameters, and $\phi(\cdot) \in \mathbb{R}^d$ is a feature function. We train

our model by maximizing the regularized conditional log-likelihood objective $\sum_{i=1}^{N} \log p_\theta(a^{(i)} \mid q^{(i)}, R^{(i)}) + \lambda \cdot ||\theta||_2^2$. At test time, we return the most probable answers based on $p_\theta(a \mid q, R)$ (details in Section 4). While semantic parsers generally return a set, in COMPLEXQUESTIONS 87% of the answers are a singleton set.

Features A candidate span a often has multiple mentions in the result set R. Therefore, our feature function $\phi(\cdot)$ computes the average of the features extracted from each mention. The main information sources used are the match between the candidate answer itself and the question (top of Table 2) and the match between the context of a candidate answer in a specific mention and the question (bottom of Table 2), as well as the Google rank in which the mention appeared.

Lexicalized features are useful for our task, but the number of training examples is too small to train a fully lexicalized model. Therefore, we define lexicalized features over the 50 most common non-stop words in COMPLEXQUESTIONS. Last, our context features are defined in a 6-word window around the candidate answer mention, where the feature value decays exponentially as the distance from the candidate answer mention grows. Overall, we compute a total of 892 features over the dataset.

4 Experiments

COMPLEXQUESTIONS contains 1,300 training examples and 800 test examples. We performed 5 random 70/30 splits of the training set for development. We computed POS tags and named entities with Stanford CoreNLP (Manning et al., 2014). We did not employ any co-reference resolution tool in this work. If after candidate extraction, we do not find the gold answer in the top-K(=140) candidates, we discard the example, resulting in a training set of 856 examples.

We compare our model, WEBQA, to STAGG (Yih et al., 2015) and COMPQ (Bao et al., 2016), which are to the best of our knowledge the highest performing semantic parsing models on both COMPLEXQUESTIONS and WEBQUESTIONS. For these systems, we only report test F_1 numbers that are provided in the original papers, as we do not have access to the code or predictions. We evaluate models by computing average F_1, the official evaluation metric defined for COMPLEXQUESTIONS. This measure computes the F_1

Template	Description
SPAN LENGTH	Indicator for the number of tokens in a_m
TF-IDF	Binned and raw tf-idf scores of a_m for every span length
CAPITALIZED	Whether a_m is capitalized
STOP WORD	Fraction of words in a_m that are stop words
IN QUEST	Fraction of words in a_m that are in q
IN QUEST+COMMON	Conjunction of IN QUEST with common words in q
IN QUESTION DIST.	Max./avg. cosine similarity between a_m words and q words
WH+NE	Conjunction of wh-word in q and named entity tags (NE) of a_m
WH+POS	Conjunction of wh-word in q and part-of-speech tags of a_m
NE+NE	Conjunction of NE tags in q and NE tags in a_m
NE+COMMON	Conjunction of NE tags in a_m and common words in q
MAX-NE	Whether a_m is a NE with maximal span (not contained in another NE)
YEAR	Binned indicator for year if a_m is a year
CTXT MATCH	Max./avg. over non stop words in q, for whether a q word occurs around a_m, weighted by distance from a_m
CTXT SIMILARITY	Max./avg. cosine similarity over non-stop words in q, between q words and words around a_m, weighted by distance
IN TITLE	Whether a_m is in the title part of the snippet
CTXT ENTITY	Indicator for whether a common word appears between a_m and a named entity that appears in q
GOOGLE RANK	Binned snippet rank of a_m in the result set R

Table 2: Features templates used to extract features from each answer candidate mention a_m. Cosine similarity is computed with pre-trained GloVe embeddings (Pennington et al., 2014). The definition of *common words* and *weighting by distance* is in the body of the paper.

System	Dev		Test		
	F_1	p@1	F_1	p@1	MRR
STAGG	-	-	37.7	-	-
COMPQ	-	-	**40.9**	-	-
WEBQA	35.3	36.4	32.6	33.5	42.4
WEBQA-EXTRAPOL	-	-	34.4	-	-
COMPQ-SUBSET	-	-	48.5	-	-
WEBQA-SUBSET	53.6	55.1	51.9	53.4	67.5

Table 3: Results on development (average over random splits) and test set. Middle: results on all examples. Bottom: results on the subset where candidate extraction succeeded.

between the set of answers returned by the system and the set of gold answers, and averages across questions. To allow WEBQA to return a set rather than a single answer, we return the most probable answer a^* as well as any answer a such that $(\phi(q, R, a^*)^\top \theta - \phi(q, R, a)^\top \theta) < 0.5$. We also compute precision@1 and Mean Reciprocal Rank (MRR) for WEBQA, since we have a ranking over answers. To compute metrics we lowercase the gold and predicted spans and perform exact string match.

Table 3 presents the results of our evaluation. WEBQA obtained 32.6 F_1 (33.5 p@1, 42.4 MRR) compared to 40.9 F_1 of COMPQ. Our candidate extraction step finds the correct answer in the top-K candidates in 65.9% of development examples and 62.7% of test examples. Thus, our test F_1 on examples for which candidate extraction succeeded (WEBQA-SUBSET) is 51.9 (53.4 p@1, 67.5 MRR).

We were able to indirectly compare WEBQA-SUBSET to COMPQ: Bao et al. (2016) graciously provided us with the predictions of COMPQ when it was trained on COMPLEXQUESTIONS, WEBQUESTIONS, and SIMPLEQUESTIONS. In this

setup, COMPQ obtained 42.2 F_1 on the test set (compared to 40.9 F_1, when training on COMPLEXQUESTIONS only, as we do). Restricting the predictions to the subset for which candidate extraction succeeded, the F_1 of COMPQ-SUBSET is 48.5, which is 3.4 F_1 points lower than WEBQA-SUBSET, which was trained on less data.

Not using a KB, results in a considerable disadvantage for WEBQA. KB entities have normalized descriptions, and the answers have been annotated according to those descriptions. We, conversely, find answers on the web and often predict a correct answer, but get penalized due to small string differences. E.g., for *"what is the longest river in China?"* we answer *"yangtze river"*, while the gold answer is *"yangtze"*. To quantify this effect we manually annotated all 258 examples in the first random development set split, and determined whether string matching failed, and we actually returned the gold answer.[2] This improved performance from 53.6 F_1 to 56.6 F_1 (on examples that passed candidate extraction). Further normalizing gold and predicted entities, such that *"Hillary Clinton"* and *"Hillary Rodham Clinton"* are unified, improved F_1 to 57.3 F_1. Extrapolating this to the test set would result in an F_1 of 34.4 (WEBQA-EXTRAPOL in Table 3) and 34.9, respectively.

Last, to determine the contribution of each feature template, we performed ablation tests and we present the five feature templates that resulted in the largest drop to performance on the development set in Table 4. Note that TF-IDF is by far the most impactful feature, leading to a large drop of 12 points in performance. This shows the importance of using the redundancy of the web for our QA system.

Analysis To understand the success of WEBQA on different compositionality types, we manu-

---

[2] We also publicly release our annotations.

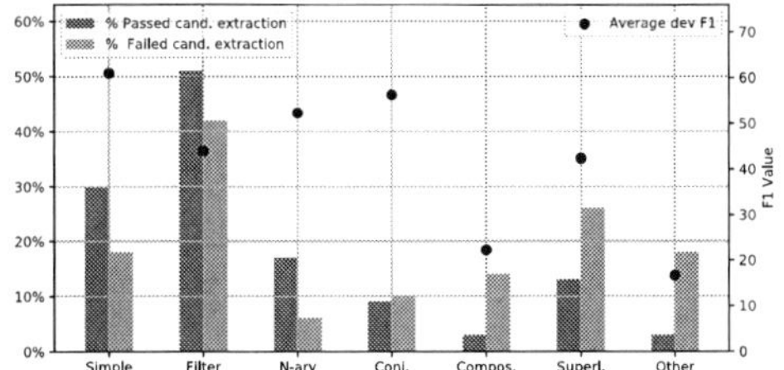

Figure 2: Proportion of examples that passed or failed candidate extraction for each compositionality type, as well as average F_1 for each compositionality type. COMPOSITION and SUPERLATIVE questions are difficult for WEBQA.

Feature Template	F_1	Δ
WEBQA	53.6	
- MAX-NE	51.8	-1.8
- NE+COMMON	51.8	-1.8
- GOOGLE RANK	51.4	-2.2
- IN QUEST	50.1	-3.5
- TF-IDF	41.5	-12

Table 4: Feature ablation results. The five features that lead to largest drop in performance are displayed.

ally annotated the compositionality type of 100 random examples that passed candidate extraction and 50 random examples that failed candidate extraction. Figure 2 presents the results of this analysis, as well as the average F_1 obtained for each compositionality type on the 100 examples that passed candidate extraction (note that a question can belong to multilpe compositionality types). We observe that COMPOSITION and SUPERLATIVE questions are challenging for WEBQA, while SIMPLE, FILTER, and N-ARY quesitons are easier (recall that a large fraction of the questions in COMPLEXQUESTIONS are N-ARY). Interestingly, WEBQA performs well on CONJUNCTION questions (*"what film victor garber starred in that rob marshall directed"*), possibly because the correct answer can obtain signal from multiple snippets.

An advantage of finding answers to questions from web documents compared to semantic parsing, is that we do not need to learn the "language of the KB". For example, the question *"who is the governor of California 2010"* can be matched directly to web snippets, while in Freebase (Bollacker et al., 2008) the word *"governor"* is expressed by a complex predicate $\lambda x.\exists z.\text{GoverPos}(x, z) \wedge \text{PosTitle}(z, \text{Governor})$. This could provide a partial explanation for the reasonable performance of WEBQA.

5   Related Work

Our model WEBQA performs QA using web snippets, similar to traditional QA systems like MULDER (Kwok et al., 2001) and AskMSR (Brill et al., 2002). However, it it enjoys the advances in commerical search engines of the last decade, and uses a simple log-linear model, which has become standard in Natural Language Processing.

Similar to this work, Yao et al. (2014) analyzed a semantic parsing benchmark with a simple QA system. However, they employed a semantic parser that is limited to applying a single binary relation on a single entity, while we develop a QA system that does not use the target KB at all.

Last, in parallel to this work Chen et al. (2017) evaluated an unstructured QA system against semantic parsing benchmarks. However, their focus was on examining the contributions of multitask learning and distant supervision to training rather than to compare to state-of-the-art semantic parsers.

6   Conclusion

We propose in this paper to evaluate semantic parsing-based QA systems by comparing them to a web-based QA baseline. We evaluate such a QA system on COMPLEXQUESTIONS and find that it obtains reasonable performance. We analyze performance and find that COMPOSITION and SUPERLATIVE questions are challenging for a web-based QA system, while CONJUNCTION and N-ARY questions can often be handled by our QA model.

Reproducibility   Code, data, annotations, and experiments for this paper are available on the CodaLab platform at `https://worksheets.codalab.org/worksheets/0x91d77db37e0a4bbbaeb37b8972f4784f/`.

Acknowledgments

We thank Junwei Bao for providing us with the test predictions of his system. We thank the anonymous reviewers for their constructive feedback. This work was partially supported by the Israel Science Foundation, grant 942/16.

References

J. Bao, N. Duan, Z. Yan, M. Zhou, and T. Zhao. 2016. Constraint-based question answering with knowledge graph. In *International Conference on Computational Linguistics (COLING)*.

J. Berant, A. Chou, R. Frostig, and P. Liang. 2013. Semantic parsing on Freebase from question-answer pairs. In *Empirical Methods in Natural Language Processing (EMNLP)*.

J. Berant and P. Liang. 2015. Imitation learning of agenda-based semantic parsers. *Transactions of the Association for Computational Linguistics (TACL)* 3:545–558.

K. Bollacker, C. Evans, P. Paritosh, T. Sturge, and J. Taylor. 2008. Freebase: a collaboratively created graph database for structuring human knowledge. In *International Conference on Management of Data (SIGMOD)*. pages 1247–1250.

A. Bordes, N. Usunier, S. Chopra, and J. Weston. 2015. Large-scale simple question answering with memory networks. *arXiv preprint arXiv:1506.02075* .

E. Brill, S. Dumais, and M. Banko. 2002. An analysis of the AskMSR question-answering system. In *Association for Computational Linguistics (ACL)*. pages 257–264.

D. Chen, J. Bolton, and C. D. Manning. 2016. A thorough examination of the CNN / Daily Mail reading comprehension task. In *Association for Computational Linguistics (ACL)*.

Danqi Chen, Adam Fisch, Jason Weston, and Antoine Bordes. 2017. Reading Wikipedia to answer open-domain questions. In *Association for Computational Linguistics (ACL)*.

K. M. Hermann, T. Koisk, E. Grefenstette, L. Espeholt, W. Kay, M. Suleyman, and P. Blunsom. 2015. Teaching machines to read and comprehend. In *Advances in Neural Information Processing Systems (NIPS)*.

D. Hewlett, A. Lacoste, L. Jones, I. Polosukhin, A. Fandrianto, J. Han, M. Kelcey, and D. Berthelot. 2016. Wikireading: A novel large-scale language understanding task over Wikipedia. In *Association for Computational Linguistics (ACL)*.

F. Hill, A. Bordes, S. Chopra, and J. Weston. 2015. The goldilocks principle: Reading children's books with explicit memory representations. In *International Conference on Learning Representations (ICLR)*.

Mandar Joshi, Eunsol Choi, Daniel S Weld, and Luke Zettlemoyer. 2017. Triviaqa: A large scale distantly supervised challenge dataset for reading comprehension. *arXiv preprint arXiv:1705.03551* .

R. Kadlec, M. Schmid, O. Bajgar, and J. Kleindienst. 2016. Text understanding with the attention sum reader network. In *Association for Computational Linguistics (ACL)*.

T. Kwiatkowski, E. Choi, Y. Artzi, and L. Zettlemoyer. 2013. Scaling semantic parsers with on-the-fly ontology matching. In *Empirical Methods in Natural Language Processing (EMNLP)*.

C. Kwok, O. Etzioni, and D. S. Weld. 2001. Scaling question answering to the web. *ACM Transactions on Information Systems (TOIS)* 19:242–262.

P. Liang, M. I. Jordan, and D. Klein. 2011. Learning dependency-based compositional semantics. In *Association for Computational Linguistics (ACL)*. pages 590–599.

C. D. Manning, M. Surdeanu, J. Bauer, J. Finkel, S. J. Bethard, and D. McClosky. 2014. The stanford coreNLP natural language processing toolkit. In *ACL system demonstrations*.

T. Onishi, H. Wang, M. Bansal, K. Gimpel, and D. McAllester. 2016. Whodid what: A large-scale person-centered cloze dataset. In *Empirical Methods in Natural Language Processing (EMNLP)*.

P. Pasupat and P. Liang. 2015. Compositional semantic parsing on semi-structured tables. In *Association for Computational Linguistics (ACL)*.

J. Pennington, R. Socher, and C. D. Manning. 2014. Glove: Global vectors for word representation. In *Empirical Methods in Natural Language Processing (EMNLP)*.

P. Rajpurkar, J. Zhang, K. Lopyrev, and P. Liang. 2016. Squad: 100,000+ questions for machine comprehension of text. In *Empirical Methods in Natural Language Processing (EMNLP)*.

S. Reddy, M. Lapata, and M. Steedman. 2014. Large-scale semantic parsing without question-answer pairs. *Transactions of the Association for Computational Linguistics (TACL)* 2(10):377–392.

M. Seo, A. Kembhavi, A. Farhadi, and H. Hajishirzi. 2016. Bidirectional attention flow for machine comprehension. *arXiv* .

E. M. Voorhees and D. M. Tice. 2000. Building a question answering test collection. In *ACM Special Interest Group on Information Retreival (SIGIR)*. pages 200–207.

Y. Yang, W. Yih, and C. Meek. 2015. WikiQA: A challenge dataset for open-domain question answering. In *Empirical Methods in Natural Language Processing (EMNLP)*. pages 2013–2018.

X. Yao, J. Berant, and B. Van-Durme. 2014. Freebase QA: Information extraction or semantic parsing. In *Workshop on Semantic parsing*.

W. Yih, M. Chang, X. He, and J. Gao. 2015. Semantic parsing via staged query graph generation: Question answering with knowledge base. In *Association for Computational Linguistics (ACL)*.

M. Zelle and R. J. Mooney. 1996. Learning to parse database queries using inductive logic programming. In *Association for the Advancement of Artificial Intelligence (AAAI)*. pages 1050–1055.

L. S. Zettlemoyer and M. Collins. 2005. Learning to map sentences to logical form: Structured classification with probabilistic categorial grammars. In *Uncertainty in Artificial Intelligence (UAI)*. pages 658–666.

Logical Metonymy in a Distributional Model of Sentence Comprehension

Emmanuele Chersoni
Aix-Marseille University
emmanuelechersoni@gmail.com

Alessandro Lenci
University of Pisa
alessandro.lenci@unipi.it

Philippe Blache
Aix-Marseille University
philippe.blache@univ-amu.fr

Abstract

In theoretical linguistics, *logical metonymy* is defined as the combination of an event-subcategorizing verb with an entity-denoting direct object (e.g., *The author began the book*), so that the interpretation of the VP requires the retrieval of a covert event (e.g., *writing*). Psycholinguistic studies have revealed extra processing costs for logical metonymy, a phenomenon generally explained with the introduction of new semantic structure. In this paper, we present a general distributional model for sentence comprehension inspired by the Memory, Unification and Control model by Hagoort (2013, 2016). We show that our distributional framework can account for the extra processing costs of logical metonymy and can identify the covert event in a classification task.

1 Logical Metonymy: Psycholinguistic Evidence and Computational Modeling

The interpretation of so-called *logical metonymy* (e.g, *The student begins the book*) has received an extensive attention in both psycholinguistic and linguistic research. The phenomenon is extremely problematic for traditional theories of compositionality (Asher, 2015) and is generally explained as a type clash between an event-selecting metonymic verb (e.g., *begin*) and an entity-denoting nominal object (e.g., *the book*), which triggers the recovery of a hidden event (e.g., *reading*). Past research work brought extensive evidence that such metonymic constructions also determine extra processing costs during online sentence comprehension (McElree et al.,

2001; Traxler et al., 2002), although such evidence is not uncontroversial (Falkum, 2011). According to Frisson and McElree (2008), event recovery is triggered by the type clash, and the extra processing load is due to "the deployment of operations to construct a semantic representation of the event". Thus, logical metonymy raises two major questions: i.) How is the hidden event recovered? ii.) What is the relationship between such mechanism and the increase in processing difficulty?

One of the first accounts of the phenomenon dates back to the works of Pustejovsky (1995) and Jackendoff (1997), which assume that the covert event is retrieved from complex lexical entries consisting of rich knowledge structures (Pustejovsky's *qualia roles*). For example, the representation of a noun like *book* includes telic properties (the purpose of the entity, e.g. *read*) and agentive properties (the mode of creation of the entity, e.g. *write*). The predicate-argument type mismatch triggers the retrieval of a covert event from the object noun qualia roles, thereby producing a semantic representation equivalent to *begin to write the paper* (see also the discussion in Traxler et al. (2002)).

On the one hand, the lexicalist explanation is very appealing, since it accounts for the existence of default interpretations of logical metonymies (e.g. *begin the book* is typically interpreted as *begin reading/writing the book*). On the other hand, Lascarides and Copestake (1998) and more recently Zarcone et al. (2014) show that qualia roles are simply not flexible enough to account for the wide variety of interpretations that can be retrieved. These are in fact affected by the subject choice, the general syntactic and discourse context, and by our world knowledge. [1]

---

[1] Consider the classical example from Lascarides and Copestake (1998): *My goat eats anything. He really enjoys*

*Proceedings of the 6th Joint Conference on Lexical and Computational Semantics (*SEM 2017)*, pages 168–177,
Vancouver, Canada, August 3-4, 2017. ©2017 Association for Computational Linguistics

An alternative view on logical metonymy has been proposed in the field of relevance-theoretic pragmatics (Sperber and Wilson, 1986; Carston, 2002). According to studies such as de Almeida (2004), de Almeida and Dwivedi (2008) and Falkum (2011), the metonymy resolution process is driven by post-lexical pragmatic inferences, relying on both general world knowledge and discourse context. The 'pragmatic hypothesis' allows for the necessary flexibility in the interpretation of logical metonymies, since the range of the potential covert events is not constrained by the lexical entry, but only by the hearer's expectations of the optimal relevance of the utterance. However, as pointed out by Zarcone and Padó (2011), the pragmatic account is not precise with respect to the mechanism and to the type of knowledge involved in the process of metonymy resolution. Moreover, it tends to disregard the fact that there are default interpretations that are activated in neutral, less informative contexts.

More recently, Zarcone and Padó (2011) and Zarcone et al. (2014) brought experimental evidence for the role of Generalized Event Knowledge (GEK) (McRae and Matsuki, 2009) in the interpretation of logical metonymies. The authors refer to a long trend of psycholinguistic studies (McRae et al., 1998; Altmann, 1999; Kamide et al., 2003; McRae et al., 2005; Hare et al., 2009; Bicknell et al., 2010), which show that speakers quickly make use of their rich event knowledge during online sentence processing to build expectations about the upcoming input.[2] The experiments on German by Zarcone et al. (2014) show that the subjects combine the linguistic cues in the input to activate typical events the sentences could refer to. Given an agent-patient pair, if the covert event is typical for that specific argument combination, it is read faster and it is more difficult to inhibit in a probe recognition task. The authors explained their results in the light of the words-as-cues paradigm (Elman, 2009, 2014), which claims that the words in the mental lexicon are cues to event knowledge modulating language comprehension in an incremental fashion.

Research in computational semantics has fo-

cused on two different aspects of the phenomenon: the first one is the retrieval of the covert event, which has been approached by means of either probabilistic methods (Lapata and Lascarides, 2003; Lapata et al., 2003; Shutova, 2009) or of distributional similarity-based thematic fit estimations (Zarcone et al., 2012), whereas the second aspect concerns modeling the experimental data about processing costs. Zarcone et al. (2013) showed that a distributional model of verb-object thematic fit can reproduce the reading times differences in the experimental conditions found by McElree et al. (2001) and Traxler et al. (2002). Their merits notwithstanding, a limit of the former studies is that they did not try to build a single model to account for both aspects involved in logical metonymy.

The goal of this paper is twofold. First of all, we present a **general distributional model of sentence comprehension** inspired by recent proposals in neurocognitive sciences (Section 2). Secondly, we introduce a **semantic composition weight** that is used to model the reading times of metonymic sentences reported in previous experimental studies and to predict the covert event in a binary classification task (Section 3).

2 A Distributional Model of Sentence Comprehension

The model we present includes a **Memory component**, containing distributional information activated by lexical items, and a **Unification component**, which combines the items in Memory to form a coherent semantic representation of the sentence.[3] This architecture is directly inspired by Memory, Unification and Control (MUC), proposed by Peter Hagoort as a general model for the neurobiology of language (Hagoort, 2013, 2016). MUC incorporates three main functional components: i.) *Memory* corresponds to linguistic knowledge stored in long-term memory; ii.) *Unification* refers to the assembly in working memory of the constructions stored in Memory into larger structures, with contributions from the context; iii.) *Control* is responsible for relating language to joint action and social interaction. Similarly to

---

your book (= eating). The event retrieval cannot be explained in terms of qualia structures, as it is unlikely that the lexical entry for *book* includes something related to *eating*-events.

[2]It should be pointed out that, unlike relevance theory which conceives world knowledge and linguistic knowledge as separate modules, GEK includes both linguistic and extralinguistic information.

---

[3]A previous version of this model has already been introduced in Chersoni et al. (2016a), the main difference being the way the complexity score component based on Memory was computed (see section 5 and 6 of the 2016 paper). Moreover, the model was applied to a different task (i.e., the computation of context-sensitive argument typicality).

MUC, we argue that the comprehension of a sentence is an incremental process driven by the goal of constructing a coherent semantic representation of the event the speaker intends to communicate. Our model rests on the following assumptions:

- the Memory component contains information about events and their typical participants, which is derived from both first-hand experience and linguistic experience. Following McRae and Matsuki (2009), we call this information **Generalized Event Knowledge** (GEK). In this paper we restrict ourselves to the 'linguistic' subset of GEK (henceforth GEK_L), which we model with distributional information extracted from corpora;

- during sentence processing, lexical items activate portions of GEK_L, and the Unification component composes them into a coherent representation of the event expressed by the sentence;

- the event representation is assigned a **semantic composition weight** on the basis of i) the availability and salience of information stored in GEK_L and activated by the linguistic input; ii) the semantic coherence of the unified event, depending in turn on the mutual typicality of the event participants;

- a sentence interpretation is the event with the highest semantic composition weight, that is the event that best satisfies the semantic constraints coming from lexical items and the contextual information stored in GEK_L.

Sentence comprehension therefore results from a "balance between storage and computation" (Baggio and Hagoort, 2011; Baggio et al., 2012) that simultaneously accounts for the unlimited possibility to understand new sentences, which are constructed by means of Unification, and for the processing advantage guaranteed by the retrieval from Memory of "ready-to-use" information about typical events and situations.

Crucially, we argue that logical metonymy interpretation shares this same mechanism of on-line sentence processing and that the covert event is i.) an event retrieved from GEK_L that is strongly activated by the lexical items, ii.) and with a high degree of mutual semantic congruence with the other arguments in the sentence. Therefore, there is no formal difference between simple and enriched forms of compositionality (Jackendoff, 1997), both being instances of the same general model of sentence processing.

2.1 The Memory Component: A Distributional Model of GEK_L

In our framework, we assume that each lexical item w_i activates a set of events $\langle e_1, \sigma_1 \rangle, \ldots, \langle e_n, \sigma_n \rangle$ such that e_i is an event in GEK_L, and σ_i is an activation score computed as the conditional probability $P(e|w_i)$, which quantifies the 'strength' with which the event is activated by w_i.

We represent **events** in GEK_L as feature structures specifying participants and roles, and we extract this information from parsed sentences in corpora: the attributes are syntactic dependencies, which we use as a surface approximation of semantic roles, and the values are distributional vectors of dependent lexemes.[4] For example, from the sentence *The student reads a book* we extract the following event representation:

$$[_{EVENT} \text{ NSUBJ:}\overrightarrow{student} \text{ HEAD:}\overrightarrow{read} \text{ DOBJ:}\overrightarrow{book}]$$

Events in GEK_L can be cued by several lexical items, with a strength depending on the salience of the event given the item. For example, the event above is cued by *student, read* and *book*. Besides complete events, we assume GEK_L to contain schematic (i.e., underspecified) events too. For instance, from the sentence *The student reads a book* we also generate **schematic events** such as $[_{EVENT} \text{ NSUBJ:}\overrightarrow{student} \text{ DOBJ:}\overrightarrow{book}]$, obtained by abstracting over one or more of the instantiated attribute values. Such representation describes an underspecified event schema involving a student and a book, which can be instantiated by different activities (e.g., *reading, borrowing*, etc.). According to this view, GEK_L is not a flat list of events, but a structured repository of prototypical knowledge about event contingencies.

It is worth remarking that the events in GEK_L are complex symbolic structures including distributional representations of the event head and its participants. Events in GEK_L are therefore modeled like a sort of **semantic frames** whose elements are distributional vectors.[5]

---

[4]We represent dependencies according to the Universal Dependencies annotation scheme: http://universaldependencies.org/.

[5]Unlike traditional semantic frames, our events are satu-

2.2 The Unification Component: Building Semantic Representations

Language can be seen as a set of instructions that the comprehender uses to create a representation of the situation that is being described by the speaker. In our framework, we make use of **situation models** (henceforth SMs),[6] defined as data structures that contain a representation of the event currently being processed (Zwaan and Radvansky, 1998). Comprehension always occurs within the context of an existing SM: during online sentence processing, lexical items cue portions of GEK_L and the SM is dynamically updated by unifying its current content with the new information. In this perspective, the goal of sentence comprehension consists in recovering (reconstructing) the event e that the sentence is most likely to describe (Kuperberg, 2016). The event e is the event that best satisfies all the constraints set by the lexical items in the sentence and by the active SM.[7]

Let $w_1, w_2, \ldots, w_n$ be an input linguistic sequence (e.g., a sentence or a discourse) that is currently being processed. Let SM_i be the semantic representation built for the linguistic input until $w_1, \ldots, w_i$, and let e_i be the event representation in SM_i. When we process w_{i+1}:

1. the GEK_L associated with w_{i+1} in the lexicon, $GEK_L[w_{i+1}]$, is activated;

2. $GEK_L[w_{i+1}]$ is integrated with SM_i to produce SM_{i+1}, containing the new event e_{i+1}.

We model semantic composition as **an event construction and update function** F, whose aim is to build a coherent *SM* by integrating the GEK_L cued by the linguistic elements that are composed:

$$F(SM_i, GEK_L[w_{i+1}]) = SM_{i+1} \qquad (1)$$

The composition function is responsible for two distinct processes:

- F **unifies** two event feature structures into a new event, provided that the attribute-value features of the input events are compatible.

Here is an example of unification:

$$[_{EVENT} \;\; \text{NSUBJ}{:}\overrightarrow{mechanic} \;\; \text{DOBJ}{:}\overrightarrow{engine}] \;\; \sqcup$$
$$[_{EVENT} \; \text{NSUBJ}{:}\overrightarrow{mechanic} \; \text{HEAD}{:}\overrightarrow{check}] = [_{EVENT}$$
$$\text{NSUBJ}{:}\overrightarrow{mechanic} \; \text{HEAD}{:}\overrightarrow{check} \; \text{DOBJ}{:}\overrightarrow{engine}]$$

The event of a *mechanic* performing an action on an *engine* and the event of a *mechanic checking* something are unified into a new event of a *mechanic checking an engine*;

- F **weights** the unified event e_k with a pair of scores $\langle \theta_{e_k}, \sigma_{e_k} \rangle$, weighting e_k with respect to its semantic coherence and its salience given the lexical cues activating it.

The score θ_{e_k} quantifies the degree of **semantic coherence** of the unified event e_k. We assume that the semantic coherence (or internal unity) of an event depends on the **mutual typicality** of its components. Consider the following sentences:

(1)   a.   The student writes a thesis.
       b.   The mechanic writes a sonnet.

The event represented in (1-a) has a high degree of semantic coherence because all its components are mutually typical: *student* is a typical subject for the verb *write* and *thesis* has a strong typicality both as an object of *write* and as an object occurring in *student*-related events. Conversely, the components in the event expressed by (1-b) have a low level of mutual typicality, thereby resulting into an event with much lower semantic coherence. Although the sentence is perfectly understandable, it sounds a little weird because it depicts an unusual situation.

We measure the mutual typicality of the components by extending the notion of **thematic fit**, which is normally used to measure the congruence of a predicate with an argument (McRae et al., 1998). In our case, instead, thematic fit is a general measure of the semantic typicality or congruence among event participants. Extending the approach by Erk et al. (2010), thematic fit is measured with vector cosine in the following way:

$\theta(\overrightarrow{a}|s_i, \overrightarrow{b})$ (the thematic fit of $\overrightarrow{a}$ given $\overrightarrow{b}$ and the role s_i) is the cosine between $\overrightarrow{a}$ and the prototype vector built out of the k top values $\overrightarrow{c_1}, \ldots, \overrightarrow{c_k}$, such that $\underset{\longrightarrow}{s_i}{:}\overrightarrow{c_z}$, for $1 \leq z \leq k$, co-occurs with $\overrightarrow{b}$ in the same event structures

---

rated structures, with participants specified for each role.

[6] SMs are akin to Discourse Representation Structures in DRT (Kamp, 2013).

[7] The idea also bears some similarities with the inferential model of communication proposed by Relevance Theory, where the interpretation of a given utterance is the one that maximizes the hearer's expectations of relevance (Sperber and Wilson, 1986).

For instance, the thematic fit of *student* as a subject of *write* is given by the cosine between the vector of *student* and the centroid vector built out of the k most salient subjects of *write*. Similarly, we assess the typicality of *thesis* as an object related to *student* (i.e., as an object of events involving student as subject) by measuring the cosine between the vector of *thesis* and the centoid vector built out of the k most salient objects related to *student*. Finally, we measure in the same way the typicality of *thesis* as an object of *write*.

Formally, the global score θ_{e_k} of an event e_k is defined as:

$$\theta_{e_k} = \prod_{a,b,s_i \in e} \theta(\overrightarrow{a}|s_i, \overrightarrow{b}) \qquad (2)$$

meaning that the degree of semantic coherence of an event is given by the product of the partial thematic fit scores between all its components.[8]

On the other hand, the σ_{e_k} score weights the **salience** of the unified event e_k by combining the weights of e_i and e_j into a new weight assigned to e_k. In this work, we compute activation of an event e simply by summing the activation scores of the single lexical items cuing it (i.e., the conditional probabilities of the event given each lexical item in the input sentence):

$$\sigma_i = P(e|i) = \frac{P(e,i)}{P(i)} \qquad (3)$$

$$F(\sigma_i, \sigma_j) = \sigma_{e_k} = \sigma_i + \sigma_j \qquad (4)$$

Thus, the score σ_{e_k} measures the degree to which the unified event is activated by the linguistic expressions composing it. Consequently, events that are cued by many constructions in the sentence should incrementally increase their salience.

To sum up, we weight unified events along two dimensions: internal semantic coherence (θ), and degree of activation by linguistic expressions (σ). The latter is used to estimate the importance of "ready-to-use" event structures stored in GEK_L and retrieved during sentence processing. On the the other hand, the θ score allows us to weight events not available in the Memory component. In fact, the Unification component can construct new event never observed before, thereby accounting

for the ability to comprehend novel sentences representing atypical and yet possible events. For instance, the event expressed by (1-a) might be expected to be already stored in GEK_L because of its high typicality, thereby having a high σ score. Suppose instead that the sentence (1-b) expresses a brand new event, and that its components never co-occurred together before. In this case, its weight will only depend on the θ score, that is on how similar are its participants to other events stored in the event repository (e.g., how *mechanic* is similar to the prototypical subjects of *write*). Therefore, the joint effect of the σ and θ scores captures the "balance between storage and computation" driving sentence processing (cf. above).

Given an input sentence s, its interpretation INT(s) is the event e_k with the highest **semantic composition weight (SCW)**, defined as follows:

$$\text{INT}(s) = \underset{e}{\text{argmax}}(\text{SCW}(e)) \qquad (5)$$

$$\text{SCW}(e) = \theta_e + \sigma_e \qquad (6)$$

We model the **semantic complexity (Semp-Comp)** of a sentence s as inversely related to the SCW of the event representing its interpretation:

$$\text{SemComp}(s) = \frac{1}{\text{SCW}(\text{INT}(s))} \qquad (7)$$

The less internally coherent is the event represented by the sentence and the less strong is its activation by the lexical items, the more the unification is cognitively expensive and the sentence semantically complex.

3 Modeling Logical Metonymy

We apply the distributional model of sentence comprehension presented in the previous section to account for psycholinguistic data about metonymic sentences. In particular, we predict that *metonymic sentences will have higher Sem-Comp scores than non-coercion sentences*, because they do not comply with the semantic preferences of the event-selecting verb. According to Zarcone et al. (2013), it is exactly the low thematic fit between verb and object that triggers complement coercion and that, at the same time, causes the extra processing load.

Additionally, we predict that the covert event in metonymic sentence is i.) strongly activated by the lexical items in the context, and is ii.) semantically coherent with respect to the participants that

---

[8]For the present study, we discarded the modifiers. However, θ scores could also be computed for measuring the coherence of modified arguments (e.g. *the angry child smiled*). We thank one of our reviewers for pointing this out.

are overtly realized. In other words, the inferred covert event is *the event that maximizes the SCW of the global event structure* representing the interpretation of the sentence.

3.1 Datasets

We used two datasets created for previous psycholinguistic studies: the **McElree** dataset (McElree et al., 2001) and the **Traxler** dataset (Traxler et al., 2002). Each dataset compared three different experimental conditions, by contrasting constructions requiring a type-shift with constructions requiring normal composition:

(2)   a.   The author was starting the book.
        b.   The author was writing the book.
        c.   The author was reading the book.

Sentence (2-a) corresponds to the metonymic condition (MET), while sentences (2-b) and (2-c) correspond to non-metonymic constructions, with the difference that (2-b) represents a typical event given the subject and the object (HIGH_TYP), whereas (2-c) expresses a plausible but less typical event (LOW_TYP). The McElree dataset was created for the self-paced reading study by McElree et al. (2001), and includes 99 sentences (33 triplets), while the Traxler dataset was used in the eye-tracking experiment by Traxler et al. (2002) and contains 108 sentences (36 triplets).[9]

3.2 Extracting GEK_L

In order to populate the repository of events in GEK_L, we followed the procedure proposed by Chersoni et al. (2016b) to extract syntactic joint contexts from a concatenation of four different corpora: the Reuters Corpus Vol.1 (Lewis et al., 2004); the Ukwac and the Wackypedia Corpus (Baroni et al., 2009) and the British National Corpus (Leech, 2013). For each sentence, we generated an event (as described in Section 2.1) by extracting the verb and its direct dependencies. In the present case, the dependency relations of interest are subject (SUBJ), direct (DOBJ) and indirect object (IOBJ), infinitive and gerund complements (XCOMP), and a generic prepositional complement relation (PREPCOMP), on which we mapped all the complements introduced by a preposition. We discarded the adjectival/adverbial modifiers

---

[9]The sentences in the same triple have the same syntactic complexity, as they differ only for the verb.

and we just keep their heads. For instance, from the joint context *director-n-subj__write-v-head__article-n-dobj* we generated the event $[_{EVENT}$ NSUBJ:$\overrightarrow{student}$ HEAD:$\overrightarrow{read}$ DOBJ:$\overrightarrow{book}]$. For each joint context, we also generated schematic events from its dependency subsets. We totally extracted 1,043,766 events that include at least one of the words of the evaluation datasets.

All the lexemes in the events are represented as distributional vectors. We built a syntax-based distributional semantic model by using as targets the 20K most frequent nouns and verbs in our concatenated corpus, plus any other word occurring in the events in the GEK_L. Words with frequency below 100 were excluded. The total number of targets is 20,560 (cf. Table 1 for the dataset coverage). As vector dimensions, we used the same target words, while the dependency relations are the same used to build the joint contexts (*SUBJ:author-n* and *DOBJ:book-n* are examples of dimensions for the target *write-v*). Syntactic co-occurrences were weighted with Local Mutual Information (Evert, 2004):

$$LMI(t, r, f) = log\left(\frac{O_{trf}}{E_{trf}}\right) * O_{trf} \qquad (8)$$

with O_{trf} the co-occurrence frequency of the target t, the syntactic relation r and the filler f, and E_{trf} their expected co-occurrence frequency.

Dataset	Coverage
McElree et al. (2001)	30/33
Traxler et al. (2002)	36/36

Table 1: GEK_L coverage for the evaluation triplets

3.3 Modeling the Processing Cost of Metonymic Sentences

The sentences in the original datasets were represented as S(subject)-V(verb)-O(object) tuples. For each sentence s, SemComp(s) was measured as in equation (7), by computing θ_e and σ_e as follows:

- θ_e is the product of the thematic fit of O given V, $\theta_{O,V}$, the thematic fit of S given V, $\theta_{S,V}$, and the thematic fit of O given S, $\theta_{O,S}$ (see Equation 2). $\theta_{O,V}$ is the cosine between the vector of O and the centroid vector built out of the k most salient direct objects of V (e.g., the cosine between the vector of *book* and the centroid vector of the most salient objects of *write*); $\theta_{S,V}$ is the cosine between the vector of S and the centroid vector built out of the

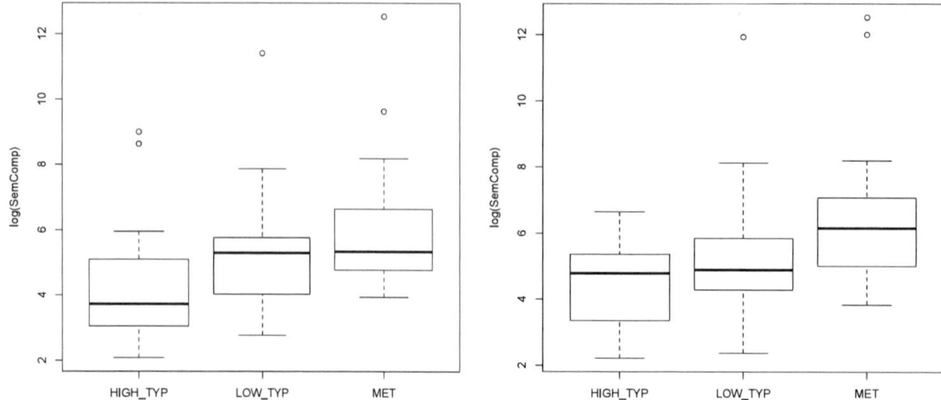

Figure 1: SemComp scores for McElree (left) and Traxler (right)

k most salient subjects of V (e.g., the cosine between the vector of *author* and the centroid vector of the most salient objects of *write*); finally, $\theta_{O,S}$ is the cosine between the vector of O and the centroid vector built out of the k most salient direct objects occurring in events whose subject is S (e.g., the cosine between the vector of *book* and the prototype vector of the most salient objects of events whose subject is *author*). Following Baroni and Lenci (2010), we used LMI scores to identify the most salient fillers of each target-specific syntactic slot and we fixed $k = 20$.

- σ_e is the salience score of the triple s, and it corresponds to the sum of the activation scores of i.) the full event represented by the triple and of ii.) the sub-events corresponding to all the partial combinations of the verb and its arguments. Each activation score is the conditional probability of the event given a lexical item in the test tuple.

Given the verb-argument triple s, the set E is the set of i events containing i.) the entire event e; ii.) all the schematic events $e_1, \ldots, e_i$ generated by abstracting over one of the lexemes of the triples (e.g., for $s = \{author - write - book\}$), $E = \{< author, write, book >, < author, write >, < author, book >, < write, book >\}$. σ_e is computed with the following equation:

$$\sigma_e = \sum_{e_i \in E} \sigma_{e_i} \qquad (9)$$

Figure 1 shows the boxplots of the log SemComp scores for three types of sentences (MET,

HIGH_TYP, and LOW_TYP) in the datasets. The Kruskal-Wallis rank sum test reveals a main effect of the sentence types on the *SemComp* scores assigned by our GEK_L-based distributional model for the McElree dataset ($\chi^2 = 17.18$, $p < 0.001$). Post-hoc tests (cf. Table 2) show that SemComp scores for the HIGH_TYP conditions are significantly lower than those in the LOW_TYP ($p < 0.05$) and MET conditions ($p < 0.001$). These results mirror exactly those of McElree et al. (2001) for the reading times at the type-shifted noun (both conditions engendered significantly longer reading times than the preferred condition).

p-values	HIGH_TYP	LOW_TYP
LOW_TYP	0.04*	-
MET	0.00046*	0.31

Table 2: Results of the pairwise *post-hoc* comparisons for the three conditions on the McElree dataset (Wilcoxon rank sum test with Bonferroni correction).

p-values	HIGH_TYP	LOW_TYP
LOW_TYP	0.31	-
MET	9.7e-06*	0.01*

Table 3: Results of the pairwise *post-hoc* comparisons for the three conditions on the Traxler dataset (Wilcoxon rank sum test with Bonferroni correction).

A main effect of sentence types on the SemComp score also also exists for the Traxler dataset ($\chi^2 = 15.39$, $p < 0.001$). In their eye-tracking experiment (Experiment 1), Traxler et al. (2002) found no significant difference between HIGH_TYP and LOW_TYP conditions, but they observed higher values for second-pass and total time data in the MET condition with respect to the other two. Interestingly, the distributional model produces sim-

174

ilar results: post-hoc tests reveal no difference between non-coerced conditions, but significantly higher SemComp scores for metonymic sentences with respect to both the HIGH_TYP ($p < 0.001$) and the LOW_TYP condition ($p < 0.05$).

3.4 Identifying the Covert Event

We assume that the interpretation of a metonymic sentence like *The author starts the book* is the following conjunction of events:

$$(3) \quad [_{EVENT} \text{ NSUBJ}:\overrightarrow{author} \text{ HEAD}:\overrightarrow{start} \text{ DOBJ}:\overrightarrow{e}]$$
$$[_{EVENT} \text{ NSUBJ}:\overrightarrow{author} \text{ HEAD}:\overrightarrow{e} \text{ DOBJ}:\overrightarrow{book}]$$

where e is the covert event to be recovered (e.g., writing). We modeled covert event retrieval as a binary classification task, as in Zarcone et al. (2012), using the following procedure: i.) for each metonymic sentence (e.g. *The author starts the book*) in the McElree and Traxler datasets, we selected as candidate covert events, E_{cov}, the verbs in the non-coercion sentences, which we refer to respectively as HIGH_TYP_EVENT (e.g. *write*) and LOW_TYP_EVENT (e.g., *read*); ii.) for each sentence $SV_{met}O$, we computed SCW(e) (cf. equation 6) of the events composing its interpretation, that is $[_{EVENT} \text{ S } V_{met} \text{ E}_{cov}]$ and $[_{EVENT} \text{ S E}_{cov} \text{ O}];^{10}$ iii.) the model **accuracy** was computed as the percentage of test items for which SCW(E_{cov} = HIGH_TYP_EVENT) is higher than SCW(E_{cov} = LOW_TYP_EVENT).

Model	McElree	Traxler
Random	50%	50%
σ	46.66%	30.55%
θ	73.3%	75%
$\sigma + \theta$	80%	77.77%

Table 4: Accuracy of model components and random baseline on the binary classification task for covert event retrieval.

The results for the covert event identification are shown in Table 4. We tested both the full model (SCW = $\sigma + \theta$) and its σ and θ components separately, to check their contribution to the task. Overall, it can be observed that the full model is the best performing one, classifying correctly just a few items more than the thematic fit-based, θ-only model. Both models are significantly better than the random baseline at $p < 0.05$ on the Traxler dataset, whereas only the full model achieves a significant advantage over the baseline

on McElree.[11]

The performance of the σ component, which makes use only of the information stored in GEK_L, is pretty weak, especially on the Traxler dataset. This is the same problem affecting purely probabilistic approaches, given also the fact that many of the words of the evaluation datasets have low frequencies in corpora. The θ component therefore plays a crucial role in the covert event prediction. In fact, θ works like a generalization component, and it serves to compute and weight new event representations when the information stored in memory is not sufficient. The strong performance of a thematic fit-based method is also consistent with the results obtained by Zarcone et al. (2012) on German data.

Interestingly, a further study by Zarcone et al. (2013) has proposed thematic fit estimation as the mechanism which is responsible also for the triggering of logical metonymy, hypothesizing that the recovery of the implicit event could be a consequence of the dispreference of the verb for the entity-denoting argument. This means, in our perspective, that the low thematic fit between verb and patient triggers a retrieval operation with the aim of increasing the semantic coherence of the event represented in the situation model. To test this claim, we compared the θ scores of the events containing the HIGH_TYP covert event (i.e., $[_{EVENT} \text{ S } V_{met} \text{ E}_{cov}] + [_{EVENT} \text{ S E}_{cov} \text{ O}]$) and the corresponding MET event (i.e., $[_{EVENT} \text{ S } V_{met} \text{ O}]$), predicting that the former events are more semantically coherent than the latter.[12] This hypothesis turned out to be correct: according to the Wilcoxon rank sum test, both in the McElree ($W = 199, p < 0.01$) and in the Traxler dataset ($W = 157, p < 0.01$) the θ of the events containing the covert events are significantly higher.

4 Conclusions

In this paper, we have presented a distributional model of sentence comprehension as an incremental process to build the semantic representation of the event expressed by the sentence. Events are represented with complex formal structures that contain the distributional vectors of its component. Sentence interpretation is carried out by unifying stored distributional information about

---

[10]Importantly, the covert events do not contribute to the σ scores, since they are not present in the linguistic input.

[11]p-values computed with the χ^2 statistical test.

[12]Since the computation of the two θs requires a different number n of factors, the scores have been normalized by elevating them to the power of $1/n$.

events, GEK_L. The event representing a sentence is the event with the highest semantic composition weight, SCW, which is in turn a function of its internal semantic coherence and the activation strength by the linguistic input. The semantic coherence of an event, measured by the θ score, depends on its similarity to stored events. Therefore, the unlimited ability of understanding new sentences can be conceived as the ability to adapt our general knowledge about events to novel situations: in brief, **productivity is adaptation**, and **adaptation is by similarity**.

The model has been successfully applied to the case of logical metonymy, accounting for two aspects of this phenomenon that have always been treated separately in the literature, namely processing costs and covert event retrieval. Given these encouraging results, we are planning to apply the model also to other semantic tasks involving event knowledge, such as the detection of anomalies (e.g. violations of selectional restrictions), the recovery of implicit arguments and of bridging inferences.

Acknowledgments

This work has been carried out thanks to the support of the A*MIDEX grant (nANR-11-IDEX-0001-02) funded by the French Government 'Investissements d'Avenir' program. We would like to thank the three anonymous reviewers for their many insightful comments and suggestions.

References

Gerry T. M. Altmann. 1999. Thematic Role Assignment in Context. *Journal of Memory and Language* 41(1):124–145.

Nicholas Asher. 2015. Types, Meanings and Coercions in Lexical Semantics. *Lingua* 157:66–82.

Giosuè Baggio and Peter Hagoort. 2011. The Balance between Memory and Unification in Semantics: A Dynamic Account of the N400. *Language and Cognitive Processes* 26(9):1338–1367.

Giosuè Baggio, Michiel van Lambalgen, and Peter Hagoort. 2012. The Processing Consequences of Compositionality. In Markus Werning, Wolfram Hinzen, and Edouard Machery, editors, *The Oxford Handbook of Compositionality*, Oxford University Press, Oxford, pages 1–23.

Marco Baroni, Silvia Bernardini, Adriano Ferraresi, and Eros Zanchetta. 2009. The WaCky Wide Web: A Collection of Very Large Linguistically Processed Web-crawled Corpora. *Language Resources and Evaluation* 43(3):209–226.

Marco Baroni and Alessandro Lenci. 2010. Distributional Memory: A General Framework for Corpus-based Semantics. *Comput. Linguist.* 36(4):673–721.

Klinton Bicknell, Jeffrey L. Elman, Mary Hare, Ken McRae, and Marta Kutas. 2010. Effects of Event knowledge in Processing Verbal Arguments. *Journal of Memory and Language* 63:489–505.

Robyn Carston. 2002. *Thoughts and Utterances*. Blackwell, Oxford.

Emmanuele Chersoni, Philippe Blache, and Alessandro Lenci. 2016a. Towards a Distributional Model of Semantic Complexity. In *COLING Workshop on Computational Linguistics for Linguistic Complexity*.

Emmanuele Chersoni, Alessandro Lenci, Enrico Santus, Philippe Blache, and Chu-Ren Huang. 2016b. Representing Verbs with Rich Contexts: An Evaluation on Verb Similarity. In *Proceedings of the 2016 Conference on Empirical Methods in Natural Language Processing*. pages 1967–1972.

Roberto G. de Almeida. 2004. The Effect of Context on the Processing of Type-shifting Verbs. *Brain and Language* 90:249–261.

Roberto G. de Almeida and Veena D. Dwivedi. 2008. Coercion without Lexical Decomposition: Type-shifting Effects Revisited. *Canadian Journal of Linguistics* 53(2/3):301–326.

Jeffrey L. Elman. 2009. On the Meaning of Words and Dinosaur Bones: Lexical Knowledge without a Lexicon. *Cognitive Science* 33(4):547–582.

Jeffrey L. Elman. 2014. Systematicity in the Lexicon: On Having your Cake and Eating it too. In Paco Calvo and John Symons, editors, *The Architecture of Cognition: Rethinking Fodor and Pylyshyn's Systematicity Challenge*, The MIT Press, Cambridge, MA.

Katrin Erk, Sebastian Padó, and Ulrike Padó. 2010. A Flexible, Corpus-driven Model of Regular and Inverse Selectional Preferences. *Computational Linguistics* 36(4):723–763.

Stefan Evert. 2004. *The Statistics of Word Co-occurrences: Word Pairs and Collocations*. Ph.D. thesis.

Ingrid L. Falkum. 2011. A Pragmatic Account of Logical Metonymy'. In *Proceedings of Metonymy 2011*. pages 11–17.

Steven Frisson and Brian McElree. 2008. Complement Coercion is not Modulated by Competition: Evidence from Eye Movements. *Journal of Experimental Psychology: Learning, Memory, and Cognition* 34(1):1–11.

Peter Hagoort. 2013. MUC (Memory, Unification, Control) and Beyond. *Frontiers in Psychology* 4(JUL):1–13.

Peter Hagoort. 2016. MUC (Memory, Unification, Control): A Model on the Neurobiology of Language beyond Single Word Processing. In Gregory Hickok and Steve Small, editors, *Neurobiology of Language*, Elsevier, Amsterdam, volume 28, pages 339–347.

Mary Hare, Michael N. Jones, Caroline Thomson, Sarah Kelly, and Ken McRae. 2009. Activating Event Knowledge. *Cognition* 111:151–167.

Ray Jackendoff. 1997. *The Architecture of the Language Faculty*. The MIT Press, Cambridge, MA.

Yuki Kamide, Gerry T. M. Altmann, and Sarah L. Haywood. 2003. The Time-course of Prediction in Incremental Sentence Processing: Evidence from Anticipatory Eye Movements. *Journal of Memory and Language* 49:133–156.

Hans Kamp. 2013. *Meaning and the Dynamics of Interpretation: Selected Papers by Hans Kamp*. Brill, Leiden-Boston.

Gina R. Kuperberg. 2016. Separate Streams or Probabilistic Inference? What the N400 can Tell us about the Comprehension of Events. *Language, Cognition and Neuroscience* 31(5):602–616.

Mirella Lapata, Frank Keller, and Christoph Scheepers. 2003. Intra-sentential Context Effects on the Interpretation of Logical Metonymy. *Cognitive Science* 27(4):649–668.

Mirella Lapata and Alex Lascarides. 2003. A Probabilistic Account of Logical Metonymy. *Computational Linguistics* 29(2):261–315.

Alex Lascarides and Ann Copestake. 1998. Pragmatics and Word Meaning. *Journal of Linguistics* 34:378–414.

Geoffrey Neil Leech. 2013. 100 Million Words of English: the British National Corpus (bnc)*.

David D Lewis, Yiming Yang, Tony G Rose, and Fan Li. 2004. Rcv1: A new benchmark collection for text categorization research. *Journal of Machine Learning Research* 5(Apr):361–397.

Brian McElree, Matthew J. Traxler, Martin J. Pickering, Rachel E. Seely, and Ray Jackendoff. 2001. Reading Time Evidence for Enriched Composition. *Cognition* 78:B17–B25.

Ken McRae, Mary Hare, Jeffrey L. Elman, and Todd R. Ferretti. 2005. A Basis for Generating Expectancies for Verbs from Nouns. *Memory & cognition* 33(7):1174–1184.

Ken McRae and Kazunaga Matsuki. 2009. People Use their Knowledge of Common Events to Understand Language, and Do So as Quickly as Possible. *Language and Linguistics Compass* 3(6):1417–1429.

Ken McRae, Michael J. Spivey-Knowlton, and Michael K. Tanenhaus. 1998. Modeling the Influence of Thematic Fit (and Other Constraints) in Online Sentence Comprehension. *Journal of Memory and Language* 38:283–312.

James Pustejovsky. 1995. *The Generative Lexicon*. The MIT Press, Cambridge, MA.

Ekaterina Shutova. 2009. Sense-based Interpretation of Logical Metonymy Using a Statistical Method. In *Proceedings of the ACL-IJCNLP 2009 Student Research Workshop*. pages 1–9.

Dan Sperber and Deirdre Wilson. 1986. *Relevance: Communication and Cognition*. Blackwell, Oxford.

Matthew J. Traxler, Martin J. Pickering, and Brian McElree. 2002. Coercion in Sentence Processing: Evidence from Eye-movements and Self-paced Reading. *Journal of Memory and Language* 47:530–547.

Alessandra Zarcone, Alessandro Lenci, Sebastian Padó, and Jason Utt. 2013. Fitting, not Clashing! A Distributional Semantic Model of Logical Metonymy. In *Proceedings of the 10th International Conference on Computational Semantics (IWCS 2013)*. pages 404–410.

Alessandra Zarcone and Sebastian Padó. 2011. Generalized Event Knowledge in Logical Metonymy Resolution. In *Proceedings of the 33rd annual meeting of the Cognitive Science Society (CogSci 2011)*.

Alessandra Zarcone, Sebastian Padó, and Alessandro Lenci. 2014. Logical Metonymy Resolution in a Words-as-Cues Framework: Evidence from Self-paced Reading and Probe Recognition. *Cognitive Science* 38(5):973–996.

Alessandra Zarcone, Jason Utt, and Sebastian Padó. 2012. Modeling Covert Event Retrieval in Logical Metonymy: Probabilistic and Distributional Accounts. In *Proceedings of the 3rd Workshop on Cognitive Modeling and Computational Linguistics (CMCL 2012)*. pages 70–79.

Rolf A. Zwaan and Gabriel A. Radvansky. 1998. Situation Models in Language Comprehension and Memory. *Psychological bulletin* 123(2):162–185.

Double Trouble:
The Problem of Construal in Semantic Annotation of Adpositions

Jena D. Hwang and **Archna Bhatia**
IHMC
{jhwang,abhatia}@ihmc.us

Na-Rae Han
University of Pittsburgh
naraehan@pitt.edu

Tim O'Gorman
University of Colorado Boulder
timothy.ogorman@colorado.edu

Vivek Srikumar
University of Utah
svivek@cs.utah.edu

Nathan Schneider
Georgetown University
nathan.schneider@georgetown.edu

Abstract

We consider the semantics of prepositions, revisiting a broad-coverage annotation scheme used for annotating all 4,250
preposition tokens in a 55,000 word corpus
of English. Attempts to apply the scheme to
adpositions and case markers in other languages, as well as some problematic cases
in English, have led us to reconsider the
assumption that an adposition's lexical contribution is equivalent to the role/relation
that it mediates. Our proposal is to embrace
the potential for **construal** in adposition
use, expressing such phenomena directly
at the token level to manage complexity
and avoid sense proliferation. We suggest
a framework to represent both the scene
role and the adposition's lexical function so
they can be annotated at scale—supporting
automatic, statistical processing of domain-
general language—and discuss how this
representation would allow for a simpler
inventory of labels.

1 Introduction

Prepositions and postpositions (collectively **adpositions**) are widespread in the world's languages as
grammatical markers expressing spatial, temporal,
thematic,[1] and other kinds of semantic relations.
Unfortunately for semantic processing, a handful
of high-frequency types carry an immense payload
by way of extreme polysemy. Thus, disambiguation of adpositional meaning is crucial to piecing
together the interpretation of a sentence (§2).

A line of previous work (Srikumar and Roth,
2013a; Schneider et al., 2015, 2016, see §2) has
developed a scheme for broad-coverage annotation

of adpositions with an eye toward building automatic disambiguation systems. Their most recent
proposal consists of an inventory of 75 categorical
labels known as **supersenses** that characterize the
polysemy of English prepositions in a lexically-
neutral and coarse-grained fashion. They envision
disambiguation as assigning a single one of these
supersenses to each preposition token.

While formalizing disambiguation via single-
label classification works well for prototypical
members of the categories, on closer examination,
we argue that it is overly simplistic for many usages. This became particularly evident when we
tried to adapt the English-centric supersense labels
to other languages.

Here we advance a more nuanced view that an
adposition can contribute a semantic perspective, or
construal, over and above the scenario relation that
its object participates in. We argue that it is essential to distinguish the contribution of the preposition itself, i.e., what the adposition **codes** for, from
the semantic role or relation that the adposition mediates and that a predicate or scene **calls** for; and as
a result, the label that would be most appropriate
is underdetermined for many tokens (§3). In our
view, the mismatch can be understood through the
lens of **construal**, and this should be made explicit
in corpora (§4).

To that end, we sketch an annotation approach
that disentangles the two elements of the meaning
while retaining the advantages of a broad-coverage
(rather than lexicographic-sense-based) scheme.
Preliminary analysis suggests that this scheme will
work well not only for English, but also for the
other languages examined. §5 surveys some of the
phenomena that our new analysis addresses with
examples from multiple languages; §6 suggests that
this added flexibility at the token level removes the
need for a great deal of complexity in the supersense inventory itself: i.e., we can get away with

---

[1] In the sense of thematic roles (agent, patient, etc.).

*Proceedings of the 6th Joint Conference on Lexical and Computational Semantics (*SEM 2017)*, pages 178–188,
Vancouver, Canada, August 3-4, 2017. ©2017 Association for Computational Linguistics

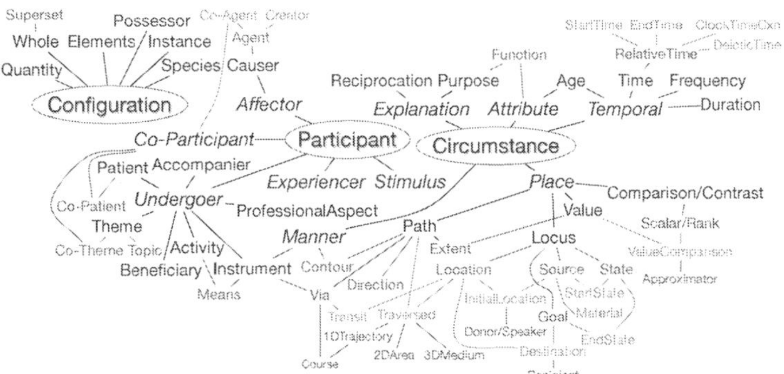

Figure 1: Preposition supersense hierarchy (from Schneider et al., 2016). Top-level categories are circled and subcategories radiate outward.

1/3 fewer semantic labels, reducing somewhat the practical concern of sparse data. Here we also discuss challenges and tradeoffs inherent in the proposed approach. We have begun testing the workability of this proposal empirically by annotating data in multiple languages, with disambiguation experiments to follow.

2 Approaches to Prepositional Polysemy

The most frequent English prepositions are extraordinarily polysemous. For example, the preposition **at** expresses different information in each of the following usages:

(1) a. It is **at** 123 Main St. (LOCATION)
    b. We met him **at** 7pm. (TIME)
    c. Everyone pointed **at** him. (GOAL)
    d. She laughed **at** my acting. (STIMULUS)
    e. He held her **at** gunpoint. (INSTRUMENT)

When confronted with a new instance of **at**, NLU systems must determine whether it marks an entity or scene's location, time, goal, or something else.

As lexical classes go, prepositions are something of a red-headed stepchild in the linguistics literature. Most of the semantics literature on prepositions has revolved around how they categorize space and time (e.g., Herskovits, 1986; Verkuyl and Zwarts, 1992; Bowerman and Choi, 2001). However, there have been a couple of lines of work addressing preposition semantics broadly. In cognitive linguistics, studies have examined abstract as well as concrete uses of English prepositions (e.g., Dirven, 1993; Lindstromberg, 2010). Notably, the polysemy of **over** and other prepositions has been explained in terms of sense networks encompassing core senses and motivated extensions (Brugman, 1981; Lakoff, 1987; Dewell, 1994; Tyler and Evans, 2001, 2003). The Preposition Project (TPP; Litkowski and Hargraves, 2005) broke ground in

stimulating computational work on fine-grained word sense disambiguation of English prepositions (Litkowski and Hargraves, 2005; Ye and Baldwin, 2007; Tratz and Hovy, 2009; Dahlmeier et al., 2009). Typologists, meanwhile, have developed *semantic maps* of functions, where the nearness of two functions reflects their tendency to fall under the same adposition or case marker in many languages (Haspelmath, 2003; Wälchli, 2010).

Preposition supersenses. Following Srikumar and Roth (2013b), Schneider et al. (2015) developed coarse-grained semantic categories of prepositions as a broader-coverage alternative to fine-grained senses, using categories similar to those appearing in semantic maps (LOCATION, RECIPIENT, etc.) rather than lexicalized senses. Schneider et al. (2015) refined their inventory of categories through extensive deliberation involving the use of dictionaries, corpora, and pilot annotation experiments. They call the categories **supersenses** to emphasize their similarity to coarse-grained classifications of nouns and verbs that go by that name (Ciaramita and Altun, 2006; Schneider et al., 2012).

The **at** examples in (1) are accompanied by the appropriate supersenses from the supersense scheme. Most supersenses resemble thematic roles (cf. Fillmore (1968)); a few others are needed to describe preposition-marked relations between entities. There are multiple English prepositions per supersense; e.g., "**in** the city" and "**on** the table" would join "**at** 123 Main St." in being labeled as LOCATIONs. We understand the supersenses as prototype-based categories, and in some cases use heuristics like paraphrasability ("in order to" for PURPOSE) and WH-question words ("Why?" for PURPOSE and EXPLANATION) to help determine which tokens are instances of the category.

The 75 supersenses are organized in a taxonomy based on that of VerbNet (Bonial et al., 2011), with

179

PARTICIPANT, CIRCUMSTANCE, and CONFIGU-RATION at the top level.[2] The taxonomy uses multiple inheritance to account for subcategories which are considered to include properties of multiple supercategories. The full hierarchy is in figure 1.

The approach to preposition annotation is *comprehensive*, i.e., every token of every preposition type is given a supersense label. The supersenses were applied to annotate a 55,000 word corpus of online reviews in English, covering all 4,250 preposition tokens (Schneider et al., 2016). For each token, annotators chose a single label from the inventory. This is not an easy task, but with documentation of many examples in a lexical resource, **PrepWiki**,[3] trained university students were able to achieve reasonable levels of inter-annotator agreement. Every token was initially labeled by at least two independent annotators, and differences were adjudicated by experts.

3 Problems with Preposition Supersenses

While the above approach works reasonably well for most English tokens, difficulties in directly applying the scheme to adpositions and case markers in other languages, as well as some of the persistent issues arising in English, have led us to conclude that perhaps the supersense hierarchy as it stands is too simplistic to provide a faithful account of the prepositions' semantic behavior. This has caused us to examine fundamental assumptions made by previous work and reevaluate what it means to semantically label an adposition.

3.1 Semantic Overlap in English

In the original English annotation (Schneider et al., 2016), a few phenomena caused much handwringing—not because there was no appropriate supersense, but because *multiple* supersenses seemed to fit. For example, it was observed that TOPIC and STIMULUS could compete for semantic territory. (2) evinces related usages of **about** with different governors:

(2)   a. I read [a book **about** the strategy].
        b. I read **about** the strategy.
        c. I knew **about** the strategy.
        d. I cared **about** the strategy.

Usages (2a–2c) could reasonably be labeled as TOPIC. This is because the **about**-PP indicates what is communicated (2a, 2b) and known (2c). The fourth example (2d), however, presents an overlap in its interpretation. On the one hand, traditional thematic role inventories include the category STIMULUS for something that prompts a perceptual or emotional experience, as in (3).

(3)   I was afraid **of** the strategy.

Surely, *cared* in (2d) describes an emotional state, so **about** marks the STIMULUS. However, much like examples (2a–2c), the semantics relating to TOPIC is still very much present in the use of **about**, drawing attention to the aspects of the caring process involving thought or judgement. This contrasts with the use of **for** in "I cared **for** my grandmother," where the prepositional choice calls attention to the benefactive aspect of the caring act.

If we are constrained to one label per argument, where should the line be drawn between STIMULUS and TOPIC in cases of overlap? In other words, should the semantic representation emphasize the semantic commonality between all of the examples in (2), or between (2d) and (3)?

Observing that annotators were inconsistent on such tokens, Schneider et al. (2016) drew a boundary between TOPIC and STIMULUS in an attempt to force consistency, stating that "TOPIC should be used if the governor is a predicate of communication or of 'higher-level' cognition—i.e., primarily mental/intellectual rather than emotional/perceptual/bodily in nature".[4] This criterion seems artificial to us; at the very least, it splits hairs in a way that would be difficult to explain to annotators.

Below, we instead argue that the idea of construal/conceptualization offers a more principled answer; in our new analysis, the TOPIC suggested by **about** and the STIMULUS suggested by *cared* can coexist.

3.2 Applying the Supersenses to Other Languages

One of the premises of using unlexicalized supersenses was that the scheme would port well to other

---

[2] These loosely correspond to event arguments, adjuncts, and adnominal complements, respectively. However, supersense organization does not make any claims with regard to coreness or the argument/adjunct distinction, as there are many phenomena that do not conform to either of the prototypes for argument and adjunct (for a review of the literature on the argument/adjunct distinction, see Hwang, 2011). We are also not convinced that a firm distinction between lexical and non-lexical/functional adpositions (Rauh, 1993) can be established, though the relevance of this distinction in the context of the construal approach merits further investigation.

[3] http://tiny.cc/prepwiki

[4] http://tiny.cc/prepwiki/index.php/Category:SST-Topic

languages (as the WordNet noun and verb supersenses have: Picca et al., 2008; Schneider et al., 2012, *inter alia*). To test this, we have begun applying the existing supersenses to three new languages, namely, Hebrew, Hindi, and Korean. Pilot annotation in these languages has echoed the fundamental problem discussed in the previous section.

Consider the Hindi examples below. In (4a), the experiencer of an emotion is marked with a postposition **kaa**, the genitive case marker in Hindi.

(4) a. [Hindi]: EXPERIENCER vs. POSSESSOR
       bipaashaa **kaa** gussaa
       Bipasha **GEN** anger
       "Bipasha's anger"

     b. [Hindi]: EXPERIENCER
       bipaashaa bahut gussaa hui
       Bipasha very angry became
       "Bipasha got very angry."

The use of **kaa** strongly suggests possession (in (4), possession of an abstract quality). However, the semantics of the phrase also includes EXPERIENCER—thus, it seems inappropriate to force a choice between EXPERIENCER and POSSESSOR for this token. (The same problem is seen in a similar phrase "the anger **of** Bipasha" in English.) There are other ways to attribute anger to Bipasha—e.g., see (4b). Here Bipasha is not construed as a possessor when the postposition **kaa** is not used.

Our preliminary annotation of Hindi, Korean, and Hebrew has suggested that instances of overlap between multiple supersenses are fairly frequent.

4   The Construal Analysis

Why do "cared **about** the strategy" in (2d) and "anger **of** Bipasha" (cf. (4a)) not lend themselves to a single label? These seem to be symptoms of the fact that no English preposition prototypically marks EXPERIENCER or STIMULUS roles, though from the perspective of the predicates, such roles are thought to be important generalizations in characterizing events of perception and emotion. In essence, there is an apparent mismatch between the roles that the verb *care* or the noun *anger* calls for, and the functions that English prepositions prototypically code for. While **about** prototypically codes for TOPIC and **of** prototypically codes for POSSESSOR, there is no preposition that "naturally" codes for EXPERIENCER or STIMULUS in the same way. Thus, if a predicate marks an EXPERIENCER or STIMULUS with a preposition, the preposition

will contribute something new to the conceptualization of the scene being described. With "cared **about** the strategy," it is TOPIC-ness that the preposition brings to the table; with "anger **of** Bipasha," it is the conceptualization of anger as an attribute that somebody possesses.

Thus, we turn to theories in Cognitive Semantics to define the phenomenon of **construal** as a means of understanding the contributions that are emerging from the adpositions with respect to the expressed event or situation. Then, we propose a method to handle the problem posed by construal and to resolve the apparent semantic overlap which is pervasive across languages.

4.1   Defining Construal

The world is not neatly organized into bits of information that map directly to linguistic symbols. Rather, linguistic meaning reflects the priorities and categorizations of particular expressions in a language (Langacker, 1998; Jackendoff, 2002; Croft and Cruse, 2004, ch. 3). Much like pictures of a scene from different viewpoints will result in different renderings, a real-world situation being described will "look" different depending on the linguistic choices made by a speaker. This includes within-language choices: e.g., the choice of "John sold Mary a book" vs. "John sold a book to Mary" vs. "Mary bought a book from John." In the process called **construal** (a.k.a. **conceptualization**), a speaker "packages" ideas for linguistic expression in a way that foregrounds certain elements of a situation while backgrounding others.

We propose to incorporate this notion of construal in adposition supersense annotation. We use the term **scene** to refer to events or situations in which an adpositional phrase plays a role. (We do not formalize the full scene, but assume its roles can be characterized with supersense labels from figure 1.) Contrast the use of the prepositions **by** and **of** in (5):

(5) a. The festival features works **by** Puccini.
     b. I'm an expert on the works **of** Puccini.

While both prepositional phrases indicate works created by the operatic composer Puccini (i.e., CREATOR), the different choices of preposition reflect different construals: **by** highlights the agency of Puccini, whereas **of** construes Puccini as the source of his composition. Thus, "works **by** Puccini" and "works **of** Puccini" are paraphrases, but present subtly different portrayals of the relationship between

Puccini and his works. In other words, these paraphrases are not identical in meaning because the preposition carries with it different nuances of construal. In this paper, we focus on differences in construal manifested in different adposition choices, and the possibility that an adposition construal complements the construal of a scene and its roles (as evoked by the governing head or predicate).

For instances like "I read **about** the strategy" in (2b) that were generally unproblematic for annotation under the original preposition guidelines, the semantics of the adposition and the semantic role assigned by the predicate are congruent. However, for examples like "cared **about** the strategy" in (2d) and "anger **of** Bipasha" in (4a), we say that the adposition construes the role as something other than what the scene specifies. Competition between different adposition construals accounts for many of the alternations that are near-paraphrases, but potentially involve slightly different nuances of meaning (e.g., "talk **to** someone" vs. "talk **with** someone"; "angry **at** someone" vs. "angry **with** someone").

Thus, the notion of construal challenges Schneider et al.'s (2015; 2016) original conception that each supersense reflects the semantic role assigned by its governing predicate (i.e. verbal or event nominal predicate), and that a single supersense label can be assigned to each adposition token. Rather than trying to ignore these construals to favor a single-label approach, or possibly create new labels to capture the meaning distinctions that construals impose on semantic roles, we adopt an approach that gives us the flexibility to deal with both the semantics coming from the scene and the construal evoked by the adpositional choice.

4.2 Formulating a Construal Analysis

We address the issues of construal by decoupling the semantics signaled by the adposition from the role expected by the scene. Essentially, we borrow from Construction Grammar (Fillmore et al., 1988; Kay and Fillmore, 1999; Goldberg, 2006) the notion that semantic contributions can be made at various levels of syntactic structure, beginning with the semantics contributed by the lexical items.

Under the original single-label analysis, the full weight of semantic assignment rested on the predicate's semantic role, with the indirect assumption that the predicate selects for adpostions relevant to the assignment. Under the construal analysis, we assign semantics at both scene and adposition lev-

els of meaning: we capture what the scene *calls* for, henceforth **scene role** and what the adposition itself *codes* for, henceforth **function**. Both labels are drawn from the supersense hierarchy (figure 1). Allowing tokens to be annotated with both a role and a function accounts for the non-congruent adposition construals, as in (6).

(6)   a.   The festival features works **by** Puccini.
         scene role: CREATOR; *function:* AGENT

       b.   I'm an expert on the works **of** Puccini.
         scene role: CREATOR; *function:* SOURCE

We recognize that both of these sentences carry the meaning represented by the supersense CREATOR at the scene level, but also recognize the construal that arises from the chosen preposition: **by** is assigned the function of AGENT and **of** is assigned the function of SOURCE.[5]

5 Applying the Construal Analysis

In this section, we discuss some of the more productive examples of non-congruent construals in English as well as in Hindi, Korean, and Hebrew. Hereafter, we will use the notation ROLE↝FUNCTION to indicate such construals. Adopting the "realization" metaphor of articulating an idea linguistically, this can be read as "ROLE is realized with an adposition that marks FUNCTION."

5.1 Emotion and Perception Construals

Scenes of emotion and perception (Dirven, 1997; Osmond, 1997; Radden, 1998) provide a compelling case for the construal analysis. Consider the sentences involving emotion in example (7):

(7)   a.   I was scared **by** the bear.
         STIMULUS↝CAUSER

       b.   I was scared **about** getting my ears pierced.
         STIMULUS↝TOPIC

Comparing examples (7a) and (7b), we notice that there are two different types of stimuli represented in otherwise semantically parallel sentences.

---

[5] We also acknowledge that there is a level of construal contributed by the verb. For example, *Alex* in *Alex sent the package to Pam* can be AGENT or SOURCE depending whether the interpretation is focused on the agency of the argument or the spatial relation it has in reference to the action described by the verb. These verb-triggered construals have been previously explored, most notably by Jackendoff (1990). Perspective can also be evident in the choice of syntactic constructions, e.g., active vs. passive voice (*I made a mistake* versus *Mistakes were made*), which can be connected to sentiment (Greene and Resnik, 2009). We specifically focus on the construal that arises from the adposition in a given sentence.

The preposition **by** gives the impression that the stimulus is responsible for triggering an instinctive fear reflex (i.e., CAUSER), while **about** portrays the thing feared as the content or TOPIC of thought.[6]

In some languages, the experiencer can be conceptualized as a recipient of the emotion or feeling, thus licensing dative marking.[7] In the Hebrew example (8a), the experiencer of bodily perception is marked with the dative preposition **l(e)-** (Berman, 1982). Similarly, in Hindi, the dative postpostion **-ko** marks an experiencer in (8b).

(8)   a.   [Heb.]: EXPERIENCER⤳RECIPIENT
          Koev l-i ha-rosh
          Hurts **DAT**-me the-head
          "My head hurts."

      b.   [Hindi]: EXPERIENCER⤳RECIPIENT
          mujh-**ko** garmii lag rahii hai
          I-**DAT** heat feel PROG PRES
          "I'm feeling hot."

Contrast this with examples where scene role and adposition function are congruent:

(9)   a.   I ate dinner **at** 7:00. TIME⤳TIME
      b.   Let's talk **about** our plan. TOPIC⤳TOPIC

In (9a) and (9b), the preposition is prototypical for the given scene role and its function directly identifies the scene role. Because the semantics of the role and function are congruent, these cases do not exhibit the extra layer of construal seen in (7) and (8).[8] In essence, our analysis helps capture the construals that characterize the less prototypical scene role and function pairings.

5.2 Professional Associate Construals

The online reviews corpus (Schneider et al., 2016) shows that, at least in English, professional relation-

---

[6]Interestingly, "scared **about**" seems to require an explicit or metonymic event/situation as the complement. Thus, "scared **about** the bear" would be felicitous to describe apprehension about some mischief that the bear might get up to. It would be less than felicitous to describe a hiker's reaction upon being surprised by a bear.

[7]English displays this to a limited extent: "It feels/seems/ looks perfect **to** me."

[8]One might object that most or all adpositions impose a spatial construal—and thus, (9a) should be annotated as TIME⤳LOCATION. We do not discount the possibility that such a metaphor can be cognitively active in speakers using temporal adpositions; in fact, there is considerable evidence that time-as-space metaphors are cross-linguistically pervasive and productive (Lakoff and Johnson, 1980; Núñez and Sweetser, 2006; Casasanto and Boroditsky, 2008). However, we do not see much practical benefit to annotating temporal **at** or topical **about** as spatial.

ships (especially employer–employee and business–client ones) are fertile ground for alternating preposition construals. The following were among the examples tagged as PROFESSIONALASPECT:

(10)   a.   My dad worked **for** a record label.
          PROFESSIONALASPECT⤳BENEFICIARY

      b.   Dr. S— **at** CVTS is not a good doctor.
          PROFESSIONALASPECT⤳LOCATION

      c.   Nigel **from** Nidd Design has always been great!
          PROFESSIONALASPECT⤳SOURCE

      d.   The owners and employees **of** this store ...
          PROFESSIONALASPECT⤳POSSESSOR

All of these construals are *motivated* in that they highlight an aspect of prototypical professional relationships: e.g., an employee's work prototypically takes place at the business location (hence "work **at**"), though this is not a strict condition for using "work **at**"—the meaning of **at** has been extended from the prototype. Likewise, the pattern "*person* {**at**, **from**, **of**} *organization*" has been conventionalized to signify employment or similar institutional-belonging relationships.

The construal analysis equips us with the ability to use the existing labels like BENEFICIARY and LOCATION to deal with the overloading of the PROFESSIONALASPECT label, instead of forcing a difficult decision or creating several additional categories. This analysis also accounts for similar construals presented by adpositions in other languages. For example, the overlap of PROFESSIONALASPECT with SOURCE, as seen in English example (10c), occurs in Hindi and Korean as well.

5.3 Static vs. Dynamic Construals

Another source of difficulty in the original annotation came from caused-motion verbs like *put*, which takes a PP indicating part of a path. Sometimes the preposition lexically marks a source or goal, e.g., **into**, **onto**, or **out of** (11a). Often, however, the preposition is prototypically locative, e.g., **in** or **on** (11b), though the object of the preposition is interpreted as a destination, equivalent to the use of **into** or **onto**, respectively. This locative-as-destination construal is highly productive, so analyzing **on** as polysemous between LOCATION and DESTINATION does not capture the regularity. The PP is sometimes analyzed as a resultative phrase (Goldberg, 2006). In our terms, we simply say that the scene calls for a DESTINATION, but the preposition codes for a LOCATION:

(11) a. Cynthia put her things **into** a box.
          DESTINATION↝DESTINATION

      b. Cynthia put her things **on** her bed.
          DESTINATION↝LOCATION

Thus, we avoid listing the preposition with multiple lexical functions for this regular phenomenon.

The opposite problem occurs with fictive motion (Talmy, 1996): a path PP, and sometimes a motion verb, construe a static scene as dynamic as seen in "A road runs **through** my property." Rather than forcing annotators to side with the dynamic construal effected by the language, versus the static nature of the actual scene, we represent both: the scene role is LOCATION (static) and the preposition function is PATH (dynamic) (i.e., LOCATION↝PATH).

5.4 Metaphoric Scenes

Finally, our analysis gives us a way to handle metaphoric scenes (Lakoff and Johnson, 1980). In (12), the locative-as-destination construal (§5.3) is layered with the states-are-locations metaphor. We annotate the scene in terms of the governing predicate's **target domain** (domain which we seek to describe), and the adposition function in terms of the **source domain** (domain from which we draw metaphorical expressions to conceptualize the target domain):

(12) The election news put him **in** a very bad mood.
          ENDSTATE↝LOCATION

Our construal analysis can capture both source and target domains by assigning the source domain meaning to the function of the preposition and the target domain meaning to the scene role.

6 Toward a Revised Hierarchy

The annotation of both scene and function levels of semantics allows us to trade more complexity at the token level for less complexity in the label set. As discussed in §4, separating the scene role and function levels of annotation will more adequately capture construal phenomena without forcing an arbitrary choice between two labels or introducing further complexity into the hierarchy.

In fact, we intend to *simplify* the current supersense hierarchy, by collapsing some of the finer-grained distinctions that can be accounted for with the construal analysis instead. Candidates for removal include the labels with multiple inheritance such as CONTOUR (inheriting from PATH and

Figure 2: Preliminary revised hierarchy of 50 adposition supersenses.

MANNER; e.g., "The fly flew **in** zig-zags") and TRANSIT (inheriting from VIA and LOCATION; e.g., "We traveled **by** bus").

A preliminary proposal for a new hierarchy appears in figure 2.[9] It weighs in at only 50 categories, a third fewer than the original 75. A significantly smaller inventory will both ease the cognitive burden on annotators and reduce the sparsity of labels in the data, which should facilitate better statistical generalizations with limited data.

The added representational complexity of construals seems justified to account for many of the phenomena discussed above, especially as the project grows to include more languages. But is the complexity worth it on balance? We consider some of the tradeoffs below.

6.1 Challenges in Function Assignment

We encountered several examples in which function labels are difficult to identify. Consider the following paraphrases:

(13) a. [Korean]: LOCATION↝LOCATION
          Cheolsu-nun undongcang-**eyse** tallyessta.
          Cheolsu-NOM schoolyard-**at** ran.
          "Cheolsu ran in the schoolyard."

      b. [Korean]: LOCATION↝?
          Cheolsu-nun undongcang-**ul** tallyessta.
          Cheolsu-NOM schoolyard-**ACC** ran.
          "Cheolsu ran in the schoolyard."

---

[9]Apart from changes enabled by the construal analysis, a number of other simplifications and enhancements are incorporated into the proposal, which space does not allow us to enumerate here: for example, collapsing LOCUS/LOCATION/STATE, SOURCE/INITIALLOCATION/INITIALSATE, GOAL/DESTINATION/ENDSTATE, and TIME/RELATIVETIME/CLOCKTIMECXN; and replacing PROFESSIONALASPECT with SOCIALREL and ORGROLE.

In (13a), "schoolyard" is accompanied by a postposition **-eyse** (comparable to English **at**), which marks it as the location of running. This is the unmarked choice. On the other hand, in sentence (13b), the noun is paired with the accusative marker **-ul**, the marked choice. The use of **-ul** evokes a special construal: it indicates that the schoolyard is more than just a backdrop of the running act and that it is a location that Cheolsu mindfully chose as the place of action. Additionally, marking the location with the accusative marker, pragmatically, brings focus to the noun (i.e., he ran in a schoolyard as opposed to anywhere else). Such construals are not limited to locations, but may also include other scene roles such as GOAL and ACCOMPANIER, in alternation with postpositions that can express those functions. Since accusative case markers generally serve syntactic functions over semantic ones, it may be difficult to identify a semantic function the accusative marker carries.

A similar phenomenon can be found in Hindi:

(14) a. [Hindi]: bare NP as DESTINATION
maiN library jaa rahii thii
I library go PROG PST
"I was going to the library."

b. [Hindi]: DESTINATION⤳?
maiN library-**ko** jaa rahii thii
I library-**ACC** go PROG PST
"I was going to the LIBRARY." [more emphasis on the library]

This suggests that, apart from spatiotemporal relations and semantic roles, adpositions can mark **information structural** properties for which we would need a separate inventory of labels.

In some idiomatic predicate–argument combinations, the semantic motivation for the preposition may not be clear (15).

(15) a. Listen **to** the violin! STIMULUS⤳?
b. What's he proudest **of**? STIMULUS⤳?
c. Unhappy **with** my meal! STIMULUS⤳?
d. I'm interested **in** politics. TOPIC⤳?

While the scene role in (15a) and (15b) is clearly STIMULUS, the function is less clear. Is the object of attention construed (metaphorically) as a GOAL in (15a), and the cause for pride as a SOURCE in (15b)? Or are **to** and **of** semantically empty argument-markers for these predicates (cf. the "case prepositions" of Rauh, 1993)? We do not treat either combination as an unanalyzable multiword

expression because the ordinary meaning of the predicate is very much present. (15c) and (15d) are similarly fraught. But as we look at more data, we will entertain the possibility that the function can be null to indicate a marker which contributes no lexical semantics.

6.2 Challenges in Scene Role Assignment

There are complications which we are not yet prepared to fully address. First, if the PP is not governed by a predicate which provides the roles—such as a verb or eventive/relational noun—the preposition may need to evoke a meaning more specific than our labels. E.g., for "children **in** pajamas" and "woman **in** black," **in** may be taken to evoke the semantics of wearing clothing.[10] The label set we use for broad-coverage annotation is, of course, vaguer, and would simply specify ATTRIBUTE for the clothing sense of **in**. Copular constructions raise similar issues. Consider "It is **up to** you to decide," meaning that deciding is the addressee's responsibility: this idiomatic sense of **up to** is closer to a semantic predicate than to a semantic role or figure-ground relation.

6.3 Multi-Construal Analysis?

In rare instances, we are tempted to annotate a chain of extensions from a prototypical function of a preposition, which we term **multiple construal**. For instance:

(16) a. Bob's boss yelled **at** him for his mistake.
RECIPIENT⤳BENEFICIARY⤳GOAL

b. Jane was angry **at** him for his mistake.
STIMULUS⤳BENEFICIARY⤳GOAL

c. I was involved **in** the project.
THEME⤳SUPERSET⤳LOCATION

"Yelled **at**" in (16a) is a communicative action whose addressee (RECIPIENT) is also a target of the negative emotion (BENEFICIARY⤳GOAL: compare the use of **at** in "shoot **at** the target"). (16b) is similar, except "angry" focuses on the emotion itself, which Bob is understood to have evoked in his boss.

With regard to (16c), the item "involved **in**" has become fossilized, with **in** marking an underspecified noncausal participant (hence, THEME as the scene role). At the same time, one can understand

---

[10]Indeed, this is the position adopted by version 1.7 of FrameNet, where **in** is listed as a lexical unit of the WEARING frame (`https://framenet2.icsi.berkeley.edu/fnReports/data/frame/Wearing.xml`).

the **in** here as motivated by the member-of-set sense (cf. "I am **in** the group"), which would be labeled SUPERSET↝LOCATION because it conceptualizes membership in terms of containment. A similar logic would apply to "people **in** the company": PROFESSIONALASPECT↝SUPERSET↝LOCATION. Effectively, the multiple construal analysis claims that multiple steps of extending a preposition's prototypical meaning remain conceptually available when understanding an instance of its use. That said, we are not convinced that this logic could be applied reliably by annotators, and thus may simplify the usages in (16) to just the first and second or the first and third labels.

6.4 The Annotation Process

Annotators are generally capable of interpreting meaning in a given context. However, it might be difficult to train annotators to develop intuitions about adposition functions, which reflect prototypical meanings contributed by the lexical item that may not be literally applicable. These distinctions may be too subtle to annotate reliably. As we are approaching this project with the goal of producing annotated datasets for training and evaluating natural language understanding systems, it is an important concern.

We are currently planning pilot annotation studies to ascertain (i) the prevalence of the role vs. function mismatches, and (ii) annotator agreement on such instances. Enshrining role–function pairs in the lexicon may facilitate inter-annotator consistency: our experience thus far is that annotators benefit greatly from examples illustrating the possible supersenses that can be assigned to a preposition.

If initial pilots are successful, we would then need to decide whether to annotate the role and function together or in separate stages. Because the function reflects one of the adposition's prototypical senses, it may often be deterministic given the adposition and scene role, in which case we could focus annotators' efforts on the scene roles. Existing annotations for lexical resources such as PropBank (Palmer et al., 2005), VerbNet (Palmer et al., 2017; Kipper et al., 2008), and FrameNet (Fillmore and Baker, 2009) might go a long way toward disambiguating the scene role, limiting the effort required from annotators.

6.5 Linguistic Utility of Annotated Data

Assuming the above theoretical and practical concerns are surmountable, annotated corpora would facilitate empirical studies of the nature and limits of adposition/case construal within and across languages. For example: Is it the case that some of the supersense labels can only serve as scene roles, or only as functions? (A hypothesis is that PARTICIPANT subtypes tend to be limited to scene roles, but this needs to be examined empirically.) Which role–function pairs are attested in particular languages, and are any universal? Thus far we have seen that certain scene roles, such as EXPERIENCER, STIMULUS, and PROFESSIONALASPECT, invite many different adposition construals—is this universally true? As adpositions are notoriously difficult for second language learners, would it help to explain which construals do and do not transfer from the first language to the second language?

7 Conclusion

We have considered the semantics of adpositions and case markers in English and a few other languages with the goal of revising a broad-coverage annotation scheme used in previous work. We pointed out situations where a single supersense did not fully characterize the interaction between the adposition and the scene elaborated by the PP. In an attempt to tease apart the semantics contributed specifically by the adposition from the semantics coming from elsewhere, we proposed a construal analysis. Though many details remain to be worked out, we are optimistic that our analysis will ultimately improve broad-coverage annotations as well as constructional analyses of adposition behavior.

Acknowledgments

We thank the rest of our CARMLS team—Martha Palmer, Ken Litkowski, Omri Abend, Katie Conger, and Meredith Green—for participating in weekly discussions of adposition semantics; Michael Ellsworth for an insightful perspective on construal, Paul Portner for a helpful clarification regarding approaches to conceptualization in the literature, and anonymous reviewers for their thoughtful comments. We also thank the participants in the AAAI Spring Symposium on Construction Grammar in NLU, held earlier this year at Stanford, where an early version of this work was presented.

References

Ruth A. Berman. 1982. Dative marking of the affectee role: data from Modern Hebrew. *Hebrew Annual Review* 6:35–59.

Claire Bonial, William Corvey, Martha Palmer, Volha V. Petukhova, and Harry Bunt. 2011. A hierarchical unification of LIRICS and VerbNet semantic roles. In *Fifth IEEE International Conference on Semantic Computing*. Palo Alto, CA, USA, pages 483–489.

Melissa Bowerman and Soonja Choi. 2001. Shaping meanings for language: universal and language-specific in the acquisition of spatial semantic categories. In Melissa Bowerman and Stephen Levinson, editors, *Language Acquisition and Conceptual Development*, Cambridge University Press, Cambridge, UK, pages 475–511.

Claudia Brugman. 1981. *The story of 'over': polysemy, semantics and the structure of the lexicon*. MA thesis, University of California, Berkeley, Berkeley, CA. Published New York: Garland, 1981.

Daniel Casasanto and Lera Boroditsky. 2008. Time in the mind: using space to think about time. *Cognition* 106(2):579–593.

Massimiliano Ciaramita and Yasemin Altun. 2006. Broad-coverage sense disambiguation and information extraction with a supersense sequence tagger. In *Proc. of EMNLP*. Sydney, Australia, pages 594–602.

William Croft and D. Alan Cruse. 2004. *Cognitive linguistics*. Cambridge University Press, Cambridge, UK.

Daniel Dahlmeier, Hwee Tou Ng, and Tanja Schultz. 2009. Joint learning of preposition senses and semantic roles of prepositional phrases. In *Proc. of EMNLP*. Suntec, Singapore, pages 450–458.

Robert B. Dewell. 1994. 'Over' again: Image-schema transformations in semantic analysis. *Cognitive Linguistics* 5(4):351–380.

René Dirven. 1993. Dividing up physical and mental space into conceptual categories by means of English prepositions. In Cornelia Zelinsky-Wibbelt, editor, *The semantics of prepositions: From mental processing to natural language processing*, Mouton de Gruyter, Berlin, pages 73–97.

René Dirven. 1997. Emotions as cause and the cause of emotions. In Susanne Niemeier and René Dirven, editors, *The Language of Emotions: Conceptualization, expression, and theoretical foundation*, John Benjamins, Amsterdam, pages 55–86.

Charles J. Fillmore. 1968. The case for case. In Emmon Bach and Robert Thomas Harms, editors, *Universals in Linguistic Theory*, Holt, Rinehart, and Winston, New York, pages 1–88.

Charles J. Fillmore and Collin Baker. 2009. A frames approach to semantic analysis. In Bernd Heine and Heiko Narrog, editors, *The Oxford Handbook of Linguistic Analysis*, Oxford University Press, Oxford, UK, pages 791–816.

Charles J. Fillmore, Paul Kay, and Mary Catherine O'Connor. 1988. Regularity and idiomaticity in grammatical constructions: the case of *let alone*. *Language* 64(3):501–538.

Adele E. Goldberg. 2006. *Constructions at work: the nature of generalization in language*. Oxford University Press.

Stephan Greene and Philip Resnik. 2009. More than words: syntactic packaging and implicit sentiment. In *Proc. of NAACL-HLT*. Boulder, Colorado, pages 503–511.

Martin Haspelmath. 2003. The geometry of grammatical meaning: semantic maps and cross-linguistic comparison. In Michael Tomasello, editor, *The New Psychology of Language: Cognitive and Function Approaches to Language Structure*, Lawrence Erlbaum Associates, Mahwah, NJ, volume 2, pages 211–242.

Annette Herskovits. 1986. *Language and spatial cognition: an interdisciplinary study of the prepositions in English*. Cambridge University Press, Cambridge, UK.

Jena D. Hwang. 2011. Making verb argument adjunct distinctions in English. Synthesis paper, University of Colorado, Boulder, Colorado.

Ray Jackendoff. 1990. *Semantic structures*. MIT press.

Ray Jackendoff. 2002. *Foundations of Language: Brain, Meaning, Grammar, Evolution*. Oxford.

Paul Kay and Charles J. Fillmore. 1999. Grammatical constructions and linguistic generalizations: the *What's X doing Y?* construction. *Language* 75(1):1–33.

Karin Kipper, Anna Korhonen, Neville Ryant, and Martha Palmer. 2008. A large-scale classification of English verbs. *Language Resources and Evaluation* 42(1):21–40.

George Lakoff. 1987. *Women, fire, and dangerous things: what categories reveal about the mind*. University of Chicago Press, Chicago.

George Lakoff and Mark Johnson. 1980. *Metaphors We Live By*. University of Chicago Press, Chicago.

Ronald W. Langacker. 1998. Conceptualization, symbolization, and grammar. In Michael Tomasello, editor, *The New Psychology of Language: Cognitive and Functional Approaches to Language Structure*, Lawrence Erlbaum Associates, Mahwah, NJ, pages 1–39.

Seth Lindstromberg. 2010. *English Prepositions Explained*. John Benjamins, Amsterdam, revised edition.

Ken Litkowski and Orin Hargraves. 2005. The Preposition Project. In *Proc. of the Second ACL-SIGSEM Workshop on the Linguistic Dimensions of Prepositions and their Use in Computational Linguistics Formalisms and Applications*. Colchester, Essex, UK, pages 171–179.

Rafael E. Núñez and Eve Sweetser. 2006. With the future behind them: convergent evidence from Aymara language and gesture in the crosslinguistic comparison of spatial construals of time. *Cognitive Science* 30(3):401–450.

Meredith Osmond. 1997. The prepositions we use in the construal of emotions: why do we say *fed up with* but *sick and tired of*? In Susanne Niemeier and René Dirven, editors, *The Language of Emotions: Conceptualization, expression, and theoretical foundation*, John Benjamins, Amsterdam, pages 111–133.

Martha Palmer, Claire Bonial, and Jena D. Hwang. 2017. VerbNet: Capturing English verb behavior, meaning and usage. In Susan E. F. Chipman, editor, *The Oxford Handbook of Cognitive Science*, Oxford University Press, pages 315–336.

Martha Palmer, Daniel Gildea, and Paul Kingsbury. 2005. The Proposition Bank: an annotated corpus of semantic roles. *Computational Linguistics* 31(1):71–106.

Davide Picca, Alfio Massimiliano Gliozzo, and Massimiliano Ciaramita. 2008. Supersense Tagger for Italian. In Nicoletta Calzolari, Khalid Choukri, Bente Maegaard, Joseph Mariani, Jan Odjik, Stelios Piperidis, and Daniel Tapias, editors, *Proc. of LREC*. Marrakech, Morocco, pages 2386–2390.

Günter Radden. 1998. The conceptualisation of emotional causality by means of prepositional phrases. In Angeliki Athanasiadou, Elżbieta Tabakowska, René Dirven, Ronald W. Langacker, and John R. Taylor, editors, *Speaking of emotions: conceptualisation and expression*, Mouton de Gruyter, pages 273–294.

Gisa Rauh. 1993. On the grammar of lexical and non-lexical prepositions in English. In Cornelia Zelinsky-Wibbelt, editor, *The Semantics of Prepositions: From Mental Processing to Natural Language Processing*, Mouton de Gruyter, New York, pages 99–150.

Nathan Schneider, Jena D. Hwang, Vivek Srikumar, Meredith Green, Abhijit Suresh, Kathryn Conger, Tim O'Gorman, and Martha Palmer. 2016. A corpus of preposition supersenses. In *Proc. of LAW X – the 10th Linguistic Annotation Workshop*. Berlin, Germany, pages 99–109.

Nathan Schneider, Behrang Mohit, Kemal Oflazer, and Noah A. Smith. 2012. Coarse lexical semantic annotation with supersenses: an Arabic case study. In *Proc. of ACL*. Jeju Island, Korea, pages 253–258.

Nathan Schneider, Vivek Srikumar, Jena D. Hwang, and Martha Palmer. 2015. A hierarchy with, of, and for preposition supersenses. In *Proc. of The 9th Linguistic Annotation Workshop*. Denver, Colorado, USA, pages 112–123.

Vivek Srikumar and Dan Roth. 2013a. An inventory of preposition relations. Technical Report arXiv:1305.5785. http://arxiv.org/abs/1305.5785.

Vivek Srikumar and Dan Roth. 2013b. Modeling semantic relations expressed by prepositions. *Transactions of the Association for Computational Linguistics* 1:231–242.

Leonard Talmy. 1996. Fictive motion in language and "ception". In Paul Bloom, Mary A. Peterson, Nadel Lynn, and Merrill F. Garrett, editors, *Language and Space*, MIT Press, Cambridge, MA, pages 211–276.

Stephen Tratz and Dirk Hovy. 2009. Disambiguation of preposition sense using linguistically motivated features. In *Proc. of NAACL-HLT Student Research Workshop and Doctoral Consortium*. Boulder, Colorado, pages 96–100.

Andrea Tyler and Vyvyan Evans. 2001. Reconsidering prepositional polysemy networks: the case of 'over'. *Language* 77(4):724–765.

Andrea Tyler and Vyvyan Evans. 2003. *The Semantics of English Prepositions: Spatial Scenes, Embodied Meaning and Cognition*. Cambridge University Press, Cambridge, UK.

Henk Verkuyl and Joost Zwarts. 1992. Time and space in conceptual and logical semantics: the notion of Path. *Linguistics* 30(3):483–512.

Bernhard Wälchli. 2010. Similarity semantics and building probabilistic semantic maps from parallel texts. *Linguistic Discovery* 8(1):331–371.

Patrick Ye and Timothy Baldwin. 2007. MELB-YB: Preposition sense disambiguation using rich semantic features. In *Proc. of SemEval*. Prague, Czech Republic, pages 241–244.

Issues of Mass and Count: Dealing with 'Dual-Life' Nouns

Tibor Kiss
Ruhr-Universität Bochum
44801 Bochum, Germany
tibor@linguistics.rub.de

Francis Jeffry Pelletier
University of Alberta
Edmonton, Canada
francisp@ualberta.ca

Halima Husić
Ruhr-Universität Bochum
44801 Bochum, Germany
husic@linguistics.rub.de

Johanna Poppek
Ruhr-Universität Bochum
44801 Bochum, Germany
poppek@linguistics.rub.de

Abstract

The topics of +MASS and +COUNT have been studied for many decades in philosophy (e.g., (Quine, 1960; Pelletier, 1975)), linguistics (e.g., (McCawley, 1975; Allan, 1980; Krifka, 1991)) and psychology (e.g., (Middleton et al., 2004; Barner et al., 2009). More recently, interest from within computational linguistics has studied the issues involved (e.g., (Pustejovsky, 1991; Bond, 2005; Schmidtke and Kuperman, 2016)), to name just a few. As is pointed out in these works, there are many difficult conceptual issues involved in the study of this contrast. In this article we study one of these issues – the "Dual-Life" of being simultaneously +MASS and +COUNT – by means of an unusual combination of human annotation, online lexical resources, and online corpora.

1 Background

The standard story of +MASS and +COUNT usually starts with some examples of nouns of both sorts.

- +COUNT: car, dog, idea, university, belief, …

- +MASS: water, garbage, advice, oil, admiration, knowledge…

These examples are usually accompanied by some syntactic tests for +MASS and +COUNT:

- Count terms can be pluralized, occur with indefinite determiner, allow numeral modifiers, occur with the quantifiers *each, every*, …. Mass terms can't do any of these.

- Always occurring in the singular, mass terms occur with "measure" terms (e.g., *much*), with the quantifiers *most, all* and the unstressed *some*, and bare in (e.g.) subject position with singular verb agreement. Singular count terms can't do any of these.

These lead to such comparisons as

(1) a. a car, four ideas, each university
    b. *a water, *four garbage, *each admiration
    c. all garbage, most water, advice is helpful
    d. *all dog, *most university, *car is fast

It can be seen from this brief (and partial) description of the +MASS/+COUNT distinction that the presumption is that the distinction applies to lexical nouns and that it is exhaustive and exclusive – every such noun is either +COUNT or +MASS, and no noun is both.

Our account will deny all these presumptions, and in doing so will open what we find to be a much more plausible account of various mysterious phenomena surrounding +MASS and +COUNT (although in this study we just examine the "dual-life" case).

2 Some Background Methodological Issues

A fundamental feature of (and, we think, a problem with) with the "usual story" is that it presumes that the locus or home of +MASS and +COUNT is the lexical *noun*. This is a feature of modern analyses as well as the older ones despite the fact that even in the oldest of the works we find remarks cautioning against this, such as (Quine, 1960)'s ambiguous *Mary put a little chicken into the salad* and cautionary remarks by others that such sentences as *We had crocodile for supper last night!* are completely normal. And to the claim that this "changes the sense" of *chicken* from +COUNT to +MASS, (Pelletier, 1975, p.456) remarked "Such a claim makes clear that either (1) surface structure is not what the criteria are talking about or (2) we need to distinguish not between mass and count *nouns* but between mass and count *senses* of nouns." This sort of remark can be found throughout the literature on +MASS/+COUNT; however, dic-

*Proceedings of the 6th Joint Conference on Lexical and Computational Semantics (*SEM 2017)*, pages 189–198,
Vancouver, Canada, August 3-4, 2017. ©2017 Association for Computational Linguistics

tionaries in fact do not usually make this distinction. The only relevant sense of *crocodile* in WordNet (Miller, 1995; Miller and Fellbaum, 2007) and *Webster's New Collegiate Dictionary* is "large voracious aquatic reptile having a long snout with massive jaws and sharp teeth and a body covered with bony plates; of sluggish tropical waters". In fact, with only a few exceptions, the relationship between an animal and its flesh used as food (when it is the same noun for each) does not generate new senses in dictionaries (nor WordNet). Somehow, both of the alleged meanings are contained in the same sense.

One might postulate (and many theorists have, e.g., (Bunt, 1985; Payne and Huddleston, 2002)) that there are some background "rules" that can apply to a basic meaning of a noun and which will generate the related sense that describes the opposite value of the +MASS/+COUNT dimension. Suggestions include rules for grinding (*armadillo all over the road*), portioning (*Order me a beer*), sorting (*eight beers on tap*), evaluating (*too much car for the average driver*) and others. However, it has seemed clear to most theorists that this sort of strategy wouldn't be able to account for all the varied ways that +MASS and +COUNT senses of a given noun might be related. Furthermore, for many so-called abstract nouns, it is not even clear what it is that makes a meaning be +MASS or +COUNT.

Another problem is that researchers looking into the issues involved in +MASS/+COUNT tend to use their own intuitions, based on a very limited number of data points (that is, a very limited group of words and their meanings). The use of large-scale resources is relatively rare (although see (Baldwin and Bond, 2003; Grimm, 2014; Katz and Zamparelli, 2012; Kulkarni et al., 2013)). And the use of dictionary resources is also rare, meaning that researchers rely on their own "intuitions into meaning" when it comes to issues of +COUNT and +MASS. Although many researchers have pointed to these sorts of limitations, none have actually investigated the actual senses of nouns as they appear in large resources (e.g., dictionaries), nor have they investigated what it means for a specific *sense* to be "dual-life" – i.e., to be both +MASS and +COUNT.

For these sorts of reasons, we have decided to investigate the possibility that the locus of +MASS and +COUNT should be a given *sense* of a noun. But a consequence of this will be that some senses are *both* +COUNT and +MASS, as for instance, our examples *beer* and *crocodile*. Even if we wish to retain the "semantic conversion/coercion" rules mentioned above and thus excuse these from being both +MASS and +COUNT, there are many others (as we will show below) that do not lend themselves to such coercions. So one of our goals is to display many *individual senses* of nouns (we call these "noun-senses") that are both +MASS and +COUNT;. The usual name for a theory that allows something to be both +MASS and +COUNT is "dual-life" – "dual-life nouns" if the locus is the noun, but "dual-life noun-senses" for our viewpoint.

3 What We Did

We used the American National Corpus (ANC: (Ide and Suderman, 2004; Ide, 2008)), parsed with the Stanford NLP Group (`http://nlp.stanford.edu`) parser (Chen and Manning, 2014). We then intersected the ANC's set of nouns with those in WordNet to form a repository of nouns for which there were definitions (in WordNet).[1] We employed four graduate linguistics students to (independently) evaluate the extent to which each of the WordNet senses thus chosen could be used in certain contexts (we call these tests the 'syntactic tests') and whether, given the answers to some of the syntactic tests, certain implications follow from their use (we call these the 'semantic tests'). There are six of these tests in all, four syntactic and two semantic, chosen for their relevance to various of the issues that are salient in the studies of +MASS and +COUNT terms. Table 1 gives the bare-bones outline of the annotators' tasks, which ask whether the annotators can construct sentences obeying the syntactic patterns specified, while maintaining the NOUN's meaning to be the one under investigation. Table 2 shows some noun-senses and how they fare with the tests. We discovered that there was very significant inter-annotator agreement in these answers. We have approximately 13,000 annotated and agreed-upon noun-senses. Inter-annotator agreement, as measured by Krippendorff's α, = 0.755, which (Artstein and Poesio, 2008, pp. 576, 591) define as highly reliable.

---

[1] We employed the ANC as a natural corpus because we also wished to investigate the actual senses in use. Our annotators characterized the MASS/COUNT feature of the various senses, but we wished then to see which of these senses were actually used in what contexts. That aspect of our research is not reported in the present paper.

Syn 1:	Can the noun-sense pair in its singular form appear together with *more*?
Sem 1:	If Syn 1 = yes, is the comparison based on number of entities, or another mode of measurement?
Syn 2:	Can the noun-sense pair in its plural form appear together with more?
Sem 2:	If Syn 2 = yes, is the sentence equivalent to a sentence with an explicit classifier?
Syn 3:	Can the noun-sense pair in its singular form and combined with an indefinite determiner be the syntactic subject of a definition or characterization?
Syn 4:	Can the noun-sense pair in its singular form but without a determiner be the syntactic subject of a definition or characterization?

Table 1: Four syntactic tests and two semantic tests annotators answered for each noun-sense

Noun	WordNet description	Syn 1	Sem 1	Syn 2	Sem 2	Syn 3	Syn 4
car#1	a motor vehicle with four wheels	no	na	yes	¬ equiv.	yes	no
fruitcake#1	a whimsically eccentric person	no	na	yes	¬ equiv.	yes	no
fruitcake#2	a rich cake containing dried fruit and nuts [...]	yes	¬ num.	yes	¬ equiv.	yes	yes
lingerie#1	women's underwear and nightclothes	yes	num.	na	na	no	yes
whiskey#1	a liquor made from fermented mash of grain	yes	¬ num.	yes	equiv.	no	yes

Table 2: Examples of Test Outcomes.

Further details on the texts, the various senses and the annotation process can be found in (Kiss et al., 2014). Some other aspects of the general research effort are in (Kiss et al., 2016).

Each noun-sense thus gets some unique pattern of answers, which we can represent as an ordered six-tuple of answers (we use the ordering given in Table 1). We extracted and processed the annotators' responses using **R** (`https:\cran.r-project.org`), allowing us not only to process the resulting answers given by our annotators, but also to aid in the inner-annotator agreement evaluation. A side effect of using **R** numerical names to the groups of senses that have the same six-tuple of answers. In this study we focus on one of these groups ("Classes"); **R** gave it the name "726", which we have kept (even though "dual-life" might have been a more informative choice of name).

There are three possible answers for each of the six Tests: yes, no, and not applicable (but we sometimes use 'num' and 'eq', together with negations), hence 729 possible classes. But the questions are not independent of one another, and in fact there are only 80 independently possible classes. Our annotators found there to be 18 ac-

tual classes to be populated with noun-senses, out of these 80 possible classes.

4 "Dual Life" senses

Remembering now that we are describing *senses* of nouns, as identified by WordNet, what sort of noun-senses manifest this duality of being *both* +MASS and +COUNT? Or put more accurately, since we test the senses by determining answers to questions that have that sense used in a full noun phrase, what sort of noun-senses manifest the possibility of occurring in both +MASS NPs and also in +COUNT NPs?

Our main group of such senses is called Class 726 by **R**. This group has the profile <yes,¬num,yes,¬equiv,yes,yes>. That is,

(2) a. This noun-sense can be used in the singular with *more*. <e.g., *John has more X than Mary*>

b. This amount of X is not based on instances of X.

c. It can be used in the plural <e.g., *John has more Xs than Mary*>

d. The Xs are not equivalent to any classifier + X <e.g., not equivalent to *more*

cups (or kinds) of X>

e. It can be used with an indefinite singular determiner definition <e.g., *An X is a (some definition)>*

f. It can be used in the singular without a determiner definition <e.g., *X is (some definition)>*

Class 726 contains 162 different senses of nouns. There are two different broad categories that we can distinguish within this group of dual-life noun-senses. The two basic types are:

1. Senses of *Nominally-Oriented nouns*

2. Senses of *Verbally-Oriented nouns*

There are 57 senses of Type 1 and 96 senses of Type 2. There are thus 8 other senses. 3 of which seem to fit into both categories equally, and 5 that do not seem to be of either Type.

4.1 Nominally-Oriented Noun Senses

We start with the Type 1 senses. Unlike the nouns that give rise to the Type 2 senses, the nouns behind these senses are not formed from other parts of speech: they are either simple nouns on their own or else nouns compounded from nouns and possibly other (non-verb) parts of speech.

Some of the Nominally-Oriented Noun senses are in groups that have been discussed in the literature before. One Nominally-Oriented noun type that has long received play in the mass-count literature is that associated with food.[2] For animal noun-senses other than *pig, cow*, e.g., *alligator*, the animal-designating "meaning" is +COUNT while the flesh-designating "meaning" is +MASS. A special version of this occurs when the particular amount or type of the meat is typically cooked or served as a unit, then such a unit gets called by a special +COUNT term and that special term acquires a +COUNT "meaning" for the meat that comprises it: *We had a steak for dinner/We had steak for dinner; Mary cooked a ham for Easter/Mary served ham for supper; George bought a large roast/George*

---

[2]As remarked above, dictionaries and other lexical sources (in particular, WordNet) take these differing ways to interpret a word like *alligator* to be parts of *one and the same sense*. Yet in writing about them, we wish to be able to discuss the differences that are *internal* to a sense. So, we have decided to use the term "meaning" (with double quote marks) when we wish to discuss the different interpretations that can be given to a single sense (or alternatively put, the different ways that a single sense can be used).

had leftover roast for a week. We give one example of a noun-sense that is in this group, and then list the nouns for the other 8 senses of the members of this subgroup.

(3) a. **fruitcake#2**: a rich cake containing dried fruit and nuts and citrus peel [...]

b. *cake#3, casserole#1, ham#1, marshmallow#1, melon#2, pizza#1, salad#1, steak#1*

(Rothstein, 2010) brought attention to a class of dual-life nouns that we may call the "fence-nouns". She was motivated by considerations like this:

(4) a. Hans Müller's ranch has more fence than Alexis Sánchez's granja.

b. A fence can be cut in half and part of it moved, and then there are two fences.

As can be seen from (4-b), Rothstein's dual-life evidence is semantic in nature, as well as the syntactic (4-a), although even in (4-b) we see the syntactic point that 'fence' can be used with an indefinite determiner. Rothstein makes a similar case for other nouns, such as *wire*. And though she does not remark on the fact that she is testing nouns, as opposed to noun *senses*, one could plausibly argue that she in fact *has* kept the sense of 'fence' (and 'wire') constant in these examples, and that is borne out by our annotators, who were just looking at individual senses. Class 726 is the home of a number of such noun senses.

(5) a. **cable#2**: a conductor for transmitting electrical or optical signals or electric power

b. **cable#3, cord#1, ribbon#4, rope#1, thread#1, wire#1**

Another identifiable subgroup of Class 726 is what we call the *-sides* dual life group. This group does not seem to have been identified in the earlier literature. Our annotators have determined that some sentence such as (6-a) is grammatical (and not due to counting the number of distinct seasides in the two locations), and as well, it is obvious that sentences like (6-b) are grammatical. And yet this is the same sense of *seaside*.

(6) a. California has more seaside than Oregon.

b. We spent our vacation on a seaside in southern England.

Our data included only 4 such senses:

(7) a. **seaside#1**: the shore of a sea or ocean regarded as a resort
   b. **hillside#1, riverside#1, roadside#1**

A final small group of the nominally-oriented dual-life senses we call the *-land* senses:

(8) a. **marshland#1**: low-lying wet land with grassy vegetation; usually is a transition zone between land and water
   b. **forest#2, marsh#1, rainforest#1, swamp#1, wetland#1**

There are many other Nominally-Oriented dual-life senses in Class 726 which do not manifest any of the preceding four types of meaning. The most common of the remaining ones are what we call "Kind-Instance" (or "Type-Token") in nature, usually where the kind-"meaning" is mass while the instance-"meaning" is count. There are 31 such senses, a few of which are:

(9) a. **drought#1**: A shortage of rainfall."Farmers most affected by the drought hope that there may yet be sufficient rain early in the growing season"[3]
   b. **mockery#3**: humorous or satirical mimicry.
   c. **brunch#1**: combination breakfast and lunch; usually served in late morning
   d. **anticoagulant#1**: medicine that prevents or retards the clotting of blood

In (9-a) we have a general term, 'drought', which has many instances such as exemplified in *A drought has bedevilled California since 1999*. So this seems a straightforward example of our Nominally-Oriented Kind-Instance dual-life senses. Things are maybe a little less obvious with (9-b), but it seems plausible to claim that it is designating a kind or sort of linguistic activity, and each particular case of a humorous or satirical mimicry is a mockery. Here we are *not* saying that the particular cases are the *result* of the activity, but rather that they exemplify the kind, mockery. With (9-c) one might wonder why it was not classified as an example of the Food subtype. In our opinion this is because brunch is not the "con-

tainer" that has the mass-stuff as its makeup, in the way that a chicken is a container for chicken(-meat). Instead, brunch is the name for a kind of activity, and each one of its manifestations is a brunch.

As we noted above, most senses here make the general "meaning" be mass, and the more individual-denoting "meaning" be count. But there are exceptions to this. *Anticoagulant#1*, for example, seems to be a mass sense for the stuff that is put into one's body to retard blood clotting, that is, this "meaning" picks out the physical manifestation of the kind term (akin to the individual-denoting "meaning" of the more usual terms). But this makes this manifestation "meaning" be mass, and the count sense seems to be a "sorting" meaning, that is, the kind "meaning" is count. Thus, 'an anticoagulant' names a kind or sort of stuff, rather like 'a beer' can name a type/kind/sort of beer. So 'anticoagulant' without an indefinite article names (something like) the stuff that is, in some particular case, doing the work of anti-coagulating.

4.2 Verbally-Oriented Noun Senses

There is a long-standing tradition claiming that "event nouns"[4] are ambiguous between a "meaning" that describes an activity, action, event, or process, on the one hand, and a "meaning" that describes the *result* of that activity, action, event, or process, on the other hand. Some clear examples of this in the literature are:

(10) a. *collection*: the activity of gathering together a group of items vs. the group that is thus gathered.
   b. *invention*: the process of generating some new type of thing vs. the actual kind of thing that has been generated.

Although some linguists would say that the fact that one "meaning" is predictable from the other "meaning", and so they shouldn't both be entered in the lexicon (e.g., (Payne and Huddleston, 2002, p. 337)), sometimes these two "meanings" are distinguished as separate senses in WordNet (and in dictionaries more generally), but sometimes not. For example, in WordNet we find

---

[3]The only other sense of *drought* in WordNet concerns any prolonged shortage: "When England defeated Pakistan it ended a ten-year drought".

[4]We use 'event' to name this group, even though there are nouns that don't seem to be derived from event verbs nor do they intuitively designate the occurrence of some event. For example, some are actions, activities, achievements, processes, etc..

(11) a. **collection#1**: several things grouped together or considered as a whole

b. **collection#2**: a publication containing a
variety of works

c. **collection#3**: a request for a sum of
money

d. **collection#4**: the act of gathering something together

Here we see the two "meanings" separated as different senses (senses #1 vs. #4). On the other hand,
sometimes the two "meanings" are merged into
the same sense. WordNet gives

(12) a. **burglary#1**: entering a building unlawfully with intent to commit a felony or
to steal valuable property[5]

b. **emission#1**: the act of emitting; causing to flow forth[6]

c. **amplification#1**: addition of extra material or illustration or clarifying detail[7]

Here we see that *burglary#1* describes both the
activity of burgling and also the result of the activity (a burglary). *emission#1* describes both the
event of causing something to flow, and also the
result of that event (an emission). Similarly, *am-
plification#1* describes both the activity of adding
extra material and the result of doing so. The former "meanings" are mass(-like) while the latter
are count(-like), as the examples in (13)–(15) suggest.

(13) a. Burglary is not a difficult activity to
carry out.

b. The Müllers' house suffered a burglary
last night.

(14) a. Methane emission in coal mines is a se-
rious health issue.

b. The cause of the miners' deaths was determined to be an emission of methane.

(15) a. The Opposition demanded amplification of the Prime Minister's remarks.

b. The Ministers for Foreign Affairs and of

Defense each provided an amplification
of the Prime Minister's remarks.

There is another relation that is, in a way,
"between" these the categories of Nominally-
Oriented Kind-Instance and Verbally-Oriented
Event-Result. It happens when an event-noun (or
state- or process-noun) designates a general term
for a kind or type that has instances or tokens
called by the same name. Note that these are *instances* or *tokens* of the kind, and not the *result* of
the event. In such cases, the event/state/process
"meaning" is usually or naturally seen as mass,
while the instance "meaning" seems usually or
naturally to be count. For example,

(16) a. **fantasy#1**: imagination unrestricted by
reality; "a schoolgirl fantasy"

b. **litigation#1**: a legal proceeding in a
court; a judicial contest to determine
and enforce legal rights

c. **silence#1**: the state of being silent (as
when no one is speaking); "there was
a shocked silence"; "he gestured for silence"

These cases seem to suggest that we have a general
term ('fantasy', 'litigation', 'silence') denoting a
type or kind, which in turn has many instances.
The instances are thus *not* effects of these kinds.
For example, "a schoolgirl fantasy", "a legal proceeding", "a shocked silence" are all instances
of their respective kinds, but not effects of them.
Nonetheless, it seems clear that these all display
the fact that the ultimate source of these noun-
senses is a verb: *fantasize, litigate, silence*, whose
WordNet senses are: "to portray in the mind", "to
engage in legal proceedings", "to cause to be quiet
or not talk". So such senses seem best classified
as Verbally-Oriented Kind-Instance senses, and as
we said, should be seen as forming a sort of middle ground between the Nominally-Oriented Kind-
Instance senses and the Verbally-Oriented Event-
Act senses. And so we call these senses *Verbally-
Oriented Kind-Instance* dual-life.

But in many cases it is difficult to determine
whether we have a case of the Verbally-Oriented
Act–Result relation or of the Verbally-Oriented
Kind–Instance relationship. For instance, with
each of the senses identified in (17), it seems that
there is no good reason to choose between viewing
the relationship as an Event-Result or as a Kind-

---

[5]This is the only sense identified in WordNet.

[6]Other senses of *emission* focus on the *kind* of material
that is released by an emission; one sense even picks out a
specific subtype of that sort of emission, namely that of water
from a pipe.

[7]The other two senses of 'amplification' indicate rather
different features: *amplification#2*: 'the amount of increase
in signal power or voltage or current expressed as the ratio
of output to input'; *amplification#3*: '(electronics) the act of
increasing voltage or power or current'.

Instance:

(17) a. **eccentricity#1**: strange and unconventional behavior

b. **idealization#2**: (psychiatry) a defence mechanism that splits something you are ambivalent about into two representations – one good and one bad

c. **imperfection#1**: the state or an instance of being imperfect

Is *eccentricity#1*, for instance, the name for a process, activity, or force, etc., that brings about an eccentricity as a result? Or is it instead the name of a kind or type of force (etc.) which has instances that are called eccentricities? What about *idealization#2*? Or *imperfection#1*? In the latter case it is explicitly defined as "either a state or an instance" and so even the definition explicitly leaves room for either interpretation. There seems to be no good reason to view any of these (and others) in one way or the other. About all that can be said is that these are Verbally-Oriented, but we can't further determine which subtype they manifest. Or maybe better put: they in fact do manifest both types equally.

Examples such as these make one want to go back to the earlier examples of Event-Result and Kind-Instance and reanalyze them also, making it become easier to see them too as perhaps exemplifying both ways in which a single sense can be simultaneously mass and count. In fact, we are tempted to say that there is some sort of "continuum" or continuity between the two ways – in the same way that one can order wavelengths of light so as to display a continuum between blue and green.

The largest subgroup in the 726 Dual-Life Class is the Verbally-Oriented Event-Result senses. (Although keep in mind that many of these also manifest at least a degree of Verbally-Oriented Kind-Instance "meaning".) There are 70 such senses in this Class; 55 of them are senses of *-tion* nominalizations from activity verbs, 2 are *-ment* nominalization, 3 are *-ing* nominalizations, and there are 15 others. A few examples of each of these types senses are in (18-a)–(18-d) .

(18) a. **acclimation#1**: adaptation to a new climate (a new temperature or altitude or environment); **deception#1**: the act of deceiving; **insertion#2**: the act of putting one thing inside another; **elimination#4**: the act of removing an unknown mathematical quantity by combining equations;

b. **embellishment#1**: elaboration of an interpretation by the use of decorative (sometimes fictitious) detail; **infringement#1**: an act that disregards an agreement or a right.

c. **borrowing#1**: the appropriation (of ideas or words etc) from another source; **ending#2**: the act of ending something.

d. **analysis#2**: the abstract separation of a whole into its constituent parts in order to study the parts and their relations; **burglary#1**: entering a building unlawfully with intent to commit a felony or to steal valuable property; **dispersal#1**: the act of dispersing or diffusing something; **influx#1**; **revival#1**; **war#1**

A group that is somewhat smaller than the just-mentioned Verbally-Oriented Event-Result senses is that of Verbally-Oriented Kind-Instance senses, with 18 members. Unlike the Verbally-Oriented Event-Result senses where one "meaning" is a name for the kind of activity and the other "meaning" is a name for a result of that activity, here we have a "meaning" as a name for the kind of activity and the other "meaning" is a name for tokens or instances of that activity, rather than a result of that activity. But unlike the Nominally-Oriented Kind-Instance noun-senses, these Verbally-Oriented senses clearly rely on a sense of a verb and not derived from a noun-sense. 10 of these noun-senses are *-tion* nominalizations, one formation is from each of *-ing, -ship, -ment*, while five are otherwise derived. A handful of the *-tion*-formations are in (19-a), the *-ing, -ship, -ment* formations are in (19-b), while the others are in (19-c).

(19) a. **elaboration#3**: a discussion that provides additional information; **intonation#1**: rise and fall of the voice pitch; **recrimination#1**: mutual accusations;

b. **looting#1**: plundering during riots or in wartime; **displacement#4**: (chemistry) a reaction in which an elementary substance displaces and sets free a constituent element from a compound; **friendship#1**: the state of being friends

(or friendly)

c. **curvature#1**: (medicine) a curving or bending; often abnormal; **fantasy#1**: imagination unrestricted by reality; **genocide#1**: systematic killing of a racial or cultural group; **silence#1**: the state of being silent (as when no one is speaking); **tribute#1**: something given or done as an expression of esteem

Here that there is always a verb-oriented situation, where the activity it describes gives rise to a mass general name for that activity, and the results are described by a count "meaning" of the same name.

4.3 Borderline Cases

Our rationales for the distinction between Kind-Instance noun-senses and Event-Result noun-senses (when they are both Verbally-Oriented) is this:

(20) If the event's happening suggests a *cause* for the result, then it is a case of Event-Result "meaning".

(21) When the event seems not to play any role in the formation, causation, occurrence, or existence of the object in question, then it is a Kind-Instance "meaning".

We think that these two explanations can merge into one another. E.g., in (22) it seems that the event is causing an instance to occur, and so we classify it in the Event-Result group, even though one can also see that the so-called result maybe is just an instance of the kind indicated by the event.

(22) a. **insertion#2**: the act of putting one thing into another
b. **encryption#1**: the activity of converting data or information into code
c. **re-creation#1**: the act of creating again.
d. **amelioration#1**: the act of relieving ills and changing for the better

Although the examples in (22) are most naturally seen as cases where an event causes some result, they could also be seen the other way. So, it seems natural to say that putting one thing into another causes there to be some result – an insertion. The activity of converting data to code (encryption) brings about an encryption of the data. But

on the other hand, one might say that the abstract kind (or type), insertion, has various specific physical manifestations – various instances or tokens of that type. As we said, we think the former is more natural here and in the other members of (22), but it also seems that the latter understanding is certainly possible.

But when there was no salient particular causation involved, and it was merely a matter of some abstract kind (or concept) which is then said to be instantiated in a particular situation, we labelled it as Verbally-Oriented Kind-Instance, as in (23):

(23) a. **elaboration#3**: a discussion that provides additional information
b. **fantasy#1**: imagination unrestricted by reality; "a schoolgirl fantasy"
c. **retraction#1**: a disavowal or taking back of a previous assertion
d. **genocide#1**: systematic killing of a racial or cultural group

Here it seems more natural to think that the noun is describing some (abstract) kind or type, and the count interpretation is a manifestation of that type. In this way, 'elaboration' seems to us to describe a type of speech act, and its manifestations or instantiations will be this or that elaboration. (Of course, one might also say that an act of elaboration is an action which will result in some specific elaboration, which makes the Event-Result reading become more prominent.)

However, there seem to be various noun senses in Class 726 that are Verbally-Oriented, but for which we find it impossible to decide whether they are more clearly Event-Result or more clearly Kind-Instance. Probably the best thing to say about them is that they are *both* Verbally-Oriented Event-Result *and* Verbally-Oriented Kind-Instance *to the same extent*. Here are two representatives:

(24) a. **defection#1**: withdrawing support or help despite allegiance or responsibility
b. **eccentricity#1**: strange and unconventional behavior

Finally, we see a very few noun-senses that seem to be equally Verbally- and Nominally-Oriented:

(25) a. **curve#1**: the trace of a point whose direction of motion changes
b. **poop#1**: obscene terms for feces

c. **regret#1**: sadness associated with some
wrong done or some disappointment

5 Concluding Remarks

We have offered some theoretical considerations
for favouring an analysis of (dictionary-defined)
senses of nouns, rather than the nouns themselves,
as the locus for explaining why a NP is +MASS or
+COUNT. We have also offered empirical evidence
in the form of a large repository of carefully annotated noun-senses. These annotated senses can
be analyzed to determine which individual ones of
them can be used only in +COUNT NPs, or only in
+MASS NPs, or in both +COUNT and +MASS NPs, or
are not usable in either +MASS or +COUNT NPs. This
paper in particular discussed a class of senses of
the third of these varieties: "Dual-life" senses –
those individual meanings that can be used in both
+MASS and +COUNT NPs.

We view the current undertaking as a necessary
step in providing a complete semantic analysis of
+MASS and +COUNT NPs. Such an account requires
both the underlying meanings of the component
nouns, and also the semantic effect of the syntactic method of forming the NP (that is, the giving
the meaning of the NP) from the noun's meaning.
However, without a detailed account of the wide
range of senses of the component nouns, it will be
impossible to give the desired group of semantic
rules. And without that, there would be no hope
for a compositional account of these phenomena.

We encourage other researchers to investigate
the resources available with the Bochum English Countability Lexicon (BECL). The BECL
2.1 database is publicly available at http://
count-and-mass.org.

Acknowledgments

We gratefully acknowledge the Alexander von
Humboldt Foundation for an Anneliese-Maier
prize and grant to Pelletier, and the Deutsche
Forschungsgemeinschaft (KI-759/5) grant to Kiss,
for their support of the work reported here and our
other reports.

References

Allan, K. (1980). Nouns and countability. *Language 56*, 541–567.

Artstein, R. and M. Poesio (2008). Inter-coder agreement for computational linguistics. *Computational
Linguistics 34*, 555–596. http://aclweb.
org/anthology/J08-4004.

Baldwin, T. and F. Bond (2003). Learning the countability of English nouns from corpus data. In *Proc.
of the 41st Annual Meeting of the Association for
Computational Linguistics*. http://aclweb.
org/anthology/PS03-1059.

Barner, D., S. Inagaki, and P. Li (2009). Language,
thought, and real nouns. *Cognition 11*, 329–344.

Bond, F. (2005). *Translating the Untranslatable: A
Solution to the Problem of Generating English De-
terminers*. Stanford: CSLI Press.

Bunt, H. (1985). *Mass Terms and Model Theoretic Semantics*. Cambridge: Cambridge UP.

Chen, D. and C. Manning (2014). A fast and accurate
dependency parser using neural networks. In *Proceedings of EMNLP 2014*. doi: 10.3115/v1/D14-
1082.

Grimm, S. (2014). Individuating the Abstract. In
U. Etxeberria, A. Fălăuş, A. Irurtzun, and B. Lefer-
man (Eds.), *Proceedings of Sinn und Bedeutung 18*,
Bayonne and Vitoria-Gasteiz, pp. 182–200.

Ide, N. (2008). The Amercian National Corpus: Then,
now, and tomorrow. In M. Haugh, K. Burridge,
J. Mulder, and P. Peters (Eds.), *Selected Proceed-
ings of the 2008 HCSNet Workshop on Designing the
Australian National Corpus: Mustering Languages*,
Summerville, MA. Cascadilla Proceedings Project.

Ide, N. and K. Suderman (2004). The Amercian National Corpus first release. In *Proceedings of the
Fourth Language Resources and Evaluation Conference (LREC)*, Lisbon, pp. 1681–1684. http:
//aclweb.org/anthology/L04-1313.

Katz, G. and R. Zamparelli (2012). Quantifying
count/mass elasticity. In J. Choi (Ed.), *Proceedings
of the 29th West Coast Conference on Formal Linguistics*, Somerville, MA, pp. 371–379. Cascadilla
Proceedings Project.

Kiss, T., F. J. Pelletier, H. Husić, and J. Poppek (2016).
A sense-based lexicon of count and mass expressions: The Bochum English countability lexicon.
In *Proceedings of LREC 2016*, Portoroz, Slovenia.
http://aclweb.org/anthology/L16.

Kiss, T., F. J. Pelletier, and T. Stadtfeld (2014). Building a reference lexicon for countability in English.
In *Proceedings of the Ninth LREC 2014*, Reykjavik. http://aclweb.org/anthology/
L14-1312.

Krifka, M. (1991). Massennomina. In A. von Stechow and D. Wunderlich (Eds.), *Semantics: An International Handbook of Contemporary Research*, pp. 399–417. Berlin: Mouton de Gruyter.

Kulkarni, R., S. Rothstein, and A. Treves (2013). A statistical investigation into the cross-linguistic distribution of mass and count nouns: Morphosyntactic and semantic perspectives. *Biolinguistics 7*, 132–168.

McCawley, J. (1975). Lexicography and the count-mass distinction. In *Berkeley Linguistic Society, Vol. 1*, pp. 314–321. Reprinted in J. McCawley (ed.) *Adverbs, Vowels, and Other Objects of Wonder*, Univ. Chicago Press, Chicago, 1979, pages 165–173.

Middleton, E., E. Wisniewski, K. Trindel, and M. Imai (2004). Separating the chaff from the oats: Evidence for a conceptual distinction between count noun and mass noun aggregates. *Journal of Memory and Language 50*, 371–394.

Miller, G. (1995). WordNet: A lexical database for English. *Communications of the ACM 38*, 39–41.

Miller, G. and C. Fellbaum (2007). WordNet then and now. *Language Resources and Evaluation 41*, 209–214. doi: 10.1007/s10579-007-9044-6.

Payne, J. and R. Huddleston (2002). Nouns and noun phrases. In R. Huddleston and G. K. Pullum (Eds.), *The Cambridge Grammar of the English Language*, pp. 323–523. Cambridge, UK: Cambridge UP.

Pelletier, F. J. (1975). Non-singular reference: Some preliminaries. *Philosophia 5*, 451–465. Reprinted in (Pelletier, 1979, pp. 1-14).

Pelletier, F. J. (Ed.) (1979). *Mass Terms: Some Philosophical Problems*. Dordrecht: Kluwer Academic Pub.

Pustejovsky, J. (1991). The generative lexicon. *Computational Linguistics 17*, 409–441. http://aclweb.org/anthology/J91-4003.

Quine, W. (1960). *Word and Object*. Cambridge, MA: MIT Press.

Rothstein, S. (2010). Counting and the mass-count distinction. *Journal of Semantics 27*, 343–397.

Schmidtke, D. and V. Kuperman (2016). Mass counts in world Englishes: A corpus linguistic study of noun countability in non-native varieties of english. *Corpus Linguistics and Linguistic Theory 12*. doi: 10.1515/clit-2015-0047.

Parsing Graphs with Regular Graph Grammars

Sorcha Gilroy
University of Edinburgh
s.gilroy@sms.ed.ac.uk

Adam Lopez
University of Edinburgh
alopez@inf.ed.ac.uk

Sebastian Maneth
Universität Bremen
smaneth@uni-bremen.de

Abstract

Recently, several datasets have become available which represent natural language phenomena as graphs. Hyperedge Replacement Languages (HRL) have been the focus of much attention as a formalism to represent the graphs in these datasets. Chiang et al. (2013) prove that HRL graphs can be parsed in polynomial time with respect to the size of the input graph. We believe that HRL are more expressive than is necessary to represent semantic graphs and we propose the use of Regular Graph Languages (RGL; Courcelle 1991), which is a subfamily of HRL, as a possible alternative. We provide a top-down parsing algorithm for RGL that runs in time linear in the size of the input graph.

1 Introduction

NLP systems for machine translation, summarization, paraphrasing, and other tasks often fail to preserve the compositional semantics of sentences and documents because they model language as bags of words, or at best syntactic trees. To preserve semantics, they must model semantics. In pursuit of this goal, several datasets have been produced which pair natural language with compositional semantic representations in the form of directed acyclic graphs (DAGs), including the Abstract Meaning Representation Bank (AMR; Banarescu et al. 2013), the Prague Czech-English Dependency Treebank (Hajič et al., 2012), Deepbank (Flickinger et al., 2012), and the Universal Conceptual Cognitive Annotation (Abend and Rappoport, 2013). To make use of this data, we require models of graphs.

Consider how we might use compositional semantic representations in machine translation

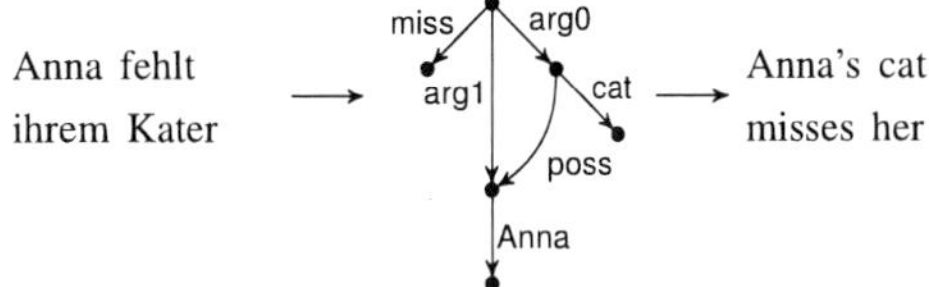

Figure 1: Semantic machine translation using AMR (Jones et al., 2012). The edge labels identify 'cat' as the object of the verb 'miss', 'Anna' as the subject of 'miss' and 'Anna' as the possessor of 'cat'. Edges whose head nodes are not attached to any other edge are interpreted as node labels.

(Figure 1), a two-step process in which semantic analysis is followed by generation. Jones et al. (2012) observe that this decomposition can be modeled with a pair of synchronous grammars, each defining a relation between strings and graphs. Necessarily, one projection of this synchronous grammar produces strings, while the other produces graphs, i.e., is a **graph grammar**. A consequence of this representation is that the complete translation process can be realized by parsing: to analyze a sentence, we parse the input string with the string-generating projection of the synchronous grammar, and read off the synchronous graph from the resulting parse. To generate a sentence, we parse the graph, and read off the synchronous string from the resulting parse. In this paper, we focus on the latter problem: using graph grammars to parse input graphs. We call this **graph recognition** to avoid confusion with other parsing problems.

Recent work in NLP has focused primarily on **hyperedge replacement grammar** (HRG; Drewes et al. 1997), a context-free graph grammar formalism that has been studied in an NLP context by several researchers (Chiang et al., 2013; Peng et al., 2015; Bauer and Rambow, 2016). In particular, Chiang et al. (2013) propose that HRG could be used to represent semantic graphs, and precisely characterize the complexity of a CKY-style

*Proceedings of the 6th Joint Conference on Lexical and Computational Semantics (*SEM 2017)*, pages 199–208,
Vancouver, Canada, August 3-4, 2017. ©2017 Association for Computational Linguistics

algorithm for graph recognition from Lautemann (1990) to be polynomial in the size of the input graph. HRGs are very expressive—they can generate graphs that simulate non-context-free string languages (Engelfriet and Heyker, 1991; Bauer and Rambow, 2016). This means they are likely more expressive than we need to represent the linguistic phenomena that appear in existing semantic datasets. In this paper, we propose the use of Regular Graph Grammars (RGG; Courcelle 1991) a subfamily of HRG that, like its regular counterparts among string and tree languages, is less expressive than context-free grammars but may admit more practical algorithms. By analogy to Chiang's CKY-style algorithm for HRG. We develop an Earley-style recognition algorithm for RGLs that is linear in the size of the input graph.

2 Regular Graph Languages

We use the following notation. If n is an integer, $[n]$ denotes the set $\{1, \ldots, n\}$. Let Γ be an alphabet, i.e., a finite set. Then $s \in \Gamma^*$ denotes that s is a sequence of arbitrary length, each element of which is in Γ. We denote by $|s|$ the length of s. A **ranked alphabet** is an alphabet Γ paired with an arity mapping (i.e., a total function) rank: $\Gamma \to \mathbb{N}$.

Definition 1. *A **hypergraph** (or simply **graph**) over a ranked alphabet Γ is a tuple $G = (V_G, E_G, att_G, lab_G, ext_G)$ where V_G is a finite set of nodes; E_G is a finite set of edges (distinct from V_G); $att_G : E_G \to V_G^*$ maps each edge to a sequence of nodes; $lab_G : E_G \to \Gamma$ maps each edge to a label such that $|att_G(e)| = rank(lab_G(e))$; and ext_G is an ordered subset of V_G called the **external nodes** of G.*

We assume that the elements of ext_G are pairwise distinct, and the elements of $att_G(e)$ for each edge e are also pairwise distinct. An edge e is attached to its nodes by **tentacles**, each labeled by an integer indicating the node's position in $att_G(e) = (v_1, \ldots, v_k)$. The tentacle from e to v_i will have label i, so the tentacle labels lie in the set $[k]$ where $k = rank(e)$. To express that a node v is attached to the ith tentacle of an edge e, we say $vert(e, i) = v$. Likewise, the nodes in ext_G are labeled by their position in ext_G. We refer to the ith external node of G by $ext_G(i)$ and in figures this will be labeled (i). The **rank** of an edge e is k if $att(e) = (v_1, \ldots, v_k)$ (or equivalently, $rank(lab(e)) = k$). The **rank** of a hypergraph G, denoted by $rank(G)$ is the size of ext_G.

Example 1. Hypergraph G in Figure 2 has four nodes (shown as black dots) and three hyperedges labeled a, b, and X (shown boxed). The bracketed numbers (1) and (2) denote its external nodes and the numbers between edges and the nodes are tentacle labels. Call the top node v_1 and, proceeding clockwise, call the other nodes v_2, v_3, and v_4. Call its edges e_1, e_2 and e_3. Its definition would state $att_G(e_1) = (v_1, v_2)$, $att_G(e_2) = (v_2, v_3)$, $att_G(e_3) = (v_1, v_4, v_3)$, $lab_G(e_1) = a$, $lab_G(e_2) = b$, $lab_G(e_3) = X$, and $ext_G = (v_4, v_2)$.

Definition 2. *Let G be a hypergraph containing an edge e with $att_G(e) = (v_1, \ldots, v_k)$ and let H be a hypergraph of rank k with node and edge sets disjoint from those of G. The **replacement** of e by H is the graph $G' = G[e/H]$. Its node set $V_{G'}$ is $V \cup V_H$ where $V = V_G - \{v_1, \ldots, v_k\}$. Its edge set is $E_{G'} = (E_G - \{e\}) \cup E_H$. We define $att_{G'} = att \cup att_H$ where for every $e' \in (E_G - \{e\})$, $att(e)$ is obtained from $att_G(e')$ by replacing v_i by the ith external node of H. Let $lab_{G'} = lab \cup lab_H$ where lab is the restriction of lab_G to edges in $E_G - \{e\}$. Finally, let $ext_{G'} = ext_G$.*

Example 2. A replacement is shown in Figure 2.

2.1 Hyperedge Replacement Grammars

Definition 3. *A **hyperedge replacement grammar** $\mathcal{G} = (N_{\mathcal{G}}, T_{\mathcal{G}}, P_{\mathcal{G}}, S_{\mathcal{G}})$ consists of ranked (disjoint) alphabets $N_{\mathcal{G}}$ and $T_{\mathcal{G}}$ of nonterminal and terminal symbols, respectively, a finite set $P_{\mathcal{G}}$ of productions, and a start symbol $S_{\mathcal{G}} \in N_{\mathcal{G}}$. Every production in $P_{\mathcal{G}}$ is of the form $X \to G$ where G is a hypergraph over $N_{\mathcal{G}} \cup T_{\mathcal{G}}$ and $rank(G) = rank(X)$.*

For each production $p : X \to G$, we use $L(p)$ to refer to X (the left-hand side of p) and $R(p)$ to refer to G (the right-hand side of p). An edge is a **terminal edge** if its label is terminal and a **nonterminal edge** if its label is nonterminal. A graph is a **terminal graph** if all of its edges are terminal. The **terminal subgraph** of a graph is the subgraph consisting of all terminal edges and their incident nodes.

Given a HRG $\mathcal{G}$, we say that graph G **immediately derives** graph G', denoted $G \to G'$, iff there is an edge $e \in E_G$ and a nonterminal $X \in N_{\mathcal{G}}$ such that $lab_G(e) = X$ and $G' = G[e/H]$, where $X \to H$ is in $P_{\mathcal{G}}$. We extend the idea of immediate derivation to its transitive closure $G \to^* G'$, and say here that G **derives** G'. For every $X \in N_{\mathcal{G}}$ we also use X to de-

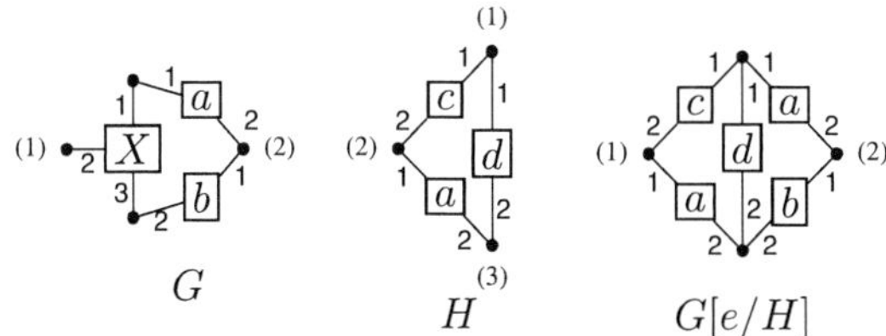

Figure 2: The replacement of the X-labeled edge e in G by the graph H.

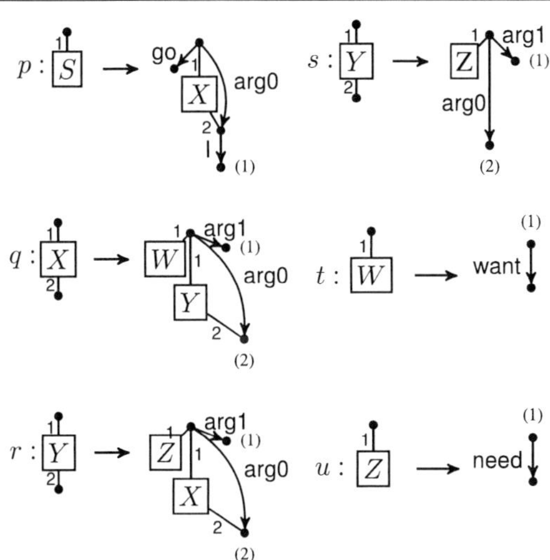

Table 1: Productions of a HRG. The labels p, q, r, s, t, and u label the productions so that we can refer to them in the text. Note that Y can rewrite in two ways, either via production r or s.

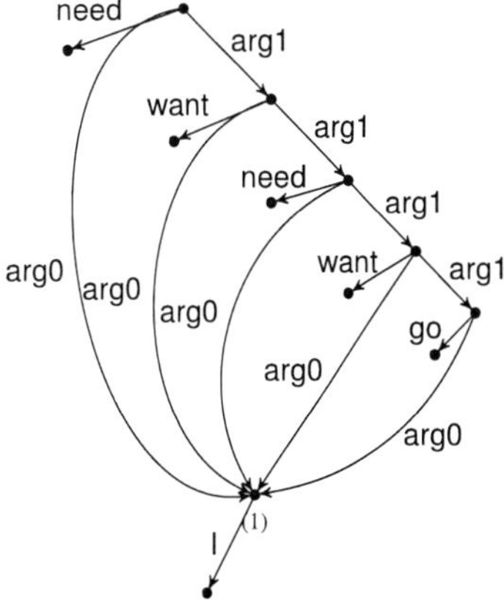

Figure 3: Graph derived by grammar in Table 1.

Figure 4: A HRG producing the string language $a^n b^n$.

(strings) by restricting the form of the productions in the grammars. Figure 4 shows a HRG that produces the context-free string language $a^n b^n$. HRGs can simulate the class of mildly context-sensitive languages that is characterized, e.g., by linear context-free rewriting systems (LCFRS; Vijay-Shanker et al. 1987), where the fan-out of the LCFRS will influence the maximum rank of nonterminal required in the HRG, see (Engelfriet and Heyker, 1991).

2.2 Regular Graph Grammars

A regular graph grammar (RGG; Courcelle 1991) is a restricted form of HRG. To explain the restrictions, we first require some definitions.

Definition 4. *Given a graph G, a **path** in G from a node v to a node v' is a sequence*

$$(v_0, i_1, e_1, j_1, v_1)(v_1, i_2, e_2, j_2, v_2)$$
$$\dots (v_{k-1}, i_k, e_k, j_k, v_k) \quad (1)$$

such that $v_0 = v, v_k = v'$, and for each $r \in [k]$, $vert(e_r, i_r) = v_{r-1}$ and $vert(e_r, j_r) = v_r$. The length of this path is k.

A path is **terminal** if every edge in the path has a terminal label. A path is **internal** if each v_i is internal for $1 \leq i \leq k - 1$. Note that the endpoints v_0 and v_k of an internal path can be external.

Definition 5. *A HRG $\mathcal{G}$ is a **Regular Graph Grammar** (or simply **RGG**) if each nonterminal in $N_{\mathcal{G}}$ has rank at least one and for each $p \in P_{\mathcal{G}}$ the following hold:*

note the graph consisting of a single edge e with $\mathrm{lab}(e) = X$ and nodes $(v_1, \dots, v_{\mathrm{rank}(X)})$ such that $\mathrm{att}_G(e) = (v_1, \dots, v_{\mathrm{rank}(X)})$, and we define the language $L_X(\mathcal{G})$ as $\{G \mid X \to^* G \wedge G$ is terminal$\}$. The **language of** $\mathcal{G}$ is $L(\mathcal{G}) = L_{S_{\mathcal{G}}}(\mathcal{G})$. We call the family of languages that can be produced by any HRG the **hyperedge replacement languages (HRL)**.

We assume that terminal edges are always of rank 2, and depict them as directed edges where the direction is determined by the tentacle labels: the tentacle labeled 1 attaches to the source of the edge and the tentacle labeled 2 attaches to the target of the edge.

Example 3. Table 1 shows a HRG deriving AMR graphs for sentences of the form 'I need to want to need to want to ... to want to go'. Figure 3 is a graph derived by the grammar. The grammar is somewhat unnatural, a point we will return to (§4).

We can use HRGs to generate chain graphs

(C1) $R(p)$ has at least one edge. Either it is a single terminal edge, all nodes of which are external, or each of its edges has at least one internal node.

(C2) Every pair of nodes in $R(p)$ is connected by a terminal and internal path.

Example 4. The grammar in Table 1 is an RGG. Although HRGs can produce context-free languages (and beyond) as shown in Figure 4, the only string languages RGGs can produce are the regular string languages. See Figure 5 for an example of a string generating RGG. Similarly, RGGs can produce regular tree languages, but not context-free tree languages. Figure 6 shows a tree generating RGG that generates binary trees the internal nodes of which are represented by a-labeled edges, and the leaves of which are represented by b-labeled edges. Note that these two results of regularity of the string- and tree-languages generated by RGG follow from the fact that graph languages produced by RGG are MSO-definable (Courcelle, 1991), and the well-known facts that the regular string and graph languages are MSO-definable.

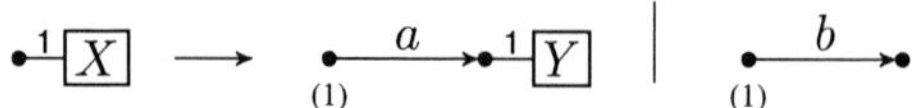

Figure 5: A RGG for a regular string language.

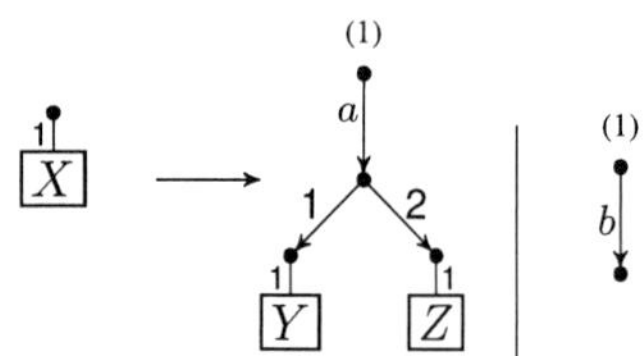

Figure 6: A RGG for a regular tree language.

We call the family of languages generated by RGGs the **regular graph languages** (RGLs).

3 RGL Recognition

To recognize RGG, we exploit the property that every nonterminal including the start symbol has rank at least one (Definition 5), and we assume that the corresponding external node is identified in the input graph. This mild assumption may be reasonable for applications like AMR parsing, where grammars could be designed so that the external node is always the unique root. Later we relax this assumption.

The availability of an identifiable external node suggests a top-down algorithm, and we take in-spiration from a top-down recognition algorithm for the predictive top-down parsable grammars, another subclass of HRG (Drewes et al., 2015). These grammars, the graph equivalent of LL(1) string grammars, are incomparable to RGG, but the algorithms are related in their use of top-down prediction and in that they both fix an order of the edges in the right-hand side of each production.

3.1 Top-Down Recognition for RGLs

Just as the algorithm of Chiang et al. (2013) generalizes CKY to HRG, our algorithm generalizes Earley's algorithm (Earley, 1970). Both algorithms operate by recognizing incrementally larger subgraphs of the input graph, using a succinct representation for subgraphs that depends on an arbitrarily chosen **marker node** m of the input graph.

Definition 6. *(Chiang et al. 2013; Definition 6) Let I be a subgraph of a graph G. A **boundary node** of I is a node which is either an endpoint of an edge in $G\backslash I$ or an external node of G. A **boundary edge** of I is an edge in I which has a boundary node as an endpoint. The **boundary representation** of I is the tuple $b(I) = \langle bn(I), be(I), m \in I \rangle$ where*

1. $bn(I)$ is the set of boundary nodes of I

2. $be(I)$ is the set of boundary edges of I

3. $(m \in I)$ is a flag indicating whether the marker node is in I.

Chiang et al. (2013) prove each subgraph has a unique boundary representation, and give algorithms that use only boundary representations to compute the union of two subgraphs, requiring time linear in the number of boundary nodes; and to check disjointness of subgraphs, requiring time linear in the number of boundary edges.

For each production p of the grammar, we impose a fixed order on the edges of $R(p)$, as in Drewes et al. (2015). We discuss this order in detail in §3.2. As in Earley's algorithm, we use dotted rules to represent partial recognition of productions: $X \rightarrow \bar{e}_1 \ldots \bar{e}_{i-1} \bullet \bar{e}_i \ldots \bar{e}_n$ means that we have identified the edges $\bar{e}_1$ to $\bar{e}_{i-1}$ and that we must next recognize edge $\bar{e}_i$. We write $\bar{e}$ and $\bar{v}$ for edges and nodes in productions and e and v for edges and nodes in a derived graph. When the identity of the sequence is immaterial we abbreviate it as α, for example writing $X \rightarrow \bullet \alpha$.

We present our recognizer as a deductive proof system (Shieber et al., 1995). The items of the

Name	Rule	Conditions
PREDICT	$\dfrac{[b(I), p : X \to \bar{e}_1 \dots \bullet \bar{e}_i \dots \bar{e}_n, \phi_p][q : Y \to \alpha]}{[\phi_p(\bar{e}_i), q : Y \to \bullet \, \alpha, \phi_q^0[\mathrm{ext}_{R(q)} = \phi_p(\bar{e}_i)]]}$	$\mathrm{lab}(\bar{e}_i) = Y$
SCAN	$\dfrac{[b(I), X \to \bar{e}_1 \dots \bullet \bar{e}_i \dots \bar{e}_n, \phi_p][e = \mathrm{edg}_{\mathrm{lab}(\bar{e}_i)}(v_1, \dots, v_m)]}{[b(I \cup \{e\}), X \to \bar{e}_1 \dots \bullet \bar{e}_{i+1} \dots \bar{e}_n, \phi_p[\mathrm{att}(\bar{e}_i) = (v_1, \dots, v_m)]]}$	$\phi_p(\bar{e}_i)(j) \in V_G \Rightarrow$ $\phi_p(\bar{e}_i)(j) = \mathrm{vert}(e, j)$
COMPLETE	$\dfrac{[b(I), p : X \to \bar{e}_1 \dots \bullet \bar{e}_i \dots \bar{e}_n, \phi_p][b(J), q : Y \to \alpha \bullet, \phi_q]}{[b(I \cup J), X \to \bar{e}_1 \dots \bullet \bar{e}_{i+1} \dots \bar{e}_n, \phi_p[\mathrm{att}(\bar{e}_i) = \phi_p(\mathrm{ext}_{R(q)})]]}$	$\phi_p(\bar{e}_i)(j) \in V_G \Rightarrow$ $\phi_p(\bar{e}_i)(j) =$ $\phi_q(\mathrm{ext}_{R(q)})(j),$ $\mathrm{lab}(\bar{e}_i) = Y,$ $E_I \cap E_J = \emptyset$

Table 2: The inference rules for the top-down recognizer.

recognizer are of the form

$$[b(I), p : X \to \bar{e}_1 \dots \bullet \bar{e}_i \dots \bar{e}_n, \phi_p]$$

where I is a subgraph that has been recognized as matching $\bar{e}_1, \dots, \bar{e}_{i-1}$; $p : X \to \bar{e}_1, \dots, \bar{e}_n$ is a production in the grammar with the edges in order; and $\phi_p : E_{R(p)} \to V_G^*$ maps the endpoints of edges in $R(p)$ to nodes in G.

For each production p, we number the nodes in some arbitrary but fixed order. Using this, we construct the function $\phi_p^0 : E_{R(p)} \to V_{R(p)}^*$ such that for $\bar{e} \in E_{R(p)}$ if $\mathrm{att}(\bar{e}) = (\bar{v}_1, \bar{v}_2)$ then $\phi_p^0(\bar{e}) = (\bar{v}_1, \bar{v}_2)$. As we match edges in the graph with edges in p, we assign the nodes $\bar{v}$ to nodes in the graph. For example, if we have an edge $\bar{e}$ in a production p such that $\mathrm{att}(\bar{e}) = (\bar{v}_1, \bar{v}_2)$ and we find an edge e which matches $\bar{e}$, then we update ϕ_p to record this fact, written $\phi_p[\mathrm{att}(\bar{e}) = \mathrm{att}(e)]$. We also use ϕ_p to record assignments of external nodes. If we assign the ith external node to v, we write $\phi_p[\mathrm{ext}_p(i) = v]$. We write ϕ_p^0 to represent a mapping with no grounded nodes.

Since our algorithm makes top-down predictions based on known external nodes, our boundary representation must cover the case where a subgraph is empty except for these nodes. If at some point we know that our subgraph has external nodes $\phi(\bar{e})$, then we use the shorthand $\phi(\bar{e})$ rather than the full boundary representation $\langle \phi(\bar{e}), \emptyset, m \in \phi(\bar{e}) \rangle$.

To keep notation uniform, we use dummy nonterminal $S^* \notin N_{\mathcal{G}}$ that derives $S_{\mathcal{G}}$ via the production p_0. For graph G, our system includes the **axiom**:

$$[\mathrm{ext}_G, p_0 : S^* \to \bullet \, S_{\mathcal{G}}, \phi_{p_0}^0[\mathrm{ext}_{R(p_0)} = \mathrm{ext}_G]].$$

Our **goal** is to prove:

$$[b(G), p_S : S^* \to S_{\mathcal{G}} \bullet, \phi_{p_S}]$$

where ϕ_{p_S} has a single edge $\bar{e}$ in its domain which has label $S_{\mathcal{G}}$ in $R(p_S)$ and $\phi_{p_S}(\bar{e}) = \mathrm{ext}_G$.

As in Earley's algorithm, we have three inference rules: PREDICT, SCAN and COMPLETE (Table 2). PREDICT is applied when the edge after the dot is nonterminal, assigning any external nodes that have been identified. SCAN is applied when the edge after the dot is terminal. Using ϕ_p, we may already know where some of the endpoints of the edge should be, so it requires the endpoints of the scanned edge to match. COMPLETE requires that each of the nodes of $\bar{e}_i$ in $R(p)$ have been identified, these nodes match up with the corresponding external nodes of the subgraph J, and that the subgraphs I and J are edge-disjoint.

We provide a high-level proof that the recognizer is sound and complete.

Proposition 1. *Let $\mathcal{G}$ be a HRG and G a graph. Then the goal $[b(G), p_S : S^* \to S_{\mathcal{G}} \bullet, \phi_{p_S}]$ can be proved from the axiom $[\mathrm{ext}_G, p_S : S^* \to \bullet \, S_{\mathcal{G}}, \phi_{p_S}[\mathrm{ext}_{R(p_S)} = \mathrm{ext}_G]]$ if and only if $G \in L(\mathcal{G})$.*

Proof. We prove that for each $X \in N_{\mathcal{G}}$, $[b(G), p_X : X^* \to X \bullet, \phi_{p_X}]$ can be proved from $[\mathrm{ext}_G, p_X : X^* \to \bullet \, X, \phi_{p_X}[\mathrm{ext}_{R(p_X)} = \mathrm{ext}_G]]$ if and only if $G \in L_X(\mathcal{G})$ where the dummy nonterminal X^* was added to the set of nonterminals and $p_X : X^* \to X$ was added to the set of productions. We prove this by induction on the number of edges in G.

We assume that each production in the grammar contains at least one terminal edge. If the HRG is not in this form, it can be converted into this form and in the case of RGGs they are already in this form by definition.

Base Case: Let G consist of a single edge.

If: Assume $G \in L_X(\mathcal{G})$. Since G consists of one edge, there must be a production $q : X \to G$. Apply PREDICT to the axiom and $p_X : X^* \to X$ to obtain the item $[\phi_{p_X}(X), q : X \to \bullet\, G, \phi_q^0[\text{ext}_G = \phi_{p_X}(X)]]$. Apply SCAN to the single terminal edge that makes up G to obtain $[b(G), q : X \to G\, \bullet, \phi_q]$ and finally apply COMPLETE to this and the axiom reach the goal $[b(G), p_X : X^* \to X, \phi_{p_X}]$.

Only if: Assume the goal can be reached from the axiom and $G = e$. Then the item $[b(e), q : X \to e, \phi_q]$ must have been reached at some point for some $q \in P_{\mathcal{G}}$. Therefore $q : X \to e$ is a production and so $e = G \in L_X(\mathcal{G})$.

Assumption: Assume that the proposition holds when G has fewer than k edges.

Inductive Step: Assume G has k edges.

If: Assume $G \in L_X(\mathcal{G})$, then there is a production $q : X \to H$ where H has nonterminals $Y_1, \ldots, Y_n$ and there are graphs $H_1, \ldots, H_n$ such that $G = H[Y_1/H_1]\ldots[Y_n/H_n]$. Each graph H_i for $i \in [n]$ has fewer than k edges and so we apply the inductive hypothesis to show that we can prove the items $[b(H_i), r_i : Y_i \to J_i, \phi_{r_i}]$ for each $i \in [n]$. By applying COMPLETE to each such item and applying SCAN to each terminal edge of H we reach the goal $[b(G), p_X : X^* \to X\, \bullet, \phi_{p_X}]$.

Only If: Assume the goal can be proved from the axiom. Then we must have at some point reached an item of the form $[b(G), q : X \to H, \phi_q]$ and that H has nonterminals $Y_1, \ldots, Y_n$. This means that there are graphs $H_1, \ldots, H_n$ such that $[b(H_i), p_{Y_i} : Y_i^* \to Y_i, \phi_{p_{Y_i}}]$ for each $i \in [n]$ and $G = H[Y_1/H_1]\ldots[Y_n/H_n]$. Since each H_i has fewer than k edges, we apply the inductive hypothesis to get that $H_i \in L_{Y_i}(\mathcal{G})$ for each $i \in [n]$ and therefore $G \in L_X(\mathcal{G})$. $\qquad\square$

Example 5. Using the RGG in Table 1, we show how we can recognize the graph in Figure 7, which can be derived by applying production s followed by production u, where the external nodes of Y are (v_3, v_2). Assume the ordering of the edges in production s is arg1, arg0, Z; the top node is $\bar{v}_1$; the bottom node is $\bar{v}_2$; and the node on the right is $\bar{v}_3$; and that the marker node is not in this subgraph— we elide reference to it for simplicity. Let $\bar{v}_4$ be the top node of $R(u)$ and $\bar{v}_5$ be the bottom node of $R(u)$. The external nodes of Y are determined

top-down, so the recognize of this subgraph is triggered by this item:

$$[\{v_3, v_2\}, Y \to\; \bullet\; \text{arg1 arg0}\; Z,$$
$$\phi_s^0[\text{ext}_{R(s)} = (v_3, v_2)]] \quad (2)$$

where $\phi_s(\text{arg1}) = (\bar{v}_1, v_3)$, $\phi_s(\text{arg0}) = (\bar{v}_1, v_2)$, and $\phi_s(Z) = (\bar{v}_1)$.

Table 3 shows how we can prove the item

$$[\langle\{v_3, v_2\}, \{e_3, e_2\}\rangle, Y \to \text{arg1 arg0} Z\; \bullet\;, \phi]$$

The boundary representation $\langle\{v_3, v_2\}, \{e_3, e_2\}\rangle$ in this item represents the whole subgraph shown in Figure 7.

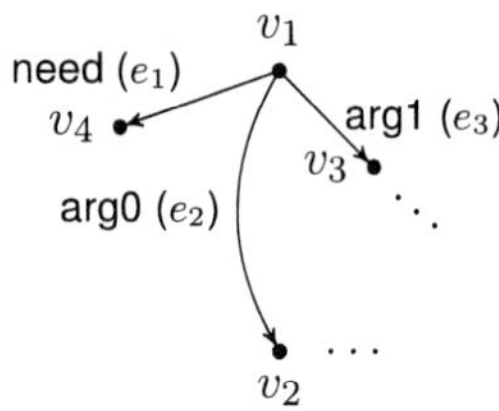

Figure 7: Top left subgraph of Figure 3. To refer to nodes and edges in the text, they are labeled v_1, v_2, v_3, e_1, e_2, and e_3.

3.2 Normal Ordering

Our algorithm requires a fixed ordering of the edges in the right-hand sides of each production. We will constrain this ordering to exploit the structure of RGG productions, allowing us to bound recognition complexity. If $s = \bar{e}_1 \ldots \bar{e}_n$ is an order, define $s_{i:j} = \bar{e}_i \ldots \bar{e}_j$.

Definition 7. *Let* $s = \bar{e}_1, \ldots, \bar{e}_n$ *be an edge order of a right-hand side of a production. Then s is* ***normal*** *if it has the following properties:*

1. $\bar{e}_1$ is connected to an external node,

2. $s_{1:j}$ is a connected graph for all $j \in [n]$

3. if $\bar{e}_i$ is nonterminal, each endpoint of $\bar{e}_i$ must be incident with some terminal edge $\bar{e}_j$ for which $j < i$.

Example 6. The ordering of the edges of production s in Example 5 is normal.

Arbitrary HRGs do not necessarily admit a normal ordering. For example, the graph in Figure 8 cannot satisfy Properties 2 and 3 simultaneously. However, RGGs do admit a normal ordering.

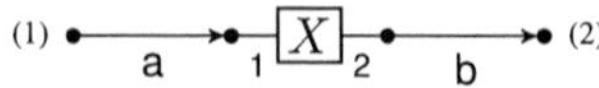

Figure 8: This graph cannot be normally ordered.

Current Item	Reason
1. $[\{v_3, v_2\}, Y \rightarrow \,\bullet\, \mathrm{arg1arg0}Z, \phi_s^0[\mathrm{ext}_{R(s)} = (v_3, v_2)]]$	Equation 2
2. $[\langle\{v_3, v_2, v_1\}, \{e_3\}\rangle, Y \rightarrow \mathrm{arg1} \,\bullet\, \mathrm{arg0}Z, \phi_s[\mathrm{att(arg1)} = (v_1, v_3)]]$	SCAN: 1. and $e_3 = \mathrm{edg}_{\mathrm{arg1}}(v_1, v_3)$
3. $[\langle\{v_3, v_2, v_1\}, \{e_3, e_2\}\rangle, Y \rightarrow \mathrm{arg1arg0} \,\bullet\, Z, \phi_s[\mathrm{att(arg0)} = (v_1, v_2)]]$	SCAN: 2. and $e_2 = \mathrm{edg}_{\mathrm{arg0}}(v_1, v_2)$
4. $[(v_1), Z \rightarrow \,\bullet\, \mathrm{need}, \phi_u^0[\mathrm{ext}_{R(u)} = (v_1)]]$	PREDICT: 3. and $Z \rightarrow \mathrm{need}$
5. $[\langle\{v_1, v_4\}, \{e_1\}\rangle, Z \rightarrow \mathrm{need} \,\bullet\,, \phi_u[\mathrm{att(need)} = (v_1, v_4)]]$	SCAN: 4. and $e_1 = \mathrm{edg}_{\mathrm{need}}(v_1, v_4)$
6. $[\langle\{v_3, v_2\}, \{e_3, e_2\}\rangle, Y \rightarrow \mathrm{arg1arg0}Z \,\bullet\,, \phi_s[\mathrm{att}(Z) = (v_1)]]$	COMPLETE: 3. and 5.

Table 3: The steps of recognizing that the subgraph shown in Figure 7 is derived from productions r_2 and u in the grammar in Table 1.

Proposition 2. *If $\mathcal{G}$ is an RGG, for every $p \in P_{\mathcal{G}}$, there is a normal ordering of the edges in $R(p)$.*

Proof. If $R(p)$ contains a single node then it must be an external node and it must have a terminal edge attached to it since $R(p)$ must contain at least one terminal edge. If $R(p)$ contains multiple nodes then by C2 there must be terminal internal paths between all of them, so there must be a terminal edge attached to the external node, which we use to satisfy Property 1. To produce a normal ordering, we next select terminal edges once one of their endpoints is connected to an ordered edge, and nonterminal edges once all endpoints are connected to ordered edges, possible by C2. Therefore, Properties 2 and 3 are satisfied. $\square$

A normal ordering tightly constrains the recognition of edges. Property 3 ensures that when we apply PREDICT, the external nodes of the predicted edge are all bound to specific nodes in the graph. Properties 1 and 2 ensure that when we apply SCAN, at least one endpoint of the edge is bound (fixed).

3.3 Recognition Complexity

Assume a normally-ordered RGG. Let the maximum number of edges in the right-hand side of any production be m; the maximum number of nodes in any right-hand side of a production k; the maximum degree of any node in the input graph d; and the number of nodes in the input graph n.

As previously mentioned, Drewes et al. (2015) also propose a HRG recognizer which can recognize a subclass of HRG (incomparable to RGG) called the predictive top-down parsable grammars. Their recognizer in this case runs in $\mathcal{O}(n^2)$ time. A well-known bottom-up recognizing algorithm for HRG was first proposed by Lautemann (1990).

In this paper, the recognizer is shown to be polynomial in the size of the input graph. Later, Chiang et al. (2013) formulate the same algorithm more precisely and show that the recognizing complexity is $\mathcal{O}((3^d \times n)^{k+1})$ where k in their case is the treewidth of the grammar.

Remark 1. *The maximum number of nodes in any right-hand side of a production (k) is also the maximum number of boundary nodes for any subgraph in the recognizer.*

COMPLETE combines subgraphs I and J only when the entire subgraph derived from Y has been recognized. Boundary nodes of J are also boundary nodes of I because they are nodes in the terminal subgraph of $R(p)$ where Y connects. The boundary nodes of $I \cup J$ are also bounded by k since form a subset of the boundary nodes of I.

Remark 2. *Given a boundary node, there are at most $(d^m)^{k-1}$ ways of identifying the remaining boundary nodes of a subgraph that is isomorphic to the terminal subgraph of the right-hand side of a production.*

The terminal subgraph of each production is connected by C2, with a maximum path length of m. For each edge in the path, there are at most d subsequent edges. Hence for the $k - 1$ remaining boundary nodes there are $(d^m)^{k-1}$ ways of choosing them.

We count instantiations of COMPLETE for an upper bound on complexity (McAllester, 2002), using similar logic to (Chiang et al., 2013). The number of boundary nodes of I, J and $I \cup J$ is at most k. Therefore, if we choose an arbitrary node to be some boundary node of $I \cup J$, there are at most $(d^m)^{k-1}$ ways of choosing its remaining boundary nodes. For each of these nodes, there are at most $(3^d)^k$ states of their attached boundary edges: in I, in J, or in neither. The total number of instantiations is $\mathcal{O}(n(d^m)^{k-1}(3^d)^k)$, linear in the number of input nodes and exponential in the degree of the input graph. Note that in the case of the AMR dataset (Banarescu et al. 2013), the maximum node degree is 17 and the average is 2.12.

We observe that RGGs could be relaxed to produce graphs with no external nodes by adding a dummy nonterminal S' with rank 0 and a single production $S' \rightarrow S$. To adapt the recognition algorithm, we would first need to guess where the graph starts. This would add a factor of n to the complexity as the graph could start at any node.

4 Discussion and Conclusions

We have presented RGG as a formalism that could be useful for semantic representations and we have provided a top-down recognition algorithm for them. The constraints of RGG enable more efficient recognition than general HRG, and this tradeoff is reasonable since HRG is very expressive—when generating strings, it can express non-context-free languages (Engelfriet and Heyker, 1991; Bauer and Rambow, 2016), far more power than needed to express semantic graphs. On the other hand, RGG is so constrained that it may not be expressive enough: it would be more natural to derive the graph in Figure 4 from outermost to innermost predicate; but constraint C2 makes it difficult to express this, and the grammar in Table 1 does not. Perhaps we need less expressivity than HRG but more than RGG.

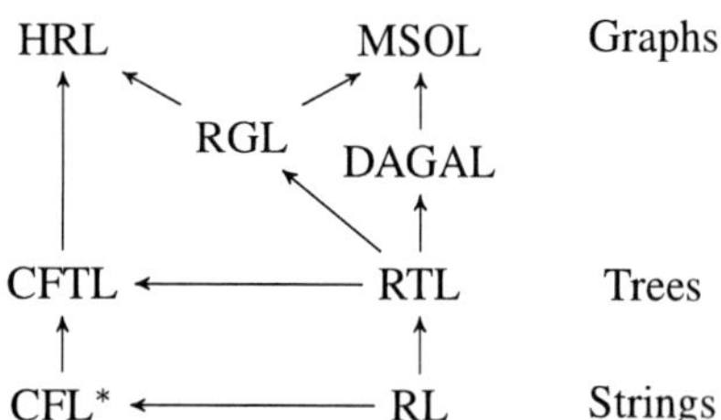

Figure 9: A Hasse diagram of various string, tree and graph language families. An arrow from family A to family B indicates that family A is a subfamily of family B.

A possible alternative would be to consider Restricted DAG Grammars (RDG; Björklund et al. 2016). Parsing for a fixed such grammar can be achieved in quadratic time with respect to the input graph. It is known that for a fixed HRG generating k-connected hypergraphs consisting of hyperedges of rank k only, parsing can be carried out in cubic time (k-HRG; (Drewes, 1993)).

More general than RDGs a is the class of graph languages recognized by DAG automata (DAGAL; Blum and Drewes 2016), for which the deterministic variant provides polynomial time parsing. Note that RGGs can generate graph languages of unbounded node degree. With respect to expressive power, RDGs and k-HRGs are incomparable to RGGs. Figure 9 shows the relationships between the context-free and regular languages for strings, trees and graphs. Monadic-second order logic (MSOL; Courcelle and Engelfriet 2011) is a form of logic which when restricted to strings gives us exactly the regular string languages and when restricted to trees gives us exactly the regular tree languages. RGLs lie in the intersection of HRG and MSOL on graphs but they do not make up this entire intersection. Courcelle (1991) defined (non-constructively) this intersection to be the strongly context-free languages (SCFL). We believe that there may be other formalisms that are subfamilies of SCFL which may be useful for semantic representations. All inclusions shown in Figure 9 are strict. For instance, RGL cannot produce "star graphs" (one node that has edges to n other nodes), while DAGAL and HRL can produce such graphs. It is well-known that HRL and MSOL are incomparable. There is a language in RGL that is not in DAGAL, for instance, "ladders" (two string graphs of n nodes each, with an edge between the ith node of each string).

Another alternative formalism to RGG that is defined as a restriction of HRG are Tree-like Grammars (TLG; Matheja et al. 2015). They define a subclass of SCFL, i.e., they are MSO definable. TLGs have been considered for program verification, where closure under intersection of the formalism is essential. Note that RGGs are also closed under intersection. While TLG and RDG are both incomparable to RGG, they share important characteristics, including the fact that the terminal subgraph of every production is connected. This means that our top-down recognition algorithm is applicable to both. In the future we would like to investigate larger, less restrictive (and more linguistically expressive) subfamilies of SCFL. We plan to implement and evaluate our algorithm experimentally.

Acknowledgments

This work was supported in part by the EPSRC Centre for Doctoral Training in Data Science, funded by the UK Engineering and Physical Sciences Research Council (grant EP/L016427/1) and the University of Edinburgh; and in part by a Google faculty research award (to AL). We thank Clara Vania, Sameer Bansal, Ida Szubert, Federico Fancellu, Antonis Anastasopoulos, Marco Damonte, and the anonymous reviews for helpful discussion of this work and comments on previous drafts of the paper.

References

Omri Abend and Ari Rappoport. 2013. Universal conceptual cognitive annotation (ucca). In *ACL (1)*. The Association for Computational Linguistics, pages 228–238. http://dblp.uni-trier.de/db/conf/acl/acl2013-1.html#AbendR13.

Laura Banarescu, Claire Bonial, Shu Cai, Madalina Georgescu, Kira Griffitt, Ulf Hermjakob, Kevin Knight, Philipp Koehn, Martha Palmer, and Nathan Schneider. 2013. Abstract meaning representation for sembanking. In *Proceedings of the 7th Linguistic Annotation Workshop and Interoperability with Discourse*. Association for Computational Linguistics, Sofia, Bulgaria, pages 178–186. http://www.aclweb.org/anthology/W13-2322.

Daniel Bauer and Owen Rambow. 2016. Hyperedge replacement and nonprojective dependency structures. In *Proceedings of the 12th International Workshop on Tree Adjoining Grammars and Related Formalisms (TAG+12), June 29 - July 1, 2016, Heinrich Heine University, Düsseldorf, Germany.* pages 103–111. http://aclweb.org/anthology/W/W16/W16-3311.pdf.

Henrik Björklund, Frank Drewes, and Petter Ericson. 2016. *Between a Rock and a Hard Place – Uniform Parsing for Hyperedge Replacement DAG Grammars*, Springer International Publishing, Cham, pages 521–532. https://doi.org/10.1007/978-3-319-30000-9_40.

Johannes Blum and Frank Drewes. 2016. Properties of regular DAG languages. In *Language and Automata Theory and Applications - 10th International Conference, LATA 2016, Prague, Czech Republic, March 14-18, 2016, Proceedings.* pages 427–438. https://doi.org/10.1007/978-3-319-30000-9_33.

David Chiang, Jacob Andreas, Daniel Bauer, Karl Moritz Hermann, Bevan Jones, and Kevin Knight. 2013. Parsing graphs with hyperedge replacement grammars. In *Proceedings of the 51st Annual Meeting of the Association for Computational Linguistics (Volume 1: Long Papers)*. Association for Computational Linguistics, Sofia, Bulgaria, pages 924–932. http://www.aclweb.org/anthology/P13-1091.

Bruno Courcelle. 1991. The monadic second-order logic of graphs V: on closing the gap between definability and recognizability. *Theor. Comput. Sci.* 80(2):153–202. https://doi.org/10.1016/0304-3975(91)90387-H.

Bruno Courcelle and Joost Engelfriet. 2011. *Graph Structure and Monadic Second-Order Logic, a Language Theoretic Approach.* Cambridge University Press.

Frank Drewes. 1993. Np-completeness of k-connected hyperedge-replacement languages of order k. *Inf. Process. Lett.* 45(2):89–94. https://doi.org/10.1016/0020-0190(93)90221-T.

Frank Drewes, Berthold Hoffmann, and Mark Minas. 2015. *Predictive Top-Down Parsing for Hyperedge Replacement Grammars*, Springer International Publishing, Cham, pages 19–34. https://doi.org/10.1007/978-3-319-21145-9_2.

Frank Drewes, Hans-Jörg Kreowski, and Annegret Habel. 1997. Hyperedge replacement graph grammars. In Grzegorz Rozenberg, editor, *Handbook of Graph Grammars and Computing by Graph Transformation*, World Scientific, pages 95–162.

Jay Earley. 1970. An efficient context-free parsing algorithm. ACM, New York, NY, USA, volume 13, pages 94–102. https://doi.org/10.1145/362007.362035.

Joost Engelfriet and Linda Heyker. 1991. The string generating power of context-free hypergraph grammars. *Journal of Computer and System Sciences* 43(2):328–360.

Dan Flickinger, Yi Zhang, and Valia Kordoni. 2012. Deepbank : a dynamically annotated treebank of the Wall Street Journal. In *Proceedings of the Eleventh International Workshop on Treebanks and Linguistic Theories (TLT11)*. Lisbon, pages 85–96. HU.

Jan Hajič, Eva Hajičová, Jarmila Panevov, Petr Sgall, Ondřej Bojar, Silvie Cinková, Eva Fučíková, Marie Mikulová, Petr Pajas, Jan Popelka, Jiří Semecký, Jana Šindlerová, Jan Štěpánek, Josef Toman, Zdeňka Urešová, and Zdeněk Žabokrtský. 2012. Announcing prague czech-english dependency treebank 2.0. In Nicoletta Calzolari (Conference Chair), Khalid Choukri, Thierry Declerck, Mehmet Uur Doan, Bente Maegaard, Joseph Mariani, Asuncion Moreno, Jan Odijk, and Stelios Piperidis, editors, *Proceedings of the Eight International Conference on Language Resources and Evaluation (LREC'12)*. European Language Resources Association (ELRA), Istanbul, Turkey.

Bevan Jones, Jacob Andreas, Daniel Bauer, Karl Mortiz Hermann, and Kevin Knight. 2012. Semantics-based machine translation with hyperedge replacement grammars. In *Proceedings of COLING*.

Clemens Lautemann. 1990. The complexity of graph languages generated by hyperedge replacement. *Acta Informatica* 27(5):399–421. https://doi.org/10.1007/BF00289017.

Christoph Matheja, Christina Jansen, and Thomas Noll. 2015. *Tree-Like Grammars and Separation Logic*, Springer International Publishing, Cham, pages 90–108. https://doi.org/10.1007/978-3-319-26529-2_6.

David McAllester. 2002. On the complexity analysis of static analyses. *J. ACM* 49(4):512–537. https://doi.org/10.1145/581771.581774.

Xiaochang Peng, Linfeng Song, and Daniel Gildea. 2015. A synchronous hyperedge replacement grammar based approach for AMR parsing. In *Proceedings of the 19th Conference on Computational Natural Language Learning, CoNLL 2015, Beijing, China, July 30-31, 2015*. pages 32–41. http://aclweb.org/anthology/K/K15/K15-1004.pdf.

Stuart M. Shieber, Yves Schabes, and Fernando C. N. Pereira. 1995. Principles and implementation of deductive parsing. *Journal of Logic Programming* 24(1-2).

K. Vijay-Shanker, David J. Weir, and Aravind K. Joshi. 1987. Characterizing structural descriptions produced by various grammatical formalisms. In *Proceedings of the 25th Annual Meeting on Association for Computational Linguistics*. Association for Computational Linguistics, Stroudsburg, PA, USA, ACL '87, pages 104–111. https://doi.org/10.3115/981175.981190.

Embedded Semantic Lexicon Induction with Joint Global and Local Optimization

Sujay Kumar Jauhar
Language Technologies Institute
Carnegie Mellon University
Pittsburgh, PA, USA
sjauhar@cs.cmu.edu

Eduard Hovy
Language Technologies Institute
Carnegie Mellon University
Pittsburgh, PA, USA
hovy@cs.cmu.edu

Abstract

Creating annotated frame lexicons such as PropBank and FrameNet is expensive and labor intensive. We present a method to induce an embedded frame lexicon in an minimally supervised fashion using nothing more than unlabeled predicate-argument word pairs. We hypothesize that aggregating such pair selectional preferences across training leads us to a global understanding that captures predicate-argument frame structure. Our approach revolves around a novel integration between a predictive embedding model and an Indian Buffet Process posterior regularizer. We show, through our experimental evaluation, that we outperform baselines on two tasks and can learn an embedded frame lexicon that is able to capture some interesting generalities in relation to hand-crafted semantic frames.

1 Introduction

Semantic lexicons such as PropBank (Palmer et al., 2005) and FrameNet (Baker et al., 1998) contain information about predicate-argument frame structure. These frames capture knowledge about the affinity of predicates for certain types of arguments, their number and their semantic nature, regardless of syntactic realization.

For example, PropBank specifies frames in the following manner:

- eat $\rightarrow$ [agent]$_0$, [patient]$_1$

- give $\rightarrow$ [agent]$_0$, [theme]$_1$, [recipient]$_2$

These frames provide semantic information such as the fact that "eat" is transitive, while "give" is ditransitive, or that the beneficiary of one action is a "patient", while the other is a "recipient".

This structural knowledge is crucial for a number of NLP applications. Information about frames has been successfully used to drive and improve diverse tasks such as information extraction (Surdeanu et al., 2003), semantic parsing (Das et al., 2010) and question answering (Shen and Lapata, 2007), among others.

However, building these frame lexicons is very expensive and time consuming. Thus, it remains difficult to port applications from resource-rich languages or domains to data impoverished ones. The NLP community has tackled this issue along two different lines of unsupervised work.

At the local token level, researchers have attempted to model frame structure by the selectional preference of predicates for certain arguments (Resnik, 1997; Séaghdha, 2010). For example, on this problem a good model might assign a high probability to the word "pasta" occurring as an argument of the word "eat".

Contrastingly, at the global type level, work has focussed on inducing frames by clustering predicates and arguments in a joint framework (Lang and Lapata, 2011a; Titov and Klementiev, 2012b). In this case, one is interested in associating predicates such as "eat", "consume", "devour", with a joint clustering of arguments such as "pasta", "chicken", "burger".

While these methods have been useful for several problems, they also have shortcomings. Selectional preference modelling only captures local predicate-argument affinities, but does not aggregate these associations to arrive at a structural understanding of frames.

Meanwhile, frame induction performs clustering at a global level. But most approaches tend to be algorithmic methods (or some extension thereof) that focus on semantic role labelling.

*Proceedings of the 6th Joint Conference on Lexical and Computational Semantics (*SEM 2017)*, pages 209–219,
Vancouver, Canada, August 3-4, 2017. ©2017 Association for Computational Linguistics

Their lack of portable features or model parameters unfortunately means they cannot be used to solve other applications or problems that require lexicon-level information – such as information extraction or machine translation. Another limitation is that they always depend on high-level linguistic annotation, such as syntactic dependencies, which may not exist in resource-poor settings.

Thus, in this paper we propose to combine the two approaches to induce a frame semantic lexicon in a minimally supervised fashion with nothing more than unlabeled predicate-argument word pairs. Additionally, we will learn an embedded lexicon that jointly produces embeddings for predicates, arguments and an automatically induced collection of latent slots. The embeddings provide flexibility for usage in downstream applications, where predicate-argument affinities can be computed at will.

To jointly capture the local and global streams of knowledge we propose a novel integration between a predictive embedding model and the posterior of an Indian Buffet Process. The embedding model maximizes the predictive accuracy of predicate-argument selectional preference at the local token level, while the posterior of the Indian Buffet process induces an optimal set of latent slots at the global type level that capture the regularities in the learned predicate embeddings.

We evaluate our approach and show that our models are able to outperform baselines on both the local and global level of frame knowledge. At the local level we score higher than a standard predictive embedding model on selectional preference, while at the global level we outperform a syntactic baseline on lexicon overlap with PropBank. Finally, our analysis on the induced latent slots yields insight into some interesting generalities that we are able to capture from unlabeled predicate-argument pairs.

2   Related Work

The work in this paper relates to research on identifying predicate-argument structure in both local and global contexts. These related areas of research correspond to the NLP community's work respectively on selectional preference modelling and semantic frame induction (which is also known variously as unsupervised semantic role labelling or role induction).

Selectional preference modelling seeks to capture the semantic preference of predicates for certain arguments in local contexts. These preferences are useful for many tasks, including unsupervised semantic role labelling (Gildea and Jurafsky, 2002) among others.

Previous work has sought to acquire these preferences using various means, including ontological resources such as WordNet (Resnik, 1997; Ciaramita and Johnson, 2000), latent variable models (Rooth et al., 1999; Séaghdha, 2010; Ritter et al., 2010) and distributional similarity metrics (Erk, 2007). Most closely related to our contribution is the work by Van de Cruys (2014) who use a predictive neural network to capture predicate-argument associations.

To the best of our knowledge, our research is the first to attempt using selectional preference as a basis for directly inducing semantic frames.

At the global level, frame induction subsumes selectional preference by attempting to group arguments of predicates into coherent and cohesive clusters. While work in this area has included diverse approaches, such as leveraging example-based representations (Kawahara et al., 2014) and cross-lingual resources (Fung and Chen, 2004; Titov and Klementiev, 2012b), most attempts have focussed on two broad categories. These are latent variable driven models (Grenager and Manning, 2006; Cheung et al., 2013) and similarity driven clustering models (Lang and Lapata, 2011a,b),

Our work includes elements of both major categories, since we use latent slots to represent arguments, but an Indian Buffet process induces these latent slots in the first place. The work of Titov and Klementiev (2012a) and Woodsend and Lapata (2015) are particularly relevant to our research. The former use another non-parametric Bayesian model (a Chinese Restaurant process) in their work, while the latter embed predicate-argument structures before performing clustering.

Crucially, however all these previous efforts induce frames that are not easily portable to applications other than semantic role labelling (for which they are devised). Moreover, they rely on syntactic cues to featurize and help cluster argument instances. To the best of our knowledge, ours is the first attempt to go from unlabeled bag-of-arguments to induced frame embeddings without any reliance on annotated data.

3 Joint Local and Global Frame Lexicon Induction

In this section we present our approach to induce a frame lexicon with latent slots. Following prior work on frame induction (Lang and Lapata, 2011a; Titov and Klementiev, 2012a), the procedural pipeline can be split into two distinct phases: argument identification and argument clustering.

As with previous work, we focus on the latter stage, and assume that we have unlabeled predicate-argument structure pairs – given to us from gold standard annotation or through heuristic means (Lang and Lapata, 2014).

We begin with preliminary notation. Given a vocabulary of predicate types $P = \{p_1, ..., p_n\}$ and contextual argument types $A = \{a_1, ..., a_m\}$. Let $C = \{(p_1, a_1), ..., (p_N, a_N)\}$ be a corpus of predicate-argument word token pairs[1]. Given this corpus, we will attempt to learn an optimal set of model parameters θ that maximizes a regularized likelihood over the corpus.

The model parameters include $V = \{v_i \mid \forall p_i \in P\}$ an $n \times d$ embedding matrix for the predicates and $U = \{u_i \mid \forall a_i \in A\}$ an $m \times d$ embedding matrix for the arguments. Additionally, assuming K latent frame slots we define $Z = \{z_{ik}\}$ an $n \times k$ binary matrix that represents the presence or absence of the slot k for the predicate i, and a latent $K \times d$ weight matrix $S = \{s_k \mid 1 \leq k \leq K\}$ that associates a weight vector to each latent slot.

The generalized form of the objective we optimize is given by:

$$\hat{\theta} = \arg\max_{\theta} \sum_{(p_i, a_i) \in C} \log \left(\sum_k Pr(a_i | p_i, z_{ik}, s_k) \right) + \log pr_\theta(Z|V) \quad (1)$$

This objective has two parts: a likelihood term, and a posterior regularizer. The former will be responsible for modelling the predictive accuracy of selectional-preference at a local level, while the latter will capture global consistencies for an optimal set of latent slots.

We detail the parametrization of each of these components separately in what follows.

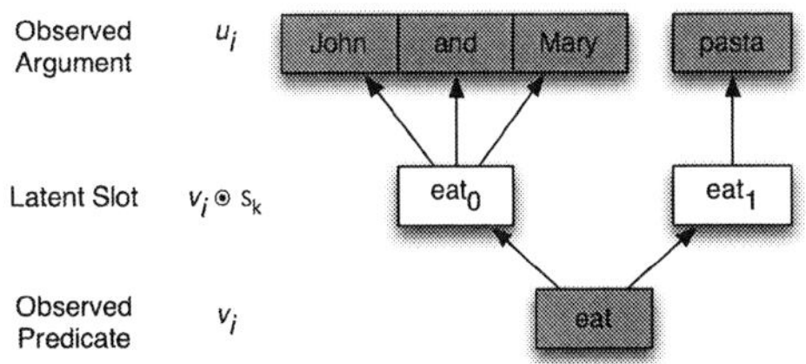

Figure 1: The generative story depicting the realization of an argument from a predicate. Argument words are generated from latent argument slots. Observed variables are shaded in grey, while latent variables are in white.

3.1 Local Predicate-Argument Likelihood

The likelihood term of our model is based on the popular Skip-gram model from Mikolov et al. (2013) but suitably extended to incorporate the latent frame slots and their associated weights. Specifically, we define the probability for a single predicate-argument pair (p_i, a_i) as:

$$Pr(a_i|p_i) = \sum_k Pr(a_i|p_i, z_{ik}, s_k) =$$

$$\sum_k z_{ik} \frac{\exp((v_i \odot s_k) \cdot u_i)}{\sum_{a_{i'}} \exp((v_i \odot s_k) \cdot u_{i'})} \quad (2)$$

where $\odot$ represents the element-wise multiplication operator. Intuitively, in the likelihood term we weight a general predicate embedding to a slot-specific representations, which then predicts a specific argument. This is graphically represented in Figure 1.

3.2 Global Latent Slot Regularization

The posterior regularization term in equation 1 seeks to balance the likelihood term by yielding an optimal set of latent slots, given the embedding matrix of predicates.

We choose the posterior of an Indian Buffet process (IBP) (Griffiths and Ghahramani, 2005) in this step to induce an optimal latent binary matrix Z. The IBP itself places a prior on equivalence classes of infinite dimensional sparse binary matrices, and is the infinite limit ($K \to \infty$) of a beta-Bernoulli model.

$$\pi_k \sim Beta(\alpha/K, 1)$$
$$z_{ik} \sim Bernoulli(\pi_k) \quad (3)$$

Given a suitable likelihood function and some

---

[1]In this work, we assume argument chunks are broken down into individual words, – to increase training data size – but the model remains agnostic to this decision.

data, inference in an IBP computes a posterior that yields an optimal *finite* binary matrix with respect to regularities in the data.

Setting the *data*, in our case, to be the embedding matrix of predicates V, this gives us precisely what we are seeking. It allows us to find regularities in the embeddings, while factorizing them according to these consistencies. The model also automatically optimizes the number of and relationship between latent slots, rather than setting these a priori.

Other desiderata are encoded as well, including the fact that the the the matrix Z remains sparse, while the frequency of slots follows a power-law distribution proportional to Poisson(α). In practise, this captures the power-law distribution of relational slots in real-world semantic lexicons such as PropBank (Palmer et al., 2005). All of these properties stem directly from the choice of prior, and are a natural consequence of using an IBP.

In this paper, we use a linear-Gaussian model as the likelihood function. This is a popular model that has been applied to several problems, and for which different approximate inference strategies have been developed (Doshi-Velez et al., 2009; Doshi-Velez and Ghahramani, 2009). According to his model, the predicate embeddings are distributed as:

$$v_i \sim Gaussian(z_i W, \sigma_V^2 \mathbf{I}) \qquad (4)$$

where W is a $K \times d$ matrix of weights and σ_V is a hyperparameter.

For a detailed derivation of the posterior of an IBP prior with a linear-Gaussian likelihood, we point the reader to Griffiths and Ghahramani (2011), who provide a meticulous summary.

3.3 Optimization

Since our objective in equation 1 contains two distinct components, we can optimize using alternating maximization. Although guaranteed convergence for this technique only exist for convex functions, it has proven successful even for non-convex problems (Jain et al., 2013; Netrapalli et al., 2013).

We thus alternate between keeping Z fixed and optimizing the parameters V, U, S in the likelihood component of section 3.1, and keeping V fixed and optimizing the parameters Z in the posterior regularization component of section 3.2.

In practise, the likelihood component is optimized using negative sampling with EM for the latent slots. In particular we use *hard* EM, to select a single slot before taking gradient steps with respect to the model parameters. This was shown to work well for Skip-gram style models with latent variables by Jauhar et al. (2015).

In the E-Step we find the best latent slot for a particular predicate-argument pair:

$$\hat{k} = \arg\max_k Pr(a_i | p_i, z_{ik}, s_k) \qquad (5)$$

We follow this by making stochastic gradient updates to the model parameters U, V, S in the M-Step using the negative sampling objective:

$$\log z_{i\hat{k}} \sigma \left((v_i \odot s_{\hat{k}}) \cdot u_i \right) +$$
$$\sum_l \mathbb{E}_{a_{i'} \sim Pr_n(a)} \left[\log z_{i\hat{k}} \sigma \left((v_i \odot s_{\hat{k}}) \cdot u_{i'} \right) \right] \qquad (6)$$

where $\sigma(\cdot)$ is the sigmoid function, $Pr_n(a)$ is a unigram noise distribution over argument types and l is the negative sampling parameter.

As for optimizing the posterior regularization component, an approximate inference technique such as Gibbs sampling must be used. In Gibbs sampling we iteratively sample individual z_{ik} terms from the posterior:

$$Pr(z_{ik} | X, Z_{-ik}) \propto Pr(X|Z) \cdot Pr(z_{ik} | Z_{-ik}) \qquad (7)$$

where Z_{-ik} is the Markov blanket of z_{ik} in Z. The prior and likelihood terms are respectively those of equations 3 and 4. Doshi-Velez and Ghahramani (2009) present an accelerated version of Gibbs sampling for this model, that computes the likelihood and prior terms efficiently. We use this approach in our work since it has the benefits of mixing like a collapsed sampler, while maintaining the running time of an uncollapsed sampler.

In conclusion, the optimization steps iteratively refine the parameters V, U, S to be better predictors of the corpus, while Z is updated to best factorize the regularities in the predicate embeddings V, thereby capturing better relational slots.

3.4 Relational Variant

In addition to the standard model introduced above, we also experiment with an extension where the input corpus consists of predicate-argument-relation triples instead of just predicate-argument pairs. These relations are observed relations, and should not be confused with the latent slots of the model.

To accommodate this change we modify the argument embedding matrix U to be of dimensions $m \times \frac{d}{2}$ and introduce a new $q \times \frac{d}{2}$ embedding matrix $R = \{r_i \mid 1 \leq i \leq q\}$ for the q observed relation types.

Then, wherever the original model calls for an argument vector u_i (which had dimensionality d) we instead replace it with a concatenated argument-relation vector $[u_i; r_j]$ (which now also has dimensionality d). During training, we must make gradient updates to R in addition to all the other model parameters as usual.

While this relation indicator can be used to capture arbitrary relational information, in this paper we set it to a combination of the directionality of the argument with respect to the predicate (L or R), and the preposition immediately preceding the argument phrase (or *None* if there isn't one). Thus, for example, we have relational indicators such as "L-on", "R-before", "L-because", "R-None", etc. We obtain a total of 146 such relations.

Note, that in keeping with the goals of this work, these relation indicators still require no annotation (prepositions are closed-class words than can be enumerated).

4 Experiments and Evaluation

In what follows, we detail experimental results on two quantitative evaluation tasks: at the local and global levels of predicate-argument structure. In particular we evaluate on pseudo disambiguation of selectional preference, and semantic frame lexicon overlap. We also qualitatively inspect the learned latent relations against hand-annotated roles. We first specify the implementational details.

4.1 Implementational Details

We begin by pre-training standard skip-gram vectors (Mikolov et al., 2013) on the NY-Times section of the Gigaword corpus, which consists of approximately 1.67 billion word tokens. These vectors are used as initialization for the embedding matrices V and U, before our iterative optimization. While this step is not strictly required, we found that it leads to generally better results than random initialization given the relatively small size of our predicate-argument training corpus.

For training our models, we use a combination of the training data released for the CoNLL 2008 shared task (Surdeanu et al., 2008) and the extended PropBank release which covers annotations of the Ontonotes (Hovy et al., 2006) and English Web Treebank (Bies et al., 2012) corpora. We reserve the test portion of the CoNLL 2008 shared task data for one of our evaluations.

In this work, we only focus on verbal predicates. Our training data gives us a vocabulary of 4449 predicates, after pruning verbs that occur fewer than 5 times.

Then, from the training data we extract all predicate-argument pairs using gold standard argument annotations, for the sake of simplicity. Note that previous unsupervised frame induction work also uses gold argument mentions (Lang and Lapata, 2011a; Titov and Klementiev, 2012b). Our method, however, does not depend on this, or any other annotation, and we could as easily use the output from an automated system such as Abend et al. (2009) instead.

In this manner, we obtain a total of approximately 3.35 million predicate-argument word pairs on which to train.

Using this data we train a total of 4 distinct models: a base model and a relational variant (see Section 3.4), both of which are trained with two different IBP hyperparameters of $\alpha = 0.35$ and $\alpha = 0.7$. The hyperparameter controls the avidity of the model for latent slots (a higher α implies a greater number of induced slots).

This results in the learned number of slots ranging from 17 to 30, with the conservative model averaging about 4 latent slots per word, while the permissive model averaging about 6 latent slots per word.

Since our objective is non-convex we record the training likelihood at each power iteration (including an optimization over both the predictive and IBP components of our objective), and save the model with the highest training likelihood.

We set our embedding size to $d = 100$ and, after training, obtain latent slot factors ranging in number from 15 to 30.

Model	α	Variant	k slots	% Acc
Skip-gram	-	-	-	0.77
pa2IBPVec	0.35	Standard	17	0.81
		Relational	15	**0.84**
	0.7	Standard	27	0.81
		Relational	30	0.81

Table 1: Results on pseudo disambiguation of selectional preference. Numbers are in % accuracy of distinguishing true arguments from false ones. Our models all outperform the skip-gram baseline.

4.2 Pseudo Disambiguation of Selection Preference

The pseudo disambiguation task aims to evaluate our models' ability to capture predicate-argument knowledge at the local level. In this task, systems are presented with a set of triples: a predicate, a true argument and a fake argument. The systems are evaluated on the percentage of true arguments they are able to select.

For example, given a triple:

resign, post, liquidation

a successful model should rate the pair "resign-post" higher than "resign-liquidation".

This task has often been used in the selectional preference modelling literature as a benchmark task (Rooth et al., 1999; Van de Cruys, 2014) .

To obtain the triples for this task we use the test set of the CoNLL 2008 shared task data. In particular, for every verbal predicate mention in the data we select a random nominal word from each of its arguments phrase chunks to obtain a true predicate-argument word pair. Then, to introduce distractors, we sample a random nominal from a unigram noise distribution. In this way we obtain 9859 pseudo disambiguation triples as our test set.

We use our models to score a word pair by taking the probability of the pair under our model, using the best latent slot:

$$\max_k z_{ik}\sigma\left((v_i \odot s_k) \cdot u_i\right) \qquad (8)$$

where v_i and u_i are predicate and argument embeddings respectively, z_{ik} is the binary indicator of the k'th slot for the i'th predicate, and s_k is the slot specific weight vector. The argument in the higher scoring pair is selected as the correct one.

In the relational variant, instead of the single argument vector u_i we also take a max over the relation indicators – since the exact indicator is not observed at test time.

We compare our models against a standard skip-gram model (Mikolov et al., 2013) trained on the same data. Word pairs in this model are scored using the dot product between their associated skip-gram vectors.

This is a fair comparison since our models as well as the skip-gram model have access to the same data – namely predicates and their neighboring argument words. They are trained on their ability to discriminate true argument words from randomly sampled noise. The evaluation then, is whether the additionally learned slot structure helps in differentiating true arguments from noise. The results of this evaluation are presented in Table 1.

The results show that all our models outperform the skip-gram baseline. This demonstrates that the added structural information gained from latent slots in fact help our models to better capture predicate-argument affinities in local contexts.

The impact of latent slots or additional relation information does not seem to impact basic performance, however. This could be because of the trade-off that occurs when a more complex model is learned from the same amount of limited data.

4.3 Frame Lexicon Overlap

Next, we evaluate our models at their ability to capture global predicate-argument structure. Previous work on frame induction has focussed on evaluating instance-based argument overlap with gold standard annotations in the context of semantic role labelling (SRL). Unfortunately, because our models operate on individual predicate-argument words rather than argument spans a fair comparison becomes problematic.

But unlike previous work, which clusters argument instances, our approach produces a model as a result of training. We can thus directly evaluate this model's latent slot factors against a gold standard frame lexicon. Our evaluation framework is, in many ways based on the metrics used in unsupervised SRL, except applied at the "type" lexicon level rather than the corpus-based "token" cluster level.

In particular, given a gold frame lexicon Ω with K^* real argument slots (i.e. the total number of

Model	α	Variant	Coarse			Fine		
			PU	CO	F1	PU	CO	F1
Syntax	-	-	0.71	0.87	0.78	0.70	0.91	0.79
pa2IBPVec	0.35	Standard	0.76	0.89	0.82	0.76	0.97	0.85
	0.35	Relational	0.73	0.90	0.81	0.73	0.97	0.83
	0.7	Standard	0.79	0.91	**0.85**	0.79	**0.98**	0.87
	0.7	Relational	**0.80**	**0.92**	**0.85**	**0.80**	**0.98**	**0.88**

Table 2: Results on the lexicon overlap task. Our models outperform the syntactic baseline on all the metrics.

possible humanly assigned arguments in the lexicon), we evaluate our models' latent slot matrix Z in terms of its overlap with the gold lexicon.

We define *purity* as the average proportion of overlap between predicted latent slots and their maximally similar gold lexicon slots:

$$PU = \frac{1}{K} \sum_k \max_{k'} \frac{1}{n} \sum_i \delta(\omega_{ik'}, z_{ik}) \qquad (9)$$

where $\delta(\cdot)$ is an indicator function. Given that the ω's and z's we compare are binary values, this indicator function is effectively an "XNOR" gate.

Similarly we define *collocation* as the average proportion of overlap between gold standard slots and their maximally similar predicted latent slots:

$$CO = \frac{1}{K^*} \sum_{k'} \max_k \frac{1}{n} \sum_i \delta(\omega_{ik'}, z_{ik}) \qquad (10)$$

Given, the *purity* and *collocation* metrics we can define the $F1$ score as the harmonic mean of the two:

$$F1 = \frac{2 \cdot CO \cdot PU}{CO + PU} \qquad (11)$$

In our experiments we use the frame files provided with the PropBank corpus (Palmer et al., 2005) as gold standard. We derive two variants from the frame files.

The first is a coarse-grained lexicon. In this case, we extract only the functional arguments of verbs in our vocabulary as gold standard slots. These functions correspond to broad semantic argument types such as "prototypical agent", "prototypical patient", "instrument", "benefactive", etc. A total of 16 gold slots are produced in this manner, and are mapped to indices. For every verb the corresponding binary ω vector marks the existence or not of the different functional arguments according to the gold frame files.

The second variant is a fine-grained lexicon. Here, in addition to functional arguments we also consider the numerical argument with which it is associated, such as "ARG0", "ARG1" etc. Note that a single functional argument may appear with more than one numerical slot with different verbs over the entire lexicon. The fine-grained lexicon yields 72 gold slots.

We compare our models against a baseline inspired from the syntactic baseline often used for evaluating unsupervised SRL models. For unsupervised SRL, syntax has proven to be a difficult to outperform baseline (Lang and Lapata, 2014).

This baseline is constructed by taking the 21 most frequent syntactic labels in the training data and associating them each with a slot. All other syntactic labels are associated with a 22nd generic slot. Given these slots, we associate a verbal predicate with a specific slot if it takes on the corresponding syntactic argument in the training data. The results on the lexicon overlap task are presented in Table 2.

They show that our models consistently outperform the syntactic baseline on all metrics in both the coarse-grained and fine-grained settings. We conclude that our models are better able to capture predicate-argument structure at a global level.

Inspecting and comparing the results of our different models seems to indicate that we perform better when our IBP posterior allows for a greater number of latent slots. This happens when the hyperparameter $\alpha = 0.7$.

Additionally our models consistently perform better on the fine-grained lexicon than on the coarse-grained one. The former itself does not necessarily represent an easier benchmark, since there is hardly any difference in the $F1$ score of the syntactic baseline on the two lexicons.

Overall it would seem that allowing for a greater number of latent slots does help capture global

Predicate	Latent Slot							
	1	2	3	5	6	8	10	12
provide	A0			A1	A2			A2
enter	A0	A1						AM-ADV
praise	A0	A1				A2		
travel	A0	A0				AM-PNC	AM-TMP	
distract	A0		A1	A2				
overcome	AM-TMP		A0	A0				

Table 3: Examples for several predicates with mappings of latent slots to the majority class of the closest argument vector in the shared embedded space.

predicate-argument structure better. This makes sense, if we consider the fact that we are effectively trying to factorize a dense representation (the predicate embeddings) with IBP inference. Thus allowing for a greater number of latent factors permits the discovery of greater structural consistency within these embeddings.

This finding does have some problematic implications, however. Increasing the IBP hyperparameter α arbitrarily represents a computational bottleneck since inference scales quadratically with the number of latent slots K. There is also the problem of splitting argument slots too finely, which may result in optimizing purity at the expense of collocation. A solution to this trade-off between performance and inference time remains for future work.

4.4 Qualitative Analysis of Latent Slots

To better understand the nature of the latent slots induced by our model we conduct an additional qualitative analysis. The goal of this analysis is to inspect the kinds of generalities about semantic roles that our model is able to capture from completely unannotated data.

Table 3 lists some examples of predicates and their associated latent slots. The latent slots are sorted according to their frequency (i.e. column sum in the binary slot matrix Z). We map each latent slot to the majority semantic role type – from training data – of the closest argument word to the predicate vector in the shared embedding space.

The model for which we perform this qualitative analysis is the standard variant with the IBP hyperparameter set to $\alpha = 0.35$; this model has 17 latent slots. Note that slots that do not feature for any of the verbs are omitted for visual compactness.

There are several interesting trends to notice

here. Firstly, the basic argument structure of predicates is often correctly identified, when matched against gold PropBank frame files. For example, the core roles of "enter" identify it as a transitive verb, while "praise", "provide" and "distract" are correctly shown as ditransitive verbs. Obviously the structure isn't always perfectly identified, as with the verb "travel" where we are missing both an "ARG1" and an "ARG2".

In certain cases a single argument type spans multiple slots – as with "A2" for "provide" and "A0" for "travel". This is not surprising, since there is no binding factor on the model to produce one-to-one mappings with hand-crafted semantic roles. Generally speaking, the slots represent distributions over hand-crafted roles rather than strict mappings. In fact, to expect a one-to-one mapping is unreasonable considering we use no annotations whatsoever.

Nevertheless, there is still some consistency in the mappings. The core arguments of verbs – such as "ARG0" and "ARG1" are typically mapped to the most frequent latent slots. This can be explained by the fact that the more frequent arguments tend to be the ones that are core to a predicate's frame. This is quite a surprising outcome of the model, considering that it is given no annotation about argument types. Of course, we do not always get this right as can be seen with the case of "overcome", where a non-core argument occurs in the most frequent slot.

Since this is a data driven approach, we identify non-core roles as well, if they occur with predicates often enough in the data. For example we have the general purpose "AM-ADV" argument of "enter", and the "ARG-PNC" and "ARG-TMP" (purpose and time arguments) of the verb "travel". In future work we hope to explore methods that might be able to automatically distinguish core slots from non-core ones.

In conclusion, our model show promise in that it is able to capture some interesting generalities with respect to predicates and their hand-crafted roles, without the need for any annotated data.

5   Conclusion and Future Work

We have presented a first attempt at learning an embedded frame lexicon from data, using no annotated information. Our approach revolves around jointly capturing local predicate-argument affinities with global slot-level consistencies. We model this approach with a novel integration between a predictive embedding model and the posterior of an Indian Buffet Process.

We experiment with our model on two quantitative tasks, each designed to evaluate performance on capturing local and global predicate-argument structure respectively. On both tasks we demonstrate that our models are able to outperform baselines, thus indicating our ability to jointly model the local and global level information of predicate-argument structure.

Additionally, we qualitatively inspect our induced latent slots and show that we are able to capture some interesting generalities with regards to hand-crafted semantic role labels.

There are several avenues of future work we are exploring. Rather than depend on gold argument mentions in training, we hope to fully automate the pipeline to leverage much larger amounts of data. With this greater data size, we also will likely no longer need to break down argument spans into individual words. Instead, we plan to models these spans as chunks using an LSTM.

With this additional modeling power we hope to evaluate on downstream applications such as semantic role labelling, and semantic parsing.

In a separate line of work we hope to be able to parallelize the Indian Buffet Process inference, which remains a bottleneck of our current effort. Speeding up this process will allow us to explore more complex (and potentially better) models.

Acknowledgments

The authors would like to thank the anonymous reviewers for their valuable comments and suggestions to improve the quality of the paper. This work was supported in part by the following grants: NSF grant IIS-1143703, NSF award IIS-1147810, DARPA grant FA87501220342.

References

Omri Abend, Roi Reichart, and Ari Rappoport. 2009. Unsupervised argument identification for semantic role labeling. In *Proceedings of the Joint Conference of the 47th Annual Meeting of the ACL and the 4th International Joint Conference on Natural Language Processing of the AFNLP: Volume 1-Volume 1*. Association for Computational Linguistics, pages 28–36.

Collin F Baker, Charles J Fillmore, and John B Lowe. 1998. The berkeley framenet project. In *Proceedings of the 36th Annual Meeting of the Association for Computational Linguistics and 17th International Conference on Computational Linguistics-Volume 1*. Association for Computational Linguistics, pages 86–90.

Ann Bies, Justin Mott, Colin Warner, and Seth Kulick. 2012. English web treebank. *Linguistic Data Consortium, Philadelphia, PA* .

Jackie Chi Kit Cheung, Hoifung Poon, and Lucy Vanderwende. 2013. Probabilistic frame induction. *arXiv preprint arXiv:1302.4813* .

Massimiliano Ciaramita and Mark Johnson. 2000. Explaining away ambiguity: Learning verb selectional preference with bayesian networks. In *Proceedings of the 18th conference on Computational linguistics-Volume 1*. Association for Computational Linguistics, pages 187–193.

Dipanjan Das, Nathan Schneider, Desai Chen, and Noah A Smith. 2010. Probabilistic frame-semantic parsing. In *Human language technologies: The 2010 annual conference of the North American chapter of the association for computational linguistics*. Association for Computational Linguistics, pages 948–956.

Finale Doshi-Velez and Zoubin Ghahramani. 2009. Accelerated sampling for the indian buffet process. In *Proceedings of the 26th annual international conference on machine learning*. ACM, pages 273–280.

Finale Doshi-Velez, Kurt T Miller, Jurgen Van Gael, Yee Whye Teh, and Gatsby Unit. 2009. Variational inference for the indian buffet process. In *Proceedings of the Intl. Conf. on Artificial Intelligence and Statistics*. volume 12, pages 137–144.

Katrin Erk. 2007. A simple, similarity-based model for selectional preferences. In *Annual Meeting - Association For Computational Linguistics*. volume 45, page 216.

Pascale Fung and Benfeng Chen. 2004. Biframenet: bilingual frame semantics resource construction by cross-lingual induction. In *Proceedings of the 20th international conference on Computational Linguistics*. Association for Computational Linguistics, page 931.

Daniel Gildea and Daniel Jurafsky. 2002. Automatic labeling of semantic roles. *Computational linguistics* 28(3):245–288.

Trond Grenager and Christopher D Manning. 2006. Unsupervised discovery of a statistical verb lexicon. In *Proceedings of the 2006 Conference on Empirical Methods in Natural Language Processing*. Association for Computational Linguistics, pages 1–8.

Thomas L Griffiths and Zoubin Ghahramani. 2005. Infinite latent feature models and the indian buffet process. In *NIPS*. volume 18, pages 475–482.

Thomas L Griffiths and Zoubin Ghahramani. 2011. The indian buffet process: An introduction and review. *Journal of Machine Learning Research* 12(Apr):1185–1224.

Eduard Hovy, Mitchell Marcus, Martha Palmer, Lance Ramshaw, and Ralph Weischedel. 2006. Ontonotes: the 90% solution. In *Proceedings of the human language technology conference of the NAACL, Companion Volume: Short Papers*. Association for Computational Linguistics, pages 57–60.

Prateek Jain, Praneeth Netrapalli, and Sujay Sanghavi. 2013. Low-rank matrix completion using alternating minimization. In *Proceedings of the forty-fifth annual ACM symposium on Theory of computing*. ACM, pages 665–674.

Sujay Kumar Jauhar, Chris Dyer, and Eduard H Hovy. 2015. Ontologically grounded multi-sense representation learning for semantic vector space models. In *HLT-NAACL*. pages 683–693.

Daisuke Kawahara, Daniel Peterson, Octavian Popescu, Martha Palmer, and Fondazione Bruno Kessler. 2014. Inducing example-based semantic frames from a massive amount of verb uses. In *EACL*. pages 58–67.

Joel Lang and Mirella Lapata. 2011a. Unsupervised semantic role induction via split-merge clustering. In *Proceedings of the 49th Annual Meeting of the Association for Computational Linguistics: Human Language Technologies-Volume 1*. Association for Computational Linguistics, pages 1117–1126.

Joel Lang and Mirella Lapata. 2011b. Unsupervised semantic role induction with graph partitioning. In *Proceedings of the conference on empirical methods in natural language processing*. Association for Computational Linguistics, pages 1320–1331.

Joel Lang and Mirella Lapata. 2014. Similarity-driven semantic role induction via graph partitioning. *Computational Linguistics* 40(3):633–669.

Tomas Mikolov, Kai Chen, Greg Corrado, and Jeffrey Dean. 2013. Efficient estimation of word representations in vector space. *arXiv preprint arXiv:1301.3781* .

Praneeth Netrapalli, Prateek Jain, and Sujay Sanghavi. 2013. Phase retrieval using alternating minimization. In *Advances in Neural Information Processing Systems*. pages 2796–2804.

Martha Palmer, Daniel Gildea, and Paul Kingsbury. 2005. The proposition bank: An annotated corpus of semantic roles. *Computational linguistics* 31(1):71–106.

Philip Resnik. 1997. Selectional preference and sense disambiguation. In *Proceedings of the ACL SIGLEX Workshop on Tagging Text with Lexical Semantics: Why, What, and How*. Washington, DC, pages 52–57.

Alan Ritter, Mausam, and Oren Etzioni. 2010. A latent dirichlet allocation method for selectional preferences. In *Proceedings of the 48th Annual Meeting of the Association for Computational Linguistics*. Association for Computational Linguistics, pages 424–434.

Mats Rooth, Stefan Riezler, Detlef Prescher, Glenn Carroll, and Franz Beil. 1999. Inducing a semantically annotated lexicon via em-based clustering. In *Proceedings of the 37th annual meeting of the Association for Computational Linguistics on Computational Linguistics*. Association for Computational Linguistics, pages 104–111.

Diarmuid O Séaghdha. 2010. Latent variable models of selectional preference. In *Proceedings of the 48th Annual Meeting of the Association for Computational Linguistics*. Association for Computational Linguistics, pages 435–444.

Dan Shen and Mirella Lapata. 2007. Using semantic roles to improve question answering. In *EMNLP-CoNLL*. pages 12–21.

Mihai Surdeanu, Sanda Harabagiu, John Williams, and Paul Aarseth. 2003. Using predicate-argument structures for information extraction. In *Proceedings of the 41st Annual Meeting on Association for Computational Linguistics-Volume 1*. Association for Computational Linguistics, pages 8–15.

Mihai Surdeanu, Richard Johansson, Adam Meyers, Lluís Màrquez, and Joakim Nivre. 2008. The conll-2008 shared task on joint parsing of syntactic and semantic dependencies. In *Proceedings of the Twelfth Conference on Computational Natural Language Learning*. Association for Computational Linguistics, pages 159–177.

Ivan Titov and Alexandre Klementiev. 2012a. A bayesian approach to unsupervised semantic role induction. In *Proceedings of the 13th Conference of the European Chapter of the Association for Computational Linguistics*. Association for Computational Linguistics, pages 12–22.

Ivan Titov and Alexandre Klementiev. 2012b. Crosslingual induction of semantic roles. In *Proceedings of the 50th Annual Meeting of the*

Association for Computational Linguistics: Long Papers-Volume 1. Association for Computational Linguistics, pages 647–656.

Tim Van de Cruys. 2014. A neural network approach to selectional preference acquisition. In *EMNLP*. pages 26–35.

Kristian Woodsend and Mirella Lapata. 2015. Distributed representations for unsupervised semantic role labeling. In *EMNLP*. Citeseer, pages 2482–2491.

Generating Pattern-Based Entailment Graphs for Relation Extraction

Kathrin Eichler, Feiyu Xu, Hans Uszkoreit, Sebastian Krause
German Research Center for Artificial Intelligence (DFKI)
Berlin, Germany
`firstname.lastname@dfki.de`

Abstract

Relation extraction is the task of recognizing and extracting relations between entities or concepts in texts. A common approach is to exploit existing knowledge to learn linguistic patterns expressing the target relation and use these patterns for extracting new relation mentions. Deriving relation patterns automatically usually results in large numbers of candidates, which need to be filtered to derive a subset of patterns that reliably extract correct relation mentions. We address the pattern selection task by exploiting the knowledge represented by entailment graphs, which capture semantic relationships holding among the learned pattern candidates. This is motivated by the fact that a pattern may not express the target relation explicitly, but still be useful for extracting instances for which the relation holds, because its meaning *entails* the meaning of the target relation. We evaluate the usage of both automatically generated and gold-standard entailment graphs in a relation extraction scenario and present favorable experimental results, exhibiting the benefits of structuring and selecting patterns based on entailment graphs.

1 Introduction

The task of relation extraction (RE) is to recognize and extract relations among entities or concepts mentioned in texts. One common approach to RE is to learn and exploit extraction patterns (e.g., based on syntactic dependency trees), which express the targeted semantic relations. In order to circumvent the manual creation of patterns, nu-

merous approaches have been investigated to derive patterns automatically. Automatic methods generally induce large numbers of unique candidate patterns, which only potentially express the target relation and need to be filtered in order to derive a subset of high-quality patterns for the relation extraction task. The task of filtering or selecting patterns can be tackled in various ways, e.g., based on frequency information, or by applying syntactic or semantic criteria.

For many RE applications, such as knowledge base population, patterns are not only relevant if they express the target relation explicitly, but also if they extract facts from which the target relation can be inferred. For example, all patterns below can be utilized for extracting pairs of people who are or were involved in a marriage relation:

P1: PERSON_1 <marry> PERSON_2[1]

P2: PERSON_1 <be widow of> PERSON_2

P3: PERSON_1 <divorce from> PERSON_2

However, only pattern P1 expresses the target relation explicitly. Patterns P2 and P3 are semantically different from P1, but express a fact that *entails* the marriage relation[2]. As being aware of these semantic relationships holding among patterns can be of help in the pattern selection process, we propose to capture and exploit these relationships using pattern-based entailment graphs and show how technology from the area of recognizing textual entailment can be adapted to automatically generate these graphs. Finally, we apply the generated knowledge for relation extraction.

---

[1] PERSON_x refers to a slot filler for a person recognized in the input from which the pattern was extracted, <text> refers to a normalized form of the text part of the extracted pattern.

[2] We ignore tense aspects for the time being, which is also the approach taken in the RTE challenges (Dagan et al., 2005).

*Proceedings of the 6th Joint Conference on Lexical and Computational Semantics (*SEM 2017)*, pages 220–229,
Vancouver, Canada, August 3-4, 2017. ©2017 Association for Computational Linguistics

2   Related Work

The task of estimating the quality of automatically learned extraction patterns has been dealt with in various ways, for example based on integrity constraints (Agichtein, 2006), frequency heuristics (Krause et al., 2012) or lexical semantic criteria (Moro et al., 2013). Another line of research in RE groups similar patterns, e.g., by merging patterns based on syntactic criteria (Banko et al., 2007; Shinyama and Sekine, 2006; Thomas et al., 2011; Angeli et al., 2015), by clustering patterns that are semantically related (Kok and Domingos, 2008; Yates and Etzioni, 2009; Yao et al., 2011), or by identifying patterns associated to a given seed relation (Bauer et al., 2014). Such approaches help gain generalization; however, their ability to express semantic relationships is limited, as they cannot capture the asymmetric nature of these relationships. For example, clustering can help us identify pattern P4 below as being semantically related to patterns P1 to P3 in section 1.

$$\text{P4: } \text{PERSON}_1 \text{ <love> } \text{PERSON}_2$$

However, it falls short of expressing that two entities linked by patterns P1 to P3 are mentions of the marriage relation, whereas this is not necessarily true of entities linked by pattern P4. Similarly, clustering can identify patterns P1 and P3 as semantically related. However, it cannot express that the relation expressed by pattern P3 entails the relation expressed by pattern P1, but not vice versa. These asymmetric relationships have been considered by Riedel et al. (2013), who learns latent feature vectors for patterns based on matrix factorization, and have also been studied extensively in the context of recognizing textual entailment (RTE). RTE is the task of determining, for two textual expressions T (text) and H (hypothesis), whether the meaning of H can be inferred from the meaning of T (Dagan and Glickman, 2004). In RE, RTE systems have been applied to validate a given relation instance (Wang and Neumann, 2008) and to extract instances entailing a given target relation (Romano et al., 2006; Bar-Haim et al., 2007; Roth et al., 2009).

As illustrated above, RE can clearly benefit from considering semantic relationships holding among extraction patterns. However, previous work in RE has either focussed on grouping related patterns without considering non-symmetric relations, or, on computing entailment decisions for individual T/H pairs. We propose to exploit entailment relationships holding among RE patterns by structuring the candidate set in an *entailment graph*. Entailment graphs are hierarchical structures representing entailment relations among textual expressions and have previously been generated for various types of expressions (Berant et al., 2010, 2012; Mehdad et al., 2013; Levy et al., 2014; Kotlerman et al., 2015). Entailment graphs can be constructed by determining entailment relationships between pairs of expressions or, as proposed by Kolesnyk et al. (2016), by generating entailed sentences from source sentences. Our work of building entailment graphs based on RE patterns is related to the work by Nakashole et al. (2012), who create a taxonomy of binary relation patterns. For their syntactic patterns, they compute partial orders of generalization and subsumption based on the set of mentions extracted by each pattern. In contrast to their work, we construct pattern-based entailment graphs using RTE technology. This is motivated by the fact that entailment is semantic and not mention-based, i.e., one pattern can entail another pattern even if they extract disjoint sets of mentions in a given text corpus.

3   Entailment Graph Generation

3.1   Pattern-Based Entailment Graphs

A pattern-based entailment graph refers to a directed graph, in which each node represents a unique RE pattern, and each edge ($\rightarrow$) denotes an entailment relationship. Bidirectional edges ($\leftrightarrow$) denote that the patterns represented by the two nodes are considered semantically equivalent. A sample subgraph for the *marriage* relation is given in Figure 1[3], which shows all entailment relations with respect to the pattern [PERSON$_1$ <marry> PERSON$_2$]. Automatic entailment graph generation is usually performed in two steps: First, entailment decisions for individual T/H pairs are computed (using an RTE engine); second, an optimization strategy is applied to derive a consistent, transitive graph (Berant et al., 2010).

3.2   RTE Engine

For recognizing entailment relations between individual T/H pairs of patterns, we make use

---

[3]For reasons of simplicity, the figure shows the text representation of the patterns, which are in fact represented as dependency structures. Since entailment is transitive, all edges are omitted that can be recovered in the transitive closure.

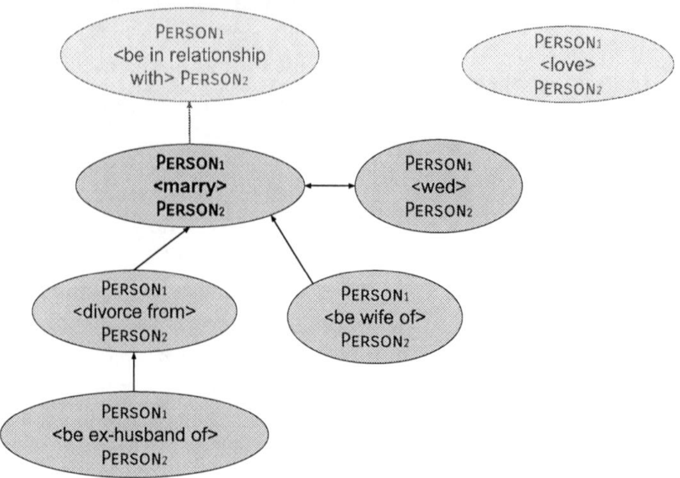

Figure 1: Subgraph showing entailment relations for the pattern [PERSON$_1$ <marry> PERSON$_2$]

of an RTE engine based on multi-level alignments. This RTE engine, referred to as *Multi-Align*, is available through the RTE platform EXCITEMENT (Magnini et al., 2014) and achieved state-of-the-art performance on several RTE corpora (Noh et al., 2015). We opted for this RTE system because it makes use of external knowledge resources and, unlike more recent systems based on neural networks (Rocktäschel et al., 2015; Bowman et al., 2015), is able to cope with the restricted amount of training data available for the task. *MultiAlign* uses shallow parsing for linguistic preprocessing and logistic regression for entailment classification. Features for the classifier are generated on the basis of multi-level alignments using four aligners: a lemma aligner (aligning identical lemmas found in T and H), an aligner based on the paraphrase tables provided by the METEOR MT evaluation package (Denkowski and Lavie, 2014), and two lexical aligners based on Wordnet (Fellbaum, 1998)[4] and VerbOcean (Chklovski and Pantel, 2004). As output, it produces a binary decision (entailment, non-entailment) along with a computed confidence score.

As the RTE engine was originally designed for sentences, rather than patterns, we converted each pattern into its textual representation. The variables expressing type and semantic role of the entities linked by the pattern were excluded in this representation, as the resulting variable alignments would skew the RTE engine's entailment decision. For our experiments, we used the original *MultiAlign* implementation as well as an adapted version, in which we made some changes to the WordNet aligner. In particular, unlike in the original implementation, which only considered the first sense of each WordNet entry, we extended this to cover all senses. This allowed us to retrieve additional relevant alignments such as *wed* ↔ *marry*. In addition, rather than retrieving rules for all words in T, we only consider rules for full verbs, nouns, and adjectives. This way, we particularly filter out rules for auxiliary verbs, which tend to produce irrelevant alignments, especially when considering all senses. A sample set of decisions produced by our RTE engine among candidate patterns for the *marriage* relation is depicted in Figure 2.

3.3 Graph Optimization

Automatically derived entailment decisions may contradict each other. For example, as illustrated in Figure 2, our RTE engine correctly decides that [PERSON$_1$ <spouse of> PERSON$_2$] → [PERSON$_1$ <'s marriage to> PERSON$_2$] and that [PERSON$_1$ <'s marriage to> PERSON$_2$] → [PERSON$_1$ <marry> PERSON$_2$]. However, it misses the entailment relation between [PERSON$_1$ <spouse of> PERSON$_2$] and [PERSON$_1$ <marry> PERSON$_2$], because the relationship between *spouse* and *marry* is not covered by the semantic resources underlying the system. This leads

---

[4]Relations considered by the WordNet aligner: synonym, derivationally related, (instance) hypernym, member / part holonym, entailment, and substance meronym.

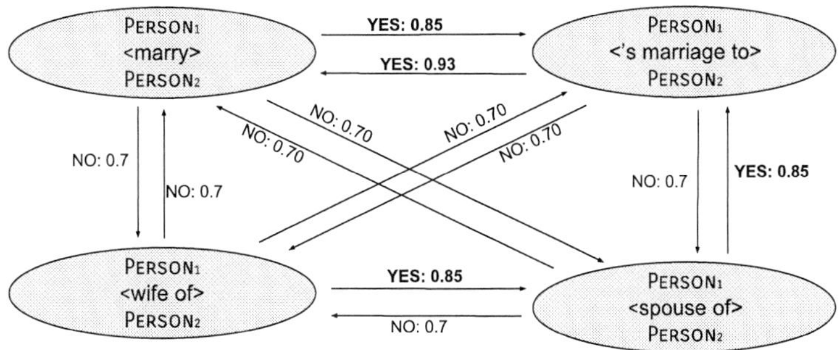

Figure 2: Sample set of RTE decisions (YES: entailment, NO: no entailment) with associated confidence

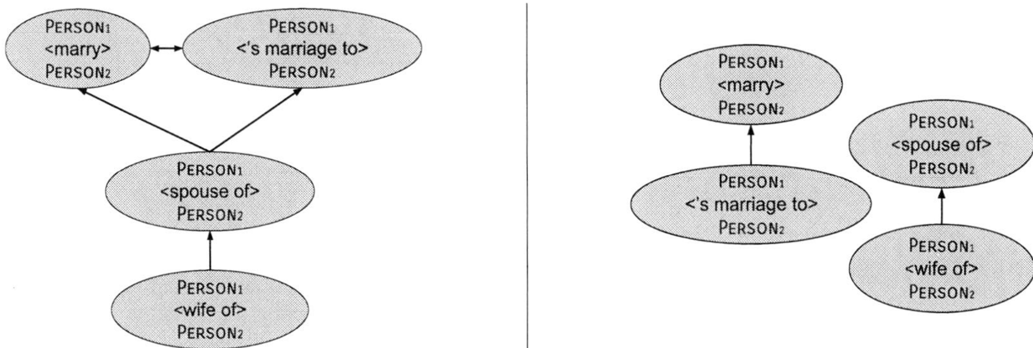

Figure 3: Sample outputs using greedy (left) and global (right) graph optimizer

to a set of decisions that is invalid given the transitivity of the entailment relation. For deriving a consistent graph, we applied two different strategies: First, a simple greedy strategy that assumes each computed positive entailment relation with a confidence exceeding a pre-defined threshold to be valid, and adds missing entailment edges to ensure transitive closure. Second, the global graph optimization algorithm by Berant et al. (2012), which searches for the best graph under a global transitivity constraint, approaching the optimization problem by Integer Linear Programming. The selection of the optimization strategy is crucial, as illustrated in Figure 3, which shows two sample outputs from each of the two strategies for the decisions in Figure 2.

4 Applying Pattern-Based Entailment Graphs for Relation Extraction

In order to exploit entailment graphs for relation extraction, we propose the following approach, which is depicted in Figure 4:

1. Create a set of candidate extraction patterns P (applying any method of choice).

2. Generate an entailment graph EG expressing entailment relations among the patterns in P.

3. Choose a base pattern[5], expressing the target relation explicitly and select all patterns entailing the base pattern according to EG.

4. Apply the selected patterns to extract relation mentions.

Given the sample graph in Figure 1 and the base pattern H: [PERSON$_1$ <marry> PERSON$_2$], our method would select all patterns entailing H, either directly or via transitivity, e.g., [PERSON$_1$ <be ex-husband of> PERSON$_2$], including patterns considered semantically equivalent, such as [PERSON$_1$ <wed> PERSON$_2$]. It would neither select [PERSON$_1$ <love> PERSON$_2$], as it has no entailment relation to H, nor [PERSON$_1$ <be in relationship with> PERSON$_2$], as it is entailed by, but not equivalent to H.

---

[5]Note that the selection of a base pattern can be done manually, but can also be automated. For example, for the relations at hand, the most frequent pattern candidate learned for a particular relation turned out to be an appropriate choice.

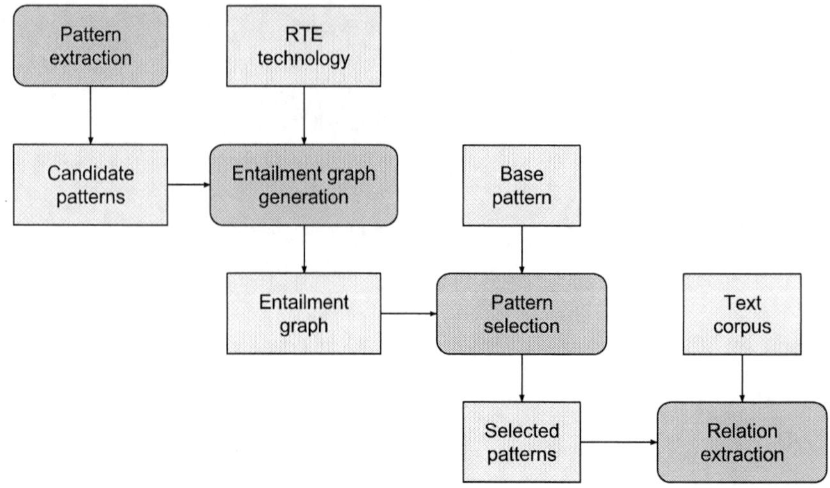

Figure 4: Procedure for relation extraction using pattern selection based on entailment graphs

5   Experiments

For evaluating our method on the relation extraction task, we conducted experiments on two freely available datasets: TEG-REP (Eichler et al., 2016) and FB15k-237 (Toutanova et al., 2015). On the TEG-REG dataset, we carried out a detailed evaluation of several pattern filtering strategies with respect to two semantic relations. On the FB15k-237 corpus, we evaluate the scalability of our method to other semantic relations.

5.1   TEG-REP

The TEG-REP corpus contains automatically derived relation extraction patterns as well as gold-standard entailment graphs created from these patterns for three relations typically considered in RE tasks: *marriage*, *acquisition*, and *award honor*. The patterns underlying this corpus are a subset of the patterns used by Moro et al. (2013) and were acquired automatically using the pattern discovery system by Krause et al. (2012). The system derives candidate patterns from dependency-parsed sentences extracted using distant supervision based on relation instances from the fact knowledge base Freebase (Bollacker et al., 2008). The TEG-REP corpus is the only available corpus of pattern-based entailment graphs and particularly suitable for our evaluation because it allows for a comparison of patterns selected based on both manually and automatically created entailment graphs. For our experiments on this corpus, we divided the full set of patterns in the corpus (around 500 per relation) into two equally-sized

portions, one for creating training data for the RTE engine, and one for evaluating pattern selection methods. For creating an evaluation dataset, we applied all patterns in the evaluation split to 14.5 million ClueWeb sentences (Lemur Project, 2009) linked to Freebase entities (Gabrilovich et al., 2013), and manually annotated around 3000 of the extracted mentions.[6] A mention was annotated as being correct if we found evidence for the target relation between the entities in the mention to hold. Evidence was drawn either from the source sentence itself, or, in cases were the source sentence did not express the relation explicitly, from external resources such as Freebase or Wikipedia.

Our experiments on the TEG-REP dataset are based on the relations *marriage* and *acquisition*[7]. For our experiments, we split the evaluation set into a development set for optimizing the graph building parameters and a test set for the final evaluation. In our experiments, we tested several strategies for selecting patterns and measured performance over the annotated relation mentions in the evaluation dataset. For evaluating the graph-based methods, we selected all patterns entailing the base patterns [PERSON$_1$ <marry> PERSON$_2$] (for *marriage*) and [ORGANIZATION$_1$ <acquire>

---

[6]The annotation was done by three annotators. About 10% of the mentions were annotated by two annotators in parallel, who achieved a very high interannotator agreement (Cohens Kappa > 0.9). The remaining mentions were annotated by a single person.

[7]We did not evaluate the *award honor* relation because the vast majority (> 98%) of mentions extracted using these patterns were correct, which would not have allowed for a meaningful evaluation.

ORGANIZATION$_2$] (for *acquisition*). In order to investigate the benefits of the graph structure, we compared the results to those achieved when computing entailment relations at a pair-wise level, i.e., using the base pattern of the relation as H and all other candidate patterns for the relation as T. We also applied the approach by Moro et al. (2013), who identify relation-relevant word senses based on lexical semantic subgraphs derived from BabelNet and filter out patterns not containing any relevant word sense. Based on a parameter k, they consider a word sense to be relevant, if it is at most k-step distant to the core word sense for the target relation.

5.2 FB15k-237

As training the RTE models requires appropriate training data, which may not be available, we ran additional experiments to investigate if the models trained on T/H pairs for one relation are general enough to be used for computing entailment relations among pattern candidates for other semantic relations. To this end, we used the FB15k-237 corpus (Toutanova et al., 2015), which contains knowledge-base relation triples and textual mentions of Freebase entity pairs. For our experiments on this corpus, we generated candidate patterns by extracting the first 1000 tuples matching a particular relation from the pattern files in the corpus, and then extracting all patterns linking any of the tuples in the textual triples used by Toutanova and Chen (2015). This way, our candidate pattern set contains both patterns expressing the target relation as well as patterns expressing other relations. For creating the entailment graph, we converted all patterns into a textual representation, removed patterns with no lexical item, and, from the remaining patterns, built an entailment graph applying the RTE engine described in 3.2 with the model trained on the *marriage* relation and the best parameter setting derived based on the TEG-REP corpus. For evaluating the result, we selected 10 relations, defined a base pattern for each of them, and checked, for each pattern in the graph, whether it entailed the base pattern according to the graph structure and whether the entailment decision was correct based on the semantics expressed by the pattern.

As in this setting, we evaluated the entailment relations expressed by the pattern graph rather than the usage of the patterns for relation extraction, the results are not directly comparable to the figures obtained on the TEG-REP corpus, but still allow for an assessment of the quality of the selected patterns.

6 Results and Discussion

6.1 TEG-REP

Table 1 shows results on the TEG-REP corpus and contains, for each of the following pattern selection methods, the computed precision, recall, and F1 scores:

- *All patterns* All patterns from the test split (baseline).

- *Lexical semantic filter (Moro et al., 2013)* Patterns selected using the lexical semantic filter.

- *Pair-wise entailment (MultiAlignAdapted)* Patterns selected based on pair-wise entailment decisions using the model of *MultiAlignAdapted*.

- *Entailment Graph (MultiAlignOriginal / MultiAlignAdapted)* Patterns selected based on entailment graphs generated with the original / adapted *MultiAlign* implementation.

- *Entailment Graph (TEG-REP gold standard)* Patterns selected based on gold-standard entailment graphs from the TEG-REP corpus.

For the lexical semantic filter method, we experimented with different levels of k and noted down the value achieving the best F1 score. The results in the table were produced setting k to 1 for the *marriage* relation and k to 5 for the *acquisition* relation. For the RTE-based methods, we experimented with the two different graph optimization strategies and, for each of them, with different confidence threshold values, and optimized these parameters based on the development split. The figures in the table show the results achieved on the test split using the parameter setting optimized on the development set: the greedy optimization strategy with thresholds of 0.71 (*MultiAlignOriginal*) and 0.77 (*MultiAlignAdapted*) for the *marriage* relation and thresholds of 0.74 (*MultiAlignOriginal*) and 0.75 (*MultiAlignAdapted*) for the *acquisition* relation. On our data, the greedy edge selection strategy produced better results than the global graph optimizer for both relations. This was because the global strategy, even with low confidence thresholds, was more restrictive and removed too many edges from the graph, thus yielding lower recall figures.

Configuration	Precision	Recall	F1
All patterns	0.15	1.00	0.27
Lexical semantic filter (Moro et al., 2013)	0.61	0.73	0.67
Pair-wise entailment (MultiAlignAdapted)	0.97	0.56	0.71
Entailment Graph (MultiAlignOriginal)	0.96	0.59	0.73
Entailment Graph (MultiAlignAdapted)	0.96	0.68	**0.80**
Entailment Graph (TEG-REP gold standard)	0.96	0.69	0.80

Table 1: Results for *marriage* relation (TEG-REP corpus)

Configuration	Precision	Recall	F1
All patterns	0.30	1.00	0.46
Lexical semantic filter (Moro et al., 2013)	0.30	0.97	0.46
Pair-wise entailment (MultiAlignAdapted)	0.82	0.49	0.62
Entailment Graph (MultiAlignOriginal)	0.81	0.53	0.64
Entailment Graph (MultiAlignAdapted)	0.59	0.93	**0.73**
Entailment Graph (TEG-REP gold standard)	0.82	0.49	0.62

Table 2: Results for *acquisition* relation (TEG-REP corpus)

For both relations, the best overall results were achieved using our proposed method based on entailment graphs generated automatically applying the adapted RTE engine. The results show that entailment-based pattern selection is in fact more powerful than the lexical semantic filter. It selects patterns yielding a much higher precision because it is able to successfully filter out non-entailing patterns, such as [PERSON$_1$ <be in relationship with> PERSON$_2$] for the *marriage* relation, which are wrongly selected using the lexical semantic filter. For the *marriage* relation, the results not only show that our RTE engine adaptations yielded a much higher recall (with almost no loss in precision) than the original implementation (thanks to an increased number of relevant alignments), but also that pattern selection can in fact benefit from the graph structure: Entailment graphs created using *MultiAlignAdapted* achieved much better performance than a selection based on pair-wise entailment computation using the same RTE model. This was due to a higher recall achieved because the graph structure allowed the algorithm to identify entailment relations that involved the combination of several inference steps and were missed when applying RTE in a pair-wise manner. An example is the relationship between *wife* and *marry*, as shown below:

$$wife \xrightarrow{\substack{hyper-\\nym}} spouse \xrightarrow{\substack{member\\holonym}} marriage \xrightarrow{\substack{deri-\\vation}} marry$$

For the *acquisition* relation, we noticed that the lexical semantic filter performed quite poorly on our corpus. The relation requires a large k-value, i.e., $k >= 5$, since there are many ways in which an acquisition can be described. A company can for instance devour, take-over or purchase another company. Each increase of k allows many additional content words, thus increasing the danger of inappropriate ones. An example is [ORGANIZATION$_1$ <trademark of> ORGANIZATION$_2$]. Where it is plausible that in the training set, an acquired company may persist as a brand of its new owner, *trademark* does not express a take-over. Although the semantic filter by Moro et al. (2013) can provide useful hints and can be applied without manually annotating training data, it is not powerful enough to discriminate content words as to whether they provide strong evidence for an acquisition or not.

Also patterns selected based on the entailment graph gold-standard performed surprisingly low on the *acquisition* relation. Here, recall was affected negatively because some of the non-entailing patterns that were filtered out were in fact able to extract correct instances with good precision. In particular, patterns expressing a planned acquisition, such as [ORGANIZATION$_1$ <plan to purchase> ORGANIZATION$_2$], [ORGANIZATION$_1$ <be to acquire> ORGANIZATION$_2$], or [ORGANIZATION$_1$ <announce intention to acquire> ORGANIZATION$_2$] extracted many cor-

Relation	Base pattern	Precision	Recall	F1
award-award_honor-ceremony	win at	0.58 (0.31)	0.73 (1.00)	**0.65** (0.47)
base-locations-continents-countries_within	country in	0.67 (0.57)	0.84 (1.00)	**0.75** (0.59)
education-education-major_field_of_study	degree in	1.00 (0.47)	0.49 (1.00)	**0.65** (0.64)
film-...-film_regional_debut_venue	premiere at	0.73 (0.13)	0.89 (1.00)	**0.80** (0.23)
film-performance-film	star in	0.97 (0.57)	0.53 (1.00)	0.69 (**0.72**)
organization-place_founded	founded in	0.83 (0.16)	0.83 (1.00)	**0.83** (0.27)
people-marriage-location_of_ceremony	marry in	0.80 (0.07)	1.00 (1.00)	**0.89** (0.12)
people-marriage-spouse	marry	1.00 (0.15)	0.58 (1.00)	**0.73** (0.26)
people-person-place_of_birth	born in	1.00 (0.41)	0.84 (1.00)	**0.91** (0.58)
people-place_of_burial	buried at	1.00 (0.33)	0.71 (1.00)	**0.83** (0.50)

Table 3: Entailment graph based pattern selection (vs. baseline) for FB15k-237 relations

rect mentions, as the acquisition in fact happened at a later stage. Nevertheless, filtering out these cases is correct from a semantic point of view, even if many of the reported plans or attempts concerning acquisitions later become a reality.

Precision on the *acquisition* gold-standard was also lower than for the *marriage* relation, due to patterns annotated as entailing in the TEG-REP corpus, which extracted comparably many incorrect instances. One such pattern is [ORGANIZATION$_1$ <takeover of> ORGANIZATION$_2$], which yields low precision values because it often occurs in sentences expressing irrealis moods, such as *the proposed Microsoft takeover of Yahoo* or *is a Pfizer takeover of BMS realistic?*, and because of its generality often extracts non-company entities, e.g., *Republican takeover of Congress*. Detecting the embedding of correct patterns in irrealis contexts is a largely unsolved problem and calls for the development of general methods for recognizing nonfactual modalities along the lines of the NegEx algorithm for detecting negations in medical texts (Chapman et al., 2001) and its later extensions.

6.2 FB15k-237

Our experiments on the FB15k-237 corpus are presented in Table 3, showing the performance of our pattern selection method based on entailment graphs (with the adapted *MultiAlign* implementation) compared to a simple baseline (all patterns). The results show that, even using an RTE model trained on a completely different semantic relation, our method achieves decent performance on selecting meaningful patterns for a wide range of relations. The figures in the table were produced with the simple graph optimization strategy, but the global graph optimizer performed very similar on this dataset, achieving the same results for eight out of the ten relations. It performed worse on the *award-award_honor-ceremony* relation (F1: 0.48), and better for the *base-locations-continents-countries_within* relation (F1: 0.91). Nevertheless, when dealing with larger numbers of patterns, the global graph optimizer should be the method of choice, as it is less prone to semantic drift.

7 Conclusions and Future Work

We presented an approach for structuring relation extraction patterns using entailment graphs and evaluated the usefulness of these graphs for pattern selection. For generating entailment graphs automatically, we employed and adapted an alignment-based entailment classifier, which makes use of external knowledge resources, and experimented with different graph optimization strategies. Our classifier was trained on a manageable amount of annotated patterns for a single semantic relation, resulting in a generic model that was shown to produce valid entailment decisions for a wide range of other semantic relations. Our experimental results suggest that meaningful pattern-based entailment graphs can be constructed automatically and that the derived knowledge is in fact valuable for selecting useful relation extraction patterns. In particular, entailment graph based filtering can help achieve higher precision than methods which do not take into account the asymmetric nature of semantic relations.

Acknowledgments

This research was supported by the German Federal Ministry of Education and Research (BMBF) through the projects ALL-SIDES (01IW14002) and BBDC (01IS14013E) and by the German Federal Ministry of Economics and Energy (BMWi) through the project SDW (01MD15010A).

References

Eugene Agichtein. 2006. Confidence estimation methods for partially supervised information extraction. In *Proceedings of the Sixth SIAM International Conference on Data Mining*. Bethesda, MD, USA, pages 539–543.

Gabor Angeli, Melvin Jose Johnson Premkumar, and Christopher D. Manning. 2015. Leveraging linguistic structure for open domain information extraction. In *Proceedings of the 53rd Annual Meeting of the Association for Computational Linguistics and the 7th International Joint Conference on Natural Language Processing*. Association for Computational Linguistics, Beijing, China, pages 344–354.

Michele Banko, Michael J. Cafarella, Stephen Soderland, Matt Broadhead, and Oren Etzioni. 2007. Open Information Extraction from the Web. In *Proceedings of the 20th International Joint Conference on Artifical Intelligence*. pages 2670–2676.

Roy Bar-Haim, Ido Dagan, Iddo Greental, and Eyal Shnarch. 2007. Semantic Inference at the Lexical-Syntactic Level. In *Proceedings of the Twenty-Second AAAI Conference on Artificial Intelligence*. AAAI Press, Vancouver, British Columbia, Canada, pages 871–876.

Sandro Bauer, Stephen Clark, Laura Rimell, and Thore Graepel. 2014. Learning a theory of marriage (and other relations) from a web corpus. In *Advances in Information Retrieval*, Springer International Publishing, pages 591–597.

Jonathan Berant, Ido Dagan, Meni Adler, and Jacob Goldberger. 2012. Efficient tree-based approximation for entailment graph learning. In *Proceedings of the 50th Annual Meeting of the Association for Computational Linguistics*. Jeju Island, Korea, pages 117–125.

Jonathan Berant, Ido Dagan, and Jacob Goldberger. 2010. Global learning of focused entailment graphs. In *Proceedings of the 48th Annual Meeting of the Association for Computational Linguistics*. Uppsala, Sweden, pages 1220–1229.

Kurt D. Bollacker, Colin Evans, Praveen Paritosh, Tim Sturge, and Jamie Taylor. 2008. Freebase: a collaboratively created graph database for structuring human knowledge. In *Proceedings of the ACM SIGMOD international conference on Management of data*. pages 1247–1250.

Samuel R. Bowman, Gabor Angeli, Christopher Potts, and Christopher D. Manning. 2015. A large annotated corpus for learning natural language inference pages 632–642.

Wendy W. Chapman, Will Bridewell, Paul Hanbury, Gregory F. Cooper, and Bruce G. Buchanan. 2001. A simple algorithm for identifying negated findings and diseases in discharge summaries. *Journal of Biomedical Informatics* 34(5):301 – 310.

Timothy Chklovski and Patrick Pantel. 2004. VerbOcean: Mining the Web for Fine-Grained Semantic Verb Relations. In *Proceedings of EMNLP*. Barcelona, Spain, pages 33–40.

Ido Dagan and Oren Glickman. 2004. Probabilistic Textual Entailment: Generic Applied Modeling of Language Variability. In *Learning Methods for Text Understanding and Mining*.

Ido Dagan, Oren Glickman, and Bernardo Magnini. 2005. The PASCAL Recognising Textual Entailment Challenge. In *Proceedings of the PASCAL Challenges Workshop on Recognising Textual Entailment*.

Michael Denkowski and Alon Lavie. 2014. Meteor Universal: Language Specific Translation Evaluation for Any Target Language. In *Proceedings of the Ninth Workshop on Statistical Machine Translation*.

Kathrin Eichler, Feiyu Xu, Hans Uszkoreit, Leonhard Hennig, and Sebastian Krause. 2016. TEG-REP: A corpus of textual entailment graphs based on relation extraction patterns. In *Proceedings of the Tenth International Conference on Language Resources and Evaluation (LREC)*.

Christiane Fellbaum. 1998. *WordNet: an electronic lexical database*. MIT Press, Cambridge, MA, USA.

Evgeniy Gabrilovich, Michael Ringgaard, and Amarnag Subramanya. 2013. FACC1: Freebase annotation of ClueWeb corpora, Version 1 (Release date 2013-06-26, Format version 1, Correction level 0).

Stanley Kok and Pedro Domingos. 2008. Extracting semantic networks from text via relational clustering. In *Proceedings of the European Conference on Machine Learning and Knowledge Discovery in Databases*. pages 624–639.

Vladyslav Kolesnyk, Tim Rocktäschel, and Sebastian Riedel. 2016. Generating natural language inference chains. *CoRR* abs/1606.01404.

Lili Kotlerman, Ido Dagan, Bernardo Magnini, and Luisa Bentivogli. 2015. Textual entailment graphs. *Natural Language Engineering* 21:699–724.

Sebastian Krause, Hong Li, Hans Uszkoreit, and Feiyu Xu. 2012. Large-scale learning of relation-extraction rules with distant supervision from the web. In *Proceedings of the 11th International Semantic Web Conference*. Springer.

The Lemur Project. 2009. Clueweb09. http://www.lemurproject.org.

Omer Levy, Ido Dagan, and Jacob Goldberger. 2014. Focused Entailment Graphs for Open IE Propositions. In *Proceedings of the Eighteenth Conference on Computational Natural Language Learning*. Ann Arbor, Michigan, pages 87–97.

Bernardo Magnini, Roberto Zanoli, Ido Dagan, Kathrin Eichler, Günter Neumann, Tae-Gil Noh, Sebastian Padó, Asher Stern, and Omer Levy. 2014. The Excitement Open Platform for Textual Inferences. In *Proceedings of the ACL 2014 System Demonstrations*. ACL.

Yashar Mehdad, Giuseppe Carenini, Raymond T. Ng, and Shafiq R. Joty. 2013. Towards topic labeling with phrase entailment and aggregation. In *Proceedings of the Human Language Technologies: Conference of the North American Chapter of the Association of Computational Linguistics*. Atlanta, Georgia, USA, pages 179–189.

Andrea Moro, Hong Li, Sebastian Krause, Feiyu Xu, Roberto Navigli, and Hans Uszkoreit. 2013. Semantic rule filtering for web-scale relation extraction. In *Proceedings of the 12th International Semantic Web Conference*. pages 347–362.

Ndapandula Nakashole, Gerhard Weikum, and Fabian M. Suchanek. 2012. PATTY: A taxonomy of relational patterns with semantic types. In *Proceedings of the 2012 Joint Conference on Empirical Methods in Natural Language Processing and Computational Natural Language Learning*. Jeju Island, Korea, pages 1135–1145.

Tae-Gil Noh, Sebastian Padó, Vered Shwartz, Ido Dagan, Vivi Nastase, Kathrin Eichler, Lili Kotlerman, and Meni Adler. 2015. Multi-level alignments as an extensible representation basis for textual entailment algorithms. In *Proceedings of *SEM 2015*. ACL.

Sebastian Riedel, Limin Yao, Andrew McCallum, and Benjamin M. Marlin. 2013. Relation Extraction with Matrix Factorization and Universal Schemas. In *Proceedings of the Conference of the North American Chapter of the Association for Computational Linguistics: Human Language Technologies*. pages 74–84.

Tim Rocktäschel, Edward Grefenstette, Karl Moritz Hermann, Tomás Kociský, and Phil Blunsom. 2015. Reasoning about entailment with neural attention. *CoRR* abs/1509.06664.

Lorenza Romano, Milen Kouylekov, Idan Szpektor, Ido Dagan, and Alberto Lavelli. 2006. Investigating a generic paraphrase-based approach for relation extraction. In *Proceedings of the 11st Conference of the European Chapter of the Association for Computational Linguistics*. Trento, Italy.

Dan Roth, Mark Sammons, and V. G. Vinod Vydiswaran. 2009. A framework for entailed relation recognition. In *Proceedings of the 47th Annual Meeting of the Association for Computational Linguistics and the 4th International Joint Conference on Natural Language Processing of the Asian Federation of Natural Language Processing*. The Association for Computer Linguistics, Singapore, pages 57–60.

Yusuke Shinyama and Satoshi Sekine. 2006. Preemptive information extraction using unrestricted relation discovery. In *Proceedings of the Human Language Technology Conference of the NAACL*. New York City, USA, pages 304–311.

Philippe Thomas, Stefan Pietschmann, Illés Solt, Domonkos Tikk, and Ulf Leser. 2011. Not all links are equal: Exploiting Dependency Types for the Extraction of Protein-Protein Interactions from Text. In *Proceedings of the BioNLP Workshop*. pages 1–9.

Kristina Toutanova and Danqi Chen. 2015. Observed versus latent features for knowledge base and text inference. In *Proceedings of the Workshop on Continuous Vector Space Models and Their Compositionality*.

Kristina Toutanova, Danqi Chen, Patrick Pantel, Hoifung Poon, Pallavi Choudhury, and Michael Gamon. 2015. Representing text for joint embedding of text and knowledge bases.

Rui Wang and Günter Neumann. 2008. Relation validation via textual entailment. In *Proceedings of the 1st International and KI-08 Workshop on Ontology-based Information Extraction Systems*. volume 400, pages 26–37.

Limin Yao, Aria Haghighi, Sebastian Riedel, and Andrew McCallum. 2011. Structured relation discovery using generative models. In *Proceedings of the Conference on Empirical Methods in Natural Language Processing*. Stroudsburg, PA, USA, pages 1456–1466.

Alexander Yates and Oren Etzioni. 2009. Unsupervised methods for determining object and relation synonyms on the web. *Journal of Artificial Intelligence Research* 34:255–296.

Classifying Semantic Clause Types: Modeling Context and Genre Characteristics with Recurrent Neural Networks and Attention

Maria Becker◇♠**, Michael Staniek**◇♠**, Vivi Nastase**◇♠**, Alexis Palmer**♣**, Anette Frank**◇♠

◇ Leibniz ScienceCampus "Empirical Linguistics and Computational Language Modeling"
♠Heidelberg University, Department of Computational Linguistics
♣University of North Texas, Department of Linguistics
{mbecker,staniek,nastase,frank}@cl.uni-heidelberg.de
alexis.palmer@unt.edu

Abstract

Detecting aspectual properties of clauses in the form of situation entity types has been shown to depend on a combination of syntactic-semantic and contextual features. We explore this task in a deep-learning framework, where tuned word representations capture lexical, syntactic and semantic features. We introduce an attention mechanism that pinpoints relevant context not only for the current instance, but also for the larger context. Apart from implicitly capturing task relevant features, the advantage of our neural model is that it avoids the need to reproduce linguistic features for other languages and is thus more easily transferable. We present experiments for English and German that achieve competitive performance. We present a novel take on modeling and exploiting genre information and showcase the adaptation of our system from one language to another.

1 Introduction

Semantic clause types, called *Situation Entity (SE)* types (Smith, 2003; Palmer et al., 2007) are linguistic characterizations of aspectual properties shown to be useful for argumentation structure analysis (Becker et al., 2016b), genre characterization (Palmer and Friedrich, 2014), and detection of generic and generalizing sentences (Friedrich and Pinkal, 2015). Recent work on automatic identification of SE types relies on feature-based classifiers for English that have been successfully applied to various textual genres (Friedrich et al., 2016), and also show that a sequence labeling approach that models contextual clause labels yields improved classification performance.

Deep learning provides a powerful framework in which linguistic and semantic regularities can be implicitly captured through word embeddings (Mikolov et al., 2013b). Patterns in larger text fragments can be encoded and exploited by recurrent (RNNs) or convolutional neural networks (CNNs) which have been successfully used for various sentence-based classification tasks, e.g. sentiment (Kim, 2014) or relation classification (Vu et al., 2016; Tai et al., 2015).

We frame the task of classifying clauses with respect to their aspectual properties – i.e., situation entity types – in a recurrent neural network architecture. We adopt a Gated Recurrent Unit (GRU)-based RNN architecture that is well suited to modeling long sequences (Yin et al., 2017). This initial model is enhanced with an attention mechanism shown to be beneficial for sentence classification (Wang et al., 2016) and sequence modeling (Dong and Lapata, 2016). We explore the usefulness of attention in two settings: (i) the individual classification task and (ii) in a setting approximating sequential labeling in which the attention vector provides features that describe the clauses preceding the current instance. Compared to the strong baseline provided by the feature based system of Friedrich et al. (2016), we achieve competitive performance and find that attention as well as context representation using predicted or gold-standard labels of the previous N clauses, and text genre information improve our model.

A strong motivation for developing NN-based systems is that they can be transferred with low cost to other languages without major feature engineering or use of hand-crafted linguistic knowledge resources. Given the highly-engineered feature sets used for SE classification so far (Friedrich et al., 2016), porting such classifiers to other languages is a non-trivial issue. We test the portability of our system by applying it to German.

*Proceedings of the 6th Joint Conference on Lexical and Computational Semantics (*SEM 2017)*, pages 230–240,
Vancouver, Canada, August 3-4, 2017. ©2017 Association for Computational Linguistics

We present a novel take on modeling and exploiting genre information and test it on the English multi-genre corpus of Friedrich et al. (2016).

Our aims and contributions are: (i) We study the performance of GRU-based models enhanced with attention for modeling local and non-local characteristics of semantic clause types. (ii) We compare the effectiveness of the learned attention weights as features for a sequence labeling system to the explicitly defined syntactic-semantic features in (Friedrich et al., 2016). (iii) We define extensions of our models that integrate external knowledge about genre and show that this can be used to improve classification performance across genres. (iv) We test the portability of our models to other languages by applying them to a smaller, manually annotated German dataset. The performance is comparable to English.

2 Semantic Clause Types

Semantic clause types can be distinguished by the function they have within a text or discourse. We use the inventory of semantic clause types, also known as **situation entity (SE) types**, developed by Smith (2003) and extended in later work (Palmer et al., 2007; Friedrich and Palmer, 2014). SE types describe abstract semantic types of situations evoked in discourse through clauses. As such, they capture the manner of presentation of content, along with the information content itself. The seven SE types we use are described below.

1. STATE (S): *Armin has brown eyes.*
2. EVENT (EV): *Bonnie ate three tacos.*
3. REPORT (R) provides attribution:
   The agency said costs had increased.
4. GENERIC SENTENCE (GEN) predicates over classes or kinds:
   Birds can fly. – Scientists make arguments.
5. GENERALIZING SENTENCE (GS) describes regularly occurring events:
   Fei travels to India every year.
6. QUESTION (Q): *Why do you torment me so?*
7. IMPERATIVE (IMP): *Listen to this.*

An eighth class OTHER is assigned to clauses without an SE label, e.g. bylines or email headers.

Features that distinguish SE types are a combination of linguistic features of the clause and its main verb, and the nature of the main referent of the clause.[1] There is a correlation between the

---

[1] The main referent of a clause is roughly the per-

distribution of SE types in text passages and discourse modes, e.g., narrative, informative, or argumentative (Palmer and Friedrich, 2014; Mavridou et al., 2015; Becker et al., 2016a).

3 Related Work

Feature-based classification of situation entity types. The first robust system for SE type classification (Friedrich et al., 2016) combines task-specific syntactic and semantic features with distributional word features, as captured by Brown clusters (Brown et al., 1992). This system segments each text into a sequence of clauses and then predicts the best sequence of SE labels for the text using a linear chain conditional random field (CRF) with label bigram features.[2]

Although SE types are relevant across languages, their linguistic realization varies across languages. Accordingly, some of Friedrich et al. (2016)'s syntactic and semantic features are language-specific and are extracted using English-specific resources such as WordNet and Loaiciga et al. (2014)'s rules for extracting tense and voice information from POS tag sequences.

Friedrich et al. (2016)'s system is trained and evaluated on data sets from MASC and Wikipedia (Section 5), reaching accuracies of 76.4% (F1 71.2) with 10-fold cross-validation, and 74.7% (F1 69.3) on a held-out test set. To evaluate the contribution of sequence information, Friedrich et al. (2016) compare the CRF model to a Maximum Entropy baseline, with the result that the sequential model significantly outperforms the model which classifies clauses in isolation, particularly for the less-frequent SE types of GENERIC SENTENCE and GENERALIZING SENTENCE.

When trained and tested within a single genre (of the 13 genres represented in the data sets), Friedrich et al. (2016)'s system performance ranges from 26.6 F1 (for government documents) to 66.2 F1 (for jokes). Training on all genres levels out this performance difference, with a range of F1 scores from 58.1-69.8.

Neural approaches to sentence classification, sequence and context modeling. Inspired by research in vision, sentence classification tasks have initially been modeled using Convolutional Neural Networks (Kim, 2014; Kalchbrenner et al.,

---

son/thing/situation the clause is about, often realized as its grammatical subject.

[2] Code and data: https://github.com/annefried/sitent

2014). RNN variations – with Gated Recurrent Units (GRU) (Cho et al., 2014) or Long Short-Term Memory units (LSTM) (Hochreiter and Schmidhuber, 1997) – have since achieved state of the art performance in both sequence modeling and classification tasks. Recent work applies bi-LSTM models in sequence modeling (PoS tagging, Plank et al. (2016), NER Lample et al. (2016)) and structure prediction tasks (Semantic Role Labeling, Zhou and Xu (2015) or semantic parsing into logical forms Dong and Lapata (2016)). Tree-based LSTM models have been shown to often perform better than purely sequential bi-LSTMs (Tai et al., 2015; Miwa and Bansal, 2016), but depend on parsed input.

Attention. Attention has been established as an effective mechanism that allows models to focus on specific words in the larger context. A model with attention learns what input tokens or token sequences to attend to and thus does not need to capture the complete input information in its hidden state. Attention has been used successfully e.g. in aspect-based sentiment classification (Wang et al., 2016), for modeling relations between words or phrases in encoder-decoder models for translation (Bahdanau et al., 2015), or bi-clausal classification tasks such as textual entailment (Rocktäschel et al., 2016). We use attention to larger context windows and previous labeling decisions to capture sequential information relevant for our classification task. We investigate the learned weights to gain information about what the models learn, and we start to explore how they can be used to provide features for a sequential labeling approach.

4 Models

We aim for a system that can fine-tune input word embeddings to the task, and can process clauses as sequences of words from which to encode larger patterns that help our particular clause classification task. GRU RNNs are used because they can successfully process long sequences and capture long-term dependencies. Attention can encode which parts of the input contain relevant information. These modeling choices are described and justified in detail below. The performance of the models is reported in Section 6.

4.1 Basic Model: Gated Recurrent Unit

Recurrent Neural Networks (RNNs) are modifications of feed-forward neural networks with recurrent connections, which allow them to find patterns in – and thus model – sequences. Simple RNNs cannot capture long-term dependencies (Bengio et al., 1994) because the gradients tend to vanish or grow out of control with long sequences. Gated Recurrent Unit (GRU) RNNs, proposed by Cho et al. (2014), address this shortcoming. GRUs have fewer parameters and thus need less data to generalize (Zhou et al., 2016) than LSTM RNNs, and also outperform the LSTM in many cases (Yin et al., 2017), which makes them a good choice for our relatively small dataset.[3] The relevant equations for a GRU are below. x_t is the input at time t, r_t is a reset gate which determines how to combine the new input with the previous memory, and the update gate z_t defines how much of the previous memory to keep. h_t is the hidden state (memory) at time t, and $\tilde{h}_t$ is the candidate activation at time t. W_* and U_* are weights that are learned. $\odot$ denotes the element-wise multiplication of two vectors.

$$r_t = \sigma(W_r x_t + U_r h_{t-1})$$
$$\tilde{h}_t = tanh(W x_t + U(r_t \odot h_{t-1}))$$
$$z_t = \sigma(W_z x_t + U_z h_{t-1})$$

$$h_t = (1 - z_t) \odot h_{t-1} + z_t \odot \tilde{h}_t \qquad (1)$$

The last hidden vector h_t will be taken as the representation of the input clause. After compressing it into a vector whose length is equal to the number of class labels (=8) using a fully connected layer with sigmoid function, we apply $softmax$.

4.2 Attention Model

We extend our GRU model with a neural attention mechanism to capture the most relevant words in the input clauses for classifying SE types. Specifically, we adapt the implementation of attention used in Rocktäschel et al. (2016) for our clause classification task as follows:

$$M = tanh(W_h H + W_v h_t \otimes e_L)$$
$$\alpha = softmax(w^T M)$$
$$r = H\alpha^T$$

where H is a matrix consisting of the hidden vectors $[h_1, ..., h_t]$ produced by the GRU, h_t is the last output vector of the GRU, and e_L is a vector of 1s where L denotes the L words of the input clause. $\otimes$ denotes the outer product of the

---

[3]Comparison of GRUs, bi-GRUs, LSTMs and bi-LSTMs on our dataset for our classification task showed that GRUs outperform the latter three, confirming this assumption.

two vectors. α is a vector consisting of attention weights and r is a weighted representation of the input clause. W_h, W_v, and w are parameters to be learned during training.

The final clause representation is obtained from a combination of the attention-weighted representation r of the clause and the last output vector v.

$$h^* = tanh(W_p r + W_x h_t) \qquad (2)$$

where W_p and W_x are trained projection matrices. We convert h^* to a real-valued vector with length 8 (the number of target classes) and apply $softmax$ to transform it to a probability distribution.

4.3 Modeling Context and Genre

Text types differ in their situation entity type distributions: Palmer et al. (2007) find that GENERIC SENTENCES and GENERALIZING SENTENCES play a predominant role for texts associated with the argument or commentary mode (such as essays), and EVENTS and STATES for texts associated with the report mode (such as news texts). (Becker et al., 2016a) find that argumentative texts are characterized by a high proportion of GENERIC and GENERALIZING SENTENCES and very few EVENTS, while reports and talks contain a high proportion of STATES, and fiction is characterized by a high number of EVENTS. N-gram analyses show that sequences of SE types differ among different genres: e.g. while ST-ST is the most frequent bigram within journal articles, the most frequent bigram in Wikipedia articles is GEN-GEN. The most frequent trigram in Jokes is EV-EV-EV, followed by ST-ST-ST, whereas in government documents the most frequent trigrams are ST-ST-ST and EV-ST-ST. These results show that n-grams cluster in texts (cf. (Friedrich and Pinkal, 2015)), and they differ among genres. This supports the choice of incorporating (sequential) context information for classification of SE types. Fig. 1 illustrates both the context and the genre information our models consider for classifying SE types, while Fig. 2 illustrates our model's architecture.

4.3.1 Context Modeling: Clauses and Labels

We develop two models that not only consider the local sentence for SE classification in model training, but also the previous clauses' token sequences or the labels of previous clauses. When attending to **tokens of previous clauses** we add one GRU model with attention mechanism for each previous clause (N denotes the number of previous clauses) and concatenate their final outputs with the final output of the GRU with attention for the current clause (cf. Fig. 2).

$$h^*_{con1} = < tanh(W_p r_1 + W_x v_1); ...; \\ tanh(W_p r_N + W_x v_N) >$$

We then transform the concatenated vector into a dense vector equal to the number of class labels and apply $softmax$.

For attending to **labels of the previous clauses**, we first transform the gold labels used during training into embeddings and apply attention as described in section 4.2 to these representations. We then concatenate the last output of the current clause with the embeddings for the labels of the previous clauses (here N denotes the number of previous labels):

$$h^*_{con2} = < tanh(W_p r + W_x v); y_{t-1}; ...; y_{t-N} >$$

where y_{t-i} is the embedding representation for the previous t-i label. At test time we use the predicted probability distribution vector as the labels of previous clauses.

4.3.2 Feature Modeling: Textual Genres

The English corpus we use consists of texts from 13 genres; the German corpus covers 7 genres (Section 5).

Information about genre is encoded as dense embeddings g of size 10 initialized randomly, and we apply attention mechanism to these representations. Adding genre information produces three new versions of the model: (i) genre+basic model: $< g; h_t >$ (h_t from eq.1), (ii) genre+attention model $< g; h_* >$ (h_* from eq.2), (iii) genre+context in form of previous labels (cf. Fig.2). Results for all three combinations are reported in Section 6.

4.4 Word embeddings

Word embeddings have been shown to capture syntactic and semantic regularities (Mikolov et al., 2013b) and to benefit from fine tuning for specific tasks. The features used by Friedrich et al. (2016) cover a variety of linguistic features – such as tense, voice, number, POS, semantic clusters – some of which we expect to be encoded in pre-trained embeddings, while others will emerge through model training. We start with pre-trained embeddings for both English and German, because this leads to better results than random ini-

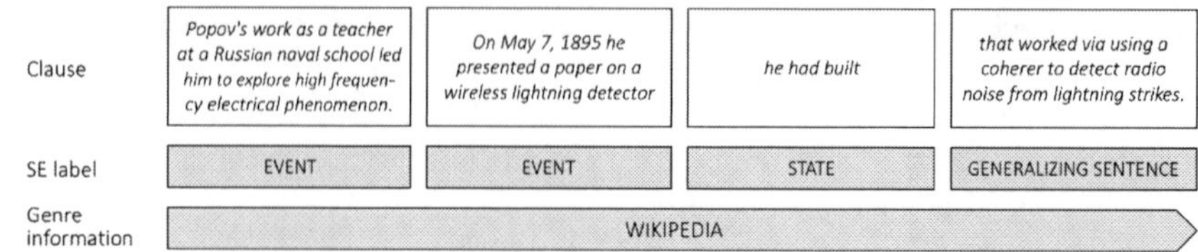

Figure 1: Context and genre information modeled in our system, example from Wikipedia

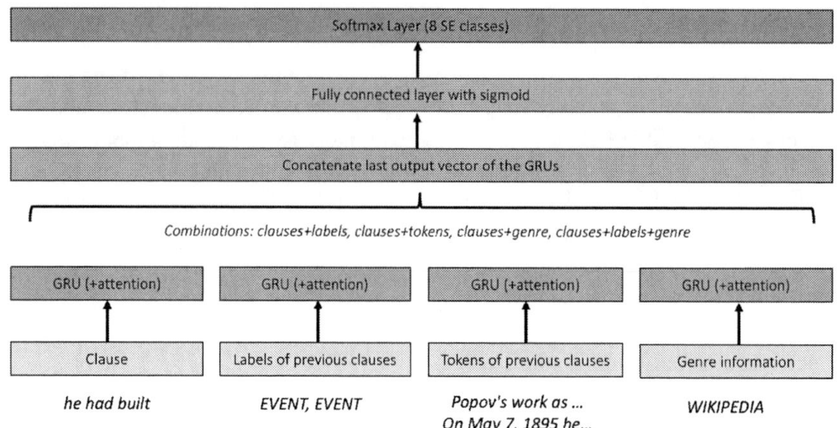

Figure 2: Model Architecture, illustrated with an example (cf. Fig. 1).

tialization. For German, we use 100-dimensional word2vec embeddings trained on a large German corpus of 116 million sentences (Reimers et al., 2014).[4] For English, we use 300-dimensional word2vec embeddings (Mikolov et al., 2013a) trained on part of the Google News dataset (about 100 billion words). The pre-trained embeddings are tuned during training.

4.5 Parameters and Tuning

Hyperparameter settings were determined through exhaustive random search using *optunity* (Bergstra and Bengio, 2012) on the development set, and we use the best setting for evaluating on the test set. We tune batch size, number of layers, GRU cell size, and regularization parameter (L2). For learning rate optimization we use AdaGrad (Duchi et al., 2011) and tune the initial learning rate. For the basic model (without attention), the best result on the development set is achieved for GRU with batch size 100, 2 layers, cell size 350, learning rate 0.05, and L2 regularization parameter (0.01). For the model using attention mechanism the parameters are identical except for L2 (0.0001).

Data set	# Clauses/SEs	# Tokens
English: MASC	30,333	357,078
English: Wiki	10,607	148,040
German: all	18,194	236,522

Table 1: Data sets with SE-labeled clauses

5 Data

We use the English dataset described in Friedrich and Palmer (2014).[5] The texts, drawn from Wikipedia and MASC (Ide et al., 2010), range across 13 genres, e.g. news texts, government documents, essays, fiction, jokes, emails. For German, we combine two data sets described in Mavridou et al. (2015) and Becker et al. (2016a) and additional data annotated by ourselves.[6] The German texts cover 7 genres: argumentative essays (Peldszus and Stede, 2015), Wikipedia, fiction, commentary, news texts, TED talks, and economic reports. Statistics appear in Table 1.

The distribution of SE types varies with the genre. For the selected English Wiki texts, 50% of the SE types are GENERIC SENTENCE clauses,

---

[4]https://public.ukp.informatik.tu-darmstadt.de /reimers/2014_german_embeddings

[5]Available at: https://github.com/annefried/sitent

[6]The data is available at http://www.cl.uni-heidelberg.de/ english/research/downloads/resource_pages/GER_SET/GER _SET_data.shtml. This dataset only contains the German data that has been annotated within the Leibniz Science campus.

	Acc	F1
Palmer07, Brown dataset	53.1	-
Fried16, set A (CRF, test)	69.8	63.9
Fried16, set B (CRF, test)	71.4	65.5
Fried16, set A+B (CRF, test)	74.7	69.3
Fried16, set A+B (CRF, CV)	76.4	71.2
Fried16, set A+B (MaxEnt+CRF, CV, seq-oracle)	77.9	73.9

Table 2: Reported results of baseline models for English (accuracy and macro-average F1 score). CV=10-fold cross validation, test=eval. on test set.

with STATES second at 24.3%.[7] For the 12 MASC genres, STATE is the most frequent type (49.8%), with EVENTS second at 24.3%. GENERIC SENTENCES make up only 7.3% of the SE types in the MASC texts. In the German data, the distributions of SE types also differ according to genre: in argumentative texts, for example, GENERIC SENTENCES make up 48% of the SE types, followed by STATES with a frequency of 32%, while in most other genres the most frequent class is STATE.

The texts of the English dataset are split into clauses using SPADE (Soricut and Marcu, 2003). For segmenting the German dataset into clauses we use DiscourseSegmenter's rule-based segmenter (edseg, Sidarenka et al. (2015)), which employs German-specific rules. Because DiscourseSegmenter occasionally oversplit segments, we did a small amount of post-processing.

6 Experiments and Evaluation

For the English dataset, we use the same test-train split as Friedrich et al. (2016).[8] The German dataset was split into training and testing with a balanced distribution of genres (as is the case for the English dataset). Both datasets have a 80-20 split between training and testing (20% of training is used for development).

We report results in terms of accuracy and macro-average F1 score on the held-out test set.

Baseline systems. The feature-based system of *Palmer07* (Palmer et al., 2007) (Palmer07 in Table 2) simulates context through predicted labels from previous clauses. Friedrich et al. (2016) (*Fried16* in Table 2) report results for their CRF-based SE

	Acc	F1
Basic GRU	66.55	46.04
Basic GRU + genre	65.82	46.32
GRU + attention	68.99	68.87
GRU + attention + genre	71.12	67.95
GRU + att + clause (1)	69.06	59.39
GRU + att + clause (2)	**70.20**	**60.01**
GRU + att + clause (3)	69.64	37.29
GRU + att + pLab (1)	69.20	61.95
GRU + att + pLab (2)	**69.37**	**62.13**
GRU + att + pLab (3)	68.77	60.85
GRU + att + pLab (4)	68.05	59.31
GRU + att + pLab (5)	68.11	60.75
GRU + att + pLab + genre (1)	71.59	**64.94**
GRU + att + pLab + genre (2)	**71.61**	64.28
GRU + att + pLab + genre (3)	70.37	63.55
GRU + att + pLab + genre (4)	70.96	63.74
GRU + att + pLab + genre (5)	70.57	63.65

Table 3: SE-type classification on English test set, with context as predicted labels (pLab).

type labeler for different feature sets, with 10-fold cross validation and on a held-out test set. To test if the context is useful they extend their classifier with a CRF that includes the predicted label of the preceding clause. In the *oracle* setting it includes the gold label of the previous clause.

Feature set A consists of standard NLP features including POS tags and Brown clusters. Feature set B includes more detailed features such as tense, lemma, negation, modality, WordNet sense, WordNet supersense and WordNet hypernym sense. We presume that some of the information captured by feature set B, particularly sense and hypernym information, may not be captured in the word embeddings we use in our approach.

Evaluation of our neural systems. Our **local** system (cf. Section 4.1) achieves an accuracy of 66.55 (Table 3). Adding *genre information* does not help, but adding *attention* within the local clause yields an improvement of 2.44 percentage points (pp). Using both *attention and genre* information leads to a 2.13 pp increase over the model that uses only attention. Adding **context information** beyond the local clause – a window of up to three previous clauses – improves the word-based attention models slightly, but a wider window (four or more clauses) causes a major drop

---

[7]The Wiki texts were selected by Friedrich et al. (2015) precisely in order to target GENERIC SENTENCE clauses.

[8]The cross validation splits of the data used by Friedrich et al. (2016) are not available.

	Acc	F1
GRU + att + gLab (1)	72.71	65.37
GRU + att + gLab (2)	72.68	**66.51**
GRU + att + gLab (3)	72.66	65.03
GRU + att + gLab (4)	72.61	64.33
GRU + att + gLab (5)	**73.40**	66.39
GRU + att + gLab + genre (1)	73.44	**66.76**
GRU + att + gLab + genre (2)	**73.45**	66.51
GRU + att + gLab + genre (3)	72.84	66.29
GRU + att + gLab + genre (4)	73.12	66.21
GRU + att + gLab + genre (5)	73.34	66.13

Table 4: SE-type classification on English test set, *sequence oracle model* using gold labels (gLab).

in accuracy.[9] Using context as predicted labels of previous clauses improves the model slightly (up to 0.38 pp), but adding genre on top of that improves the model by up to 2.62 pp compared to the basic model with attention. The oracle model (cf. Table 4), which uses the gold labels of previous clauses, gives an upper bound for the impact of sequence information: 73.40% accuracy for previous 5 gold labels. Combined with genre information, the upper bound reaches 73.45% accuracy when using the previous 2 gold labels.

The best accuracy on the English data (ignoring the oracle) is achieved by the model that uses 2 previous predicted labels plus genre information (71.61%). This model outperforms Friedrich et al. (2016)'s results when using standard NLP features (feature set A) and their model using feature set B separately. Our model comes close to Friedrich et al.'s best results obtained by applying their entire set of features, particularly considering that our system only uses generic word embeddings.

Window size as hyper-parameter? We achieve best results when incorporating two previous labels or two previous clauses (cf. Table 3). This is in line with Palmer et al. (2007) who report that in most cases performance starts to degrade as the model incorporates more than two previous labels. A window size of two does not always lead to best performance on the German dataset (cf. Section 7), where the model using predicted labels from the maximum window size (5) performs best. When adding genre information, we achieve best results with window size two (cf. Table 5 and 6). This inconsistency can possibly be traced back to the fact that we applied the best-performing vari-

---

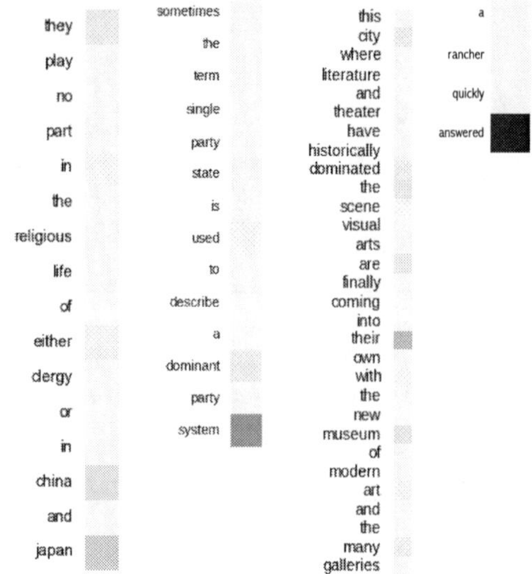

Figure 3: Visualization of attention for ST, GS, GEN. and REP.

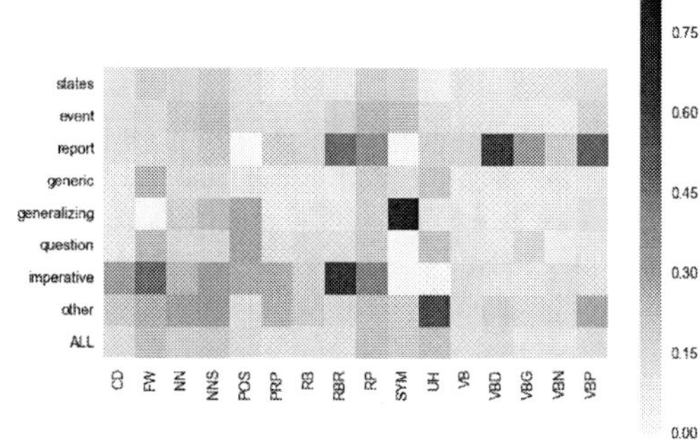

Figure 4: Mean attention scores per POS tags on English dataset. POS tags from PTB.

ations of our system developed on English data to our German dataset without further hyperparameter tuning.

Results for single classes. Fig. 6 shows macro-average F1 scores of our best performing system for the single SE classes. The scores are very similar to the results of Friedrich et al. (2016). Scores for GENERALIZING SENTENCE are the lowest as this class is very infrequent in the data set, while scores for the classes STATE, EVENT, and REPORT are the highest. In addition, we explored our system's performance for binary classification (Fig. 6): here we classified STATE vs. the remaining classes, EVENT vs. the remaining classes etc. Binary classification achieves better performance and can be helpful for downstream applications which only need information about specific

236

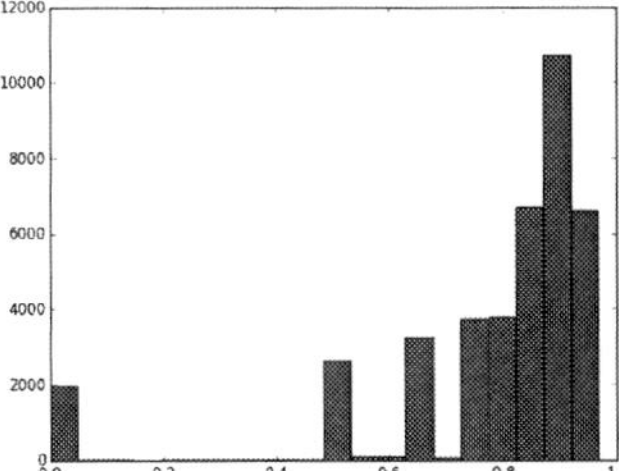

Figure 5: Position of words with maximum attention within clauses. x-axis represents the normalized position within the clause, y-axis the number of words with maximum attention at that position.

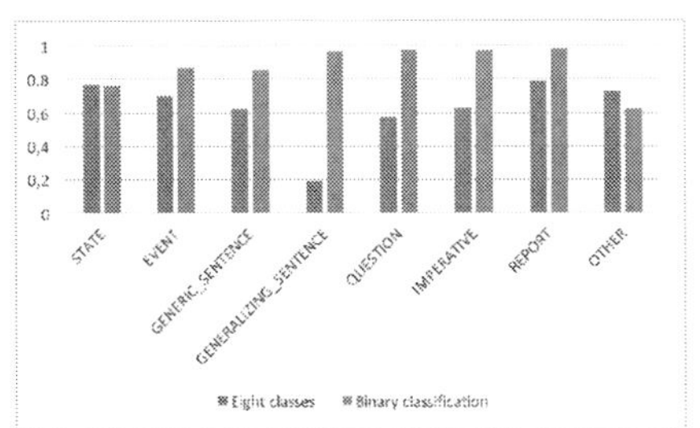

Figure 6: Macro-average F1 scores of our best performing system for single SE classes, multiclass vs. binary classification.

SE types, for example for distinguishing generic from non-generic sentences.

Analysis of attention. Attention is not only an effective mechanism that allows models to focus on specific parts of the input, but it may also enable interesting linguistic insights: (1) the attention to specific words or POS for specific SE types, (2) the overall distribution of attention weights among POS tag labels and SE types, and (3) the position of words with maximum/high attention scores within a clause.

Fig. 3 shows example clauses with their attention weights. In the first clause, a STATE, the model attends most to the nouns "China" and "Japan". In the next clause, a GENERALIZING SENTENCE, the noun "system" is assigned the highest attention weight. The highest weighted word in the GENERIC SENTENCE is the pronoun "their", and in REPORT it is the verb "answered".

Fig. 4 visualizes the mean attention score per POS tag for all SE types (gold labels).[10] Interestingly, attention seems to be especially important for classes that are rare, such as IMPERA-

TIVE or REPORT, each less than 5% of the English dataset. The heat map indicates that the model especially attends to verbs when classifying the SE type REPORT. This is not surprising, since REPORT clauses are signaled by verbs of speech. GENERALIZING SENTENCE attend to symbols, mainly punctuation, and genitive markers such as "'s". The OTHER class, which includes clauses without an assigned SE type label, attends mostly to interjections. Indeed, OTHER is frequent in genres with fragmented sentences (emails, blogs), and numerous interjections such as "wow" or "um".

Fig. 5 shows the relative positions of words with maximum attention within clauses. The model mostly attends to words at the end of clauses and almost never to words in the first half of clauses. This distribution shifts to the left when considering more words with high attention scores instead of only the word with maximum attention – words with 2nd (3rd, 4th, 5th) highest attention score can often be found at the beginning of clauses. The model seems to draw information from a broad range of positions.

We explored the impact of the attention vectors as inputs to a sequence labeling model – each clause is described through the words with the highest attention weights and these weights, and used in a conditional random field system (CRF++[12]). The best performance was obtained when using the attention vector of the current clause (and no additional context) – 61.68% accuracy (47.18% F1 score). CRF++ maps the attention information to binary features, and as such cannot take advantage of information captured in the numerical values of the attention weights, or the embeddings of the given words.

7 Porting the System to German

One advantage for developing NN-based systems that do not rely on hand-crafted features is that they can be used with different language data. We use the system described above with German data, only adjusting the size of the input embeddings.[13] Compared to the English dataset, the German dataset is smaller (44% in size) and less diverse with respect to genre (7 genres). The genres in the German dataset (argumentative texts, wikipedia, commentary, news, fiction, report, talk)

---

[10]We post-process our data with POS tags using *spaCy*[11] with the PTB tagset (Marcus et al., 1993).

[12]https://taku910.github.io/crfpp/

[13]The different size of the embeddings (for English and German cf. section 4.4, may have an impact on the results.

	Acc	F1
Basic GRU	72.67	61.55
Basic GRU + genre	72.08	66.33
GRU + attention	72.31	72.23
GRU + attention + genre	73.75	65.69
GRU + att + clause (1)	**73.49**	**63.99**
GRU + att + clause (2)	70.21	58.66
GRU + att + clause (3)	49.31	47.01
GRU + att + pLab (1)	69.83	44.31
GRU + att + pLab (2)	70.12	44.33
GRU + att + pLab (3)	70.50	44.91
GRU + att + pLab (4)	72.16	45.12
GRU + att + pLab (5)	**72.85**	**45.52**
GRU + att + pLab + genre (1)	72.19	53.22
GRU + att + pLab + genre (2)	**73.98**	**54.78**
GRU + att + pLab + genre (3)	70.78	46.25
GRU + att + pLab + genre (4)	72.88	48.94
GRU + att + pLab + genre (5)	72.60	45.98

Table 5: SE-type classification on German test set.

	Acc	F1
GRU + att + gLab (1)	71.33	58.32
GRU + att + gLab (2)	72.23	59.43
GRU + att + gLab (3)	73.81	59.12
GRU + att + gLab (4)	75.74	60.39
GRU + att + gLab (5)	**76.32**	**61.01**
GRU + att + gLab + genre (1)	74.79	59.34
GRU + att + gLab + genre (2)	**77.97**	**61.47**
GRU + att + gLab + genre (3)	74.28	59.84
GRU + att + gLab + genre (4)	74.10	59.70
GRU + att + gLab + genre (5)	74.96	58.18

Table 6: SE-type classification on German test set, *sequence oracle model* .

are more similar to one another than the ones in the English dataset. The results comparing the effectiveness of integrating context and genre information are in Table 5. The results of the oracle model using gold labels for previous clauses are in Table 6. Compared to English, the models achieve higher performance, but attention by itself does not improve the results, and neither does the inclusion of genre information. Used jointly, attention and genre information yield a moderate increase of 1.06 pp. accuracy compared to the basic GRU. Attention may need more data and possibly more diversity to be learned effectively, and we will explore this in future work.

Modeling context seems to have a larger impact:

compared to the basic GRU using attention, information about the current and the previous clauses improves the model by up to 1.67 pp. More contextual information leads to higher accuracy.

8 Conclusion

We presented an RNN-based approach to situation entity classification that bears clear advantages compared to previous classifier models that rely on carefully hand-engineered features and lexical semantic resources: it is easily transferable to other languages as it can tune pre-trained embeddings to encode semantic information relevant for the task, and can develop attention models to capture – and reveal – relevant information from the larger context. We designed and compared several GRU-based RNN models that jointly model *local and contextual* information in a unified architecture. Genre information was added to model common properties of specific textual genres. What makes our work interesting for linguistically informed semantic models is the exploration of different model variants that combine local classification with sequence information gained from the contextual history, and how these properties interact with genre characteristics. We specifically explore attention mechanisms that help our models focus on specific characteristics of the local and non-local contexts. Attention models jointly using genre and context information in the form of previous predicted labels perform best for our task, for both languages. The performance results of our best models outperform the state of the art models of *Fried16* for English when using either off-the-shelf NLP features (set A) or, separately, hand-crafted features based on lexical resources (set B). A small margin of ca. 3 pp accuracy is left to achieve in future work to compete with the knowledge-rich models of (Friedrich et al., 2016).

Acknowledgments. We thank Sabrina Effenberger, Jesper Klein, Sarina Meyer, and Rebekka Sons for the annotations, and the reviewers for their insightful comments. This research is funded by the Leibniz Science Campus Empirical Linguistics & Computational Language Modeling, supported by Leibniz Association grant no. SAS-2015-IDS-LWC and by the Ministry of Science, Research, and Art of Baden-Württemberg.

References

Dzmitry Bahdanau, Kyunghyun Cho, and Yoshua Bengio. 2015. Neural machine translation by jointly learning to align and translate. In *ICLR*.

Maria Becker, Alexis Palmer, and Anette Frank. 2016a. Argumentative texts and clause types. In *Proceedings of the 3rd Workshop on Argument Mining*. pages 21–30.

Maria Becker, Alexis Palmer, and Anette Frank. 2016b. Clause Types and Modality in Argumentative Microtexts. In *Workshop on Foundations of the Language of Argumentation (in conjunction with COMMA)*. Potsdam, Germany, pages 1–9.

Y. Bengio, P. Simard, and P. Frasconi. 1994. Learning long-term dependencies with gradient descent is difficult. *Trans. Neur. Netw.* 5(2):157–166. https://doi.org/10.1109/72.279181.

James Bergstra and Yoshua Bengio. 2012. Random search for hyper-parameter optimization. *Journal of Machine Learning Research* 13(Feb):281–305.

Peter F. Brown, Peter V. Desouza, Robert L. Mercer, Vincent J. Della Pietra, and Jenifer C. Lai. 1992. Class-based n-gram models of natural language. *Computational Linguistics* 18(4):467479.

Kyunghyun Cho, B van Merrienboer, Dzmitry Bahdanau, and Yoshua Bengio. 2014. *On the properties of neural machine translation: Encoder-decoder approaches*.

Li Dong and Mirella Lapata. 2016. Language to logical form with neural attention. In *Proceedings of the 54th Annual Meeting of the Association for Computational Linguistics (Volume 1: Long Papers)*. Association for Computational Linguistics, Berlin, Germany, pages 33–43. http://www.aclweb.org/anthology/P16-1004.

John Duchi, Elad Hazan, and Yoram Singer. 2011. Adaptive subgradient methods for online learning and stochastic optimization. *Journal of Machine Learning Research* 12(Jul):2121–2159.

Annemarie Friedrich and Alexis Palmer. 2014. Situation entity annotation. In *Proceedings of the Linguistic Annotation Workshop VIII*.

Annemarie Friedrich, Alexis Palmer, and Manfred Pinkal. 2016. Situation entity types: automatic classification of clause-level aspect. In *Proceedings of the 54th Annual Meeting of the Association for Computational Linguistics (Volume 1: Long Papers)*. Berlin, Germany, pages 1757–1768. http://www.aclweb.org/anthology/P16-1166.

Annemarie Friedrich, Alexis Palmer, Melissa Peate Sørensen, and Manfred Pinkal. 2015. Annotating genericity: a survey, a scheme, and a corpus. In *The 9th Linguistic Annotation Workshop held in conjuncion with NAACL 2015*. page 21.

Annemarie Friedrich and Manfred Pinkal. 2015. Discourse-sensitive Automatic Identification of Generic Expressions. In *Proceedings of the 53rd Annual Meeting of the Association for Computational Linguistics (ACL)*. Beijing, China.

Sepp Hochreiter and Jürgen Schmidhuber. 1997. Long short-term memory. *Neural computation* 9(8):1735–1780.

Nancy Ide, Christiane Fellbaum, Collin Baker, and Rebecca Passonneau. 2010. The Manually Annotated Sub-Corpus: A community resource for and by the people. In *Proceedings of the ACL2010 Conference Short Papers*. pages 68–73.

Nal Kalchbrenner, Edward Grefenstette, and Phil Blunsom. 2014. A convolutional neural network for modelling sentences. In *Proceedings of the 52nd Annual Meeting of the Association for Computational Linguistics*. Baltimore, Maryland, pages 655–665.

Yoon Kim. 2014. Convolutional neural networks for sentence classification. In *Proceedings of the 2014 Conference on Empirical Methods in Natural Language Processing (EMNLP)*. Doha, Qatar, page 17461751.

Guillaume Lample, Miguel Ballesteros, Sandeep Subramanian, Kazuya Kawakami, and Chris Dyer. 2016. Neural architectures for named entity recognition. In *Proceedings of the 2016 Conference of the North American Chapter of the Association for Computational Linguistics: Human Language Technologies*. Association for Computational Linguistics, San Diego, California, pages 260–270. http://www.aclweb.org/anthology/N16-1030.

Sharid Loaiciga, Thomas Meyer, and Andrei Popescu-Belis. 2014. English-french verb phrase alignment in europarl for tense translation modeling. In *Proceedings of The Ninth Language Resources and Evaluation Conference (LREC)*.

Mitchell Marcus, Beatrice Santorini, and Mary Ann Marcinkiewicz. 1993. Building a large annotated corpus of english: The penn treebank. In *Proceedings of the Annual Meeting of the Association for Computational Linguistics*.

Kleio-Isidora Mavridou, Annemarie Friedrich, Melissa Peate Sorensen, Alexis Palmer, and Manfred Pinkal. 2015. Linking discourse modes and situation entities in a cross-linguistic corpus study. In *Proceedings of the EMNLP Workshop LSDSem 2015: Linking Models of Lexical, Sentential and Discourse-level Semantics*.

Tomas Mikolov, Ilya Sutskever, Kai Chen, Greg S Corrado, and Jeff Dean. 2013a. Distributed representations of words and phrases and their compositionality. In *Advances in neural information processing systems*. pages 3111–3119.

Tomas Mikolov, Wen-tau Yih, and Geoffrey Zweig. 2013b. Linguistic regularities in continuous space word representations. In *Proceedings of the 2013 Conference of the North American Chapter of the Association for Computational Linguistics: Human Language Technologies*. Association for Computational Linguistics, Atlanta, Georgia, pages 746–751. http://www.aclweb.org/anthology/N13-1090.

Makoto Miwa and Mohit Bansal. 2016. End-to-end relation extraction using lstms on sequences and tree structures. In *Proceedings of the 54th Annual Meeting of the Association for Computational Linguistics (Volume 1: Long Papers)*. Berlin, Germany, pages 1105–1116. http://www.aclweb.org/anthology/P16-1105.

Alexis Palmer and Annemarie Friedrich. 2014. Genre distinctions and discourse modes: Text types differ in their situation type distributions. In *Proceedings of the Workshop on Frontiers and Connections between Argumentation Theory and NLP*.

Alexis Palmer, Elias Ponvert, Jason Baldridge, and Carlota Smith. 2007. A sequencing model for situation entity classification. In *Proceedings of ACL*.

Andreas Peldszus and Manfred Stede. 2015. An annotated corpus of argumentative microtexts. In *Proceedings of the First European Conference on Argumentation*.

Barbara Plank, Anders Søgaard, and Yoav Goldberg. 2016. Multilingual part-of-speech tagging with bidirectional long short-term memory models and auxiliary loss. In *Proceedings of the 54th Annual Meeting of the Association for Computational Linguistics (Volume 2: Short Papers)*. Association for Computational Linguistics, Berlin, Germany, pages 412–418. http://anthology.aclweb.org/P16-2067.

Nils Reimers, Judith Eckle-Kohler, Carsten Schnober, Jungi Kim, and Iryna Gurevych. 2014. Germeval-2014: Nested Named Entity Recognition with neural networks. In *Proceedings of the 12th Edition of the KONVENS Conference*. page 117120.

Tim Rocktäschel, Edward Grefenstette, Karl Moritz Hermann, Tomáš Kočiský, and Phil Blunsom. 2016. Reasoning about entailment with neural attention. In *Proceedings of the 4th International Conference on Learning Representations (ICLR)*. San Juan, Puerto Rico.

Uladzimir Sidarenka, Andreas Peldszus, and Manfred Stede. 2015. Discourse Segmentation of German Texts. In *Journal for Language Technology and Computational Linguistics*. volume 30, pages 71–98.

Carlota S Smith. 2003. *Modes of discourse: The local structure of texts*, volume 103. Cambridge University Press.

Radu Soricut and Daniel Marcu. 2003. Sentence level discourse parsing using syntactic and lexical information. In *Proceedings of the 2003 Conference of the North American Chapter of the Association for Computational Linguistics on Human Language Technology.*.

Kai Sheng Tai, Richard Socher, and Christopher D. Manning. 2015. Improved semantic representations from tree-structured long short-term memory networks. In *Proceedings of the 53rd Annual Meeting of the Association for Computational Linguistics and the 7th International Joint Conference on Natural Language Processing (Volume 1: Long Papers)*. Association for Computational Linguistics, Beijing, China, pages 1556–1566. http://www.aclweb.org/anthology/P15-1150.

Ngoc Thang Vu, Heike Adel, Pankaj Gupta, and Hinrich Schütze. 2016. Combining recurrent and convolutional neural networks for relation classification. In *Proceedings of the 2016 Conference of the North American Chapter of the Association for Computational Linguistics: Human Language Technologies*. San Diego, California, pages 534–539. http://www.aclweb.org/anthology/N16-1065.

Yequan Wang, Minlie Huang, xiaoyan zhu, and Li Zhao. 2016. Attention-based LSTM for Aspect-level Sentiment Classification. In *Proceedings of the 2016 Conference on Empirical Methods in Natural Language Processing*. Association for Computational Linguistics, Austin, Texas, pages 606–615. https://aclweb.org/anthology/D16-1058.

Wenpeng Yin, Katharina Kann, Mo Yu, and Hinrich Schütze. 2017. Comparative study of cnn and rnn for natural language processing. *CoRR* abs/1702.01923.

Jie Zhou, Ying Cao, Xuguang Wang, Peng Li, and Wei Xu. 2016. Deep recurrent models with fast-forward connections for neural machine translation. *Transactions of the Association for Computational Linguistics* pages 371–383.

Jie Zhou and Wei Xu. 2015. End-to-end learning of semantic role labeling using recurrent neural networks. In *Proceedings of the 53rd Annual Meeting of the Association for Computational Linguistics and the 7th International Joint Conference on Natural Language Processing (Volume 1: Long Papers)*. Association for Computational Linguistics, Beijing, China, pages 1127–1137. http://www.aclweb.org/anthology/P15-1109.

Predictive Linguistic Features of Schizophrenia

Efsun Sarioglu Kayi[1], Mona Diab[1], Luca Pauselli[2], Michael Compton[2], Glen Coppersmith[3]
[1]Department of Computer Science, George Washington University
{efsun, mtdiab}@gwu.edu
[2]Medical Center, Columbia University
{mtc2176@cumc.columbia.edu, pausell@nyspi.columbia.edu}
[3]Qntfy
glen@qntfy.com

Abstract

Schizophrenia is one of the most disabling and difficult to treat of all human medical/health conditions, ranking in the top ten causes of disability worldwide. It has been a puzzle in part due to difficulty in identifying its basic, fundamental components. Several studies have shown that some manifestations of schizophrenia (e.g., the *negative symptoms* that include blunting of speech prosody, as well as the *disorganization* symptoms that lead to disordered language) can be understood from the perspective of linguistics. However, schizophrenia research has not kept pace with technologies in computational linguistics, especially in semantics and pragmatics. As such, we examine the writings of schizophrenia patients analyzing their syntax, semantics and pragmatics. In addition, we analyze tweets of (self proclaimed) schizophrenia patients who publicly discuss their diagnoses. For writing samples dataset, syntactic features are found to be the most successful in classification whereas for the less structured Twitter dataset, a combination of features performed the best.

1 Introduction

Schizophrenia is an etiologically complex, heterogeneous, and chronic disorder. It imposes major impairments on affected individuals, can be devastating to families, and it diminishes the productivity of communities. Furthermore, schizophrenia is associated with remarkably high direct and indirect health care costs. Persons with schizophrenia often have multiple medical comorbidities, have a tragically reduced life expectancy, and are often treated without the benefits of sophisticated *measurement-based care.*

Similar to other psychoses, schizophrenia has been studied extensively on the neurological and behavioral levels. Covington et al. (2005) note the existence of many language abnormalities (in syntactic, semantic, pragmatic, and phonetic domains of linguistics) comparing patients to controls. They observed the following:

- reduction in syntax complexity (Fraser et al., 1986);

- impaired semantics, such as the organization of individual propositions into larger structures (Rodriguez-Ferrera et al., 2001);

- abnormalities in pragmatics which is a level obviously disordered in schizophrenia (Covington et al., 2005);

- phonetic anomalies like flattened intonation (aprosody), more pauses, and constricted pitch/timbre (Stein, 1993).

A few studies have used computational methods to assess acoustic parameters (e.g., pauses, prosody) that correlate with negative symptoms, but schizophrenia research has not kept pace with technologies in computational linguistics, especially in semantics and pragmatics. Accordingly, we analyze the predictive power of linguistic features in a comprehensive manner by computing and analyzing many syntactic, semantic and pragmatic features. This sort of analysis is particularly useful for finding meaningful signals that help us better understand the mental health conditions. To this end, we compute part-of-speech (POS) tags and dependency parses to capture the syntactic information in patients' writings. For semantics, we derive topic based representations and semantic role labels of writings. In addition, we add more semantics by adding dense features using clusters that are trained on online resources. For pragmatics, we consider the sentiment that exists in writings, i.e. *positive* vs. *negative* and its intensity. To

*Proceedings of the 6th Joint Conference on Lexical and Computational Semantics (*SEM 2017)*, pages 241–250,
Vancouver, Canada, August 3-4, 2017. ©2017 Association for Computational Linguistics

the best of our knowledge, no previous work has conducted comprehensive analysis of schizophrenia patients' writings from the perspective of syntax, semantics and pragmatics, collectively.

2 Predictive Linguistic Features of Schizophrenia

2.1 Dataset

The first dataset called LabWriting consists of 93 patients with schizophrenia who were recruited from sites in both Washington, D.C. and New York City. This includes patients that have a diagnosis of schizophreniform disorder or first-episode or early-course patients with a psychotic disorder not otherwise specified. All patients were native English-speaking patients, aged 18-50 years and cognitively intact enough to understand and participate in the study. A total of 95 eligible controls were also native English speakers aged 18-50. Patients and controls did not differ by age, race, or marital status, however, patients were more likely to be male and had completed fewer years of education. All study participants were assessed for their ability to give consent, and written informed consent was obtained using Institutional Review Board-approved processes. Patients and controls were asked to write two paragraph-length essays: one about their average Sunday and the second about what makes them the angriest. The total number of writing samples collected from both patients and controls is 373. Below is a sample response from this dataset (text from patients rendered verbatim as is including typos):

The one thing that probably makes me the most angry is when good people receive the bad end of the draw. This includes a child being struck for no good reason. A person who is killed but was an innocent bystander. Or even when people pour their heart and soul into a job which pays them peanurs but they cannot sustain themselves without this income. Just in generul a good person getting the raw end of deal. For instance people getting laid off because their company made bad investments. the Higher ups keep their jobs while the worker ants get disposed of. How about people who take advantage of others and build an Empire off it like insurance or drug companies. All these good decent people not getting what they deserved. Yup that makes me angry.

In addition, we evaluated social media messages with self-reported diagnoses of schizophrenia using the Twitter API. This dataset includes 174 users with apparently genuine self-stated diagnosis of a schizophrenia-related condition and 174 age and gender matched controls. Schizophrenia users were selected via regular expression on *schizo* for a close phonetic approximation. Each diagnosis was examined by a human annotator to verify that it seems genuine. For each schizophrenia user, a control that had the same gender label and was closest in age was selected. The average number of tweets per user is around 2,800. Detailed information on this dataset can be found in (Mitchell et al., 2015). Below are some tweets from this dataset (they have been rephrased to preserve anonymity):

this is my first time being unemployed. please forgive me. i'm crazy. #schizophrenia

i'm in my late 50s. i worry if i have much time left as they say people with #schizophrenia die 15-20 years younger

#schizophrenia takes me to devil-like places in my mind

2.2 Approach and Experimental Design

We cast the problem as a supervised binary classification task where a system should discriminate between a patient and a control. To classify schizophrenia patients from controls, we trained support vector machines (SVM) with linear kernel and Random Forest classifiers. We used Weka (Hall et al., 2009) to conduct the experiments with 10-fold stratified cross validation. We report Precision, Recall, F-Score, and Area Under Curve (AUC) value which is the area under receiver operating characteristics curve (ROC).

2.2.1 Syntactic Features

To capture the syntactic information from writings, we produce the POS tags and dependency parse trees using Stanford Core NLP (Manning et al., 2014). To use these as features to the classifier, we calculate the frequency of each POS tag and dependencies from parse trees. For the Twitter dataset, we use a parser (Kong et al., 2014) and POS tagger (Gimpel et al., 2011) that are specifically trained for social media data.

2.2.2 Semantic Features

To analyze the semantics of the writings, we consider several sources of information. As a first approach, we use semantic role labeling (SRL). Specifically, we use Semafor (Das et al., 2010) tool to generate semantic role labels of the writings and then calculate the frequency of the labels as features for the classifier. For Twitter dataset, due to its short form and poor syntax, we were not able to compute SRL features.

In addition to SRL, we analyzed the topic distribution of writings using Latent Dirichlet Allocation (LDA) (Blei et al., 2003). With this approach, we want to see the possibility of different themes emerging in the writings of patients vs. controls. Using LDA, we represent each writing as a topic distribution where each topic is automatically learned as a distribution over the words of the vocabulary. We use the MALLET tool (McCallum, 2002) to train the topic model and empirically choose number of topics based on best classification performance on a validation set. The best performing number of topics is 20 for LabWriting dataset and 40 for Twitter dataset.

Finally, we compute dense semantic features by computing clusters based on global word vectors. Specifically, for LabWriting dataset, we use word vectors trained on Wikipedia 2014 dump and Gigaword 5 (Parker, 2011) which are generated based on global word-word co-occurrence statistics (Pennington et al., 2014). For Twitter dataset, we use Twitter models trained on 2 billion tweets.[1] We, then, create clusters of these word vectors using the K-means algorithm (K= 100, empirically chosen) for both datasets. Then, for each writing, we calculate the frequency of each cluster by checking the existence of each word of the document in the cluster. With this cluster based representation, we aim to capture the effect of semantically related words on the classification.

2.2.3 Pragmatic Features

For pragmatics, we wanted to see whether patients exhibit more negative sentiment than controls. For that purpose, we use the Stanford Sentiment Analysis tool (Socher et al., 2013). Given a sentence, it predicts its sentiment at five possible levels: *very negative, negative, neutral, positive,* and *very positive.* For each writing, we calculate the frequency of sentiment levels. Additionally, sentiment inten-

---

[1] http://nlp.stanford.edu/projects/glove/

sities are produced at the phrase level. Rather than categorical values, this intensity encodes the magnitude of the sentiment more explicitly. As such, we calculate the total intensity for each document as sum of its phrases' intensities at each level. For Twitter dataset, we use a sentiment classifier that was trained for social media data (Radeva et al., 2016). Its output includes three levels of sentiment *negative, neutral,* and *positive* without intensity information.

2.2.4 Feature Analysis

To be able to better evaluate best performing features, we analyze them based on two feature selection algorithms: Information Gain (IG) for Random Forest and Recursive Feature Elimination (RFE) algorithm for SVM (Guyon et al., 2002). The Information Gain measure selects the attributes that decrease the entropy the most. The RFE algorithm, on the other hand, selects features based on their weights based on the fact that the larger weights correspond to the more informative features.

3 Results

The list of syntactic, semantic and pragmatic features are presented in Table 1 for both datasets. Tables 2 and 3 illustrate our results for the LabWriting dataset and Twitter dataset, respectively. The majority baseline F-Score is 34.39 for the LabWriting and 32.11 for Twitter dataset. The top performance for each dataset and classifier is shown in bold. The corresponding ROC plots for features are shown in Figures 1 and 2 for LabWriting and Twitter datasets respectively. In each ROC plot, true positive rate (recall) is plotted against true negative rate where SVM is shown in magenta and Random Forest is shown in blue. The diagonal line from bottom left to upper right represents random guess and better performing results are closer to upper left corner. Overall, Random Forest performs better than SVM even though for some feature combinations, SVM's performance is higher. This could be due to bootstrapping of samples that takes place in Random Forest since both of the datasets are on the smaller side. For LabWriting dataset, the best performing features according to F-Score are syntactic: POS+Parse (syntax) for SVM and syntax + pragmatics features for Random Forest. According to AUC, best performing feature is POS for both classifiers. For Twitter dataset, the best performing features according to

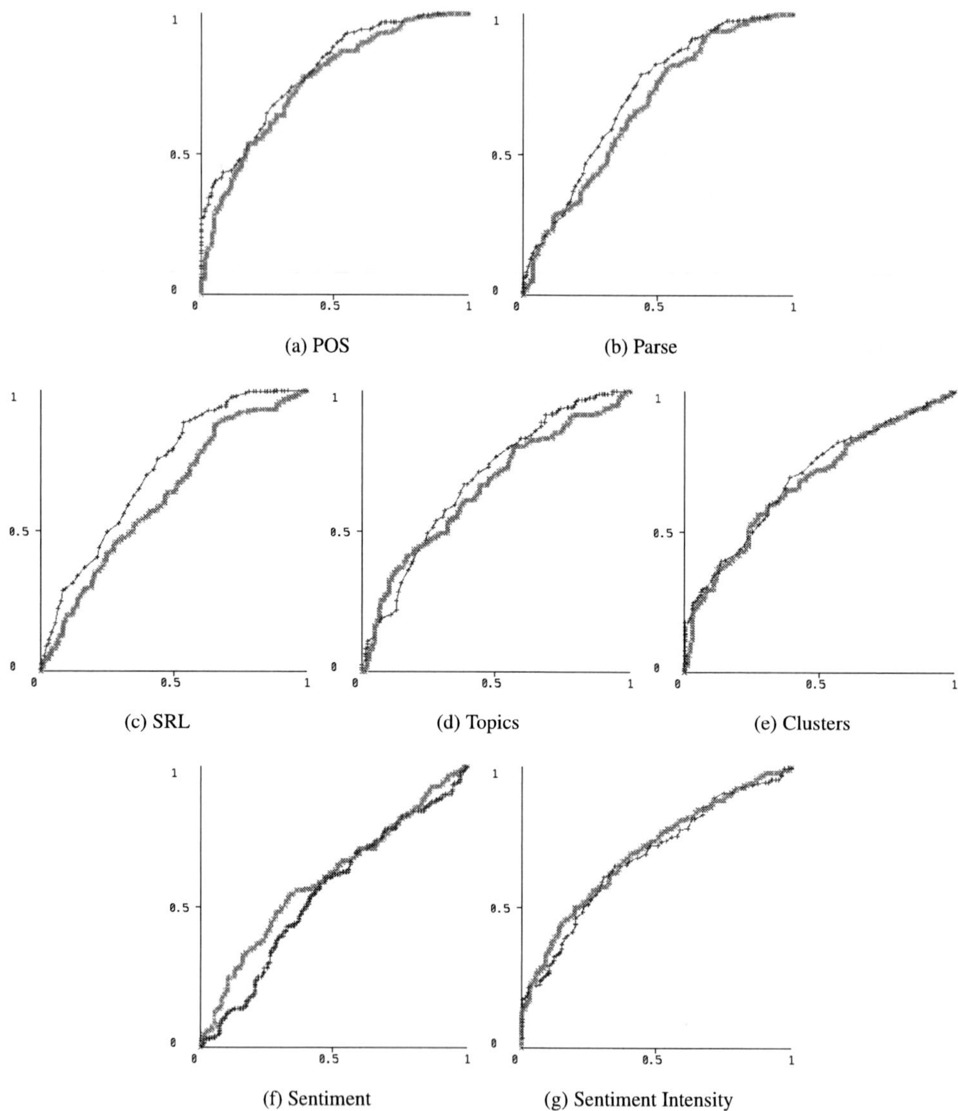

(a) POS
(b) Parse
(c) SRL
(d) Topics
(e) Clusters
(f) Sentiment
(g) Sentiment Intensity

Figure 1: ROC Plots for LabWriting Dataset

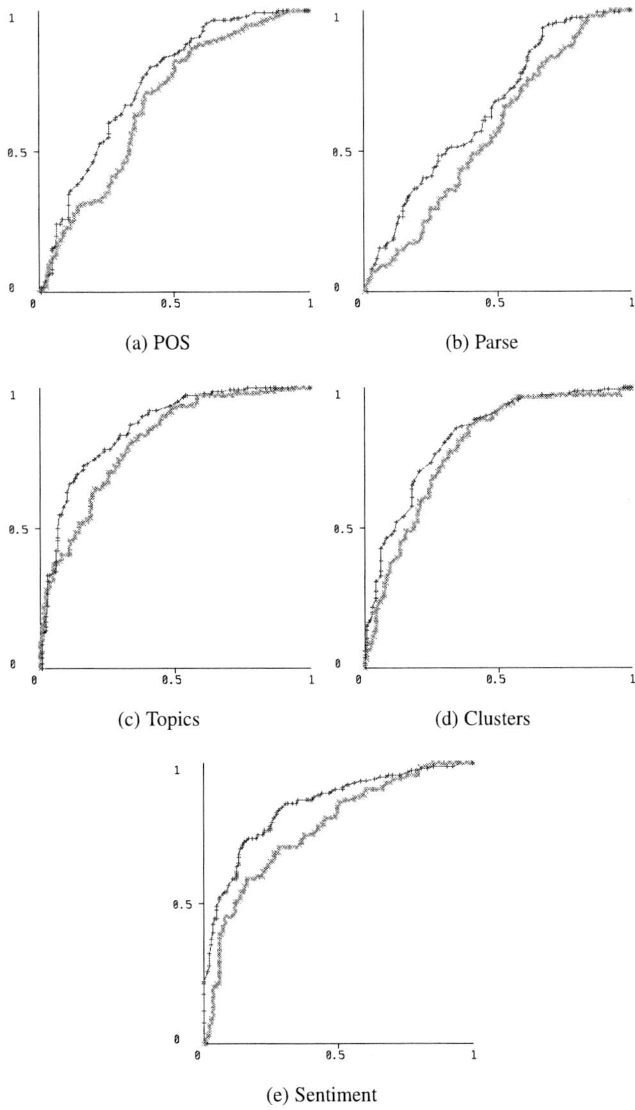

(a) POS

(b) Parse

(c) Topics

(d) Clusters

(e) Sentiment

Figure 2: ROC Plots for Twitter Dataset

Table 1: **Feature Categories**

Category	Writing Samples	Twitter
Syntactic	POS, Dependency Parse	POS, Dependency Parse
Semantic (Sem.)	SRL, Topics, Clusters	Topics , Clusters
Pragmatic (Prag.)	Sentiment, Sentiment Intensity	Sentiment

Table 2: **Classification Performance of LabWriting Dataset**

	SVM				Random Forest			
Features	AUC	Precision	Recall	F-Score	AUC	Precision	Recall	F-Score
POS	**75.72**	68.89	68.07	68.48	**78.92**	70.11	69.41	69.76
Parse	65.34	60.15	59.23	59.69	66.68	66.74	65.16	65.94
SRL	64.25	58.65	58.24	58.44	70.62	65.22	64.64	64.93
Topics	66.49	63.52	63.17	63.34	68.26	62.77	62.34	62.55
Clusters	69.68	65.12	64.85	64.98	68.43	65.38	64.62	65.00
Sentiment	60.23	54.99	53.83	54.40	56.27	57.97	57.66	57.81
Sentiment Intensity	69.98	64.20	64.07	64.13	69.39	65.31	64.62	64.96
Syntax	74.17	69.38	68.38	**68.88**	75.78	69.25	68.09	68.67
Semantics	66.46	61.59	61.05	61.32	69.16	64.39	63.72	64.05
Pragmatics	68.95	62.67	62.45	62.56	69.59	67.57	66.78	67.17
Syntax + Sem.	68.24	66.36	66.12	66.24	76.60	71.24	69.36	70.29
Syntax + Prag.	73.43	68.14	67.28	67.71	78.75	71.74	70.52	**71.12**
Sem.+ Prag.	68.01	63.98	63.46	63.72	72.09	65.75	64.81	65.28
All	70.11	66.94	66.66	66.80	77.57	71.18	69.91	70.54

both F-Score and AUC are the ones that include most of the combination of features: semantics + pragmatics for Random Forest and all features for SVM. Typically, essays, such as the ones in LabWriting dataset, are expected to have better syntax than informal tweets and as such syntactic features were not as predictive for tweets. We also analyze top performing features according to Information Gain measure and SVM RFE algorithm in Sections 3.1, 3.3, 3.2 and explain the differences of results for the two datasets in Section 3.4.

3.1 Top Syntactic Features

Syntactic features perform well mainly for Lab-Writing dataset. Between POS tags and dependence parses, the former perform better for both datasets. For LabWriting dataset, the top POS tag is *FW*, (Foreign Word). When we look at the words that were tagged *FW*, they correspond to misspelled words. Even though this could be considered a criterion for schizophrenia patients, it may also depend on patients and controls' education and language skills which we expect it to be similar but it may still show some differences. Another top POS tag is *LS*, (List item marker),

which was assigned to small case *i* which in reality refers to pronoun *I*. This could imply that the patients prefer to talk about themselves. This coincides with several other studies (Rude et al., 2004; Chung and Pennebaker, 2007) which found that use of first person singular is associated with negative affective states such as depression. Because of the likelihood of comorbidity of mental illnesses, this requires further investigation as to whether this is specific to schizophrenia patients or not. Finally, another top POS tag is *RP*, adverbial particle and top parse tag is *advmod*, adverb modifier. This could mean the ratio of adverbs used could be a characteristic of patients. Finally for Twitter dataset, the top POS tag is # corresponding to hash tags. This could be an important discriminative feature between patients and controls as patients use less hashtags than controls.

3.2 Top Semantic Features

For classification using semantic features, clusters, topics and SRL perform comparably. For Lab-Writing dataset, top SRL features consist of general categories and some specific ones that could be relevant for schizophrenia patients. General la-

Table 3: **Classification Performance of Twitter Dataset**

| | **SVM** | | | | **Random Forest** | | | |
Features	AUC	Precision	Recall	F-Score	AUC	Precision	Recall	F-Score
POS	69.34	67.83	59.14	63.19	75.17	69.48	68.92	69.20
Parse	58.63	44.76	54.06	48.97	63.72	60.94	60.63	60.78
Topics	79.88	74.85	73.66	74.25	83.48	79.38	78.77	79.07
Clusters	78.02	73.87	71.27	72.55	82.54	74.80	73.76	74.28
Sentiment	75.79	65.15	60.50	62.74	85.28	80.00	79.50	79.75
Syntax	74.87	68.16	62.13	65.01	74.35	67.72	67.47	67.59
Semantics	80.29	70.81	70.34	70.57	85.62	75.00	74.72	74.86
Syntax+Sem.	81.47	73.02	72.55	72.78	86.35	78.30	78.02	78.16
Syntax+Prag.	82.16	75.61	72.22	73.88	83.55	75.89	75.52	75.70
Sem.+Prag.	80.99	74.52	74.05	74.28	**88.98**	82.01	81.30	**81.65**
All	**82.58**	75.18	74.39	**74.78**	88.01	78.81	78.40	78.60

bels are *Quantity* and *Social Event*. More specific labels are *Morality Evaluation, Catastrophe, Manipulate into Doing* and *Being Obligated*. Words that are labeled as such are listed in Table 4. These two different sets of labels could be due to the type of questions asked to the patients. One question is neutral in nature talking about their daily life whereas the other is about the things that make them angry and more emotionally charged. A second semantic feature is the topic distributions of writings. The top words from the most informative topics are listed in Table 5. For LabWriting dataset, one of the top topics consist of words about typical Sunday activities corresponding to one of the questions asked. The second top topic, on the other hand, consist of words that show the anger of the author. For Twitter dataset, one of the topics consist of schizophrenia-related words and the other consist of hate words. Again, the top topics seem to contain relevant information in analyzing schizophrenia patients' writings and classification using topic features perform comparably well. As a final semantic feature, we use dense cluster features. The classification performance of cluster features is similar to classification performance using topics. However, cluster features' analysis is not as interpretable as topics, since they are formed from massive online data resources.

3.3 Top Pragmatic Features

When it comes to pragmatic features, top sentiment features are *neutral*, *negative* and *very negative* (LabWriting only). For sentiment intensity, *neutral intensity*, *negative intensity* and *very negative intensity* are more informative which is consistent with sentiment categorical analysis. In general, neutral sentiment is the most common for a given text and for patients, we would expect to see more negative sentiment and this was confirmed by this analysis. However, negative sentiment could also be prominent in other psychiatric diseases such as post-traumatic stress disorder (PTSD)(Coppersmith et al., 2015), as such, by itself, it may not be a discriminatory feature for schizophrenia patients. For classification purposes, sentiment intensity features performed better than sentiment features. This could be due to the fact that intensity values are more specific and collected at word/phrase level in contrast to sentence level.

3.4 Effect of Datasets' Characteristics

The two datasets have some commonalities and differences and present different challenges. The LabWriting dataset was collected in a more controlled manner and follows a structure that can be expected from a short essay. Accordingly, NLP tools applied to these writings are successful. On the other hand, the Twitter dataset consists of combinations of short text that include many abbreviations that are not standard, e.g. users' own solutions to fixed length limit imposed by Twitter. It is also very informal in nature and thus lacks proper grammar and syntax more frequently than LabWriting. Hence, some machine learning approaches for NLP analysis of these tweets are limited even though social media specific tools were used such as POS tagger (Gimpel et al., 2011), dependency parser (Kong et al., 2014), sentiment analysis tool (Radeva et al., 2016), and Twitter

Table 4: **Top Discriminative SRL Features**

Label	Sample Words/Phrases
Quantity	several, both, all, a lot, many, a little, a few, lots
Social Event	social, dinner, picnics, hosting, dance
Morality Evaluation	wrong, depraved, foul, evil, moral
Catastrophe	incident,tragedy, suffer
Manipulate into Doing	harassing, bullying
Being Obligated	duty, job, have to, had to, should, must, responsibility, entangled, task

Table 5: **Discriminative Topics' Top Words**

Method	Dataset	Top Words
IG	Writing	church sunday wake god service pray sing worship bible spending thanking
IG&RFE	Writing	i'm can't trust upset person lie real feel honest lied lies judge lying steal
IG&RFE	Twitter	god jesus mental schizophrenic schizophrenia illness paranoid medical evil
IG&RFE	Twitter	don love people fuck life feel fucking hate shit stop god person sleep bad die

models for dense clusters. For instance, even though we were able to compute POS tags and parse trees for tweets, the tag set is much smaller than PennTree Bank tags set. Similarly, some approaches such as SRL were not successful on tweets. On the other hand, both datasets consist of patients and controls with similar demographics (age, gender, etc), thus we largely expect patients and controls to have similar linguistic capabilities. In addition, for LabWriting dataset, patients and controls were recruited from the same neighborhoods. We have no such explicit guarantees for the Twitter dataset, though they were excluded if they did not primarily tweet in English. Accordingly, any differentiation these classification methods found can largely be attributed to the illness. Finally, LabWriting dataset had many spelling errors. We elected not to employ any spelling correction techniques (since misspelling may very well be a feature meaningful to schizophrenia). This likely negatively influenced the calculation of some of the features which depend on correct spelling such as SRL.

4 Related Work

To date, some studies have investigated applying Latent Semantic Analysis (LSA) to the problem (Elvevag et al., 2007) of lexical coherence and they found significant distinctions between schizophrenia patients and controls. The work of (Bedi et al., 2015) extends this approach by incorporating syntax, i.e., phrase level LSA measures

and POS tags. In the latter related work, several measures based on LSA representation were developed to capture the possible incoherence in patients. In our study, we used LDA to capture possible differences in themes between patients and controls. LDA is a more descriptive technique than LSA since topics are represented as distributions over vocabulary and top words for topics provide a way to understand the theme that they represent. We also incorporated syntax to our analysis with POS tags and additionally dependency parses. Another work by (Howes et al., 2013) predicts outcomes by analyzing doctor-patient communication in therapy using LDA. Even though manual analysis of LDA topics with manual topics seems promising, classification using topics does not perform as successful unless otherwise additional features are incorporated such as doctors' and patients' information. Although, we had detailed demographic information for LabWriting dataset and derived age and sex information for Twitter dataset, we chose not to incorporate them to the classification process be able focus solely on writings' characteristics.

The work of Mitchell et al. (2015) is, in many respects, similar to ours by examining schizophrenia using LDA, clustering and sentiment analysis. Their sentiment analysis is lexicon-based using Linguistic Inquiry Word Count (LIWC) (Tausczik and Pennebaker, 2010) categories. In our approach to sentiment analysis, we utilized a machine learning approach. Lexicon-based approaches generally have higher precision at the cost of lower recall. Having coverage of more of the content may be beneficial for analysis and interpretation, so we opt to use a more generalizable machine learning approach. For clustering, they used Brown clustering; whereas, we used clusters trained on global word vectors which were learned from large amounts of online data. This has the advantage that we could capture words and/or semantics that may not be learned from our dataset. Finally, their use of LDA is similar to our approach, i.e. representing documents as topic distributions, and their analysis does not include syntactic and dense cluster features. They had their best performance with an accuracy value of 82.3 using a combination of topic based representation and their version of sentiment features. In our analysis, combination of semantic and pragmatic features performed the best with an accuracy value of 81.7. Due to possible differences in preprocessing, parameter selection, and randomness that exist in the experiments, the results are not directly comparable, however, this also shows that the difficulty of applying more advanced machine learning based NLP techniques for Twitter dataset.

5   Conclusion

Computational assessment models of schizophrenia may provide ways for clinicians to monitor symptoms more effectively and a deeper understanding of schizophrenia and the underpinning cognitive biases could benefit affected individuals, families, and society at large. Objective and passive assessment of schizophrenia symptoms (e.g., delusion or paranoia) may provide clarity to clinical assessments, which currently rely on patients' self-reporting symptoms. Furthermore, the techniques discussed here hold some potential for early detection of schizophrenia. This would be greatly beneficial to young people and first-degree relatives of schizophrenia patients who are prodromal (clinically appearing to be at high risk for schizophrenia) but not yet delusional/psychotic, since it would allow targeted early interventions.

Among the linguistic features considered for this study, syntactic fetures provide the biggest boost in classification performance for LabWriting dataset. For Twitter dataset, combination of features such as semantics and pragmatics for SVM and syntax, semantics and pragmatics for Random Forest have the best performance.

In the future, we will be focusing on the features that showed the most promise in this study and also add new features such as level of committed belief for pragmatics. Finally, we are collecting more data and we will expand our analysis to more mental health datasets.

References

Gillinder Bedi, Facundo Carrillo, Guillermo A Cecchi, Diego Fernández Slezak, Mariano Sigman, Natália B Mota, Sidarta Ribeiro, Daniel C Javitt, Mauro Copelli, and Cheryl M Corcoran. 2015. Automated Analysis of Free Speech Predicts Psychosis Onset in High-Risk Youths. *Npj Schizophrenia* 1.

David M. Blei, Andrew Y. Ng, and Michael I. Jordan. 2003. Latent Dirichlet Allocation. *J. Mach. Learn. Res.* 3:993–1022.

Cindy K Chung and James W Pennebaker. 2007. Social Communication .

Glen Coppersmith, Mark Dredze, Craig Harman, and Kristy Hollingshead. 2015. From ADHD to SAD: Analyzing the Language of Mental Health on Twitter through Self-Reported Diagnoses. In *NAACL Workshop on Computational Linguistics and Clinical Psychology*.

Michael A Covington, Congzhou He, Cati Brown, Lorina Naci, Jonathan T McClain, Bess Sirmon Fjordbak, James Semple, and John Brown. 2005. Schizophrenia and the Structure of Language: The Linguist's View. *Schizophr Res* 77(1):85–98.

Dipanjan Das, Nathan Schneider, Desai Chen, and Noah A. Smith. 2010. Probabilistic Frame-semantic Parsing. In *Human Language Technologies: The 2010 Annual Conference of the North American Chapter of the Association for Computational Linguistics*. pages 948–956.

Brita Elvevag, Peter W Foltz, Daniel R Weinberger, and Terry E Goldberg. 2007. Quantifying Incoherence in Speech: An Automated Methodology and Novel Application to Schizophrenia. *Schizophr Res* 93(1-3):304–316.

W I Fraser, K M King, P Thomas, and R E Kendell. 1986. The Diagnosis of Schizophrenia by Language Analysis. *Br J Psychiatry* 148:275–278.

Kevin Gimpel, Nathan Schneider, Brendan O'Connor, Dipanjan Das, Daniel Mills, Jacob Eisenstein, Michael Heilman, Dani Yogatama, Jeffrey Flanigan, and Noah A. Smith. 2011. Part-of-speech Tagging for Twitter: Annotation, Features, and Experiments. In *Proceedings of the 49th Annual Meeting of the Association for Computational Linguistics: Human Language Technologies: Short Papers - Volume 2*. Association for Computational Linguistics, Stroudsburg, PA, USA, HLT '11, pages 42–47.

Isabelle Guyon, Jason Weston, Stephen Barnhill, and Vladimir Vapnik. 2002. Gene Selection for Cancer Classification Using Support Vector Machines. *Mach. Learn.* 46(1-3):389–422.

Mark Hall, Eibe Frank, Geoffrey Holmes, Bernhard Pfahringer, Peter Reutemann, and Ian H. Witten. 2009. The WEKA Data Mining Software: An Update. *SIGKDD Explor. Newsl.* 11(1):10–18.

Christine Howes, Matthew Purver, and Rose McCabe. 2013. Using Conversation Topics for Predicting Therapy Outcomes in Schizophrenia. *Biomed Inform Insights* 6(Suppl 1):39–50. https://doi.org/10.4137/BII.S11661.

Lingpeng Kong, Nathan Schneider, Swabha Swayamdipta, Archna Bhatia, Chris Dyer, and Noah A Smith. 2014. A Dependency Parser for Tweets .

Christopher D. Manning, Mihai Surdeanu, John Bauer, Jenny Finkel, Steven J. Bethard, and David McClosky. 2014. The Stanford CoreNLP Natural Language Processing Toolkit. In *Association for Computational Linguistics (ACL) System Demonstrations*. pages 55–60.

Andrew Kachites McCallum. 2002. MALLET: A Machine Learning for Language Toolkit. Http://mallet.cs.umass.edu.

Margaret Mitchell, Kristy Hollingshead, and Glen Coppersmith. 2015. Quantifying the Language of Schizophrenia in Social Media. In *Proceedings of the 2nd Workshop on Computational Linguistics and Clinical Psychology: From Linguistic Signal to Clinical Reality*. pages 11–20.

Robert et al. Parker. 2011. English Gigaword Fifth Edition LDC2011T07.

Jeffrey Pennington, Richard Socher, and Christopher D. Manning. 2014. GloVe: Global Vectors for Word Representation. In *Empirical Methods in Natural Language Processing (EMNLP)*. pages 1532–1543.

Axinia Radeva, Mohammad Rasooli, and Kathleen McKeown. 2016. Columbia Language Independent Sentiment System. Technical report, Columbia University.

S Rodriguez-Ferrera, R A McCarthy, and P J McKenna. 2001. Language in Schizophrenia and Its Relationship to Formal Thought Disorder. *Psychol Med* 31(2):197–205.

Stephanie Rude, Eva-Maria Gortner, and James Pennebaker. 2004. Language Use of Depressed and Depression-Vulnerable College Students. *Cognition and Emotion* 18(8):1121–1133.

Richard Socher, Alex Perelygin, Jean Y. Wu, Jason Chuang, Christopher D. Manning, Andrew Y. Ng, and Christopher Potts. 2013. Recursive Deep Models for Semantic Compositionality Over a Sentiment Treebank. *Conference on Empirical Methods in Natural Language Processing (EMNLP)* .

J Stein. 1993. Vocal Alterations in Schizophrenic Speech. *J Nerv Ment Dis* 181(1):59–62.

Yla R. Tausczik and James W. Pennebaker. 2010. The Psychological Meaning of Words: LIWC and Computerized Text Analysis Methods. *Journal of Language and Social Psychology* pages 24–54.

Learning to Solve Geometry Problems from Natural Language Demonstrations in Textbooks

Mrinmaya Sachan   **Eric P. Xing**

School of Computer Science
Carnegie Mellon University
{mrinmays, epxing}@cs.cmu.edu

Abstract

Humans as well as animals are good at *imitation*. Inspired by this, the *learning by demonstration* view of machine learning learns to perform a task from detailed example demonstrations. In this paper, we introduce the task of *question answering using natural language demonstrations* where the question answering system is provided with detailed demonstrative solutions to questions in natural language. As a case study, we explore the task of learning to solve geometry problems using demonstrative solutions available in textbooks. We collect a new dataset of demonstrative geometry solutions from textbooks and explore approaches that learn to interpret these demonstrations as well as to use these interpretations to solve geometry problems. Our approaches show improvements over the best previously published system for solving geometry problems.

1 Introduction

Cognitive science emphasizes the importance of *imitation* or *learning by example* (Meltzoff and Moore, 1977; Meltzoff, 1995) in human learning. When a teacher signals a pedagogical intention, children tend to imitate the teacher's actions (Buchsbaum et al., 2011; Butler and Markman, 2014). Inspired by this phenomenon, the *learning by demonstration* view of machine learning (Schaal, 1997; Argall et al., 2009; Goldwasser and Roth, 2014) assumes training data in the form of example demonstrations. A task is demonstrated by a teacher and the learner generalizes from these demonstrations in order to execute the task.

In this paper, we introduce the novel task of *question answering using natural language*

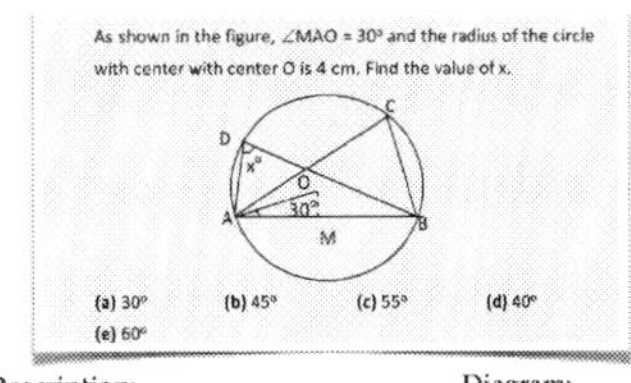

Text Description:

measure(∠MAO, 30°)
isCircle(O)
radius(O, 4 cm)
?x

Diagram:

liesOn(A, circle O), liesOn(B, circle O),
liesOn(C, circle O), liesOn(D, circle O)
isLine(AB), isLine(BC), isLine(CA), isLine(BD), isLine(DA)
isTriangle(ABC), isTriangle(ABD), isTriangle(AOM)
measure(∠ADB, x), measure(∠MAO, 30°)
measure(∠AMO, 90°)
...

Figure 1: Above: An example SAT style geometry problem with the text description, corresponding diagram and (optionally) answer candidates. Below: A logical expression that represents the meaning of the text description and the diagram in the problem. *GEOS* derives a weighted logical expression where each predicates also carry a weighted score but we do not show them here for clarity.

demonstrations. Research in question answering has traditionally focused on learning from question-answer pairs (Burger et al., 2001). However, it is well-established in the educational psychology literature (Allington and Cunningham, 2010; Felder et al., 2000) that children tend to learn better and faster from concrete illustrations and demonstrations. In this paper, we raise the question – "Can we leverage demonstrative solutions for questions as provided by a teacher to improve our question answering systems?"

As a case study, we propose the task of learning to solve SAT geometry problems (such as the one in Figure 1) using demonstrative solutions to these problems (such as the one in Figure 2). Such demonstrations are common in textbooks as they help students learn how to solve geometry problems effectively. We build a new dataset of demonstrative solutions of geometry problems and show that it can be used to improve *GEOS* (Seo et al., 2015), the state-of-the-art in solving geom-

*Proceedings of the 6th Joint Conference on Lexical and Computational Semantics (*SEM 2017)*, pages 251–261,
Vancouver, Canada, August 3-4, 2017. ©2017 Association for Computational Linguistics

1. Sum of interior angles of a triangle is 180^0

=> $\angle OAM + \angle AMO + \angle MOA = 180^0$

=> $\angle MOA = 60^0$

2. Similar triangle theorem

=> $\triangle MOB \sim \triangle MOA$

=> $\angle MOB = \angle MOA = 60^0$

3. $\angle AOB = \angle MOB + \angle MOA$

=> $\angle AOB = 120^0$

4. Angle subtended by a chord at the center is twice the angle subtended at the circumference

=> $\angle ADB = 0.5 \times \angle AOB$

$\qquad = 60^0$

Figure 2: An example demonstration on how to solve the problem in Figure 1: (1) Use the theorem that the sum of interior angles of a triangle is 180°and additionally the fact that $\angle$AMO is 90° to conclude that $\angle$MOA is 60°. (2) Conclude that $\triangle$MOA $\sim$ $\triangle$MOB (using a similar triangle theorem) and then, conclude that $\angle$MOB = $\angle$MOA = 60°(using the theorem that corresponding angles of similar triangles are equal). (3) Use angle sum rule to conclude that $\angle$AOB = $\angle$MOB + $\angle$MOA = 120°. (4) Use the theorem that the angle subtended by an arc of a circle at the centre is double the angle subtended by it at any point on the circle to conclude that $\angle$ADB = 0.5×$\angle$AOB = 60°.

etry problems.

We also present a technique inspired from recent work in situated question answering (Krishnamurthy et al., 2016) that jointly learns how to interpret the demonstration and use this interpretation to solve geometry problems. We model the interpretation task (the task of recognizing various states in the demonstration) as a semantic parsing task. We model state transitions in the demonstration via a deduction model that treats each application of a theorem of geometry as a state transition. We describe techniques to learn the two models separately as well as jointly from various kinds of supervision: (a) when we only have a set of question-answer pairs as supervision, (b) when we have a set of questions and demonstrative solutions for them, and (c) when we have a set of question-answer pairs and a set of demonstrations.

An important benefit of our approach is 'interpretability'. While *GEOS* is uninterpretable, our approach utilizes known theorems of geometry to deductively solve geometry problems. Our approach also generates demonstrative solutions (like Figure 2) as a by-product which can be pro-

vided to students on educational platforms such as MOOCs to assist in their learning.

We present an experimental evaluation of our approach on the two datasets previously introduced in Seo et al. (2015) and a new dataset collected by us from a number of math textbooks in India. Our experiments show that our approach of leveraging demonstrations improves *GEOS*. We also performed user studies with a number of school students studying geometry, who found that our approach is more *interpretable* as well as more *useful* in comparison to *GEOS*.

2 Background: GEOS

GEOS solves geometry problems via a multi-stage approach. It first learns to parse the problem text and the diagram to a formal problem description compatible with both of them. The problem description is a first-order logic expression (see Figure 1) that includes known numbers or geometrical entities (e.g. 4 cm) as constants, unknown numbers or geometrical entities (e.g. O) as variables, geometric or arithmetic relations (e.g. *isLine, isTriangle*) as predicates and properties of geometrical entities (e.g. *measure, liesOn*) as functions. The parser first learns a set of relations that potentially correspond to the problem text (or diagram) along with confidence scores. Then, a subset of relations that maximize the joint text and diagram score are picked as the problem description.

For diagram parsing, *GEOS* uses a publicly available diagram parser for geometry problems (Seo et al., 2014) that provides confidence scores for each literal to be true in the diagram. We use the diagram parser from *GEOS* to handle in our work too.

Text parsing is performed in three stages. The parser first maps words or phrases in the text to their corresponding concepts. Then, it identifies relations between identified concepts. Finally, it performs *relation completion* which handles implications and coordinating conjunctions.

Finally, *GEOS* uses a numerical approach to check the satisfiablity of literals, and to answer the multiple-choice question. While this solver is grounded in coordinate geometry and indeed works well, it has some issues: *GEOS* requires an explicit mapping of each predicate to a set of constraints over point coordinates. For example, the predicate *isPerpendicular*(AB, CD) is mapped to the constraint $\frac{y_B - y_A}{x_B - x_A} \times \frac{y_D - y_C}{x_D - x_C} = -1$. These con-

Axiom	Premise	Conclusion
Midpoint Definition	midpoint(M, AB)	length(AM) = length(MB)
Angle Addition	interior(D, ABC)	angle(ABC) = angle(ABD) + angle(DBC)
Supplementary Angles	perpendicular(AB,CD) $\wedge$ liesOn(C,AB)	angle(ACD) + angle(DCB) = 180°
Vertically Opp. Angles	intersectAt(AB, CD, M)	angle(AMC) = angle(BMD)

Table 1: Examples of geometry theorems as horn clause rules.

straints can be non-trivial to write and often require manual engineering. As a result, *GEOS*'s constraint set is incomplete and it cannot solve a number of SAT style geometry problems. Furthermore, this solver is not interpretable. As our user studies show, it is not natural for a student to understand the solution of these geometry problems in terms of satisfiability of constraints over coordinates. A more natural way for students to understand and reason about these problems is through deductive reasoning using well-known axioms and theorems of geometry. This kind of deductive reasoning is used in explanations in textbooks. In contrast to *GEOS* which uses supervised learning, our approach learns to solve geometry problems by interpreting natural language demonstrations of the solution. These demonstrations illustrate the process of solving the geometry problem via stepwise application of geometry theorems.

3 Theorems as Horn Clause Rules

We represent theorems as horn clause rules that map a premise in the logical language to a conclusion in the same language. Table 1 gives some examples of geometry theorems written as horn clause rules. The free variables in the theorems are universally quantified. The variables are also typed. For example, *ABC* can be of type *triangle* or *angle* but not *line*. Let $\mathcal{T}$ be the set of theorems. Formally, each theorem $t \in \mathcal{T}$ maps a logical formula $l_t^{(pr)}$ corresponding to the premise to a logical formula $l_t^{(co)}$ corresponding to the conclusion. The demonstration can be seen as a program – a sequence of horn clause rule applications that lead to the solution of the geometry problem. Given a current state, theorem t can be applied to the state if there exists an assignment to free variables in $l_t^{(pr)}$ that is true in the state. Each theorem application also has a probability associated with it; in our case, these probabilities are learned by a trained model. The state diagram for the demonstration in Figure 2 is shown in Figure 3. Now, we describe the various components of our *learning from demonstrations* approach: a se-

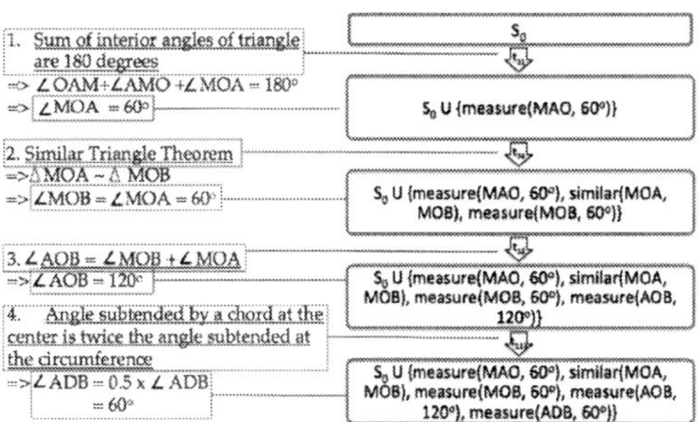

Figure 3: State sequence corresponding to the demonstration in Figure 2. Theorems applied are marked in green and the state information is marked in red. Here S_0 corresponds to the state derived from question interpretation and each theorem application subsequently adds new predicates to the logical formula corresponding to S_0. The final state contains the answer: measure(ADB, 60°). This annotation of states and theorem applications is provided only for illustrative purposes. It is not required by our model.

mantic parser to interpret the demonstration and a *deductive solver* that learns to chain theorems.

4 Approach

4.1 Interpretation via Semantic Parsing

We first describe a semantic parser that maps a piece of text (in the geometry question or a demonstration) to a logical expression such as the one shown in Figure 1. Our semantic parser uses a part-based log-linear model inspired from the multi-step approach taken in *GEOS*, which, in-turn is closely related to prior work in relation extraction and semantic role labeling. However, unlike *GEOS*, our parser combines the various steps in a joint model. Our parser first maps words or phrases in the input text x to corresponding concepts in the geometry language. Then, it identifies relations between identified concepts. Finally, it performs relation completion to handle implications and coordinating conjunctions. We choose a log-linear model over the parses which decomposes into two parts. Let $p = \{p_1, p_2\}$ where p_1 denotes the concepts identified in p and p_2 denotes the identified relations. The relation completion is performed by using a similar rule-based approach as in GEOS. The log-linear model also

253

factorizes into two components for concept and relation identification:

$$P(p|x;\boldsymbol{\theta}_p) = \frac{1}{Z(x;\boldsymbol{\theta}_p)} \exp\left(\boldsymbol{\theta}_p^T \boldsymbol{\phi}(p,x)\right)$$

$$\boldsymbol{\theta}_p^T \boldsymbol{\phi}(p,x) = \boldsymbol{\theta}_{p1}^T \boldsymbol{\phi}_1(p_1,x) + \boldsymbol{\theta}_{p2}^T \boldsymbol{\phi}_2(p_2,x)$$

$Z(x;\boldsymbol{\theta}_p)$ is the partition function of the log-linear model and $\boldsymbol{\phi}$ is the concatenation $[\boldsymbol{\phi}_1\ \boldsymbol{\phi}_2]$. The complexity of searching for the highest scoring latent parse is exponential. Hence, we use beam search with a fixed beam size (100) for inference. That is, in each step, we only expand the ten most promising candidates so far given by the current score. We first infer p_1 to identify a beam of concepts. Then, we infer p_2 to identify relations among candidate concepts. We find the optimal parameters $\boldsymbol{\theta}_p$ using maximum-likelihood estimation with L2 regularization:

$$\boldsymbol{\theta}_p^* = \underset{\boldsymbol{\theta}_p}{\arg\max} \sum_{(x,p)\in Train} \log P(p|x;\boldsymbol{\theta}_p) - \lambda||\boldsymbol{\theta}_p||_2^2$$

We use L-BFGS to optimize the objective. Finally, relation completion is performed using a deterministic rule-based approach as in *GEOS* which handles *implicit concepts* like the "Equals" relation in the sentence "Circle O has a radius of 5" and *coordinating conjunctions* like "bisect" between the two lines and two angles in "AM and CM bisect BAC and BCA". We refer the interested reader to section 4.3 in Seo et al. (2015) for details.

This semantic parser is used to identify program states in demonstrations as well as to map geometry questions to logical expressions.

4.1.1 State and Axiom Identification

Given a demonstrative solution of a geometry problem in natural language such as the one shown in Figure 2, we identify theorem applications by two simple heuristics. Often, theorem mentions in demonstrations collected from textbooks are labeled as references to theorems previously introduced in the textbook (for example, "Theorem 3.1"). In this case, we simply label the theorem application as the referenced theorem. Sometimes, the theorems are mentioned verbosely in the demonstration. To identify these mentions, we collect a set of theorem mentions from textbooks. Each theorem is also represented as a set of theorem mentions. Then, we use an off-the-shelf semantic text similarity system (Šarić et al., 2012) and check if a contiguous sequence of sentences

in the demonstration is a paraphrase of any of the gold theorem mentions. If the degree of similarity of a contiguous sequence of sentences in the demonstration with any of the gold theorem mentions is above a threshold, our system labels the sequence of sentences as the theorem. The text similarity system is tuned on the training dataset and the threshold is tuned on the development set. This heuristic works well and has a small error ($< 10\%$) on our development set.

For state identification, we use our semantic parser. The initial state corresponds to the logical expression corresponding to the question. Subsequent states are derived by parsing sentences in the demonstration. The identified state sequences are used to train our deductive solver.

4.2 Deductive Solver

Our deductive solver, inspired from Krishnamurthy et al. (2016), uses the parsed state and axiom information (when provided) and learns to score the sequence of axiom applications which can lead to the solution of the problem. Our solver uses a log-linear model over the space of possible axiom applications. Given a set of theorems $\mathscr{T}$ and optionally demonstration d, we assume $\mathbf{T} = [t_1, t_2, \ldots t_k]$ to be a sequence of theorem applications. Each theorem application leads to a change in state. Let s_0 be the initial state determined by the logical formula derived from the question text and the diagram. Let $\mathbf{s} = [s_1, s_2, \ldots s_k]$ be the sequence of program states after corresponding theorem applications. The final state s_k contains the answer to the question. We define the model score of the deduction as:

$$P(\mathbf{s}|\mathbf{T},d;\boldsymbol{\theta}_{ex}) =$$

$$\frac{1}{Z(\mathbf{T},d;\boldsymbol{\theta}_{ex})} \prod_{i=1}^{k} \exp\left(\boldsymbol{\theta}_{ex}^T \boldsymbol{\psi}(s_{i-1},s_i,t_i,d)\right)$$

Here, $\boldsymbol{\theta}_{ex}$ represents the model parameters and $\boldsymbol{\psi}$ represents the feature vector that depends on the successive states s_{i-1} and s_i, the demonstration d and the corresponding theorem application t_i. We find optimal parameters $\boldsymbol{\theta}_{ex}$ using maximum-likelihood estimation with L2 regularization:

$$\boldsymbol{\theta}_{ex}^* = \underset{\boldsymbol{\theta}_{ex}}{\arg\max} \sum_{s\in Train} \log P(\mathbf{s}|\mathbf{T},d;\boldsymbol{\theta}_{ex}) - \mu||\boldsymbol{\theta}_{ex}||_2^2$$

We use beam search for inference and L-BFGS to optimize the objective.

4.3 Joint Semantic Parsing and Deduction

Finally, we describe a joint model for semantic parsing and problem solving that parses the geometry problem text, the demonstration when available, and learns a sequence of theorem applications that can solve the problem.

In this case, we use a joint log-linear model for semantic parsing and deduction. The model comprises of factors that scores semantic parses of the question and the demonstration (when provided) and the other that scores various possible theorem applications. The model predicts the answer a given the question q (and possibly demonstration d) using two latent variables: $\mathbf{p}$ represents the latent semantic parse of the question and the demonstration which involves identifying the logical formula for the question (and for every state in the demonstration when provided) and $\mathbf{s}$ represents the (possibly latent) program.

$$P(\mathbf{p},\mathbf{s}|q,a,d;\boldsymbol{\theta}) \propto f_p(p|\{q,a,d\};\boldsymbol{\theta}_p)$$
$$\times f_s(\mathbf{s}|\mathbf{T},d,;\boldsymbol{\theta}_s)$$

Here, $\boldsymbol{\theta} = \{\boldsymbol{\theta}_p, \boldsymbol{\theta}_{ex}\}$. f_p and f_s represent the factors for semantic parsing and deduction. $f_p(p|\{q,a,d\};\boldsymbol{\theta}_p) \propto \exp\left(\boldsymbol{\theta}_p^T\boldsymbol{\phi}(p,\{q,a,d\})\right)$ and $f_s(\mathbf{s}|\mathbf{T},d,;\boldsymbol{\theta}_s) \propto \prod_{i=1}^{k}\exp\left(\boldsymbol{\theta}_{ex}^T\boldsymbol{\psi}(s_{i-1},s_i,t_i,d)\right)$ as defined in Sections 4.1 and 4.2. Next, we describe approaches to learn the joint model with various kinds of supervision.

4.4 Learning from Types of Supervision

Our joint model for parsing and deduction can be learned using various kinds of supervision. We provide a learning algorithm when (a) we only have geometry question-answer pairs as supervision, (b) when we have geometry questions and demonstrations for solving them, and (c) mixed supervision: when we have a set of geometry question-answer pairs in addition to some geometry questions and demonstrations. To do this, we implement two supervision schemes (Krishnamurthy et al., 2016). The first supervision scheme only verifies the answer and treats other states in the supervision as latent. The second scheme verifies every state in the program. We combine both kinds of supervision when provided. Given supervision $\{q_i,a_i\}_{i=1}^{n}$ and $\{q_i,a_i.d_i\}_{i=1}^{m}$, we define the following L2 regularized objective:

$$\mathscr{J}(\boldsymbol{\theta}) = v\sum_{i=1}^{n} log \sum_{\mathbf{p},\mathbf{s}} P(\mathbf{p},\mathbf{s}|q_i,a_i;\boldsymbol{\theta}) \times \mathbb{1}_{exec(\mathbf{s})=a_i}$$
$$+ (1-v)\sum_{i=1}^{m} log \sum_{\mathbf{p},\mathbf{s}} P(\mathbf{p},\mathbf{s}|q_i,a_i,d_i;\boldsymbol{\theta}) \times \mathbb{1}_{\mathbf{s}(\mathbf{d_i})=\mathbf{s}}$$
$$- \lambda||\boldsymbol{\theta}_p||_2^2 - \mu||\boldsymbol{\theta}_{ex}||_2^2$$

For learning from answers, we set $v = 1$. For learning from demonstrations, we set $v = 0$. We tune hyperparameters λ, μ and v on a held out dev set. We use L-BFGS, using beam search for inference for training all our models. To avoid repeated usage of unnecessary theorems in the solution, we constrain the next theorem application to be distinct from previous theorem applications during beam search.

4.5 Features

Next, we define our feature set: $\boldsymbol{\phi}_1$, $\boldsymbol{\phi}_2$ for learning the semantic parser and $\boldsymbol{\psi}$ for learning the deduction model. Semantic parser features $\boldsymbol{\phi}_1$ and $\boldsymbol{\phi}_2$ are inspired from *GEOS*. The deduction model features $\boldsymbol{\psi}$ score consecutive states in the deduction s_{i-1}, s_i and the theorem t_i which when applied to s_{i-1} leads to s_i. $\boldsymbol{\psi}$ comprises of features that score if theorem t_i is applicable on state s_{i-1} and if the application of t_i on state s_{i-1} leads to state s_i. Table 2 lists the feature set.

5 Demonstrations Dataset

We collect a new dataset of demonstrations for solving geometry problems from a set of grade 6-10 Indian high school math textbooks by four publishers/authors – *NCERT*[1], *R S Aggarwal*[2], *R D Sharma*[3] and *M L Aggarwal*[4] – a total of $5 \times 4 = 20$ textbooks as well as a set of online geometry problems and solutions from three popular educational portals: *Tiwari Academy*[5], *School Lamp*[6] and *Oswaal Books*[7] for grade 6-10 students in India. Millions of students in India study geometry from these books and portals every year and these materials are available online. We manually

---

[1] http://epathshala.nic.in/
e-pathshala-4/flipbook/
[2] http://www.amazon.in/
Books-R-S-Aggarwal/
[3] http://www.amazon.in/Books-R-Sharma/
[4] http://www.amazon.in/
Books-Aggarwal-M-L/
[5] http://www.tiwariacademy.com/
[6] http://www.schoollamp.com
[7] http://www.oswaalbooks.com

	Feature	Description
ϕ_1	Lexicon Map	Indicator that the word or phrase maps to a predicate in a lexicon created in *GEOS*. *GEOS* derives correspondences between words/phrases and geometry keywords and concepts in the geometry language using manual annotations in its training data. For instance, the lexicon contains ("square", *square*, *Is-Square*) including all possible concepts for the phrase "square".
	Regex for numbers and explicit variables	Indicator that the word or phrase satisfies a regular expression to detect numbers or explicit variables (e.g. "5", "AB", "O"). These regular expressions were built as a part of *GEOS*.
ϕ_2	Dependency tree distance	Shortest distance between the words of the concept nodes in the dependency tree. We use indicator features for distances of -3 to 3. Positive distance shows if the child word is at the right of the parentâĂŹs in the sentence, and negative otherwise.
	Word distance	Distance between the words of the concept nodes in the sentence.
	Dependency edge	Indicator functions for outgoing edges of the parent and child for the shortest path between them.
	Part of speech tag	Indicator functions for the POS tags of the parent and the child
	Relation type	Indicator functions for unary / binary parent and child nodes.
	Return type	Indicator functions for the return types of the parent and the child nodes. For example, return type of *Equals* is boolean, and that of *LengthOf* is numeric.
ψ	State and theorem premise predicates	Treat the state s_{i-1} and theorem premise $l_{t_i}^{(pr)}$ as multi-sets of predicates. The feature is given by $div(s_{i-1}\|l_{t_i}^{(pr)})$, the divergence between the two multi-sets. $div(A,B)$, the divergence between multi-sets A and B is given by $\sum_k \frac{\min(A_k,B_k)}{B_k}$ which measures the degree to which the elements in A satisfy the pre-condition in B.
	State and theorem premise predicate-arguments	Now treat the state s_{i-1} and theorem premise $l_{t_i}^{(pr)}$ as two multi-sets over predicate-arguments. The feature is given by $div(s_{i-1}\|l_{t_i}^{(pr)})$, the divergence between the two multi-sets.
	State and theorem conclusion predicates	Now treat the state s_i and theorem conclusion $l_{t_i}^{(co)}$ as two multi-sets over predicate-arguments. The feature is given by $div(s_i\|l_{t_i}^{(co)})$, the divergence between the two multi-sets.
	State and theorem conclusion predicate-arguments	Now treat the state s_i and theorem conclusion $l_{t_i}^{(co)}$ as two multi-sets over predicate-arguments. The feature is given by $div(s_i\|l_{t_i}^{(co)})$, the divergence between the two multi-sets.
	State and theorem conclusion predicates	Treat the state s_i and theorem conclusion $l_{t_i}^{(co)}$ as two distributions over predicates. The feature is the total variation distance between the two distributions.
	State and theorem conclusion predicate-arguments	Now treat the state e_i and theorem conclusion $l_{t_i}^{(co)}$ as two distributions over predicate-arguments. The feature is the total variation distance between the two distributions.
	Product Features	We additionally use three product features: $\psi_1\psi_3\psi_5$, $\psi_2\psi_4\psi_6$ and $\psi_1\psi_2\psi_3\psi_4\psi_5\psi_6$

Table 2: The feature set for our joint semantic-parsing and deduction model. Features ϕ_1 and ϕ_2 are motivated from *GEOS*

marked chapters relevant for geometry in these books and then parsed them using Adobe Acrobat's *pdf2xml* parser. Then, we manually extracted example problems leading to a total of 2235 geometry problems with demonstrations. We also annotated 1000 demonstrations by labeling the various states and theorem applications. We manually collected a set of theorems of geometry by going through the textbooks, and wrote them as horn clause rules. A total of 293 unique theorems were collected. Then, we marked contiguous sentences in the demonstration texts as one of these 293 theorems or as states. An example annotation for the running example in Figures 1 and 2 is provided in Figure 3. Note that the annotation of states and theorem applications is not used in training our models and is only used for testing the accuracy of the programs induced by our model.

6 Experiments

We use three geometry question datasets for evaluating our system: practice and official SAT style geometry questions used in *GEOS*, and an additional dataset of geometry questions collected from the aforementioned textbooks. We selected a total of 1406 SAT style questions across grades 6-10. This dataset is approximately 7.5 times the size of the datasets used in Seo et al. (2015). We split the dataset into training (350 questions), development (150 questions) and test (906 questions) with equal proportion of grade 6-10 questions. We also annotated the training and development set questions with ground-truth logical forms. *GEOS* used 13 types of entities, 94 functions and predicates. We added some more entities, functions and predicates to cover other more complex concepts in geometry not covered in *GEOS*. Thus, we obtained a final set of 19 entity types and 115 functions and predicates. We use the training set to train our semantic parser with expanded set of entity types, functions and predicates. We used Stanford CoreNLP (Manning et al., 2014) for linguistic pre-processing. We also adapted the *GEOS* solver to the expanded set of entities, functions and predicates for comparison purposes. We call this system *GEOS++*.

6.1 Quantitative Results

We evaluated our joint model of semantic parsing and deduction with various settings for training: training on question-answer pairs or demonstra-

	P	O	T
GEOS	61	49	32
GEOS++	62	49	44
O.S. (QA Pairs)	63	52	47
O.S. (Demonstrations)	66	55	56
O.S. (QA + Demonstrations)	**67**	**57**	**58**

Table 3: Scores of various approaches on the SAT practice (P) and official (O) datasets and a dataset of questions from the 20 textbooks (T). We use SATâĂŹs grading scheme that rewards a correct answer with a score of 1.0 and penalizes a wrong answer with a negative score of 0.25. O.S. represents our system trained on question-answer (QA) pairs, demonstrations, or a combination of QA pairs and demonstrations.

tions alone, or with a combination of question-answer pairs and demonstrations. We compare our joint semantic parsing and deduction models against *GEOS* and *GEOS++*.

In the first setting, we only use question-answer pairs as supervision. We compare our semantic parsing and deduction model to *GEOS* and *GEOS++* on practice and official SAT style geometry questions from Seo et al. (2015) as well as the dataset of geometry questions collected from the 20 textbooks (see Table 3). On all the three datasets, our system outperforms *GEOS* and *GEOS++*. Especially on the dataset from the 20 textbooks (which is a harder dataset and includes more problems which require complex reasoning supported by our deduction model), *GEOS* and *GEOS++* do not perform very well whereas our system achieves a very good score.

Next, we only use demonstrations to train our joint model (see Table 3). We test this model on the aforementioned datasets and compare it to *GEOS* and *GEOS++* trained on respective datasets. Again, our system outperforms *GEOS* and *GEOS++* on all three datasets. Especially on the textbook dataset, this model trained on demonstrations has significant improvements as our semantic parsing and deduction model trains the deduction model as well and learns to reason about geometry using axiomatic knowledge.

Finally, we train our semantic parsing and deduction model on a combination of question answer-pairs and demonstrations. This model trained on question-answer pairs and demonstrations leads to further improvements over models trained only question-answer pairs or only on demonstrations. These results (shown in Table 3) hold on all the three datasets.

We tested the correctness of the parses and the

	P	R	F1
GEOS	0.82	0.63	0.71
O.S. (Parser)	0.88	0.75	0.81
O.S. (Joint)	**0.89**	**0.80**	**0.84**

Table 4: Precision, Recall and F1 scores of the parses induced by *GEOS* and our models when only the parsing model or the joint model is used.

	Deduction	Joint
QA Pairs	0.56	0.61
Demonstrations	0.64	0.68
QA + Demonstrations	0.68	**0.70**

Table 5: Accuracy of the programs induced by various versions of our joint model trained on question-answer pairs, demonstrations or a combination of the two. We provide results when we use the deduction model or the joint model.

	Interpretability		Usefulness	
	GEOS++	*O.S.*	*GEOS++*	*O.S.*
Grade 6	2.7	**3.0**	2.9	**3.2**
Grade 7	3.0	**3.7**	3.3	**3.6**
Grade 8	2.7	**3.6**	3.1	**3.5**
Grade 9	2.4	**3.4**	3.0	**3.6**
Grade 10	2.8	**3.1**	3.2	**3.7**
Overall	2.7	**3.4**	3.1	**3.5**

Table 6: User study ratings for *GEOS++* and our system (O.S.) trained on question-answer pairs and demonstrations by a number of grade 6-10 student subjects. Ten students in each grade were asked to rate the two systems on a scale of 1-5 on two facets: 'interpretability' and 'usefulness'. Each cell shows the mean rating computed over ten students in that grade for that facet.

deductive programs induced by our models. First, we compared the parses induced by our models with gold parses on the development set. Table 4 reports the Precision, Recall and F1 scores of the parses induced by our models when only the parsing model or when the joint model is used and compares it with *GEOS*. We conclude that both our models perform better as compared to *GEOS* in parsing. Furthermore, our joint model of parsing and deduction further improves the parsing accuracy. Then, we compared the programs induced by the aforementioned models with gold program annotations on the textbook dataset. Table 5 reports the accuracy of programs induced by various versions of our models. Our models when trained on demonstrations induces more accurate programs as compared to the semantic parsing and deduction model when trained on question-answer pairs. Moreover, the semantic parsing and deduction model when trained on question-answer pairs as well as demonstrations achieves an even better accuracy. Our joint model of parsing and deduction induces more accurate programs as compared to the deduction model alone.

6.2 User Study on Interpretability

A key benefit of our axiomatic solver is that it provides an easy-to-understand student-friendly demonstrative solution to geometry problems. This is important because students typically learn geometry by rigorous deduction whereas numerical solvers do not provide such interpretability.

To test the interpretability of our axiomatic solver, we asked 50 grade 6-10 students (10 students in each grade) to use *GEOS++* and our best performing system trained on question-answer pairs and demonstrations as a web-based assistive tool. They were each asked to rate how 'interpretable' and 'useful' the two systems were for their studies on a scale of 1-5. Table 6 shows the mean rating by students in each grade on the two facets. We can observe that students of each grade found our system to be more interpretable as well as more useful to them than *GEOS++*. This study supports the need and the efficacy of an interpretable solution for geometry problems. Our solution can be used as an assistive tool for helping students learn geometry on MOOCs.

7   Related Work

Solving Geometry Problems: Standardized tests have been recently proposed as 'drivers for progress in AI' (Clark and Etzioni, 2016). These tests are easily accessible, and measurable, and hence have attracted several NLP researchers. There is a growing body of work on solving standardized tests such as reading comprehensions (Richardson et al., 2013, inter alia), science question answering (Clark, 2015; Schoenick et al., 2016, inter alia), algebra word problems (Kushman et al., 2014; Roy and Roth, 2015, inter alia), geometry problems (Seo et al., 2014, 2015) and pre-university entrance exams (Fujita et al., 2014; Arai and Matsuzaki, 2014).

While the problem of using computers to solve geometry questions is old (Feigenbaum and Feldman, 1963; Schattschneider and King, 1997; Davis, 2006), NLP and vision techniques were first used to solve geometry problems in Seo et al. (2015). While Seo et al. (2014) only aligned geometric shapes with their textual mentions, Seo et al. (2015) also extracted geometric relations and built *GEOS*. We improve *GEOS* by building an axiomatic solver that performs deductive reasoning by learning from demonstrative problem solutions.

Learning from Demonstration: Our work follows the *learning from demonstration* view of machine learning (Schaal, 1997) which stems from the work on social learning in developmental psychology (Meltzoff and Moore, 1977; Meltzoff, 1995). *Learning from demonstration* is a popular way of learning policies from example state to action mappings in robotics applications. *Imitation learning* (Schaal, 1999; Abbeel and Ng, 2004; Ross et al., 2011) is a popular instance of *learning from demonstration* where the algorithm observes a human expert perform a series of actions to accomplish the task and learns a policy that "imitates" the expert with the purpose of generalizing to unseen data. Imitation learning is increasingly being used in NLP (Vlachos and Clark, 2014; Berant and Liang, 2015; Augenstein et al., 2015; Beck et al., 2016; Goodman et al., 2016a,b). However, all these models focus on learning respective NLP models from the final supervision e.g. semantic parses or denotations. However, we provide a technique to learn from demonstrations by learning a joint semantic parsing and deduction model. Another related line of work is Hixon et al. (2015) who acquire knowledge in the form of knowledge graphs for question answering from natural language dialogs and (Goldwasser and Roth, 2014) who propose a technique called *learning from natural instructions*. *Learning from natural instructions* allows human teachers to interact with an automated learner using *natural instructions*, allowing the teacher to communicate the domain expertise to the learner via natural language. However, this work was evaluated on a very simple Freecell game with a very small number of concepts (3). On the other hand, our model is evaluated on a real task of solving SAT style geometry problems.

Semantic Parsing: Semantic parsing is the NLP task of learning to map language to a formal meaning representation. Early semantic parsers learnt the parsing model from natural language utterances paired with logical forms (Zelle and Mooney, 1993, 1996; Kate et al., 2005, inter alia). However, recently indirect supervision, such as denotations (Liang et al., 2011; Berant et al., 2013, inter alia) and natural language directions for robot navigation (Shimizu and Haas, 2009; Matuszek et al., 2010; Chen and Mooney, 2011, inter alia) are being used to train these semantic parsers. In most of the above examples, the execution model is fairly simple (e.g. execution of a SQL query in a database, or binary feedback for interaction of the robot with the environment). However, our work uses demonstrations such as those given in textbooks for learning a semantic parser. Furthermore, our work learns the semantic parser along with the execution model. In our case, the execution model is a program sequence constructed from a set of theorem applications. Thus, our work provides a way to integrate semantic parsing with probabilistic programming. This integration has been pursued before for science diagram question-answering on food-web networks (Krishnamurthy et al., 2016) – which is closely related to our work. Technically, our deductive solver and the approach of learning from different kinds of supervision are the same as the execution model in Krishnamurthy et al. (2016). While Krishnamurthy et al. (2016) only has two program encodings, our work involves a much larger number of programs. We also provide an approach for learning from demonstrations.

8 Conclusion

We described an approach that learns to solve SAT style geometry problems using detailed demonstrative solutions in natural language. The approach learns to jointly interpret demonstrations as well as how to use this interpretation to deductively solve geometry problems using axiomatic knowledge. Our approach showed significant improvements over the best previously published work on a number of datasets. A user-study conducted on a number of school students studying geometry found our approach to be more *interpretable* and *useful* than its predecessors. In the future, we would like to extend our work in other domains such as science QA (Jansen et al., 2016) and use our work to assist student learning on platforms such as MOOCs.

Acknowledgments

We thank the anonymous reviewers for their valuable comments and suggestions. This work was supported by the following research grants: NSF IIS1447676, ONR N000141410684 and ONR N000141712463.

References

Pieter Abbeel and Andrew Y Ng. 2004. Apprenticeship learning via inverse reinforcement learning. In *Proceedings of the twenty-first international conference on Machine learning*. ACM, page 1.

R.L. Allington and P.M. Cunningham. 2010. Children benefit from modeling, demonstration, and explanation .

Noriko H Arai and Takuya Matsuzaki. 2014. The impact of ai on education–can a robot get into the university of tokyo? In *Proc. ICCE*. pages 1034–1042.

Brenna D Argall, Sonia Chernova, Manuela Veloso, and Brett Browning. 2009. A survey of robot learning from demonstration. *Robotics and autonomous systems* 57(5):469–483.

Isabelle Augenstein, Andreas Vlachos, and Diana Maynard. 2015. Extracting relations between nonstandard entities using distant supervision and imitation learning. In *Proceedings of the 2015 Conference on Empirical Methods in Natural Language Processing*. Association for Computational Linguistics, pages 747–757.

Daniel Beck, Andreas Vlachos, Gustavo Paetzold, and Lucia Specia. 2016. SHEF-MIME: word-level quality estimation using imitation learning. In *Proceedings of the First Conference on Machine Translation, WMT 2016, colocated with ACL 2016, August 11-12, Berlin, Germany*. pages 772–776.

Jonathan Berant, Andrew Chou, Roy Frostig, and Percy Liang. 2013. Semantic parsing on freebase from question-answer pairs. In *Proceedings of the 2013 Conference on Empirical Methods in Natural Language Processing, EMNLP 2013, 18-21 October 2013, Grand Hyatt Seattle, Seattle, Washington, USA, A meeting of SIGDAT, a Special Interest Group of the ACL*. pages 1533–1544.

Jonathan Berant and Percy Liang. 2015. Imitation learning of agenda-based semantic parsers. *Transactions of the Association for Computational Linguistics* 3:545–558.

Daphna Buchsbaum, Alison Gopnik, Thomas L Griffiths, and Patrick Shafto. 2011. ChildrenâĂŹs imitation of causal action sequences is influenced by statistical and pedagogical evidence. *Cognition* 120(3):331–340.

John Burger, Claire Cardie, Vinay Chaudhri, Robert Gaizauskas, Sanda Harabagiu, David Israel, Christian Jacquemin, Chin-Yew Lin, Steve Maiorano, et al. 2001. Issues, tasks and program structures to roadmap research in question & answering (q&a) .

Lucas P Butler and Ellen M Markman. 2014. Preschoolers use pedagogical cues to guide radical reorganization of category knowledge. *Cognition* 130(1):116–127.

David L. Chen and Raymond J. Mooney. 2011. Learning to interpret natural language navigation instructions from observations. In *Proceedings of the 25th AAAI Conference on Artificial Intelligence (AAAI-2011)*. pages 859–865.

Peter Clark. 2015. Elementary School Science and Math Tests as a Driver for AI:Take the Aristo Challenge! In *Proceedings of IAAI*.

Peter Clark and Oren Etzioni. 2016. My computer is an honor student - but how intelligent is it? standardized tests as a measure of ai. In *Proceedings of AI Magazine*.

Tom Davis. 2006. Geometry with computers. Technical report.

Edward A Feigenbaum and Julian Feldman. 1963. *Computers and thought*. The AAAI Press.

Richard M Felder, Donald R Woods, James E Stice, and Armando Rugarcia. 2000. The future of engineering education ii. teaching methods that work. *Chemical Engineering Education* pages 26–39.

Akira Fujita, Akihiro Kameda, Ai Kawazoe, and Yusuke Miyao. 2014. Overview of todai robot project and evaluation framework of its nlp-based problem solving. *World History* 36:36.

Dan Goldwasser and Dan Roth. 2014. Learning from natural instructions. *Machine Learning* 94(2):205–232.

James Goodman, Andreas Vlachos, and Jason Naradowsky. 2016a. Noise reduction and targeted exploration in imitation learning for abstract meaning representation parsing. In *Proceedings of the 54th Annual Meeting of the Association for Computational Linguistics (Volume 1: Long Papers)*.

James Goodman, Andreas Vlachos, and Jason Naradowsky. 2016b. Ucl+ sheffield at semeval-2016 task 8: Imitation learning for amr parsing with an α-bound. *Proceedings of SemEval* pages 1167–1172.

Ben Hixon, Peter Clark, and Hannaneh Hajishirzi. 2015. Learning knowledge graphs for question answering through conversational dialog. In *NAACL HLT 2015, The 2015 Conference of the North American Chapter of the Association for Computational Linguistics: Human Language Technologies, Denver, Colorado, USA, May 31 - June 5, 2015*. pages 851–861. http://aclweb.org/anthology/N/N15/N15-1086.pdf.

Peter Jansen, Niranjan Balasubramanian, Mihai Surdeanu, and Peter Clark. 2016. What's in an explanation? characterizing knowledge and inference requirements for elementary science exams. In *COLING 2016, 26th International Conference on Computational Linguistics, Proceedings of the Conference: Technical Papers, December 11-16, 2016, Osaka, Japan*. pages 2956–2965. http://aclweb.org/anthology/C/C16/C16-1278.pdf.

Rohit J Kate, Yuk Wah, Wong Raymond, and J Mooney. 2005. Learning to transform natural to formal languages. In *Proceedings of AAAI-05*. Citeseer.

Jayant Krishnamurthy, Oyvind Tafjord, and Aniruddha Kembhavi. 2016. Semantic parsing to probabilistic programs for situated question answering. In Jian Su, Xavier Carreras, and Kevin Duh, editors, *Proceedings of the 2016 Conference on Empirical Methods in Natural Language Processing, EMNLP 2016, Austin, Texas, USA, November 1-4, 2016*. The Association for Computational Linguistics, pages 160–170.

Nate Kushman, Yoav Artzi, Luke Zettlemoyer, and Regina Barzilay. 2014. Learning to automatically solve algebra word problems. In *Proceedings of the Annual Meeting of the Association for Computational Linguistics*.

Percy Liang, Michael I Jordan, and Dan Klein. 2011. Learning dependency-based compositional semantics. In *Proceedings of the 49th Annual Meeting of the Association for Computational Linguistics: Human Language Technologies-Volume 1*. Association for Computational Linguistics, pages 590–599.

Christopher D. Manning, Mihai Surdeanu, John Bauer, Jenny Finkel, Steven J. Bethard, and David McClosky. 2014. The Stanford CoreNLP natural language processing toolkit. In *Association for Computational Linguistics (ACL) System Demonstrations*. pages 55–60. http://www.aclweb.org/anthology/P/P14/P14-5010.

Cynthia Matuszek, Dieter Fox, and Karl Koscher. 2010. Following directions using statistical machine translation. In *2010 5th ACM/IEEE International Conference on Human-Robot Interaction (HRI)*. IEEE, pages 251–258.

Andrew N Meltzoff. 1995. Understanding the intentions of others: re-enactment of intended acts by 18-month-old children. *Developmental psychology* 31(5):838.

Andrew N. Meltzoff and M. Keith Moore. 1977. Imitation of facial and manual gestures by human neonates. *Science* 198(4312):75–78. https://doi.org/10.1126/science.198.4312.75.

Matthew Richardson, Christopher JC Burges, and Erin Renshaw. 2013. Mctest: A challenge dataset for the open-domain machine comprehension of text. In *Proceedings of Empirical Methods in Natural Language Processing (EMNLP)*.

Stéphane Ross, Geoffrey J. Gordon, and Drew Bagnell. 2011. A reduction of imitation learning and structured prediction to no-regret online learning. In *Proceedings of the Fourteenth International Conference on Artificial Intelligence and Statistics, AISTATS 2011, Fort Lauderdale, USA, April 11-13, 2011*. pages 627–635.

Subhro Roy and Dan Roth. 2015. Solving general arithmetic word problems. In *Proceedings of EMNLP*.

Stefan Schaal. 1997. Learning from demonstration. In M. I. Jordan and T. Petsche, editors, *Advances in Neural Information Processing Systems 9*, MIT Press, pages 1040–1046.

Stefan Schaal. 1999. Is imitation learning the route to humanoid robots? *Trends in cognitive sciences* 3(6):233–242.

Doris Schattschneider and James King. 1997. *Geometry Turned On: Dynamic Software in Learning, Teaching, and Research*. Mathematical Association of America Notes.

Carissa Schoenick, Peter Clark, Oyvind Tafjord, Peter D. Turney, and Oren Etzioni. 2016. Moving beyond the turing test with the allen AI science challenge. *CoRR* abs/1604.04315. http://arxiv.org/abs/1604.04315.

Min Joon Seo, Hannaneh Hajishirzi, Ali Farhadi, and Oren Etzioni. 2014. Diagram understanding in geometry questions. In *Proceedings of AAAI*.

Min Joon Seo, Hannaneh Hajishirzi, Ali Farhadi, Oren Etzioni, and Clint Malcolm. 2015. Solving geometry problems: combining text and diagram interpretation. In *Proceedings of EMNLP*.

Nobuyuki Shimizu and Andrew R. Haas. 2009. Learning to follow navigational route instructions. In *IJCAI 2009, Proceedings of the 21st International Joint Conference on Artificial Intelligence, Pasadena, California, USA, July 11-17, 2009*. pages 1488–1493.

Andreas Vlachos and Stephen Clark. 2014. A new corpus and imitation learning framework for context-dependent semantic parsing. *Transactions of the Association for Computational Linguistics* 2:547–559.

Frane Šarić, Goran Glavaš, Mladen Karan, Jan Šnajder, and Bojana Dalbelo Bašić. 2012. Takelab: Systems for measuring semantic text similarity. In *Proceedings of the Sixth International Workshop on Semantic Evaluation (SemEval 2012)*. Association for Computational Linguistics, Montréal, Canada, pages 441–448. http://www.aclweb.org/anthology/S12-1060.

John M. Zelle and Raymond J. Mooney. 1993. Learning semantic grammars with constructive inductive logic programming. In *Proceedings of the 11th National Conference on Artificial Intelligence. Washington, DC, USA, July 11-15, 1993.*. pages 817–822.

John M Zelle and Raymond J Mooney. 1996. Learning to parse database queries using inductive logic programming. In *In Proceedings of the Thirteenth National Conference on Artificial Intelligence*.

Ways of Asking and Replying in Duplicate Question Detection

João Rodrigues, Chakaveh Saedi, Vladislav Maraev, João Silva, António Branco
University of Lisbon
{joao.rodrigues,chakaveh.saedi,vlad.maraev,
jsilva,antonio.branco}@di.fc.ul.pt

Abstract

This paper presents the results of systematic experimentation on the impact in duplicate question detection of different types of questions across both a number of established approaches and a novel, superior one used to address this language processing task. This study permits to gain a novel insight on the different levels of robustness of the diverse detection methods with respect to different conditions of their application, including the ones that approximate real usage scenarios.

1 Introduction

Automatic detection of semantically equivalent questions is a language processing task of the utmost importance given the upsurge of interest in conversational interfaces. It is a key procedure in finding answers to questions. For instance, in a context of customer support via a chat channel, with the help of duplicate question detection, previous interactions between customers and human operators can be explored to provide an increasingly automatic question answering service. If a new input question is equivalent to a question already stored, it can be replied automatically with the answer stored with its recorded duplicate.

Though it has been less researched than similar tasks, duplicate question detection (DQD) is attracting an increasing interest. It can be seen as belonging to a family of semantic text similarity tasks, which have been addressed in SemEval challenges since 2012, and which in the last SemEval2016, for instance, included also tasks like plagiarism detection or degree of similarity between machine translation output and its post-edited version, among others. Semantic textual similarity assesses the degree to which two textual segments are semantically equivalent to each other, which is typically scored on an ordinal scale ranging from semantic equivalence to complete semantic dissimilarity.

Paraphrase detection can be seen as a special case of semantic textual similarity, where the scale is reduced to its two extremes and the outcome for an input pair is yes/no. DQD, in turn, could be seen as a special case of paraphrase detection that is restricted to interrogative expressions.

While SemEval2016 had no task on yes/no DQD, it had a "Question-Question" graded similarity subtask of Task 1. The top performing system in this subtask (0.74 Pearson correlation) scored below the best result when all subtasks of Task 1 are considered (0.77), and also below the best scores of many of the other subtasks (e.g. 0.84 in plagiarism detection (Agirre et al., 2016)).

While scores obtained for different tasks by systems trained and evaluated over different datasets cannot be compared, those results nonetheless lead one to ponder whether focusing on pairs of interrogatives may be a task that is harder than paraphrase detection that focuses on pairs of non-interrogatives (e.g. plagiarism pairs), or at least whether it needs different and specific approaches for similar levels of performance to be attained.

When checking for other research results specifically addressing DQD, pretty competitive results can be found, however, as in Bogdanova et al. (2015). These authors used a dataset that included a dump from the Meta forum in StackExchange (a source that would be explored also in SemEval2016) and a dump from the AskUbuntu forum, and reported over 92% accuracy.

The pairs in these datasets are made of the textual segments that are submitted by the users of the forums to elicit some feedback from other users that may be of help, and that will pile up in threads of reactions. They have two parts, known as "ti-

*Proceedings of the 6th Joint Conference on Lexical and Computational Semantics (*SEM 2017)*, pages 262–270,
Vancouver, Canada, August 3-4, 2017. ©2017 Association for Computational Linguistics

tle" and "body". The title tends to be a short segment identifying the issue being addressed, and the body is where that issue is expanded, and can be several paragraphs long.

To avoid a maze of exactly duplicate questions, and thus of duplicate threads, which would hamper the usability of the forums, for the same issue, all duplicates except one are removed, leaving only near duplicates—that are marked as such and cross-linked to each other, and may be of help in addressing the same topic from a different angle.

The pairs of duplicate segments included in the experimental datasets mentioned above are the titles and bodies of nearly duplicate threads. The pairs of non-duplicate segments are made of titles and bodies that are not near duplicate.

While these "real life" data are important for the development of DQD solutions that support the management of these community forums, their textual segments are quite far from expressions in clean and clear interrogative form. The short supply of this sort of datasets has been perhaps part of the reason why the DQD has not been more researched. This may help to explain also the lack of further studies so far on how the nature of the questions and the data may impact the performance of the systems on this task.

The experiments reported in this paper aim to address this issue and help to advance our understanding of the nature of DQD and to improve its application. We will resort to previous datasets used in the literature, just mentioned above, but we will seek to explore also a new dataset from Quora, released recently, in January 2017.

The pairs of segments in this Quora dataset concern any subject and are thus not restricted to any domain. The segments are typically one sentence long, clean and clear interrogative expressions. Their grammatical well-formedness is ensured by the volunteer experts that answer them and that, before writing their replies, can use the editing facility to adjust the wording of the question entered by the user if needed.

This is in clear contrast with the other datasets extracted from community forums. The forums are organized by specific domains. The segments may be several sentences long and are typically offered in a sloppy wording, with non-standard expressions and suboptimal grammaticality.

By resorting only to data of the latter type, Bogdanova et al. (2015) confirmed that systems trained (and evaluated) on a smaller dataset that is domain specific can perform substantially better than when they are trained (and evaluated) on a larger dataset from a generic domain.

In this paper, we seek to further advance the understanding of DQD and possible constraints on their development and application. We assess the level of impact of the length of the segments in the pairs, and study whether there is a difference when systems handle well-edited, generic domain segments, versus domain specific and sloppy ones.

As the datasets with labeled pairs of segments are scarce, to develop a system to a new specific domain lacking a training dataset, the natural way to go is to train it on a generic domain dataset. We also study the eventual loss of performance in this real usage scenario.

These empirical contrasts may have a different impact in different types of approaches to DQD. The present study will be undertaken across a range of different techniques, encompassing a rule-based baseline, a classifier-based system and solutions based on neural networks.

To secure comparability of the individual results, the experimental datasets used are organized along common settings. They have the same volume (30K pairs), the same training vs. testing split rate (80%/20%), and the same class balance (50%/50% of duplicates and non-duplicates).

This paper is organized as follows. In Section 2, the datasets used are described. Sections 3, 4 and 5 present the experimental results of a range of different detection techniques, respectively, rule-based, supervised classifiers and neural networks. In section 6, the results obtained are discussed, and further experiments are reported in Section 7, approximating a real usage scenarios of application. Sections 8 and 9 present the related work and the conclusions.

2 Datasets

We used two datasets, from two sources:[1] (i) from the AskUbuntu online community forum where a query entered by a user (in the form of a title followed by a body) is answered with contributions from any other user (which are piled up in a thread); and (ii) from Quora, an online moderated question answering site where each query introduced by a user, typically in a grammatical inter-

---

[1]Datasets are available from https://github.com/nlx-group/dqd

1	**Q** How is the new Harry Potter book 'Harry Potter and the Cursed Child'?
	Q How bad is the new book by J.K Rowling?
0	**Q** Should the toothbrush be wet or dry before applying the toothpaste?
	Q What is the cheapest toothpaste?
1	**Q** Can I install Ubuntu and Windows side by side?
	Q How do I dual boot Windows along side Ubuntu?

Figure 1: Three example question pairs and their labels from the Quora dataset

1	**Q** Why is more than 3GB of RAM not recognised when using amd64?
	Q Ubuntu 10.04 LTS 64bit only showing 2.9GB of memory
1	**Q** How can I fix a 404 Error when updating packages?
	Q What does this mean & what impact does it have: Failed to download repository information
0	**Q** hiphop, nginx, spdy
	Q print xlsx file from command line using ghostscript and libreoffice

Figure 2: Three example segment pairs (titles only) and their labels from the AskUbuntu dataset

rogative sentence, receives an answer often from a volunteer expert. For either dataset, the language of the textual segments is English.

We resorted to the first Quora dataset, released by the end of January 2017.[2] It consists of over 400k pairs of questions labeled 1 in case they are duplicates of each other, or 0 otherwise. The pairs in the dataset released were collected with sampling techniques and their labeling may not be fully correct, and are not restricted to any subject (Iyer et al., 2017).

The other dataset used here is similar to one of the datasets used by Bogdanova et al. (2015). It is made of queries from the AskUbuntu forum,[3] which are thus on a specific domain, namely from the IT area, in particular about the Ubuntu operative system. We used AskUbuntu dump available, from September 2014,[4] containing 167,765 questions, of which 17,115 were labeled as a duplicate.

A portion with 30k randomly selected pairs of title+body was extracted, the same size as the portion used by Bogdanova et al. (2015). This portion is balanced, thus with an identical number of duplicate and non-duplicate pairs. To support the experiments described below, it was divided into 24k/6k for training/testing, an 80%/20% split.

The textual segments in this dataset contain both the title and the body of the query in the corresponding thread, and this dataset is referred to as AskUbuntuTB, while its counterpart with titles only—obtained by removing the bodies—is referred to as AskUbuntuTO.

To support comparison, a portion with 30k randomly selected pairs was extracted also from the Quora release, with the same duplicate vs. non-duplicate balance and the same training vs. test split rates as for the AskUbuntu dataset.

The average length of the segments in number of words is 84 in AskUbuntuTB. Its counterpart AskUbuntuTO, with titles only, represent a very substantial (10 times) drop to 8 words per segment on average, which is similar to the 10 words per segment in the Quora dataset.

The vocabularies sizes of AskUbuntuTB, AskUbuntuTO and Quora are 45k, 16k and 24k items, respectively, and their volumes are 5M, 500k and 650k tokens, respectively. Concerning the 400k pair Quora release, in turn, it contains 9M tokens and a 125k item vocabulary.

3 Rule-based

As a first approach experimented with, inspired by (Wu et al., 2011), we resorted to the Jaccard Coefficient over n-grams with n ranging 1 to 4.

Before applying this technique, the textual segments were preprocessed by undertaking (i) tokenization and stemming, using the NLTK tokenizer and Porter stemmer(Bird, 2006); and (ii) markup cleaning, whereby markup tags for references, links, snippets of code, etc. were removed.

To find the best threshold, we used the training set in a series of trials and applied the best results for the test sets. This led to the thresholds 0.1, 0.016, 0.03 for Quora, AskUbuntuTO and AskUbuntuTB, respectively.

This approach obtains 72.91% accuracy when applied over AskUbuntuTB.[5]

When running over AskUbuntuTO, its performance seems not to be dramatically affected by the much shorter segment length, suffering a slight decrease to 72.35%. Interestingly, a clear drop of the accuracy of over 3 percentage points is observed when it is run over Quora, scoring 69.53%.

These results seem to indicate that while this technique is quite robust with respect to the short-

Title: vsftpd not listing large directory from WAN interface **Body:** I have vsftpd running on my Ubuntu server, which is behind an Asus RT-N66U router. Port 21 is forwarded to the server. I can connect via my public IP address to the server *(81 more words omitted)*
Title: hiphop, nginx, spdy **Body:** I'm about a month young at linux and brand new to ubuntu. I can do this to install hiphop https://github.com/facebook/hiphop-php/wiki/Building-and-installing-HHVM-on-Ubuntu-12.04 *(69 more words omitted)*
Title: No wireless ubuntu13.10 **Body:** Installed ubuntu 13.10 yesterday no internet connection.12.10 ok and dongle ok,13.4 no dongle, nothing now. Compac mini 110c, broadcom 4313 (AR8132 Q.Atheros.) Only have ubuntu on notebook.

Figure 3: Three example segments (titles and bodies) from AskUbuntu dataset

ening of the length of the segments, it is less robust when its application changes from a specific to an unconstrained domain.

4 Classifier

4.1 Basic features

To set up a DQD system resorting to an approach based on a supervised machine learning classifier, we resorted to supporting vector machines (SVM), following its acknowledged good performance in this sort of tasks and following an option also taken by Bogdanova et al. (2015). We employed SVC (Support Vector Classification) implementation from the sklearn support vector machine toolkit (Pedregosa et al., 2011)

For the first version of the classifier, a basic feature set (FS) was adopted. N-grams, with n from 1 to 4, were extracted from the training set and the ones with at least 10 occurrences[6] were selected to support the FS

For each textual segment in a pair, a vector of size k was generated, where k is the number of n-grams included in the FS. Each vector encodes the occurrences of the n-grams in the corresponding segment, where vector position i will be 1 if the i-th n-gram occurs in the segment, and 0 otherwise. Then a feature vector of size $2k$ is created by concatenating the vectors of the two segments. This vector is further extended with the scores of the Jaccard coefficient determined over 1, 2, 3 and 4-grams. Hence, the final feature vector representing the pair to the classifier has the length $2k + 4$.

This system achieves 70.25% accuracy[7] when trained over the AskUbuntuTB. Its accuracy drops some 1.5 percentage points, to 68.88%, when trained with the shorter segments of AskUbuntuTO, and drops over 5 points, to 64.93%, when

trained with Quora, also with shorter segments than AskUbuntuTB but from a broader, all-encompassing domain.

4.2 Advanced features

To have an insight on how strong an SVM-based DQD resolver resorting to a basic FS like the one described above may be, we proceeded with further experiments, by adding more advanced features. We used Princeton WordNet (Fellbaum, 1998) to bring semantic knowledge to the system and used further text preprocessing to have more explicit lexical information, namely the text was normalized, e.g. "n't" was replaced with "not", etc., and POS tagged, with NLTK.

Lexical features The vector of each segment was extended with an extra feature, namely the number of negative words (e.g. *nothing*, *never*, etc.) occurring in it. And, to the concatenation of segment vectors, one further feature was added, the number of nouns that are common to both segments, provided they are not already included in the FS. Any pair was then represented by a vector of size $2(k + 1) + 4 + 1$.

Semantic features Eventually, any pair was represented by a vector of size $2(k + 1) + 4 + 2$, with its length being extended with yet an extra feature, namely the value of the cosine similarity between the embeddings of the segments in the pair.

For a given segment, its embedding, or distributional semantic vector, was obtained by summing up the embeddings of the nouns and verbs occurring in it, as these showed to support the best performance after experiments have been undertaken with all parts-of-speech and their subsets.

The embeddings were based on WordNet synsets, rather than on words, as these were shown to lead to better results after experimenting with both options. We employed word2vec word embeddings (Mikolov et al., 2013) and used Autoex-

---

[6]We tried thresholds ranging from 5 to 15.

[7]We tried also with another implementation of SVM, namely SVM-light (Joachims, 2006), and the same score 70.25 was achieved.

tend (Rothe and Schütze, 2015) to extract synset embeddings with the support of WordNet. We adopted the same configuration as in that paper and used version 3 of WordNet, which contains over 120k concepts, represented by synsets. The main advantage of synset embeddings over word embeddings in duplicate detection is the fact that synonyms receive exactly the same distributional vectors, which helps to appropriately take into account words in the segments of the pair that are different in linguistic form but are synonyms.

Results The resulting system permitted an improvement of over 5 percentage points with respect to its previous version trained with basic features, scoring 75.87% accuracy when running over AskUbuntuTB.

This advantage is not so large when it is run over the datasets with shorter segments. It scored 70.87% with AskUbuntuTO (positive delta of almost 2 points relative to the previous basic version), and 68.56% with Quora (over 3.5 points better).[8]

5 Neural Networks

We experimented with three different architectures for DQD resolvers based on neural networks. The first experiment adopts the architecture explored in one of the papers reporting the most competitive results for DQD, and the second adopts the neural architecture of the top performing system in the "Question-Question" subtask of SemEval2016. The third system adopts a hybrid architecture combining key ingredients of the previous two.

5.1 Convolutional

The architecture of convolutional neural network (CNN) to address DQD was introduced by Bogdanova et al. (2015). First, the CNN obtains the vectorial representations of the words, also known as word embeddings, in the two input segments. Next, a convolutional layer constructs a vectorial representation for each one of the two segments. Finally, the two representations are compared using cosine similarity, whose value if above an empirically estimated threshold, determines that the two segments are duplicate (diagram in Figure 4).

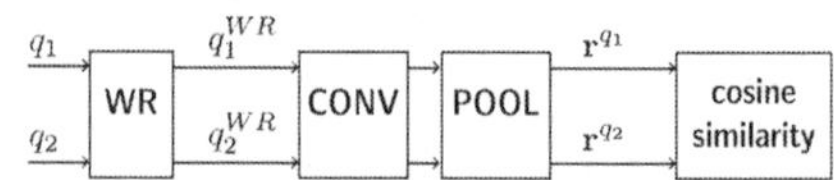

Figure 4: CNN architecture: word representation (WR), convolution (CONV), pooling (POOL) and cosine similarity measurement layers.

To replicate this approach, we resorted to Keras (Chollet, 2015) with Tensorflow (Abadi et al., 2015) back-end for training and evaluating the neural network. The hyper-parameters either replicate the ones reported by Bogdanova et al. (2015) or are taken from vanilla CNN architecture as it is implemented in the above libraries.

The DeepLearning4j[9] toolkit was used for creating the initial word representations. Bogdanova et al. (2015) specify only the skip-gram neural network architecture and the embeddings dimensionality of 200 as training parameters for their best run. In our experiment, besides these parameters, all the other hyper-parameters were taken from a vanilla version of *word2vec* implemented in DeepLearning4j. In this experiment, to train word embeddings, we used the 38 million tokens of the September 2014 AskUbuntu dump available.[10]

When trained over AskUbuntuTB, the system performs with 73.40% accuracy. An improvement of over 1 point, to 74.50%, was obtained with a slight variant where the CNN was run without pretrained word embeddings, and with a random initialization of the embeddings using uniform distribution.

The drop in performance observed in the systems presented above when moving to shorter segments is also observed here, with a much greater impact with Quora, coming down almost 15 points, to 59.90%, than with AskUbuntuTO, which comes down less than half a point, to 74.10%. This seems to indicate that the CNN is less robust than previous approaches when moving from a specific to a generic domain.

The score of 73.40%, obtained with settings similar to Bogdanova et al. (2015), is inferior in almost 20 percentage points to the score reported in that paper. This led us to look more carefully in the two experiments.

As indicated in previous sections, in our experi-

---

[8]This score was obtained resorting to 1- to 4-grams. Experiments with 1- to 3-grams and with 1- to 5-grams delivered worst scores, respectively 68.38% and 68.42%.

[9]http://deeplearning4j.org

[10]Bogdanova et al. (2015) used 121 million tokens from the May 2014 dump available to them.

ments the datasets were submitted to a preprocessing phase, including markup cleaning by means of which tags for references, links, snippets of code, etc. were removed. One of these tags is rendered to the reader of a thread in the AskUbuntu forum as "Possible duplicate: <title>", where <title> is instantiated with the title of the other thread that the present one is a possible duplicate of, and is linked to the page containing that other thread.

As we hypothesized that this might be a reason for the 20 point delta observed, we retrained our CNN-based system over AskUbuntuTB slightly modified just to keep that "Possible duplicate <title>" phrase. Accuracy of 94.20% was obtained, in the same range of the 92.9% score reported by Bogdanova et al. (2015).[11]

5.2 Deep

MayoNLP (Afzal et al., 2016) was the top performing system in the "Question-Question" subtask of SemEval 2016 Task 1 (Agirre et al., 2016).

Its architecture is based on Deep Structured Semantic Models, introduced by Huang et al. (2013), whose first layer is a 30k dense neural network followed by two hidden multi-layers with 300 neurons each and finally a 128 neuron output layer. All the layers are feed-forward and fully connected (diagram in Figure 5).

This neural network was used to process text and given the huge dimension of the input text (around 500k tokens), a word hashing method was used that creates trigrams for every word in the input sentence: for instance, the word *girl* would be represented as the trigrams *#gi, gir, irl and rl#*, including the beginning and end marks. This permitted to reduce the dimension of the input text to 30k, which is represented in the first neural layer.

The MayoNLP system adopts this architecture with the difference that the two hidden layer become a 1k neuron layer and the output layer is adapted to the SemEval2016 subtask, which is a graded textual similarity classification.

We resorted to the Keras deep learning library to replicate this architecture. Given that the dimension of the input in our task was smaller, we used one neuron for each word in our vocabulary and it was not necessary to resort to word hashing for dimensionality reduction. Hence, an input layer with approximately the same size of neurons was

---

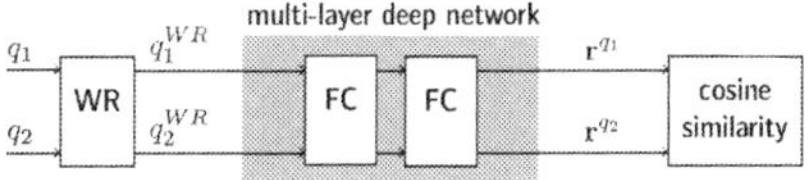

Figure 5: DNN architecture: word representation layer (WR), fully connected layers (FC) and cosine similarity measurement layer.

created: 63k for the AskUbuntuTB dataset, 16k neurons for AskUbuntuTO and 24k for Quora.

When evaluating the resulting system, the same overall pattern as with previous approaches emerges. The best accuracy is obtained with AskUbuntuTB, 78.65%, which has a slight drop with AskUbuntuTO, to 78.40%.

These scores are in contrast with the accuracy of 69.53% obtained with Quora, indicating that also here moving to a generic domain imposes a substantial loss of accuracy, of over 8 points.[12]

5.3 Hybrid DCNN

We also experimented with a novel architecture we developed by combining the convoluted and deep models discussed in the previous sections. By resorting to the Keras deep learning library, the key ingredients of the convoluted and the deep networks (DCNN) were implemented together.

The hybrid DCNN starts with the same input structure as the CNN, obtaining the vectorial representations of words in two input segments. It then connects each of them to a shared convolutional layer followed by three hidden and fully connected layers, whose output is finally compared using the cosine distance. Both the convolutional and the deep layers share the same weights for the two sentences input, in a siamese network (diagram in Figure 6).

The vectorial representation uses an embedding layer of 300 randomly initiated neurons with uniform distribution which are trainable. The convolution layer uses 300 neurons for the output of filters with a kernel size of 15 units, and each deep layer has 50 neurons.

Differently, from previous approaches, the resulting DQD resolver scores better over AskUbuntuTO, scoring 79.67%, than over AskUbuntuTB, for which it gets a 79.00% accuracy score. This

---

[11]Our attempt to reach the authors to obtain a copy of the dataset used in their paper remained unreplied.

[12]In the "Question-Question" subtask of SemEval 2016, thus with different datasets and for the different task of 0 to 5 graded similarity classification task, the MayoNLP system scored 0.73035 in terms of Pearson correlation coefficient (Agirre et al., 2016).

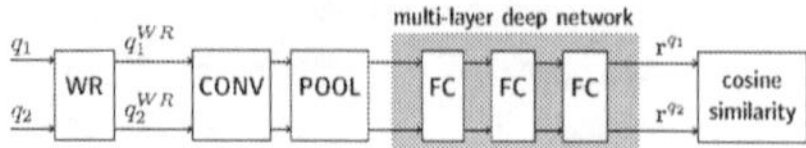

Figure 6: DCNN architecture.

may be an indicator that, when using the title and body, the neural network could perform better but may be failing due to the sparseness of the data, which requires possibly a higher number of neurons in the deep layer.

As for the result with Quora, in turn, the same pattern is observed as in previous systems. There is a substantial drop of over 8 points, to 71.48%.

6 Discussion

The experimental results reported in the previous sections are summarized in Table 1. The performance of each approach or architecture for DQD was assessed in the respective section. Putting all results side by side, some patterns emerge.

Shortening the length of the segments (from 84 words per segment on average, with AskUbuntuTB, to 8 or 10 words, respectively with AskUbuntuTO or Quora) has an overall negative impact on the accuracy of the systems, except for DCNN. For AskUbuntuTO, the negative delta ranges from 0.25 points, with DNN, to over 5 points, with SVM-adv.

NN-based solutions seem thus to be more robust to the shortening of the length of the segments than SVM-based ones, even to the point where the more sophisticated DCNN approach inverts this pattern, and performs better for shorter segments than for longer ones with AskUbuntu.

As the average length of segments in AskUbuntuTO and Quora are similar, the contrast between their scores permits to uncover yet another pattern. Moving from a specific to a generic domain has an overall negative impact on the accuracy of the systems, which is wider than with the shortening of the segments. The negative delta ranges from less than 3 points, with Jaccard or SVM-base, to over 14 points, with DNN.

The level of the impact seems to be inverted here. It is the non NN-based solutions that appear as more robust to the generalization of the domain than the NN-based ones, to the point that the superiority shown by NN-based ones with the specific domain is reduced or even canceled with the general domain.

It is interesting to note that, for the generic domain, the CNN approach offers the worst result. The DNN overcomes the best SVM approach by less than 2 points. And only the DCNN overcomes the overall second-best, but also by a modest margin.

It is also very interesting to note that, for general domain, the rule-based approach is one of the two second best, thus challenging the immense sophistication of any other approach, including the NN-based ones.

7 Cross-domain application

Given the scarcity of labeled datasets of pairs of interrogative segments, in real usage scenarios systems tend to be trained on as much data as possible from all sources and different domains. We experimentally approximated this scenario by training the best DQD system of each approach over the generic dataset (Quora) and evaluating them over the focused dataset (AskUbuntuTO).

The rule-based, the advanced SVM and the DCNN perform, respectively, with accuracies of 57.63% (dropping almost 15 points), 53.50% (dropping over 17 points) and 56.42% (dropping over 15 points).

Interestingly, leaner systems seem to be more robust in this approximation to its application in real-usage scenarios than more sophisticated ones. Importantly, however, for all types of systems, accuracy is observed to degrade and comes close to random decision performance.[13]

Given these results, it is interesting to check, for the generic domain, how this challenge may evolve when the training set is substantially enlarged, namely to the largest dataset available at present, that is to the over 400K pairs of the full Quora release. We picked the more lean technique (rule-based) and more sophisticated one (DCNN).

Interestingly their accuracy scores evolved towards opposite directions when compared to the scores obtained with the (over 13 times) smaller experimental Quora dataset, with 30k pairs. The rule-based solution scored 66.74% accuracy, dropping over 2 points, while the DCNN scored 79.36%, progressing almost 8 points.[14]

---

[13] Recall that in our experimental conditions, the 30k datasets are balanced with 50% duplicate pairs and 50% non-duplicate, but the 400k Quora release is not. To confirm this trend, we collected yet another data point for CNN, which scored 50.20%, in line with the other systems.

[14] Given the huge volume of the Quora release, we imple-

	Jcrd	SVM-bas	SVM-adv	CNN	DNN	DCNN
AskUbuntu						
title and body	72.91	70.25	75.87	74.50	78.65	79.00
title only	72.35	68.88	70.87	74.12	78.40	79.67
Quora	69.53	64.93	68.56	59.90	69.53	71.48

Table 1: Accuracy of the 6 systems (columns) over the 3 datasets (lines)

8 Related work

An interesting approach to DQD was introduced by Wu et al. (2011). It resorts to the Jaccard coefficient to measure similarities between two segments in the pair. Separate coefficients are calculated, and assigned different weights, for the segments. A threshold is empirically estimated and used to determine whether two threads are duplicates. An f-score of 60.29 is obtained for the titles only, trained with 3M questions and tested against 2k pairs taken from a dataset obtained from Baidu Zhidao, in Chinese. This approach is used as a baseline by Bogdanova et al. (2015). This system inspired one of the architectures used in our experiments, presented in detail in Section 5.1.

The recent SemEval-2016 Task 1 included a "Question-Question" subtask to determine the degree of similarity between two interrogative segments. The MayoNLP system (Afzal et al., 2016) obtained the best accuracy in this task. This system inspired one of the systems used in our experiments, presented in detail in Section 5.2.

Regarding the Quora dataset released 2 months ago, to the best of our knowledge, up to now there is only one unpublished paper concerning that task (Wang et al., 2017). It proposes a multi-perspective matching (BiMPM) model and evaluates it upon a 96%/2%/2% train/dev/test split. This system is reported to reach an accuracy of 88.17%.

Other draft results concerning Quora dataset are available only as blog posts[15,16] and are based on the model for natural language inference proposed by Parikh et al. (2016).

9 Conclusions

The experiments reported in this paper permitted to advance the understanding of the duplicate question detection task and improve its application. There is consistent progress in terms of the accuracy of the systems as one moves from less to more sophisticated approaches, from rule-based to support vector machines, and from these to neural networks, when its application is over a narrow, specific domain. The same trend is observed for the range of support vector machines solutions, with better results obtained for resolvers resorting to more advanced features. And it is observed also for the range of neural network architectures experimented with, from convoluted to deep networks, and from these to hybrid convoluted deep ones. *Overall, the novel neural network architecture we propose presents the best performance of all resolvers tested.*

The rate of this progress is however mitigated or even gets close to be canceled when one moves from a narrow and specific to broad and all-encompassing domain. Under our experimental conditions, the gap of over 11 points from the worst to the best performing solution with a narrow domain is cut to almost half, and the more sophisticated solution, with the best score, overcomes the leanest one just by less than 2 points when running over a generic domain.

Interestingly, when one moves, in turn, from longer to (eight times) shorter segments, only minor drops in performance are registered.

Given the scarcity of labeled datasets of pairs of interrogative segments, in real usage scenarios, systems are trained on as much data as possible from all sources and different domains and eventually applied over narrow domains. We experimentally approximated this scenario, where the accuracy of the systems was observed to degrade and come close to random decision performance.

In future work, we will extend our experimental space to further systems and conditions, including larger datasets, and languages other than English.

---

mented a lean version of DCNN to run this experiment, which used a vectorial representation of 25 neurons randomly initiated, followed by a convolution layer which uses 10 neurons for the output of filters and with a 5 kernel size. The deep layers were reduced to two layers each with 10 neurons. A 70%/30% randomly extracted for training/testing was used both for the experiment with the DCNN and with the rule-based approach.

[15] https://engineering.quora.com/Semantic-Question-Matching-with-Deep-Learning

[16] https://explosion.ai/blog/quora-deep-text-pair-classification

Acknowledgements

The present research was partly supported by the CLARIN and ANI/3279/2016 grants.

References

Martín Abadi, Ashish Agarwal, Paul Barham, Eugene Brevdo, Zhifeng Chen, Craig Citro, Greg S. Corrado, Andy Davis, Jeffrey Dean, Matthieu Devin, Sanjay Ghemawat, Ian Goodfellow, Andrew Harp, Geoffrey Irving, Michael Isard, Yangqing Jia, Rafal Jozefowicz, Lukasz Kaiser, Manjunath Kudlur, Josh Levenberg, Dan Mané, Rajat Monga, Sherry Moore, Derek Murray, Chris Olah, Mike Schuster, Jonathon Shlens, Benoit Steiner, Ilya Sutskever, Kunal Talwar, Paul Tucker, Vincent Vanhoucke, Vijay Vasudevan, Fernanda Viégas, Oriol Vinyals, Pete Warden, Martin Wattenberg, Martin Wicke, Yuan Yu, and Xiaoqiang Zheng. 2015. TensorFlow: Large-scale machine learning on heterogeneous systems. Software available from tensorflow.org. http://tensorflow.org/.

Naveed Afzal, Yanshan Wang, and Hongfang Liu. 2016. MayoNLP at SemEval-2016 task 1: Semantic textual similarity based on lexical semantic net and deep learning semantic model. In *Proceedings of the 10th International Workshop on Semantic Evaluation (SemEval-2016)*. pages 1258–1263.

Eneko Agirre, Carmen Banea, Daniel M. Cer, Mona T. Diab, Aitor Gonzalez-Agirre, Rada Mihalcea, German Rigau, and Janyce Wiebe. 2016. Semeval-2016 task 1: Semantic textual similarity, monolingual and cross-lingual evaluation. In Steven Bethard, Daniel M. Cer, Marine Carpuat, David Jurgens, Preslav Nakov, and Torsten Zesch, editors, *Proceedings of the 10th International Workshop on Semantic Evaluation, SemEval@NAACL-HLT 2016, San Diego, CA, USA, June 16–17, 2016*. The Association for Computer Linguistics, pages 497–511. http://aclweb.org/anthology/S/S16/S16-1081.pdf.

Steven Bird. 2006. NLTK: the natural language toolkit. In *Proceedings of the COLING/ACL on Interactive presentation sessions*. Association for Computational Linguistics, pages 69–72.

Dasha Bogdanova, Cícero Nogueira dos Santos, Luciano Barbosa, and Bianca Zadrozny. 2015. Detecting semantically equivalent questions in online user forums. In Afra Alishahi and Alessandro Moschitti, editors, *Proceedings of the 19th Conference on Computational Natural Language Learning, CoNLL 2015, Beijing, China, July 30–31, 2015*. ACL, pages 123–131. http://aclweb.org/anthology/K/K15/K15-1013.pdf.

François Chollet. 2015. Keras. https://github.com/fchollet/keras.

Christiane Fellbaum. 1998. *WordNet*. Wiley Online Library.

Po-Sen Huang, Xiaodong He, Jianfeng Gao, Li Deng, Alex Acero, and Larry Heck. 2013. Learning deep structured semantic models for web search using clickthrough data. In *Proceedings of the 22nd ACM International Conference on Information & Knowledge Management*. ACM, pages 2333–2338.

Shankar Iyer, Nikhil Dandekar, and Kornél Csernai. 2017. First quora dataset release: Question pairs. https://data.quora.com/First-Quora-Dataset-Release-Question-Pairs.

Thorsten Joachims. 2006. Training linear SVMs in linear time. In *Proceedings of the 12th ACM SIGKDD International Conference on Knowledge Discovery and Data Mining*. pages 217–226.

Tomas Mikolov, Wen-tau Yih, and Geoffrey Zweig. 2013. Linguistic regularities in continuous space word representations. In Lucy Vanderwende, Hal Daumé III, and Katrin Kirchhoff, editors, *Human Language Technologies: Conference of the North American Chapter of the Association of Computational Linguistics, Proceedings, June 9-14, 2013, Westin Peachtree Plaza Hotel, Atlanta, Georgia, USA*. The Association for Computational Linguistics, pages 746–751. http://aclweb.org/anthology/N/N13/N13-1090.pdf.

Ankur P. Parikh, Oscar Täckström, Dipanjan Das, and Jakob Uszkoreit. 2016. A decomposable attention model for natural language inference. In Jian Su, Xavier Carreras, and Kevin Duh, editors, *Proceedings of the 2016 Conference on Empirical Methods in Natural Language Processing, EMNLP 2016, Austin, Texas, USA, November 1–4, 2016*. The Association for Computational Linguistics, pages 2249–2255. http://aclweb.org/anthology/D/D16/D16-1244.pdf.

F. Pedregosa, G. Varoquaux, A. Gramfort, V. Michel, B. Thirion, O. Grisel, M. Blondel, P. Prettenhofer, R. Weiss, V. Dubourg, J. Vanderplas, A. Passos, D. Cournapeau, M. Brucher, M. Perrot, and E. Duchesnay. 2011. Scikit-learn: Machine learning in Python. *Journal of Machine Learning Research* 12:2825–2830.

Sascha Rothe and Hinrich Schütze. 2015. Autoextend: Extending word embeddings to embeddings for synsets and lexemes. *arXiv preprint arXiv:1507.01127* .

Zhiguo Wang, Wael Hamza, and Radu Florian. 2017. Bilateral multi-perspective matching for natural language sentences. *CoRR* abs/1702.03814. http://arxiv.org/abs/1702.03814.

Yan Wu, Qi Zhang, and Xuanjing Huang. 2011. Efficient near-duplicate detection for Q&A forum. In *Fifth International Joint Conference on Natural Language Processing, IJCNLP 2011, Chiang Mai, Thailand, November 8–13, 2011*. The Association for Computer Linguistics, pages 1001–1009. http://aclweb.org/anthology/I/I11/I11-1112.pdf.

Author Index

António Rodrigues, João, 262
Apidianaki, Marianna, 12, 84
Asghar, Nabiha, 78

Becker, Maria, 230
Berant, Jonathan, 161
Bhatia, Archna, 178
Bhavsar, Virendrakumar, 54
Blache, Philippe, 168
Boleda, Gemma, 104
Branco, António, 262
Bravo-Marquez, Felipe, 65

Callison-Burch, Chris, 12, 84
Carpuat, Marine, 33
Chen, Ao, 44
Chersoni, Emmanuele, 168
Cocos, Anne, 84
Compton, Michael, 241
Cook, Paul, 54
Coppersmith, Glen, 241
Cotterell, Ryan, 97

Dagan, Ido, 155
Diab, Mona, 241
Drozd, Aleksandr, 135

Eichler, Kathrin, 220

Farmer, Stephanie, 1
Feng, Yukun, 91
Ferraro, Francis, 97
Finley, Gregory, 1
Frank, Anette, 230

Geva, Mor, 161
Gharbieh, Waseem, 54
Gilroy, Sorcha, 199
Gupta, Abhijeet, 104

Han, Na-Rae, 178
Hirschberg, Julia, 110
Hovy, Eduard, 209
Husic, Halima, 189
Hwang, Jena D., 178

Jauhar, Sujay Kumar, 209
Jiang, Xin, 78

Kiss, Tibor, 189
Korhonen, Anna, 22
Krause, Sebastian, 220

Lenci, Alessandro, 168
Levitan, Sarah Ita, 110
Li, Bofang, 135
Li, Hang, 78
Liu, Chunhua, 91
Lopez, Adam, 199

Maneth, Sebastian, 199
Maraev, Vladislav, 262
Maredia, Angel, 110
Medić, Zoran, 115
Modi, Ashutosh, 121
Mohammad, Saif, 65

Nastase, Vivi, 230
Nguyen, Dai Quoc, 121
Nguyen, Dat Quoc, 121

O'Gorman, Tim, 178
Ostermann, Simon, 128

Padó, Sebastian, 104, 115
Pakhomov, Serguei, 1
Palmer, Alexis, 230
Pauselli, Luca, 241
Pelletier, Francis Jeffry, 189
Pinkal, Manfred, 121, 128
Poliak, Adam, 97
Ponti, Edoardo Maria, 22
Poppek, Johanna, 189
Poupart, Pascal, 78

Rajana, Sneha, 12
Rogers, Anna, 135
Roth, Michael, 128

Sachan, Mrinmaya, 251
Saedi, Chakaveh, 262
Sarioglu Kayi, Efsun, 241

Schechtman, Kara, 110
Schneider, Nathan, 178
Shutova, Ekaterina, 149
Shwartz, Vered, 12, 155
Silva, João, 262
Šnajder, Jan, 115
Srikumar, Vivek, 178
Staniek, Michael, 230
Stanovsky, Gabriel, 155
Sun, Maosong, 44

Talmor, Alon, 161
Thater, Stefan, 121, 128

Uszkoreit, Hans, 220

Van Durme, Benjamin, 97
Vulić, Ivan, 22
Vyas, Yogarshi, 33

Wundsam, Andreas, 149

Xing, Eric, 251
Xu, Feiyu, 220
Xu, Jian, 91

Yannakoudakis, Helen, 149
Yu, Dong, 91